SEVENTEENTH CENTURY FRANCE

SEVENTEENTH CENTURY FRANCE

by

G. R. R. Treasure, M.A.

Assistant Master at Harrow School

RIVINGTONS LONDON

Published by
RIVINGTONS (PUBLISHERS) LIMITED
Montague House, Russell Square, London W.C.1

© G. R. R. Treasure 1966
First Published 1966

Set in 11 on 12 pt. Garamond and printed in Great Britain by
T. AND A. CONSTABLE LTD., HOPETOUN STREET, EDINBURGH
27/225   PR.3024

CONTENTS

LIST OF ILLUSTRATIONS

Between pages 244 and 245

vii

Anne of Austria   *P. P. Rubens*

Fénelon   *J. Vivien*

For permission to reproduce the photographs in this book the
author and publishers are indebted to the Bibliothèque Nationale,
Réunion des Musées Nationaux, Photographie Giraudon and
Archives Photographiques, Paris. The portraits of Richelieu
on the jacket and between pages 244 and 245 are reproduced
by courtesy of the Trustees, The National Gallery, London.

PREFACE

LARGE gaps still exist between the specialist monographs and the more general histories of the European nations. Nowhere are such gaps so evident and so striking as in the case of Seventeenth Century France. There is a surprising difference between the intensive treatment which has been accorded to the last years of the *ancien régime* and to the Revolution, and the rarity of books about the *Grand Siècle*, when France exercised a dominating influence in Europe, but when also, in the problems of the time, the origins of future crisis and revolution can be seen. Perhaps it is just because this is a great subject that historians have been chary of presenting a general account of the age, perhaps because so much work is being done upon the period which is still altering the picture. Whatever the cause, the effect has been to force the reader, if he has tried to pursue the subject among English writers, to receive incomplete accounts which sometimes rely too heavily upon the evidence of contemporary memoirs, unbalanced or Whiggish interpretations of the period. The difficulty of obtaining a fair picture is aggravated by the fact that, until recently, French historians have tended to study the period from an avowed political standpoint, monarchist, Buonapartist or republican, Catholic or anti-clerical. This book does not pretend to be a work of scholarship or a definitive account of the age. It is offered rather as a provisional narrative history of France in a century of rich and varied achievement. If it introduces the reader to the findings of some of the historians who have been doing seminal work upon the period, if at the same time it interests him in the age and provides him with a platform from which he may explore further, it may serve a useful purpose.

The theme of the book is the evolution of the centralised state in France: what one writer has called, misleadingly I think, the baroque state, and which I prefer to call, in a safer tradition, the absolute state. It is this theme, more than anything else, which gives coherence to an age of grand and prolific achievement. I have been concerned particularly with the nature and growth of royal administration in the face of the surviving manifestations of the feudal spirit. I have looked also for characteristic expressions of the outlook and temper of the time, and have found these in the religious conflicts of the century, as well as in the more conventional areas of war and diplomacy. It may seem that the chapters which deal with Jansenism and Huguenotism are disproportionately full. I find these subjects exceptionally interesting, but there is a more compelling reason for dealing with them in detail. In this century religious questions were of deep and central significance. From a narrative account we can learn much about the way men thought—and what they thought important.

Campaigns, battles and treaties also take up a considerable part of the book. It was tempting to deal with the wars of the time through a brief analysis. But the history of the state must be, to some extent, the history of those matters which occupied the attention of the statesmen. It may be, too, that I am not alone in finding history without story as unsatisfactory to read as it is difficult to teach. In Aristotle's words, 'history is what Alcibiades did and suffered'. The narrative then is provided substantially by those military and diplomatic events which loomed so large in the lives of men who accepted war as part of the natural order of things.

I have tried to give some account of the cultural achievement of France in this century of genius, and in so doing have been more than usually aware of my inadequacies of knowledge and understanding. One is oppressed too, of course, by the inherent difficulty which faces the writer of a book that aims, in any way, to be comprehensive: how to maintain a balance and at the same time to be reasonably complete, without being trite. Writing, for example, about such men as Pascal, Descartes or Bossuet, in the compass of a page or so presents acute problems of selection and compression, and leaves often a sense of frustration at being unable to pursue in depth more than a few of the great subjects which present themselves.

This is in no sense a history of Europe. But it has, more even than a history of England in this century, to take account of the contemporary developments and events in the leading countries with which France had to deal. I have tried to put France properly in the context of Europe, by reference to what was happening outside her own frontiers and by analogies and comparisons, where these may be helpful or appropriate. Only in one period does the history of France so merge with the history of Europe that the account has to broaden out into the latter—the Thirty Years War, when French diplomacy is unintelligible without a full explanation of the war which provided Richelieu with the opportunities to lay the foundation for the later dominance of France in Europe. Throughout, however, the reader who wishes to have a complete understanding of the European history of the time will need to have some other work to hand; fortunately there is no shortage of these.

I am acutely aware of what is missing in this book. I have made no attempt to present a thorough or particular analysis of French society, for I feel that this is properly the work of a native historian or of one who is so steeped in the records that he can write significantly about the lives of Frenchmen in the seventeenth century. I gave been concerned only with such aspects of society and economy as seem to have affected public events and to throw light upon our knowledge of the political and administrative problems of the time. I have made little attempt, and then in the most cautious way, to deal with differences in manners and material living, between classes, provinces, town and country, north and south.

I am deeply indebted throughout to the many historians whose researches have provided the raw material for this work. They are listed in the short bibliography, but it is fitting that a writer who has done none of the spadework himself should acknowledge what he owes to those who have laboured before him. These apart, I am especially grateful to my colleague Roger Ellis, who when he found that other commitments prevented him from completing what was originally to have been a joint work, handed over several finished sections, and much other material, for incorporation in this book. His help has made my work materially easier. I wish also to thank my friend Francis Pearson for his meticulous work upon the copy, proofs and index. What is still wrong, in fact or interpretation is, I need hardly say, my work alone.

1 PROLOGUE

The Three Henries

On August 1, 1589, a monk, Jacques Clément, plunged his knife into the stomach of Henry III at Saint-Cloud, where the king and his brother-in-law, Henry of Navarre, were planning to attack Paris, with the support of most moderate and peace-loving men and with every prospect of subduing the city. When, to the surprise of his physicians, the king died early the following morning, the nobles had to decide whether or not to swear allegiance to a Huguenot. In life Henry had presided fitfully over the decomposition of France; in his last year he had sunk religious differences and acted with some resolution to recover his capital; now dying, he bequeathed his kingdom to his Huguenot ally. The situation for which the Catholic League had been preparing had arrived.

In 1584, the League, led by the Guise family, had set itself up as an independent body inside France with the avowed aim of excluding Henry of Navarre from the throne and substituting the old Cardinal Bourbon. To achieve this they had enlisted the support of Philip II of Spain who promised, by the Treaty of Joinville, to give the League 50,000 crowns a month. The League in turn promised to reduce heresy, not only in France but also in the Netherlands. With the blessing of Pope Sixtus V, who issued a bull depriving Henry of Navarre of his rights, they took their place in the imperial design of the Spanish king: the destruction of heresy, and the promotion of Spanish power throughout Europe.

Wealthier than the king, and strong in the provinces, especially in the north, east, and around Paris, the League had forced the king to abandon the policy of religious concession, to grant complete control of the eastern provinces to the Guises and even to provide subsidies for the League's attacks on the Huguenots. Henry III had personal as well as political reasons for disliking the virile Henri de Guise, the leader of the faction who put their religious and family interests before their duty to France. Guise was a standing reproach to the king's neurotic personality, his inconstant whims and fears and his makeshift policies. Henry III's mother, Catherine de Médicis, was nearing the end of her devious efforts for survival; her reputation was stained by the murderous treachery of St. Bartholomew's Eve, and she had to pay 50 per cent interest for her loans from the bankers of Lyon. She advised Henry to give way, but she and her son put their faith now in Henry of Navarre and urged him to change his religion. This he would not yet do, fearing to lose the support of the Huguenots without gaining that of the Catholics; he too had to play a waiting game. The League were however afraid that something might come from the *rapprochement* of France and Navarre, and they determined to win control of Paris. In the largest city in Europe, the various discontents of the townsfolk, the theological orthodoxy of the Sorbonne, the fanaticism of monks and *curés* and the traditional rowdiness of the streets crystallised round the organisation of the craft guilds into a revolutionary force. The *Seize* was a secret organisation, with one member from each of the sixteen sections of the city, preparing now to overthrow the loyal leaders of *Parlement* and of the magistracy, and even to assassinate the king. With the *Seize*, Guise now allied. When he entered Paris in 1588 against the king's orders, they provoked such a demonstration in his favour that Henry slipped out of Paris with four friends and established his court at Chartres. Even there he appeared ready to conciliate, to sign the Edict of Union promising no peace for the heretics; he summoned the States-General to the great hall at his château of Blois in October.

The operations of this States-General, and the king's reaction to it, mark the nadir of monarchy in France, at least since the English invasions of the fifteenth century. Guise took no chances with its composition. The great part of the church and nobility were with him for he stood for Roman Catholicism without concession, and for the immunity of the aristocracy from crown interference in the provinces. The *bourgeoisie* tended, however, to be hostile and Guise carried out something of an election campaign. 'Having sent out into every province trustworthy men, I think I have arranged that the majority of deputies will be for us and devoted to our cause', he wrote to the Spanish ambassador, Mendoza, who was by now accredited to the League rather than to the king. The *tiers état* elected as their President, La Chapelle-Marteau, one of the *Seize*, and joined wholeheartedly with the other two estates in making extreme demands of the king: royal favourites were to be dismissed, the subsidy granted to the king was to be controlled by a special commission elected from the estates and edicts were to be entitled 'sovereign' before they had been signed by the king.

The estates encouraged themselves by claiming that they were following the example of the English Parliament, but Queen Elizabeth would have turned apoplectic if she had had to suffer such treatment. Henry met the attacks on his prerogative with the last weapon of weakness. He had the duc de Guise assassinated by his bodyguard of fourteen Gascons in his royal apartments adjoining the Great Hall where the States-General met. He killed Guise's brother the next day, arrested La Chapelle-Marteau and Brissac, respectively the Presidents of the *tiers* and the Nobility. This was not only an act of personal vendetta but a *coup d'état* as well. It led to open war between the king and all extreme Catholics for, as the dying Catherine de Médicis is said to have prophesied when her son brought her the news of his stroke, in another part of the château: 'You can cut but you cannot sew.' To the Parisians, Henri de Valois became, anagrammatically, *Vilain Herodes*.

This was the situation which Henry of Navarre inherited. The League had lost some of its leaders but it commanded the support of most of the nobility and of the church, of Paris and many other important towns. It was in alliance with Spain whose armies were still the most formidable in Europe. It was the champion of the States-General and of its claim to be 'the brain' of the state. Provinces such as Provence, towns such as Marseilles, were virtually independent of royal authority. Henry was indeed king only in name; his achievement should be measured against this background.

The Politique king

The new king was 43 years old; in 1572, the year of his marriage to Marguerite de Valois and of the massacre of St. Bartholomew's Eve which provided the grisly postscript to the wedding, he had been 26. The intervening years had been a hard schooling in the arts of war and diplomacy. He had learned to thread his way amongst the treacheries, perjuries and acts of violence that were a commonplace of the age of Catherine de Médicis and, so doing, he had acquired a mature and cynical judgment of men and measures. He was still however something of a *hobereau*, a southerner and a soldier, and he was foreign to the sophisticated manners of the château-belt of the Loire valley and the Île de France. His long sharp face, tailing into a beard which, he said, had been turned grey with bad news, was dominated by a huge hooked nose. His sharp tongue, his bonhomie, his endurance and accessibility, his constant love-affairs, even his notorious slovenliness about dress and washing, made him a popular figure among the troops, with whom he spent much of the first decade of his reign. In those years was born the legend of the father of his country who had his people's interests at heart. He gained, of course, enormously from the contrast with his effete and neurasthenic predecessor, but solid virtues contributed to his success: imagination, common sense and courage. He used promises and congratulations more often than gifts, for he had little to give; indeed he made his poverty a point of pride, boasting of the fact that he only had five handkerchiefs when he arrived in Paris in 1594. It is interesting to see how many of his traits reappeared in his grandson, Charles II of England, who, like him, learned in adversity to assess men as colleagues and rivals before they could hide behind the mask of the courtier. Like Charles, he was easy-going, except where his sovereign rights were concerned, preferring power itself to the appearance of power. He had the conveniently bad memory which enabled him to forget grudges, and the generosity to forgive with a frankness that won over an enemy from fear, through relief, to a delighted gratitude. The duchesse de Montpensier, who had stayed in Paris throughout its siege and helped to inspire its resistance, was also popularly believed to have sent Jacques Clément to kill Henry III. When she met his successor she was asked not for an account of her misdeeds, but for a sugared apricot. Some of his best servants, for instance Jeannin and Villeroi, had been Leaguers; there was that about him which made men want to serve him. Even his vices contributed to his popularity. His love of gambling was a profitable sideline for some of his courtiers. The court was tolerant, too, of his *amours* until they led, as with Gabrielle d'Estrées and Henriette d'Estragues, to scheming for the advancement of a large and unpleasant family (Gabrielle's was known at court as 'The Seven Deadly Sins'). Here was Henry IV's Achilles' heel; here his judgment was fallible, and sometimes the political repercussions were serious.

For three years Henry made little progress. Of the forty thousand troops with the late king and himself, nearly half deserted after the assassination, and only a minority of the aristocracy remained loyal, despite his promise that he would not extend the rights of the Huguenots. He adopted therefore a policy of caution and bluff, moving his army from Saint-Cloud, not southwards to his own country, but north to Normandy; this province, until the fall of Paris in 1594, he made his headquarters. Thus he was able to threaten the capital constantly, and to keep in touch with the English, his chief allies, since they were already at war with Spain; the previous year the English navy and Atlantic gales had destroyed the Spanish Armada. The League armies advanced to destroy Henry in Normandy, at least twenty-five thousand strong, outnumbering him by two to one; they were commanded by the duc de Mayenne, younger brother of the murdered duc de Guise, self-styled Lieutenant General of the realm, acting regent for the old Cardinal Bourbon who was a prisoner in Henry's hands. Men contrasted the two opponents by saying that Henry spent less time in bed than Mayenne did at table. Though idle and greedy, the latter was also ambitious and hoped to be the power behind the throne, if not king himself. He was conscious of the privileges of high birth but too stolid to enjoy the esteem of his brother; now his reputation suffered further from two defeats in the field. At Arques, his army failed to press home an attack against a fortified position which lasted intermittently for twenty-three days, and eventually had to retreat, leaving the way open for Henry to try an unsuccessful surprise attack upon Paris. In the following spring, March 14, 1590, the two armies met again, with the same odds, at Ivry. Rallying his troops round his *panache blanc*, Henry made his name as a leader and tactician in this brief but spectacular engagement.

Though these victories won over some of the nobility, including Épernon and Nevers, and led the moderate Pope Sixtus V to withhold his condemnation, they were the limits of Henry's success. The siege of Paris which followed showed him how stubborn was the opposition. Mayenne had left the city with his temporary government; the city was ill-prepared and had food supplies for only a month, yet it held out for four, from May to September. There were no Spanish troops as yet, though the old Spanish ambassador, Mendoza, remained at his post, mustered his staff on the walls, turned his courtyard into a soup-kitchen and inspirited the defenders by his example. Thirteen hundred monks remained in the city, far from useless mouths, encouraging the garrison with services and processions. The Sorbonne and the *Seize*, academics and demagogues, were determined to hold out till relief came. They would not submit, as they put it in a pamphlet, to a king who was not worthy of his God-given office. Henry had no intention of storming his capital; his army was too small, and, even if he effected surprise entry, he feared the struggle over the barricades and the blood that would be shed. He did not want to spoil his reputation on his way to the throne.

Relief came in September, not from Mayenne but from Parma with the Spanish army from the Netherlands, the best-trained troops in the world. Henry could only withdraw, leaving the citizens to ponder the implications of the presence of foreign troops. The same bitter experience happened to him outside Rouen in 1592, after a siege prolonged unnecessarily by the attitude of Biron, his general, one of a number who wanted the war to go on because they feared losing their authority when it ended. Henry at this juncture was distracted from military affairs by his interest in Gabrielle d'Estrées. In truth, however, he was not strong enough to defeat the League, and the Spanish, who could come into action whenever the American convoys got through with their gold to pay Parma's men. English diversions in his favour, and their increasingly efficient efforts in the Netherlands, were peripheral, not decisive. In the provinces there was stalemate. Henry could win his kingdom only by a change of heart in his leading subjects.

Paris worth a Mass

There had never been lacking men who considered the religious arguments to be of less importance than the political, who saw that France was being torn apart by the fanatics; these men were the *politiques*, whose motto might have been the saying of Michel l'Hôpital, Catherine de Médicis' Chancellor (1505-77): 'A man does not cease to be a citizen because he is excommunicated.' They believed that the first priority was the safety of the state, the community which framed and nourished the lives and faiths of its individual citizens. They did not underestimate the vitality of the warring creeds but they realised the vulpine nature of a struggle that was tearing France apart. Evoking the feudal quarrels of the families of Guise and Châtillon-Montmorency, the anonymous writer of the *Satire Ménippée* exclaimed: 'For all the bloody tragedies which have been played out on this pitiful French stage arose from these first quarrels, and not from differences of religion.' Decadent feudalism, writhing under the centralising tendencies of monarchy, was Henry's enemy; the reaction from its factious destructiveness was his ally. The menace of Spain, so evidently concerned to exploit the divisions of France, was the rallying point of the *politiques*. Men like Villeroi and Jeannin from the Leaguers, Duplessis Mornay from the Huguenots, now stressed the importance of hereditary monarchy and opposed alike Spanish interference in French territory and Papal interference in the Gallican church. They were supported by all who wanted to travel and trade without fear, and to grow crops which would not be plundered.

Since the end of the Siege of Paris, the *Seize* had pressed on towards their own conception of revolutionary power. They denounced the League and Mayenne, who had allowed the siege to take place and had done nothing to end it. They denounced too, but less fairly, the lawyers of *Parlement* and appointed a special committee of ten, Jacobin-wise, to extirpate their enemies who were divided into three groups, marked P, D and C—*pendu*, *dagué* and *chassée*. In November 1591, *Parlement* failed to convict one of the accused, whereupon they seized Brisson, *Premier Président*, hanged him, with two other leading officials, and carried their naked bodies in procession through the streets. This demonstration did not have the looked-for results and Mayenne returned to Paris and punished the offenders, with popular support. So the monks and the *Seize* lost ground together. Mob rule and religious fanaticism were regarded with suspicion by the nobles and the lawyers.

Meanwhile Spain's demands were pressing. Cardinal Bourbon died in 1590, and the Leaguers had not yet produced an official candidate for the throne to replace him, because Mayenne did not feel strong enough to put his chances to the test, yet would not give up his claim. Now Philip who, through Parma, had saved Paris and Rouen, and had since provided Paris with a garrison, proposed that his daughter, Isabella should succeed; she was the niece of Henry III. Immured in the Escorial, he relied upon the reports of his ambassadors that good Catholics still put creed before country. His demands were unfortunately timed. The leaders of *Parlement* were roused by this threat to the Salic Law, one of those fundamental laws of the realm which they conceived to be their responsibility. The *politique* argument was strengthened. Mayenne was paralysed. The only hope for the Spanish proposal was that Isabella should marry a French prince of the Catholic party; this was too much for Spanish diplomacy to swallow, and the girl was allotted more conventionally to the Archduke

Ernest, likely heir to the Holy Roman Empire. The glorious possibility of being ruled by such a combination did not appeal to the French nobility, who were further alarmed by reports that Philip intended to dismember the country, giving Brittany to Isabella, Provence to Charles-Emmanuel of Savoy, Béarn and Gascony to Henry, Picardy and Flanders to the Spanish Netherlands and the remainder to the duc de Guise.

In January 1593, the States-General met in Paris to provide a national policy for the League. There were only 128 delegates, instead of the 505 at Blois in 1588, largely because Henry had done his best to prevent representatives from getting there; several indeed made special wills before setting out on their journey, and churches echoed with prayers for their safety. Those who came demanded the publication of the decrees of the Council of Trent, a reduction in taxes, a guarantee of provincial liberties and a Catholic, French king.

This was the moment chosen by Henry to announce his intention of changing his religion. The timing was admirable. For years he had refused to take this step because, having already been forced once to abjure, after St. Bartholomew's Eve, in peril of his life, he was afraid that he would get a reputation for insincerity, as well as losing the only loyal support he had, that of the Huguenots. Dogmatic differences meant little to him and it is unlikely that he had many religious scruples about the operation. He always, however, paid fair tribute to the God of Battles; thus he pointed out a religious moral to his troops after the victory of Arques and ascribed his entry into Paris to a divine miracle. He made a show, too, of concern about the theological issues, but this may have been merely a tactful demonstration to the Sorbonne and the French clergy that he was in earnest. The conversion was really a matter of political expedience; indeed it was inevitable. Since the people would not be of the religion of the prince, the prince must be converted to the religion of the people; no other solution was acceptable by the standards of the sixteenth century: *cuius regio, eius religio*. Now that a compromise was desired by the nobility, the States-General, the church, even many of the Huguenots, he had to emerge as the champion of the *politiques* before another candidate could be chosen. Paris was indeed 'worth a Mass'—whether he actually said so or not. The Pope's opposition and an assassination attempt by Le Baru, a leading Catholic, only served to increase Gallican support for him. After a four-day debate at Saint-Denis with leading Bishops, he was received into the Catholic church on July 25, 1593. Early in 1594 he was crowned, not at Reims, which was still in the hands of the League, but in Chartres cathedral, where he was anointed with oil from a fresh supply, found in the abbey of Marmoutiers and took the oath, which included a promise to hunt out heretics. A month later, in March, he entered Paris, almost without fighting. The *coup* by which this was achieved was the result of a conspiracy between the governor, Brissac, the head of *Parlement*, Huillier, and many local commanders of the *milice*. The Parisians seem to have been delighted. Ever since the previous summer, when Henry had allowed them out under truce into the countryside, they had taken to making catcalls at the preachers, and even at the leaders of the *Seize*. Henry sealed his victory by allowing the mob to crush round him wherever he went in Paris, and by refusing to execute or even to imprison a single opponent, typical and rewarding displays of confidence. Doubting Catholics, suspicious of his conversion, were reassured when he displayed his kingly healing powers over the scrofulous. In 1595 he was absolved by Pope Clement VIII; in official parlance, as in the hearts of his subjects, he was now 'His Most Christian Majesty'.

Until 1594, Henry had been fighting as one claimant for the throne against another. From 1594 until 1598, when he settled accounts with the Spanish by the Peace of Vervins, and the Huguenots by the Edict of Nantes, he was leading the French monarchy against its enemies. On paper, these were formidable, but over all hung the pall of exhaustion. If they could not beat Henry as a partisan without Paris they had little chance against him as a king. Parma was dead. Philip II was an old man who wished to leave his empire at peace; he was bankrupt, and he was quarrelling with the Pope, who saw with distress that the Catholic powers were weakening themselves as England and Holland grew stronger and richer. The war was only prolonged because Philip still hoped to subdue the Low Countries; for this purpose his French allies, Mercoeur in Brittany and Mayenne in Burgundy, were of some use. Henry, by declaring war on Spain, tainted these men with treason. Mayenne lost his hold on Burgundy, although Henry nearly threw everything away at the battle of Fontaine-Française in 1595, after marching precipitantly to help the citizens of Dijon. When he found that Mayenne and the Spanish outnumbered him by five to one, he refused to retreat, indulged in a dramatic thrust against their advance guard and should have been captured by the main army. The Spanish general however refused to advance, suspecting a trap, and Henry galloped away to boast of his *gasconnade*. Mayenne, despairing of allies even more cautious than himself, joined Henry, and was so well received that he became his loyal servant. Joyeuse, Guise and Charles of Lorraine all gave up as well; Nemours died. When in 1597 the final crisis of the war against Spain was reached, only Mercoeur was holding out. He could achieve nothing in Brittany and made his submission in the following year, soothed by the arrangement of a marriage between his daughter and Henry's illegitimate son, César de Vendôme.

In 1597, Amiens, in the centre of the great plain stretching from Paris to the north-east, and the supply depot for Henry's forthcoming war against the Spanish Netherlands, was surprised and captured by Portecarrero. Henry and Sully, who was by now managing his finances, had to raise forced loans, sell offices, bargain away taxes for years ahead in exchange for money, and even offer Calais to Elizabeth in order to fit out a sufficient army to recapture it. When the Archduke Albert led his 28,000 men to the relief of his garrison, he did not feel strong enough to fight. Philip was then at last ready to negotiate.

It is remarkable how little in the way of territory Henry had lost in the course of his struggle to become effective king of France. By the Treaty of Vervins in 1598 France kept all the territory she had held after the Peace of Cateau-Cambrésis in 1558, that is before the Wars of Religion had started. Charles-Emmanuel of Savoy, who had been trying to establish himself in the Rhône valley, which was still frontier territory, gained nothing except the right to continue negotiations about Saluzzo, a French enclave up in the mountains of his own lands. England, a greedy friend, was left out of the treaty and lost her chance of regaining Calais, fortunately perhaps for James I, who was to succeed Elizabeth in 1603: it would have been as much an embarrassment to him as Dunkirk was later to Charles II.

The great princes did not go unrewarded for their return to allegiance. Henry's policy had been to spend money freely in buying them over since, as he argued when Sully objected, it would be ten times more expensive to fight them. Guise cost him 3,706,000 *livres*, Joyeuse and Brissac 1,500,000 each, according to Sully, who may have been exaggerating. In order to pay these sums he had to sell crown lands, for which he compensated by bringing his own property in Navarre to the crown. The nobles had spent huge sums during the war and it would be false to think of them as a class grown wealthy at the expense of the king; many of them suffered the encumbrance of debts that was the common lot of grandees all over Europe, when expenditure was habitually based upon expectations rather than upon income. Several gained important provincial posts, Mayenne for example becoming Governor of the Île de France. Henry firmly maintained that a Governor's job was a military one, and that he should have nothing to do with justice or finance. This was to be the chief issue between the crown and the nobility in the seventeenth century. Henry had the sense to see that it would be so, and the toughness to hold his position, always in theory and usually in practice.

The Edict of Nantes

In the same year as the Peace of Vervins, Henry IV came to terms with the Huguenots. The settlement took the form of an Edict, but it was more like a treaty between two independent powers. To the determined minority of the French Calvinists Henry was forced to make large concessions; they were in a strong bargaining position, while he was prepared to pay highly for an end to religious schism. Sentiment towards his late co-religionaries, and his own moderate views, played their part in the settlement, but he was not a free agent; the Huguenots could not be reduced by mere force.

Calvin had given to his movement an ideology and organisation especially well suited to thrive in revolutionary conditions. In Geneva, on the border of France, he had constructed a new sort of polity which embodied the principles contained in the *Christianæ Religionis Institutio*, first published in Latin in 1536 and in a French edition in 1541. He had taken to its extreme the doctrine of predestination, present always in modified form in mediaeval Catholicism, and re-stated by Luther. His followers, fortified by the idea that they were the elect of God, accepted the discipline of a church-state which cut across frontiers of race and language. The episcopate was replaced by a hierarchy of local consistories, regional colloquies and national synod; ministers and lay elders shared the government of a body which claimed to control every aspect of the life of the faithful. Where Lutheranism remained amorphous and was everywhere subservient to the secular authority for want of a viable organisation, Calvinism confronted the Roman church with a rival administrative machine. The dedication and missionary spirit of its members and the toughness and flexibility of the organisation provided a hard core of resistance to church and state. In Scotland, in England, in the Netherlands and in France, Calvinists were a small minority, but wielded an influence disproportionate to their numerical size; round the fanatics who were ready to fight and die for their faith clustered the discontented who wanted to better their political and social condition.

The majority of French Huguenots (the name may be derived from the name of Hugues, leader of a Swiss Protestant confederation formed in 1526, or from the French use of the name Hugues to mean 'bogey') were peasants. A relatively high proportion however came from educated, influential or noble families. The rigorous logic of Calvinism appealed to the university mind, trained to think analytically, and especially to the lawyer; the faith was nourished by regular reading of the Bible rather than by those ceremonies and symbols which interpreted faith to the illiterate. The *bourgeois* was attracted by the ethics of Calvinism, which stressed the merits of thrift and enterprise; everywhere this class tended to anti-clericalism, not least in France where the Gallican church, in its higher reaches, presented a displeasing image of aristocratic wealth and privilege. The lesser *noblesse*, struggling to maintain its status in the face of diminishing rents and new-rich *bourgeois* land-purchasers, were in a mood to seek drastic solutions to their problems. The great territorial magnates, princes of the blood like Condé and Anthony de Bourbon, King of Navarre and Henry IV's father, and old families like the Montmorencies and Colignies resented the encroachments of the crown upon their control of estates and provinces. Many who had a quarrel with authority, or who looked covetously upon the lands of the church had turned to the uncompromising affirmation of Calvin that God was sovereign over all secular interests, Pope and prince included; some of these were mere fellow-travellers with the new church, others accepted and lived by its austere principles. Though there were Huguenot communities and families all over France by the end of the century, Huguenotism was strongest in the towns which had traditions of autonomy or special reason for jealousy of

Catholic Paris, places such as Lyon, Tours, La Rochelle and Nîmes. Just as in the Netherlands the Calvinists came to be concentrated in the north as the result of the revolt against Spain and the artificial frontier which geography and strategy imposed there, so in France the religious wars accentuated the north-south religious division of the country. The majority of Huguenots lived south of the Loire, in the provinces of the Dauphiné, Languedoc, Gascony, Guyenne and Saintonge; in some of these a tradition of resistance to church and crown may be traced back to the Albigensian 'crusade'.

Calvin's own view had inclined to non-resistance, though he had conceded in a letter to Gaspard de Coligny that revolt might be lawful if it had some established authority, such as that of *Parlement*, behind it. The Huguenot leaders were careful to maintain the fiction that they were fighting against the bad advisers of the crown, notably the Guise family; at least until St. Bartholomew's Eve this claim was justified by the apparent neutralism of Catherine de Médicis, who was wholly unfitted to perceive the differences of principle which divided the parties. The Huguenots were never, however, prepared to compromise as Catherine wished; they had in mind the example of John Knox in Scotland, who had in 1560 presided over a violent and successful revolution against the Catholic monarch. They wished, for a start, to establish an independent and defensible position, and at the Peace of St. Germain in 1570 secured the concession of four 'guarantee towns' which they might garrison by way of security. They intended further to link up with the international crusade against Catholicism; it was Catherine's fear that Coligny would engineer war against Spain that led her to plan his assassination, and so to the more desperate expedient of general massacre. After 1573, the crown was obviously committed to the Catholic side and the Huguenots moved correspondingly into an avowed revolutionary stance. The author of the *Vindiciae contra tyrannos*, one of many such treatises, claimed that rebellion by the 'magistrates' of the kingdom against an unjust sovereign was lawful in the eyes of God; the argument was to be used by both sides to justify war and even tyrannicide. In 1576 the crown had returned wearily to the policy of compromise, but it was unable to maintain this position in the face of the fanaticism of the Guises and the League. The reign of Henry III ended with the alliance of the Most Catholic King and the leader of the Huguenots, Henry of Navarre: an anomalous position to say the least. After his conversion, the new king had to give the million and a half Huguenots a degree of toleration and security, without offending the Catholic majority of his subjects. By this time the Huguenots had entrenched themselves. Protestant France was divided into nine areas, with an elected council in each; an elected assembly, drawn from these, was to meet each year. That of Saumur, in 1595, demanded that there should be as many Huguenots as Catholics in each *parlement*. Its successor, in 1596, had sent agents to negotiate separately in London and Amsterdam. Some Huguenot nobles had served notice upon the king when they abandoned his army in a critical stage of the war against Spain. Anxious to avoid the further hardening of schism at a time when he and the League were exhausted, Henry therefore conceded most of their demands.

The Edict of Nantes, signed in April 1598, a few weeks before the Peace of Vervins, allowed the Huguenots to worship publicly in all places where they had been doing so during the previous two years, except within five leagues of Paris (after 1608, Parisian Huguenots, of whom there were at one stage as many as thirty thousand, worshipped at Charenton, the old national lunatic asylum). Nobles were to be allowed to worship privately at court. All were granted complete civil rights, with free access to the professions and to the universities. They thus obtained the ordinary rights of the French citizen which, by contemporary standards, they should have forfeited by refusing to accept the religion of the state. They were also given special privileges. *Chambres de l'édit*, on which there had to be Huguenot representatives, were added to the *parlements* of Paris, Grenoble and Bordeaux, to try cases in which Huguenots were involved. The system of assemblies, which they had evolved to help themselves, now received official sanction. They were allowed to fortify one hundred towns, *places de sûreté*, for eight years, including such stout natural bastions as Montauban and La Rochelle; the garrisons of these towns were to be maintained at the expense of the state.

This was not an essay in toleration but an armed truce. Neither side accepted the Edict as final; zealots in both camps saw it as a point of departure for new missionary activity; even those who considered that schism was irremediable, deplored it. All over France men confronted each other over lines of demarcation; in Huguenot towns Catholics, in Catholic towns Huguenots, ground their teeth and prayed for right to prevail. Henry himself accepted the Edict as a makeshift, for want of a happier solution; French kings had to become used to enclaves of privilege, and this was only the largest of special situations where the crown had to compromise with local interests. He may have envisaged the crown's remaining neutral: 'We are all French and citizens of the same country.' He appointed Huguenots as ministers and tried to draw the two religions together at court. But in the cold war of texts and lawsuits which followed the settlement, the Most Catholic King could not be entirely indifferent. He had a Jesuit confessor, Père Coton, and extended his favour to that order which was in the van of the Catholic counter-attack all over Europe. By the end of his reign he was listening to sermons at court denouncing the Huguenots.

2 FRENCH SOCIETY: SOME CHARACTERISTICS

The nobility

French society was very far from static during the seventeenth century; conditions varied widely from province to province. The structure of the classes and their relationships were more subtle than is sometimes conveyed by the notion of three strata: upper, middle and lower; nobleman, *bourgeois* and peasant. For these reasons, general statements about 'the nature of society' should be treated with caution; they should nevertheless be attempted if the history of the century is to be understood.

It became Louis XIV's deliberate policy to encourage the *noblesse* to come to court, but even in his reign only a minority were anything more than occasional visitors. At the start of the century the distinction which came later to be drawn between the *noblesse de la cour* and the *noblesse campagnard* would hardly have been understood. Many noblemen of the highest rank kept away from court; the ordinary *seigneur* would only come up to pay his respects to the king upon some great occasion, unless he had some office or were a determined adventurer or hanger-on. The antics of Henry III's circle of personal friends and the casual manners of Henry IV's household did nothing to promote the idea of the court as the apex of society. The first *salon* was founded by Mme de Rambouillet to provide an escape from the court, not in imitation of it.

The *noblesse de l'épée*, the feudal aristocracy of France, had been more successful than their counterparts in England in retaining their privileged status. Even so they were far from being an absolutely closed caste; the highest ranks could be conferred and there were ways of by-passing the genealogical rules which in theory protected the old families from new patents. Nor could anything resist the process by which the rich *bourgeois* bought the estates of impoverished noblemen and the *droits de seigneur* that went with them.

The powers to which the *seigneur* was entitled included *lods et ventes*, a tax of around ten per cent on any land changing hands among their tenants; *redevances en nature*, a percentage tax in kind on all crops raised on *seigneurial* land; the *aveu*, a document exacted from every new tenant, listing his property and the obligations attached to it; *péages*, or tolls on goods passing through their estates; the *corvée*, entitling them to claim the labour of peasants on their domain land for a few days each year; the *banalités*, by which they compelled each tenant to bring his grain and grapes to their mills and wine presses; and varying petty perquisites, such as the rainwater which fell on the manorial roads, or the tongues of all animals killed by their tenants.

The tenants of the big estates were possibly the worst off, where the bailiff was responsible for the collecting of feudal dues; even if he were honest, it was his job to screw as much as possible from the peasantry. The great noble was seldom seen by his tenants. Over the feudal courts, which should have been the hub of lordly justice and protection, where all cases between tenants were heard, or where the lord's own interests were involved, the nobles were forbidden, by the Ordinance of Moulins (1566), to preside. Instead they appointed officials, often second-rate men who could not succeed in the royal courts, whom they underpaid; what should have been the greatest benefit of *seigneurial* rule, became instead its greatest curse. Criminal jurisdiction had largely been removed from the manorial courts but they could still deal with a large number of civil cases. The processes of feudal justice were at this late stage in its development proliferous, chaotic and expensive, involving appeal after appeal.

Some tenants saw their lords and protectors only when they came to hunt. Such occasions were well prepared. Bailiffs saw to it that the tenant had not erected any inconvenient fences or walls which might spoil the sport, thus preventing any of the enclosures which the English gentry, who knew more about farming, were developing enthusiastically. Harvesting before mid-summer was also forbidden, so that the game should be kept feeding in the fields until the hunting season. Sometimes hay crops were ruined, and farmers had to watch the pigeons settling on to their corn while the keepers preened themselves on the excellence of their lofts. Then came the great days when the nobles trampled across the fields, plunging into the thickest crops to drive out the game. An edict of 1669 forbade hunting over land when the corn was in stalk, but at the same time renewed the ban on hunting by all *roturiers*, even on their own land. The prohibition was ineffective, like so much paternalist legislation of the time and did nothing to lessen the odium of the *droit de chasse*.

The peasant might be no better off on a smaller estate where the *seigneur* was resident. Even if the *seigneur* was content to live in rustic simplicity, he would probably have a family to maintain; often large, perhaps not all legitimate. A commission in a regiment, a university education, or, for a girl, a dowry for a place in a convent, the expenses of clothes and servants in an age when some ostentation was expected of every man of rank; these necessities compelled the *seigneur* to make the most of his patrimony. His plight was made worse by the social taboos that stood in the way of a career in trade or law. He might take to soldiering and leave the estate to the bailiffs, but even if he were not disabled by wounds, he must live somewhere between campaigns or after he was forced to retire. The inflation of prices, which had gnawed at the landowners' position throughout the sixteenth century in every country in Western Europe, had its worst effects upon the small landowner. As early as 1569 the Venetian ambassador had written of the *noblesse* 'crippled by debts'. François de la Noue voiced a nostalgia typical of his class of *noblesse campagnard* for the reigns of 'our good kings Louis XII and Francis I', and he was precise about the misfortunes of the nobility: out of ten noble families one would find eight inconvenienced by the alienation of some portion of their property, by mortgage or other forms of debt. Like their contemporaries in Spain where, as the source of inflation, this was worst, and in England, where the effects were less severe but still bad enough to merit consideration as a cause of the Great Rebellion of the 1640's, the rural nobility was a depressed class. Often rents were fixed in cases where the land had been let in perpetuity in the mediaeval years of labour shortage to prevent the land going out of cultivation altogether. The *seigneur* would not often farm the land himself; more than half the land was let out *en métayerie*, the *métayer* being a peasant farmer. The *seigneur* advanced the capital for stock and seed and the peasant worked the land and paid a percentage. This was a precarious income, dependent upon the vagaries of the weather and the probity of the *métayer*. It is not surprising that the landowner pursued his ancillary feudal dues with ingenuity and often with harshness.

Relations between *seigneur* and peasant could be amicable; in some cases there was little to differentiate the farmer who did not, in theory, work, who wore a sword and paid no *taille*, from the peasants among whom he lived; he might have been to the same school, he went to the same church. Some of the larger landowners took their duties seriously. The *Devoirs des Seigneurs*, written by the duc de Luynes and published in 1668, may fairly represent these: he advises the *seigneur* to live economically so that he may have money to spare for charity, to visit the poor and to keep in touch with the peasants' area of outlying estates, to behave modestly and piously. Some followed his advice in practical ways, building sick-houses, paying for a doctor, providing *fêtes*. In Brittany especially, contemporaries commented on the existence of idyllic communities, where the village bell was rung when the *seigneur* was going hunting and the villagers went to the château to join in the sport, or where the whole village joined in feasts and dances. There were other less fortunate places where, as the *jours d'Auvergne* revealed, the *seigneur* could be a gangster and racketeer with impunity. Much of course depended upon the character of the *seigneur*, something perhaps upon that of the *curé*, usually a man of peasant stock himself. There were, however, evils in the system which tended to poison relations between the classes even where the intentions were good. In a society of cash relationships feudal privileges had no sort of *raison d'être* and their existence could only make for bitterness. When, as the century advanced, the state, in the form of the *intendant* and his *subdélégué*, encroached more and more upon his powers (for instance in 1693 he lost his right of appointing the village judge), the position of the *seigneur* became ever more blatantly an anachronism. When, especially in the *pays d'élection*, the peasant paid a heavy *taille* on top of his feudal dues, the exemption of his superior rankled.

At court, even at the start of the century, the lives of its *habitués* was much concerned with etiquette. Competition for precedence was almost as fierce in the rough and tumble of the courts of Henry IV and Louis XIII as it was in the more ordered splendour of Versailles. A *prince du sang* came before a *prince légitimé* (legitimised or illegitimate); the latter class became more numerous as Henry IV's reign proceeded; foreign princes, holding land feudally inside France, but also possessing foreign property, the foreign princes whose outside principalities were not large enough to gain official recognition, dukes, peers, and any others whose titles were derived from their estates followed in order. As it became more obvious that promotion and pensions could only be won at court, nobles came there to offer their services and were drawn into the circle of privilege, while the administrative control of the provinces slipped away from them. They stepped from the restrictive life of the country into a society which bore the hall-marks of crowded and idle isolation; detailed rules of etiquette, secret societies, gossip and scandal, jealousy, quick quarrels upon point of honour, affectations of accent and dress. In a drawl which turned the old French words *paroisse* and *souleil* into *paresse* and *soleil*, they discoursed on the difficulties of obtaining money, on the social pretensions of their creditors, on the distribution of royal favours, on their military exploits in the past and their hopes for the future, on the duels with which they satisfied their tempers and dispelled their boredom. Only in wartime could they be effectively employed, and this was one of the strongest arguments in favour of war as a means of settling the problems of the state.

Life at court did nothing to ease the financial distress of the great nobility, though individuals here and there might have windfalls: gambling profits or an estate or pension for some valuable service to the crown. In the first carefree days of the Regency there were handsome rewards for those fortunate enough to be able to put pressure on Marie de Médicis. Many courtiers seem however to have found themselves financially embarrassed in some degree. They had large households to maintain; the grandest families indeed had miniature courts of their own. Military duties involved them in enormous personal expense, especially those who commanded regiments or fortresses which the government often expected them to equip. Court life meant opulent clothes, expensive lodgings, spectacular entertainment and constant gambling. Princes from the provinces turned beggars, in debt to rich *bourgeois*, just as the value of money was becoming stabilised at last, and the debtor lost the advantage of having the real value of his fixed interest reduced every year. In 1627, a contemporary described them as being 'in the most pitiable condition they have ever been in. Poverty overwhelms them, enforced idleness makes them vicious, oppression has reduced them practically to despair.'

In these circumstances a profitable marriage was often the only way in which a nobleman could put his affairs in order again and avoid the danger of retreat to the country life of the *hobereau*. As the century went on, a *mésalliance* into the family of a creditor became common. Such was the prestige that attached to ancient names that *bourgeois* were often prepared to bid high for the right to become the father-in-law of a nobleman. The proudest families soon accepted *bourgeois* alliances. Mme de Sévigné's grandfather on her mother's side was a wealthy tax farmer; her grandmother on her father's side came from a family of *noblesse de la robe*.

The bourgeoisie

Although French industry and commerce had not developed so rapidly as that of Elizabethan England, the *bourgeoisie* were growing steadily more prosperous. Their usual ambition was to climb in society; the first step was often the acquisition of some official post, a *charge* in the administration or in the law courts. Between 1600 and 1650, it is estimated that about 50,000 new offices had been created to meet this demand; many of them were shared by two or more people. The government was unable to resist the temptation of making quick and easy money by selling new offices; the *bourgeois* came to have a vested interest in the prosperity of the régime. He also invested money in government loans (*rentes*), if he became sufficiently well-to-do he bought an estate; once landed, he might well be within sight of a title. In this manner the capital of the country was diverted from productive use to the sterile enterprises of social advancement.

The best *charges* to be had were in the *parlements*; membership of the Paris *Parlement* carried with it political influence. Fouquet was prepared, in the middle of the century, to pay 150,000 *livres* to become its *procureur général*. The rest were concerned with local justice or municipal government, bodies designed to keep order, like the *milice* of Paris, or the *maréchaussée* of the provinces. Strictly speaking, municipal posts were held by men who had been elected to them, but the government interfered frequently and their nominees rarely lost an election. There were also posts to be bought in the guilds, which the government also took over as it gained control of the municipalities. Almost every place in the royal law-courts had become a *charge* and these became swamped with hungry advocates who had bought themselves in, and now wanted some means of subsistence; inevitably cases were spun out and passed from court to court. In 1620, Louis XIII issued an edict that no new *procureurs* were to be made without his approval; the fact that the number of *procureurs* in the Paris *Parlement* doubled between 1621 and 1629 gives therefore some idea of the pressures to which monarchy was subject.

A *bourgeois*, technically, was an inhabitant of a *bourg*, but not any inhabitant; he enjoyed not only the rights of the citizen which belonged to any person who lived in the town, but special municipal rights as well. To become a *bourgeois*, it was necessary to spend a qualifying period of residence of at least five years; in

Paris a *bourgeois* forfeited his rank if he spent more than five months a year outside the city. The new *bourgeois* usually had to take some oath of allegiance to the city. He was a corporate-minded person in a corporate-minded age. The noble was largely excluded from residence or influence over the town. He regarded it as a privileged and foreign body, exempt from the laws and customs which made him supreme in the countryside, rather than the social and economic centre of the neighbourhood. Occasion-ally some grandee held sway over a town: the duc de Grammont for instance was hereditary mayor of Bayonne. On the whole, however, they affected to despise the town, its inhabitants and their occupations. This division of interests was of service to the crown, for its policies of centralisation could have been thwarted by a common front of the privileged classes in the provinces. The substantial citizen of one of the larger towns often had the best of both worlds. He was exempt from the *taille*, he might have hunting rights in the *banlieue*, the surrounding villages; he enjoyed a fair share of power in a relatively independent community; if he committed an offence he might be tried by a special tribunal. During the century, the government tried to secure some degree of control over the towns, often with little success; everywhere, the elective principle survived, even if it were of little use in practice.

The town was an organised, hierarchical and status-conscious community. It had its own aristocracy of high officers of justice and administration, financiers and members of the *parlement*, if there was one; beneath them, its middle class of merchants and shopkeepers, divided into their own trade *corps*; in Paris for instance there were six of these: drapers, grocers, haberdashers, furriers, hosiers and goldsmiths, all under their own *prévôt des marchands*, who was the senior city magistrate. The bulk of the population would be artisans, who belonged to *corporations*; as *compagnons* of one of these, they enjoyed a recognised legal status. In Paris, by 1673, there were sixty of these. Both *corps* and *corporations* had their elected officers, their own distinctive rules, their own patron saint and their communal Mass. Presiding over the affairs of the whole town was some sort of elected body, the *corps de ville* which varied widely in composition and duties. There was always a mayor, under some name, a body approximat-ing to the English aldermen, and councillors. There was a *procureur du roi* who was the officer of the crown when the council sat as a law court and was also supposed to represent the interests of the citizens when necessary against the council. Beneath him was a *greffier*, a sort of town clerk, a permanent and usually hereditary official. The council of a medium-sized town was not usually idle; such matters as billeting, a dreaded imposition in the days before the provision of proper barracks, local defence, again important for the towns of the frontier province, the care of hospitals and schools, the regulation of local manufacturers and markets, the care of roads and sanitation—the latter not taken very seriously by modern standards—all came within its range.

The peasantry

Peculiar difficulties face the historian who tries to discover the condition of agriculture and the peasantry in the seventeenth century. The lot of the peasant varied from province to province, from estate to estate, from year to year. To the courtier this class of producers and tax payers was the *lie du peuple*, a phrase which sometimes even appears in official correspondence. Most villages, however, had their more affluent peasants: the *fermier*, a tenant-farmer who owned or rented enough land to live comfortably, was superior to the *métayer*, a share-cropper; the most wretched *métayer* counted himself fortunate not to be a *journalier*, a landless labourer. Then there were artisans, cobblers, masons or smiths, inn-keepers, millers, corn-dealers. Some were able to supplement their incomes by home industries such as lace-making or weaving; some had considerate landowners or were able to take advantage of slack bailiffs to poach the lord's streams and woods; many may have bamboozled the tax-collector by a false appearance of poverty and kept their hoards intact. A peasant was especially unfortunate if he lived on an estate that was run as an investment designed by the landowner, often a new one, to provide a good return in rents and dues, or if he lived in a frontier province in wartime, or in one of the *pays d'élection*—the larger part of France—where the *taille* was arbitrarily assessed and ruthlessly exacted.

The 'peasant problem' was not the subject of serious study till the turn of the century, when Boisguillebert and Vauban both incurred disgrace for their analysis and criticism, and no radical remedies were attempted till the time of the *physiocrates* towards the end of the eighteenth century. The life of the court and of the *salons* is so vividly and amply portrayed that it is sometimes difficult to realise that Paris or Versailles was not France, that when Saint-Simon talks about 'all France', he has in mind at most about fifty thousand people. The annals of the poor are less copious, the evidence is inevitably patchy and unreliable; it has to be gleaned from tax-returns, from the incidence of famines and revolts, the relief work of men like Vincent de Paul, from the reports of *intendants* and ministers and, most unsatisfactory of all, from the occasional memoir of travellers like Evelyn or Locke or of native writers. It is tempting to quote the latter and leave the subject with a few impressionistic strokes: Mme de Sévigné's account of the peasant who arrived with heavy bags of what turned out to be worthless coin, or La Bruyère's of the peasants scrabbling like animals in the fields. But even at the risk of being misleading it is worth trying to establish some reasons for the facts: one, that French agriculture was backward, not only in relation to conditions across the Channel or in Holland, but also by comparison with current developments in manufactures during the period; two, that the condition of the bulk of the peasantry was a degraded one, which if anything grew worse during the century.

The land was divided into small holdings. The nobility possessed more than half in the west, about a third in Burgundy, in some provinces, such as Dauphiné, no more than a tenth. This domain was often largely woodland, or reserved for *la chasse*; most of the rest was let off in small lots. The peasants, apart from the land which they thus rented, also owned a remarkably larger amount, from a fifth in Brittany to a half in Languedoc. A high proportion of the land was uncultivated, because of shallow soil, or bad drainage or the need for common grazing land (in places war was a cause, as in those parts of Burgundy where the peasant proprietor disappeared and whole villages were depopulated). The rest was farmed on the strip system, with fields lying fallow for one or sometimes even two years out of three. Small holdings meant lack of capital for improvements, so ploughs remained wooden and crude, and the soil was poorly manured for want of cattle. Because of the almost entire absence of root crops, such as the turnip, stock was usually killed off in the winter and there was therefore no chance of improvement of the herd by selective breeding. There were few sheep, despite the complaints of drapers, and few horses. Wheat was considered a luxury product and most peasants grew rye, maize or, in the Limousin, a form of buckwheat that was too coarse to be made into bread but was used in oatcakes, or in a sort of porridge, more suitable for horses. The potato, which gives high bulk and protein returns for a small area of land, the peasant refused to cultivate.

Few attempts were made to specialise. Bad communications and the crippling effect of local customs barriers made it necessary for each province to be self-supporting. In some years, peasants might be starving in one province while grain stores went bad in a neighbouring province which had been more fortunate in its weather. In Louis XIV's reign efforts were still being made to grow vines in the north of France, where the climate, similar to that of England, was unsuitable, because of the expense of transporting wine from Burgundy and Bordeaux. Often the crown officials would order peasants to divide their already small acreage into three, one to lie fallow, one for corn and the third for hay, so as to ensure a balanced production. A few enlightened men appreciated that the private landowner could do more than the state to increase the productivity of the land. Henry IV's attempts to interest the nobility in the cultivation of their estates met with little response. One of the most important differences between England and France at this time can be seen in the reluctance of the French *noblesse* to reside on their estates and to concern themselves with the practical and profitable business of farming. The depredations and nuisances of hunting, the pressure of feudal dues were enough alone to account for the stagnation of farming; on top of these, however, the peasant had to endure a system of taxation which might have been especially designed to impoverish the land.

Taxation

The chief direct tax in France was the *taille*. As a permanent tax this had been established in 1439. At the beginning of the sixteenth century it yielded some 3 million *livres*; by 1640 more than 40 million. There were two types: the *taille personelle*, which was estimated on the wealth of the person, and the *taille réelle*, on the value of his property. The latter, obviously a fairer and more stable system in the absence of any proper bureaucratic machinery for assessing income, was to be found only in the *pays d'état*, provinces such as Brittany and Languedoc, where the estates still had some say in the annual tax estimates. In the *pays d'élection* however the *taille* was fixed arbitrarily by the central government.

No accounts were published, nor indication given of the method by which the sum was decided; inevitably, the *taille* was increased with every emergency. At the one end of the process, the figure decided would probably be the government's estimate of what the province could bear without revolt; *surintendant* or *contrôleur général* would be subject to a number of pressures from interested parties, landowners for instance who feared a fall in rents from over-taxed peasants. In turn the *intendant* or his equivalent in the *généralité* was lobbied by local parties while he tried to decide how to divide the total between the *élections*; the least influential *élection* might receive an unfair amount, so might the poorest village. At the other end of the process was the unfortunate *élu*, the man chosen annually by the village to raise the money. He had to be both honest and brave if he were to do his duty fairly; if he were desperate he had the right to call for troops to be billetted on defaulters' houses, to distrain their goods. If he failed to collect the required total, he had to pay himself or go to gaol during the government's pleasure. The intrinsic unfairness of this system, the scope that it gave to bribery and favouritism and the positive discouragement to enterprising agriculture were unhappy features of this tax. Add the exemptions of the wealthiest citizens, the nobility, the church, large numbers of office-holders and other bourgeois, and the disastrous picture is complete. It is not surprising that it was the peasant's dream to save enough, not to improve his land but to buy some snug office that carried with it exemption from the *taille*; nor that the government was forced, as early as 1646, to decree that any peasant settling in a town must pay *taille* in his former village for the next ten years.

An argument in favour of direct taxation is that it can be scaled to the varying wealth of those who pay it. In this period the indirect taxes were more equitable since, at least in theory, they fell upon all; in practice however they fell almost entirely upon the Third Estate, since the nobility and clergy had gained exemption in the fifteenth century for the products of their demesne lands. The *gabelle* was not really an indirect tax anyway, since the consumer of salt was not free to take the quantity he pleased. Salt was needed by everybody, especially for preserving fish and meat. An extra payment was made on this and all other eating salt; any other salt, designed for purposes such as tanning, was carefully poisoned. There were extraordinary variations in the amount of duty paid. Those living in the *pays de grande gabelle*, which roughly extended from Normandy and Picardy in the north to Touraine in the west and Burgundy in the east, had to pay twenty-five times as much for their salt as those in the areas exempted altogether, down the west coast, while other areas paid the *petite gabelle*. Of course there was smuggling, and this became a major preoccupation of local officials. Decrees such as that condemning to death any dog caught carrying salt were naturally ineffective, and the government was from time to time driven to order people to make compulsory purchases at the full price. To collect the tax *regratteurs* were employed, who bought the salt off the government in Tours coinage and were empowered to demand the equivalent in Paris coinage, worth 25 per cent more, when they resold it. In 1641, the income of the French government from salt alone was 20 million *livres*, which was twice the total average annual income of Charles I of England between 1631 and 1641.

The *aides*, the other important indirect tax, levied on drink, again had some features which would be condemned by the modern economist. It embraced the whole process of production and distribution, from the grape to the innkeeper. For its collection a small army of functionaries was required. It lent itself to fraud and inefficiency of every sort. It was controlled by the *cour des aides* in Paris. Its exactions were not exempt from the law of diminishing returns: wine was surprisingly expensive in France in the seventeenth century, and drinking was not heavy among the poorer classes. Transport costs and customs—the *douane* which might be levied on the border of town, province and even *seigneurie*—were responsible for huge differences of price; between distant provinces, the cost of the internal movement of produce could be as much as four times the saleable value of the commodity.

Projects of reform

Men were ready by Henry IV's time to abandon their local rivalries and religious enthusiasms, and accept the rule of a compromise king, because they wanted peace and the assistance of the royal government. Bridges were broken, roads dangerous, bands of peasants out everywhere, with different names in different areas, *gautiers* maybe or *croquants*, but all with the same idea, to earn by pillage the living which they could not make by agriculture, and to fight for themselves instead of for the local nobility. Trade stagnated. Without a home market, the silk-masters at Tours dropped from 800 to 200, while in Paris the dye industry declined by five-sixths during the Wars of Religion. In these circumstances foreign trade was needed, but there was no fleet to protect merchant ships from the attacks of Barbary or English pirates. Building a merchant fleet was thus not worth while, and the French lagged far behind the Spanish, the Dutch and the English, giving their Atlantic rivals a lead which they did not recover. In 1635, Admiral Sir John Pennington, in command of the first Ship Money fleet in the Channel, recorded in his diary that he had met 60 Dutch ships sailing from La Rochelle, laden with French salt.

All this Henry was expected to put right. It was an age when government interference in the economic affairs of the country was expected. The doctrines of mercantilism, which were treated and enforced as a body by Colbert, were already under discussion individually in Henry's reign, and men approached economic problems in a mercantilist frame of mind. They wanted unity, the central control that made this possible, and the national power and prosperity which it would bring. The phrase 'political economy' is said to have been coined by Montchrétien in the *Treatise of Political Economy* which he wrote in 1615.

Montchrétien, a Norman, was born in 1575 and killed during a Huguenot rising in 1621. He became rich by marriage to a wealthy widow. It was not of her but of France, however, that he wrote in his *Treatise of Political Economy* (1615): 'Gold is shining on her clothes, brilliants in her hair, pearls on her neck, diamonds on her fingers, and everyone, attracted from afar by this luxurious magnificence, comes to make love to her and attempts, while caressing her, to rob her of something.' He urged France to build ships, to recover her Turkish markets, to drive the decadent Spanish out of her American colonies, to fish for her own herrings instead of buying them off the Dutch. There were 600 French ships employed catching cod off Newfoundland. Why could not the same number catch herrings in the North Sea? France was the richest nation in western Europe, best placed geographically. She could carry all before her overseas, if only she would spend the money on ships instead of silk stockings, and if only her people would work. For the idle, he advocated workhouses.

Barthélemy Laffemas (1545-1612) was an influential figure at court. Like many who stayed with Henry when he became King of France, he started in the court of Navarre, where, after holding the position of court tailor for a time, he was given financial duties. Many of his schemes were disastrous, for he was ahead of his times, and made experiments in credit when the general confidence on which credit relies was lacking. But his mind bulged with theories, and he pushed them forward so insistently that Henry allowed him to preside over an 'Assembly of Commerce', which contained seventeen of the most prominent economic pundits at court, held 176 sessions between 1602 and 1604, and aired the ideas of Laffemas himself and the more moderate ones of the Assembly of Notables, which had been discussing the same problems in 1597. Laffemas believed that new industries must be encouraged at all costs, by protecting them against foreign competition, by giving them monopolies at home, by letting raw materials into the country duty free, and by learning new techniques from foreigners, who should be encouraged to work in France with a school of French apprentices. So, later, Richelieu was to send Jean du Chastelet to Hungary to learn mining techniques, and put him in charge of all mining research when he returned. So too, an expert from Milan under Henry IV had the monopoly of making gold and silver thread, but in return for this he promised that half his apprentices should be French. Laffemas also wanted the taxes on all home-produced goods to be dropped, or, as was eventually achieved, to be simplified into one fixed tax on all of them, instead of an accumulation of duties imposed in different areas at different dates, for the benefits of private nobles as well as for the state. 'Simplify and centralise' was his theme. He urged uniform weights and measures, and a system of guilds to cover the whole country.

In 1597 an edict was produced, on the lines of an earlier and less effective one of 1581, which laid down the rules to be observed by all craftsmen. In theory this edict was a liberal one, because, it put new crafts on the same footing as the old ones, whose masters had kept the upstarts in an inferior position by preventing them from starting a guild at all. But what the edict really did was to extend restrictive practices, for the guild rules which the newer crafts now adopted prevented men from becoming 'Masters' of their trade until they had completed their *chef d'œuvre*, which they could not do until they had served a long period of apprenticeship, and made payments of a size big enough to keep out the poor.

If the spread of the guilds proved restrictive, it also provided the government with an extremely important weapon for controlling the industrial life of the country. The Bourbons rapidly gained control over the guilds. *Intendants* worked with guild officials, who were themselves often indirectly royal nominees, since most of them were municipal authorities whose elections were managed by the crown. All cases connected with guilds were tried, in accordance with Roman Law, by royal courts. Special crown officials were appointed in 1626 to supervise particular industries. There was one in each *bailliage* where iron was produced, to inspect its quality and to stamp it 'D' for *doux*—good quality—and 'A' for *aigue*. With the aid of town councils, the government steadily extended its control over prices and methods of manufacturing. An edict of 1571, for instance, fixed the price of every kind of cloth throughout the realm.

Through the guilds, the Bourbons pursued a policy of keeping down the buoyant capitalists, who were giving their Stuart contemporaries such troubles. They limited the number of apprentices to be employed, and saw to it that the apprentices were fairly treated. In England the apprentices were rioting, in France it was the masters who protested, an interesting commentary on the enforcement of apprenticeship Statutes in the two countries. They kept the different crafts separate, and prevented the same man from making his own cloth and dyeing it. They fixed the maximum size of looms and the maximum hours of work. Admittedly, they allowed masters to pay their workers very small wages, by following a policy of fixed wages regardless of prices. But this had the effect of encouraging journeymen to become masters as soon as they could, even if it meant borrowing money. A large majority of industrial workers were masters and apprentices, only a minority wage-workers; of these, most could look forward to becoming masters themselves. Inspectors could keep a check on the masters because of the system of written contracts between master and apprentice which prevailed in France.

Some industries were royal monopolies. Roman Law held that the rulers of the land were the owners of the minerals in it. This was extended in France to gunpowder, to the mines, and to salt. Sully, as Master of Artillery from 1599 until 1610, watched over the production of gunpowder, which was in the hands of royal contractors, who handed out the capital they obtained from government officials to private individuals. Each of these produced what gunpowder he could from the saltpetre earth he had found for himself, and handed it in to the contractors. Nobody made a fortune out of this operation, but the crown got plenty of gunpowder. The mines were organised by three important edicts in Henry IV's reign, those of 1597, 1601 and 1604, which strengthened the national administration of them already in existence under the Valois; soon there were at least thirty-seven officials in charge of this one department. Neither Henry nor Laffemas showed much interest in coal or iron, which were dug for locally by groups of peasants. Henry, indeed, taxed blacksmiths and insisted on a royal licence for every new forge. But France was rich in other minerals, with gold, silver and copper on the slopes of the Pyrenees, lead in the Cevennes, silver at Carcassonne, precious stones in Foix, and silver and tin in Normandy. These were taxed at source, the crown taking the royalties to which it was entitled by Roman Law. Their production was encouraged by allowing the workers exemption from the *taille*, and efforts were made to start the nobles mining on their own land. Mining was declared not to be a disqualification from nobility; but example is more potent than legislation in the world of fashion, and the great nobles would not give a lead. If they had, the French Revolution might have been controlled, and not merely started, by the aristocracy. As it was, the government was more worried about getting enough out of the mines than about preventing other people from making too much money out of them. With salt, however, the problem was over-production. Sully was so anxious to keep smuggling down by keeping output down that he gave money to owners of salt marshes to persuade them to keep their production to a given maximum, and also encouraged its export. Salt was the supreme example of the government's exploitation of its rights over minerals. There were salt houses in all towns, and in some villages, where it had to be stored. There was a large staff for collecting it, for supervising the collectors and for preventing smuggling. There was enough money to be raised from both salt and gunpowder to pay for a large administrative staff and to leave a profit over.

In England, the money made out of church land, the great trading companies, the mines, the cloth industry and piracy went into the pockets of the aristocracy, and the middle classes, already in control of local government, determined to keep clear of crown interference. Guild rules were never applied to new industries, and the old ones were fast freeing themselves from them. They asked for crown help, but refused to submit to crown control. But, while the Elizabethans had been speculating and accumulating, in France the church clung to its land. The Wars of Religion had kept the nobles busy and had drained the money from their pockets; when they were over, etiquette forbade them to enter trade and the military leadership needed in a country with such a long land frontier kept their attentions on unprofitable matters. The nobles, or some of them, were the only people strong enough to stop the crown from extending its economic powers, to qualify the mercantilist ideas which were emerging, and to prevent the spread of a crown-controlled bureaucracy. In France, they had not acquired the wealth or the interest to play this part.

Modern times have proved one of Marx's theses correct. In economics, the good big concern will always defeat the good little one. So the policy of keeping industrial undertakings small, while helping the crown politically, damaged the industry of the country. There were also many in Henry IV's reign who were not anxious to see industries developing at all. There was a fierce struggle between the new silk-producers at Tours and the city of Lyon. Lyon relied for much of its wealth on trade up the Rhône valley from the Mediterranean. It held seven fairs a year, and extracted tolls on all goods passing through. Laffemas, to protect the silkworms of Tours, persuaded Henry, in 1599, to forbid the import of foreign silk. Eventually the Lyon merchants were too strong for him, and the edict was repealed. They had found an ally in Sully, who was a steady opponent of the silkworm. He regarded it as a rival to corn and the vine, and as a soft luxury. He insisted that any expenses incurred in starting it should be paid for by an increase in the *taille*. Being a fierce guardian of the pennies, he allowed little capital to be spent on this or any new ventures.

Sully

The Huguenot nobleman, Maximilien de Béthune, marquis de Rosny and later duc de Sully, was the most important of Henry IV's advisers; he was interested in every side of France's economy except the development of industry. Like Laffemas, he had been a figure at the court of Navarre, but he was rather more than a bursar. He had won the king's friendship as a soldier; at the battle of Coutras, in command of the royal artillery, he handled his cannons with much resource. At Ivry he was wounded in the calf by a lance, on the head and the hand by a sword, and in the hip and the thigh by musket balls. He was, not surprisingly, considered to be dying as he was taken from the field. But he was in action again next year, fit enough to receive, and survive, a bullet which entered his mouth and emerged at the back of his neck, a wound which, as a biographer put it 'caused him all his life painful inconveniences'. He emerged from these experiences somewhat soured. Although unquestioningly loyal to Henry, and a man who loved his work, he had all the weaknesses of complete self-confidence; he respected no man, was rude and obstinate. Although seven years younger than Henry, he talked to him like a grizzled grandfather. He was so disliked by his fellow-councillors that they all turned on him as soon as Henry died, and had him ousted from office, so that he retired to live on for thirty years in splendour, and to complicate history by writing his own version of it.

The extent of his influence is uncertain. Henry had ideas of his own on almost every subject, and took counsel from many others besides Sully. He was made a Councillor in 1596, was put in charge of fortifications and communications in 1597, and became *surintendant des finances* in 1599. But in 1600 the Venetian ambassador could still write: 'The chancellor [Pomponne de Bellièvre] and Villeroi do everything, and M. de Rosny looks for and finds the money, and for that is much disliked.' Sully and Bellièvre were old enemies and Bellièvre attempted to obtain more control for the Council over the administration. For this he was eventually disgraced, and from about 1604 onwards, Sully appears to have been able to by-pass the Council when he could not control it. But Henry remained the active king. He and Sully thought very much alike on most topics, but they disagreed over industrial development, and Henry ignored Sully's advice. Not only did he give Laffemas many chances to experiment, but he set up in the grand gallery of the Louvre a school for fine arts and industrial experiment, exempting its workers from the guild rules, lending them money, and urging them to pass on their discoveries to pupils. There worked de la Garde, clockmaker, sculptor and jeweller, Roussel, who made scent, Varronier the cutler, Raulin, who designed mathematical instruments. None of this was Sully's work. Henry had started a Bourbon tradition, their patronage of the arts.

Both Henry and Sully were enthusiastic for agricultural

improvements. While he was still fighting for his throne, Henry had looked after the interests of the peasants. He billeted his troops in towns and not in villages, he forbade nobles to force men to join their armies, or to obtain money by taking peasants for forced labour and then holding them to ransom. He tried to stop nobles from riding across corn between March 1st and harvest time, and promised compensation to peasants who had had cattle driven off. Later, he and Sully set about getting some of France's marshland drained. Humphrey Bradley was brought in from Bergen-op-Zoom, and undertook to drain land, in exchange for half the land thus rendered fit for cultivation, with the assistance of its owners, who were to keep the other half. Henry hoped to open their eyes to the chances of wealth available, but he was disappointed. Only in the days of Richelieu did the duc de Ventadour, the enterprising founder of the Company of the Holy Sacrament, give a lead which a few others followed. Until then, foreign capital was used. The biggest operations went on in Bordeaux, and met with guerilla opposition from fishermen and reed-slashers.

An edict of 1597, a busy legislative year, revived the forest rules, which had ceased to be effective during the wars. A licence was now needed to fell trees, and particular ones were to be marked for preservation. The wolf-trappers had to report their successes to a forest official every three months.

Free trade in corn was one of the ways in which Sully hoped to stimulate agriculture. As long as the harvest was good, export was encouraged, and, although it was forbidden in bad years, prices should then be high enough to ensure a living for the farmers. Unfortunately, bad roads and high customs duties prevented the ready circulation of corn. Sully was well aware of this problem, and embarked on an ambitious canal scheme, to join the Saône to the Loire, the Loire to the Seine, and the Seine to the Meuse, thus linking the Mediterranean, the Atlantic and the Channel coasts of France by internal navigation. By 1610, seven of the nine leagues between the Seine and the Loire had been covered by the Briare canal. When Sully was dismissed, the work was stopped, to be finished only in 1642. The canal joining the Saône and the Loire was not completed until 1793. In this sphere, Sully's interests and ambitions were more enlightened than those of his contemporaries. He also worked to improve the roads, obtaining labour by starting the royal *corvée* which extended the feudal custom of forced labour to a national scale. Peasants found themselves planting trees, designed partly, as now, to shade the traveller, but also to mark the limits of the road, whose surface was not always easily distinguishable from the surrounding countryside. The trees became symbols of hated work, and, after the duc de Biron had been executed, were often savagely lopped with the comment: 'There's a Rosny. Let's make it a Biron.' But, for all Sully's work, we still read of merchants making a detour of up to a hundred miles because a road was impassable. The practice of mercantilism would fall far short of its theories in these circumstances, however determined the ruler. It was difficult to treat France as a single economic unit.

A book published in 1600 became fashionable at court for a time, the *Théâtre d'Agriculture et Mesnage des Champs*, by Olivier de Serres, a Huguenot country gentleman, who lived a peaceful life on his estates. It was the work of a domesticated farmer, one of the eight parts being devoted to gardens. It showed how different crops affected the land in which they were grown, and, full of practical advice, should have been the forerunner of a system of rotation without waste. Henry IV read it for half an hour after dinner every day for four months. It may have acted as a soporific, but it caught the fashion, and was in circulation until the reign of Louis XIV, when it vanished, to be hailed as a re-discovery shortly after Louis XVI came to the throne. But it was a book for theorists only; Henry and Sully never managed to persuade men of rank and money to stay on the land. Even the *bourgeoisie*, who had taken over the lands of nobles bankrupted during the wars, lived in the towns, and treated their lands as social rather than financial assets. Taxation relief was the only way to break the conservative, hand-to-mouth life on the land, and that was what Sully would not consider. It was unfortunate that the minister and the king most interested in farming were more interested still in making money.

'As soon as you speak to him of money, all other reasoning ceases,' remarked the Venetian ambassador of Sully. Although he realised in theory that the wealth of the crown was synonymous with the prosperity of the nation, he could never bring himself to part with temporary profit for the sake of lasting gain. He was a masterly financier. He increased Henry's annual revenue from 27 to 60 million *livres*. He reduced the crown debt from 300 to 196 million *livres*. He left a reserve of about 20 million *livres*, and an armoury and a fleet equipped for a war against the Hapsburgs; all this despite the fact that, in the year before he took over, expenditure far exceeded income. He made good use of the years of peace which Henry provided during his term of office.

Much of this was achieved by close accountancy and hard work. He produced, for the first time in French history, an estimated account in which defined expenditures were balanced by income from a specified source. He improved collection by cutting out all the links in the tax-farming chain, and making every farmer pay directly to the crown. A tax-farmer had to hand over his accounts to his successor, who was held liable for any previous malpractices, and so took good care to spot them before he started his duties. A special court was set up in 1601 to deal with such offenders, and those who had done so well for themselves during the wars only avoided appearing before it by lending the king money at a low rate of interest. Those who had obtained the farm of crown land had it taken away from them, but much of it proved irrecoverable, as the farmers had pawned the land. Those who had obtained noble privileges between 1578 and 1598 had to pay for them again since it was alleged that the crown had not been 'in its right mind' during this period. Men who had lent money to the government were divided into two classes: those who had failed to see that the documents covering the transaction had been drawn up legally lost their money. For the others, Sully had a scheme, in 1605, to pay off arrears of interest out of a special fund, so as to keep the encumbrance off his budget. But the *rentiers*, thoroughly suspicious by now, thought that was the first step towards ignoring all past debts. Henry told Sully to drop it, so that, in 1611, Sully was still paying the interest for the year 1600.

Sully was a man for ever gazing into a kaleidoscope. He shook it, and the pattern under the glass altered, but the pieces of coloured paper were still the same. He thought that he could solve the problems of the nation's finances without using any new taxes. His only innovation, the *paulette*, was a disaster. But he was successful in almost all that he was called upon to do, and he managed to camouflage, though not to remove, the need for more radical adjustments. His parsimony assumes the look of statesmanship when it is set against the contemporary longing for extravagance that found expression in the cornucopia courts of Philip III of Spain and James I of England.

The crown

'The greatest of all evils is civil war. The evil to be feared from a fool who succeeds by right of birth is not as considerable nor as certain.' Few of Pascal's contemporaries would have disagreed with his view of the necessity of strong authority vested in a hereditary king. Royalist sentiment was not usually however expressed in such negative terms. Archbishop Embrun, an ambassador at the court of Madrid, observed that the 'Spanish love their state more than their rulers, while the French love their sovereign personally'. This intimacy of loyalty was as old as the family of Capet, the long dynasty of protectors. The king was the head of the family of his people, and he was expected to be a familiar figure. There had been an outcry when, in the sixteenth century, the customary prefix of Majesty had been introduced: 'what are these mimicries, these idolatries, these barbarous fashions?' The king stood also for continuity: 'In France the king does not die' was the characteristic formula of the jurists. When the king did actually leave the mortal scene, the Chancellor of France, personifying his authority, did not go into mourning. Finally, he represented the unity of the nation. In the age between the passing of feudal society, with its personal and contractual notions of allegiance, and the growth of a conception of national sovereignty, awareness of the *patrie* was a vague sentiment rather than a compelling force. In the absence of any visible organic unity, only the person of the king truly unified France. The eighteenth century Jacobin might say, after the execution of Louis XVI, as the philosophers had been urging for some time, that he was only a man after all. He was only a man—but the people had wept for joy at his coronation at Reims, the oil from the sacred phial of Clovis damp upon his head. He had been the rallying point for twenty millions and the vacuum that he left behind has never since been satisfactorily filled.

The experiences of the civil wars during the last embarrasssed years of the Valois kings focussed attention upon the nature of kingship. The country had come near to disintegration when other loyalties overrode the political loyalty of subject to king, local allegiance to feudal *seigneur*, or confessional loyalty to one of the rival creeds of Catholic and Calvinist. Calvin himself, in 1540, had told a young woman who was contemplating emigration to Geneva: 'we should prefer to our country any part of the world where God is adored in purity'. In 1593, the extremists of the League spoke in similar sense: 'if the king is a devout Catholic and sent by God, it is a matter of indifference to us to which nation he belongs. We are not concerned with the nation but with religion.' A natural consequence of these higher loyalties was the spread of ideas about the deposition of unjust sovereigns, elective monarchy, even tyrannicide. That these ideas were potent was very plain to the age which witnessed the assassination of two successive kings of France by religious fanatics.

A reaction was inevitable. In 1595 Gérard François, Henry IV's doctor, defined the position of many people of his condition: 'as by God's will I was born a true *François* both in name and nationality, and consequently a very humble servant of their Majesties and very devoted to the welfare of my country . . . in compassion for her plight, I could do no less than offer her all the help that every well-born child naturally owes to his mother'. Chancellor de Thou recalled later the patriotism to which he had been brought up: 'I brought this state of mind to the administration of affairs, being of the opinion of the ancients, that one's country is a second divinity, that laws come from God and that those who violate them are sacrilegious parricides.' The *politiques*, who undertook to consider only the political aspect of the wars, are represented by Pithou in the *Satire Ménippée*: 'we want a king so that we may have peace, but we do not want to imitate the frogs. We want a natural, not an artificial king, already made and not still to be made. In this matter we do not wish to take the advice of the Spaniards, who are our inveterate enemies and who wish to tutor us by force. . . . The king we ask for has already been made by nature. He was born in the real garden of the flowers of France, a straight green shoot from the stem of St. Louis. Those who speak of making another are mistaken. We can make dozens of Marshals and Peers, but not a king. He alone must be born of himself.'

Lawyers had long been in the forefront of patriotic awareness, since they were schooled in the use of political abstractions and in a special view of sovereignty. The Roman law was exacting with regard to civic duties and exalted in its view of the ruler's prerogative. Since the time of Philip the Fair, lawyers had been the natural allies of the crown against the pretensions of the

Papacy. The interference of Rome in the Religious Wars revived the old Gallican arguments in a fury that derived as much from nationalist feeling as from jurisdictional jealousies. When the Pope released Frenchmen from their loyalty to a Huguenot king, two bishops even declared that the Bulls had no power over them, as they came from foreigners who were enemies of France. When Henry IV was excommunicated, the magistrates declared the Bulls to be 'worthless, damnable, full of sacrilege and imposture'. It did not need the king to become Catholic to secure the allegiance of the mass of the *bourgeois*, who saw in hereditary monarchy the surest defence of property and order; but his action quieted the conscience of the clergy and won the fanatic people of Paris, secured the loyalty of the mass of the population and exposed the Huguenot minority as reluctant rebels.

'The king of France is Emperor in his realm': this lawyers' formula is older than the sixteenth century. It served once to stress that the Holy Roman Emperor had no sway in France, but it had come by the start of the seventeenth century to be a fair definition of the nature of royal power. He enjoyed *pleine puissance*. He was the sole proprietary of the land of France, though it was left to Louis XIV to amplify this in full ownership of goods, as well as of land. He was almost free from any obligations to the Estates, and he was the supreme financial authority, though it was not yet accepted that he could of his own accord raise permanent taxes. He was the highest judicial authority; the only source of the law, which is always administered in his name. He was the living law; in lawyers' old French: '*si veult le roi, si veult la loi*'. 'He held direct from God', in the words of a *Parlement* of 1489. Divine Right was to be interpreted with different emphases by the theorists of church and state, and there was disagreement about the power that this gave him over the church. But that he was absolute in all matters which did not affect the Pope was conceded by the majority.

The claims made on behalf of the king were imposing, although they had not yet received their highest embellishment. The sentiment which royalty attracted was a potent force. If theory and sentiment were to be transformed into a real and received authority, the crown had to find means of establishing its sovereignty, at the centre first, then in the provinces. This process, the creation of an administrative monarchy, was to be the work of the century.

To the question, 'What, at the start of Henry IV's reign, was the government?' there could be only one answer: 'The king.' The institutions which are, to the modern mind, inseparable from the term government, scarcely existed. Government was personal, and its arrangements were haphazard to an extraordinary degree. This is why, as the conspicuous failure of the later Valois had emphasised, so much depended upon the personal qualities of the king, and why men so feared the accession of a minor to the throne. In a Minority those who could helped themselves to the proceeds of a government which was not sufficiently mature to enjoy immunity from political upheavals. The word administration has today a meaning of its own: it is the machinery of government. But to the Frenchman of 1589, the word did not stand on its own. He might talk of the administration of justice, or of finance, but the word by itself was meaningless, since the forms that it now stands for did not exist. The king, it was understood, rendered justice, raised taxes and, when order was gravely upset, established order. He did not have full control over either the armed services or over civil government, for these were both private worlds of privilege and immunity. Since public order and the preservation of the frontiers were largely in the hands of the one, and the raising of revenue and the administration of justice in the hands of the other, it will be plain that the king was not truly master in his own house.

The councils and ministers

Henry IV's government was in every sense personal. The traditional phrase *pour le roi en son conseil* was not just a polite legal fiction, for commands issued in the king's name were the only effective political authority in the land. Even when Richelieu's dominating position in Louis XIII's reign gave him a certain independence of action, his requests to the other ministers and secretaries were always made in the name of the king. The sovereign courts waited for a letter from the king before they would execute a minister's order. In times of severe crisis, only the king's presence would do. Louis XIII was frequently compelled to go out into the provinces to quell disturbances or to coerce an obstinate *parlement*.

The king was aided by *ministres d'état*, whom he convoked when and how he pleased; these formed the *conseil d'affaires*. He might also hear the advice of others who received by *brevet* the title of *conseilleurs du roi en ses conseils*. When these met, the Council was entitled the *conseil d'état et des finances*, or the *conseil d'en haut*. The arrangements were haphazard and the king always took the initiative, at least in form. The council was hardly, at the beginning of the century, an institution, though by usage it was growing into one. There was no regular council room or time of sitting. It might meet in the king's *chambre de travail*; or a group of ministers, meeting together, might consider themselves *en conseil*. But these ministers did not possess delegated powers as did those of Louis XIV, merely rights which allowed them to act in a way that was conditioned by their own ability and the favour of the king. During the Minority, Marie de Médicis opened up the council to include *princes du sang* and grandees who were impatient of the ways of Henry IV's old ministers. But an inner group survived, since the more important business was usually prepared and decided upon beforehand. In 1616 Condé demanded, and obtained, titular recognition as head of the Council while, after the murder of Concini, Louis resolved to rule by himself. After 1624, until 1642, the prevailing influence was that of Richelieu; under his management slightly more regularity appears in proceedings, because he deliberately fostered a group of loyal supporters who worked in his interests.

At the heart of the business of government, even at the start of the century, there were always a few who might be called professionals, with family traditions of service to the crown. For instance the Loménie family produced *secrétaires d'état* under Henry IV, Louis XIII and Louis XIV; a forebear had been a secretary to Charles IX and killed in the massacre of Saint Bartholomew. The Neuville family was another whose members had served the Valois kings; Nicholas de Neuville, better known from his title as Villeroi, added prestige to the secretaries' office through his favour with Henry IV. These offices were not hereditary, since the crown held the reversion, but bureaucrats' fortunes were frequently invested in the continuity of high office. Government papers were also private papers; an incoming secretary might be unable to lay his hands on vital documents which his predecessor had filed away in his family archives.

Villeroi was perhaps the first of the secretaries to bear any resemblance to the later specialised and authoritative *secrétaires d'état*. As late as 1588 a *règlement* (one of a series of statements of the powers and functions of the king's servants) depicted the secretary as a confidential clerk, like his equivalent in Philip II's Spain. But it was inevitable that the extension of the king's authority should be accompanied by a development of the scope and authority of those who enjoyed his confidence. Along with the *surintendant des finances*, the *secrétaire d'état* is the key figure in the rise of absolute monarchy. His importance came from his central position between the provincial officials and the king. The four secretaries shared the *secret*, taking in turns of a month the duty, which this phrase implies, of signing the royal acts. They reported every day to the king with the despatches of their departments. After the tradition established by the Valois kings they divided responsibility for the provinces between them; the *règlement* of Henry III reserved the right to rotate these departments every year, a measure designed to prevent the establishment of dangerous blocs of political interest. Even after the growth of specialisation, notably in war and foreign affairs, this system persisted. It has a clumsy look of decentralisation to modern eyes; it seems to be a half-way house between feudal France, controlled by the king by separate treatment of individual provinces, and modern centralised government. It reflects the problems of the crown at a time when there was no machinery of central government in the provinces, and when the royal will was expressed by letter; it was government by courier. It had practical disadvantages. If an army crossed from one province to another, it was the duty of the secretaries to decide who should convey the king's orders to the commanding officers. Troops in the field, in Richelieu's day, came under the authority of the secretary for war; but garrison troops were under the authority of whichever secretary controlled the province they occupied. Against this, however, must be set an important advantage. When the secretary, attended council meetings, he was not a mere reporter or recorder; he could speak from first-hand knowledge of the conditions in the provinces. At a time when accurate knowledge of the conditions of the people was of prime importance in government, in the assessment of taxation for example, the secretary's contact with provincial governors, churchmen and officials of all sorts was the crucial factor in his rise to independent responsibility. By the end of Richelieu's régime this was an accomplished fact, though one that has been obscured by the traditional interpretation of Richelieu as dictator and master-administrator. Chavigny, his confidant and supporter, whose prime task was to represent his interests with the king, can be described as a foreign secretary; he prepared the despatches to ambassadors abroad, and received and informed foreign ambassadors at home; in this department the boundaries of action were fixed by the end of Louis XIII's reign. Sublet de Noyers, in the same period, is recognisable as a war minister, specialising in army affairs and working towards the establishment of royal authority over the complex of private rights and duties that opposed it. Noyers and Chavigny had constant access to the *conseil d'en haut*. They attended as experts; they were establishing the rights and traditions of a department. They were able to insist that all royal correspondence passed through their hands, and they were informed of everything.

Throughout this period, however, the key figure was that of the *surintendant*, of whom there were usually two. Their work as supervisors of the finances, 'the nerves of war', brought them into constant contact, not only with king or cardinal, but with the secretaries, whose work depended upon the money that they could provide. In Henry IV's reign the constructive work of Sully showed what powers a *surintendant* could wield; there was no such pre-eminent figure again until Colbert, who absorbed the role in his capacity as *contrôleur général*. The *surintendant* had only supervisory control over the finances; he was responsible only to the king, and to his conscience, for the way in which he treated with the private agents, *traitants*, who managed the actual collection of the taxes. He was responsible, with the Chancellor, for the liaison with the sovereign courts whose privilege it was to register edicts. He watched over the monetary policy of the Mint. He planned new ways of raising revenues, the creation of offices for example, and ways of curtailing expenditure, such as the cutting down of pensions. Wealth and prestige accrued to this office. The first of the *surintendants*, Semblançay, was disgraced by Francis I for presuming too far; so was the last, Fouquet, by Louis XIV.

In terms of status, the Chancellor, usually also Keeper of the Seals, who presided in council during the king's absence, ranked highest among the great officers of the crown. The edicts of the council were not legal without his signature. The high dignity of this politico-judicial figure was a source of mistrust to Richelieu; in turn he secured the exile of Marillac and Châteauneuf. The arrival of Séguier at the chancellorship in 1630 was an important event in the course of this office. As a devoted creature of Richelieu, Séguier seems to have been content to see the extension of the authority of the central government so long as the interests of the judiciary were preserved. The Chancellor was the last governmental survivor of the great officers of the feudal monarchy, which still proliferated in the shape of an enormous court, fixed in numbers, by a statute of 1578, at 1,517. The high dignitaries, Constable, Marshal and Lieutenants-General, were still important, too, in the military sphere.

Local administration and justice

While the feudal officers had lost their power and dignities at court, the spirit of feudalism persisted in the office and function of the provincial governor. The terms of appointment might speak of 'the public welfare', but the attitude of governors reflected more of the tradition of the time when the feudal estates were coalescing but slowly into France. The official view might be that Normandy, Picardy and Brittany were 'provinces', but the landed wealth and influence of the great families and the tendency of governorships to become hereditary made them look sometimes more like separate fiefs. An *ordonnance* of 1545 declared the theoretical position, that governorships were not hereditary dignitaries, and Henry II reduced and regrouped them. But in the Civil War they fell apart in the hands of the magnates of both sides; only in name was a Montmorency in Languedoc, or a Longueville in Normandy, a representative of the king. The governor's powers were supposed to be primarily military, but they were, in fact, almost what he made of them; a determined governor could control finance and justice in his province. His real power came from his extensive clientage, from the hundreds of lesser men who looked to him for promotion or protection rather than to the distant and ineffective king. These means of influence persisted into the seventeenth century long after peace and nominal order had been restored. Even in Richelieu's day it was necessary for a royal official to have a covering letter from the governor if his order were to carry weight. Richelieu struck hard at the local power of the magnates. In 1614 there were 16 provincial governorships; Condé in Berry, Vendôme in Brittany, Nevers in Champagne, Guise in Provence, and so on; the full list is a roll call of the *élite* of the old aristocracy. At his death there were only four of these left. Louis XIV finally made the office in most cases a nominal one, with a duration of only three years. The royal nominees were made to dance attendance at court, while the new men, the *intendants*, carried out the duties of government in their province.

In the absence of what we would call a royal administration, to a very large extent the king's subjects governed themselves. There was a local administration, based upon local communities. Every municipality had its magistrates. Paris had its *prévôt des marchands*, with *échevins* (roughly the equivalent of aldermen), other towns a *maire* and *échevins*; in the south there were *consuls*, in Toulouse *capitouls*, in Bordeaux *jurats*, different titles for magistrates. The terms might vary, but there were certain things in common. These officers were elected, usually by some narrow clique of municipal office-holders; not a very democratic process, but free from government supervision until Colbert's administrative revolution and the extension of the powers of the *intendants*. The magistrate's powers differed from town to town, but all had police functions and some form of jurisdiction exercised through *greffiers* who were the custodians and enforcers of judicial decisions, contracts of apprenticeship, bye-laws concerning markets or taverns or other local concerns. The village too could form an *assemblée générale* and in every village a *syndic* was chosen to represent his fellows. Villages and towns alike had their communal property, the proceeds of which were supposed to maintain the community. They might also obtain royal authorisation to levy taxes, for instance the *octroi* on the entry of merchandise, and to defray exceptional expenses they might even tax themselves.

Over these numerous little republics the crown exercised such authority as it could through its *officiers*, of whom two categories may be distinguished: *officiers de finance* and *officiers de judicature*. At the lowest level of the former there were simple cashiers and clerks without any administrative powers; then there were officials for special taxes, the *grènetier de sel*, for instance, for the administration of the salt tax, the *officiers d'élection*, primarily occupied with the *tailles*. At the top, in the capital of each *généralité*, stood the *trésoriers de France*, a meeting of whom constituted a *bureau de finance*. The latter had been set up towards the end of the sixteenth century with the prime responsibility of allocating the direct taxes. New offices were constantly being created by the government, as much to raise money from their sale as to answer new administrative needs. At the head of the Bureau was a *président*; with him and the *trésoriers* might sit a *lieutenant*, a *procureur du roi*, the king's legal representative, other *procureurs* (barristers), *avocats*, *huissiers* and *greffiers*. These weighty tribunals were entrusted, after an edict of 1570, with the conservation of the *domaine royal* in their *généralités*, which involved them at some very sensitive points of the subject's existence, fishing, pasturage and woodcutting on the royal lands. They might hear pleas upon such matters as the reduction of the *taille*, after some famine or fire. The *trésoriers* also looked after the affairs of the municipal bodies, checking upon local taxation; they had in fact some of the responsibilities which later devolved upon the *intendant*. The government was largely dependent upon them, and when they acted together with the local *parlements*, they could form a tiresome resistance to royal will.

The conception of justice, which was the province of the other category of *officiers*, was a broad one: '*une bonne police*', the maintenance of good order and security. No distinction was made between 'police' work and 'judicial' work. The former was the province of the *prévôts*, the junior royal judges, along with the *baillis*; the latter were left now with largely honorary functions, but they dealt with appeals from *prévôt* cases and acted as a court of first instance for some civil pleas about property, inheritances etc. Some of the *bailliages* had a wider competence and were called *présidiaux*; in towns where there was one of the latter, its officials shared the policing of the town, not usually in harmony with the municipal authorities. Alongside this ladder there existed, from the middle of the sixteenth century, the *maréchaussée*, whose function was more strictly judicial, and whose principals, the *prévôts des maréchaux* had to judge all cases of violence in the countryside and on the roads. At the summit of this complex structure were the *parlements*, whose officers had the surveillance of some affairs, such as markets, or were liable to take over in times of plague or similar emergencies; and the greatest conflict of authorities can be seen in *parlement* towns. Paris actually had four separate jurisdictions: the municipality, the *prévôt des marchands* and his *échevins*; the *châtelet*, only another name for the *présidial* of Paris; a sort of *maréchaussée* in the shape of an official entitled the *chevalier de guet*; finally *Parlement*, represented by its *Premier Président*.

Parlements

There were a number of *parlements* besides Paris, in provincial capitals, such as Toulouse in Languedoc, and Rennes in Brittany.

New courts were started in the seventeenth century in provinces acquired by conquest; Besançon, in Franche-Comté, in 1676, and Douai, in Flanders, in 1686. All varied in size and character, as they sprang from local institutions and local needs, but they had certain privileges and features in common. Their functions were primarily legal: they acted as final courts of appeal under the king and took a limited number of cases into their own jurisdiction (choosing their own). Nearly all offices were purchaseable, and these increased both in number and in price as the century proceeded. That *parlements* could be tenacious of local rights is demonstrated by the struggle of the *parlement* of Bordeaux against the maritime classes of Colbert. All showed a tendency to become more conscious of status and more fashionable in composition. At Rennes, for instance, *parlement* would only admit people 'of noble condition or living as a noble lives'. They were centres of hereditary privilege.

The *Parlement* of Paris was by far the most important of these bodies, with an area of jurisdiction stretching over a third of France. It had been, from its beginnings in the end of the thirteenth century, a court of law, staffed by lawyers. The right of registering royal edicts was developed, as was the money right of the English Commons, into the right of examination, and hence of approval, but it did not acquire a political role in any way analogous to that of Parliament in England. If its influence was wider than its strictly legal functions should have allowed, this was owing in part to the right of remonstrance, by which the magistrates of *Parlement* could point out to the king faults in a law, some detail which clashed with precedent or which was harmful to the state. This right did not extend beyond objection, and if the sovereign wished the edict to be registered, *Parlement* could do nothing about it. From this practice of remonstrance, however, and from political theories based upon the notion of a contract between the king and the people, derived the pretensions of *Parlement* in the seventeenth century.

By the end of the seventeenth century the *Parlement* of Paris had eight permanent chambers, of which the Great Chamber, the original from which the rest proliferated, was the most important. This dealt with matters affecting disputes of Princes of the Blood, crimes committed by noblemen, the king's rights in such matters as the *régale*. Princes and peers were counsellors by right and took their places in the Great Chamber. New laws were discussed there by the magistrates, and formal ceremonies enacted, the chief of which was the solemn assembly, when the king himself was present as the fount of justice and *Parlement* lapsed into a purely consultative body. Magistrates bought their offices from the king and received the right to pass them on to their heirs; this was assured by a law of 1604. *Parlement* thus kept alive its pretensions; a sense of political importance was passed down from one generation to the next, surviving the heavy hand of Richelieu and of Louis XIV. The purchase of office carried with it noble status, and the magistrate was therefore privileged and exempt from the normal taxes and dues. Most were wealthy, as they needed to be in the first place, to have made this considerable investment in a highly competitive and restricted market. A typical magistrate would have both town house and country estate and maybe investments in the *rentes* larger than the emoluments of his office; a large part of the land round *parlement* towns such as Dijon was bought up by magistrates. He was indeed a member of an exclusive legal club. Men like the Harlays, Molés and Arnaulds were among the first names of France, providing leading figures in the church and state, sometimes even royal ministers. Their head was the *Premier Président*, and his office alone was at the king's disposal, neither to be bought nor inherited. He was flanked by nine other *présidents*, and there were about thirty other permanent *conseilleurs* in the Great Chamber, of whom a third would be churchmen; the full complement of all the chambers was about 250. In theory these should be at least 25 years of age, have a degree in laws and have no relatives already possessing office in *Parlement*. In fact, dispensations were common by the end of the century for both age and kinship, while the examination in law was often a farce. Mme de Sévigné wrote of one youthful *président* of a provincial *parlement*: 'for forty thousand francs he has bought himself all the experience he needs to be at the head of one of the highest courts in the country'.

Struggles between the king and this privileged body were inevitable. In 1597, *Parlement* required for the king that he should choose his Council from a list of names submitted by them. In 1617, a magistrate claimed the right to refuse registration. Richelieu fought to reduce their pretensions and devalued the institution by creating for sale new councillorships. The biggest blow to the powers of *parlements* in the provinces was the establishment of the *intendants*, forced through the *Parlement* of Paris by *lit de justice*. In 1641 *Parlement* was ordered to confine itself to judicial matters. The preamble to the edict contains a fair definition of the monarchical state which 'cannot suffer any hand to be laid upon the sceptre of the sovereign, or to share his authority'. The words seem almost to be a challenge; if so, one that was accepted during the Fronde, when for a short time *Parlement* enjoyed a positive political role, demanding the reduction of taxes and the reform of government. Louis XIV gave short shrift to such demands. The hopeful theory that no law was valid unless it had been freely registered lay dormant after the edict of 1673 which forbade remonstrances to be made until after a royal edict had been registered. But the taste for politics was too strong to destroy, even if it could not be gratified till after the king's death.

Bureaucratic offices

The bulging edifice of officialdom did not amount to a civil service. It was rather a species of bureaucratic feudalism; a world in which public office and private property were indistinguishable. Office was regarded as a form of investment, providing social position, immunities from the more distressing forms of taxation, perquisites which could be substantial and a property to pass on to the holder's descendants. The jurist Hotman, writing in the sixteenth century, thought that the most serious cases of multiplicity of offices occurred in the Roman Law countries, which took as their model the elaborate hierarchy of Byzantium. Office hunting may have been the peculiar vice of the *petite bourgeoisie* of France, who would do anything to clamber from the ignorance and servility of the *roturier* class. But Common Law England saw a roughly parallel development; there, though on a smaller and less organised scale, the sale of office was openly practised. Its extension in France to the point in which the government could not exist without it owed something to special factors in France's character and history.

Sale of office was first systematised in 1522, when the *bureau des parties casuelles* was set up to act as a clearing house for this desirable form of property. Selling became general and could not for long be confined to the financial offices for which it was at first intended. Reversion came to be allowed and flourished, despite attempts to limit it by stipulating that it should take place within forty days of the seller's death. By an edict of 1604, the forty days' rule was waived, in return for the payment of a small annual charge to the crown, which thereby gained a regular revenue in place of irregular windfalls. This new system of sale on easy terms was soon called the *paulette*, after Charles Paulet, the official entrusted by Henry IV with its farm. Since office promised quicker and safer returns than most forms of commerce, as well as the nearest thing that the seventeenth century could provide in the way of a gilt-edged security, it is not surprising that it was much in demand. A large operator could build himself a private empire of *charges*; in 1622, seventeen Commissioners for the *taille* in Normandy shared 969 offices between them. In response to what was at all times an enthusiastic demand, at times a sordid scramble, prices rose steadily, as much as 600 per cent in some offices in the first twenty years. Though Henry IV had envisaged the *paulette* as providing a steady but modest revenue, it could not fail also to become a pillar of royal finance and the first expedient of war budgets. In 1610 Henry IV anticipated later form by putting a block of new offices upon the market; Richelieu constantly employed the same means. Loyseay estimated that about 50,000 offices were created in the first half of the seventeenth century; 'today half the inhabitants of towns are officials . . . it provides a manna that never fails'. By 1633, the returns from the *bureau* provided rather more than half the total revenue of the state.

The state gained more than revenue in this gigantic market; it bought political security. In the previous century, office had come into the hands of great private patrons, who could use their wealth and influence to secure the allegiance of well-placed clients. Richelieu considered that Henry IV had been influenced more by his experience of the power of the Guises in this field than by necessities of revenue; this is supported by the generous terms of his bargain with the office-holders. Now, through the expanding market provided and controlled by the state, the *bourgeois* had a growing interest in the stability of the state, which paid, but could also withhold, his dues. Condé discovered this, when he failed, in 1615, to win the sympathy of *Parlement* for his naïve campaign against venality. Richelieu, who had started his term of power by considering its abolition, came to make indiscriminate use of the convenient system.

The Cardinal justified his failure in his *Testament*: 'prudence does not admit action of this sort in an old monarchy, whose imperfections have passed into custom, and whose disorder forms part of the order of the state'. The last words express his dilemma perfectly. Order was purchased at the price of disorder, just as a quick capital was realised at the expense of steady income loss. In some years, losses to the office-holders, in the shape of remitted taxation and dues, outweighed payments by them to the *bureau*. If the crown tried to recoup its losses by bleeding the office-holders, it risked revolts; if on the other hand it flooded the market by creating too many new offices, their price fell. At Richelieu's death many offices were unsold and returns had fallen off catastrophically, while the revolt of the Fronde, six years later, was in part at least an expression of office-holders' discontent with the government's policy. The cost of the policy cannot however be measured in terms of revenue or revolts; it was paid in the small coin of everyday defaults in efficiency and justice, in friction, favouritism, bribery and delay. The government's policy of using offices to raise money created a huge vested interest in misgovernment. It was, as Richelieu himself saw, 'prejudicial to your authority and to the purity of justice'.

4 FRANCE: A EUROPEAN POWER ONCE MORE

Outside Europe

The range and success of Henry IV's diplomatic operations after the Peace of Vervins is the surest sign of the strength of his position at home. The administrative machinery at his disposal was adequate to produce the money required by a nation which, unlike Spain, had no permanent foreign commitments. The experience of the Wars of Religion was a warning to Huguenots against trying to improve upon their reasonably favoured position, and Henry had solid support in enlightened opinion whenever he had to deal with the plots of restless and independent-minded nobles. He was thus able to intervene effectively as mediator in a number of disputes in Germany, Italy and the Netherlands, and to build up a series of alliances which strengthened his position against the Hapsburgs. Since the Peace of Cateau-Cambrésis in 1559, French influence in foreign affairs had diminished to a point at which she had almost ceased to exist as a European power. During this period, the Hapsburgs dominated Western Christendom.

In the east, the Russia of Ivan the Terrible, after spectacular successes against the Mongol tribes to the east and south, had met with a decisive check in her efforts to break out to the west through the Baltic. Despite the trading contacts established by way of the White Sea by Chancellor, the consequent formation in England of a Muscovy Company and the rumoured desire of Ivan for a western bride, Sully reflected the general feeling in the west when he wrote of Russia in his *Grand Dessein* as a power whose interests lay in Asia rather than in Europe. During the seventeenth century, Russia was at first absorbed in succession problems, which began when Ivan hit his son over the head with an iron bar. This 'Time of Troubles', whose most intense phase, from 1610 to 1613, saw Muscovy exposed to the invasion of marauding bands of Poles, Swedes, Cossacks and Tartars, ended with the succession, in 1613, of Michael Romanoff.

Michael was a significant figure, not only because he started a long and remarkable line of Czars, but because he stood for national unity and the Orthodox Faith: through him was ended the Polish attempt to bring Russia into Western Christendom, as a Roman Catholic power under a Polish sovereign. This was a check to the Counter-Reformation, for the Jesuits now dominated

Poland, which had once briefly succumbed to Lutheranism. Russia only emerged as a diplomatic force of any account in the west after Peter the Great's victories over Sweden in the Great Northern War at the end of the seventeenth century.

Sully classed Muscovy and Turkey together, as powers against which crusades should be launched. At the same time as Ivan was conquering Kazan and attaching the aristocracy to the service of the state, Suleiman the Magnificent (1520-1566) was exploiting his victory of Mohacz, overrunning Hungary, extracting tribute from Transylvania and turning the eastern Mediterranean into a Turkish lake. The decline of the Ottoman Empire started, not with the Mediterranean battle of Lepanto (1571), for Don John's alliance fell apart after the battle, but with the death of the Grand Vizier, Mohammed Sokolli, in 1579. There followed a period during which the Empire and Venice might well have taken advantage of the administrative incompetence and lack of central direction in the Balkans to regain lost ground. But Venice was fully absorbed in maintaining her commercial interests, and preferred to keep the Turk at peace, so as to prevent yet more goods from the east being diverted along other routes. The rulers of the Empire, as we shall see, only looked east when they had to, for their full attention was devoted to their problems in Germany.

There was, then, comparatively little interference from non-European powers in the diplomacy of the first half of the seventeenth century. It was not possible for Henry IV to revive the policy of Francis I and use Turkish power against the Hapsburgs. Without it, his prospect must have seemed unpromising. The Treaty of Vervins restored France to the position she had reached at the Treaty of Cateau-Cambrésis (1559). But, while France had been surviving the Wars of Religion, the Counter-Reformation had been restoring much of Europe to something different from the passive acceptance of traditional rule and thought—to a vital, militant Roman Catholicism. The diplomatic history of this movement is full of wranglings, particularly between the Popes and the Kings of Spain. Philip II, who identified the glory of God very clearly with the glory of Spain, was mistrusted at Rome. But the church militant required soldiers as well as martyrs, and for these she had to rely ultimately on the Hapsburgs. While Henry IV might favour the Jesuits, and use his influence to help the Popes to extend their temporal dominions, he could not shake the traditional leadership of the Counter-Reformation which Spain

C

and Austria had established. It was a Catholic dagger that killed him, to thwart his avowed purpose of setting out to lead a Protestant alliance against a Catholic power.

The challenge of Spain

Austria and Spain were thus supported by all those who put their Roman Catholic faith higher than any temporal loyalty. Of these powers Spain was by far the greatest. Englishmen, justly proud of the successes of Elizabethan seamen, tend to forget the grandeur of Spain's position even at the very end of the sixteenth century. Territorially her power was dominating. She had not yet acknowledged the independence of the United Provinces. In the Spanish Netherlands she held the strategic heart of Europe, from which her armies could invade either Germany or France. Franche-Comté, nominally imperial, tenaciously independent and anti-French, gave her a route to these, via the Rhine and Rhône valleys, so long as she could retain the friendship of Savoy. In Italy she held Milan, Naples, Sicily, Sardinia and the armed ports of Tuscany and was thus able to control the southern entrances into the Alpine valleys, the northern ends of which debouched into Austria. Here, only the co-operation of the groups of tribes inhabiting the valleys themselves was required. In every court her envoys took diplomatic precedence, a matter of such importance throughout the seventeenth century that Louis XIV was ready to invoke war in order to assert the precedence of French envoys. Indeed, at the beginning of the century Spain was the only one of the larger nations to possess anything like what we should now term a Foreign Office, and her diplomatic service attracted some distinguished men; under the weak rule of Philip III, the ambassador to Venice practically achieved a *coup d'état* on his own, while the power of Gondomar over James I aroused the fury of Englishmen of the day and was probably responsible for the death of Sir Walter Raleigh.

The wealth of Spain had largely evaporated by 1600. But her potential wealth remained considerable, and this is the explanation of the apparently paradoxical situation of a country which had been forced since 1557 into successive bankruptcies but was yet able, mainly on foreign credit, to finance large-scale and non-stop military operations. Spain continued to guard the trade with the Indies jealously and, by the accession of Philip II to Portugal in

1580, she lost a rival and gained a fleet. Her methods of guarding her treasure fleets were improving. Drake's last voyage was a failure, and in 1591 Sir Richard Grenville went down with the *Revenge* in an attempt to intercept the treasure convoy off the Azores. The Dutch, although given the right to trade in Spanish waters by the terms of the twelve-year truce signed in 1609, were not allowed to encroach upon the Indies trade. Spanish military successes in the second half of the sixteenth century had been such that until the very end of his reign (he died in 1598) Philip II had been able to dream of restoring Western Europe to the new Catholicism under Spanish hegemony. Her generals, Don John, Parma, Spinola, had earned world-wide fame, her soldiers, though increasingly drawn from Northern Italy and Franche-Comté, had seldom been beaten, and her tactics and, more surprisingly, her methods of naval construction, were studied to considerable profit by France and England. Her influence on high society survived throughout the seventeenth century. The French nobility copied the elaborately courtly behaviour of their Spanish counterparts, and the punctilious code of gallantry which sprang from the book *l'Astrée* by d'Urfé owes its origin to Spain. It can truly be said therefore that the second half of the sixteenth and even the first half of the seventeenth centuries form an age of Spanish preponderance.

Only in the field of economic theory and practice can Spain be said to have contributed nothing—except an example to be avoided. The attitude of the typical *hidalgo* (these were a nobility but not an aristocracy, comprising about one in ten of the population) towards any form of work was one of disdain. Much of the soil of Spain is very dry and shallow, particularly in the central regions. Communications are also bad in those parts where the hills are high and only broken by furrowed rocky valleys. Only in the coastal regions, especially around Valencia, was the land profitably farmed, by a race despised and loathed by all good Spaniards, the unfortunate Moriscoes, the survivors of the Moorish occupation of Spain. More than a quarter of a million of these were expelled from Spain in 1609 and, although there was no immediate change in prices and so, presumably, no startling drop in production, the long-term effect of this on Spanish agriculture was bad. The most profitable form of agriculture in Spain was sheep farming. But here, too, bad old customs prevailed. Because of the remarkable change of climate in the centre of the country

(Madrid's winters are as cold as Moscow's), the good grazing land in those parts could only be used temporarily and the sheep had to be driven down to warmer coastal regions every winter. In order to preserve their lands at each end of this trek, the Spanish sheep-owners banded together in a single union, called the *Mesta*, and this was backed by the government. Thus sheep farming remained nomadic, while the effect of monopoly was to restrict the number of sheep and to raise their price.

Spain largely depended for its wealth, therefore, upon imports of foreign silver and its Indies trade. But for various reasons this was inadequate to finance her huge European commitments. At the turn of the century there was a significant decline in bullion imports. Potosi, the mountain of silver upon which Spanish greatness had rested since 1540, was being worked out. Moreover, the value of the precious metals was naturally declining as more and more gold and silver circulated Western Europe as a result of the payments made by Spain to her foreign mercenaries and creditors. In addition, Spanish exports to the Indies were so few that her colonies, despite their close and organised relationship with the old country, were naturally tempted to trade elsewhere whenever this was possible, and this too increased the amount of precious metal circulating in Europe. The very extent of Spanish commitments, the very purpose for which Philip II desired to use his gold, ruined his own conception of wealth by flooding Europe with it. It is when one judges Philip and his successors by their purposes that they appear weak. Spain was a great power, but she could not re-create Christendom. Yet this is what her rulers determined to do. So the whole wealth of Spain and Portugal was pledged to allies or spent on Spanish armies. The contents of the treasure fleets were pledged in advance—and to foreigners. Inevitably, they found their way eventually to the chief trading powers, the greatest enemies to the ideals for which Spain was fighting.

To deal with frequent financial crises, the Spanish government employed eccentric and unsuccessful measures, though it must be said in their defence that they had to meet greater financial difficulties than any power before them except for the Papacy, at a time when no reliable statistics were available. Philip II first declared himself bankrupt (that is, defaulted from his creditors) in 1557, and this method of wiping the slate clean was used six times in the next century. But it made borrowing impossible for the next few years, and on each occasion forced Spain to bring to an end the war she was fighting at the time.

The alliance between Spain and Austria remained close; although after Charles V's withdrawal into a monastery the Hapsburg dominions had been split, successive marriages tightened the bonds: Philip II of Spain married the daughter of Emperor Maximilian II, their son Philip III married the sister of Emperor Ferdinand II, and Philip III's daughter married Ferdinand's son—and so it was to go on. It was clear to almost every European statesman, except James I of England, that Spain was ready to support Austria with all her resources in the Counter-Reformation.

The grand design

Henry IV prided himself, justly, on being a man of common sense, with a clear view of essentials and of priorities. There was attributed to him by Sully, in his memoirs, a *grand dessein* for the future of Europe. According to this, it was his aim to reorganise the whole continent, excluding Muscovy and the Turks. There were to be six hereditary monarchies—England, France, Spain, Sweden, Denmark and Lombardy; six elective monarchies—Venice, Austria, Poland, Hungary, Bohemia and Rome (the Papal States together with Naples); and three republics—Switzerland, Belgium and Italy (north of the Papal States, and excluding Venice and Lombardy). The affairs of Europe were to be conducted by six local councils and one central council which was to have representatives from all the member states; the latter was to remain in permanent session. War was to be restricted to a campaign against the Turk, and for this a composite army would be raised under the auspices of the supreme council. Apart from this there was to be general disarmament. On the strength of this *grand dessein*, embodying an original theory of international co-operation and an enlightened re-thinking of the nature and consequences of war, Henry has been proclaimed a statesman of Napoleonic imagination and the highest ideals. Moreover, his foreign policy has been treated as if it was all subservient to the Design. Consequently, there has been some misunderstanding of his intentions. For the Design was Sully's, and even Sully never intended it to be read as a coherent whole. It consists of a collection of excerpts from his memoirs, put together as one chapter by an admiring *abbé* in

1745. It is fortunate indeed that the whole was coherent, as Sully's memoirs, written and rewritten over thirty years, are unreliable. For instance, he wrote of an embassy undertaken by him to England in 1601, of which there is no mention at all in any of the English state papers. As a record of fact, the memoirs are worthless, and the Design is a construction of Sully's imagination, appearing in the later parts of the memoirs, when Richelieu had made it seem possible; Sully may have fathered it on to Henry because he felt that it would thus be more credible to a country which already looked fondly upon Henry's name.

The *Grand Dessein* has been misleading in that it has contributed to the common illusion that Spain was at the mercy of France— another 'sick man', with rival surgeons waiting to carve him up. But, as the dream of a retired statesman in the 1630's, it has more than a passing interest. In the first place, it is interesting to see that the conservative Sully showed a respect for old traditions and forms. The republicanism of the Low Countries and Switzerland matched the elective monarchies of Bohemia and Poland. Only three types of religion were to be recognised—Lutheranism, Calvinism and Roman Catholicism—and no country could contain more than one of these. The idea that it was possible for one state to contain two religions co-existing peacefully and with equal rights was not yet acceptable even to a Huguenot—an interesting commentary on the French attitude towards their great religious problem. Then, it is worth noticing that Sully had already grasped the idea of the natural frontiers that was to affect the theories, if not the practice, of French foreign policy from the reign of Henry IV to the time of Napoleon. Explaining why France would not wish to extend her territories into Italy, he wrote that it had a 'climate, laws, manners and language different from ours; seas and chains of mountains almost inaccessible are all so many natural barriers, which we may consider as fixed even by nature'.

He was reflecting views which Henry IV appears to have shared, for his Italian policy, as we shall see, was to allow Savoy to spread east into the Po valley, while France occupied her western possessions, to bring the French frontier away from the Rhône valley up to the Alps. It is possible, even while discounting the Design as a whole, to find hints in it of the policy which Henry steadily pursued during the twelve years of peace between the Treaty of Vervins and the Clèves-Julich affair. Sully, crafty even in his dreams, realised that it was possible to envisage a complete reorganisation of Europe only on the basis of a share-out of some worthwhile spoils. He selected the Empire as his public prey, and he intended to push the Hapsburgs out of Italy as well. Here, it has been pointed out, the influence of Richelieu is marked. But there is other evidence to show that this was also the aim, far distant perhaps, towards which the efforts of Henry IV were bent. Whether arranging for a truce in the Netherlands sufficiently indecisive to keep Spanish forces tied down in that fatally expensive area, or sending his envoys round the Protestant princes in Germany, or wooing Savoy and Venice and the Papacy, or corresponding with desperate Moriscoes, all the king's diplomatic activities were anti-Hapsburg. In a conversation with Lesdiguières in 1609, he said that he wanted ten more years to use the alliances that he had built up. There was ultimately nothing pacific about his policy, and he was consciously planning to bring to an end the Hapsburg supremacy in Western Europe.

Italy

In Italy, his aim was to dispute with Spain the control of the routes running north from the Mediterranean, to Austria, the Franche-Comté and the Netherlands. The best ally he could have for this purpose was Savoy. But, unfortunately, Savoy was fairly firmly attached to Spain. Emmanuel Philibert had owed his restoration to his Duchy to Philip II, after distinguishing himself in battle against the French at Saint-Quentin in 1557. His son, Charles-Emmanuel, an unhealthy child, who had somehow survived the physical training given him by an unusually tough father and had emerged all muscle and spirit, succeeded in 1580; he married Philip II's second daughter, and now posed as a leader of the Counter-Reformation, trying to enlarge his Duchy by occupying Geneva, or interfering in the French Wars of Religion with the vague idea of reviving the old Kingdom of Arles. It was indeed a sign of the shifting balance of power that, by 1610 this ambitious and restless schemer should have come to the conclusion that he could get more out of a French alliance. There were causes for quarrel between France and Savoy at the start of Henry IV's reign. In 1590, Charles-Emmanuel had entered Aix-en-Provence at the request of the Leaguers, where he had stayed for nearly a year, fighting Lesdiguières, and it was not his fault that Spanish troops did not come to help him. Then, finding the

Leaguers divided and his flank dangerously exposed, he retired to his mountains, where he set about occupying the marquisate of Saluzzo. At the Treaty of Vervins, no solution could be reached about the future of Saluzzo, and the matter was referred to Papal arbitration. The Pope found his task impossible, so Charles-Emmanuel went to Paris in person, and agreed to spend not more than three months deciding on terms suggested by Henry. While in Paris, however, he got in touch with Biron and other malcontents, and thought that he had arranged for a large-scale diversion, and even a revolt. As Biron was commanding troops at Lyon, he naturally took no notice of the three-month limit. But Henry, his position and his finances strengthened by his match with Marie de Médicis, niece of the rich Grand Duke of Tuscany, launched a vigorous and successful campaign, and Sully's artillery train proved so devastating that Biron remained loyal. By the Treaty of Lyon (1601), Charles-Emmanuel was forced to a definite conclusion. In exchange for ceding Bresse, Bugey and Gex to Henry, he was allowed to keep Saluzzo. So France gained by a useful extension of her south-eastern frontier, with nearly all the land north of the Rhône, and avoided the involvements that might have come with possession of land beyond the Alps. Considering that all Savoy had once been occupied by the French, Charles-Emmanuel had good reason to be satisfied. Henry's plan to concentrate on strengthening his natural mountain frontier, instead of extending his power directly into Italy, although temporarily losing him influence over the North Italian princes, had the effect of pushing Savoy up against Spain in the Milanese. Charles-Emmanuel could only expand at the expense of the Swiss to the north or the Spanish to the east.

Such was the influence of Spain that Charles-Emmanuel, in spite of their failure to help him in Provence and in spite of the disappointing legacy of his father-in-law, Philip II—one crucifix and one statue of the Virgin—decided in 1602 to attack Geneva, hoping for Spanish support and risking French opposition. The attack was unsuccessful, a night surprise being prematurely exposed before dawn, and a combination of Genevese, Bernese and French volunteers carried the war into Savoy. But French influence in Italy seemed very slight. With Savoy hostile, Mantua and Modena feeling abandoned to Spain by Henry's surrender at Saluzzo and, in the Val Telline, the Gray League (Grisons) refusing to renew its French alliance, Henry had no power beyond the Alps.

But his diplomats were active. Already, in 1597 they had helped to secure for Pope Clement VIII the succession to the estates of the Este family in Ferrara. The tradition of the Venetian oligarchy was liberal. They did not accept the claims of the Papacy embodied in the decrees of the Council of Trent. There was a constant bone of contention in the neighbouring Duchy of Ferrara, which had become a Papal fief in 1597, on the extinction of the family of Este, with the aid of French diplomacy. Clement VIII was delighted at the return of his prodigal son, which left him less at the mercy of the Hapsburgs. As for Venice, she had been the first power to recognise Henry as King of France. Both could be useful allies to France, for both were anxious to preserve some sort of balance in Italy. Venice was also the first to lend Henry money.

In 1606 a violent quarrel broke out between the two. The Council of Ten in Venice claimed the right to punish priests guilty of secular crimes; then it published decrees controlling gifts of land to the church. Paul V, new to his office and in his mid-fifties, reacted strongly. Henry, instead of backing Venice, sent Joyeuse to mediate. A proud doge, who described Paul as 'young and inexperienced', was persuaded to withdraw the offensive edicts, and the Pope preferred the diplomacy of France to the military support of Fuentes, the Spanish governor of Milan.

Venice was already proving a good ally in a vital area. As a result of French gains from Savoy in the Rhône valley at the Treaty of Lyon, Spanish communications with Flanders and the Franche-Comté had been pushed eastwards, and the passes of the Val Telline had assumed a new importance. These were dominated by the Grisons, a federation of Protestant tribes with republican governments.[1] In 1603, they had come to an agreement with the Venetians and, thus supported, were strong enough to prevent the Spanish from using the Val Telline as a supply and troop route between Milan and Austria. Fuentes had built a fortress near Lake Como to block the mouth of the valley but, although there was a considerable Catholic population there, he could not get his men through.

Slowly, Charles-Emmanuel came to realise that Spanish domination of North Italy was not inevitable. Henry's diplomats continued to circulate busily, pointing out the independence of the Spanish rulers of Naples and Lombardy, the lack of interest shown by Philip III away in Valladolid, and the effects of Henry's

[1] See also pages 116-17.

marriage in 1600 with Marie de Médicis. Marie was the niece and heiress of the Grand Duke of Tuscany, and brought with her a dowry of 600,000 *sous*. In spite of his infidelities, and although he failed to fulfil the expectations of the generous Duke by repaying debts contracted before the marriage and the dowry, Henry's new connection helped to maintain his influence in northern Italy.

Charles-Emmanuel, disappointed in Switzerland, began to look east. He made alliances with Mantua and Modena. In 1608, he imprisoned and executed the leader of the Spanish party in Savoy. By 1609 he was negotiating again for a French alliance. Henry was near to achieving a powerful combination of North Italian supporters.

The Netherlands

But, before this was completed, relations between France and Spain had deteriorated seriously over the settlement of a truce between Spain and the United Provinces. The revolt of the Netherlands, started forty years earlier, had developed into a war of attrition between the northern provinces, effectively led by the Calvinists, and the Spanish in the south. Geography imposed a military frontier which neither side seemed to have any hope of penetrating. The Spanish had consolidated their hold upon the Walloon and Flemish provinces. The Dutch, now led by Maurice, William the Silent's energetic and imaginative soldier son, were secure and prosperous in the north. This division was to become permanent, and is marked today by the borders of Holland and Belgium, but it was an unnatural one, with some Protestants and Dutchmen south of the border, and some Catholics and French-speaking Walloons north of it, and it marks what was meant to be only a temporary compromise, fixed originally as a Twelve Years Truce in 1609. In the negotiations which led up to this truce, Henry IV played a prominent part and angered the Spanish.

Philip II had handed the Spanish Low Countries over to his daughter Isabella, as part of her dowry when she married her cousin, the Archduke Albert, but there were no children from the marriage, and it seemed likely that they would eventually revert to the Spanish crown. Albert and Isabella tried in vain to combine a rule beneficial to the provinces with a policy satisfactory to

Spain. It was one thing to patronise Flemish artists and encourage Rubens to return from Mantua, and to employ native officials in the government of the country, but quite another to make a peace which recognised the independence of any part of the provinces; this was as unacceptable to Madrid as it was essential to the welfare of the Netherlands. If there was to be a peace, the Dutch would want to trade with the Spanish Indies and to coerce Roman Catholics in the independent provinces. These were points which made negotiation futile until a point of exhaustion had been reached. But Albert and Isabella were determined to seize every opportunity for a settlement.

Until 1607, Henry IV did not take the possibilities of a truce seriously, but believed that he could gain most by offering his services as a friend, at a price. The Dutch were in a weak position. They had lost their chief ally when James I signed the Peace of London with Spain in 1604. In the same year, the Genoese Spinola, the most capable of a long line of Spanish generals in the Netherlands, captured Ostend and turned north for further advances. In these circumstances, Henry offered to help the Dutch in return for Flanders and all French-speaking parts of the Netherlands, and even asked upon what terms they would accept him as their sovereign. But the Dutch knew that Henry could not allow them to be overrun by the Spanish, and that he would not want a treaty arranged behind his back. They therefore side-stepped his demands, and arranged an eight months' truce direct with the Archduke Albert. Henry reacted promptly and promised to help the Dutch to win their independence, preferably by peaceful means. Jeannin was put in charge of the negotiations, and told to arrange things on as temporary a footing as possible. A truce was to be preferred to a treaty, and boundary grievances should be left which France might exploit in the future. The negotiator who is instructed to shelve the outstanding problems starts at an advantage. Jeannin was notably successful.

The Spanish were driven to terms in 1609 by pressure from the Archduke and shortage of money; a Dutch naval victory at Gibraltar and the extravagance of Lerma's regime at Madrid contributed to this. They accepted the independence of the United Provinces for twelve years, by the Treaty of Bergen-op-Zoom. The Dutch were to have trading rights in Spanish waters, but not in the Indies. The Spanish were unable to extract a guarantee of freedom of worship for Catholics under Dutch rule. All this was a terrible blow to their pride, and they blamed France for it; they were not ready yet to accept the strategic facts of the war, and felt that it was only fear of French intervention that made the Archduke so anxious for peace and encouraged the Dutch to keep their terms so high. They were bitter, too, at having missed an opportunity for a much more favourable settlement in the previous year, when the Pope had tried to arrange a marriage between Philip III's second son, Don Carlos, and a daughter of Henry IV, with the Low Countries as a dowry. Lerma had ruined this scheme by choosing a pig-headed ambassador, and giving him too rigid instructions. It was natural that he should now vent his spleen against France.

Germany

There were no signs that this truce-making in the Low Countries was part of a general pacification. On the contrary, enmity between Protestants and Catholics in Germany was hardening, and it was clear to Henry that he would not be able to keep out of the struggle. There were disparities of aim on both sides; between the Calvinist and Lutheran Princes in the Protestant camp and, among the Catholics, between Maximilian of Bavaria and Spain. The Austrian Hapsburgs were drifting irresolutely. The Emperor Rudolph was finally displaced by his brother Matthias in 1611, but not before Hungary had won religious independence, and a new force had appeared in European diplomacy: the Principality of Transylvania, a border state between the Empire and the Turks, ruled by the Calvinist Stephen Bocskai, forerunner of Bethlen Gabor. Matthias was old and Philip III and Henry IV were both thinking that the next emperor would have to be found in another family. But there was one young aspirant whom they underestimated, Ferdinand of Styria, a junior cousin, who was destined to win renown for Austria and for his faith.

Henry IV tried to exploit these divisions among the Catholics by lining up with Maximilian of Bavaria, a Wittelsbach, in the hope that dynastic rivalry would prove stronger than religious zeal. But Maximilian's unprepossessing person and habits concealed great efficiency as an administrator and caution as a diplomat; he was never prepared to attempt what he was not certain of achieving. In 1607 he made his position clear when he obeyed the Imperial command to occupy the rebellious town of Donauworth, whose Protestant magistrates had authorised an attack with sticks and stones on a Catholic procession. This drove the Protestant princes, Calvinist and Lutheran alike, to form the Evangelical Union in 1608, a ten years' defensive alliance, whose members ran an army from a common exchequer, presenting a united front at all meetings of the Imperial Diet, and looked to Henry for patronage.

So Henry was compelled to alter his German policy. Hitherto he had been on poor terms with the Protestant Princes, to the frustration of his envoy Bongars, who had a roving commission in Germany. In the test case of Strasbourg, where Protestants and Catholics had clashed over the appointment of a new Bishop, he had allowed the Catholic candidate, Charles of Lorraine, a Hapsburg, to win the position, and to fob off John George, Protestant grandson of the Elector of Brandenburg, with a pension. He was much displeased with the Protestants for the way in which they had supported the duc de Bouillon, a rebellious Huguenot noble who had defied Henry from his principality of Sedan. More deeply, he felt the dangers of intervening on the Protestant side with the religious settlement so raw in his own country; there was always a strong party at court which opposed any anti-Catholic moves in Germany. However, Bouillon had surrendered in 1606 and now, with the Hapsburg quarrels settled and Maximilian on the Imperial side, Henry had little choice but to side with the Protestants in the event of a fresh crisis.

The Clèves-Julich affair

Long expected, this came in 1609. On March 25th, the Duke of Clèves-Julich-Berg died after a lingering illness. He had no children and four sisters, and a problem was created which taxed the resources of the diplomats to the full. Indeed, only Henry's assassination prevented war. The territories of the late Duke were a bundle of estates with different rules of inheritance and different family connections. As far back as 1483, the Emperor had promised to the Elector of Saxony the reversion of Clèves if the male line failed. Others claimed the county of Mark separately. The children of the four sisters demanded the entire estates. Of these, the most important were the Elector of Brandenburg and the Count of Neuburg, and they also had the best claims, being descended from the two eldest sisters. But there was sufficient confusion to give the Emperor an excuse to intervene and take the decision himself; there were sound precedents for the arbitration of the highest authority within the German constitution. Since the Reformation, however, no internal dispute could remain isolated from the ambitions of the protagonists of the rival creeds.

Clèves-Julich-Berg formed an unusually compact collection of lands, including a stretch of the rivers Rhine and Ruhr, along the communication lines of the Spanish and near the frontiers of France. It was the position of Clèves which had tempted Thomas Cromwell to negotiate the marriage between Henry VIII and 'The Flanders mare', Anne of Clèves. The soil was rich, the population largely Catholic, while both Brandenburg and Neuburg, the two chief claimants, were Protestants. The Emperor might take it as a challenge to his authority and his religion alike. The Evangelical Union might treat it as their first test case, while the French and the Dutch might see in it a chance to reduce further the powers of the Spanish in the Low Countries. A large number of small princes were ready to buzz enthusiastically around a rich carcase. Henry and the Protestant princes were determined to do better than over Strasbourg, while the Emperor and Spain found common cause with each other, and with the new Catholic League, formed to counter the Evangelical Union, and led at first by Maximilian of Bavaria, the religious confrontation was almost complete. The Emperor was clearly planning to reject the claims of both Protestants, and either divide the dominions or impose a compromise Catholic ruler.

Henry's diplomacy in the first stages of the dispute was of a type familiar in the modern world of east-west block alliances. He did not want a war unless he could be sure of Catholic support in France, for, having failed to detach Maximilian, he could not prevent any war from taking on the appearance of a religious struggle. But he was determined to negotiate from strength, and to avoid a war by making it clear that he was not afraid to wage it. The two Protestant claimants had arranged for a joint occupation of the territories, and the Emperor had sent Archduke Leopold to seize them, while he decided on the merits of the case. So Henry set about building up an alliance, negotiating with Switzerland, the Dutch, the Evangelical Union and Savoy. The Duke of Savoy would make the war a general one by spreading it into Italy, and Henry kept these negotiations going slowly, as an unfulfilled threat, to be dropped when a satisfactory settlement of the Clèves-Julich affair had been reached. He prepared for war, but at the same time declared himself a man of peace.

In November 1609 an incident occurred which affected the timing, even if not the intention, of Henry's actions. The 16-year-old Charlotte de Montmorency, dancing before him as one of Diana's nymphs, had coyly aimed her Cupid's bow at his heart. She was more successful than she may have intended. He cancelled her engagement to one of his more handsome courtiers, and arranged for her to be married to the plain prince de Condé so that he might the more successfully lay siege to her heart. He then launched his attack with all the paraphernalia of gallantry prescribed by the fashions of the day. Condé's reply was abrupt. He 'absconded', as Henry rather unfairly put it, with his own wife, and put her under the protection of the Infanta at Brussels.

Henry was roused as lover and as sovereign. If Condé were not brought to heel the Bouillons of the realm would find encouragement in the sight of a Hapsburg protecting a rebellious subject. From the beginning of 1610, there was no mention in the letters of Henry and his diplomats of the 'desire for general European peace' which had previously qualified all their threats of war. Sully was told to provide for an army of 30,000 men, more than three times as big as that previously contemplated, and Henry told both the Papal legate and Père Coton, his Jesuit confessor, that the peaceful settlement of the Clèves-Julich dispute depended on the return of the prince and princesse de Condé. He prepared to start a general European war with few allies, and in the face of much opposition at home. Villeroi wrote that the struggle 'would set fire to the four corners of Christendom', and Henry pressed forward more speedily with his negotiations. But James I, bargaining with Parliament to modernise his income by the 'Great Contract', was not prepared to abandon his role of the man of peace; the Dutch promised to supply 8,000 men for action in Clèves-Julich only; the Pope and the Venetians remained neutral; and Charles-Emmanuel of Savoy, once he realised how much Henry needed his help, drove a hard bargain, getting 18,000 men from France to help him, and conceding only three towns which were still to be won from the Spaniards.

By the beginning of May 1610, Henry was ready to set out to lead his army, leaving a Council of Regency under his wife, Marie de Médicis. Like a man with a bandage over his eye, as Richelieu was later to say, he was in a preoccupied and uncertain mood; he was after all 57, by the standards of the age on the threshold of old age. He was on his way to pay a farewell visit to Sully in the Arsenal when a man leaped on to his carriage as it was held up in a narrow street, and stabbed him through the heart with a carving-knife. This was Ravaillac, Catholic priest and schoolmaster, who saw visions, believed he possessed a fragment of the true cross, and thought himself to be the saviour of the Catholic church at a moment of crisis. There is no evidence of a Jesuit plot, as was once alleged, notably by Michelet. But the fact that Père Coton felt it necessary to publish a refutation of attacks upon the order is evidence for the temper and suspicion of the time. The Spanish Jesuit, Mariana, had recently published his exposition of tyrannicide: in sum, a lawful sovereign could be slain if he did not serve the interests of the Faith. He may have represented the opinion only of a minority of the Jesuits, but he had a willing disciple in Ravaillac. He was one of the very few assassins in history who did not overestimate their own importance. He postponed the outbreak of a European war for eight years; he changed the foreign policy of France from militant hostility to close co-operation with Spain; he staved off a crisis in Austria so that, when the war did come, Ferdinand of Styria, a determined bigot, had gone far towards reuniting his family dominions; and he aroused once more all the suspicions which the Protestant Princes of Germany felt for a French alliance.

The Queen-Mother

The history of France between the accession of Henry IV and the death of Louis XIV contains three periods when the authority of the crown was uncertain: from Henry's accession until the Peace of Vervins, the Regency of Marie de Médicis, and the Fronde. Of these, the Regency was the least violent. This was due partly to the ineptitude of the opposition, partly to the policy of non-intervention which Marie's government pursued, and not least to Marie's own incurious habits of buying off awkward enemies and postponing awkward decisions. She was a woman who, in Richelieu's phrase, 'ran after malcontents to satisfy them'.

The ample figure and florid features of the Italian Queen have been preserved for posterity by the generous brush of Rubens; thanks to his genius, Marie dominates a whole room in the Louvre today, but she has no other claim to fame. She was simply a self-indulgent woman, petty and frivolous, incapable of large designs, pleased enough with the perquisites and toys of monarchy but incapable of rising to its responsibilities. She had no interest in administration or finance and knew nothing of her husband's foreign schemes. Indeed she had never been close to Henry, remained a foreigner in Paris, and learned little from him of the arts of governing. As became the heiress to a family of Florentine bankers, she thought of money as something to be spent upon the arts, upon good living and her friends; as the niece of the Duke of Tuscany, she looked on Spain as her friend.

She began comfortably enough. Henry had already arranged that she should be regent while he was away at the wars. The chief princes of the blood were out of Paris; Condé was with the Spanish and Soissons was in the country, where he had been sulking ever since his wife had been forbidden to wear one more row of *fleur de lys* on her dress than the wife of Henry's bastard son, Vendôme. The military crisis was pressing, *Parlement* was in session, and within two hours it had confirmed Marie's regency. Henry's old ministers were kept, the Edict of Nantes was confirmed within a week, and the army duly honoured Henry's obligations by marching into Juliers.

Marie could not however have pursued Henry's policy even if she had wished to. The great nobles, upon whom France still relied for military success, flocked back to Paris to parade the streets with their retainers, to demand confirmation of their old rights and see how they could exploit the new situation. Henry's ministers urged her to give up any idea of a large-scale war and to use the money provided for it to sweeten the temper of the more formidable nobles. In 1611 Sully retired, assailed from all sides. Bouillon wanted to replace him as the undisputed leader of the Huguenots, Soissons was angry at having been deprived of a profitable tax on cloth sales, and the other princes chose to regard him as responsible for Henry's cavalier treatment of his legitimate relations. All wanted to see him release his clutch of the purse strings. Sully himself felt that there was no future for him in an extravagant, Catholic court and retired to brood upon his Grand Design.

His departure symbolised rather than caused a fundamental change of policy, for Marie had already decided not to go further than Juliers and to leave Savoy, France's ally, to make the best peace it could. She then signed the Treaty of Fontainebleau (1611) which arranged for a double marriage, between Louis XIII and the Spanish Infanta, and Marie's daughter Elizabeth and the heir to the Spanish throne. It also provided for a ten-year mutual defensive alliance between the two countries, against internal revolt as well as against external attack. Thus Marie could get help from Spain against rebellious nobles or Huguenots, but did not commit France to helping Spain against the Netherlands rebels, for the twelve-year truce between Spain and Holland was not due to end until 1621. This elaborate agreement was justly celebrated in Paris, with fireworks and cannon, coloured lanterns, a parade of elephants and rhinoceroses. The government could now face the trouble-makers at home unhampered by the certain expense and probable humiliation of foreign war. It was one of the more sensible acts of policy in this century of war.

The States-General of 1614

Administrative and even constitutional bodies live because they are fed with work. The States-General in France was already moribund by 1614, while its counterparts in Poland, Sweden, Hungary and many German states were noisily alive, because it had ceased to have any relevance to contemporary needs. The nobility looked to obtain what they wanted through pressure at court, or power at home. The clergy had their own assembly and could hope to influence the king through the confessional. The privileged members of the *tiers état* could make themselves felt through the *parlements*, or in some provinces, the *pays d'état*; the latter gave a modicum of power and position to nobles, clergy and *bourgeois* alike. The crown, which in England had fostered parliament by summoning it often, neglected the States-General. Kings in other parts of Europe used representative assemblies to hear grievances, to give judgments, to instruct voluntary upper-class local administrators, to ask for money, and to rally support. In France the only function the States-General was needed to perform was the first, and occasionally the last. Judgments were given in *parlements*, administration was the work of local officials; the French, schooled by a system of law which stressed the duties rather than the liberties of the individual, paid their taxes without giving consent through a representative body. The great hall at Blois, where the States-General met in the sixteenth century, still shows how this body acted as an extension of royal power; the staircase leading down into it from the royal palace descends straight into the middle of the hall, so that kings could make their entry like some Jupiter from the upper storey. But it was no longer useful even for demonstration purposes. Henry IV had never summoned it because he knew that it was too divided to be the *afforcement* which Henry VIII and Elizabeth had found parliament in England. When it met in 1614 its futility was again exposed, so unmistakably that no one pressed for its revival until the virtual bankruptcy of the state in 1788 revived interest in a forgotten institution.

Marie summoned the States-General after the treaty of Sainte-Ménéhould; this was part of the agreement with the princes. Condé issued a manifesto listing the grievances of all the classes. The *noblesse* were jealous of the education, the wealth and the increasing political power of the *bourgeoisie*; these were personified by the institution of the *paulette* which had established the heredi-tary principle in office-holding and with it the *noblesse de la robe*. They therefore proposed that the *paulette* should be abolished, and that any office-holder who wished to dispose of his office should sell it at least forty days before he died. The *paulette* was not universally popular among the *tiers état*, even though two-thirds of those elected in 1614 were office-holders. They therefore agreed to its abolition, but suggested that the 1,600,000 *livres* thus lost to the government should be made good by a corresponding reduction in pensions. Savaron, their spokesman, contrasted the vast sum spent on pensions, amounting to 5 million *livres* a year, with the poverty of many of the provinces and people of France; such a voice was not to be heard again in public until the Revolution. The nobles, who received nearly all the pensions, were enraged, and the joint attack on the government's conduct of the nation's finances was weakened.

All the Estates were agreed, however, that the national finances should be more closely supervised. A bishop compared tax-collectors to the seraphim, making heavy play with the double meaning of the word *voler*. A court was set up to deal with corruption, but the States-General only met for four months, and it would have taken as many years, or a committee of experts to get to the bottom of the government's fiscal arrangements. When there was a demand for the reduction of the *taille* by a quarter, Jeannin explained that it could not be done, and produced a few figures; he might have made them up for all anyone could do to check them. Sully had set about the problem in the right way, by shortening the lines of communication between government and collectors and supervising them closely. The nobility, however, had no intention of either administering the taxes themselves or of contributing to them. There was no budget and no control over how the money was spent. The clergy deplored the idea of public budget. If the state was the body, they argued, its finances were its nerves, and the nerves must be hidden beneath the skin—a conceit all too typical of the golden age of the metaphor.

The *tiers état* was not a homogeneous body; upon one issue however all agreed, and there was an eruption of Gallican sentiment to embarrass the clergy. Since the Concordat of Bologna, the relationship between the king and the French church had remained close. The Counter-Reformation, based politically on an alliance between the Papacy and Spain, had led inevitably to a certain coolness between the French king and the Pope, and certain features of it, the more extreme decisions of the Council of Trent, the use of the Inquisition and the activities of the Jesuits were not popular in France. In 1594 Pierre Pithou had produced a theory that the king, anointed with holy oil, was personally responsible to God for the church in his lands. The assassination of Henry IV was widely thought to have been, like that of Henry III, the work of the Roman Catholic ultramontane enemies of the king. In 1610,

Mariana's book, justifying the assassination on religious grounds, was burned by the Sorbonne; at the same time they banned Bellarmine's book claiming temporal power for the Pope. In 1611 Edmond Richer, head of the Faculty of Theology in Paris, published a treatise in which he asserted the supreme importance of bishops: 'a bishop in his diocese is the real ruler of his church', and further, 'bishops are an essential part of the church and the Pope an accessory'.

Though Richerism was too strong for most people, Gallican views found acceptance among some of the princes, for they cast doubt upon the authority of the Council of Trent in France, and it was by virtue of the Tridentine decrees that the Pope had invalidated the marriage of Henry IV and his first wife Marguarite de Valois. If the marriage had not been legally invalidated the legitimacy of Marie de Médicis' children, including Louis XIII, was brought into question. Since all Henry's other children were undoubtedly illegitimate, the junior line of Bourbon princes, Condé and Soissons, saw in this new-found claim to the throne a useful bargaining counter in their dealings with Marie de Médicis.

The Gallican sentiment of the lay estates placed the clergy in a delicate position. The majority came to the States-General in an ardent mood, demanding the reception of the decrees of the Council of Trent, and the coercion of the Huguenots. But they would not go so far as to seem to impinge upon the rights of the king, by Gallican tradition, or to question his Divine Right. Their influence secured the rejection of a motion of the *tiers état* to place on record, as a fundamental law of the state, the declaration that 'the king is sovereign in France, holds his crown only from God, and that no power, spiritual or temporal, can deprive him of the obedience of his subjects'. The formula may have been rejected but the spirit of the words obtained. The *tiers état* had reacted from aristocratic irresponsibility to Divine Right; constitutionalism was dead. The boy king was made to reply that he thanked the *tiers état* for their good feeling, but that he reserved action upon their Gallican resolutions to his own discretion, since they concerned him personally. The king's advisers found it easy to play a defensive role since their privileged critics could find no common cause. Royal prerogative had little to fear when every debate revealed the misunderstandings and jealousies which divided the classes between and within themselves. So they refused to lower the *taille*, to reveal the details of the pension list or of other fields of expenditure. After a vague promise to examine their *cahiers*, the deputies found themselves, on the morning after the royal session of February 23, 1615, standing before locked doors. They had no option but to go home, and many may have been relieved to do so.

Concini and de Luynes

Louis XIII owed his survival more to the disunity of the aristocratic opposition than to the firmness of his ministers; still less to the dominant family at court, first the Concinis, then the duc de Luynes and his brothers. The administration was left for some years to the old ministers of Henry IV: Jeannin, the *président*; Sillery, Chancellor, and Villeroi, who specialised in foreign affairs; their age and caution earned them the name of *barbons*, greybeards. Jeannin appears to have been a political soporific, a man whose words were as full of warmth and comfort as the furs of office which he always wore. Concini secured the *barbons*' removal in 1616, and promoted the young bishop of Autun, Richelieu, to the post of Secretary, with responsibility for foreign policy. After Concini's murder, however, they came back again and stayed in power till Richelieu's return in 1624. They were men who knew how to follow the path of least resistance, but they did not do badly; negative policies are not always the most disastrous.

The first seven years, at court at least, belonged to Concini, a Florentine adventurer who had slipped into a place behind the throne by marrying Leonora Galigai, the queen's foster-sister and confidante. His pleasing appearance and heroic manner appealed to the impressionable queen; she was, after all his countrywoman. Concini makes an enigmatic figure; beyond a certain aptitude for diplomacy there is nothing to suggest that he had either the ambitions or the gifts of the statesman. But his pretensions were bound to arouse the jealousy of the magnates, and his bloody end comes as no surprise. The man who profited most from his murder in 1617, was Charles d'Albret, duc de Luynes. Concini was the queen's favourite, Luynes the adolescent Louis XIII's. Luynes had come up from Provence to be a page of Henry IV; he became Louis XIII's master of falcons. He had the skill to exploit the lonely king's love of horses and hunting, but his own interests seem to have been as limited as his intellect. After 1617 he rose as swiftly as one of his hawks.

What is surprising in this troubled period is not that there were revolts but that these revolts did not assume the proportions of a general civil war. Marie and her son, squabble as they might, always realised that ultimately their interests were the same; it seems too that with the gathering impetus of the religious revival which was making its mark upon church and court, all Catholics were ready to join together to fight the Huguenots. The memory of the Wars of Religion was still uncomfortable, and the prestige of Henry IV's reign had survived his death. When his son appeared in the field, the armies of the nobles tended to disperse without putting up a fight. It was the crown's good fortune too that its most dangerous opponent was one of the most unpopular men in France.

Henri de Bourbon, prince de Condé, was a cousin of the king and heir-presumptive to the throne. In Voltaire's opinion, his greatest achievement was to be the father of the victor of Rocroi. He was a conspirator who could not keep trust with his confederates and a general who would never pay his troops. He tried to ally with the Huguenots and then fought against them, flaunting his piety; he took bribes from the queen-mother and then denounced her for mis-spending the nation's money; he raged against Henry IV for trying to seduce his wife, but was notoriously unfaithful himself. He was indeed a prime example of the overmighty subject, unable to see beyond the interests of his caste, uneasily aware that he must do something to protect its prerogatives, but unable to follow a consistent plan. The Huguenots, Spain, the States-General, any cause that promised to be useful he would make his own; in the final analysis, however, he represented nothing but himself and his house.

The Huguenots were only going to be a serious threat to the crown when they found a champion in one of the great princes; such a man was Henri de la Tour-d'Auvergne, duc de Bouillon. His power straddled the frontier, where as lord of the principality of Sedan, he was virtually an independent ruler. Some of his possessions he held of the Bishop of Liège, and the latter was a Prince of the Empire. He had already essayed a revolt against royal authority when he joined the cabal of Montmorency and Biron in 1601. Since then he had adopted the stance of a persecuted Protestant for the benefit of the Germans, but in 1614 he made no bones about joining with the Catholics, Mayenne (the son of Henry IV's old foe), Soissons and Épernon in their protest against the Concinis. The pacification of Sainte-Ménéhould in May 1614 bought them off; the lavish pensions and promises which were the price of allegiance then, and in 1616, when a further cabal was followed by more bribes, shows that they were not disinterested in their actions. They wished to have the best of both worlds: independence in the province and pensions at court, influence over policy without the daily drudgery of administration.

In 1615, trying to stop the Spanish marriage, even at the last moment, to get back to the good old days when Spain sent arms to help rebellions, Condé and Bouillon bid for Huguenot support. The Huguenots were, however, too cautious to fight and Condé, with an army of his own to keep happy, allowed them to live off the country in lieu of pay, which aroused the worst memories of the Wars of Religion and lost him popular support. He did not succeed in preventing the marriage, and Louis XIII and the Infanta, Anne of Austria, were wedded at Bordeaux; both bride and bridegroom were aged 15. Having achieved this, Marie decided to give Condé enough rope to hang himself. By the Treaty of Loudun, 1616, he got 1½ million *livres* and a place on the Council which he accepted without consulting his fellow-rebels or Mayenne. Once on the Council, Condé talked openly of taking the throne. By this time he had alienated every faction of any significance and Marie was able to arrest him without causing any disturbance by smuggling soldiers into the Louvre in bales of Italian silk.

Marie made no effort to see that the king was properly educated, and he became bored and frustrated; he was left to expend his energies on hawking and hunting. He hunted regularly three days a week; out except in the very worst of weather, and then indoors, watching sparrows dashing themselves against the walls to escape his hawks. He liked no one so much as his falconer, de Luynes, and to him in the evening he confided his grievances and his longing for real and recognised authority. Concini, after Condé's arrest, had become a changed man. Where he had been timid and anxious, like his wife, to build up a fortune without being involved directly in the ruling of the country, he now started to swagger and to assert his powers. He received petitions wherever he went, began to collect provincial governorships, styled himself the Maréchal d'Ancre and was rumoured to have his eye upon the high feudal office of Constable. Richelieu estimated his importance so highly that he accepted office at his hands. His increasing interest in affairs of state led to a firmer government attitude towards rebellions, so that when the duc de Nevers threatened revolt, an army was at once gathered together and sent against him. Luynes realised that a *coup d'état* to overthrow this aggressive upstart would please others besides the king. On April 24, 1617, Vitry, the Captain of the Guard, arrested Concini as he was surrounded by a crowd of petitioners in a courtyard of the Louvre. When Concini cried out for help, he was stabbed to death. His wife, as befitted a woman who was rumoured to be a sorceress and a tool of the Jews, was burned at the stake. With this barbaric rite the Regency of her friend and foster-sister was over, ended as it had begun in violence.

Marie thus paid for her neglect of her awkward son, for they remained estranged and were always uneasy in each other's presence. She was often in future to be found stirring up trouble, but wherever she was involved rebellion was half-hearted; she knew her interests to be those of the crown, even if not those of her son. Now she went to Blois and, with her, Richelieu, as chaplain, while the king installed Luynes in Concini's place; the falconer knew even less about state affairs than his predecessor, and supplied no effective leadership in council. At the height of the crisis which precipitated the Thirty Years War, he is said to have asked, in full council, whether Bohemia was on the sea. It is not surprising that between the new favourite and the old ministers, France played an insignificant role in the first phase of the war.

In 1619, Marie escaped from her captivity and defied the king. The skill of Richelieu brought about an agreement at Angoulême, in April, but her gesture served as the pretext for a mustering of the nobles which required stronger action. All the most important of the grandees were in the conspiracy, except Condé, whom the rest dared not trust; it was ostensibly directed against the duc de Luynes who was loathed and despised. The duc de Longueville in Normandy, his hereditary governorship, Vendôme in Brittany, Mayenne with Guise money and troops around Bordeaux, and the promise of Spanish help: these seemed a formidable threat. Louis had only a small army. It was big enough however, and one battle, such an anti-climax that it became known as the *drôlerie de Ponts-de-Cé*, was enough to finish the whole rebellion. The fiasco is noteworthy because it reveals the weakness of all the forces rallied against the monarchy and presages the age of Richelieu,

Mazarin and Louis XIV. The rebels, with their strength in the provinces, were not prepared to join together; they had seen what had happened to Condé when he had led his troops away from home, and the irresponsible plundering which he had sanctioned in order to keep his army together without pay. So Longueville stayed in Normandy and Mayenne refused to move north from Bordeaux, and neither was present at Ponts-de-Cé on the Loire. Marie was no more capable of leading them than she was of helping her son. Influential churchmen constantly urged noble and crown to sink their differences and set about the serious business of stamping out heresy. Most significantly this rebellion illustrates the strength of the crown, at what was apparently its feeblest hour. Everyone testified to the effect of Louis' own presence on the battlefield. To fight against the king was treason. 'I saw', said Richelieu afterwards, 'that those who fight against the power of the state will always be defeated by their own imagination, since behind the enemy they cannot help seeing the executioner.'

Huguenotism in arms

The easy victory of the crown emboldened Luynes and Louis to embark upon a long-contemplated stroke: the restoration of Béarn to Catholicism. Henry IV's native county had remained Huguenot despite the fusion of Navarre and France. The restoration of this province to the Faith had been one of the conditions upon which Pope Clement VIII had granted Henry absolution. Now the bishops of Oloron and Lescar claimed the restoration of the property of the church in their dioceses, and they had the support of Catholics throughout France. What they demanded was what was soon to be done, on a larger scale, in Germany. Luynes' action too was in line with the government's foreign policy; they looked with equanimity on the misfortunes of Protestants in Germany (the battle of the White Mountain was fought in November 1620) and they abandoned the cause of the Grisons in the following year. Luynes' action was both popular and successful. In the autumn of 1620, Béarn was forcibly reunited with the crown, the sovereign councils of Béarn and Navarre were merged into one, and the practice of Catholicism restored.

The militant party among the Huguenots chose to regard this act as a challenge to their position. They were not unprepared.

At the Assembly of Saumur in 1610 they had organised themselves into 'circles' after the example of their German brethren. Between 1598 and 1620 they held nine general assemblies, two of them, 1617 and 1620, without royal consent. The Huguenots of the north, and especially those of Paris, an exposed and defenceless minority, preferred to avoid trouble, but the spirit of the Religious Wars was still alive in the south, where the communities were larger and more confident. Some of the Huguenots felt themselves to be committed to the international struggle; they could not remain passive spectators while their co-religionaries were being destroyed in Germany. The fiery pronouncements of Church Assemblies and the Catholic zealots at court, the missionary activities of Capucins and Jesuits, seemed to indicate that the decisive struggle was coming. There were arguments for striking first. The party of action found a leader in the ambitious family of Rohan, Henri de Rohan, Sully's son-in-law, and his brother Soubise. A war of religion occupied the king's army in 1621-2. Luynes, now Constable, captured Saumur and Saint-Jean d'Angély, both *places de sûreté*, but died in December of scarlet fever soon after his first check at Montauban. Two servants were caught playing picquet on his coffin; a not inappropriate memorial to the favourite's career. The town, high and encased in thick-ribbed walls, resisted heroically, stiffened no doubt by reports of persecution in other parts of France; the bitterness that had lain dormant for twenty years came to the surface in a number of cases of violence and insult. But the crown was more cautious than the spokesman of the church; and shrank from the effort and expense of war to the death. Montauban held out till terms were made, between Condé, enjoying his brief hour of success, and Lesdiguières, Louis XIII's commander, who had inherited the Constable's sword from Luynes, and abandoned his Huguenotism to do so. The crown dealt with the Huguenots as it had with other rebels, by the distribution of honours and pensions. La Force and Châtillon received marshal's batons. A substantial pension did not however deter Rohan from pursuing his design of making the area round La Rochelle into an independent republic, under the auspices of England.

Abuses and reforms

Throughout the seventeenth century, politics and diplomacy were being conducted under religious banners. That this was to some extent a convention will be realised by anyone who has studied the history of England in the seventeenth century where the Puritans were not all dogmatic zealots. Clarendon was probably stating a truism when he observed that 'religion was made a cloak to cover all manner of impious designs'. The decline of Papal influence in the diplomatic field, the secular tendencies of policies such as Richelieu's and the loss or confusion of the religious impulse in the Thirty Years War may all be quoted to show that the religious banners meant little. Yet did they? The banners were still being waved vigorously at the end of the century. In England Titus Oates aroused passions which were none the less deep for being ignorant; religion was the staple of domestic politics in the age of Marlborough. In France, the repeal of the Edict of Nantes was the consummation, as it seemed to the majority of Frenchmen, of the crusade of a century. The great contests between Jansenist and Jesuit, between Bossuet and Fénelon, were followed with rapt attention by a fashionable and committed audience. Though the ground was being prepared for the anti-clericalism of the eighteenth century by the increasing control of the state over the church, and by the scientific discoveries, with their consequent stress on the material world, this was only apparent, even at the end of the century, from sceptical trends in a small section of society.

The seventeenth century was the great age of the church in France. Whether one considers the personalities and careers of the remarkable churchmen of the time, the intellectual and moral grandeur of the great debates, or the passionate seriousness of a large number of lay men, the conclusion is the same: this is 'the great age of souls'. Religious enthusiasm is reflected in the improvements which took place in most Catholic countries in the century which followed the reforms of the Council of Trent, and the French church, which received the reforms late and suspiciously, is only the outstanding example of a general process. But when Rome fell somewhat short of the example that might be expected of the head of the post-Tridentine church, when Germany was occupied in religious war and Spain sunk in intellectual and spiritual isolation, the counter-reformation in France shone with all the greater lustre.

When Henry IV was established on the throne, the church was for various reasons an unedifying spectacle. Here and there, as Brémond has shown, there were ardent spirits waiting for the hour of reform. But the demoralising effects of the Wars of Religion, the effort of Catherine de Médicis to achieve a *politique* compromise between extremes whose ardour she could not understand, the close connection between the church and the nobility, the lack of any system of instruction or test of entry for the lower clergy, all helped to make a church which could not, without reform, engage the sympathy of those even who fought for it. The real battle was left to be fought.

The church must inevitably reflect the conditions of society, and efforts towards reform could not alter this, except in points of detail. Thus the church continued to reflect the feudalism of an age when it had been intimately concerned with the feudal arrangements of society, and it served at the same time the needs of the monarchy; for the king was always in practice and, after the Concordat of Bologna, in theory as well, for purposes of appointments and discipline, the head of the church in France. So we find a strange situation; alongside the spiritual richness of the period there persists a worldliness and laxity which seem to make nonsense of the efforts of the reformers. Saint Vincent de Paul sits in the *conseil de conscience* with Cardinal Mazarin, who was a Cardinal before he became a priest. Bishop Bossuet rubs shoulders in the Church Assembly with Bishop de Coislin, who received his first abbey at the age of four, and became bishop of Orléans (a good one apparently) at 21. These are the anomalies that become inevitable when the church is also a department of state, and when the highest appointments are part of a system of patronage more attuned to the economic needs of the nobility than to the spiritual needs of the people. The spiritual quality of the French church is all the more astonishing when it is realised that the conditions of the church encouraged the bishop to be a courtier and degraded the *curé* to the level of the peasant.

The Council of Trent had closed the doors of the church to the inroads of Protestant theology. The notion that the individual could find his own way was rejected in favour of the traditional assumption that salvation came through the mediation of the church. The celibate priesthood, the monastic ideal, transubstantiation and other traditional orthodoxies, the old ritual and the use of Latin, were given the definitive force and sanction of a council of the church. But the Council was essentially Mediterranean in character, the majority of its members Italian and Spanish, heavily weighted by the religious orders and notably by the Dominicans. The Gallicanism of the French church and the conditions of the Religious Wars delayed the acceptance of the council's decrees. When the French king showed that he was willing to be a true Catholic, and not merely a heretic in disguise, by accepting a Jesuit confessor, when the religious orders were streaming back into France and the clergy pressed the crown to accept the decrees, it still refused. Indeed the Council of Trent was never accepted by the crown, right up to 1789. This would have involved a sacrifice of an authority over the church which was one of the most important assets of the crown. Therefore, although every reform in France was guided by the ideas of Trent, its decrees continued to be a battleground, not only between Catholic and Protestant, but between Gallican and Ultramontane.

The upper clergy were largely aristocrats who had chosen *le noir* rather than *le rouge* because they were physically more suited to it, or intellectually inclined, or because it was expedient to keep a profitable endowment in the family. Richelieu himself became bishop of Luçon for this reason; if he had lived fifty years earlier it is unlikely that he would have shown the religious energy that he did, in fact, display. Some received preferment for services rendered to the crown. The King of France had exceptional powers of appointment; the Gallican church was more independent of the Pope than the English church ever was before the Reformation. In 1714, the last mediate right of appointment went when the duc de Nevers lost his control of the small diocese of Clemency; long before that the king controlled all important appointments. He could give profitable positions to favourites with a good conscience, since the right of holding an abbey *in commendam* allowed the holder to pass on the responsibility of performing the duties while keeping a large percentage of the emoluments. Sully, a Huguenot, held four abbeys in this way, and Richelieu, normally scrupulous about appointments, gave one to Desportes for writing elegant love verses. The rules were broken regularly even by the Papacy. The celebrated Mère Angélique began her career as abbess of Port Royal at the age of seven, her parents excusing her uncanonical age by claiming that she had the spiritual age of 21. Indeed she was to prove exceptional, one of the foremost among the many reforming abbesses of the time; but the breaches of the rules were not always so satisfactory. Henry IV could not be relied upon for discretion in these matters; he installed his bastard son, Henri de Verneuil, as bishop of Metz at the age of 11, having previously failed to persuade the Pope to accept him at the age of 6. On appointing the 4-year-old Charles de Lévis bishop of Lodève, he wrote cheerfully to Marie de Médicis that he would be able to get absolution on easy terms from such a confessor. Such scandals occur from time to time throughout the century. Saint-Simon's choice gallery of worldly bishops shows that the episcopacy was still open to men who took their social duties more seriously than their sees. But when one considers the system one is struck by the number of conscientious ones. A good courtier was not necessarily a bad diocesan. De Coislin, bishop of Orleans, for instance, bishop at 21, had the courage to stand out against the brutalities of the *dragonnades* when everyone was still applauding the Revocation. Henri de Sourdis, a typical Richelieu appointment, man of action and administrator, was a vigorous Archbishop of Bordeaux. Richelieu still retained enough of the *dévot* to be scrupulous about his appointments, and Louis XIII insisted upon scrutinising them. Louis XIV took this part of his *métier* as seriously as any other; so, good and bad, the episcopacy reflected a society in which high seriousness and utter cynicism existed side by side.

Between bishop and *curé* there was a deep gulf fixed. In towns the *curé* tended to have some standing, but in the village he was too often a peasant among peasants, often almost indistinguishable from them in education or in his manner of life. He was miserably paid. The tithe which was a major part of the income of the church, being in some provinces as large a levy on the peasant as the *taille* and which was thus bitterly resented, often did not go direct to him, but to a monastery or chapter which controlled his parish; they then paid him a wage, the *portion congrue*. Some of the most important work of the reformers of the church in this period concerned the parish priest, providing for his training in seminaries, missions to the countryside, the issuing of popular manuals of devotion. But nothing could overcome the basic evil of the system; the class-structure of the church which divided the two worlds of upper and lower clergy, so that promotion from one to the other was rare and a proper working relationship between the hierarchy and the parish difficult to achieve.

The state of the monasteries left much to be desired at the beginning of the century. Poverty, indiscipline and a lack of true vocation were among the complaints of reformers. Henry IV remarked of the monks of Saint-Denis, 'our souls will be a long time in purgatory if they depend on these gentlemen to get them out'. Monks left their monasteries at will, treating them as free houses more than places of devotion; tonsures were overgrown, robes discarded, offices unsung. During the civil wars many monasteries became military centres, and not necessarily Catholic ones. Martial habits were not easily discarded in time of peace, as Bérulle found when he was instructed to visit the Augustinians in Paris to investigate the condition of their House. They met him with showers of stones and, when eventually he got inside, several tried to hit him with candlesticks seized from the altar. Determined efforts were made to reform the old orders during the seventeenth century, led by Cardinal de la Rochefoucauld, who was put at the head of a special commission by Louis XIII, and by Richelieu, who became himself general of the Cistercians in 1635. The new generation was prepared to accept the rigours of the Benedictine rule, but attempts to make the older monks do so usually failed. The tradition that monasteries were places for unathletic gentlemen persisted. Eventually Alexander VII accepted the situation and a Bull of 1666 provided for two sorts of Cistercian, the one following a 'strict', the other, euphemistically, a 'common' observance. In the historian Mabillon, in the second half of the century, the Benedictines did produce one of the most remarkable scholars of this or any age, and in the ascetic de Rancé, and his severe Trappist fraternity, an extreme interpretation of the monastic ideal.

The Benedictines did not play a major part in the religious revival, but there was no lack of response to the ideal of the religious life. Brémond compared Christian France in the time of Henry IV to 'a part of the mission field in the first years of advance'. New houses and new orders were founded pell mell without waiting for the jurists of *Parlement* or the curia of Rome. In 1631 the *parlement* of Rouen declared that 'in the last twenty or thirty years more religious orders have been founded than in the last thousand years'. This seems to be no exaggeration. In the single diocese of Coutances there were six foundations in twelve years. Almost every order flourished, Franciscans, Dominicans, Capucins (Franciscans of a strict observance), Calvarists and Feuillants among the Benedictines, Premonstratensians, Carmelites and, most conspicuously, the Jesuits. The Carmelites represent the Spanish influence upon the devotional revival. When Henry IV succumbed in 1602 to the pressure of the group led by Mme Acarie and gave leave for the foundation of a French Carmelite house, he was acting against all his instincts as a *politique*; when in the following year he went further and admitted the Jesuits, the Counter-Reformation had indeed triumphed.

The Jesuits

Without doubt the Jesuits were the most powerful single force in the French Counter-Reformation. They belonged to an exceptional order, for they had an exceptional aim: to intervene in the world, not to withdraw from it, to fight for the souls of men, not merely to pray for them. They were the Church Militant, trained and equipped for religious war. Their statutes, which they were allowed to change themselves, enabled them to speak in public and gave them freedom from ecclesiastical jurisdiction, save that of the Pope himself. Their training stressed obedience before everything, poverty and chastity: these the novice vowed; then later, when he was judged fit to bear the spiritual and physical dangers which it might involve, a father vowed to devote himself to missionary work against heretics and infidels. Their organisation was autocratic, with an all-powerful general at the top and a council of four to assist him. Since there was only one church, there was only one order; there were no national subdivisions. The power of the Jesuits came from their internationalism, their heroic vision, their love of souls; their chief weapons were the school and the confession box.

The Jesuits had had a chequered career in France since Saint Ignatius Loyola had founded the order in 1540. They had a Provincial there as early as 1552, and a College in the Palace of Clermont in Paris in 1564; thence they had spread to the provinces, founding eleven schools in the next fifteen years. Catherine de Médicis, not interested in souls, disliked their part in the Council of Trent and their close connection with Spain. So they were banished from the country; as late as 1594 the Paris *Parlement* had re-affirmed their banishment. For motives which remain obscure Henry IV allowed them to return in 1603; was he trying to ingratiate himself with the Papacy? Or did some stir of religious feeling touch him? At the time it did not seem a major concession. Although the order had been officially banished it had continued to do its work while, in the decree re-establishing it, it was stipulated that only in Lyon, Dijon and la Flèche could the Jesuits open new colleges beyond those already in existence. Their right to speak outside their own buildings was subject to the licence of the local bishop. All Jesuits in France had to become naturalised Frenchmen and to take an oath that they would plan nothing against church or state. They were excluded from the Sorbonne. A permanent Jesuit representative had to be kept at court to answer for any breach of these rules.

The Jesuits were not thus to be contained. The rules restricting Jesuit colleges were flouted and they spread so rapidly as to arouse frequent but unavailing protests from the Sorbonne and the *parlements*. Their excellent education was designed to attract the upper classes. The Jesuits, searching for influential converts, did not neglect the social graces. The young Frenchmen were given a good grounding in deportment, dress and elocution, important elements in the education of the future courtiers or diplomat. Nor were they required to mix with anybody of lower social status than the *bourgeoisie*. Jesuit education was upper-class education (and, in a century when the nobility was as conscious of its privileges as any nobility in history has ever been, it was tempting for Huguenot nobles to abandon a religion which involved kneeling with the lower orders in a temple like Charenton, and to set up their private Catholic chapels). The teaching was good and the subjects taught enlightened. A group of six Jesuits, each from a different country, had worked for fourteen years to produce the *Ratio Studiorum*, the guide for curriculum and methods of instruction. The mediaeval schoolmen, with their textual twists, were abandoned, and a return was made to the pure stream of the classics themselves; this was in accord with the principles of the Huguenots and was not original. The emphasis moreover was entirely on style, and ideas were not discussed. It was hoped that by the time the student had reached the age when he could grasp ideas, his trust in his teacher would be so great that he would approach them in the spirit, not of criticism, but of acceptance.

This trust was vital to the Jesuits and the foundation on which they built their whole movement. For so personal a task only the choicest were found worthy, and these were instructed to replace the parents in the lives of their pupils. Were chastisement needed, as it often was in schools where discipline was strict, it must be administered by a servant, while the master shook his head in solemn sorrow and comforted the afflicted. So, when the youthful minds became restless, they could turn to one who commanded the affection due to a parent, as well as the respect required by a teacher.

From the Jesuit schools there entered into French Society a steady stream of devout laymen, and these did not lose contact with their masters when they left school. Many of them joined fresh organisations—congregations which often served as an effective counter to the Huguenot parish synods. But the most powerful body of Catholic laymen was the Company of the Holy Sacrament. In about 1630, the duc de Ventadour, *lieutenant général* of the king in Languedoc, founded this *cabale des dévots*. He was one of many who were affected at this time by the influence of the Spanish mystics; he meditated daily on St. Theresa's masterpiece, *Introduction à la vie dévote*. He decided that, except as a brother, he should not live with his beautiful wife. She went, therefore, to a convent of the Carmelites, while he set about drawing influential associates into his movement for Catholic action. By 1658 there were fifty-two branches, each centred upon a different town. Only the central bureau could elect new members, and these had to go through a mysterious rite before being admitted. All members were laymen, except a few of the founders; they included some of the greatest in the land. There was much more to this formidable body than the cloak and dagger of secrecy. It undertook work of social importance, often in close alliance with St. Vincent de Paul, starting hospitals, giving legal help to the poor, improving conditions among the prisoners who manned the Mediterranean galleys. During the Fronde they organised relief for those whose land had suffered. They employed their considerable wealth in financing missionary ventures. They also took as their province the morals of the nation, launching campaigns against swearing and duelling amongst the nobility and improper dressing amongst the women of Marseilles. They kept a particular check upon the leaders in church and state, any doubtful character having a special card kept up to date among their records. Mazarin was constantly embarrassed by their attentions.

But perhaps the most important of their activities was their struggle against the Huguenots; in this they were true disciples of the Jesuits. They excluded Huguenots from all their charitable works and kept them out of jobs, notably in the medical profession. They issued a stream of pamphlets, planning their propaganda on a regional basis, translating canticles into the local dialect and designing picture postcards for the less theologically minded. They encouraged religious processions which sometimes led to open brawls in the streets between Huguenot and Catholic. Mazarin, who had good reason to dislike them, took the chance to strike when it was discovered that they had been arresting and trying people privately. In December 1660 *Parlement* declared illegal the existence of any society not authorised by royal patent. The leaders of the society then burned their papers and declared themselves dissolved, but continued to meet and to exert pressure on the government; the importance of this cannot be gauged.

The special powers of absolution granted to the Jesuits were used to gain the ear not only of many leading nobles and ministers but also of the king himself. By a neat twist of the clauses designed to restrict their powers, they managed to instal Père Coton, their representative appointed to be responsible at court for any breach of the agreement, as confessor to Henry IV. This was no sinecure, as the king became ever more outrageous in his behaviour as he grew older, but he had an ungrudging affection for the gentle priest. All through the century, after Père Coton, a Jesuit held this key position at court, all the more important because both Louis XIII and Louis XIV were men of sensitive conscience. The influence exerted on policy by the counsel of the confessional was inestimable because it was secret; it was partly a fear of the unknown, partly dislike for what was known of Jesuit methods of argument and absolution that aroused opposition. To the traditional suspicion of *Parlement* for a body which was believed to represent the interests of Spain was added that of Jansenism, a puritan movement inside the church. The Jansenists can only be understood if it is realised that their chief motive was opposition to the Jesuits. This is the one thread that runs through the complicated story of their relations with Pope and king. The two greatest controversial works that they produced, Arnauld's

De la Fréquente Communion and Pascal's *Lettres Provinciales* were attacks on the Jesuits. This great force in the religious revival was born in opposition and nourished in the fury of debate.

The Jansenists

Jansenism is more resistant than most subjects to the summary treatment required by a book of this sort. Like other religious themes of the seventeenth century, it has been chronicled in minute detail. If a series of disputes on intellectual and spiritual matters, conducted by men of the highest ability and followed with intense interest by the educated public, is evidence of a great age, then the seventeenth century is indeed the *grand siècle*; and of these disputes, without question the greatest was that of Jansenist and Jesuit. It cannot be skimped. The story may be seen as an extension of the theological arguments and attitudes of the reformation, as a separatist movement inside the church, or as a form of puritanism which did not, unlike its counterpart in England, spread out beyond the practice and precept of a perfectionist minority. It is all these, and more. Jansenism defies analysis because it is as much an attitude of mind as a set of beliefs or a movement. It has a significance beyond the small group who composed the two houses of Port Royal. From the time when Saint-Cyran first attracted the suspicious attention of Richelieu, to the last battles round the promulgation of the Bull *Unigenitus*, at the end of Louis XIV's reign, Jansenism was never far from the agenda of government, the debate of theologians or the conversation of society.

Cornelius Jansen was a Flemish theologian who had been rewarded by the Spanish for his services in the Netherlands with the bishopric of Ypres. His life's work was the re-establishment of Saint Augustine, in whose writing he saw the true principles which Christendom needed against the dangers that followed from the humanist revival—formal and mechanical practices of devotion, and strictly rational or merely ethical approaches to problems of faith. The *Augustinus*, Jansen's life work, published in 1640, two years after his death, presented the saint's views in the most comprehensive form. He had read the anti-Pelagian passages thirty times to ensure that he missed nothing. It is arguable, however, that in his devotion to the letter he missed the spirit of the saint's work. Augustine's doctrine of Grace emerged from the reflections of an ardent soul upon the miracle of his own conversion. The Roman church has honoured Augustine for his insistence upon the depravity of man and his consequent dependence upon Divine Grace while it has tempered, in the light of Christ's teaching in the Gospels, some of Augustine's extreme conclusions: notably that Grace was given to those for whom it was predestined, and correspondingly withheld from others who suffered in this way the penalty of man's original fall. Jansen lifted Augustine's view of the limitations of Grace from the context of his life and teaching and presented the result of his selections as the pure ideal from which the church had fallen, by its neglect, for over a thousand years. Although the work was scrupulous in detail, it was therefore misleading in its entirety, and as much a work of propaganda as of scholarship. Jansen, who believed that theology was an exercise in memory, not in understanding, believed that he had done justice to his subject, and died as he had lived, in the assurance of orthodoxy.

It was his friendship with Saint-Cyran, and the part that the book played in Saint-Cyran's personal mission, that was to draw attention to the possible heresies contained in the *Augustinus*. Even so, the book trod heavily upon embattled ground when it treated of Grace and free will.

The terms require some amplification. Man's relation with God, after and because of the original fall, involves the problem of free will. The orthodox Catholic view, expressed by the Council of Trent, is that man's will, although corrupted and weakened, was not extinguished by the Fall, *minime extinctum . . . viribus licet attenuatum et inclinatum*. Grace therefore, which is essentially God's love, is not wholly unaffected by the will of the recipient. The respective parts played by the human being's natural effort and by the unpredictable workings of supernatural Grace are left open to some freedom of interpretation. Heresy comes however with too great a stress upon one, to the detriment of the other. The Pelagians emphasised the part of human effort, erring too far in the way of free will. Augustine refuting them, and drawing upon Saint Paul rather than the teaching of Christ, minimised the part played by human will; Grace was irresistible, effecting the Divine purpose irrespective of man's participation or will; it was withheld from the mass of men whose damnation was foreknown although not fore-ordained by God. Calvin had pressed Augustine's logic to its awful and heretical conclusion that the majority whom Grace did not touch were deliberately and irrevocably damned.

Within the Catholic camp dispute had raged between the Jesuits and the Dominicans. The former, led by Molina, Professor of Theology at Evora in Portugal (1535-1601), projected a middle way between Augustinian and Pelagian extremes, holding that Grace was efficacious only so far as the will co-operates. God, omniscient beyond and out of time, can predict the future by His awareness of all the circumstances that will bear upon it; He can execute His plans, yet leave to man his freedom of will, man being able to resist Grace which, without His co-operation, is powerless. The Dominicans opposed this with a variant of Augustinian theory: sufficient Grace is a Divine premonition given to all, preparing the souls for Efficient Grace which is needful for man's acts to be justified before God. For years, (1594-1605, in the Congregation *de Auxiliis*) the matter was debated at Rome, without conclusion, though the Jesuits seem to have been fortunate to escape without condemnation. The seventeenth century Catholic was left therefore to choose between the Dominican view which stressed the prerogative of an omnipotent God, and the Jesuit insistence upon the will of man. There was value in both views when they were not forced too far in the hothouse of academic disputation. The fatalistic Spanish Dominicans were prepared to be rigid; the guardian order of the Inquisition was ready for purity's sake to accept the view that the elect of God were few. The missionary Society of Jesus required, by contrast, a practical solution of the problem, even a working hypothesis, if that would give them scope for their work of conversion.

Duvergier de Hauranne, a Basque of good family, born in 1581, became in 1620 Abbé of Saint-Cyran; he first came into contact with Port Royal in 1633, was imprisoned by Richelieu in 1638 and died soon after release in 1643. He may be revered as a saint or dismissed as a crank; neither view can be accepted without qualification. Indeed he illustrates in their most extreme forms the traits which made Jansenism remarkable, admirable and detestable. His theory rested upon the need to stand aside and let the Grace of God operate through the passive spirit; yet upon occasions he could be affected, morbid and intolerably self-important. He was devoted, prayerful and ascetic. His ecstasies arouse in the reader the same mingling of awe and embarrassment as the more tasteless art-forms of this period; he may properly be envisaged against a baroque design of flowing draperies, adoring angels and trumpeting cherubs—only the design should be in black and white. The followers of his preaching and spiritual direction saw him as a man of God; these included Bérulle, founder of the Oratory, and Vincent de Paul with whom he helped to create the charitable organisation of *Saint-Lazare*. Richelieu, as might be expected, looked more coldly upon his raptures: 'His entrails are on fire and they send into his head vapours which he mistakes for inspiration.' His alleged opinions were disturbing enough: that there had been no church for five or six centuries and that the Council of Trent had been 'an assembly of scholastics'. Furthermore, the Jesuits, for whom Saint-Cyran had no love, were able to accuse him of planning to overthrow the church; his plot, the *affaire Pilmot*, takes its name from one of the cypher words used in his correspondence with Jansen about the purification of the church. In the face of such trifles, the Cardinal's action is testimony to Saint-Cyran's force of personality, and its mystery; as Richelieu observed to a friend: 'If Luther and Calvin had been clapped into a gaol the moment they started dogmatising, the nations would have been saved a lot of trouble.' Not the least important of Saint-Cyran's legacies to Jansenism was the taint of separatism and sedition.

Saint-Cyran had met Jansen at Louvain, and the theologian and the obsessed student, who had nothing in common but their veneration for Saint Augustine, became fast friends. Jansen stayed for long periods at Saint-Cyran's home in the south, and there they planned the regeneration of the church. The theologian's convictions about the nature of Grace gave backbone to Saint-Cyran's passionate puritanism. The latter went further even than Calvin in his philosophy of damnation for the masses, and self-denial for the chosen but uncertain few. (The only mortals who could be sure of salvation were baptised children who died in infancy.) Mortifying self-discipline was the lot of the presumably saved, and eschewal of the world and its vanities; these included the imaginative arts as well as the more obvious bogeys of dancing and gambling. Conversion, the process by which the few had intimation that they were saved was a violent, Pauline process, a sudden impact of Grace upon the soul. Saint-Cyran, backed by the massive theology of his mentor, devoted himself, as confessor and preacher, to the needs of those of whose conversion he saw evidence. An offshoot of this mission, founded in 1637, a year after Saint-Cyran had first entered the nunnery of Port Royal in Paris, was the group of male solitaries at Port Royal des Champs. The dominant figure at the Paris house was Jacqueline Arnauld; the first of the solitaries was Antoine le Mâitre, her nephew, who abandoned a promising career in law for a hermit's cell outside the deserted buildings of Port Royal des Champs.

It was almost inevitable that Saint-Cyran would have fallen foul of the Society of Jesus, whose aims, theology and outlook were so different from his own. But it was chance that brought him personally into contact with the leaders of the Gallican opposition to the Jesuits, in the shape of the Arnauld family. Antoine Arnauld the elder, father of twenty, himself a lawyer, a Catholic of Gallican convictions but the son of a Huguenot who had been Catherine de Médicis' *procureur général*, may be said to have founded the family tradition with his oratorical denunciation of the Jesuits upon the charge of complicity in the assassination of Henry IV; now he led the opposition of the University of Paris to the admission of the Jesuits. In 1643, after the death of Richelieu, the struggle was won. In the same year, Antoine Arnauld, his youngest son, published his anti-Jesuit treatise, *De la Fréquente Communion*.

Antoine's sister Jacqueline had become Abbess of Port Royal at the age of 7 (her sister Agnes had found similar preferment at the age of 5). At 11 she assumed control, with the aid of a prioress, of the rheumatic and demoralised community. A sermon by a wandering friar, Père Basile, converted her at 17 to a stricter view of the office. With a purposefulness characteristic of the Arnaulds, and a flair for self-dramatisation which was peculiarly her own, she began her work of reform, turning Port Royal into a model house, regular and austere. Her prowess as a reformer led to her installation in the notorious house at Maubouisson where Mme d'Estrées, the abbess, had been entertaining lavishly and had set up a household of her illegitimate children. In 1626, Mme Arnauld, her widowed mother, took the veil but, being reluctant to live at swampy Versailles, transferred the entire house to a new establishment in the Faubourg Saint-Jacques. Zamet the zealous and modest bishop of Lângres was the spiritual director, and through his influence the house was removed from the Cistercian order and placed under the Archbishop of Paris. In 1633 Mère Angélique (Jacqueline) became the Superior of a religious house established for the adoration of the Holy Sacrament. Zamet introduced Saint-Cyran, who had supported him over the use of a devotion, the *Chapelet secret*, to her. When in 1636 the two houses were merged, with Jacqueline's sister Agnes as abbess and herself novice-mistress, Zamet was excluded and Saint-Cyran had full sway. Up to this point, Port Royal and the Arnaulds had not been committed in character or doctrine.

The life of the male community at Port Royal lends itself to adjectives such as idyllic and pastoral, but the realities were unromantic enough. The rules of the house had to fit the needs of about thirty *bourgeois*, educated, independent-minded persons who had little in common except their wish to be out of the world. Port Royal was indeed more of a permanent retreat house than a monastery, for the inmates took no vows; they lived however to a strict code, observing prayer times, living and sleeping on bare boards, eating sparingly. They worked outside, draining the malarious marshes, gardening (under the direction of an obscure English gentleman called Jenkins); they transcribed manuscripts, worked on the printing press, studied and taught in the *petites écoles*. They had retired from the world, not merely to pray for it but to do penance and find salvation undistracted from the world. They were free to come and go; sympathisers like Pascal came to stay without commitment; they busied themselves during the Fronde with practical works of mercy. Their outside interests possibly saved them from the worst penalties of their escapism and their gloomy theology, but an air of joylessness was inevitable in this oasis of the saved in a world largely composed of damned persons—not to speak of an anxiety lest they should be wrong. The heroism and the high-mindedness of the solitaries and the nuns (for they had much beside the Arnaulds in common, and habitually acted together) command our admiration. But Port Royal was not entirely unworldly; its inmates displayed at times the sort of priggishness which is liable to follow from such a narrowly selected and inbred environment, The Arnaulds saw themselves in the front line against worldliness, but they were committed to one side of a controversy which was political as well as theological. They dominated the two houses. In the Paris house, by 1640, beside Mme Arnauld and her six daughters, one of whom, Mme le Maître, was married and widowed, there were the latter's four daughters. Three le Maître sons were also solitaries, as well as Arnauld d'Andilly, now the eldest male member of the family. Antoine, his younger brother, was very much in the world but might be described as a corresponding member of the society which was otherwise largely composed of Arnauld friends and associates. It is not surprising if Port Royal seems sometimes to display an air of corporate complacency; nor that others besides the Jesuits came to think that Port Royal was a family conspiracy against the established order.

Jansen's *Augustinus* appeared two years after his death, in 1640; on the opening pages, the Fleming attacked the Jesuit theory of Grace. Saint-Cyran, from his prison, hailed the book and called for action to recover purity of doctrine and morals. The youngest of Arnauld's twenty children, Antoine, an able and persistent lawyer, accepted his charge to lead the campaign. The outline was clear. Port Royal and the Arnaulds were committed against the Jesuits, the Sorbonne, the Court, Rome, to defend the *Augustinus*.

In 1643 Antoine published his *De la Fréquente Communion*; this amounted to a declaration of war. The pretext of the work was the alleged practice of a Jesuit confessor who allowed worldly pursuits, such as dancing, on condition that confession, absolution and the sacraments followed every lapse. The idea of regular communion as a form of insurance was embodied in his treatise which was popular with ladies who wished to keep in with both worlds. It was a perversion of Molinist teaching about free will, but typical, the Jansenist thought, of the philosophy of salvation on easy terms that came from such teaching. The *Fréquente Communion* did not attack the practice of regular communion, but laxism, the easy-going counsel of confessors who recommended communion as spiritual medicine without care for preparation, or for the state of mind of the communicant. Arnauld's book stressed the cost and discipline of Christian life; that it fulfilled a need can be seen from its avid reception. A Jesuit Cardinal at Rome praised the book, but the Jesuits in France saw it in the context of Saint-Cyranism, not merely as an appeal for reverence towards the Eucharist but as an assault upon the methods of the Society. Arnauld's manner was indeed unfortunate; always more of a lawyer than a theologian, he wrote in a combative vein, sometimes seeming to be more concerned with proving a case than with the delicate task of establishing truth. There was danger in his case too, if carried too far, as it was by some Jansenists who made a merit of denying themselves communion.

The Jesuits counter-attacked through the influence of the court and insinuated that the book was an heretical attack upon the doctrine of the Eucharist; they contrived, therefore, to obscure the great merit of the work: its statement of an ideal of uncompromising virtue, unsupported by mechanical aids to devotion.

The *Fréquente Communion* was only the spearhead of an attack whose solid force lay in the *Augustinus*, and its view of Grace. If this was allowed to stand, then the Jesuits must be in the wrong. So the *Augustinus* was examined clause by clause by the Syndic of the Theological Faculty in the Sorbonne, Nicholas Cornet, himself an ex-Jesuit and official censor of theological works. He found five propositions which he declared heretical. Jansen's unbalanced work perhaps deserved this treatment; it is arguable that Cornet was less unfair to Jansen than Jansen had been to Augustine. The doctrines embodied in the Five Propositions were, as Bossuet later admitted, the soul of the book. They amounted to a reasonable criticism of its extreme views: that some lack grace to obey the Divine Commandments; that Christ did not die for all men without exception; that man could neither control nor resist his Grace since his will had no free part to play.

Pascal

The Five Propositions were condemned by a Bull of Innocent X on May 31, 1653. Jansenism was then officially a heresy. The heretics took the lawyer's line of defence. The church had the *right*, which they conceded, to condemn the five propositions. But these they repudiated for the *fact* of the matter was that these propositions, which were *résumés* rather than literal extracts, were not to be found in this form in the *Augustinus*. Thus was evolved the celebrated distinction between *fait* and *droit* which was to be the crux of the ensuing battle.

The Jesuit Almanac of January 1652 celebrated their triumph in its frontispiece: the Pope, under the heavenly dove, cast down the mitred Jansen who sped, on bats' wings, towards the corner where Calvin was making himself agreeable to a bespectacled Jansenist nun. They had reason indeed for satisfaction. For the next two years, Arnauld, tainted with the damaging suspicion of Calvinism, fought against the Jesuits, the Chancellor Séguier and a packed jury of the Sorbonne, to defend his position. On January 31, 1656, he was censured; degradation followed. The struggle had attracted attention in a society whose appetite for theological debate was wilting under the boring reiteration of technical detail. Now it broke suddenly upon a wider audience, the issues were lifted on to a larger plane; genius intervened. On January 23, Pascal had published the first of the *Lettres Provinciales*.

Blaise Pascal was 32 years old, the son of a high legal official and an Auvergnat, two points of identity with Arnauld. He had been a prodigious child, observant, inventive, sensitive. Before he left school he had written an essay on conics which laid the foundations of integral calculus; at 20 he had invented and constructed a calculating machine; three years later the publication of his work upon the vacuum contributed to the solution of the problem which stood in the way of great advances in physics. After chance acquaintance with the devout and philanthropical Deschamps brothers, his family, who had been brought up in the humanist Montaignist tradition, became immersed in the religious awakening. His charming and brilliant sister Jacqueline developed the vocation for the religious life which was to take her to Port Royal. His own response was more complicated. He studied the Bible intently; as early as 1645 he could write: 'corporeal things are only an image of spiritual things and God has represented the invisible in the visible', and elsewhere, 'we ought to consider ourselves as criminals in a prison entirely full of images of their liberator and of the instructions necessary for them to emerge from their servitude'. His heart yearned for the certitudes of faith, but his mind was a scientist's. He pursued experiments on the frontier of knowledge which the Deschamps regarded as morally dangerous and distracting. In 1647, largely from overwork, he suffered one of those collapses in health which have led historians to emphasise his physical debility. After his death it was indeed discovered that he had a bony ridge on the skull which must have been the cause of his tormenting headaches. His disposition was fretful and restless; 'the extraordinary vivacity of the temper of M. Pascal made him sometimes so impatient that it was difficult to please him'. Suffering, physical and mental, was never far from Pascal, and it may be held to account for his obsessions with original sin and the misery of man. The man who was disturbed to see children kissing their parents, who wore a spiked girdle round his waist, did much to settle the Jansenists in that mood of despair which was already implicit in their theology. But the portrait of an invalid genius, with its inference that the sting of his attacks upon the Jesuits came from the sick imagination of an embittered man, is misleading. Pascal accomplished a huge amount of work in his short life; never did he lose lucidity, seldom in the heat of debate did he resort to invective for its own sake. His passion was subdued by the operation of a scrupulous mind and a sensitive conscience. Pascal's problem was not a new one; faith and reason have always tugged in opposite directions; if his dilemma seems modern, it may be because his was an age of scientific revolution, and he was one of its pioneers. To a person as sensitive as Pascal the opposition of views was agonising: one, that the truths of Christianity could be established by reasons; two, that Grace must work independently of the intellect. His personal problem was that of the practising scientist; should his energies be employed upon matters of the senses, whose validity he could never repudiate? The contacts of a successful man with the fashionable world and its polite debates about belief and reason were not helpful to his peace of mind—'a man of the world among ascetics, and an ascetic among men of the world'. But he was rather especially interested in the study of human nature. 'Pascal had,' wrote Sainte-Beuve, 'in its most intense degree, the feeling of the human being.' When the issue of *Fait* and *Droit* was being fought at the Sorbonne, Pascal seems to have been immersed in the study of Montaigne, whose stoical qualities seemed to offer a basis for higher standards of social conduct, but whose sceptical view of religion as something venerable and remote appeared to him to be inadequate.

By training and instinct Pascal accepted the finer parts of Montaigne's evaluation of man, but refused to accept his verdict: that he was virtually self-sufficient. If so, what then separated him from the beasts? It was characteristic of Pascal that he should probe further, to find in his study of Epictetus the stoic, the idea of man as an instrument of God's purpose, of resolute and contented acquiescence in his will. His sister's portrait is not exaggerated: 'All his powers were consecrated to the knowledge and practice of Christian morality, to which he bent all the talents with which God had endowed him.'

On November 23, 1654, Pascal underwent his second conversion in a mystical experience of which he has left detailed record; on his death, it was found sewn into his coat. It was the climax of a period of void and mental struggle; towards the end he had been paying visits to Jacqueline, more serene than himself, reading

Saint John's Gospel. This was not however a conversion of gradual persuasion, but a sudden overwhelming conviction, of which he has left vivid record: 'certitude, joy, peace, forgetfulness of the world and of everything except God' were its compelling notes. The proofs of this mystical experience are to be found in his subsequent life and writing. The basis of Pascal's new way of life was indeed the Jansenist view that fallen man was bound by the chain of his sins. But he was always a Jansenist with a difference, for he did not, as is often asserted, surrender the intellect. In one of the *Pensées* he summarises the belief to which he remained faithful: 'it is the way of God who does all things gently to put religion into the mind by reasons, and into the heart by grace'. He believed that there was function for the human will which the Jansenists did not allow, and which was Montaignist in its origin; custom, the repetition of acts of devotion, could put a man on the road to realising the truths implicit in these habits.

Pascal was not bound to Port Royal though he went on retreat there and paid occasional visits. On one such occasion he met Arnauld, near the end of his fight to vindicate himself and looking for someone to present his case in terms which the world could understand. Could Pascal expose the unfairness of the attack? The answer was a letter, written by a *provincial* to 'one of his friends'. Pascal was moved by the spectacle of Arnauld crushed by the professional establishment of the Sorbonne; he responded recklessly, with all his gifts, in the confidence of his new-found faith and his intellectual power. He used the technique of the innocent outsider, the provincial gentleman, who wishes to discover the truth of the matter he hears so much about. In so doing he penetrates to the hollowness of the charge against Arnauld and uncovers the unholy alliance of Thomist and Jesuit against him. His irony, his raillery, his occasional deep thrusts into the absurdities of the situation found a rapturous audience. It was his special strength as a controversialist that he was most logical when he was most aroused. The man, the formula, and the audience, weary and confused, were perfectly matched. In the third letter Pascal demolished the ground upon which Arnauld had been condemned a few days before: his *provincial* was surprised to find that the Sorbonne's judgment rested upon an utterance of Arnauld's which was a direct quotation from Saint Augustine and Saint Chrysostom; what then made them heretics? The answer must be votes, for 'monks are in better supply than arguments'. So M. Arnauld was heretical, not in his opinion but in his person, and 'Saint Augustine's doctrine of grace can never be true while M. Arnauld defends it; its one chance is for him to attack it. That would work, and the only way to destroy Molinism is to induce him to embrace it.'

Indignation at the treatment of a good man had been Pascal's point of departure. But the Jesuits did not intend to let their attack upon Jansenism rest with the condemnation of Arnauld. Pascal may not have been wrong in thinking that Port Royal was fighting for its life; he was fighting for the Jesus of his recent conversion, in the heat and passion of that event. His anger was reinforced by his further study of Jesuit moral theology. As a puritan he suspected the spirit of these works of 'easy devotion' which were alien to his own narrowness and intensity of will and feeling: '*Seigneur, je vous donne tout*'. Restraint was for Pascal as much a part of art and living as it was a condition of faith. As a logician he was repelled by the sloppy thinking of the Jesuits: 'to refuse to love truth is to refuse to love God'. So the next thirteen letters, appearing at intervals throughout 1656, anonymously from one printing press after another, so that the government could not track them down, were directed against the organisation and confessional practices of the Jesuits. Voltaire wrote of them that the earlier ones were as witty as Molière, the latter as grand as Bossuet. The Society of Jesus winced before his barbs, and a large part of clerical and lay opinion was swayed against their practices. Casuistry, a sort of moral case law upon which the priest could draw for the judgment of particular problems of conscience, and Probabilism, the acceptance as provable (not probable) of some opinion on a moral case which is held to be proved (when there is more than one case the penitent could plead the more lenient): these were held up to scorn.

The Jesuits were ill-served by the feeble and pedantic efforts of their apologists; the order was not strong in Paris and the intellectual ascendancy of the Jansenists is as notable as their moral initiative. But the case for the defence ought not to go unregarded.

First, the abuses of a few fashionable confessors should not be held to be typical of the practices of the whole order. Second, it may be urged that the Jesuits, if they were to operate efficiently in the world must use its weapons: *humanum nihil a me alienum puto* was not an ignoble motto. To the order which sent missionaries to Malabar, to Paraguay and to Japan, the little clique of Port

Royal must have seemed to be wrapping themselves in a philosophy of retreat from the world; and the world was the province of the Jesuits. The Jesuits wished to catch many fish; they must cast their net wide. The church of the Counter-Reformation was moving out to meet people who seemed to be abandoning their traditional faith. The Jesuits were the great convertors of the church, trying to adapt Christian beliefs to the fast-moving world of science and literature. They were prepared to go half way to meet rationalism, just as the affair of the Malabar rites showed that they were prepared to go half way to meet paganism. They loved God: did they also love truth? Pascal's answer was: 'To refuse to love truth is also to refuse to love God.' This is the crux of the matter: the Jansenist view of single-standard Christianity and absolute standards of morality over against the insidious idea of the relative—the end justifies the means. There is of course room for both views inside the church, and it may be regarded as tragic that the two attitudes became caricatured in the passions of the duel. Pascal turned a blind eye to the great quality of the Jesuits, their positive concern and adventurous quest for souls. He may too have been slightly infected by the combativeness of Port Royal, their deficiencies of charity, when he accused the Jesuits of spiritual power-politics. But he was confronted by a large array: an international organisation, favoured by Rome, supported by the court and, for the time being, by a majority in the law courts and the Sorbonne. Against this, stood a pamphleteer whose identity might be betrayed at any time, a small body of solitaries and nuns, a few uninfluential friends. In the circumstances the temptation to dramatise must have been powerful, and the wonder is that his invective was so restrained. Ultimately the justification of the *Lettres* is their truthfulness. Pascal knew, as a mathematician, that hours of working could be invalidated by a single mistake of fact; he did not make any. The Jesuits cried *menteur*, but they could prove nothing.

In October 1656, Alexander VII's Bull, *Ad Sacram Sedem*, extended the condemnation of the Five Propositions to the *Augustinus*; the book was banned. How was the question of Papal authority to be faced, when it condemned the book which Jansenists held to be fundamentally true in its reading of Augustine? Fortunately, there was no need for further distinction between *fait and droit*, for *Parlement* refused, upon Gallican grounds, to register the Bull. In December 1660, Louis XIV, weary of the tug-of-war between the Jesuit fathers and 'these Gentlemen of Port Royal', ordered a closure: the Bull *Ad Sacram* was to be enforced, the Formulary signed. The clergy and nuns faced the crisis: was the answer to be martyrdom or a saving clause? Most signed, since the accompanying pastoral letter allowed them to accept the doctrines contained in the Bull, while keeping their peace as to the facts contained in it. Pascal may have helped a sympathetic Vicar-General to draw up the helpful pastoral; ironically his sister Jacqueline was the leader of those who were affronted by the deceit of it, and refused to sign: 'where bishops are showing the courage of girls, it is time for girls to show the courage of bishops'. Her brother persuaded her to accept the olive branch, but its humiliation broke her and she died thirteen weeks later. Then the king forbade the pastoral letter; the Jesuits had manœuvred their opponents into an impasse.

Pascal now held out for integrity and against compromise. Tired of the legalism of Port Royal, stirred by his sister's courage, he waited for his end in God's time, writing his *Pensées* when he could. His last illness came in June, when he asked to be transferred to a hospital for the incurable poor where he could find the real presence of Christ as truly as in the Eucharist. On August 18 he died. His will, dated a few days before, defined his position: 'good Christian, Catholic, Apostolic, Roman'.

Some of the nuns of Port Royal at first refused to sign the Formulary and found support from several bishops, Caulet of Pamiers and Pavillon of Alet amongst them. Port Royal was not recommended to the king by the partisanship of the disreputable de Retz, largely on account of the sympathetic treatment which they had received, during his exile, from his Vicars-General. De Retz had never been a Jansenist, but Mme de Longueville, another *frondeur* and libertine, now adopted them. So Jansenism took on a political tinge which was as suspect to Louis and Mazarin as it was irrelevant to their main ideals.

In 1664, Archbishop Péréfixe attempted to destroy what remained of Port Royal by removing the abbess and the more spirited of the nuns. But in 1669, two years after the accession of Pope Clement IX, a new Formulary was devised by which the nuns, signing 'purely and simply' instead of 'sincerely', were allowed to return to their convent. This was the 'Peace of the Church', achieved ironically by a word-play of which any casuist might be proud.

Leaders of the Counter-Reformation

This dramatic contest must be prominent in any picture of the French church. But the Jesuits kept apart from the regular life of the church in France, and the Jansenists were never more than a tiny minority. Inevitably they stand outside the main currents of Catholic activity at this time: the foundation of a new school of spirituality, the reform of the priesthood and the development of a new approach and method in works of charity. To understand the significance of these we must select a few from the extraordinarily large number of holy and thoughtful people who contributed to this great age of the church in France: Cardinal Bérulle, Mme Acarie, Vincent de Paul and François de Sales.

As Brémond has shown in his study of mysticism in this period, the ecstasies and visions of the great Spanish mystics, St. John of the Cross, St. Theresa and Ignatius Loyola had some worthy followers in France: Catherine de Jésus and Jean de Saint-Samson to name only two. In the hands of Bérulle (1575–1629), writer, preacher and teacher, Spanish mysticism acquired a new and Gallic look. The ideal of all mystics, the giving of self to Christ, or what Bérulle called 'adherence to Christ', was as powerful for Bérulle as it had been for any of his precursors. But with him there enters a characteristic rationality and method, so that his theocentricism seems almost sophisticated. This mystic was also the *honnête homme*. It was not for nothing that Bérulle admired the young Descartes and wished to use his rational approach to serve the interests of religion. Bérulle's contacts were wide; he was a friend of both Saint-Cyran and Jansen; had he lived he would probably have taken the side of the Jansensist in the great controversy. Saint François de Sales, Saint Vincent de Paul and Bishop Bossuet were among those who were proud to be disciples of Bérulle, 'teacher of so many teachers, master of so many saints'. When in 1611 he founded the French Oratory, his object was to establish a new ideal of spiritual life and a new model for the priesthood. The Oratory was opposed by the Jesuits because its looseness of organisation and its teaching mission seemed to imply criticism of their own methods. Indeed Bérulle had intended to wrest from the Jesuits what appeared to be their unhealthy monopoly of Catholic education. Bérulle, for all his gentleness and his moments of *naïveté* was a politician as well as a priest. But the mainspring of his life was a mystical devotion to

God, revealed in the Incarnation; it was this theocentric spirit as much as the practical works that he achieved that made his contribution so important.

Another central figure in the religious revival was Bérulle's cousin, Mme Acarie, 'La Belle Acarie' (1566-1618). The gay and dauntless wife of a prominent Leaguer who had signed the letter inviting the king of Spain to the French throne, she found herself bankrupt at the end of the Wars of Religion, with children to educate and a husband in exile. Within ten years her house had become a social centre of an unusual type: a sort of religious *salon*. The casual visitor might find himself in a group with a royal councillor, a doctor of the church, a woman of the town and a young gentleman of the court. Père Coton was often there; so were Bérulle, Marillac, Richelieu's opponent at court, and Mme de Sainte-Beuve who founded the Ursulines in 1604. Such a hostess must have had quite exceptional power to please and inspire; she was a mystic who could lose herself for many hours in adoration of the Blessed Sacrament and who may have received the stigmata; at the same time she was the most practical of persons who, seems to have moved naturally from the carpet brush to the cross. Certainly she had a talent for getting the best out of people. She played an important part, with Bérulle, in persuading Henry IV to allow her to introduce the Carmelite order into France, and even to devote his gambling profits of a year to its endowment. To one of the Carmelite convents she retired herself, after the death of her husband, a cantankerous person who found life with a *dévot* somewhat trying. Other contemporaries however saw in her the living type of the 'sublime' towards which so many in this age felt vaguely called.

Among the occasional visitors to Mme Acarie's house was one who, although not strictly speaking a Frenchman, must have a prominent part in any history of France: St. François de Sales (1567-1622). He was born in a castle near Annécy, then part of Savoy; his father, a gentleman, had him educated at the Jesuit College of Clermont in Paris for seven years, and then at Padua, where he read law as for a political career. But he rejected his father's plans and devoted himself instead to the service of the church. He accepted a commission of Charles-Emmanuel of Savoy to carry out a mission to the province of Chablais, Calvinist since it had been seized by Berne in 1634. For the first two years he worked in hostile country, without much help from his patron.

There were attempts to assassinate him, and he spent winter nights out in the open, unable to obtain shelter, one of them precariously balanced on the branch of a tree, with wolves howling below. There were few converts, but he prepared the ground well by his heroism and intelligence. Calvinist ministers shook the faith of their patrons when they refused to meet him in open debate. Then Charles-Emmanuel came to his aid with the resources of his state. Protestant books were confiscated, legal documents signed by Protestants were declared invalid and troops quartered on leading Calvinist families, veterans of campaigns against the Indians in Mexico being reserved for the most important. St. François, a gentle humanist, was in no doubt about his Christian duty when he was confronted by sectarianism; he was ready, in his own significant words, to exile Protestant leaders who 'follow their heresy rather as a party than as a religion'.

In 1602 François de Sales became bishop of Geneva, and he remained there until his death despite efforts of both Henry IV and Louis XIII to bring him to France. From his mountain diocese he influenced a large following by his spiritual direction and the grace and lucidity of his writing. With Mme de Chantal, a young widow who became his devoted follower, he founded the Order of the Visitation, especially designed for 'strong souls with weak bodies', for those in fact who did not have the physique to undergo the full strain of monastic life. It was for her, and her *Visitandines*, that he wrote the *Traité de l'aamour de Dieu*, a handbook to mysticism which has become a spiritual classic. More important still was perhaps his *Introduction à la vie dévote*, published in 1609. This work saw so deeply into the problems of the man of the world trying to live in the presence of God that it became the treasured possession of thousands of Catholic laymen, running into forty editions by 1656. Here was the Catholic answer to Luther's 'priesthood of all believers', for St. François held that mystical experience of God was available to all good Catholics. The importance of such a work in preparing the way for lay groups like the Company of the Holy Sacrament does not have to be stressed. Mère Angélique wanted to join his order, St. Vincent de Paul made his followers read a chapter of the *Introduction* every day. François was a saint in the popular reckoning before his death; the process of canonisation was begun only four years after his death, more quickly than that of any other saint in the Church.

Today, perhaps, St. Vincent de Paul (1576-1660) is even better known than St. François, the Christian humanist. He was the man of action of the Counter-Reformation, who believed that the best way to live as a Christian was to work as one. He was a mystic who wished to pursue his mystical experience in the world. So he wrote in one of his lectures: 'Love is divided into affective and effective love. Affective love is a certain flow of the person who loves into the beloved, or the goodness and tenderness one feels for the thing one loves, as the father for his child. Effective love consists in doing those things commanded or desired by the person one loves.' For Monsieur Vincent affective and effective love were inseparable; he was a mystic of action. As Brémond said: 'it was not charity that made him a saint, but his saintliness that made him charitable.' His instructions to his Daughters of Charity reveal his approach to life: 'for your monastery use the houses of the sick, for your chapel, the parish church, for your cloister, the streets of towns or the rooms of hospitals'.

The son of a peasant from a poor village of the Landes, he was given an education with the local Franciscans and then at the University of Toulouse—his father sold a pair of oxen to send him there. Soon after he was ordained he fell into the hands of some Barbary pirates; finding himself the slave of an apostate monk from Annécy, he secured his release and the conversion of his master at the same time. He was for a time the chaplain of the great family of Gondi, tutor of their sons and chaplain of the royal galleys which General de Gondi commanded. Once when a slave collapsed, he is said to have seized his chains and oar and rowed on himself. Then briefly he was a *curé* in a dilapidated village, Châtillon-sur-Lombes, where he was reminded of the spiritual neglect and physical poverty that was the lot of millions of peasants. This he did not forget when he moved back into the pious circle of the Gondis and of the queen herself. For the rest of his life he devoted himself to enlisting the money and aid of the rich and influential in his work for the underprivileged. Like Olier, the founder of Saint Sulpice, and St. John Eudes, the great missioner of Normandy, he recognised that a properly trained priesthood was the prime need. The squalor that he had seen in the countryside indicated an ignorant as well as a negligent clergy. In 1625, with money from the Gondis, he started a college of priests for the specific purpose of evangelising the country districts. This again was not a new idea. At the end of the previous century, the Jesuit fathers Auger and Régis had shown what could be achieved by preaching missions. Michel le Nobletz was active at this time in Brittany. But Vincent de Paul carried the idea of the mission a stage further than these pioneers by creating a new sort of order. From their residence at Saint-Lazare, they went all over France, preaching and catechising, living close to the people as their founder directed. The Lazarists worked in teams, led sometimes by Vincent de Paul himself. Bossuet was later to testify to the immense impact made upon him by Monsieur Vincent when he heard him as a boy. The headquarters at Saint-Lazare was used for retreats for ordinands, where future priests could be formed in their theology and devotional practices. The importance of this development is not lessened by the fact that it spread all over France and was soon followed by the general introduction of seminaries for the training of priests. Cardinal Richelieu himself asked Monsieur Vincent to take over the first of these new seminaries; at his death over four hundred priests were coming from his seminaries every year. This transformed the church in France.

Vincent de Paul is best known perhaps for his *Filles de Charité*, founded to help 'our lords the poor'. Ten years after the founding of the first group at Châtillon in 1517 there were over a hundred; their members included famous names, princesse Montmorency, duchesse de Nemours. Anne of Austria herself went to the poorest hospitals. The Ladies of Charity soon became the Daughters of Charity. Wearing a greyish dress and the white *cornette* typical of peasant clothes of the time, they took the concept of Christian charity out into the darkest places of France; they founded hospitals for incurables, looked after stray children whom they often found dumped at the door of churches, and sent missionaries and nurses to the troops. During the Fronde they set up soup kitchens, nursed the sick and buried the dead. Because he disliked the segregation of most of the religious orders, Monsieur Vincent used lay help whenever he could. He created a lively sense of the obligations of charity amongst the French laity. So the fervour of the devotional revival of the time found practical expression in service to the poor and the outcasts of society. He taught others, as he had taught himself, to live the Lord's Prayer.

One of the activities of this versatile man was to send missionaries to North Africa, to follow up his good work when he had been a slave. There, his Lazarists worked alongside Capucins and Jesuits in one small part of a world-wide outpouring of missionaries from France. There has perhaps been no single period in the history of the church when its message was spread so far so quickly. French missionaries went to Canada, Morocco, Egypt, Syria, Turkey, Abyssinia, Madagascar, India, China, Tibet and Japan. In the East, they were working with or alongside the Spanish and Portuguese, who followed the pioneer, St. Francis Xavier, who had died there in 1552. Père de Rhodes, who wrote a description of his travels around China and the Indies when he returned in 1649, describes how the Jesuits were admitted to the court of the Emperor of China, in Eastern robes, and how they instructed the Chinese in mathematics. One of them, indeed, later became the imperial astronomer. In 1658, the duchesse d'Aiguillon endowed, with some of the money left her by Richelieu, a French bishopric at Tonkin. In the Middle East, the Capucins led the way. Père Joseph, *l'éminence grise*, dreamed all his life of a crusade against the Turks. Frustrated in this, he had none the less organised missions in every part of the Turkish Empire outside Europe, and had persuaded the king to instruct French diplomats there that it was their duty to protect all Christians of whatever nation. But the sphere which the French had all to themselves was Canada, a colony 'born in the very heart of Catholic France'. Champlain claimed that 'the salvation of one soul is worth more than the conquest of an Empire'. Without the Jesuits, French Canada would have been nothing more than a few trading-posts. It was their aim to follow the traditions of Spain in converting the races of the lands they occupied. But they actually went further than this, by outstripping the other settlers, and going to live alone among the natives. Their task was formidable. The Red Indians formed vagrant hunting tribes, worshipped witch doctors, and treated their many wives as chattels. Their cruelty to each other was reflected in their treatment of their would-be converters. One Jesuit, bound to a stake, had one eye removed and a burning piece of wood pushed into the empty socket. Another saw strips of his own flesh eaten in front of him. Friendship with one tribe meant the hatred of another. The Hurons and the Iroquois were bitter enemies, and the Jesuits found themselves taking a leading part in their battles. The rigidity of their religious discipline was an asset in the missionary field, where men of action, with courage based on faith, carried the Cross into hostile lands, and, by bringing them medical comforts, showing them where to settle and how to farm, attracted the Indians to the Christianity which they advertised in so practical a manner. They were followed by the Ursulines and the Hospitalières, teachers and nurses, gallant women, one of whom, Madame de la Peltrie, was so enthusiastic when she saw a group of converted Hurons that she fell on their necks and embraced them severally. The barbarians, commented an on-looker, were surprised and edified. With such people alongside the trappers and fishermen, the French won esteem for the care with which they treated their natives and found them grateful allies in the following century. Perhaps the absence of any colour difficulties in France today is in part due to this.

The full significance of the French missionaries can only be realised by considering French influence, since the seventeenth century, in the areas in which they operated. Canada, Indo-China, Madagascar, Morocco, Egypt, Turkey—wherever the French Empire is or has been, or French diplomatic influence has been strong, there the missionaries went. They played a notable part, for France, in the expansion of Europe.

Taken by itself, this chapter would seem to give the impression of a nation transformed into a Church Militant. It is probably true, however, that all religious movements are minority move-ments. Of course, false values, worldliness and insincerity persis-ted. But, when all qualifications have been accepted, two facts remain to be stressed. First, the Gallican church was stronger, from top to bottom, in 1700 than it was in 1600. It had such a hold over the people that it survived all that a sceptical aristocracy and *bourgeoisie* could do to it, to emerge strong under Napoleon, and triumphant after his fall. The true war of religion was won. Secondly, this revival was of inestimable value to the French crown. In England, the enemies of the government seemed to have a monopoly of moral uplift. Laud battled almost alone against the tide. Such enthusiasm as was displayed by the Church of England in the seventeenth century was largely political, and Anglicanism did not come to life until it became Tory, under Clarendon and Danby. Even then, it was embarrassing to the king, for it was a Parliamentary, and not a royal, church. The Stuarts always dreaded the 'religious' enthusiasms of their subjects. But the Bourbons welcomed them. Secure in the knowledge that the Huguenots were already on the wane, Louis XIII and Richelieu could happily grant them toleration. The energies of Jesuits and

Capucins, Oratorians and Sulpicians, congregations and seminaries, were all being devoted to the greater power and glory of a church of which the King of France was the temporal head, and to the extermination of his enemies at home. The Catholic church was one of the most powerful props of the French monarchy at its greatest period.

His early career

Armand du Plessis de Richelieu was born in 1585, in Paris, the third son of a Poitevin noble. His mother, Suzanne de la Porte, came from a prominent legal family. His father, at the time of Armand's birth, was Grand Provost at the court of Henry III. His son's christening was made the occasion of a fine entertainment to the king and court; over the child's cot was emblazoned the motto: 'Armand for the king'. It was to prove an apt dedication.

The political fortunes of the family were made by his father, François. When he was young, at the prompting of his mother, François had carried out a vendetta murder to avenge his brother, ambushed after a squabble over precedence in church. He had attached himself to the court of Henry III and earned himself the reputation of a fine fighter, a sound Catholic, and a king's man above all. After serving on the committee which investigated the crime of Jacques Clément, he transferred his allegiance to Henry IV. For this he was rewarded with the bishopric of Luçon. This unregarded benefice, in the heart of Poitou, the quarterings of the family coat of arms and the fierce and proud tradition they represented, and a parcel of debts, was the extent of his legacy to his sons when he died, prematurely, in 1590.

François' widow brought up her family in a country château to know pride, in the person of her formidable mother-in-law, and the poverty that was the lot of so many of the nobility in these years of declining rents and fierce competition for place and pension. She had not brought the Richelieu family the riches they may have hoped for when they contracted a *mésalliance* with the daughter of a *bourgeois*, but her gift to Armand was something as important, qualities of self-control, industry and intelligence that early marked him as someone out of the ordinary. At the age of 17 he was required to make a sacrifice of personal inclinations. The elder son was trained at court for the responsibilities of head of the family, the second was destined for the bishopric but suddenly resolved to become a friar. So Armand gave up a hopeful career as a soldier and courtier to be bishop of Luçon.

'I will accept all for the good of the Church and the glory of our house', he wrote to his mother, but this was no mere act of passive obedience. From the start he displayed a lofty seriousness of purpose. He may have wanted to be a soldier and may have been appalled at the restraints and discomforts of a remote bishopric. But it is typical of him that he was resolved to be a good bishop, putting all his nervous energy and administrative ability to the service of his see. For several years before he went for consecration to Rome he studied theology and philosophy. In his diocese, he impressed a people, inured to neglect and exploitation, by his preaching and by his attention to administrative and social questions. He was concerned with prestige and outward appearance and lost no time in improving the amenities of his palace. But he also persuaded the local *parlement* to give funds for the repair of his decayed cathedral. He secured a reduction in the tax-assessment of his people, and produced a special catechism for the poor. Despite ill-health, the migraines, nervous headaches and bad circulation which discomfited him all his life, he travelled in all weathers to outlying parts of his swampy diocese.

Though he might be a model bishop, and single-minded in his concern for his diocese, Richelieu was never truly a *dévot*. His temperament was unmystical and practical; he always thought like a politician. But his faith was deep and coherent, and he befriended and corresponded with some of the most prominent figures of the spiritual revival. His tutor in philosophy had been the English Jesuit Richard Smith, of whom Robert Parsons once said: 'I never dealt with a man in my life more heady and resolute in his opinions'. Later, when these opinions got Smith into trouble in England, Richelieu gave him a home in his palace and a sinecure abbey. A very different person was his correspondent Antoinette d'Orléans, who had become a nun at the nearby abbey of Frontrevault; she founded later her own order, the Daughters of Calvary. Richelieu was not unresponsive to such ardours, which had touched his own family when his brother became a Capucin. The greatest of the Capucins of the day, François le Clerc du Tremblay, an aristocrat like himself and only a few years older, met him through the agency of Antoinette. Richelieu was well acquainted with the problem of heresy, for the Huguenots were strong in Luçon in the heart of Poitou. Père Joseph had a sympathetic ear when he unfolded his ardent designs for war against heresy and his dream of a new crusade. Bérulle, the moving spirit of the Oratory in Paris, was another of Richelieu's contacts, and he founded his second Oratory for the training of young priests in Luçon during Richelieu's episcopate. Even before he came to power the *dévots* were looking to Richelieu's intellect and ambition to further their cause.

His career at court started in the States-General of 1614, when he was selected by the order of clergy to compose the address to the throne. His comprehensive survey of the political scene left his audience in no doubt about his powers of analysis and maturity of judgment. Nor would they miss the point of his remarks about the special fitness of the clergy to serve the state: their vocation required them to cultivate learning and to live honourably, while, since they were celibate, they must be uninterested in material rewards. Recognised by the clergy, he was now used by the Queen-Mother, but at an inopportune time for him, since her Regency was soon to end. He was used on a mission to pacify the rebellious Condé and was designated as ambassador to Spain; before his departure, he was given a place on the Council. There he was involved in the policy of alliance with Spain which was being promoted by the Queen-Mother and the *dévot* party and was sealed by the double marriage of 1615. Richelieu was sympathetic with the *dévot* view that France should line up with Spain in the Catholic front against heresy, but he mistrusted the intentions of Spain. Were they any more disinterested than they had been in Philip II's reign, when they exploited the disunity of France in the name of religion? He made, in fact, a tentative step towards a different policy by informing the princes of Europe that the alliance of France and Spain should not be interpreted as a menace to France's older friendships.

Richelieu habitually took long views. The murder of Concini in April 1617 was not wholly disastrous for him because he had taken care to cultivate the coming man, the duc de Luynes. So he did not go to the Bastille, but to the provinces, to act as Marie's agent during her exile from court. He kept in touch with the government by informing the king of her plans and movements, but did not earn Louis' confidence. He had acquired the reputation of being clever and ambitious, and Louis' entourage talked of him as an enemy. For a time therefore he resumed his duties at Luçon; owing to the suspicion of Luynes, he also spent some months in exile at Avignon. He was frustrated but not inactive. In 1619 he negotiated the Settlement of Angoulême between Marie and the king, and in 1620, after the debacle of the battle at

Ponts-de-Cé, the Peace of Angers. For this service he was rewarded, not with a place on the council, but with Louis' recommendation of a Cardinal's hat; he got it in 1622. He was fortunate in the obvious incompetence of the ministers and the disintegration of their Spanish policy; while they trailed ineffectively in the wake of Spain, and the Bohemian revolt developed into a European war, Richelieu pressed his views through the voice of the Queen-Mother, now reconciled with the king, and the pens of pamphleteers. The most notable of these, Fancan, wrote in 1622, after the failure of French policy in the Val Telline and the Articles of Milan: 'the passage of the Rhine is now in the power and disposition of the Marquis Spinola. . . . In a night he can be at the gates of Strasbourg. . . . On the other side, Spain has seized the passes of the Val Telline . . . the realm of France will be entirely blockaded.'

Père Joseph had meanwhile been disillusioned by the collapse of his plan for a crusade against the Turk. The duc de Nevers was to have been its leader; he had founded a new order, the Christian Militia, for this purpose, approached the Pope, the Duke of Tuscany and some German princes. In 1618 he had been raising troops and securing ships, while Père Joseph preached the message of Holy War, when Philip III suddenly refused leave to the Christian Militia to recruit in Spain. Spain was more interested in the Palatinate than in the crusade; without Spain, the crusade was impracticable. Père Joseph accepted the logic of a situation which was as old as the history of the crusades. Before a Holy War could be launched, Europe must be united. Spain would not think in these terms, therefore France must take her place. From this time he worked for a new orientation of the great powers, as a good Catholic and patriotic Frenchman. As a first step he used his influence to secure the appointment of Richelieu to the Council. In April 1624, despite the manœuvres of La Vieuville, the king concurred.

La Vieuville had been brought in by the Brûlarts as a financial expert whom they expected to take measures to rescue the crown from bankruptcy. He soon showed greater ambition, accused them of taking a share of the subsidy which was being sent to help Maurice of Nassau, and secured their dismissal. Rather than accept Richelieu, Louis then tried to make a chief minister out of La Vieuville. But he had no more experience of state affairs than had Luynes. He was a financier, but even in this sphere he had been successful only because his uncle was a large tax-farmer who had given him useful information on the methods of his friends. Now he floundered. He failed to pay the nobles their pensions punctually, a tactless method of reform by default. He ignored the rest of his council. He also neglected the interests of the church in foreign policy; it was towards this last aspect of his work that Richelieu directed his fire. The Treaty of Compiègne settled the terms of French support for the Dutch against the Spanish. La Vieuville failed to obtain from the Dutch a guarantee of freedom of worship for Roman Catholics. Again, in the summer of 1624, negotiations were opened for a marriage between Prince Charles of England and Henrietta Maria, Louis' sister. Since in the previous year, Charles had actually been proposing to the Spanish Infanta in Madrid, these negotiations were a feather in La Vieuville's cap; their successful conclusion, on top of the Dutch treaty would bring him prestige. Richelieu, approving the match, at the same time contrived to use it against the minister; he urged that the English ought to be made to concede the same rights to Roman Catholics in England as they had been made to concede during the negotiations in Madrid. These very concessions had outraged opinion in England and there was little hope that Buckingham could be made to bend again. The *dévot* party were delighted with Richelieu; La Vieuville had good reason to complain that 'these infernal priests will spoil everything'. His rearguard action was in vain, for he was undermined by a virulent campaign of pamphlets. Fancan's *La Voix Publique au Roi* accused him of corrupt practices; he was hoist with his own petard. Already Richelieu had insisted that his rank, as Cardinal, gave him precedence in council. In August 1624, when La Vieuville was arrested, this became accomplished fact.

The Val Telline

Richelieu inherited a weak, and deteriorating situation, in which it appeared that France was invested by the Hapsburg powers and that they were, in Germany at least, irresistible. The last German Protestant forces were being chased from the field; there was a prospect of further trouble from the Huguenots at home; the Val Telline was open to the passage of Spanish troops. Only by a successful exercise in the latter theatre could Richelieu damage the Hapsburg interests without involving France in war. War he knew, because of the weakness of the armed forces, the irresponsible powers of the nobility and the truculent independence of the Huguenots, he must avoid. Moreover, he was by no means yet committed to the full-blooded anti-Hapsburg policy with which he was credited by the active propagandists—*bon français*—of the type of Fancan. His position in council was precarious, dependent on the favour of the king, and therefore, to some extent, upon the good-will of Marie de Médicis and the Spanish Queen, Anne of Austria. He could not afford to jettison immediately the support of the *dévots*. If his goal was indeed fixed, and sure, in the first months of power, he took pains to conceal it. He trod warily and watchfully. He listened to the voice of Bérulle, who saw in the English match the beginning of a crusade to reconquer England for the Faith, as well as to that of Fancan. At the first sign of revolt at home, he withdrew from his campaign in the Val Telline, resolved to play no further part in the European struggle until he had dealt with the Huguenot problem. This at least was uncontroversial and engaged the sympathy of all parties. A successful assault upon this state within the state would do more than anything to please the *dévots* and satisfy the king; then he might move more confidently into Europe.

The French were already involved in the struggle for the control of the 60-mile-long stretch of the Val Telline. A glance at the map will show the importance of this valley which runs north and then east from Lake Como, and turns north again when it reaches the Tyrol. Along its southern side lies Venetian territory, and to the north, Switzerland. Since the great Spanish base of Milan is only a few miles south of Como, it was the link between the Hapsburg powers, involving a ten days' journey from Milan to Vienna. It was the only route through the Alps which did not involve breaking the neutrality of Venice or Switzerland, and thus marching through land dominated by a potentially hostile power. Its control therefore interested both the Hapsburgs and their enemies. The Venetians had the additional worry that it was the only land route for their trade to Western Europe which did not pass through Hapsburg territory. Finally the valley was a notable recruiting ground, for its men lived hard and had to look abroad for wealth; Henry IV had raised 10,000 men there.

The Val Telline's population of 80,000 was ruled by a federation of Leagues of mountain dwellers, known as the Grisons, or Gray Leaguers. The Leagues ran their domestic affairs through democratically elected officers, but they governed the unfortunate inhabitants of the Val Telline through unpaid officials who were expected to extract what they could from their subjects. The Reformation had greatly increased the perils of this overlordship. The population of the valley was Roman Catholic, but the Grisons Federation was divided, one League being Catholic, one Zwinglian, the third divided within itself. Furthermore the league had a constitutional procedure which actually encouraged the intervention of foreign powers. Any group of 300 could meet together on a plea of public danger, in a *Strafgericht* or tumultuous assembly. From the death of Henry IV until 1621, French influence was exerted on the Spanish side, in accordance with the pro-Hapsburg policies of Marie and her ministers. In 1620 the Val Telline was essential to Spain, as Spinola was building up his army for an invasion of the United Provinces at the end of the Truce, and valuable also to the Emperor, who needed Spanish support for his operations in the German war. Fortunately for them, the Protestant Leagues had provided them with a plausible excuse for occupying the valley, by murdering the head of the Catholic family of Planta, the Duke of Feria. The new Spanish governor of Milan organised a counter-murder plot, and then put the warring valley under Spanish protection.

Thus far the French general Guiffier had co-operated with the Spanish. But the interests of France required toleration for the Roman Catholics, not domination by Spain. In 1621, Marshal Bassompierre and the Pope succeeded in getting all parties to sign the Treaty of Madrid, which achieved French ends. The Grisons were restored to their control of the valley, but were forbidden to persecute Catholics. Unfortunately this Treaty needed a guarantor, and none could be found; so war broke out again, the Spanish moved 18,000 men into the valley fortresses and all was to be done again. La Vieuville negotiated the Treaty of Paris between France, Savoy and Venice, who all agreed to force the terms of the Treaty of Madrid on to the combatants. But the Spanish were now unwilling to go back to this, since their commitments in the west now included the Palatinate, which Spinola occupied while the Elector Frederick was busy in Bohemia. Eventually the Pope agreed to act as guarantor of the Madrid settlement. But this proved to be a solution more satisfactory to the Spanish than it was to the French, since Papal troops in the valley allowed the Spanish free transit. The Pope was only too delighted to see the armies marching north towards the battlefields of Germany and away from papal territory in Italy; as he politely indicated, he did not wish to see them come back the way they had gone. Eventually, the French decided to end this unsatisfactory state of affairs. In the summer of 1624 the marquis de Coeuvres led 7,000 French and 4,000 Swiss troops into the valley, the Pope's forces withdrew and the triumphant French decreed that the Val Telline's inhabitants should be ruled by their own officials, paying a tribute of 25,000 crowns to the Grisons. This solution could however only be upheld against the Grisons by French troops permanently stationed in the valley.

The marquis de Coeuvres' intervention was part of a cautious incursion by France into European affairs, the first direct use of French troops in the war which had started when the Elector Palatine had accepted the crown of Bohemia. It had soon become apparent that the future of Protestantism in Germany was at stake; if the Protestants in Germany lost, Austria gained; if Austria, then Spain too. France could not therefore be indifferent to the outcome of the war. At first, negotiations had been carried out under the direction of Père Joseph to build up a Roman Catholic party; the hollow face, red beard and sandals of the Capucin became familiar in the courts of Europe. Savoy and Venice were already allies with France over the Val Telline, and it was now proposed to bring in Maximilian of Bavaria. This failed over the question of the Palatine Electorate, which had been forfeited by Frederick and granted by the Emperor to Maximilian of Bavaria. The Emperor's arbitrary action embarrassed the French government, since Henrietta Maria had just married Charles, Prince of Wales, and brother-in-law of the displaced Elector. So Bavaria had to be left out, and the alliance took on a deeply Protestant tinge. La Vieuville then signed the Treaty of Compiègne with the Dutch, and planned to bring in the English as well.

Meanwhile other anti-Hapsburg Protestant alliances were made, which were mutually encouraging: Lutheran Sweden and Denmark, Calvinist Brandenburg and the United Provinces. In the formation of this group too, the French had played a modest part, but it would be misleading to pretend that they had constructed it, or that it was the work of Richelieu, who was not in power until after it had been completed, and who disliked its Protestant aims.

Indeed, Richelieu's attitude was equivocal. In 1626, it was by no means certain that he was not going to fall in with the policy of Bérulle and the *dévots* and join an alliance of the Catholic crowns against heresy. The treaty of Monçon, by which Richelieu accepted the withdrawal of French troops from the Val Telline, has often been represented as the result of 'a stab in the back' by the Huguenots or by the Chalais conspiracy; it is quite possible that Richelieu was relieved to have a pretext to call off an operation whose unpopularity at court threatened to destroy him.

The great siege

Since the death of Henry IV there had been a deep division amongst Huguenots about the attitude that they should adopt in the face of the avowed hostility of the *dévots*. The *prudents*, amongst whom Bouillon was now prominent, thought that safety lay in loyalty. The *fermes*, led by the Rohan family, urged active resistance, while the crown was still weak, to restore the Huguenot courts attached to the *parlements*, and to secure guarantees of all the rights won by the Edict of Nantes, including the fortifications originally promised for only eight years. They were encouraged in this view by the heroic defence of Montauban in the war of 1621-2, and by the relative insufficiency of the royal troops in the campaigns of those years. They also had no reason to suppose that Richelieu was not under the influence of Bérulle; his reputation was still that of the representative of the *dévots*, whose support had helped him to obtain power. They have been blamed for disrupting Richelieu's attempt to relieve the pressure on their co-religionaries in Germany. But it is understandable that they may have thought, in this dark hour of Protestantism in Europe, that the Cardinal Minister would consolidate his place by a general assault upon the Huguenots, a policy which they knew would be acceptable to the king. They had no reason to be pessimistic about the outcome of war. The number of Huguenots was steadily increasing, by about a quarter of a million since the beginning of the century; there were at least 30,000 in Paris alone. There was a steady change in the leadership of the movement; the feudal outlook of the nobility was being slowly transformed in the face of the new prestige of the monarchy, the subtle pressures of fashion, and the ardour of the church. Though many of the great names remained to the movement, Bouillon, La Trémoille, La

Force and Châtillon, the most influential Huguenots were *bourgeois*, men like the financiers Laffemas and Tallement, lawyers like the Hérouards, men who had everything to lose by military revolt. When it came to the point, the revolt was a minority affair of hot-heads. The Huguenots could not put a large army in the field, and relied upon old loyalties and walled cities. The greatest of these was La Rochelle. Its gallant resistance in a fourteen-month siege shows how formidable the revolt would have been it if had been more widely supported. The revolt of the Rohans may have been misjudged; but it was neither the forlorn adventure, nor the stab in the back, that it has sometimes been called.

An irresponsible piece of piracy by Soubise was the occasion for war. He siezed five ships belonging to the duc de Nevers in the harbour of La Rochelle, and sailed them off to England. The moment was chosen when Louis and Richelieu were far away in the Alps. In London the Duke of Buckingham was party to the plot, and Charles I was ready to play his minister's game. La Rochelle was a famous Huguenot centre, with a sturdy tradition of privateering and a chronic grievance against the government. Soubise was the brother of Rohan, the hero of the last Huguenot war, one of the most appealing figures amongst the French aristocracy, not least perhaps because he spent most of his life fighting in the service of a lost cause. After the treaty of Montpellier he had retired to his estate at Castres where a contemporary described him as leading a single life in a huge house, drinking only water, breaking in his own horses and helping his tenants. He had not been consulted by his brother about the *coup* at La Rochelle, but he now determined to turn it into a major effort to secure the rights won by the Edict of Nantes. He went round the towns of Languedoc, the Holy Scriptures carried before him by a pastor, preaching unity and war.

The leading citizens of La Rochelle were by no means certain that they wanted war. In fact they were forced to fight largely because Buckingham decided to 'rescue' the town before it was even attacked. He had been disappointed in the marriage he had arranged between Charles I and Louis XIII's sister Henrietta Maria. So in July 1627 he appeared off La Rochelle with a fleet and an army to help the citizens in their struggle. The old duchesse de Rohan persuaded them to be amenable to the English, for they had actually gone so far as to bar their gates against them and English troops landed on the neighbouring island of Rhé. Only three months later did hostilities break out between the town itself and the French army which had been gathering outside it, for Richelieu wanted the Rochellois to make the first move.

He staked everything on the siege of La Rochelle, and there were not wanting Cassandras to remind him, as it dragged on, how Luynes had taken the same risk at Montauban. Richelieu understood the importance of winning wars by concentrating forces at the vital point; if La Rochelle fell, nothing else would stand against him for long. His problem was to keep the royal army together, for the siege lasted from September 1627 until October 1628. Louis had given him authority over the noble generals but had not expected him to be able to exert it. 'They are as likely to obey him as to obey the kitchen boy,' was his comment. He himself remained at the siege all the winter, but in February went off to hunt; some were surprised when he returned in April and remained with the army till the end, but he found the siege operations absorbing, and knew the moral value of his presence. Meanwhile Richelieu ensured that the troops were well paid and that they were reminded, by the holding of daily services, of the religious significance of their mission. The fact that the army was static made it easier to arrange for its supplies and to supervise the conduct of the troops. None the less, a siege lasting over a year was a remarkable undertaking, and Richelieu never left it. He was faced with the risk of a large English reinforcement for the garrison, and he had to starve the town, since he could not storm it, because of the bulky new fortifications and impassable salt marshes which baffled the king's artillery. He had no navy. To keep out English or other food-ships, he built a stone dyke across the mouth of the port 647 fathoms long, based on sunken ships held to the bottom of the sea by thick wooden stakes.

Buckingham's original landing ended humiliatingly. He had laid siege to Fort Saint Martin on the island of Ré, held by a small royalist garrison. Confident that it would soon surrender, he exchanged presents with its general, island melons for his bottles of scented orange water; the garrison held out, however, and Richelieu gathered an army on the mainland. Buckingham tried to take the fort by storm, but his ladders were too short. Finally Richelieu managed to get his army across to the island in small boats, locally commandeered, surprised the English and pushed them off the island. Future English expeditions were fatally inhibited by memories of this disaster. A fleet under Denbigh arrived off the dyke in May, before it was completed, and the garrison got their flags out and celebrated with double rations. But Denbigh could not persuade his captains to make the attack and sailed away. A third expedition, under Lindsay, sailing after Buckingham had been assassinated, ended in the same way. Leaky ships, bad food, and the intense political unpopularity of her government, led England to one of the more unhappy experiences in her history, and dramatically lowered her prestige abroad.

There seemed to be little chance that the Rohan family would succeed where the English had failed. Soubise was inside La Rochelle, avoiding front-line action on the orders of his mother; when the English sailed away, he went with them. Meanwhile Rohan was struggling to raise an army in the south and west. But at this critical time, the Huguenots were found wanting; Richelieu was not. Luynes had allowed himself to be distracted by Rohan's activities outside Montauban, but Richelieu stayed where he was, and Rohan could not muster a force strong enough to lead against him. This was partly because of the scale of Richelieu's preparations, but also because of the inherent weakness of the Huguenots. No longer would peasant bands muster at the call of their feudal lord. So Rohan had to content himself with fortifying other positions and waiting to see the strongest fortress of all give up its keys.

This did not happen until All Saints Day 1628. The resistance could not have been more determined. The old duchesse de Rohan fared better than some; her household ate first the carriage horses, and then the harness. Others died of starvation, while the mayor, Jean Guiton, always protesting loyalty to the crown, tried to bargain for the rights of his city and its religion. When the end came, Richelieu showed a magnanimity which recalls his words to the Huguenots of Luçon, when he first came to his diocese: 'I hope that we shall be one in love, and I shall do all in my power to make it so, for that will be best for us and most pleasing to the king.' The siege had been of unprecedented length, and the rule that a fallen city should be sacked was accepted in France, as elsewhere. The complete discipline shown here by the royal army was a remarkable tribute to the king's control over the nobility: even the food which was transported into the starving, but still wealthy, town was sold at the same price as in the camp. The port was soon able to resume its old prosperity, but its political independence was smashed. The walls were rased, every church was given back to the Catholics, and the special privileges of the town were revoked. Guiton, whose fierce civic pride had kept the resistance going against mounting opposition in his own council, who had twice fainted from hunger in church services, went off into exile. On November 1st the king made his formal entry, and the Cardinal who had worn the buff coat and cuirass of a soldier throughout the siege, now a priest again, offered the sacrament to the kneeling generals of the king.

The end of Huguenot resistance elsewhere came in more ordinary fashion. During the siege, Condé, in the orthodox way, had been rampaging about Languedoc, putting inhabitants of Huguenots towns to the sword, or sending them to the galleys. He temporarily increased his difficulties by frightening doubtful consistories into determined resistance. But the fall of La Rochelle gave the half-hearted the chance to lay down their swords. Rohan could not hold the towns together, even though he managed to sign a treaty with Spain. All he could do was to persuade Richelieu to deal with each town separately. In 1629 the Peace of Alais was signed. All Huguenot fortifications were to be destroyed; they lost their rights as a separate political organisation, their privileged towns, magistracies and lawcourts. Complete religious toleration was however to be observed. For this Richelieu was attacked by the *dévots*; it marks his complete breach with that interest. He shared with them the desire for uniformity, and he had no respect for *Messieurs les prétendus réformés*. But he looked ahead to a time when he might have to fight in Europe with Protestant allies. The duc de Rohan was moreover a brave man; not disloyal to the king either, according to his idea of loyalty. Driven to desperation by the behaviour of one Huguenot Consistory, he shouted out in a rage 'you are all republicans'—the worst insult he could think of. Rohan belonged to an obsolete tradition in that he thought that subjects could negotiate with their king, and he was prepared to look for the support of foreign powers. This was not odd behaviour; Turenne and the younger Condé were to do the same in the Fronde. Richelieu was anxious to conciliate him by granting the toleration that he sought, and Rohan was soon to prove one of his most efficient generals. His judgment was sound. The vital difference between the Wars of Religion and the Fronde was that, during the Fronde, the Huguenots, when they fought at all, fought on the side of the king.

From 1629 the struggles of the Monarchy against the nobles were not complicated by religion. Richelieu was right, too, in judging that toleration would not strengthen Protestantism in France. He believed that missionaries could succeed where force might fail. Time, as well as truth, he felt, was on his side.

8 RICHELIEU AND THE FRENCH ARISTOCRACY

The Chalais conspiracy

In 1629, Richelieu initiated negotiations with Gustavus Adolphus of Sweden, through his ambassador Charnacé, which were to lead to alliance with a Lutheran power, with the express object of saving the German Protestant states from the dominion of the Emperor. This new alignment was loathed by the *dévots* and the Spanish party at court. They had an alternative programme to offer, and their opposition to the Cardinal, which came to the boil in the critical years 1629-30, had a serious political content. Not all the enemies of Richelieu could claim, however, that they had a constructive purpose. The loves, hates, poses and ambitions of the great feudal magnates, their wives and mistresses, do not add up to a responsible opposition. But they had motives for disliking the Cardinal, for he was bent upon reducing their independence, in the province as Governors, in court as councillors and officers of the household. Richelieu's opponents were united in one thing only: their desire to destroy him before he destroyed them.

The Chalais conspiracy of 1626 can be traced to two immediate causes: the Cardinal's edict of that year ordering the destruction of private fortresses, and the projected marriage of Gaston d'Orléans and Marie de Montpensier. In part, a furious reaction against the authority of the Cardinal, and in part a tangle of personalities and private ambitions, it is typical of the domestic crises which Richelieu had to face and which made it difficult for him to pursue a consistent or effective foreign policy. Orléans was 18 in 1626. As the younger brother of the king, he was heir-apparent, a position which would have made him the centre of court intrigue, even if Louis XIII had been more robust. If he had been strong-minded, or unambitious, he might have played a distinguished or honourable role. He was, unfortunately, both ambitious and cowardly. He seems to have had no consistent idea or policy: his life is characterised by a chronic restlessness, dishonesty and sense of grievance. He was a bad enemy, because he did not have the nerve to pursue a dangerous policy, a bad friend, because in a crisis his first recourse was always to save himself by accusing others.

These faults, which have made him a figure of contempt in

French history, may not have been evident when marriage was planned for him with Marie de Bourbon, duchesse de Montpensier the richest heiress in France. He did not want the match; the duchesse was unamusing. His tutor, the Maréchal d'Ornano, also wanted to prevent him marrying for he was in love with the duchesse himself, or professed to be so. The comte de Soissons, a representative of the Bourbon line, was another candidate for Mme de Montpensier's hand. Anne of Austria, childless after ten years of marriage, was anxious lest her own position should suffer if the young princess were to have children. The Queen's intimate friend, the duchesse de Chevreuse, 'so brilliant that her ideas seemed like a flash of lightning, yet so sagacious that no great man in any century would have disavowed them', induced her lover, the marquis de Chalais, to join the conspiracy. Condé of course was in it, and so was the duc de Vendôme, Gaston's own illegitimate half-brother, who went so far as to suggest that 'the Crown would look well on Monsieur's head'. The conspirators did not reckon with the efficiency of Richelieu's intelligence service. When rumours reached him, he acted with typical promptitude and disregard of noble privilege: d'Ornano was sent to the fortress of Vincennes. Chalais then panicked and revealed the plot: the next day Richelieu was to be killed at a banquet in the presence of Monsieur. Vendôme was imprisoned and was deprived for ever of his governorship of Brittany. Gaston, declaring his affection 'to all those whom His Majesty will honour with his confidence', made a humiliating confession, the first of many. For reward he was given an income of 100,000 *livres*, a pension of 560,000 *livres*, and an escort of eighty guards in velvet liveries embroidered with his initials in gold. This was the cost to France of his vanity, but it did not satisfy Gaston, who promptly embarked on a further plot. Mme de Chevreuse, who would not concede defeat, persuaded Chalais to approach him with a plan to put himself at the head of the Huguenots and claim the throne. Again Richelieu was informed, again Gaston confessed. He accepted the Montpensier marriage in return for restoration of his properties and favour at court. Mme de Chevreuse was exiled, and Chalais was executed. The fact that he was a member of the important Talleyrand family did not deter Richelieu. Chalais certainly suffered for his offence. Gaston sought to save him by bribing the executioner to stay away. An amateur headsman was therefore employed, a prisoner who was provided with a cooper's axe. It was only at the thirty-fourth stroke that he managed to sever the head.

Two policies

There was slightly more coherence about the next challenge to Richelieu's power. It centred round Marie de Médicis, who alone had the power to influence the king against Richelieu, and it was directed by two very different men, Cardinal Bérulle and Michel Marillac. Bérulle was no politician; in the world of affairs he was lost. His mother had removed the family estates from his care after she discovered that he could not distinguish between one type of coin and another. His interests in matters of state was only roused when he believed that the interests of the church were involved, and his opposition to Richelieu was in no way personal. Richelieu himself wrote of him that 'he did not know what it was to hate anybody'. His saintly personality commanded great respect at court, and it was embarrassing for Richelieu to have his foreign policy condemned by the founder of the Oratory, his own adviser and benefactor. Bérulle's death, in October 1629, may well have altered the result of the affair, for Marillac's motives for opposition, though understandable to us, were less convincing in Louis XIII's court.

Marillac was an old man who had obtained political power late in life; Richelieu made him *surintendant* in 1624, when he was 61, and Keeper of the Seals in 1626. In the latter capacity he presided over the Assembly of Notables, where he championed naval reform. During the next four years he showed that he was an efficient administrator making some useful improvements in the working of the councils. He also displayed a mind of his own; he was not prepared to submit entirely to the Cardinal's direction. A devout Roman Catholic, he had a private cell in the forecourt of a Carmelite monastery. He also opposed Richelieu's foreign policy on grounds of expense and, less surely, of strategy. This rift had been allowed to harden because of the long absences of the king and Cardinal in the wars of 1627-30, when the Council was divided.

Marie acted as regent of the north during the siege of La Rochelle, and of the whole country during the Italian campaign. Marillac was always at her side. He disliked the anti-Hapsburg drift of Richelieu's Italian campaign, and his negotiations in Germany. He feared that the Hapsburgs would retaliate by invading France from the Spanish Netherlands or from Lorraine. He knew more than Richelieu of the condition of people, and the domestic dangers of this policy. As he wrote to Richelieu in 1630: 'France is full of sedition. The *parlements* do not punish anybody. The king sends judges to do so, and *Parlement* refuses to ratify their judgments. So sedition is officially authorised.' In 1628 there had been riots at Amiens, caused by a rumour that there was to be a tax on goods bought and sold in the town, to pay for some new offices that had just been created. They were incited by the small manufacturers and their apprentices. Neither mayor nor *parlement* would act to suppress them, for they disliked the new office-holders and the tax. The Governor of Picardy wrote that he could not raise enough troops to restore order, and the royal official, who had been sent to organise the tax, gave up the attempt. Opposition of this sort often won its point, but it was usually local and unco-ordinated. In 1630, however, there was trouble throughout Languedoc and Provence, and amongst the wine growers of Burgundy, when the government tried to substitute royal for provincial agents to collect their taxes. Here the pride and the vested interests of the *pays d'état* were roused. In Languedoc, the governor, Montmorency, stood by the Estates; action of this sort emphasised the limitations of the central government when local authority lay with an unco-operative grandee. In Lyon itself, when the Queen and Queen-Mother were in residence, troops had to be called out to deal with the mobs. It is not surprising to find Marillac demanding that the war should be brought to an end. He possessed neither the Cardinal's political vision nor his stoical indifference to social discontents.

By 1630 he had completely won over Marie de Médicis to his way of thinking. She had a new personal grudge to excite her. As a Médicis she had a low opinion of the Italian house of Gonzague. Now French armies had invaded Italy in order to defend the claim to Mantua of the duc de Nevers; the duke was a member of the Gonzague family, of Italian blood, though a French subject. At the same time, Gaston d'Orléans, whose first wife had died soon after giving birth to a daughter, now set his heart on another member of the house. To lure him away from this match she made promises of governorships, which Richelieu persuaded the king not to ratify; since the provinces in question were Burgundy and Champagne, on the vulnerable eastern frontier, it is not surprising. Richelieu threatened to resign on the issue; after a tearful reconciliation, Louis confirmed his status by giving him the official title of Principal Minister. Marie was now his open enemy.

The struggle in Italy, which Louis and Richelieu took up with urgency immediately after the siege of La Rochelle, drew the French army twice across the Alps to the valley of the Po. Nevers claimed, in Mantua and Montferrat, lands which lay between Savoy and Milan, in the heart of the rich open plain of North Italy, land that the Hapsburgs had to hold if Spanish armies were to be able to march to Germany. So Spain pressed Charles-Emmanuel of Savoy, aged 77 and in the last year of his life, to join in throwing out Nevers. In 1629 the French invaded Savoy, forced Charles-Emmanuel to change sides, and left a garrison in Casale. The Hapsburgs reacted by sending two armies to take Casale and reduce Savoy to a satellite. In December 1629 Richelieu again led an army, this time without Louis, to the rescue of Casale. He captured Pinerolo, a fortress on the very edge of the Po valley; there, with the snowy Alps behind him, he looked out across the level fields to the horizon where stood Milan. This was the moment for decision. It was not often that Richelieu and Louis were apart; in a state governed from the centre by a very few people, the rulers seldom need to write to each other. This occasion therefore offers us a rare chance to study the way in which Louis and Richelieu reached their decisions. In his long memorandum, Richelieu set out the arguments for and against continuing the war. He advised Louis to consult responsible persons at home to find out the truth about conditions inside the country. He then presented the two possibilities abroad: a respectable peace, with Savoy intimidated and Nevers installed in his lands, but with the Hapsburgs still dominating the Po valley, their war effort in Germany unimpeded; or war, in alliance with Savoy, to overthrow this dominion. Richelieu warned Louis of the expense, the revolts he might expect at home, the hazard of Hapsburg attack on the eastern frontier, which might be all the worse if it coincided with a disturbance by Gaston. Louis discussed this memorandum with his council, and joined Richelieu in the Alps.

Day of Dupes

Richelieu judged the peace party's chance of success slight so long as the war was successful, because a large part of the nobility was employed in it. It was a maxim of his that the nobility should devote themselves to arms in the state's service; he thought rightly that war was something that they would respond to. Trouble came when the army caught the plague and Louis had to come home for fear of catching it. Desertions followed at once, another of the problems of the commanders of the day. There were *dévots* among the generals, Marillac's brother among them. Casale was still enduring siege, while the Imperialists overran Mantua. Then Louis fell ill, not of the plague but with an internal abscess. He had been unwell throughout the year, and his physician had bled him forty times in twelve months. He became delirious and the guard was instructed to arrest Richelieu as soon as he died; but the abscess burst and he recovered. Marie and Anne nursed him back to health and insinuated their point of view; they hoped that Louis, devout in his way, and given to introspection at the best of times, would realise that it was mortal sin to fight against the Catholic cause. Queen, Queen-Mother and Confessor accompanied him to Paris, where, in the Louvre early in November, was enacted the famous scene which was the prelude to the 'Day of Dupes'. Marie was pressing her case against Richelieu when he walked in, through an unlocked door, to a passage leading to her private chapel. Marie, 'froth and venom, spat herself abroad'; Richelieu, for once not master of himself, fell on his knees before the king; Louis retired in confusion, without a word. Marie and her friends interpreted his silence to indicate assent and began to appoint new ministers, anticipating the Cardinal's disgrace. He, too, may have thought that he was lost, and considered flight to Le Havre, of which place he was governor. But luckily for him, he obeyed the king's summons.

Richelieu's courage had been tried severely this year. The danger from Lorraine had become acute, as Francis, Duke Charles's brother and bishop of Verdun, had fled to Germany to appeal to the Emperor for help in dislodging the French from his bishopric. At the Diet of Ratisbon, Père Joseph, thinking to disembarrass his master, had signed away Casale and Montferrat, in a treaty with the Emperor. Richelieu rejected his agent's work in a fury. But this was not the worst. A treaty could be, and was, repudiated; the loss of Louis XIII's favour would be the end. At Versailles he knelt before the king to await his sentence. Louis raised him; the witnesses left the room. In affirming his support of the Cardinal, Louis had made a gesture of independence which was to be of the greatest importance. 'I honour my mother,' he said, 'but my obligations to the state are greater than towards her.' Richelieu was effusively grateful: 'I shall have no greater happiness in this world than in making known to Your Majesty by ever-increasing proofs, that I am the most devoted subject and most zealous servant that ever king or master had in this world.'

Louis XIII

Louis XIII has some claim to be called a great French king. Perhaps his most important contribution to his country was his steady support of the Cardinal in the face of pressures from his family and court. But he was no mere cypher. He did not hand over all executive authority to his principal minister. He had a lofty view of the calling of a king, and he did not shrink from the labours and responsibilities of absolute government.

His personal characteristics were not appealing. Indeed, as a young man, he was a figure of some pathos, one whom people tended to treat with contempt, until they felt the lash of his tongue or came to appreciate his latent determination. After a boyhood of harshness and neglect, it is not surprising that he was shy and inhibited, especially in the presence of women. He was capable of love-affairs, as with Mme de Hautefort and Mme de la Fayette, but in these relationships, as in those with young men like Luynes and Cinq Mars, he displayed a certain inadequacy. Incapable of sustained and level friendship, he seemed to revel in emotional scenes, as if he wanted to be humiliated. Mme de Motteville said of him that the only tender spot in him was the capacity for appreciating his own sufferings. This is of a piece with a masochistic tendency which showed itself in sudden acts of insensate violence; it was said that he took pleasure in squashing the head of young sparrows in his hand. When he was a boy he had an almost ungovernable temper; for this his father's invariable penalty was whipping, administered by his governess. Throughout his life he was subjected to *mauvaises humeurs*, moods of hysterical depression when he was almost unapproachable. He found release from his cares in the hunting field, where he excelled, for he was an intrepid rider, in supervising the operations of his troops, even in shoeing a horse at his private forge. He cared little for the formalities of court life and liked to bury himself in retreats like his hunting-box at Versailles, with a few chosen companions, amongst whom was usually his loyal and sensible equerry Saint-Simon.

But Louis was neither simple-minded nor an escapist. He took his *métier du roi* seriously. He had an excellent head for the details of government, taking special interest in military matters. He was always angry when he discovered that his ministers were being casual in their dealings with him, using his name for some act that he had not authorised, or not keeping him properly informed. Ministers might not like him, but they learned to respect his zeal and watchfulness. He worked daily with at least one of the Secretaries of State, attended Councils frequently and was always ready to work on correspondence far into the night. He was also conscientious in personal appearances, on occasions such as awkward meetings of *parlements*, when only his presence would make his instructions effective. He earned the soubriquet 'just', partly because of the number of executions that took place in his reign, but also because of his care for the rights and traditions of his subjects. In more than one crisis he showed a firmness of will that was truly royal. In the year of Corbie, when Richelieu advised him to evacuate Paris, he refused to do so, as if he knew instinctively that a French king must not abandon Paris; this was precedent for Louis XIV's similarly staunch conduct in 1709.

Montmorency and Cinq Mars

The affair of Montmorency illustrates plainly the dangers of Richelieu's position and the nature of his problem. Since the Day of Dupes, the position of the Queen-Mother had been uncomfortable. Richelieu seemed to be secure in the favour of the king, who would not easily forgive the humiliating behaviour of his mother; from her confinement in the country, in July 1631, Marie fled to Brussels. Gaston meanwhile had been occupying himself in Lorraine, making love to the duke's sister, whom he married, and engaging the support of the unstable duke for a new adventure. He found a more formidable ally in Henri de Montmorency, aged 37, governor of Languedoc and Constable of France.

Languedoc, a *pays d'état*, remote from Paris and notorious for its Huguenotism and its independence, had been restive for some time. The Estates feared the loss of their privileged position, and the peasants the increase of taxation that would follow from it. The governor had hitherto been loyal to the court; he had been rewarded with a marshal's baton in 1629, and in 1630 he was one of the commanders in Italy. The family claimed by hereditary right the Constable's sword, and flattered themselves with the title of *premier baron chrétien*; their tradition was one of loyal service to the crown, but service essentially in the feudal manner. The 'great constable', a leading protagonist in the Religious Wars, was Henri's great grandfather; Henri himself was more than governor of Languedoc, for by virtue of his great estates in the area, his private force of tenants, servants and friends, and his influence with the Estates, he was virtual ruler of the province. His rising in 1632 may be seen therefore as one of the last gestures of a vanishing feudal society. It turned out to be futile. The year was not a hard one, the peasants did not rise, and the time was past when the *bourgeois* could feel any enthusiasm for the feudal banners even of a Montmorency. His small force was defeated at Castelnaudary by the royal troops, and Montmorency was taken prisoner. He had tried to die honourably in the field, for he had no illusions about the fate of a rebel, but the surgeons kept him alive to face the judges of the *parlement* of Toulouse. They had recently been protesting against the burdens of war taxation, but when it came to a case of treason they did not hesitate to apply the inflexible logic of Roman law: *quod principi placet legis vigorem habet*. Montmorency was sentenced to death and all the pleas of his friends could not save him. He attracts sympathy more by the manner of his trial and death than by the merits of his case.

Montmorency stood, in his dignified if futile way, for an obsolete cause; Cinq Mars stood for no recognisable principle but his own advancement. The problem of this embarrassing young man was partly, however, of Richelieu's own making. He always felt it necessary to control the king's private life; even after the unexpected birth of the dauphin, in September 1638, and that of a second son two years later had put Gaston d'Orléans at two removes from the succession, he did not relax his vigilance. He chose the dauphin's governess, Mme de Lansac, in the teeth of the queen's opposition. When the king seemed to be becoming dangerously attached to the *dévot* Mme de la Fayette, Richelieu used his influence to persuade her to take the veil. Louis XIII was deeply attached to Saint-Simon, who served him in such a disinterested way that Richelieu had no ground for suspicion; but he had him dismissed in the nervous year of 1636 when it was found that he had given a friendly warning to an acquaintance about to be arrested for treason. Saint-Simon left a large gap in the king's affections, and there is little doubt that Richelieu acted deliberately in promoting the Marquis de Cinq Mars, the 17-year-old son of a leading official in the treasury, into the entourage of the king. Louis was delighted with the boyish grace and vitality of Cinq Mars, and soon he was hopelessly spoiled by the flattery of hopeful courtiers, the interest of women and the slavish affection of the king. *Grand écuyer* by title, known everywhere as *Monsieur le Grand*, he exploited his power without restraint or tact. The ageing king's chaste, devout temperament was at his mercy; emotional quarrels were followed by humiliating reconciliations. So long as the king was ready to submit to his favourite's whims, there was danger for Richelieu, for it was not long before Cinq Mars began to play politics in the nest of Richelieu's enemies. His pretext was Richelieu's refusal to allow him to marry the daughter of the duc de Nevers, Marie de Gonzague. Gaston had nothing to lose, in reputation or prospects, by disloyalty; the fact that France was at war with Spain was only added inducement. Soissons and Bouillon were inveterate rebels, and neither shrank from negotiating for troops and money from Spain, nor from plotting the assassination of the Cardinal. Gaston was to raise the revolt in Bouillon's frontier principality of Sedan, while Bouillon was to put the army of Italy at the disposal of the rebels: Spain was to provide 18,000 troops.

Spain was however in no position to support the conspirators since her position in Flanders was crumbling and Catalonia was in open rebellion. Soissons was killed in a small action at Marfus, when the Spanish general Lamboy defeated the Maréchal de Châtillon. The plot to kill Richelieu, when he was travelling south to join the royal armies at Perpignan, miscarried; he was too well guarded by his musketeers. His own sick body was now Richelieu's greatest enemy; the king travelled on alone to campaign with his army, while Richelieu turned to make his weary journey back to Paris and death. As his state barge sailed up the Rhône, the Cardinal, lying in splendour and pain, his body covered with ulcers, his right arm already paralysed, worked as if he realised that his time was short. Through his confidants, the secretaries Noyers and Chavigny, he kept in close contact with the king and went on relentlessly collecting evidence to incriminate Cinq Mars. When he had in his hands the text of the treaty by which the conspirators undertook to hand back to Spain all France's conquests in the war, Chavigny was sent to the king at Narbonne. Cinq Mars confirmed his guilt by attempting to hide in the town; he was arrested, and the king returned to Paris. Richelieu's task was made easier by Gaston, who gave a full description of the plot, while Bouillon bought his freedom by the cession of Sedan to France. On September 5th, 1642, Richelieu arrived at Lyon; as usual, part of the wall of a house had to be broken down so that his litter could be lifted into his bedroom. On September 10th, Cinq Mars broke down and made a full confession. He could not save his life, but persisted in his pride to the end, refusing to die on the same scaffold with Monsieur le Thou, his friend and fellow-conspirator—but a commoner. On the same day, couriers brought word to Richelieu that Perpignan had fallen. As he had travelled on to Paris, he knew that he had accomplished his life's work: 'Perpignan is in the king's hands, and Monsieur le Grand is in the other world . . . these are two results of God's goodness towards the king and the state.'

The over-mighty subject

A narrative of Louis XIII's reign, with its emphasis upon war abroad and revolt at home, can convey only one side of the greatness of Richelieu. He is seen as the determined opponent of the Hapsburgs, the scourge of over-mighty subjects, the brave and subtle minister: his achievement essentially a negative one. What cannot so easily be realised is that in under twenty years, indeed in only twelve years of real power (for not until after 1630 did he have the chance to shape the executive in the way he wanted), he transformed certain aspects of French government and society. Richelieu, not Henry IV, for all the latter's skill and good sense, was the man who made possible the absolute government of Louis XIV. In the words of Hanotaux, his principal biographer, 'he was the greatest public servant that France ever possessed'.

The aristocratic plots and revolts of the reign were made more dangerous by special factors: the dastardly conduct of the duc d'Orléans, the real offence given to *dévots* by Richelieu's anti-Hapsburg policy, and the social distress caused by war taxation. Even without these incitements, however, Richelieu's policy of centralisation was bound to conflict with the feudal tradition still alive amongst the *noblesse*, and the separatism of the provinces. Richelieu had no illusions about this. He was an aristocrat himself, aware of the plight of his class and sympathetic to their claims for privileged treatment in the harsh world of the aftermath of the price-revolution. Land sales to new men, the decline of ancient families to the status of peasants, failures in the scramble for promotion and pension, these distresses were known to the Cardinal, who showed none of the levelling tendencies of Colbert and Louvois in the next reign. If anything, his prejudices were against the *officier* class who thrived on the fiscal needs of the state. He only took measures against individual nobles when the safety of the state required them, though, in the chronic insecurity of his position, the Bastille was usually well tenanted with noble prisoners who could not be tried because the charge was too vague even for a special tribunal. As a man he might listen to the requests of the Assembly of Notables for measures to re-instate their class: they wanted especially to see nobles appointed to the councils, the sale of offices abolished, and means of education provided for their sons. But as a statesman he saw the disadvantage of the presence of great magnates in councils and the impracticability of stopping the sale of offices. He did wish, however, to found an academy for the education of the sons of impoverished nobles, and he recommended the king to curtail the extravagance of court life where so many nobles were ruined by the dictates of fashion in dress and gambling.

Richelieu had his own ideal notion of the place of the nobility in the state. They should be devoted, obedient and ready to serve the king; their valour should find its outlet in fighting for the country; at home they should conform peaceably to the law. The disorders of the religious wars, which had had their echo in the years of the minority, he considered to have been as damaging to the nobility as to the crown. He was deeply conscious of the fate that had nearly overcome France in the bad days of the League, when it had seemed that some of the remoter provinces might break away altogether. The tradition of feudal independence and this separatism were combined in the institution of the Provincial Governors, and these were a prime object of Richelieu's surgical operations. In his *Testament* Richelieu defined the problem with characteristic lucidity: the expenditure entailed by the office resulted in its being given to the greatest in the land; such men did not accept or inherit governorships for altruistic reasons alone, but for the power that they conferred. The command of troops in the king's name, the patronage and the prestige that belonged to the governorship of a province, only confirmed the great in their conviction that they could be a law unto themselves. Richelieu was convinced, however, that there would be no security against civil war until the will of the king was enforced in the provinces by his own officials. The solution did not lie in the abolition of the office so much as in a change of attitude in the aristocracy and a strengthening of the organs of central government. They must be taught that defiance did not pay.

In 1614 there were sixteen local governorships; the name and fates of their occupants tell their own story. Brittany was ruled by Vendôme; he was sent to the Bastille for his share in the Chalais plot. The turbulent Soissons held the important province of Dauphiné; he had already lost it before he was killed at the beginning of the Cinq Mars affair. Guise was deposed for encouraging revolts in his province of Provence, Montmorency executed for his part in the rebellion of 1632. At Richelieu's death only four of the original sixteen survived. Harsh punishment awaited any grandee who resisted the king's authority or that of his officials. The duc d'Épernon fell out with Henri de Sourdis, Archbishop of Bordeaux and Richelieu's commander of the local naval forces; he was forgiven only after a solemn and public humiliation. When his son, the duc de la Valette, was later tried and executed for alleged neglect of his military duty, Richelieu may have been striking at the father through the son. De Sourdis seemed to be fated to arouse the rage of governors; in 1636, for striking him with a cane, de Vitry, governor of Provence, was sent to the Bastille. Richelieu was consistent in his attitude to these over-mighty subjects, but there is no pattern in his actions. He gave some provinces to men who were willing to please him, Chevreuse for example. Brittany he took for himself. Others he left without governors, like Champagne after the retreat of Soissons to Sedan, and Guyenne after the disgrace of d'Épernon; their provinces were entrusted to loyal lieutenant-generals, such as the comte de Praslin and the marquis de Montespan.

'In judging crimes against the state it is essential to banish pity': it will already be apparent that Richelieu did not neglect his own maxim. He also wrote that 'to make a law and not to see it carried out is to authorise what you have yourself forbidden'. In February 1626, a royal edict forbade the duel under penalty of death. Montmorency-Bouteville, a notorious dueller, with twenty-two deaths to his credit, promptly fought a duel under the Cardinal's window in the Place Royale. He was arrested and duly sentenced, but he awaited the king's pardon with confidence; duelling still had an honourable place in the nobleman's code of conduct. The king wavered before a flood of appeals, but Richelieu advised him to stand by his law: 'the question is,' he asked, 'do you wish to make an end of duelling or of your own power?' In June 1627, Montmorency-Bouteville was executed. The incident may seem a small one, but it provides an instructive view of the Cardinal's method; he did not so much innovate as see that things were done. There had been edicts against duelling before, containing the uncompromising words *le roi seul a droit du glaive*, but they had not been enforced. Not many contemporaries saw the duel in the romantic light that has been later shed upon it. It was a wasteful and vicious practice. Professional duellists who picked quarrels on slight points of supposed honour were little better than murderers; using not the rapier but the more deadly short sword, they fought to kill, often with the support of professional seconds. Responsible writers such as Savaron averred that few of the noble families of France escaped losses of life from duelling in the first half of the seventeenth century; Richelieu's eldest brother had been killed in a duel a few years before. Some were ready, however, to defend the custom as a form of controlled blood-letting, and the judicial element in the duel, as a means of settling quarrels which could not otherwise be resolved, persisted after the Bouteville case; the edicts of both Richelieu and Louis XIV provided for a special court, the *tribunal de maréchaux*, to deal with such quarrels. Whatever Richelieu's own view of the practice, justice was not his prime concern. He wished to teach the aristocrats of France, among whom he counted himself, that there was only one law, the king's, which all must obey. The development of absolute monarchy can be charted in terms of the reduction of privilege and exemption, and the Bouteville case is a landmark in this process.

The pretensions of Parlement

Richelieu was involved, on behalf of the king, in a series of quarrels with *Parlement* which are of special interest to the English reader who may find analogies with the contemporaneous struggle between the Stuart Kings and their parliaments. The analogy cannot be pressed far, of course, for the *Parlement* of Paris was a sovereign court, not elective but a closed corporation. It could not claim or expect support from the country at large, for it did not represent anything except a legal tradition, and it could find no solid or convincing precedent even for its claim to control legislation by registering edicts. It was powerful only in its privileges, and these were themselves a weakness, for a sharp thrust against these by a determined crown was enough to make a venal oligarchy reconsider its constitutional demands. Only a determined leadership or, as in the Fronde, an exceptionally popular issue, could make anything significant of the opposition of *Parlement*. Richelieu was too intelligent to rush into headlong collision with the lawyers so long as it could be avoided by tact. He did not approve of the pretensions of the wealthy caste of *officiers*, or of their obstreperous and legalistic Gallicanism. The delays and perversions of justice that stemmed from a system of magistracy by purchase were indefensible. But he did recognise that the purchase of office gave *Parlement* a certain independence, making it difficult for great nobles to fill it with their partisans and dependents. A common front between *Parlement* and a faction of the aristocracy was never a real danger, although it was briefly achieved during the Fronde.

In 1631 *Parlement* demurred at registering an edict directed against the accomplices of Gaston and Louis took the opportunity of telling them that neither '*Parlement* nor any other *officier* might take cognisance of state affairs, administration and government of the realm, but only the king himself, established and protected by God to whom alone he rendered account'. When several leading magistrates were exiled to the provinces, the *avocat général*, Omer Talon, represented that no *officier* 'could be prevented or deprived of his charge except by forfeiture pronounced after a hearing of the case by a properly constituted court'. The exiled magistrates were allowed to return, but the struggle was soon resumed over Richelieu's new court, the *chambre de l'arsenal*, set up in 1631 to deal with crimes against the state. *Parlement* demanded that members of the court should be chosen from its own body while the crown intended to choose them from the *conseil d'état* and the *maîtres des requêtes*. When the *Premier Président* Le Jay protested to the king about his suspension of certain magistrates who had been involved in a remonstrance against the new court, comparing his behaviour in a tactless manner with that of Louis XI, he met with a stinging answer: 'You exist for no other reason than to judge disputes between Master Peter and Master John ... and if you continue to venture beyond this, I will cut your nails to the quick.'

After a declaration of war with Spain in 1635, Richelieu raised urgently-needed money by the creation of twenty-four new offices of *conseilleur*; thus he hoped both to raise money and to devalue the privilege. After a protracted struggle in the course of which several leading members of *Parlement* were exiled and imprisoned, a compromise was reached; *Parlement* agreeing to register the creation of seventeen instead of the original twenty-four. In 1640, there was another tussle over new creations, and further exiles and imprisonments; this time the government decided to deal a decisive blow to the opposition and define exactly the limits within which they might enjoy freedom to speak and act. In February 1641, Louis held a *lit de justice* and pronounced an edict limiting the activities of *Parlement* to judicial matters. The preamble consisted of a lecture on the history of the previous fifty years, the disorders of the League, the recovery of royal authority under Henry IV, when France became 'the perfect model for accomplished monarchies', the subsequent lapses of the minority when *Parlement* presumed too much, and the second recovery of royal authority in the person of Louis XIII. Richelieu's view of history emerges plainly from the discourse and the moral that it pointed: it was only when the royal power was wholly established that 'France recovered her true strength'. *Parlement* should not touch matters of state, but were allowed the right of remonstrance about matters of finance, 'if they find any difficulty in verifying them', they might not however use the words 'we cannot, or ought not' which were derogatory to the authority of the prince. Even after the edict had been registered, further representations were allowed. So it was not yet established that there was no right to deliberate. A gate was left open through which, in the Fronde, *Parlement* could trample once more into the forbidden fields.

The Estates

It was again financial considerations, rather than any theoretical desire for uniformity for its own sake, that embroiled the king with the Estates of the *pays d'état*. Because they were privileged to levy taxes at their own rate, the six *pays d'état*, Languedoc, Brittany, Burgundy, Provence, Normandy and the Dauphiné, in size and wealth a third of France, paid only a tenth of the whole *taille* (about 4 out of 40 millions). For this reason Richelieu attempted to impose the hated *élections* upon the *pays d'état*. There is no reason to suppose that he had any dislike of the particularism of these provinces. As governor of Brittany he wrote to his cousin, La Meilleraye, the king's representative at the meeting of the Estates, that he was to restore the Estates to their former liberty, 'allowing each man who has the right of attending to come freely and vote on matters raised without any obstacle direct or indirect.' It seems to be a mistake to attribute to the pragmatic Cardinal the love of uniformity for its own sake that is typical of some later reformers. But it is equally wrong, in the afterglow of de Toqueville, to make too much of the liberty enjoyed by the *pays d'état* by comparison with the bondage of the *pays d'élection*; the former paid less in taxes, but their Estates were narrow and conservative in constitution and spirit, and ready to resist the reforms as well as the tax demands of the central government.

Dijon, a town that prided itself upon its municipal liberties, providing its own artillery, militia, elective town government and criminal justice, was the seat of the Estates of Burgundy. When the government tried in 1630 to establish *élections* there were revolts amongst the local wine-growers. The town magistrates were perhaps more alarmed than the king, who promptly entered the city with troops and exacted full submission. The liberties of the town were reduced, but in the following year the *élections* were quashed in return for a gift of 400,000 *livres*. The same process occurred in Provence, where the estates were allowed to continue unmolested in their tradition of violent debate, uninterrupted by royal spokesmen.

In Languedoc, again, the impression left is that the Cardinal's prime objective in proposing the *élections* was to obtain money in return for their abandonment. This large province was paying substantially less than its reasonable share of taxation, but an attempt after the Peace of Alais, in July 1629, to impose a *bureau d'élection* in each of the twenty-two dioceses of the province, caused a flurry of protest, and was one of the main reasons for the ill-fated decision of Montmorency to join the revolt of Gaston d'Orléans. Montmorency got little support from the southerners, however, and after his defeat at Castelnaudary the government secured a large increase in the contributions of the province. Only one *pays d'état* actually ceased to exist in this period, and this for special reasons: Protestant Dauphiné. Some years later, in 1655, the Estates of Normandy petered out from lack of local interest. The remaining four survived the rationalising tendencies of successive ministers until the Revolution, to provide Montesquieu and de Toqueville with object lessons on the virtues of representative institutions.

Ministers and intendants

Just as Richelieu insisted upon carrying through any measure of policy once it had been decided by the king, so he was reluctant to interfere with anything unless he knew that it was essential and until he felt he was on sure ground. This explains both the successes and the limitations of his work. He struck at the Estates of Dauphiné because he knew that the aristocracy and the town governments of the province were so divided that, if either Estate made a fuss, the other would fall into line with the crown. Normandy however, which after the revolt of the *Va nu-pieds* invited severe measures of repression, was left to enjoy its rights as a *pays d'état* which, Richelieu knew, were of little significance. He showed no remarkable interest in administrative reform and the great achievement of the period in this direction, the *Code Michaud*, whose 461 articles covering a wide area of justice and finance embodied many of the requests of the Assemblies of Notables of 1625 and 1626, was the work of Michel de Marillac and little to do with the Cardinal. In some ways, however, he promoted the efficiency of government. At the top, in a series of *règlements*, the most important of which was in 1630, and by his deliberate choice as ministers of men who would conform to his methods of government, he created a new sort of executive, more compact and more specialised than the old. In order to safeguard his power the Cardinal-minister worked his own associates into the key positions. These *créatures* (the word implies dependants and is not otherwise derogatory) supported him loyally since their offices depended upon it, and there was thus a unity about the executive which had been notably lacking until 1630. It is a myth that Richelieu was a dictator of almost superhuman powers who ruled France virtually alone in the name of the king. On the one hand the king insisted upon having the last word in all decisions made in his name. On the other hand, while conforming carefully to the dictates of the Cardinal in general matters of policy, the Secretaries of State, *surintendants* and the Keeper of the Seals all enlarged their own province of authority. This was not because Chavigny, Sublet de Noyers, Bullion, Bouthillier or Séguier were anything more than competent administrators, but because they acted in the king's name with ever-increasing authority as Richelieu made the king's authority feared in the land. So we see the work of Richelieu and his *créatures* preparing the way for the more developed bureaucratic structure of the next reign. At the same time it becomes clear that the dominance of the Cardinal was essentially personal, resting on his influence with the king and his authority over the other ministers rather than upon any genius for administration—which he did not claim and certainly did not possess.

It has been observed that for all Richelieu's intellectual grasp of the problems of government, his swiftness of mind and decision, he made little effort to remodel the institutions of France. There is no paradox here however. For it is precisely because he was able to ensure the smooth workings of the *conseil* that he did not consider the need to create a new machinery. The logical corollary of the drive against the old-style governor of the province was a permanent body of royal officials; these, the *intendants*, were not a system until the reign of Louis XIV. Richelieu used agents on special mission, *maîtres des requêtes* and *intendants* for specific purposes, but he did not regularise their use, or give them resident status. It is probable that this was deliberate since he preferred to rule through men whom he could control.

Church and state

Richelieu the churchman was inevitably subordinated after 1624 to Richelieu the statesman. He had been an admirably vigorous bishop, but there is little to show that he was an unusually spiritual person. His outlook was practical and materialistic; he judged by results and seems to have been immune from the exalted attitudes of some contemporary churchmen. He did on occasion betray an almost superstitious faith, as when he had the relics of St. Fiacre brought from Meaux to cure him of piles. He was not out of touch with the true piety of the time: his own brother had followed his vocation to the monastic life, the Oratorian Bérulle had been his friend, the charitable works of St. Vincent de Paul received his support, and he built a hospital for the galley slaves at Marseilles. But it is characteristic that the man closest to his ideal, the priest who really knew his mind and devoted himself to his interests, was the Capucin diplomat, Père Joseph. This austere, fanatical friar believed that the power of France was one with the good of the church; he wanted a holy war, led by France, once France was supreme in Europe; he did not shrink from the methods of the world, for lies, bluff, bribes all served their part in the Holy War. Richelieu understood and shared the outlook of 'his Ezekiel'; so long as Père Joseph lived he intended him to be his successor. No greater contrast can be imagined than that between the sandalled friar and the suave Italian who took his intended place: churchman in name only, Cardinal Mazarin.

It came naturally to Richelieu to speak in terms of the call of God; he wanted power, he said, 'for the glory of God and the honour of France'. There was no conscious hypocrisy in such language. But to all outward appearances his duties to God were always performed in the light of his duty to France. He broke with the *dévot* party when he resolved upon support of the Protestants in Germany, and he secured the dismissal of Père Caussin, the king's confessor, when that good man became scrupulous about the question of the sin of treating with heretics. He moderated between the extremes of Gallican and Ultramontane, being convinced that the church could only perform its social and political duties properly if its own image was one of conformity and obedience. He was careful in his appointments of clergy for high office, preferring men of good birth and administrative ability to scholars, *dévots*, or men who had risen from the ranks. He appointed a *conseil de conscience* to advise the king on episcopal appointments; he supervised with care General Assemblies of the church, even appointing their place of meeting. Unorthodox churchmen, such as the wild enthusiast Saint-Cyran, or the unfortunate Bishop Grandier, met with no sympathy. Saint-Cyran he imprisoned on the grounds, urged by the Jesuits, that *l'affaire Pilmot* was a plot to overthrow the church: he was a Basque, so he had 'hot entrails'. Grandier was burnt in 1634 after an unfair trial in which he had pleaded not guilty of the alleged offence of afflicting the notorious nuns of Loudon with demoniac possession. The real offence of the priest may have been his resistance to the government in the person of the *intendant*, Labardemont, who conducted the trial, in matters concerning his see.

The cultivated autocrat

During Richelieu's time there was a great increase in the circulation of pamphlets and periodicals. The first printed periodical, the *Strassburger Zeitung*, appeared in 1609; during the Thirty Years War, the productions of Protestant and Catholic publicists kept the fires of religious hatred burning. Richelieu has some claim to be the first statesman to exploit the possibilities of propaganda as an instrument of state. He had used the redoubtable pamphleteer Fancan, in the years before he came to power, to advertise the deficiencies of the regime of La Vieuville, and he went on using the pamphlet to state French aims and claims; for some time Fancan and Cassan, leading exponents of the art of political journalism, were retained as official publicists. A more regular means of influencing opinion at home was provided by the government newspapers, *Mercure* and the *Gazette* (the latter started as a private venture by a doctor, Théophraste Renandot); these dressed up small victories, toned down disasters and sustained dutiful notes of praise for the Cardinal's policies, in a way familiar to the twentieth century reader. Other semi-official productions took the war of ideas on to a loftier plane: the *Prince* of Balzac (1631) adapted Machiavelli to the needs of the time with its bald statement of the new morality of the state, and Lebret's *De la souveraineté du Roy* (1632) expounded a view of Divine Right almost as advanced as the most extreme developments of the next reign. In this way the literate Frenchmen was conditioned to accept the demands and the methods of the absolute state: the right of the sovereign to make, interpret, unmake laws; to make wars (just ones); to make, and when *raison d'état* required, to break, treaties; to raise taxes, which benefited the people as leeches did a swollen body, and to strike, if necessary upon mere suspicion, against the enemies of the state. The phrase *raison d'état* is often credited to Richelieu, and whether he coined it or not, he certainly acted upon it in such a way as gave new force to the idea, in itself not new, that acts that would be immoral in a private person might be condoned if they contributed to the good of the state.

The Cardinal himself was indeed no mean author. He wrote several *Maximes d'État*, inspired the *Testament Politique* which is a statement of his philosophy of life and politics, and at least part probably of the *Mémoires* which were edited after his death by a bishop who had been one of his household. Because of this literary ability, we know more about the ideas and thoughts of Richelieu than about those of any comparable figure. It is interesting to place the maxims of the Cardinal alongside his actions: 'secrecy is the first essential in affairs of state', and 'in popular opinion, matters falsely presented in fine words are very readily accepted as true', for instance; the reader does not have to look far to find illustration of these remarks. Richelieu is indeed outstanding among statesmen for his rigour and consistency in the application of intellectual solutions to political problems. But too much should not be made of his maxims of state. The writing of maxims was a popular diversion of the time; the art of putting deep truths and penetrating advice in a nutshell was cultivated in the *salons* which

Richelieu himself frequented from time to time. His terse, nervous style cannot be compared with the best that the *salons* could produce, any more than his verses, in which he took some pleasure, could stand up against professional competition. But he was writing skilfully in a literary form which demanded compression and neatness rather than ample development of a theme, and he himself knew better than to suppose that statesmanship was a mere academic exercise. In words which James I would have done well to have read, he wrote: 'nothing can be more dangerous in a state than those who will govern kingdoms by the maxims they find in books'. The real interest of Richelieu's writings, his letters and memoranda excepted, is in the light they throw on his mind and personality.

He was the most civilised of men, something of an aesthete as well as an intellectual, and he used his power to patronise the arts more intelligently and more generously than Louis XIV after him. Like Louis XIV and Colbert he recognised the political value of regulated art. There may have been political calculation in his building of the *Palais Cardinal* to house a court as splendid as the king's, and in the rebuilding of the church of the Sorbonne which was to house his tomb. But he built for a love of building, just as he patronised playwrights for a love of the theatre. There is an element of the dictatorial in his patronage, of course. His foundation of the *Académie Française* can be seen as an extension to literature of the characteristic centralising tendencies of the time; a large part of its work was the standardisation of the language and the codifying of laws for prose and verse. But this was the expression of an academic approach to literature which would have been just as strong without Richelieu. His contribution was in interest, money, and the various forms of help which a minister could give—a title of nobility for instance to Corneille's father—at a time when France was about to enjoy her years of artistic achievement. The fact that France was dominated, at this time, by an aristocratic churchman who listened every day to a short concert by his private musicians, who met writers like Corneille at the salon of Mme de Rambouillet, who even contributed some lines himself to one of his plays, who was painted by Philippe de Champaigne and who entertained the best society of Paris to plays and concerts in his palace when the court of Louis XIII could offer nothing better than talk of dogs and hawks, was of great significance in the artistic development of France.

The economics of grandeur

Richelieu never made it his primary concern to plan for the economic development of the country. The fiscal problem he saw increasingly in the light of the pressing needs of the army, and successive *surintendants de finance*, notably his loyal and close *'créatures'*, joint *surintendants* after 1632, Bullion and Bouthillier, were primarily tax-raisers and manipulators engaged in an ever more desperate search to find the means of fighting a war without bankruptcy or revolt. The period of Richelieu, studied against the constructive achievements of Sully before and Colbert afterwards, seems therefore to be barren of achievement in the economic sphere. There was a large increase in the rate of taxation, and little radical reform of inefficiencies of assessment and collection. Richelieu became notably careless about the effects of his short-term expedients for raising money, especially the sale of offices, and the penalty was paid in the Fronde. He was also brutally explicit in his statement of the priorities of statesmanship; indeed he denied, in his *Testament*, any particular intention of bettering the lot of the people, who 'must be compared to mules which, being used to burdens, are spoiled more by rest than by labour' (the remark of a man who was himself a delicate person sustained by an iron will, a glutton for work and an ascetic amidst the splendour of his household). There were moments when ready cash simply was not available to send to the armies; then in the *service du roi* Richelieu would himself advance money or pledge his name for loans. Money he regarded loftily as a means to a greater end: 'for no sum of money is the safety of the state too dearly bought'. He readily confessed his own incapacity for finance, as to Bullion for example: 'I confess fully my ignorance on financial matters and realise that your knowledge is so vast that the only advice I can give you is to use those people whom you will find most useful to the king's service, and I assure you that I will second you in every way'. It was unfortunate that his *surintendants*, though resourceful financiers, were conservative and unimaginative men.

Richelieu was too intelligent, however, not to be aware of the importance of developing the economic resources of the country, and several of his projects show what he might have achieved if he had not been so preoccupied with war. He established stage coaches and state posts throughout the country. He revived the project of Henry IV, the great canal of Briare, which had been abandoned; it was too much for the resources of the state, but was completed by contractors. As a good mercantilist and disciple of the influential Montchrétien he tried to prevent the flow of bullion out of France by restrictive legislation, aimed against imports in foreign ships and commercial transactions with foreigners. He believed that he could stimulate home industries by curbing the importation of luxury goods; fortunately perhaps this was a task beyond the resources of the administration. With the same combination of the conventional and the grandiose, he designed schemes for new colonies and trading companies. The *Compagnie du Morbihan*, founded for trade with Canada, the West Indies and Russia, the *Compagnie de la Nacelle de St. Pierre Fleur de lysée* with aims as splendid as its title, were short-lived ventures. Of other companies, only the *Compagnie des Indes* survived to have a more prosperous future. The *Compagnie des Îles d'Amérique* secured for France the islands of St. Kitts and San Domingo before expiring, from bankruptcy, in 1651. During this period a small colony was established at the mouth of the St. Lawrence, but this owed more to the discoveries, and the subsequent governorship, of Champlain than to Richelieu's directives. The colony was captured by the English in 1627 but handed back in the treaty of 1633. It was treated by the French as a mission station; at Richelieu's death it had a convent, a hospital, a girls' school and a school for young Indians, but only 200 inhabitants in all. At a time when colonies were being started in other parts of the continent by Englishmen who wished to escape from the dictates of the established church, the French government was refusing to allow Huguenots to settle in America. Thus the French were denied the great colonising motive of the period. New France could only have flourished as a missionary and trading venture if it had received money and troops to fight the Iroquois Indians, well supplied with firearms by the rival Dutch. The missionary spirit which inspired the French government was more admirable than the crude commercial designs of the Dutch. But starved of capital, and of constructive support from home, New France represented nothing more than wasted opportunity.

In 1639, Claude Bullion, *surintendant des finances*, wrote: 'expenditure in cash is up at least forty millions, the *traitants* are abandoning us, and the masses will not pay either the new or the old taxes. We are now at the bottom of the pot. . . . I fear that our foreign

F

war is degenerating into a civil war.' It seems that Bullion was not exaggerating, and that 1639, the year of the rising of *Va nu-pieds*, was not an exceptionally bad year for the royal finances. In 1640, for instance, about 43 million *livres* were received, 116 million *livres* spent; interest on the public debt, rising inexorably, was about 20 million *livres*. The fact is that no European state, with the exception of mercantile Holland, which was for this reason the envy of England and France alike, was able to fight a war and to make ends meet. The fate of Spain is only the most spectacular example of a common difficulty. An attempt to impose the prayer book on Scotland broke down when the English government ran out of funds; in England of course the situation was exceptional because the key to the taxable wealth of the country was held by a parliament determined to use it to their political advantage. In France, where the rich were largely exempt, there was no such difficulty; the problem was to wrest money from the peasant without actually driving him to revolt. The *sous* of the peasant were the foundation of France's war effort, his sufferings were its cost, his revolts the only effective protest. Not the least of Richelieu's problems was that of peasant revolts which forced him to divert troops from the front.

In 1636, there were widespread risings in the Limousin and in Poitou; bands of several thousand roamed the countryside, aimless but desperate, killing tax-collectors where they could find them; the revolt spread to Gascony and Périgord; the government, in the year of Corbie, could do little. In the following year the duc de la Valette, governor of Guienne, put the rebels down; over a thousand of them were killed. Then in 1639 Normandy was shaken by the rising which took its name from an obscure priest from Avranches, Jacques Va nu-pieds. Because the insurgents were protesting against the excessive rates of *taille* and *gabelle* being paid by the province, a *pays d'état* which regarded itself as privileged in these matters, they enjoyed wide support, even from some of the *noblesse*. But the movement was discredited by indiscriminate violence, one of their victims being a government supervisor in the local cloth industry. In August there was street fighting in Rouen when local *bourgeois* took strong measures to protect their homes; but they could not escape their responsibility so easily. The government seized the opportunity not only to punish the insurgents, whose leaders were broken on the wheel, but to humble the province. When Chancellor Séguier arrived he took the law out of the hands of the municipality of Rouen. The *hôtel de ville* was razed to the ground, the privileges of the mayor and of the sovereign courts were revoked.

When Richelieu died he left France a greater country, if not a happier one, than he found her. The authority of the king was more widely and more readily obeyed at home; abroad his armies were about to enter upon a new phase of victory. Contemporaries were in no doubt as to the nature of his achievement, even before the victory of Rocroi advertised to the world the collapse of Spanish power: 'France he subdued, Italy he terrified, Germany he shook, Spain he afflicted,' wrote an English pamphleteer of the man who was 'the torment and the ornament of the age'. It is a tribute to his reputation that wherever there was a political crisis, his agents were held to be responsible: in Scotland in 1637, in Catalonia in 1640 (the latter was true). The French peasant might not regard himself as specially blessed by the Cardinal's work, especially if he lived in Burgundy or some other province on the route of the contending armies. But the sufferings of France, of which we have vivid evidence in the charitable labours of St. Vincent de Paul, have to be set in the context of Europe in the later stages of the Thirty Years War: Germany, where up to a third of the population may have perished; England, soon to endure civil war; Holland, battered after sixty years of war. Much of the fighting had been done by subsidised allies of France; during the period when France was involved, the war only affected limited areas of the eastern frontier. If the Cardinal were given the chance to state his case at the bar of history, might he not have answered: 'my first consideration had to be the order and safety of the state'?

The Protestant front disintegrates

The invasion of the Val Telline was the first direct use of French troops since the start of the European war. Richelieu realised, when he came to power in 1624, that France could not afford merely to watch while the Hapsburgs enforced their will in Germany. By then the Protestant party had almost disintegrated; only in Holland was the battle in full vigour.

The Protestant front was in fact cracked from the start, though this was not apparent during the critical winter of 1619, when Bethlen Gabor, the half-civilised prince of Transylvania, and since October 1619 elective king of Hungary, a Calvinist after his own naïve fashion, laid siege to Vienna. This was because, between Lutheran and Calvinist, there were basic differences of belief and method. The Lutheran prince, typified by the sluggish but honest Elector John George of Saxony, believed that international Calvinism, uncompromising in its assertion of the sovereignty of God over all secular princes, revolutionary in its cellular organisation and fanatical in its crusading ideas, was destructive of law and order as embodied by the Empire. The Empire, for the last sixty years, had been a conveniently poor and lax master so that in practice the princes had steadily enriched themselves by the acquisition of church lands and enhanced their local authority. When the brash young Elector Palatine, influenced more than he realised by the adventurer Christian of Anhalt, accepted the crown offered him in 1618 by the Bohemian rebels, John George and his habitual ally George William, Elector of Brandenburg, decided that no good would come of it. It was a dangerous precedent, and it threatened the balance of power within the Empire. When Bethlen Gabor was forced to retreat from Vienna after a five-month siege, and when Frederick was defeated at the battle of the White Mountain in November 1620, they therefore hastened to congratulate the Emperor upon his escape from the foe 'Turco-Calvinismus', as if he had been fighting the infidel himself. In all its humiliations there was left a residue of respect for the House of Austria as the bulwark of peace and order in Germany. It is significant that Ferdinand's election to the Empire, in August 1619, had been unanimous. While, however, the princes expected the Emperor to be strong enough to ward off

Transylvanians and suppress Calvinist upstarts, they also trusted that he would be too weak to assert the interests of his house and Faith.

The Emperor had neither men nor money enough from his hereditary lands to be a formidable military power on his own. The victory of the White Mountain was in fact won by Tilly, the devout and efficient general of Maximilian of Bavaria. This ambitious prince, enjoying ample revenues from his fertile and well-administered lands, was, like Ferdinand, a pupil of the Jesuits. Ferdinand's crisis had provided him with a wonderful opportunity to assume the leadership of the Catholics in Germany and to add to his possessions; at the same time he wanted to be an elector and to gain the Upper Palatinate, and this was the price the Emperor paid for Tilly's army. In February 1623, the Imperial Diet swallowed the arbitrary transfer of the Palatine Electorate to Maximilian, but with reluctance. Saxony and Brandenburg, as well as Spain, opposed the move. Already the Emperor's dilemma was becoming clear; to be effective in his role of champion of the Counter-Reformation in Germany, he had to have an army; to secure this he had to act unconstitutionally. The only alternative was to surrender his freedom of action entirely and accept the orders of Madrid. Already Protestant propagandists were alleging that Germany was dancing to the pipe of Olivarez. Spinola had prefaced the imminent end of the truce with the Low Countries in 1621, with the invasion of the Lower Palatinate. Ultimately the interdependence of Austria and Spain was to be plain for all to see; meanwhile the dynastic interests were confused by the din of Germany's battles, fought upon the religious issue of Catholic against Calvinist. The ruthless subjugation of Bohemia, given over to the Jesuits whose efficiency and missionary zeal were making the proud kingdom into a German and Catholic satellite of Austria, was a grim example of what Protestants elsewhere might expect if Catholicism triumphed. Frederick did have some allies: Mansfeld, unable to pay or discipline his plague-ridden troops, Christian of Brunswick who professed a romantic attachment to Frederick's queen Elizabeth, and the faithful old Calvinist the Margrave of Baden-Durlach. But Tilly's victories at Wimfen and Hoechst disposed of these princes in the summer of 1622. Mansfeld lunged into the Lower Palatinate in the same year, then went off to help Maurice of Nassau raise the siege of Breda, leaving Tilly to reconquer the Palatinate, and capture Heidelberg in

September. In December of the following year, Tilly pursued Mansfeld into the Netherlands and routed the discredited mercenary at Freisoythe, after defeating Christian again at Stadlohn. By 1624, there was therefore no German leader left in the field.

The years of Wallenstein

When Richelieu came to power, the Counter-Reformation seemed to have triumphed. He could see however that if the military situation was bleak, there was still hope for diplomacy. For, if the Emperor persisted in his apparent design of recovering the lost lands of the church, he must either use Spanish troops, or find himself a commander who could maintain an army from his own resources. In either case he would offend the princes of the constitutional party, who had so far remained loyal to him, but who did not want to lose their lands or their independence. One important prince outside Germany had a finger too in this pie; as Duke of Holstein, Christian of Denmark was also a German prince, and his son was administrator of Verden and planned to secure Minden and Halberstadt as well. Denmark's motives were not disinterested; neither were those of the Catholic Cardinal who encouraged him to intervene; nor those of the new Imperial Commander who now confronted him. A Bohemian landowner who had made a fortune from land speculations after the subjugation of his country, a *condottiere* who brought a new thoroughness to the business of mercenary war, man of business and dreamer, a fierce soldier and an eccentric, a fatalist who looked to the stars for guidance and a realist who acknowledged no faith, the enigmatic Wallenstein was to be the agent of Ferdinand's dream of making a Catholic Germany. At this point, the pattern of parties and events is bewildering; the religious issue has never been plain, but it is now inextricable from the mêlée of personal and family interests, while the relatively simple lines of dynastic conflict have not yet emerged. But it is certain that Richelieu was not unique in appraising the struggle from a political standpoint. It is often said that it was his alliance with Gustavus Adolphus in 1631 that turned a primarily religious into a primarily dynastic war. The trend was in fact implicit in the events of 1624. For if the Emperor Ferdinand was unable, or found it convenient not to distinguish between religious conviction and political convenience, then

Richelieu was bound to do so. For one thing to him was sure: a Hapsburg Germany was a threat to France.

In 1625, Christian of Denmark secured the alliance of Ernest of Saxe-Weimar and the Duke of Mecklenburg, amongst others whose interests lay in North Germany. By 1626 he had a force of 30,000 men at his disposal, and counted on the support of England, France and Holland. Unfortunately for him, none of these powers could be of much assistance. No English money was forthcoming, for Buckingham had already overspent in many directions and the English Parliament was unwilling to vote supplies for Mansfeld, whom they rightly regarded as a poor investment. In 1626, by an absurd turn-about, the new king, Charles I, and Buckingham found themselves at war with the French on behalf of the La Rochellais. Richelieu was crippled by the Huguenot revolt and the Chalais conspiracy. He had intended to further the anti-Hapsburg policy by blocking the Val Telline and by helping the Duke of Savoy in his attack on Genoa, the port for Spanish armies coming to Italy and for the Spanish fleet bringing gold from America. Opposition was mounting, however, at court against France's association with the Protestant powers, and Richelieu was not yet strong enough to impose his will regardless of such opinion. 'The interests of our allies and even of ourselves', wrote Marillac, 'weigh little against the destruction of heresy.' Richelieu turned therefore, and perhaps not unwillingly, to the attack on the Huguenots. In order that he might be free to do so, his agents made the Peace of Monçon in March 1626. Fargis, his envoy at Madrid, made the initial agreement which allowed Papal troops to reoccupy the valley and which gave what amounted to free passage to Spanish troops. Without consulting his allies Savoy and Venice, he abandoned the Grisons whom he was pledged to support, and left the Hapsburg lifeline open for several crucial years. He had little choice, but Richelieu's own complacent comments on the treaty in his memoirs should not delude the reader. This was a disaster for France and for Protestant Germany, expiated finally on the field of Nordlingen, the great Spanish victory of 1634. Holland, finally, was in one of the troughs of her long struggle. Maurice of Nassau, whose energies had been failing him, had died in April 1625. In the following year Breda at last fell to Spinola. Velasquez's famous picture of the scene of the surrender shows the grizzled commander, triumphant but weary, amidst the courtesies of the day;

the great feat of arms caught the imagination of Europe, but it did not take Spain appreciably nearer to the conquest of Holland.

Three Protestant armies took the field in 1626, but they failed to combine. Christian of Denmark was routed by Tilly at the battle of Lutter in August. Mansfeld had already been defeated by Wallenstein in April at Dessau, but he went, according to plan, to join forces with Bethlen Gabor in Hungary, only to find the wily Transylvanian making his peace with the Emperor. He died obscurely in the Bosnian mountains, where he had gone to raise a Slav revolt. The German princes grew lukewarm after these disasters and Christian himself was disheartened. Soon his own lands of Schleswig and Holstein were invaded by Wallenstein and Tilly. The two soldiers were hardly however allies, for Wallenstein was pursuing a haughty line of his own. In 1626, his principality of Friedland was made a hereditary duchy, in 1628 he was given Mecklenburg; he wanted to make the Emperor, that is himself as representing the Emperor, a great military power in Germany, and to this end he was prepared to turn North Germany into a vast armed camp. He was contemptuous of the interests of the German princes, Catholic and Protestant alike. A Diet in October 1627 complained bitterly of the ravages of his troops, but the Emperor was not yet disenchanted with his new instrument of power. In the years of Wallenstein's grip, the illusion that the Empire existed either to protect the princes, or to leave them alone, persisted. The Emperor turned again to the Catholic League in 1629, after the failure of Wallenstein's siege of Stralsund in the previous year. By then he had forfeited the support of Saxony and Brandenburg, for whom neutrality had proved to be unrewarding. Only the Edict of Restitution, issued by the Emperor in March 1629, was needed to complete their discomfiture. In the new war which followed from the determination of the Emperor to recover the alienated lands of the church, the Emperor was to provide the opportunity and the pretext for the entry of Gustavus Adolphus: a formidable enemy and, for Richelieu, a formidable ally.

Gustavus Adolphus

The king of Sweden had come to his throne in 1611 at the age of 17 and had been at war ever since, against Denmark, Russia and latterly against Sigismund of Poland, who still claimed the Swedish throne. He had found time to create a centralised bureaucracy and he had persuaded his nobles to run it; nor had he neglected the economy of Sweden. In relation to its size, his country was the most efficient in Europe. The dogged war-effort of Sweden in the fifteen years that followed his death is sufficient tribute to the constructive side of his work. His army was, however, his instrument of power and his claim to fame: the first truly national army in Europe, shaped into a coherent force by his heroic personality and by the tie of a common faith, for all his men were Protestant. The prayer book which Gustavus issued to every man may have been as important a factor of victory as the improved fire power of their muskets, or their commander's original tactics. Gustavus Adolphus was a convinced Lutheran, and a man of intelligence. He wished to employ his army to serve Protestantism in Germany, but in his own time, and on his own terms. Since Denmark still possessed Skania, a province at the south end of the Swedish peninsula, and Sweden was starting to acquire land on the south coast of the Baltic, the rivalry of the two countries was stronger than their common interest. It therefore suited the Lutheran Gustavus to see the Lutheran Christian IV defeated at Lutter in 1626 while he pursued his private war against the king of Poland. His avowed purpose in crossing into Europe in 1630 was to defend the 'liberty' of Germany and to restore the lands of ousted princes such as the Duke of Mecklenburg, but the North German princes knew too that he wanted to make the Baltic a German lake, and were as sceptical of his promises as they were luke-warm about his victories. After his victory at Breitenfeld in April 1631, he declared that his ultimate aim was to create a new evangelical confederation in Germany that would be strong enough to resist the Emperor, and independent of outsiders, France or Spain. There will always be speculation about Gustavus' intention, especially as to his next move if he had survived the battle of Lutzen. But his prime motives are no mystery: anxiety for Protestantism and desire for land and influence in Germany to recompense Sweden for the expenses of his campaigns. He was a man of his century in believing that religious security could be guaranteed only by the possession of territory. By his premature death he was spared the disillusionment that came to others from the discovery that, to a foreigner, these aims were incompatible, for it was only against a foreigner that the chaotic powers of Germany would combine.

F*

The port of Stralsund had held out in the summer of 1628 against Wallenstein; it was attached, so Protestants said, 'by chains, to heaven', but the supplies shipped in by Gustavus contributed to its salvation. He realised that the time had come to intervene. The Edict of Restitution, in March 1629, threatened to make the Hapsburgs supreme in northern Germany, by the restoration to Catholicism of Magdeburg, Bremen, Minden, Halberstadt, Verden and Lubeck, to name only the more important towns which had lapsed since 1555. It was not only Sweden who shuddered at the thought of the ascendancy of a military empire, directed by Wallenstein and a Jesuit junta at Vienna. Wallenstein himself saw that Sweden's entry was imminent and instigated a parley with Christian of Denmark which led to the peace of Lubeck in May 1629. In December of the same year, Gustavus came to terms with Sigismund of Poland at Altmark. The French diplomats needed no special skill to persuade Gustavus to become their ally. By the terms of the treaty of Bar-wälde, signed in January 1631, France pledged the sum of a million *livres* a year, for five years, in return for which Gustavus promised to keep an army of 30,000 infantry and 6,000 cavalry in the field. The Roman Catholic faith was everywhere to be tolerated, and Gustavus was not to attack Bavaria. The somewhat vague provisions of this document reflect Richelieu's embarrassed concern to preserve appearances. Between the Hapsburg menace in Germany and the ultra-montane Catholics at court he had to steer a delicate course. The Treaty of Barwälde left untouched the most awkward problem: while Gustavus promised France that he would not attack Bavaria, he was at the same time pledged to restore the Palatine to the dispossessed ex-Elector Frederick. It was in fact a pragmatic bargain. France hoped for a swift war to cut the Hapsburgs down to size, and trusted to luck that Gustavus would not go too far. Meanwhile French diplomacy had been active at the Diet of Ratisbon, in July 1630, and French troops had taken the initiative in Italy with the capture of Pinerolo in the same year.

The Diet of Ratisbon amounted to a conference between the Emperor and the Catholic princes of Germany, since the Protestant electors refused to come. It was called to consider the complaints of the princes against Wallenstein, the election of a King of the Romans, the title accorded to the recognised heir to the Empire, and the succession to the duchy of Mantua. In the latter

question France had a vital interest. Three years before, the last of
the Gonzague dukes of Mantua had died. The nearest heir to this
block of lands, which included the important fortresses of Mantua
and Casale, was Charles, duc de Nevers, a Gonzague, but a
Frenchman by upbringing and sympathy. He urged Richelieu to
take up his cause and challenge the place of Spain in Italy. Spain
in turn backed the claim of another member of the family, the
Duke of Guastalla, attached the slippery Duke of Savoy to their
cause by talk of partition of the lands, and sent Gonsalvo de
Cordova to besiege Casale. In December 1628, Louis XIII's
armies entered La Rochelle and at last Richelieu was free to think
of action abroad. He accompanied his king on a swift march
through the winter snows of the Mont Cenis pass and arrived
before the fortress, to break up the siege in March. At the beginning of this year, Richelieu had written to the king: 'it is necessary
to have a perpetual design to stop the progress of Spain'. Officially
the two countries were not at war, but the effect was the same.
He appreciated that the fate of Germany and of France turned
upon the fate of these fortresses in North Italy and risked the fury
of the Hispanophiles and *dévots* at court to secure them. Towards
the end of 1629 the French troops had to withdraw from Italy to
deal with a fresh Huguenot insurrection, but in 1630 they crossed
the Alps again, moved into Savoy and captured Pinerolo. At
Ratisbon, Richelieu's envoy Brûlart, and his 'theological adviser'
Joseph du Tremblay, pressed for a solution. Wallenstein was their
ally, for he was a friend of the duc de Nevers, and was already sore
at having lost some of his troops to the Italian theatre. The Diet
took the view that the Emperor's jurisdiction in Italy was a
mediaeval anachronism, and Ferdinand was forced to concede the
right to both Mantua and Montferrat to the duc de Nevers. In
July 1630, the matter was formalised at the Treaty of Cherasco,
where France promised to hand back Pinerolo to Savoy. In
September 1631, the place was solemnly returned to Savoy before
representatives of the Emperor and Spain. No sooner had these
dignitaries left than a company of French soldiers coolly took over
the citadel, for by a secret treaty earlier in the year, the Duke of
Savoy had sold Pinerolo to France.

In the other questions before the Diet the French were less
directly concerned. The Diet refused to elect Ferdinand's son
King of the Romans, an outcome which Brûlart and Père Joseph
wanted but did little to effect. It promised to help the Emperor

against the Swedish armies but came to no decision about the Edict of Restitution. Most important, the princes persuaded the Emperor to dismiss Wallenstein ; in this the private dealings of Père Joseph, who had instructions, concealed even from Brûlart, to make an alliance with Bavaria, were influential. In March 1630 Maximilian pledged himself and the Catholic League not to assist the enemies of France, to fight against the Dutch or to oppose the claims of the ousted Dukes of Mecklenburg.

Richelieu professed himself dissatisfied with the settlement of Ratisbon and disowned its authors on the grounds that they could have obtained better terms in Italy. Privately, however, he may have felt content, for he had secured the benevolent neutrality of Germany's strongest Catholic ruler; once he had tied Gustavus to his cause as well, he could look forward to the defeat of the Hapsburgs without having to commit a single French soldier to the struggle. Diplomacy had done much, but its limitations were soon to be revealed. The envoys of Saxony and Brandenburg, in conference at Leipzig in March 1631, shied away from French proposals for the union between Sweden and the Protestant princes which Richelieu saw as the corollary of the Treaty of Barwälde. They did not think that the Cardinal could control the King of Sweden, and they proved to be right.

While Gustavus was treating with Saxony and Brandenburg for leave to pass through their lands, Tilly and Pappenheim were besieging the old Hanse town of Magdeburg, strategically important in its site on the banks of the Elbe and claimed by the Emperor in furtherance of the Edict of Restitution. The Swedish general who had been sent to help organised a stout resistance. But Gustavus failed to reach it in time, for reasons which remain controversial, and on May 31st it fell to Pappenheim's desperate assault. The famished citizens who survived the six-month siege were unlucky, for there ensued one of the worst incidents of military history. The fury of rape, murder and fire, which killed 20,000 and left the city a shambles, shocked the most war-hardened. For days the swollen bodies floated down the Elbe while Protestant writers plied their pens: this was what the Protestants of Germany were to expect from the Emperor's dream of reconversion. 'Magdeburg mercy' was something more than a propaganda point; it was the corner of the war. Saxony, Hesse-Cassel and Saxe-Weimar joined Gustavus as he marched south; the Margrave's protests were brushed aside as Swedish soldiers seized the garrisons of Brandenburg. Whether they liked it or not, the North German states were now involved. Brandenburg became a Swedish barracks, Saxony a battleground. At Breitenfeld, near Leipzig, in September 1631, Gustavus met Tilly and Pappenheim. Fresh troops and new tactics destroyed the weary Imperialists, fighting in the old Spanish manner; Ferdinand's position in Germany crumbled at the blow. But Gustavus, not Richelieu, was the victor. The Cardinal expected Gustavus to march upon Austria; instead he turned to the Rhine, to winter at Frankfort and Mainz. The electors of the rich and vulnerable Rhineland electorates implored aid from Richelieu, but the paymaster had lost control. Maximilian realised that he must fend for himself, and refused to give the French envoy Charnacé an assurance that he would continue to respect the neutrality of Sweden. He trusted in Tilly, but the death of this great soldier early in 1632 was followed by a ruthless invasion of his lands. When he produced half a million thalers to buy off the Swedes, Gustavus could afford to snap his fingers at the threats of France.

Meanwhile Wallenstein had been waiting sardonically for his call. He now emerged, on the pleas of the Emperor, with the army that he had been nursing in Bohemia, mediated between Ferdinand and John George, joined forces with the remnants of Tilly's army, and confronted Gustavus at Nuremberg. Here he checked him, and then, while Gustavus faltered, prepared to go, with Pappenheim, into winter quarters. Gustavus seems to have decided that he must deal with him before he could march on Vienna, and attacked him at Lutzen on the misty morning of November 16, 1632. Pappenheim rallied the Imperialists as they were giving way to the first assault, but then he was killed. Wallenstein's musketeers, shooting up from their ditches at the bellies of the Swedish horses, checked another advance. The Swedes held the field but could not celebrate a victory, for the naked body of their king was found in a pile of corpses. A lucky bullet had saved the Emperor from his enemy, and Richelieu from his ally.

Richelieu enters the war

Of the three generals, Wallenstein alone survived, but without credit. Every man's hand was against him, as he negotiated successively with Sweden, Saxony and France. He did nothing, in 1633, to show what use he meant to make of his power, but his very inactivity roused suspicion at Vienna. In January 1634, he was relieved of his command, then declared guilty of treason. At Eger, on the Bohemian frontier, he asked for Swedish help. To prevent the city falling into Swedish hands the governor, with the connivance of Ferdinand, planned his murder. On February 27th, with his generals, he was killed by one of his Irish mercenaries. Gallas, seldom sober, but obedient after his rough fashion to the dictates of Vienna, took his place as commander of the Imperial armies, and laid siege to Nordlingen. It was to save this town that Bernard of Saxe-Weimar offered battle to the combined forces of Austria and Spain, commanded nominally by the young Hapsburg cousins, Ferdinand, son of the Emperor, and Ferdinand, the Cardinal-Infant of Spain. The decisive Hapsburg victory that followed ended the German war. The Elector of Saxony, agile for once, made his peace with the Emperor at Prague, in June 1635. Of the German princes, only Bernard of Saxe-Weimar refused to submit, and he was now in Richelieu's pay.

At the battle of the White Mountain, the soldiers of Tilly had fought under banners inscribed: '*Sancta Maria*'. At Nordlingen, the imperialist device was '*Viva Espana*'. The dynastic quarrel was no longer masked by religious considerations. At Prague the Emperor virtually abandoned the Edict of Restitution: there was no longer therefore any reason for the war to continue, except the enmity of France and Spain. The Swedes would, of course, continue to fight to secure bargaining counters for negotiation: Bavaria would try to make the most of any war that was going. The Emperor was tied, after Nordlingen, to the policy of Spain, and Spain was still committed to the Dutch War.

On May 21st, 1635, in the Grande Place of Brussels, a French herald proclaimed with mediaeval pomp that the Most Christian King Louis XIII declared war upon His Catholic Majesty Philip IV of Spain. After the years of war by proxy, France had entered the lists in person. Richelieu was too subtle a statesman to commit his armies wildly, but by 1635 diplomacy had done all that was possible, and further advantage could only be won by military means. Sweden and Bernard of Saxe-Weimar might be useful auxiliaries, but they could not be expected to bear the brunt alone. The fundamental interests of France, the security of her eastern frontier and her influence in Germany, now required action. Thus the end of the German war, on the field of Nordlingen and in the conference chamber at Prague, was the start of the most intense phase of Hapsburg-Bourbon rivalry; the ensuing war was to make Germany a battleground for another thirteen years.

In April 1635, Oxenstierna had come to Paris to negotiate in person with the French, whose manner he found 'very strange and depends much on finesse'. Richelieu had known that Oxenstierna needed his alliance, and that he had little to offer for it but mutinous armies and an empty purse. But the experienced Swede could point to the Spanish armies on the Rhine, to the defection of Saxony, to the menace of court intrigues between Anne of Austria and her brother the Cardinal Infant. That Richelieu himself had realised the dangers is shown by his hurried agreement with Holland in February, by which he offered troops to the Prince of Orange. At Compiègne, on April 20th, they had come to terms. The French recognised Sweden as an equal ally, agreed to make no peace without her, made fresh subsidies and took over the left bank of the Rhine from Breisach to Strasbourg. A few days later Vienna published the terms of the Peace of Prague, the constitutionalist John George of Saxony's great contribution to the political problems of his time, and by now completely irrelevant. This 'Peace' of Prague, as it came to be called, open to all who wished to subscribe, became in effect an alliance for war, on behalf of the House of Austria, against the outside powers of Sweden and France. 'Saxony has made his peace', wrote Richelieu, 'but that will have no effect on us save to make us renew our efforts to keep everything going.'

As the religious issues faded from sight, as the struggle wandered about in its dreary and erratic course, one thing stood out plainly from the tangle of private and national interests. On the battlefields of Flanders, the Rhine and Germany, France and Spain would fight it out until one side or other established some decisive advantage. The Peace of the Pyrenees in 1659 was to proclaim in unmistakable terms the decline of Spain and the arrival of a greater political and military force. That this would be the outcome was not however, in 1635, as obvious as it has subsequently seemed.

Richelieu was under no illusions about the magnitude of the struggle, and his preparations had been thorough. In September 1633, Lorraine had been ceded by its incurious Duke, Charles of Lorraine, and French troops had entered Nancy. France had Philippsburg, on the Rhine, from Sweden, and further land on the middle Rhine by treaty with the bishop of Basle; she controlled the Moselle by arrangement with the Elector of Trier and her troops were on the edge of Franche-Comté. Her treaty with Holland was followed in July by the Treaty of Rivoli with Savoy, ceding the fortresses of Mantua and Montferrat. Finally, Bernard of Saxe-Weimar promised to maintain his army in return for four million *livres*, a personal allowance, and the secret grant of the Landgravate of Alsace.

The army and navy

France had not been engaged in a major war since the sixteenth century, and her armies went to war in the spirit of Marignano; they had been spectators of the military revolution of Maurice of Nassau and Gustavus Adolphus. The strategic position of France was strong, but her troops were disproportionately weak, in organisation, tactics and equipment. The fresh troops who marched to the frontier through yet unspoiled lands made a pretty contrast with the shabby veterans of Austria and Spain. But they had to learn experience of the new conditions of war in bitter and humiliating reverses.

The army at this time was neither national nor feudal; it can best be described as a mercenary force under royal direction. The government licensed officers to raise troops. Some of these officers were nobles, warriors by tradition and upbringing, but many were not, producing soldiers by virtue of their licence and not as part of any feudal service; once a troop had been raised it could be sold as personal property. There was, of course, no compulsory military service. When there was a crisis men might be urged to turn out, but this was not, and could not be, an order. In 1636 there was a *levée en masse* of the *ban*, a local militia, but this was a defensive weapon of little use. Richelieu, who had a low opinion of the fighting spirit of the French, urged Feuquières to recruit in Germany, and he tried, like Henry IV, to entice the peasants of the Val Telline to serve in the French army.

The clothes and food of their troops were the responsibility of the officers who had found them. The system belonged to the days when campaigns were short and infrequent and was too hand-to-mouth for the needs of modern war. An English mercenary, already eleven years a campaigner in the Thirty Years War, remarked on the difference between the French army at the start of its first season of war, the cavalry crested with feathers and resplendent in scarlet and silver lace, and the ragged deserters who stole away, officers as well as men, before the end. The serious consequence of an inadequate supply system is revealed by the following letter, from La Valette to Père Joseph, in the year of Corbie, 1636, when he was required to initiate a winter campaign. 'Our troops are weak; we have been given no money for supplies; we have no horses to pull our large artillery train, which we must have if we are to enter enemy country entirely laid waste, in which such meagre supplies as there are have been collected in strong points which can only be taken with the aid of cannon.' Richelieu made some reforms by his own astonishing energy and command of detail. He began to provide fresh clothes and weapons for any soldiers who had served for a season, although he docked their pay accordingly. He had large carts copied from those used in the Imperial armies to transport supplies. The Jesuits helped to organise rudimentary medical attention, for these polyglot armies were a challenge to the consciences of churchmen of the day. Richelieu himself set out a scheme for an Hôtel des Invalides to be built and staffed with money from the abbeys, whose traditional responsibility it was to provide for the aged who had no homes. But the abbeys were unenthusiastic and the scheme foundered for want of funds.

New weapons and formations had to be introduced if the French were to hold their own against troops who had fought at Breitenfeld and Nordlingen. The arquebus with its pronged stand was giving way to the musket, which could be fired from the shoulder. To exploit this Gustavus had trained his musketeers to fight in five ranks. The first two fired together, front kneeling, second standing; these then moved to the rear so that the intervals for reloading were reduced to a minimum. The cavalry were now usually armed with pistols, but these were less effective in their hands than the sword. Despite these and other changes, there was little drill, no administrative department for the provision of weapons, or arms-making factory in France. Richelieu did however spend money on the development of artillery. He bought the office of Grand Master of the Artillery from old Sully, who was still clinging on to it in retirement, and gave it to one of his own cousins, La Meilleraye, a sure sign with him that he wanted to keep a close personal control over it. He started a foundry at Le Havre, employed skilled foreigners to forge and use the guns, and persuaded the king to make them regular officers in the army.

For all his efforts Richelieu did not go very far towards solving the basic problem of authority over the army. He made one important move in the right direction however by his use of the *intendant*, representative of the crown and responsible to it, attached to an army for purposes of administration. They managed the pay, billeting and feeding of the troops. Inevitably they were treated, as representatives of the Cardinal and as civil servants amongst soldiers, with varying degrees of dislike and contempt. They used their authority tentatively, were often blamed for doing too little and seldom for doing too much. One *intendant* of whom more was to be heard, was Michel Le Tellier. From his assignment in Piedmont, he learned at first hand of the problems of discipline and supply which in years to come, as war minister, he was to do so much to solve. The military revolution of France was his work, and his son's; all that was done in the Thirty Years War was to paper over the cracks.

The army may have been ineffective; the navy did not exist. The cost of maintaining a regular fleet was prohibitive. Every country relied to some extent on temporary fleets, collected from merchants in times of emergency, and on privateers whose activities were made legal by the issue of letters of mark from their government. In these circumstances the French were less effective than their neighbours. The English tradition of seamanship could not be killed even by James I, though he did his best to deprive his irregulars of a living by refusing to issue letters of mark; his son showed a greater awareness of English naval needs than his father—or those of his subjects who refused to pay Ship Money. The Netherlands could survive only as a maritime power, and customs duties were regularly ear-marked for the construction of new vessels. The Spanish had to keep a navy permanently afloat to protect their convoys of American gold, and the *Casa de Contracion*, set up in 1503 to control all trade with the Indies, had become, amongst other things, one of the greatest centres of navigational research in Europe. But the French, despite their long coastline, had never had the same urgent political argument for a strong navy, and had never had to nationalise their privateers, even temporarily.

By 1629, the need for some sort of French navy seemed to Richelieu to be pressing. Henry IV did not have a ship which he could call his own; worse, he hardly had any coastline either. Richelieu's agents, sent out in 1629 and 1633 to investigate the

Atlantic and Mediterranean coasts, reported that almost all the beaches and harbours of France had been bartered away to members of the nobility and the church, who exploited their privileges, as elsewhere. Thus, the duc de Nevers laid a tax on every ship which was built in his port of Saint-Valery; off the coast of Brittany, *curés* demanded the value of one fish for every twenty caught. The authority of the Admiral of France did not run in any coastal province except Normandy and Picardy; elsewhere, the governors would be admirals in their own provinces, if there was a fleet to be admiral of. Meanwhile, the Mediterranean coastline of France was being exposed to attacks from the great Spanish galleys and from the Barbary pirates who were regularly carrying off Frenchmen as slaves to North Africa. An opportunity too was being missed so long as it was left to the Dutch to cut the golden lifeline of Spain which stretched across the Atlantic, and the Western Mediterranean, from Gibraltar to Genoa.

Richelieu's actions were characteristic; he struck at the power of the nobles which strangled the initiative of the state. He became himself *'surintendant général de la navigation et commerce de France'*. He bought the rank of Admiral of France from Montmorency and the command of the galleys from Gondi. He abolished the special naval privileges of the governors, and swept away private coastline rights in the *ordonnance de la marine*. Then he created a fleet. Every port had to build one ship for royal services, so that by 1642, the combined Atlantic and Mediterranean fleets, assembled off Toulon, mustered 65 sail and 22 galleys, the former of modern design, with better hull lines and greater displacement than their rivals. The show-piece, *La Couronne*, drew 2,000 tons, while Charles I's *Sovereign of the Seas*, the pride of the Ship Money fleet, drew only 1,500. They had been built in haste, however, and a contemporary described many of them as 'open to the sea'.

To man this fleet an effort was made to start a naval training college for young nobles. The scheme did not however attract young bloods, who preferred to fight on land or to sail against the Turks and pirates as 'Knights of Malta'. To get naval ratings needed either violence or bribery on the largest scale. Colbert was eventually to resort to a form of conscription, but Richelieu contented himself with ordering all French seafarers who had settled abroad to return home, on pain of death if they were captured in foreign service; at the same time he tried to develop a French navy by forbidding foreign ships to unload in French ports, a measure as impracticable as it was heavy-handed. Richelieu did not understand the economic facts of life.

The new fleet had a brief life, but not an inglorious one. Henri de Sourdis, Archbishop of Bordeaux, was Richelieu's Admiral and one after the Cardinal's heart; a priest who hankered for a life of action, a man of courage and intelligence who would not be deflected from his purpose by the obstinacy of governors or the shortage of sailors. Sourdis justified his unclerical appointment by swift success. In May 1637 he recaptured the Lerin islands, whence the Spanish threatened the Provençal coast. In August 1638 he defeated the Spanish in a full-scale fleet action, when they tried to escape from the blockade of the Pyrenean fortress of Fuentanabia. The Spanish lost fourteen capital ships, and the French navy came of age.

The year of Corbie

In the engagements of 1635, the French drew first blood. The Spanish were worsted in a small encounter near Namur, Franche Comté was invaded without disaster, and the Huguenot Rohan, a shrewd choice to command amongst the Swiss, kept a firm grip on the Val Telline against all Spanish attempts. 1636, however, brought crisis. The Imperialists, encouraged by reports of peasant revolts in Gascony, Anjou and Normandy, planned a double invasion which, they hoped, would lead to the capture of Paris and force Richelieu to sue for peace. In mid-summer, the Cardinal-Infant and the Bavarian general Werth joined forces in Picardy, overran the flat country between the Somme and the Oise and, in August, occupied the important fortress of Corbie, near Amiens. Further south, Imperial soldiers, under Gallas and Charles of Lorraine, poured through the Belfort gap in the Vosges mountains and occupied Franche-Comté. When Werth thrust on to Compiègne, only forty miles from Paris, there was panic in the city and an outcry against Richelieu. The Cardinal was calm, but his advice was depressing: the line of the Seine should be held, but Paris evacuated. Louis XIII, who had already expressed himself forcibly about the 'slackness and carelessness' of his troops, defied his councillors and rode off to join the army at Senlis. His instinct was sound; defeatism did not become the son of Henry IV. The gesture put new heart into his troops, but they were really saved by Bernard of Saxe-Weimar, who blocked Gallas in the south until plague and desertion among his soldiers, on top of news of a Swedish attack on Brandenburg, compelled the Austrian to retire. The Cardinal-Infant would not risk further advance without him, and hesitated fatally, a step short of a triumph which would have put Nordlingen in the shade; in November, Werth was withdrawn by Maximilian of Bavaria. Corbie was recaptured in November, but the shocks of 'the year of Corbie' could not easily be forgotten. Richelieu put an inscription on two fountains at his country house, boasting that he would shed as much Spanish blood as they shed water. His *Gazette* broke into obedient panegyrics at every minor French advantage. But such gestures and propaganda could not conceal the shortcomings of French troops, or the alarming ease with which France could be invaded through

Picardy and Champagne. Not for the last time Frenchmen were reminded of the perilous proximity of Paris to the frontier, about a hundred miles of as easy going as could be found in Europe.

Les Misères de Guerre

In December 1636, the young King of Hungary and co-victor of Nordlingen was elected King of the Romans. Only two months later his father died, happy in the apparent triumph of his policies. For the first time since the Bohemian Revolt he had the solid backing of the leading princes of the Empire. The Elector Palatine was a forlorn and stateless fugitive. The opposition of Holland, Sweden, France and a few German princelings did not seem to amount to much. The Val Telline was secure and the right bank of the Rhine occupied. He had, since the death of Wallenstein, acquired his own army. The new Emperor, Ferdinand III, could reasonably look forward to prosperous years; if parchment were sufficient, his authority should have been beyond question. In truth, however, the armies ruled. It was now a soldiers' war, in which political decisions counted for less and less, in which even the generals could not always be answerable for the conduct of their polyglot armies. There may be some doubt about who was winning the war at this stage; there can be none about who was losing. No words can convey the desolation of Germany in these years, when generals like Werth made a point of burning everything they found in hostile country, when strategy was dictated as much by the search for food in still unravaged territories as by the movements of the enemy. Stories of torture and cannibalism were bruited about and anything could be believed: that the Swedes sprinkled gunpowder upon their prisoners' clothes before setting fire to them, that some Imperialists had boiled a woman in her own cauldron, that men kept guard over graveyards in the Rhineland against robbers who sold the flesh of the newly buried for food. The English ambassador on his way to Regensburg was appalled at the scenes he witnessed, peasants 'found dead with grass in their mouths' and towns 'miserably battered'. The population of central Germany seemed to have dissolved into one vast refugee movement. France now had her share of these horrors. In the so-called 'war of the two Burgundies', the nobility and peasantry of the Spanish provinces joined with Gallas'

Spaniards and Croats to make systematic war and pillage upon their French neighbours. After the soldiers came plague, typhus and famine. The Lorraine artist Callot provides us with some documentation of the sufferings of a frontier province in this period. In one of his etchings, a priest stands on a ladder, giving absolution to a man about to join a row of gallow-birds, who hang like stiff scarecrows from a tree in the middle of a wide ring of soldiers. His famous series, *Les Misères de Guerre*, was actually executed in 1633, the year of Richelieu's invasion of Lorraine; they serve as an artist's commentary upon the unpleasantness of seventeenth century war.

Bernard of Saxe-Weimar

The Treaty of Compiègne had enabled Oxenstierna to reassert his authority in Stockholm, release the little Queen Christina from her virtual imprisonment in the hands of the Queen-Mother and despatch orders and money to his marshals. Baner's victory at Wittstock in October 1636 did something to restore the morale of the Swedish army, crippled the military power of the Saxons and prevented the Imperialists from following up their successes in the west. There, in October 1637, after a prodigious siege of nearly twelve months, the great fortress of Breda on the Dutch border fell to Prince Frederick Henry of Orange. This was a serious blow to the plans and prestige of the Cardinal-Infant and it made possible a new thrust from Bernard who, for the last two years, had been nursing his resources and resisting the demands of the French government. At Rheinfelden, in March, he battered an Imperialist army and captured its general Werth. By June he was before Breisach, a natural fortress on a rocky eminence over the Rhine. With Philippsburg and Rheinfelden in French hands, Breisach—commanding a vital bridge—alone remained between Bernard and control of the Rhine. Richelieu recognised its crucial importance and French troops under Turenne were hurried up to assist. The town was doomed after October, when Charles of Lorraine was defeated by Bernard while trying to relieve the town, but its citizens clung on grimly. By December its inhabitants were dropping dead of hunger and there were stories of cannibalism. In Paris, Père Joseph, whose policies had done so much to bring about this situation, lay dying. Day after day they waited for news of Breisach's surrender; surely resistance was hopeless. Legend says that Richelieu, in a rare tender moment, pretending joy, leant over the friar's bed and called: 'Breisach is ours'. Though he did not know it, it had fallen on December 17, 1638.

The fall of Breisach precipitated the breach between Richelieu and Bernard. Richelieu was essentially concerned with Flanders and the Rhine; for him it was a war of the frontier. His success depended, however, on his ability to persuade his allies that it was worth their while to continue the war on his terms. Sweden had already tried to break away and only the Emperor's unwillingness to cede Pomerania kept her in the war. Now, in the spring of 1639, Bernard made his stand against the French crown. He demanded that he should be given Alsace outright, in fulfilment of the treaty promise of 1635, without any consideration of French claims, and he announced that he would hold Breisach, since it had surrendered not to the king of France but to him. Upon his claim that he was standing as a German prince upon German soil rests the reputation that he has enjoyed as a German patriot. It is true that he was a man of conscience and principle and as such stands out from other mercenaries. But the problem that he posed to Richelieu was not much different from that of Wallenstein to the Emperor ten years before; he was another soldier of fortune who wanted to capitalise his success and settle down to the life of a territorial prince. For months there was deadlock and then suddenly, in July, the obstinate young Protestant died. He was only 35 and his death was so convenient for Richelieu that there were murmurs of poison. We may ignore them, but we must notice Richelieu's double good fortune: first Gustavus, now Bernard, the embarrassingly powerful instrument of policy, dies when he has done his paymaster's work. Richelieu was lucky again when Charles Lewis, the Elector Palatine, who had succeeded to the titles—but not to the lands of his unhappy father, the Winter Prince—chose rashly to travel across France on his way to the Rhine to claim Bernard's army for himself. He was seized at Moulins and forced to languish in gaol while Bernard's second-in-command, Erlach, prepared to sell his army to the best bidder. In October the Bernardines were taken over by the French; in return for French pay they would from now follow the orders of the French general. Though Hesse-Cassel might continue to make gestures, this agreement ended effective German participation in the Bourbon-Hapsburg war.

The collapse of Spain

The marvel of the Spanish disaster in the 1640's was not that it happened but that it had not happened before. Nordlingen had shown Spanish valour and discipline unimpaired; in the Cardinal-Infant, Olivarez had a general and a statesman in the best tradition of Spanish Imperialism. Olivarez himself has some claim to be regarded as the Spanish Richelieu and there is a superficial resemblance in their policies. He tried to tighten the control of the central government over a loose assemblage of provinces, to extinguish their cherished privileges and to enforce uniform laws. But he did not possess Richelieu's sense of the possible or his wary reluctance to be drawn into adventures beyond the strength of the state. In a grandiose foreign policy which aimed simultaneously at the subjugation of the Dutch, the support of the Emperor and the destruction of the French military strength, there was no thought, either of the danger of a war on three fronts, Flanders, the Rhine, and Italy, or of its cost. So the resources of the state which should have been concentrated upon one limited object, were dissipated upon the ever-lengthening fronts of the European war. Once only, at Nordlingen, did Olivarez' policy seem to be entirely justified and the Hapsburg axis to dominate Europe. But it was the very success of this battle which encouraged Madrid to persist and compelled Richelieu to enter the war.

The Empire which had made Europe tremble in 1618 was now ready for dissolution. The court was hectically gay. Philip IV, devout, melancholy and psychic, lavished money upon his bull-fights and his mistresses while his commanders begged for pay for their mutinous troops. Olivarez had abandoned all pretence of administrative reform, while by tampering with the currency he only made worse an inflation so terrible that the people were falling back on barter. There was serious depopulation in the inland parts of Castile which had been the nursery of Spain's finest soldiers. About three-quarters of the goods which came to Spanish ports were carried in Dutch ships. The sick economy was kept going by injections of bullion, upon which all now depended, but often the ships took their precious cargoes straight to the bankers of Genoa. In October 1639, the great disaster came, when the annual South American treasure fleet was trapped by the daring action of Van Tromp in English waters, attacked in defiance of maritime law, and destroyed. Seventy ships were taken or sunk at this battle of the Downs, and the Englishmen who watched with envy from their cliffs witnessed the end of Spanish power, not only at sea. After this the position of the Cardinal-Infant in the Netherlands was desperate, for the Dutch ships controlled the sea routes and the Rhine was blocked by the French at Breisach. From Madrid, he received no money or supplies, only orders, counter-orders and then frantic appeals to send back arms to the home country to use against the Catalan and Portuguese rebels. He died in November 1641, in all the bitterness of squandered toils and hopes. By then French troops were firmly installed on French soil.

The revolt of the Catalans was due mainly to their hatred of the Castilian officials imposed by Olivarez; its immediate cause was the billeting of Neapolitan troops brought up to the province by the Marquis de los Balbases for defence against the French invaders of Rousillon. When Olivarez refused to receive a deputation of the rebels because they would not speak Castilian, they made a treaty with the French and elected Louis XIII Duke of Barcelona. In September 1642, the operations of the French in Catalonia were crowned by the capture of Perpignan. Since 1580 Portugal had been in sullen submission to Spain and had seen her navy, trade and colonies shrink. Olivarez had tried by administrative changes to make the union more real, and now, in his hour of crisis, he paid the price. There had already been a revolt in 1637, led by John of Braganza; in 1641, with the support of the Archbishop of Lisbon, most of the native nobility, and Richelieu, he was proclaimed John IV, king of independent Portugal. The war to realise that independence was to go on till 1667; meanwhile France had another invaluable ally. The Portuguese and Catalan revolts were to be the cause of Olivarez's disgrace in 1643. Richelieu had paid him back with interest for his complicity in the internal plots against his rule. After the last of these, the affair of Cinq Mars, Richelieu asked Louis XIII's permission to resign.

The death of Richelieu

He was a dying man, but the king would not accept it; instead he came to his bedside, and fed him with the yolk of eggs. The clumsy, tender scene was a fitting end to a remarkable partnership. Inhibited and unhappy in the intimacies of marriage and the pomp of kingship, Louis XIII nevertheless had the common sense to do what abler men have failed to do, to recognise greatness in a minister, and support him through a sea of troubles. In the face of the criticism and derision of the court, this had required moral courage. Now as the Cardinal lay dying, his confessor, the *curé* of Saint-Eustache, urged him to forgive his enemies. 'I have no enemies but those of the state,' he replied. The words are a good epilogue for a man whose personality was sunk in the service of the state, who scarcely seemed so much a human being as an impersonal force of intellect and will. On December 4, 1642, he died. In five months his king followed him to the grave.

What had Richelieu achieved? He had resisted the temptation to enter the war before the time was ripe; thus, in relation to the other powers, France was still fresh and in a position to take advantage of their exhaustion. He had enlarged the frontier to the Pyrenees. He had secured bridgeheads on the Rhine and he had prevented the effective union of the two branches of the House of Hapsburg. He lived long enough to see the beginning of the collapse of Spain, and to know that the German princes were demanding peace. In the further war with Spain, and in the negotiations for a German peace, there would be rich opportunities for France. He did not live to see the greatest triumphs of French arms and diplomacy, but he died confident that they would come. Not the least of his legacies to France was the supple diplomat, Mazarin, who succeeded to his executive powers. The victories of Rocroi and Lens, and the peace treaties of Westphalia and the Pyrenees, were Mazarin's harvest; Richelieu had sown the crop.

Rocroi

The shadow of the king's last illness lay over the operations of the French commanders in 1643. On the day before he died, he woke from a short sleep to see his cousin Condé watching him. 'Monsieur de Condé,' he said, 'I dreamed that your son had won a great victory.' Condé's son Enghien, better known by the name that he inherited, was the principal of the three commanders of the army of Flanders. He was only 22; a freakish personality, though very intelligent; impulsive and arrogant, a man who might win or lose a war in a few hours. The Spanish commander, Don Francisco de Melo, was besieging Rocroi, a strong frontier fortress, and Enghien resolved either to relieve the town or, if Melo did not withdraw, to fight him where he stood. The veteran l'Hôpital disapproved his plan to entice Melo into action, but Enghien seemed to be justified when the Spanish commander allowed the whole French army of 22,000 to debouch unmolested from the woods into the open plain. Melo had superior numbers and, more important, the finest infantry in Europe, the undefeated troops of the Cardinal-Infant. He hoped to destroy the French army entirely since its escape was cut off by the broken ground and woods behind them. At dawn of the 19th of May, Enghien's cavalry broke through the Spanish right, but on the left, l'Hôpital was driven back, while in the centre the infantry could hardly hold their own against the Spanish. Enghien's swift response to this unpromising situation decided the course of the battle. He led his cavalry through the second and third lines, the reserve of Italian, German and Walloon infantry, who gave way in consternation. His white-plumed hat, for he refused to wear a helmet, was to be seen wherever the battle was fiercest, and his mad ardour inspired his troops. When he came round to the further side of the field, Melo's horsemen scattered and the Spanish infantry were left, some eight thousand of them, on a slight rise in the centre of the field. Their last stand has caught the imagination of posterity, as has the figure of Enghien, in Bossuet's phrase, 'a young prince of the blood who carries victory in his eyes'. Three times he attacked with infantry and cavalry, only to be driven back. Then the crippled Fontaine, who commanded them from a litter, was killed and his officers signalled for a truce. Some Spaniards fired under the impression that the French were advancing again to attack and Enghien's furious troops converged on the Spanish position, killing without mercy those who could not break out. Their victory was total. The Spanish lost 8,000 killed and 7,000 prisoners, and these mostly Spaniards, the best troops; the *élite* had gone and there were few left to train new armies.

The Peace of Westphalia

In June 1643, the Emperor sanctioned the beginning of peace negotiations with France and Sweden. For the next five years the diplomats wrestled with the innumerable complications of boundary and status; meanwhile the armies went on fighting. Their campaigns were merely diplomatic gambits, intended to secure pawns for the conference table. The war was prolonged because the emissaries at Munster and Osnabrück were always prepared to delay business in the hope of some last-minute military advantage. The Austrians showed that patient optimism in adversity for which they were to become famous. The French, under less severe economic and military pressure than their allies, made it plain that they could hold on for ever. To encourage this belief, their chief ambassador planted a garden round his lodgings.

The Congress did not open until December 1644. Because of the difficulties of precedence which would have arisen if they had met in one place, two towns were chosen for separate talks. The French had been furious when they arrived at Munster to find a Spanish delegate along with the Imperial, because the last thing that Mazarin wanted was for Spain to escape the war through a general peace. The French solution was ingenious; they simply announced that they could not treat with the Spanish envoy since his credentials referred to 'the King of Spain and Portugal', while they recognised John of Braganza as King of Portugal. A further delay was caused by a sudden Swedish attack on Denmark, which was then promptly supported by the Emperor, but the accession of Queen Christina to active rule, at the age of 18 in September 1644, made Sweden less obstructive.

The first six months of the Congress were devoted to deciding where the delegates should sit, and in what order they should enter the rooms. The Papal mediator set the tone by refusing to sit in the same room as heretics. Longueville would not enter at all until he was given the title of *altesse* and, throughout the Congress, could never meet the chief Spanish ambassador because the necessary formalities could not be arranged. The real business was however done by d'Avaux, able but conceited, and seldom on speaking terms with his colleague de Sablé, who was Mazarin's personal agent. The French of course refused to treat with the Emperor's agent, Isaac Volmar, because he was only a lawyer, and it was not until the arrival in November 1645 of Trautsmandorff, friend and first minister of Ferdinand, and a man of unpretentious good sense, that negotiations could begin in earnest.

The diplomats soon found that they did not really know what the war was about, so they held a debate to clarify the issues and list the subjects for negotiation. Briefly these came under four headings. First, the complaints of the Imperial estates: for instance, the cases of Donauworth, Clèves-Julich, and all those places affected by the Edict of Restitution, whose future had been put into cold storage at the 'peace' of Prague. Second, the position of the 'rebels': notably the Elector Palatine. Third, the satisfaction of allies: was Sweden to have Pomerania, or France Alsace? Fourth, the matter of compensation: for instance to the Elector of Brandenburg should he have to cede Pomerania to Sweden.

The Spanish had hoped that the death of Richelieu would be the signal for a period of anarchy. The previous minority was a good precedent for this. Now all was propitious again: a Spanish queen-mother, who bore superficial resemblance to Marie de Médicis; a 5-year-old king and an apparently insignificant Italian minister. They could not foresee that Anne of Austria would come to rely upon and support the minister with authority and affection, or that the minister would prove to be an adequate successor to the great Cardinal. The vain and sleek Sicilian had none of the personal grandeur of Richelieu; he was acquisitive and sly. But he was versed in the language and habits of diplomacy, and a master of courtly intrigue. He had the rare ability to pursue and to utilise the digressions and trifles of diplomacy without losing sight of its larger aims; these he understood and tracked with patience and tenacity. 'Time and I', he might have said, more appropriately than Philip II, 'are a match for anyone.'

In the service of Richelieu, Mazarin had learned, diplomatically speaking, to be a good Frenchman. His understanding of the interests of France is revealed by his instructions to his ambassadors. They were to recover the Low Countries for an 'impregnable barrier' to Northern France, for only then would Paris be truly 'the heart of France'. To secure Luxembourg and the Old County of Burgundy, they should be prepared, if need be, to sacrifice Rousillon and Catalonia. On the German frontier they should reach to the Rhine by the acquisition of Alsace and Lorraine. Thus would France be re-inforced in her dealings with Holland, and with England, who 'is naturally jealous of our grandeur', and have advantages too in Germany, in relation to the Emperor's diminished prestige.

In some respects, France lost ground in the year after Rocroi. One blow was the death of the aged Pope Urban VIII, who had been the firm ally of France since the affair of the Mantuan Succession. His successor, Innocent X, whose pontificate was to see a further decline in the political authority of Rome and was notable mainly for the scandalous activities of an ambitious sister-in-law, did not provide the same useful sanction to the old alliance of Protestant powers under a Catholic paymaster. But he did not remove Cardinal Chigi, Urban's mediator at Munster, and he had practically no influence upon the negotiations. Another problem was a worsening of relations with the Dutch, primarily because of the vexed question of the Dutch Catholics. Suspicions were aroused by a tactless speech of d'Avaux about toleration for these Catholics. A growing party favoured a rapprochement with Spain and an independent peace, and opposed anything that might lead to the aggrandisement of France; in the light of future events their fears are intelligible. Mazarin could not be sure, either, of Sweden's position. After the reckless attack on Denmark, he cut off supplies from Torstensson's army. Queen Christina, who early showed that she had a mind of her own, was understood to be working for peace above everything. Mazarin did not want the northern powers to be too influential in Northern Germany but preferred to work through a group of Catholic states, based upon Maximilian of Bavaria, as a counter-poise to the Emperor. Maximilian played the weathercock, swinging wildly from the Emperor to France and back again, but gained nothing from this but the devastation of his lands by the rival armies. His debacle in 1646-7 illustrates clearly the extent to which the statesmen were powerless in the face of the armies—which did not wait upon the decencies of diplomacy.

The Emperor's hopes of military success were thwarted by the martinet Torstensson, Baner's successor in the Swedish command; his victory of November 1642, at the second battle of Breitenfeld, had been almost the Austrian Rocroi. Ferdinand had had to send Piccolomini, his ablest soldier, to the Spanish Netherlands; now the relationship of the Hapsburg partners was altered and it was Spain that hung like a millstone round Austria's neck. After the eclipse of Gallas in 1644, Ferdinand relied largely on Maximilian of Bavaria, whose excellent generals, Werth, recently released from a French prison, and Mercy, inflicted a sharp defeat upon the French under Guébriant, at Tuttlingen in the autumn of 1643. The death of Guébriant brought Turenne to the fore, a thoughtful and patient strategist, and a good foil to the more flamboyant Enghien.

These two generals won a Pyrrhic victory against Mercy at Freiburg in July 1644. They were fortunate also in the renewed efficiency of Torstensson's Swedes, who inflicted a severe defeat upon the Imperialists and destroyed most of the famous Bavarian cavalry, at Jankau, in Bohemia, in February 1645. Even so, Werth managed to surprise Turenne near Mergenthau and send him rolling back towards the Rhine. This delayed the French invasion which, with the Swedish attack on Bohemia, was expected to deliver the *coup de grâce* to the Austro-Bavarian alliance. When they did invade they found themselves held up by Mercy's Bavarians, entrenched in hill country near Nordlingen. On July 24th Enghien rashly ordered a frontal attack; the *élan* of the charge carried his troops through the Bavarian guns but their casualties were heavy and they were unable to follow up the victory. In the following year Torstensson's successor Wrangel plunged into Bavaria, and this time nothing could save its green pastures from the consequences of its Elector's policy; by the spring of the next year, 1647, he was suing for peace.

A new marriage compact with Spain by which Philip IV, recently widowed, married his own niece, Maria Anna, Ferdinand's daughter, seemed to be poor compensation to the Emperor for the loss of Bohemia. But it was a blow to Mazarin, who still hoped to isolate Spain. He could only blame himself for his next set-back, for the truce between the United Provinces and Spain, at the end of 1646, was entirely due to the Dutch discovery of French plans to marry the Infanta of Spain to Louis XIV and to take Flanders in exchange for Catalonia. To complete Mazarin's discomfiture, Werth refused to accept Maximilian's enforced neutrality and marched off to join the Emperor; soon his master was back again in the Imperial camp. Then the remainder of the Bernardines, ordered to march with Turenne to Flanders, mutinied and slouched off to enlist with Wrangel.

In January 1648, Spain and the United Provinces completed their separate peace of Munster. The main casualty of the peace was in fact Antwerp, since the Spanish conceded the closing of the Scheldt which ruined the city's trade. The French had therefore to postpone their designs upon Flanders, and Turenne marched instead to join Wrangel in a last onslaught upon Bavaria. At Susmarshausen near Augsburg, in May 1648, the superior Franco-Swedish army defeated the last troops of Austria and Bavaria, hampered it is said by a horde of camp-followers, four to every combatant. While Turenne and Wrangel despoiled the Bavarian countryside, a second Swedish army marched to invest Prague; but still Ferdinand refused to sign the peace terms. Did he hope that his brother, with the Spanish army now rid of their Dutch foes, might win some miraculous victory against the French? At Lens, in August, the Archduke Ferdinand was trapped by Condé. At last the Emperor abandoned his religious scruples and authorised the peace. They argued for weeks about the order in which the treaties should be signed. On October 24th, while the citizens of Prague were making their last desperate stand in the city where thirty years before the trouble had all started, the various treaties which, with the earlier treaty of Munster, have been given the name of the Peace of Westphalia, were signed; for all the muddle and delay which had preceded it, this was no mean settlement.

A survey of the peace terms shows that France's overall gain was substantial. The Austrian character of the Empire was enhanced by the consolidation of the Hapsburg lands: Bohemia held in hereditary sovereignty, and Upper Austria regained. At the same time its moral influence over the German states declined to almost nothing, despite the empty words of the claim which laid down that all major questions of war and law should be referred to an assembly of all the states of the Empire. The German princes were allowed to make alliances outside, or among themselves, without the consent of the Emperor. Thus the 'German liberties' were recognised, to the enormous benefit of France, which towered, a unitary and relatively coherent state, over the 'constitutional anarchy' of independent sovereignties large and small which made up the expression 'Germany'.

Sweden became an important German power by her acquisition of West Pomerania, Bremen and Verden, with a secure hold on the south shore of the Baltic. Brandenburg was significantly aggrandised, by the skill and good timing of her young Elector Frederick-William and by the patronage of France. It suited Mazarin's purpose to 'compensate' the wasted state of the Hohenzollerns by the additions of Eastern Pomerania, the bishoprics of Minden, Halberstadt and Cammin, and the reversion to Magdeburg, all of which, with her existing lands in Brandenburg, Prussia and Clèves-Julich, formed the nucleus of a potential middle power between Austria and Sweden. From all his shifts and sallies, Maximilian of Bavaria emerged only with what he had got twenty-five years before, the Upper Palatinate and the electoral hat. To satisfy Charles Lewis, who was restored to the Lower Palatinate, an eighth electorate was created. It was easy now to tinker with the constitution of a body which was no longer either 'Holy, nor Roman, nor an Empire'.

For herself, France secured two valuable concessions. First, the Emperor had abandoned Spain and consented to the exclusion of the Burgundian circle—which included the Spanish Netherlands—and Lorraine from the scope of the negotiations; the fate of these territories was thus left to be decided by the sword. Second, he ceded Metz, Toul and Verdun, Moyenvic, Breisach, and the right to garrison Philippsburg; also in name, Alsace; France actually obtained the 'landgraviate' of Upper and Lower Alsace, in full sovereignty, and the 'provincial prefecture' of the 'Ten Alsatian towns'. These towns however, along with certain monasteries and the nobility of Lower Alsace, were to be left in full possession of their privileges, though none of these were to impair the full sovereignty. What lies behind this studied ambiguity? Mazarin had two considerations in mind: militarily, the use of the garrisons, roads and bridges of the country; diplomatically, the extension of French influence into Germany. The Emperor was willing to concede full sovereignty, but Mazarin preferred to have Alsace as an Imperial fief, so that France might have a seat in the Diet. In the end the French envoys were instructed to decide the matter quickly because of alarming outbreaks of revolt at home; hence this hasty compromise which gave rise to so much trouble. Did the landgraviate bring territorial or merely feudal rights? D'Avaux rightly prophesied that the transference of this uncertain sovereignty would be a 'continual cause of wars'. Not till the '*réunions*' in the eighties was the tangle of land and law straightened out, and then in so draconian a manner as to provoke hostile alliances and war.

The Papal Nuncio denounced the whole settlement in forthright terms as being contrary to the interests of the church; it did indeed fall far short of the great hopes aroused by the Edict of Restitution in the full flush of Hapsburg victory. Yet there was no advance towards any expressed idea of toleration, and the principle followed was still *cuius regio, eius religio*, with the rider that Calvinism was now recognised officially as an alternative form of heresy. Notions of toleration in fact crept in, because of the growing mistrust of force as a means of resolving religious differences, and also the serious depopulation which made most princes reluctant to expel subjects who would not conform. There were to be no more 'religious wars'.

The germ of a new principle can be seen in the terms of West-phalia: the balance of power. The politicians were feeling their way towards the idea of a single equilibrium among states which could be found and maintained by diplomacy. This idea has the merit of admitting the basic fact of political life, namely that every state wishes to extend its power at the expense of its neighbour, and it afforded the means by which aggressive aims could be neutralised. If an aggressor were checked and brought to terms, the balance could be restored, not necessarily by return to the *status quo*, but by a reconstruction, with such annexations as were required to preserve the required proportions of the great powers. These might be called 'compensations', or they might be more elaborate and take the shape of 'partitions'. The diplomats of Munster may not have foreseen the character of the wars of the next century. But their settlement came to be considered as a great instrument of public law and created the standard arrange-ments for the European states until the Revolution. Even the Peace of Utrecht was regarded as an adjustment of the Westphalia settlement. France always pretended that her diplomatic and military forays into Germany were designed to maintain its provisions and, in 1791, in the middle of the Revolution which was creating a new Europe, it was one of the complaints of Burke against the Revolutionary politicians that they regarded the treaty as an antiquated fable.

The Peace of the Pyrenees

For three years, during the Fronde, royal government almost ceased to exist, and the military advantages of Rocroi and Lens were dissipated through the reckless sabotage of civil war, a war of mock heroics, of gutters and chamber pots. The Spanish army found itself opposed, not by the strong front and central purpose of former years, but by several and inconstant factions. In 1650, the great Turenne led his troops against the French king. In 1653, Condé, now just another soldier of fortune, bound by treaty to Spain and Lorraine, marched with Spanish troops to besiege Rocroi, the scene of his, and his country's, greatest triumph. For four years the Spanish armies played the role of patron—as Parma had played it in the last years of the Valois monarchy—to whoever was prepared to pay the price of their alliance. How the situation would have rejoiced the heart of Olivarez! In March 1649, a

Spanish envoy was admitted to Paris by the rebels of *Parlement*. In the following year, Turenne made an alliance with the Archduke Leopold, governor of the Spanish Netherlands, invaded Picardy and won the battle of Rethel against royal troops. The princesse de Condé established herself as an independent ruler in Bordeaux and would have traded the city to the Spanish if the burghers had allowed. From February 1651, when Condé was released from imprisonment, till the end of the year when Mazarin re-purchased the services of Turenne, the Cardinal could only try to govern France by correspondence, and the Spanish troops could deploy on the frontiers unopposed. After the defeat of his troops by Turenne at Étampes in May, Condé called them in to help him. While the battle of the Faubourg St. Antoine was fought out, straw against green scarf, and the *Grande Mademoiselle* had her moment of glory on the walls of the Bastille, the Spanish overran Picardy, the Lorrainers Champagne. By August they were within a few miles of Paris. But Condé had overplayed his hand and allowed Mazarin and Turenne to win public support as the guardians of the frontiers and public order. In October he was forced out, to go off and offer his sword to Spain. Mazarin resumed control of the war, which rumbled on its uneventful course of desultory sieges, marches and counter-marches on the frontier. The diplomats were more active than the generals.

Mazarin's peculiar strength was his lack of sentiment. He would not lend aid to a losing cause—such as the House of Stuart seemed to be—but rather draw advantage from a new force, even if it were a republic and born in blood and illegality. He was drawn to an alliance by admiration of the military efficiency and naval strength of England under the Protectorate. The path was smoothed by the commercial antagonism between England and Holland, which had already led to war between these countries and by Cromwell's own old-fashioned Elizabethanism, his craving for a knock-out war against Spain. In November 1655, a commercial convention was signed between the two countries and Mazarin promised that he would give no aid to the exiled Stuart. Then when he wanted to put pressure on the Spanish negotiators and bring the war to a sharp end, he made in 1657 a formal military alliance with Cromwell, which helped him to bring off his cherished design, the grand marriage alliance with Spain.

Peace talks had started in 1656, the year of the calamitous defeat of the Spanish troops by the Portuguese at Badajoz. In 1657,

French and English troops began operations against Dunkirk and Mardyke on the Flemish coast. In 1658, the isolation of Spain was taken a step further, when Mazarin joined the League of the Rhine. Mazarin was cynical about the idealistic peace aims of Philip von Schörnborn, Elector of Mainz and the inspiration of the League, but he was quick to realise its usefulness as a counterweight to Vienna among the German states. In June of this year Turenne won his victory of the Dunes. He had been besieging Dunkirk, with the aid of a contingent of Cromwellian troops, while English ships blockaded the town. The Spanish army, led by Don John, son of Philip IV and an actress, and Condé, with the Duke of York and a number of English royalists in its ranks, was routed when it tried to raise the siege. Louis XIV made formal entry into the town before it was handed over to the English. (They did not keep it long, for one of the first actions of the Restoration government was to sell it back to France.) The Dunes forced the issue; for Madrid, it was either peace or a war of attrition which could have only one end. Then they heard that the French court had come to Lyon to attend the engagement of Louis XIV to the Duke of Savoy's daughter. This elaborate *Mazarinade* brought the Spanish to terms with uncharacteristic haste. The redundant princess was disposed of somehow, for human feelings could not be allowed to stand in the way of high diplomacy. Nor was Marguerite the first sacrifice on this altar, for Mazarin had already prevented the love match of Louis and his own niece Marie. Now round this fine match of king and Infanta, with all that it implied for the future of their countries, the Peace of the Pyrenees was made. The emissaries, led by Lionne and de Haro, neatly avoided the difficulties of precedence by meeting upon the Island of Pheasants in the River Bidassoa, which flows between France and Spain, and on this unoffending ground, in November 1659, the terms were signed; it was essentially a postscript to Westphalia. It is typical that nine articles were concerned with the re-instatement of the renegade Condé; the Spanish had to pay, with several towns, the price of his pardon and de Haro's misplaced chivalry. France acquired almost all of Artois, with some Flemish towns, Gravelines and Landrecies; some places in Hainaut and Luxembourg, notably Thionville by the Moselle. Charles IV of Lorraine was restored, but France took Moyenvic and Stenay and, for all the independence that the poor Duke was to enjoy, she might have taken it all, for Louis retained the right to march his troops across the Duchy, which had already been cruelly pillaged. In the south, long-occupied Rousillon became part of France while Catalonia was abandoned. Portugal was left to fight on alone for her independence. Finally and, as was to prove, most important, Maria Theresa renounced her claim to the Spanish succession, on condition that her dowry of 500,000 crowns was paid within eighteen months of her marriage. The wedding was celebrated in June 1660 amidst fitting scenes of splendour— but the dowry was never paid. And by then a sickly child had been born to Philip IV by his second wife, the future Charles II, whose uncertain life was to stand between France and the Spanish succession for forty years.

12 MAZARIN AND THE FRONDE

The general crisis

On August 26, 1648, the victory of Lens was celebrated with the singing of the *Te Deum* in Notre Dame. The same night, the barricades were erected in the streets of Paris in protest against the arrest of the leaders of *Parlement*. The domestic conflict which incapacitated Mazarin's government for four years had entered its first violent phase. To call it a civil war is misleading, for the military operations were negligible and their pattern uncertain. Condé, who should have known, said that it should be recorded only in burlesque verse. Its name comes from the *fronde* or catapult with which Parisian urchins liked to pelt the carriages of the rich. Its symbols were straw and paper, worn in hats or carried on fans. It is, however, inadequate to dismiss the Fronde as a sort of political comic opera. The upheaval which brought so much froth to the surface came from profound disorders in every level of society. The selfish clamour of vested interests and the antics of the nobility should not be taken to represent the whole extent of the crisis of the monarchy. For the Fronde does not stand by itself but was one of a number of revolutions which troubled Europe in the middle of the seventeenth century.

Some historians have gone so far as to talk of a 'general crisis' with features common to all the main countries: in Trevor-Roper's words, 'not merely a constitutional crisis, nor a crisis of economic production' but 'a crisis in the relations between society and the state'. The clue to this, he suggests, is to be found in the expansion and the wastefulness of a parasitic state-apparatus, and in the size and expense of the court. This may be valid for England, where by 1649, a year after the outbreak of the Fronde, the English completed their own unique revolution by executing their king, under pseudo-legal forms. In France, however, the situation was different. The Fronde was not simply a rising of the country against the court and the bureaucracy; office-holders both provoked the revolts and played an important part in them.

Neither the nobility who wished to recover the privileges which they had lost at the hands of Richelieu, nor the lawyers of *Parlement* who claimed a new role in a constitutional and elective Monarchy, contemplated a republic; but they toyed with revolution at a dangerous time. The crown had been overspending in such a way as to make it dependent, through *offices* and *rentes*, upon the money and good-will of the richer bourgeois, a dependence which was, however, to some extent mutual. At the same time a large number of office-holders were aggrieved, by the crown's creation of too many offices, which lowered their value, and by the steady reduction of salaries and fees; meanwhile state *commissaires* usurped their functions.[1] The crown had also been levying taxation, which largely fell upon the peasantry, at an unprecedentedly high rate. This was more serious because of the prolonged subsistence crisis of these years, which may be said to date back to 1629-30, when there was a severe outbreak of plague and which was aggravated by a number of bad harvests. The rising of the *Nu-pieds* of Normandy in 1639 had been a reminder of the menace that lay in an oppressed peasantry: recruits for a rebel commander, and, it might be, material for a general *jacquerie*. Peasant risings after this, such as that of the *croquants* of Villefranche de Rouergue in 1643, were fomented and supported by aggrieved officials.

Cabale des importants

There was only one aim upon which all the Frondeurs could agree: the removal of the hated first minister. The subsequent troubles had been anticipated in 1643 by the *cabale des importants* which sought to overthrow him. By Louis XIII's will, Anne of Austria was appointed Regent, but her powers had been limited by the condition that she should act only upon the advice of a Council, consisting of herself, Gaston d'Orléans, now furbished with the resounding title of Lieutenant-Governor of the Kingdom, the prince de Condé and Mazarin. These in turn were assisted by officials, Séguier the Chancellor, Bouthillier, *surintendant*, and Chavigny, Secretary of State. Of this number, Mazarin had special claims upon the queen's interest. He had been designated by Richelieu to carry on the government, and he alone could take up all the threads of war and diplomacy without break or delay. But the queen, who had never been conspicuous for her support and understanding of Richelieu's aims when he was alive, had other reasons for promoting his protégé after his death. It is uncertain whether they were actually lovers or whether they were at any

[1] The *élus*, finance officers, alleged in 1648 that they had paid over 200 million *livres* since 1624 'for confirmation of an imaginary right or grant of a fictitious increment'.

time secretly married, but it seems that they were more than ordinarily fond of each other and that they acted as partners at all times. Their political liaison was fortunate for France, as the alternative might have been catastrophic. Minorities usually breed disturbances, and a Council which contained the names of Condé and Gaston does not suggest stable or co-operative government. The regency of Marie de Médicis provided a recent warning of the disadvantages of the want of a recognised first minister, and now there were the additional strains which came from Richelieu's uncompleted efforts to strengthen the executive. A reaction against this policy was inevitable, accompanied by the usual divisions and squabbles for precedence. Orléans and Condé were violently jealous of each other and could agree upon nothing except their distaste for Mazarin and the officials of the council. This provided the queen and Mazarin with their opportunity; 'divide and rule' might have been their motto, as it was their only hope. The subtle hand of Mazarin can be seen in the queen's adroit tactics. She lulled suspicion by talk of dismissing him, offended and divided the Council by seeming to favour such lightweights as Beaufort, and then flattered *Parlement* by asking them to grant her the full regency. It acted its part obediently and Anne assumed full power, whereupon she promptly made Mazarin First Minister. The regime had begun in the way that it was to continue, with a trick, exploiting the divisions and vanities of the opposing forces, when it could not vanquish them by frontal attack.

The *importants* were so called from the self-important and mysterious way in which they conducted their squalid intrigue. They included two bitter enemies of Richelieu, the ducs de Mercoeur and de Vendôme, Mme de Chevreuse, who had been exiled by Richelieu for her part in the Chalais conspiracy and was now an assiduous agent of Spain, and the absurd figurehead, Beaufort, Vendôme's son, who wanted the governorship of Brittany which his father had forfeited. Their political aim was the reversal of French foreign policy, something which they could reasonably hope for from the Spanish queen-regent, and support for Charles I against his enemies of the English Parliament. Ironically Mazarin owed his rescue to Gaston, who happened to give him a lift in his coach on the night that he was to be assassinated. The plot was revealed and Beaufort imprisoned; his confederates fled to continue their subversions from the enemy's camp. The victory of Rocroi stilled intrigue for a time, but Mazarin had received a foretaste of trouble to come.

The brilliant success of Condé soon palled in the years of indeterminate fighting and negotiation that ensued. Mazarin had inherited mounting financial deficits and exhausted credit. By 1643 the percentage of revenue from office had fallen to a mere eight per cent, as a result of the persistent over-creation of new offices by Richelieu. His hand-to-mouth finance was his worst legacy to his successor, who could only look forward to further expedients and further unpopularity since he did not have the authority to make radical changes. The French war effort was maimed at a time when it was vital to finish the war with some decisive campaign; the failure to do so brought grievances to a head in the shape of the Fronde.

The Fronde of Parlement

Omer Talon, *avocat général*, at a *lit de justice* in January 1648, spoke in words which would have been recognised outside the comfortable assembly of lawyers in *Parlement*. 'For ten years the country has been ruined, the peasants reduced to sleeping on straw, their furniture sold to pay the taxes, so that to maintain luxury in Paris millions of innocent persons are forced to live on bread made of bran and oats.' The words might be dismissed as a conventional oratorical prelude to the main point by the *avocat général*, his denial of the right of the crown to impose its will upon *Parlement* by a *lit de lustice*, were it not confirmed by the evidence from the provinces. 1648-51 were peak famine years. In some of the frontier provinces, such as Burgundy, the independent peasant proprietor had disappeared and villages were depopulated. Tax collectors' reports repeated a grim refrain: 'there are here only those who are useless for taxation'. But nearer to the minds of those who listened to Talon's defiance were the new measures of Mazarin's unpopular *surintendant*, Particelli d'Emeri. It was difficult for Mazarin to secure the acceptance of new taxes when his financiers were exploiting the public need to make themselves private fortunes. D'Emeri, the most blatant of these, in 1644 imposed a tax, the *toisé*, upon dwelling-houses built just outside the walls of the city, and revived a statute of the sixteenth century which had, for military purposes in the exceptional situation created by the League, prohibited the building of houses within a certain distance of Paris. This sort of antiquarian chicanery invited 'constitutional' opposition from those whose pockets it affected. But this and the new tax, *les aisés*, imposed in the same year, were only pinpricks compared to the assault upon the national *rentes*, issued by the Hôtel de Ville. These were the nearest thing to a government security that existed, but they were by no means gilt-edged; on the contrary, they fluctuated violently with the ups and downs of government credit. Since in a bad year an investment might yield as much as 50 per cent, Mazarin and d'Emeri may have felt themselves justified in using these funds to help government finance. But they chose a bad time to tamper with a widespread vested interest with a capital stake of many millions of *livres*. By suspending the payment of interest upon the *rentes*, they caused the capital value to fall; they then bought up large amounts cheaply, paid interest again, watched the stock rise and then sold. They could hardly expect the *rentiers* to swallow indefinitely a method which looked more like private speculation than state finance. The Fronde of the *Parlementaires* was a revolt of the privileged, on behalf of privilege; but narrow as its aims were, it could claim some justification from the contemptuous conduct of the administration. Mazarin provoked further ill-feeling by the *édit du rachat*, which was designed to screw more money from the *paulette*, from his attempt to take over the municipal *octrois* and by the creation of more offices in *Parlement*. He lacked Richelieu's instinct for the temper of public opinion and he did not sense the danger that lay in the moves of Paul de Gondi to exploit the opposition of the *rentiers* and *officiers* who saw their prestige and their pockets impaired by a government which they despised.

On May 13, 1648, *Parlement*, in the *arrêt d'union*, decided upon a meeting of the four sovereign courts, the *chambre des comptes*, the *cour des aides*, the *grand conseil* and *Parlement* itself, in the *chambre de Saint Louis* to draw up a plan of reform. Mazarin promptly withdrew their rights from the *paulette*. They then demanded a guarantee of personal liberty and the withdrawal of *intendants* and *commissaires*, except on the frontiers; amongst other financial proposals, the regular payments of the *rentes*, the abolition of monopolies, the lowering of the *taille* and a special tribunal for the treatment of dishonest financial officers; the authorisation of all taxes by *Parlement*. There are three distinct elements in this important document; reaction against the recent extension of the powers of the state, concern for the monetary interests of merchants and *officiers*, and a constitutional demand for some sort of limited monarchy. This latter derived from the view of contract which had enjoyed some vogue during the Wars of Religion—that there had been an original agreement between king and people which guaranteed separate rights for the contracting parties; *Parlement* being the representative of the people. At the same time mention of the rights of freedom from arrest and control of taxation seems to echo the stirring events across the Channel. But there is only a slight analogy between the Great Rebellion in England and the Fronde of the *parlementaires*. The latter were in no sense representative of anything except their own class; they were a close and privileged corporation fighting for certain tangible reforms, for sound finance in so far as this was compatible with their own rights. They had neither the experience nor the organisation to sustain their protest or to carry it on into a war of principles. They were fond of allusions to the republican spirit of Rome, but they could never seriously imagine themselves deprived of the authority of the king upon which their status depended. They lacked too the dynamic of religious feeling which gave strength to English Puritanism. They were too well insured to be successful rebels.

Mazarin was not a man to stand for long upon untenable ground, but preferred to retreat and wait for advantages to accrue, from the mistakes of his critics and the division of their interests. Anne therefore yielded to *Parlement* on nearly every point, though nothing was said of personal liberty. When he heard of Condé's victory at Lens on August 20th, Mazarin felt that he could take advantage of public celebrations to decapitate the opposition. While Notre Dame adorned with seventy-three banners of Spain and the Empire was echoing with Condé's triumphal *Te Deum*, prominent leaders of *Parlement* were arrested, including Blancmesnil and the septuagenarian Pierre Broussel, a venerable and popular figure amongst Parisians. The clumsy stroke served to give *Parlement* the popular support that it had hitherto lacked. The next day, the 26th, the barricades were going up, chains, benches, paving-stones, anything that would block the narrow streets; when the royal troops arrived they were pelted with stones. A delegation marched to the Palais Royal, the *Premier Président* at their head, to demand redress. Once again

Mazarin leaned before the storm; the prisoners were released and the court left Paris, first for Rueil, formerly Richelieu's domain, then for Saint-Germain. The Declaration of Saint-Germain, October 22nd, embodied all the reforms demanded by the *chambre de Saint Louis*. The next day, Servien, Mazarin's agent, was instructed to bring the peace negotiations at Munster to an end. But his great achievement of diplomacy roused little interest amidst the tumult of affairs at home. Condé who had done most to make it possible was brought home and with his troops and the promised support of Gaston, Mazarin decided to strike again. On January 5th, Anne left Paris for the discomforts of Saint-Germain and *Parlement* was ordered to betake itself to Montargis. The two acts were regarded by *Parlement* as a declaration of war. Mazarin believed that Condé's troops, who had defeated the professional armies of Spain, could soon quell Paris. But *Parlement* now had allies.

While Condé set about the siege of Paris, with 8,000 men but without conspicuous energy, the spirit of the city was being stirred up by aristocratic leaders who saw that the time had come to secure the benefits that they thought to be their due. They sustained the city by their Corneillian heroics, but they embarrassed the opposition, led by Matthieu Molé, into seeking a compromise settlement. The peace of Rueil was signed on April 1, 1649; most of the concessions already granted were confirmed by Mazarin and registered by *Parlement*. So ended the Fronde *parlementaire*. Militarily it amounted to two small battles, in which Conti and Beaufort were defeated at Longjumeau and Charenton; constitutionally it resulted in the acquisition of rights which could mean very little if the crown was determined not to honour them.

The Fronde of the nobles

The true nature of the alliance of the *noblesse* with the city fathers can be seen in the claims that they made for themselves when they pledged support to *Parlement* in January 1649. The duc de Beaufort, *le roi des halles*, wanted the governorship of Brittany and compensation for his losses under Richelieu. The duc de Bouillon wanted Sedan, or its equivalent in money, the governorship of Auvergne and recognition of himself and his family as princes of France. The prince de Conti wanted the recall of Mme de Chevreuse, a *tabouret* for the princesse de Marsillac and a *place forte* for himself in Champagne. The marquis de Vitry wanted to be made *duc*. The spokesmen for the *noblesse* confronted the failings of absolute monarchy with a catalogue of personal grievances; they spoke the language of decadent feudalism. They saw France as the sum of their local territorial interests, and her government as a fund which existed for their exclusive benefit. They were united only in their hatred of Mazarin, who stood between them and the proper flow of pensions and privileges. They could express their aims best in the *Mazarinades*, the *chansons* and pamphlets which gave them common interest with the guttersnipes of Paris. Their patriotism could not rise above denigration of the Italian minister.

If any man could have made anything of this unsatisfactory alliance, it was Paul de Gondi, the garrulous and busy co-adjutor of the Archbishop of Paris, himself Italian in origin, but an enemy of Mazarin since he had refused him the Cardinal's hat. His memoirs reveal the journalist's eye for a scene and a telling phrase, along with a heroic disregard for the truth; they show also that he was intelligent enough to see through the motives of his fellow-countryman. He looked now for the sort of control in the city that had once belonged to the family of Guise. He had some ideas about the direction of a rebellion, largely derived from his readings of Roman history, and he did see that the revolt must fail if he could not cement the alliance of aristocracy and *Parlement*. But he had little to contribute beyond a certain tactical *finesse*, for he was actuated too blatantly by private ambition. He dramatised his role as uncrowned king of Paris, deceiving himself more than he deceived others.

Mazarin's position was not a happy one. He had twice made concessions when he knew himself to be weak and reacted when he thought himself to be strong. But this strength consisted merely in the army of Condé, an independent force of lax discipline, under the command of an impetuous and arrogant grandee, whose closest relations, Conti, his brother, and Longueville, his brother-in-law, were the Cardinal's enemies. It was too much to expect that in this situation Condé would show either moderation or modesty. Urged on by Conti and Longueville, he demanded that the comte de Jarzé should take the place of Mazarin. Behind this unimportant man, chosen it seems because he had recently offended the queen by some rude advance, he expected to dominate affairs. He did his best to embarrass Mazarin, demanding that

Longueville should be given the governorship of Pont de l'Arche to add to his governorship of Normandy and that Mazarin's own nieces should marry men of his choice. He required the status of Prince of the Blood for his nominees, the cherished *tabouret* for certain ladies. Mazarin knew that his pretensions and his temper made him much disliked, especially, for different reasons, by the rival house of Vendôme, by Mme de Chevreuse and Paul de Gondi. The latter may have been behind the strange affair of December 11th, 1649, when Condé had been shot at in the streets of Paris after a fake assassination attempt upon Guy Joly, a supporter of Gondi, had led to uproar in the city. Mazarin then brought matters to a head. On January 18th, Condé, Conti and Longueville were arrested and despatched to the fortress of Vincennes. 'Ah Madame, what have you done? They are Princes of the Blood' was the shocked reaction of *Premier Président* Molé. Mme de Motteville recorded the astonishment that this stroke aroused. It was the beginning of the second and aristocratic phase of the Fronde, more dangerous than the first. Condé at large would have had few friends outside his immediate circle, but Condé imprisoned was a rallying point for all who opposed Mazarin.

It could well be called the Fronde of the women. Mme de Longueville was not the pattern of conjugal fidelity, but she was happy to fight for her husband; she dashed off to raise his province of Normandy. In Paris, the princesse Palatine, Mme de Chevreuse and Mme de Montbazon stirred up feeling in the *salons* and the streets. The demure princesse de Condé astonished her tough relations by going to Bordeaux and putting the city into a state of defence to such good purpose that its capture occupied the court army for most of the summer. What these women thought they were achieving can be seen in the *Mémoires* of Mme de Motteville, usually the most balanced of critics, who thought that women were ordinarily the chief cause of disorders in states, and that wars which brought ruin to kingdoms were most often provoked by the malice or beauty of women. Several things may be held to contribute to the rule of the petticoat in these years, the dominance of the great hostesses in the *salons*, the conventions of a literature in which women habitually struck classical and heroic poses, the spirit of a few strong-minded individuals. It provides a comment upon the effeminate tone of aristocratic society, rapt in its suicidal pursuit of place and privilege and unable to rise to any disinterested conception of the needs of the state.

Through the mouthpiece of *Parlement*, the clique of de Retz now demanded the release of the princes and the expulsion of Mazarin. He, seeing that his presence on French soil only served to diminish the credit of the court party, retreated to Breuil in the Archbishopric of Cologne, where he devoted himself to governing France by letters, principally to Le Tellier, and to negotiating with Turenne, Bouillon's nephew, who had been in arms with the Spanish. The princes were released on February 11th, 1651, entered France in triumph and proceeded to the Palace of Luxembourg to hold a national convention of princes and *Parlement*. The monarchy itself seemed to be rocking as the Convention discussed the establishment of a council of twenty representing the Three Estates, the summons of a States-General and the deprivation of Anne of Austria. Orléans, who, in the opinion of de Retz, 'had everything necessary for an *honnête homme* except courage', whose career of revolt and betrayal had scarcely fitted him for national leadership, could not hold the rival interests together. Pride of birth asserted itself against pride of office; when Gondi talked of raising the barricades, Condé announced that he would not take part in 'a war of gutters and chamber pots'. Since he took no action to secure the crown, Condé's real aims must remain a matter of conjecture; he may have wanted to crown himself, or even Mademoiselle Gaston's daughter.

The position of Anne and her son, whose majority was declared this year, was both difficult and dangerous. On one occasion a crowd of Parisians forced their way into the Palais Royal and clamoured to see the king, who, they feared, would be taken away as he was before. Anne seems to have played the waiting game assigned to her by Mazarin with skill and a certain indolent dignity. First Turenne, after his defeat at the battle of Rethel in December 1650; then Gondi, who had found that Condé was an impossible ally and now hoped for his Cardinalate from the queen, came over to the court. *Parlement* was edging away from the party of anarchy, though the queen could not be sure of it so long as she corresponded with Mazarin. In October 1651, placated by the dismissal of Mazarin's more unpopular ministers, they declared Condé guilty of treason; by the end of the year the Fronde had narrowed down to Condé's adherence amongst the nobility. In January 1652, Mazarin felt emboldened to return with hired troops and he joined the court at Poitiers. *Parlement* was content with placing a price on his head, after the precedent of Charles IX in respect of Coligny; honour satisfied, they awaited the outcome of the military operations of the year which were of a somewhat inglorious nature; the common people, as usual, were the principal sufferers (Rouen lost 17,000 inhabitants in one year). Turenne occupied himself with a desultory campaign in the district of the Loire, in which both sides seemed reluctant to commit themselves too far. A moment of high farce came when Mademoiselle de Montpensier, the hoydenish daughter of Gaston d'Orléans who had at last declared himself for Condé, anticipated Turenne's move and captured the city of Orléans before him. The first important action, on April 8th, came when Condé, who had joined forces with Beaufort and Nemours, defeated the royalist troops at Bléneau. But he made the mistake of his life when he went on to Paris instead of following up his victory. Turenne was thus able to put his army between Paris and the rebels, whom he proceeded to defeat at Étampes on May 4th. Condé accepted the logic of his position and called in foreign troops, Spanish into Artois and Picardy, Lorrainers into Champagne. He had entirely lost the sympathy of the Parisians, who now witnessed the extraordinary spectacle of street fighting between France's two greatest soldiers. In the Faubourg St. Antoine on July 2nd, Condé won a scrambled victory with the aid of Mademoiselle. Her father was paralysed with the indecision that overcame him on important occasions, so she secured the mobilisation of the city, turned the guns of the Bastille upon Turenne's troops and achieved the relief of the princes. Condé then assumed dictatorial power in the city, forcing a rump of *Parlement* to confirm Orléans as Lieutenant-General of the kingdom and entrusting the management of the city to a committee of nobles under the governorship of Beaufort. The latter chose this time to pick a quarrel with his brother-in-law and brother-in-arms, Nemours, over a matter of precedence, and killed him in the subsequent duel.

Mazarin was not the man to allow his pride to stand in the way of sound policy, and when an army of Spaniards and Lorrainers approached Paris in August, he slipped out of the country again. When deputations of Parisians came to beg the court to return to Paris, therefore, the queen was able to negotiate without the embarrassment of his presence. A party of *Parlement* were now calling themselves the party of peace, wearing white ribbons in their hats to signify their opposition to the straw emblems of the princes, and the queen could count upon a great resurgence of loyalty amongst the mass of the ordinary citizens of Paris. In October, Condé left Paris to offer his sword to Spain; the queen and Louis XIV entered the city amidst public effusions.

The Fronde had been two revolts in one. In one aspect it was the protest of the old feudal aristocracy, under political and economic duress; in another, the mutiny of the privileged leaders of the *bourgeoisie*, the *noblesse de la robe* which had benefited as the *noblesse de l'épée* had declined. This class had secured footholds in the establishment from which the old aristocracy was excluded. The *offices* and the *rentes* made up a corpus of privilege, much of it already hereditary, which amounted to a new feudalism. The old feudalism had blocked the advance of the state, the new had grown cankerwise, from and with it. The Fronde had been overcome because the minority of the nobility who revolted was unequal to the military resources of the crown, and because the *bourgeois* were ultimately more interested in security and profit than in the glamorous disorders of civil war. The victory of the crown was however worthless unless it could be followed by the reduction of both privileged orders which robbed the state of its authority.

The old aristocracy was vulnerable, its outlook obsolete and its resources sapped by the depression of rents. Prevented by its traditions from sharing, except by marriage, in the new wealth to be gained from banking and trade, it was a declining class. For this the state was to evolve a clear-cut solution, in the development of the court as the matrix of a dependent aristocratic life, and in the extension of the powers of the *intendant* in the province. The protest of the *rentiers* on the other hand, while less spectacular, had tap roots which the government could not easily reach. It came from a class which was accruing capital, investing in land and offices, and looking for social opportunities. *Bourgeois* affluence is an aspect of seventeenth century life which is sometimes overlooked amongst the more obvious splendours of court life. It is easy to see France in the reflections of the *salon des glaces*. The other France must be looked for in the great houses that men built for themselves in Paris, in other *parlement* towns such as Bordeaux, Aix-en-Provence, in purchases of rich agricultural land round provincial capitals like Dijon, in the new theatres which they patronised, in the titles they bought for themselves, in the noble marriages they contracted for their daughters, the offices they bought for their sons. In the growing towns there were opportunities for the lucky few, in finance, merchandising and shipping. In proportion to their wealth they might seem to have little direct political power; the monarchy of Versailles which could afford to ignore the protests of *Parlement* presided over a court and culture which was still aristocratic in tone. There was no representative system to allow them the share in the formulation of policy which the equivalent class enjoyed in Holland and England. But they had battened upon the economy and administration of the country in such a way as to represent an important negative influence upon its policy, a drain upon the government's capital resources and a check upon its freedom of action.

13 THE YOUNG KING

The education of the king

On March 9th, 1661, Cardinal Mazarin died, leaving with regret his superb pictures, his fortune (the revenue from his estates at his death was four million francs) and a quiescent France. His royal protégé, 23 years old but already versed and confident in the manners of royalty, did not falter. Le Tellier, the Chancellor, had been confidently spoken of as successor to the Cardinal. But when the Secretaries of State came to ask to whom they were to apply for instructions, Louis answered simply 'To me'. Before his ministers and courtiers and, the following day, before the Assembly of Clergy, he declared solemnly that he would be 'his own first minister'. Six months before he had snubbed the lawyers of *Parlement*, warning them to confine themselves henceforth to questions of law. Now the note of authority was heard again. Upon the young king who walked so imperturbably into his responsibilities were focused the aspirations of many of his countrymen. But few can have guessed how seriously he would take his role, or what conscientious study he would give to the business of being an autocratic king.

Louis had been king in title since the age of 5. The unsettled life of the court was a distracting background to his childhood, and his education had been haphazard rather than deliberately neglected. The stress was upon the practical royal virtues rather than academic training. Under the guardianship of Villeroi, a casual and acquiescent grandee, the young prince was entrusted to a staff of tutors led by Hardouin de Péréfixe, later Archbishop of Paris, and Fr. Paulin, his first confessor and the head of the Jesuit order in Paris. Péréfixe himself, in his daily summaries of the more edifying parts of French history, and particularly from his own history of Henri le Grand, presented him with an idealised portrait of his grandfather which Louis never forgot. He pointed out that since a king is almost entirely concerned with actions, 'he must be taught primarily to perform decisive actions'. Louis responded properly to this pragmatic counsel, promising 'to follow the example of the most generous of his ancestors, particularly abhorring Louis the Idle'. He was given a guide to conduct in the form of a royal commonplace book of moral tags, Péréfixe's *Institutio Principis*, which he had to translate daily from the Latin.

Many of these maxims were later passed by Louis to his son and it is interesting to see the origin of Louis' remark that 'the profession of a king is a majestic, noble and delightful one' in Péréfixe's: 'a king should delight in his calling'. The path to learning was indeed a royal one. By his writing-master he was made to copy out the sentence, 'homage is due to kings; they may do as they please'. Ordinary manuals of geography, rhetoric, logic and ethics were prepared for him, but he may have learned more from the specially designed playing-cards from which he could ponder improving gobbets of history and mythology. He never enjoyed reading, although Saint-Simon's statement that he could barely read or write is a characteristic exaggeration. His range probably included *Don Quixote*, Caesar's *Commentaries* and the *Mémoires* of Commines and he is related to have had his valet read to him in bed from Mézeray's popular *History of France*; the same valet perhaps, La Porte, who minced before him with his hat on, to teach the finer points of kingly decorum.

The circumstances of Louis' boyhood were a hard school in themselves. He never forgot the straits to which the Fronde reduced the monarchy, the hurried journeys to exile, temporary billetings in the country palaces and poverty of court life under the close rule of Mazarin; nor the spectacle of Frenchmen fighting outside Paris itself, at the battle of the Faubourg St. Antoine. After one cold night-ride to unfurnished Saint-Germain, some Parisians, in their spite, had stopped the carts carrying the furniture from the Palais Royal. Two years later, in 1651, a mob of citizens had forced their way into the Palais to see the supposedly sleeping prince. Such affronts scarred his memory with prejudice against the capital. The Fronde, and all that it implied, seemed to reinforce the lessons of French history. 'From my childhood', he recorded, 'I loathed the mention of kings of straw and mayors of the palace.' His own first noteworthy political action was the imprisonment of du Retz, whom Mazarin would have pardoned, 'an ugly but necessary act of dissimulation' which delighted the Cardinal. The king learned from the Fronde that to avoid being a mere 'king of straw' he must break the independent power of the great nobles. When he was in exile at Bruhl in 1651, Mme de Lansac, a personal enemy of Mazarin, had given him letters in which Catherine de Médicis outlined a political programme for her weak son, Henry III. Louis listened 'with close attention', but he hardly needed the prompting of Catherine's advice to her son to assume personal and autocratic control of the government. He realised that so long as the king's minister was considered a public enemy, the king's own popularity was enhanced; until however he governed himself, his power would not be secure. The Fronde which revealed the bankruptcy of the various forces of opposition helped to form Louis' political ideas and especially his leaning towards a new form of state socialism. In Lavisse's words: 'an upheaval in which every man acted for himself ended fatally in the king for all'.

Royalist sentiment

Signs of this new ardour for monarchy were not lacking. The king whose birth had been hailed as a miracle could not appear in public without scenes of spontaneous joy. Evelyn declared, after witnessing his coming of age ceremony in 1651, that the French were 'the only people in Europe who idolise their sovereign', a prince of 'grave yet sweet countenance'. Already, wrote a Parisian, Guy Patin, the *bourgeois* of Paris 'feel violent inclination beyond what they normally feel for their prince'. Beside the conventional adulation there is a note of awe in the contemporary accounts of Louis' character and appearance. Louis was indeed an admirable prince, 'beautiful as an angel', precociously grave and composed upon public occasions such as the Thanksgiving at Notre Dame for his recovery from the smallpox, or his coronation at Reims in June 1654. The child was father to the man in the studied grace of demeanour, the control of gesture and expression that was to become habitual. Mme de Motteville noticed with amazement that 'in his games and play the king never laughed'. In his own words he wished 'to be perfect in all things' and feared 'to be found to fail in anything'. He learned to translate his idea of majesty into terms of manners and deportment which a courtier could understand. So the amiable boy grew into the politest king in Europe.

It is not surprising that Anne of Austria doted upon the child of her middle age. A little lethargic and very devout in the Spanish manner, seeking in religion an escape from the weariness of politics, she instilled in Louis habits of the strictest piety: daily Mass and observance of the principal festivals. At her instance, following the shadowy precedent of Clovis, the young king was allowed the special privilege of making his first communion at Christmas rather than at Easter. Anne enjoyed showing him off to the crowds and she appreciated the value of ceremonies which focussed public attention upon him. Louis seems to have repaid his mother with one of the few spontaneous affections of his life. Mazarin's was however a greater influence on his adolescence. It was a favourite criticism of the *frondeurs* that the Cardinal neglected or subdued the young king. In fact he protected him, regarding him as his heir, and initiated him in the skills and deceits of statecraft. He kept him away from the bawdy talk of courtiers and, with less success, from the gaming table. The practical lessons taught by the Italian master at Council meetings, which he was encouraged to attend, were of the utmost value. Mazarin noted his apt intelligence in Council and his mastery of detail. He prophesied that he could become one of the greatest princes in the world, having 'the stuff of four kings; a slow beginner, he will go further than any'. The restrained prophecies of the old diplomat are of more interest than the panegyrics later in fashion.

The last stroke of the old minister was the occasion for a remarkable display of loyal sentiment by the citizens of Paris. As well as the marriage of Louis to the Infanta of Spain, they celebrated, on August 26, 1660, the rare state of peace in Europe, after the treaty between France and Spain, and the more recent treaties of Oliva and Copenhagen which had brought to an end the Northern War. Outside the walls of Paris, in the *place du trône* —as it was subsequently called—Louis received the homage of the representatives of the city, the clergy processing behind their crosses, chanting litanies of the saints, the doctors and professors of the Sorbonne in their robes and hoods, the merchants of the guilds, judges, members of the Mint, the Excise, *Parlement*; spokesmen for these bodies spoke rapturously of the young queen, peace, and the glory of the crown which lay principally in maintaining peace. In the afternoon the king entered the city, at the tail of a procession of his court, his household troops, the Chancellor and the officers of the crown, and Princes of the Blood. The latter included the renegade Condé; all was harmony. The procession took four hours from the *place du trône* to the Louvre, passing under a series of triumphal arches which had been planned with elaborate symbolism to represent such subjects as the Glory of Literature and the Union of France and Spain. These huge monuments of canvas and wood painted to look like stone were mostly broken up the next day, with their clusters of allegorical figures, emblems, friezes and decorative motifs of every sort.

But the significance of all this was not so soon lost upon the people who craned their necks to study the designs or read pamphlets distributed with translations of the Latin texts and interpretations of the somewhat academic symbolism. It was not a court function but a city fête, as spontaneous as such demonstrations can be after months of planning. The decorations were splendid. The arch of the Faubourg Saint Antoine, 60 by 48 feet, professed to rival the greatest ruins of antiquity; it had an internal staircase by which the oboists could reach the entablature whence they serenaded the king. Le Brun created the arch in the Place Dauphiné which seemed to be made of white marble and was crowned with an obelisk. The ingenuity and resource of the artists, the lavish expenditure on these transitory objects are impressive; equally so, amongst all the jingoism and festival gaiety, the reaction that they evoked. Some may have grumbled at the cost of so much sham baroque, but many seem to have welcomed the chance to express their loyalty and their more than conventional desire for the blessings of peace.

Court life

Assessments of Louis usually derive from the later part of the reign and are heavily tinged with the comments of Saint-Simon upon a figure of almost inhuman kingliness. By then, the unrelaxing pose had become second nature in the formal grandeur of Versailles. But some note must be taken of an early period, before Saint-Simon was born, when Versailles was all earthworks and scaffolding and when the healthy, greedy young Bourbon was enjoying the first fruits of power. Court life in the first decade of the reign was emancipated and extravagant. Particularly after the death of Anne of Austria, restraints were cast aside as the king indulged his taste for pageantry and fêtes. The birth of the Dauphin in 1662 was made the occasion for a typical celebration at the Tuileries, at which Louis himself appeared, in the garb of a Roman Emperor, followed by squadrons of 'Persians' under Monsieur, 'Turks' under Condé, 'Indians' under Enghien and 'American Indians' under Guise. The barbaric display, half circus and half ballet, is a cameo of the spirit of the time, splendid, arrogant and dangerously naïve. In May 1664, the court was invited to the royal hunting-box at Versailles for the *plaisirs de l'île enchantée*, a three-day event planned round the theme of Roland Furieux, and as it turned out, a feast of art, charade and decorative nonsense. Cavalcades, declamations, tilting, ballets, allegorical tableaux, plays (the *Princesse d'Elide* and *Tartuffe*, by Molière), music composed and arranged by Lulli, fireworks, banquets—the frivolities of this baroque festival were something more ingenious and lavish than anything the French court had seen before. They expressed the mood of a lusty heir to a rich inheritance. Those who shared in his bounty were unlikely to criticise his performance.

In all the free rites of the spring of his reign Louis was chief reveller and the cynosure of all eyes. He was generally accounted handsome, with commanding features, the long Capet nose, a sensuous mouth, fine brown eyes and chestnut hair which he long refused to subdue to a wig. But details scarcely mattered. He was only five foot four inches, but even without the blocked shoes that he often wore, men thought him tall. He seems to have had a royal presence and manner which commanded an instinctive deference and kept men at arm's length. As Mme de Motteville saw him, he was 'agreeable personally, polite and easily approachable, but with a lofty and serious air which impressed all with respect and awe and prevented even his confidential advisers from forgetting his position when they talked privately to him'. He spoke slowly and chose his words with care. With easy but measured politeness he made the right remark to the right person. The performance was not yet continuous, but he already showed the actor's poise; he never fluffed a line or an entry. There was more than a hint of the *roi du théâtre* about him. In an ordinary person, the manner that invested the most trite remark with a special meaning would be merely boring. But in the king it was suitable. We may suspect that some of the courtiers were lacking in a sense of humour, but there is no doubt that they were delighted and impressed. The king was never ridiculous.

Already he showed signs of pre-occupation with the theme of *la gloire*. 'As God was infinitely jealous of his Glory so should the king be.' Glory was not so much a matter of state policy as a personal response to the challenge of power. The ideal was a projection of his own extrovert temperament. The word which to modern ears has something barbaric about it, suggesting the morality of Valhalla or of Nuremberg, was to Louis almost sacred. He wrote himself that it took precedence over all other passions in his soul. In a typical passage in his *Mémoires*, he explained that it was a passion 'requiring the same delicacy of touch as the love of a woman' and a matter of daily care: 'although I was enthusiastic to make a name for myself, I was fearful of failure and since committing the slightest fault filled me with a deep sense of shame, I decided to take the greatest possible care in my behaviour'. Passages such as this have led historians to write as if all his policies followed from an odious obsession with his personal fame. It is true that considerations of prestige were always important and sometimes given disproportionate weight. But Louis' concern for glory amounts to little more than a sort of perfectionism. The word *gloire*, like *amour*, with which it was often coupled, had a conventional meaning in the period. Louis was only echoing the themes that his subjects urged upon him. One should set his values in the context of the Classical Age, when art and literature took feats of heroism and sacrifice in war and love as their usual field. When writers and painters wished to express their orthodoxy, they outdid their king in the praise of what they imagined to be the virtues of the Romans and what were, in fact, nearer to a debased form of the code of chivalry, with the humility left out. So Racine spoke of himself and his fellow-writers in the Academy as being 'mere instruments whose duty it is to administer to the glory of our august protector'. Boileau's *Discours au Roi* addresses the 'young and valiant hero . . . who alone, without minister, after the manner of the Gods, sustains everything by yourself, sees all with your own eyes'. The theologians added their gloss to this, explaining his remarkable condition by Divine approval and accepting the ideas of war and conquest as legitimate so long as they did not exclude concern for the glory of God. Even allowing for the flattery of artists who worked for an aristocratic public—Racine, Le Brun, Coysevox were all in their ways 'commissioned' artists—we may believe that they accepted the prevailing values as readily as the simplest courtier. As for him, what hope was there of distinction, what interest in life for an energetic man, except in feats of war? Only the consolation of *galanterie*, the subtleties of the campaign amongst the gentler sex, with its own rules and conventions. This was Louis' world too; it came naturally to him to speak of *gloire* and *amour*—but we should be wary of taking the words too seriously.

Women played a large part in Louis' life, but to the historian they are relatively unimportant because of his unwavering determination to keep his emotional life in a separate compartment. There is nothing of the Pompadour situation about Louis' private life, for none of his mistresses exerted any political power. Romantic novelists have delighted to exploit a situation in which a handsome king chose freely from a court where married women would assert that to give oneself to one's prince was no sin in the eyes of God. In fact, there was little that was romantic about Louis' relations with women. He was indifferent to the difficulties of his mistresses, when court convention required concealment of pregnancy. This callousness appears more marked by contrast with the exquisite courtesy upon which he prided himself; he would always take off his hat to a maid. Before he married, only one affair had caused any concern to Mazarin, his infatuation for Marie de Mancini, Mazarin's own niece and one of five girls originally brought to court to be playmates for the young king. Louis and the pretty girl were for a time inseparable and read Italian novels together. It was probably platonic but serious enough to threaten Mazarin's plans; in the end it served only as a lesson in the self-control required of kings. When Marie was sent off, in 1660, to marry an Italian nobleman, Count Colonna, the king saw her into her carriage. 'He uttered a sigh, but did not say a word; then he bowed deeply over the carriage door in honour of the princess.'

The political marriage which followed in June 1660 to the Infanta of Spain could not be expected to arouse his enthusiasm and he showed the naïve girl only passing attention. He was touched by her passion for him and formally tender, but his affection did not prevent him from seeking mistresses, nor his courtesy from giving them equal status with the queen. Louis' sense of the proprieties was curiously missing too in his dalliance with Henriette d'Orléans, the adored and amusing sister of Charles II of England, and his brother's wife. At Fontainebleau, in high summer, Louis and 'Minette' played out the comedy of Carydon and Amaryllis to the accompaniment of bathing parties, supper on the canal, woodland lit by fairy lamps, the tender music of Lulli, and Monsieur, conceited and futile in the role of cuckold. But it was Henriette's maid-in-waiting, brought to the king's notice to distract the attention of the court, who became Louis' first acknowledged mistress, a daughter of the provincial *noblesse*, shy and dazzled by the glare of court life. Her delicate beauty and disinterested love for Louis make Louise de la Vallière a sympathetic figure. Worn out by child-bearing and the ravages of an uneasy conscience, forced to stay at court for five years after

Louis had deserted her for Mme de Montespan, she was at last allowed to retire to a convent, where the sensible Carmelites remarked that she had already done much to expiate her sins. Her gentle and undemanding personality stresses, by contrast, the insensitivity of the king. In Mme de Montespan, amusing and self-assured, he found a more equal partner. As a shrewd contemporary remarked, he felt it his due to have the most beautiful woman in France for his mistress.

The case of Fouquet

Louis was faced at the outset of his personal rule with a living challenge in the person of Fouquet, Mazarin's *surintendant des finances*, whom he had admitted, with Lionne and Colbert, to his inmost confidence as Minister of State. His drastic fate was an object lesson for all in the meaning of the new order. Nicholas Fouquet was a man of many and splendid gifts. Born in a well-established family of the *noblesse de la robe*, he had risen swiftly to great power. At the age of 37 he had stood in charge of the finances of France. He had Colbert's awareness of big issues beyond the range of day-to-day accountancy, but he was in every other way the opposite of his successor. He had a wide understanding of law and diplomacy. The acknowledged leader of intelligent society, a discerning patron of artists, a lover of fine buildings and women, equally at home in the *salon* and at court, he seemed to stand secure in his talents and his friends. But his very wealth and influence invited Louis' criticism. He was casual about financial details in an office which gave scope for marginal profits on a colossal scale. He had acquired the dangerous habit of confusing the credit of the state with his own which, to do him justice, was common form. When he pleaded Mazarin's orders as his excuse for financial peccadilloes, the king seemed to accept and to favour him. But his wealth was ostentatious and his influence and following might seem to cast some shadow on the throne. At the party to which the king invited himself at Fouquet's new palace of Vaux-le-Vicomte, the king was given further food for thought, with Colbert at his elbow to point the moral. Nearly 6,000 guests came to the *château* to enjoy a week of festivity. The table service was of gold, there was music by Lulli, a play by Molière; no effort was spared to please and impress the king with a magnificence which his own palaces lacked.

Louis had already undermined Fouquet's position by persuading him to give up the post of *procureur général* to *Parlement*. The post carried with it, besides intangible influence, the right to be tried only by his colleagues of *Parlement*, and Louis had not forgotten *Parlement*'s part in the Fronde. Then two months after the fête, the minister was arrested for treason and his office was abolished. A special picked court was set up to try him and papers, probably forged, were produced which seemed to show that Fouquet was planning to collect a party of adherents and start a new Fronde.

Fouquet defended himself with courage in a trial which dragged on for nearly three years (one may note how differently things are done by the totalitarian state of today!). Public opinion was not unsympathetic and some of his friends stood by him. La Fontaine composed an ode urging clemency towards him; other friends smuggled a written defence out of prison and secretly printed and distributed it. The court, whose first president had been dismissed for impartiality in the conduct of the trial, failed to come to a clear-cut verdict and sentenced him to banishment for his careless administration. The king had hoped for a sentence of execution which Richelieu might by more drastic measures have secured; he now ordered imprisonment for life. From the Bastille Fouquet went to distant Pinerolo to expiate his faults by life imprisonment. The legend of the 'iron mask'—it was in fact velvet—and his supposed love for la Vallière have tinged the case with romance.[1] But to contemporaries the affair was serious enough. The result of the trial could never be much in doubt, once begun, for the ever-mighty subject was incompatible with the new autocracy. His private power had touched both worlds, aristocratic insolence and the entrenched privilege of *Parlement*; both were displeasing to the king.

[1] He is only one of a number of possible claimants to the 'mask', supposed to have been worn by a prisoner in Pinerolo and subsequently in the Bastille, which has been the subject of much controversy. Others include the 'twin-brother of Louis XIV' (Dumas), a mysterious d'Auger, possibly a poisoner, the spy Mattioli and, among the more fantastic, a 'son of Cromwell.' A balanced review of the evidence and, in particular, of the strong case for d'Auger, is made by Rupert Furneaux in his book, *The Man Behind the Mask*.

14 YEARS OF OPPORTUNITY

The state of the powers

The true strength of France, at this opportune time, can best be gauged through a survey of the other powers of Europe. Outstanding is the decline of the Empire, both as an ideal and as a reality. In Voltaire's words, the Emperor 'was neither more powerful nor more rich than a doge of Venice'. More recently he has been compared to the incumbent of a poor living who had to have private means—the hereditary lands of the House of Austria. The Empire which had started the Thirty Years War in bold championship of the Catholic cause, ended it struggling to maintain her dynastic interests against the outside powers of France and Sweden. The political settlement of Westphalia left Austria stronger, but only by the abandonment, for practical purposes, of the idea of Empire in the west.

The Emperor Leopold I was elected in 1658; he died in 1705. In this reign, nearly as long as that of Louis XIV, his personality was important. A man of some taste and learning, gentle, interested in the arts and in music, he proved a careful but uninspired ruler. He was anxious to be, like his cousin of Versailles, his own first minister, but he was too pedantic and too self-conscious to make an effective autocrat. Pomponne wrote of 'his natural timidity' which made him 'always dependent upon his ministers'. More brutally, another French diplomat, Grémonville, dismissed him as a 'clock which always requires re-winding'. Even his physical appearance suggested irresolution, for he had the projecting jaw and slack mouth of the Hapsburgs. At every turn of the long Hapsburg-Bourbon struggle, he appeared to lack confidence in his own judgment.

His situation was not an enviable one. The Jagellon crown of Hungary sat uneasily on his head. At the end of the Thirty Years War, the provinces of Transylvania and Hungary were both out of Hapsburg control; Bethlen Gabor and George Rakoczy had maintained an independent Magyar state. The main theme of Leopold's reign was to be the struggle of Austria and Turkey for the control of these marcher lands of Europe, and the struggle for autonomy between cross and crescent, of the Magyar peoples. To this all else came second. Leopold was personally devout, but he compromised with Protestantism in Germany, as in the case of

Saxony. Edicts of Restitution belonged to the past. He resented his loss of influence in the Rhineland, in Alsace and the Three Bishoprics, where his authority ran counter to the rivalry of France, but he could do nothing to regain it. Through both his mother and his wife, the younger daughter of Philip IV, he looked to the succession to the throne of Spain, but even here he would have at first to compromise—in the shape of partition. So Louis began with the great advantage that the Emperor's hands were tied behind his back.

Spain seemed now to await dissolution and her survival would depend on the ability of her kings to produce a male heir. There seemed little prospect of this, for Charles II who succeeded in 1665 was a chronic invalid, not expected to live long, let alone have children. In this century, Spain's population fell from eight to six millions. The power of the crown declined while the wealth of the great estates, and the church, rose. Violent price movements had wrecked currency and trade. Behind the iron curtain of the Pyrenees, she was isolated, decadent and sunk in fatalism. She had no means of protecting her Burgundian inheritance and, nearer home, was unable to suppress the revolt of the Portuguese against her feeble rule. This embarrassment gave Louis an immediate opening.

In Germany, some of the princes had seemed to gain in strength and independence of action from the decay of Imperial authority; notably Bavaria and Brandenburg. Within their states the princes had certainly accrued power; everywhere for instance the estates had lost control of taxation. New absolutisms grew out of the waste land and were consecrated by the peace of Westphalia. A host of princeling landowners made up a static and petrified society, without the means or will to produce a common front. Even the few states big enough to have a policy pursued only local aims, and when they joined European combinations it was to get German lands and titles. France had long had her client states in Germany, and Richelieu's memorial, arguing the necessity for French intervention in German affairs, had become a permanent rule of her diplomacy. A French diplomat called Westphalia 'one of the finest jewels in the French crown'—and with reason, for the peace which divided Germany into three hundred and thirty-four sovereign units left Louis free to act, if he wished, as overlord and patron of German politics.

At the Imperial election of 1658, the electors were warned

against the dangers of letting the Imperial crown become hereditary in one family. Their 'freedom' was slipping away from them!
The German princes in fact preferred the Hapsburg, for the sound
if cynical reason that his penury was the surest guarantee of their
real freedom. France, or a French-backed Emperor, might try to
make the Empire work again! After France had failed at this
election of Leopold, by pushing forward the Elector of Bavaria as a
rival candidate, they then opposed the Emperor with an organised
party, the League of the Rhine. This originated with the intelligence and patriotism of Philip von Schönborn, Elector of Mainz.
The Elector, who was an idealist as well as a practical politician,
hoped that his League, based on the three ecclesiastical electorates,
would not only stop aggression in the Rhineland but would also
lead the opinion of Europe to more lasting peace by a system of
general guarantee. The League had a council which sat at Frank-
fort-on-Rhine, to arbitrate in the disputes of its members.
Schörnborn believed that the scheme would only work under the
patronage of a great foreign country and wished to bring in
Sweden and France. Mazarin was wholly unimpressed by the
pacifist aims of the League which he thought were 'fooling', but
he saw that it gave France a new foothold in Germany. The
French agent who had been sent to seduce the electors at Ratisbon
now went on a tour of Germany on behalf of the League. The
propagandist line of France was that the Hapsburgs were the real
enemy of German 'liberty' and to this Leopold responded by
treating the League, from the start, as the tool of France. The
League was the crux of the Cardinal's machinations in Germany
and gave to Louis the assurance of German neutrality, and so a free
hand in his designs against the Hapsburgs.

Cromwell's strenuous and partisan policy, leading to the
victory of the Dunes, may have helped deceive Mazarin about the
real strength of the Protectorate in England. Certainly he did not
expect the restoration of Charles II to his throne in 1660 and, so
far from helping Charles, he rebuffed him and rejected out of hand
his offer to marry Hortense de Mancini. After the restoration the
Cardinal proposed his niece, but it was then Charles's turn to
refuse. This miscalculation did not prove serious for France, for
Charles was to prove a tame and pliable neighbour. After the
affronts and hazards of exile, Charles II was more interested in
comfort than in glory. Public opinion, reacting from Cromwell's
militarism, was strongly opposed to a standing army and Charles's

hereditary revenue was barely enough for day-to-day administration, let alone for troops. Even the navy was at times neglected, as the disaster of the Medway was to show. Worse, the king could only raise supplies through a critical Parliament. Perfidious and unstable Albion, a land of heretics and republicans, presented the greatest contrast to the 'well conditioned' state of France. Charles both admired and envied the French system and to get French money he was ready to play the role of 'poor cousin'. So long as Parliament allowed, he was a faithful ally of France. Even with the representatives of the governing class in Parliament, mercantile jealousy of the Dutch, brought into the open by the Navigation Act of 1651 and already the cause of one war, was a stronger sentiment than enmity towards France.

A different case was presented by the other great trading and Protestant power, the seven northern provinces which made up the state of Holland. They had finally secured Spanish recognition of their independence in 1648. This achievement was to some extent owing to the patronage of France, and Mazarin was furious when they contracted out of the war against Spain by a separate peace. But the decline of Spain had compelled the realistic burghers to re-appraise their situation. The attitude of John de Witt, Grand Pensionary of Holland, was summed up in the phrase: *Gallum amicum sed non vicinum*. In fact he wished to maintain the Spanish Netherlands in some independent form, as a barrier between Holland and France. Already Mazarin's project for exchanging Cerdagne and Rousillon for the Spanish Netherlands had aroused Dutch suspicion. From the French viewpoint, the wealth of Holland could not be ignored. The enterprise of Dutch seamen and promoters had won already a far-flung eastern empire. The trader-state was solvent and prosperous, and Amsterdam's bank and exchange was the heart of the world's finance and trade. Independent and tolerant, an asylum for the refugees of more conformist countries, this federation of burgher oligarchies, whose policy was first and last the advancement of trade, was most displeasing to Louis and his ministers. Colbert, who admired the business values of the people, saw them also as the chief rivals to France, in the competitive race for wealth. Louis saw hope in the House of Orange through which they might return to the fold of respectable monarchies. The irony of events was to bring this about through Louis' aggression in 1672 and to make the Orange faction the heart of resistance to France.

Since Richelieu had first called in Gustavus Adolphus to redress the balance of Europe, Sweden had been a firm ally of France. By the time of the Peace of Oliva in 1660, Sweden had become masters of the Baltic, controlling all the great ports, with the exception of Danzig and Hamburg, from the mouth of the Weser to the Gulf of Finland. Her possession of Western Pomerania gave her the standing of a province of the Empire and involved her perforce in German politics. Her hold on this bridgehead was precarious and was in the end to prove her undoing. Sweden had destroyed, in the pursuit of aggrandisement, the power of Denmark and Poland. Now in turn, bled nearly dry, she had to withstand the rivalries of the army-state of the Elector of Brandenburg and the vast, yet unschooled, Slav mass of Peter the Great's Russia. The spoilt child of French diplomacy, she was scheduled to be the northern link of the great chain of alliances which France tried to hold round the Empire.

In Brandenburg, by the single-minded statecraft of the Elector Frederick William, a strong and compact state was emerging from the near-eclipse of the Thirty Years War. The objects of his long reign (1640-88) were to weld together his lands, scattered from Clèves-Julich to Pomerania, to crush the estates of Brandenburg and Prussia and to make a completely reliable army. The army, twenty-five thousand strong and the best in Germany, was the real frontier of Frederick-William's Prussia. From it germinated the civil service; whereas in France the state came to control the army, in Prussia the army ran the state. At Westphalia, Frederick-William had obtained Eastern Pomerania with the potent help of France. If he was the most ambitious prince in Europe, he was also the most unpredictable; he was very ready to receive French money when it suited him but he was, at best, only an uncertain ally against the Emperor. Eventually the ambitions of Brandenburg-Prussia ran up against those of Sweden, and France had to choose between them.

Of other states, Poland had for long had a large place in French policy since her elective crown offered regular opportunities of manipulation. Through the exploits and personality of John Sobieski, Poland was yet to have a brief heroic period, but the flaws of her constitution already forecast the disintegration of the next century. Polish politics were erratic and incalculable, for she had not moved a step along the route of most western states towards the concentration of power at the centre and the growth of administrative machinery. The monarchy was elective, while in her Diet, where a single nobleman could veto any proposal, constitutional liberty reached its *reductio ad absurdam*. Inevitably, Poland was the vortex of successive crises in northern Europe, the first of Louis' reign being that caused by the election of 1668. Here French diplomacy failed to prevent the election of a native noble, Michael Wisniowieski, who, like his successor John Sobieski, maintained the Austrian connexion. John's fateful march to save Vienna in 1683 exposed the failure of French diplomacy to find an ally in this promising field.

In Turkey they were more fortunate. Since the beginning of the previous century, France had been extending her trade within the Ottoman Empire. The unholy connexion had already acquired something of the status of a tradition. Turkey was now, by forcing the Emperor to war on a second front, to play some part in the French scheme. Despite the crushing defeat of her soldiers at St. Gothard in 1664, when a French volunteer contingent played no small part, the Turks were to prove their value as allies when they came so near, in 1683, to capturing Vienna itself. The alliance was of more than nuisance value. Constant pressure from the Turks on Leopold's eastern frontiers prevented his having a strong policy in the west. Furthermore, the alliance ensured the economic leadership of France in the Levant.

A striking feature of the European scene had been the decline of the Papacy as a political force. In Louis XIV's reign it was to adhere to its traditional policy of mediation; a policy natural to its sacred office but ineffectual when it conflicted with the interests of a great state. It had lost, with the Reformation, its moral right to speak for an undivided Christendom, and its authority continued to shrink with that of the Empire. At Westphalia, represented by the nuncio Chigi, it could do no more than protest against the treaties there made. At the Pyrenees, the Pope, the same Chigi, now Alexander VII, was not even represented. By the end of the period, at the Treaty of Utrecht, the Papal fiefs of Sicily and Sardinia were disposed of as if the Papacy had not existed. This decline was not without its effect on the political conduct of France.

The strength of France

It is evident then that the condition of Europe offered France unprecedented opportunities: for security, influence and expansion. France had been for two centuries, potentially, the greatest of the power aggregates of Europe, but at the same time too large and amorphous to be governed effectively from a single centre. Now after the work of the Cardinals, her size was beginning to prove an advantage; after the Fronde, she could make war without fear of internal revolt. The process of centralisation had a long way to go, but already the administration and army of France was superior to that of any rival. The treaties of Westphalia and the Pyrenees had advertised a new predominance, new in the sense that its form was not international. Where Philip IV and Leopold I wore several crowns and embodied various forms of sovereignty, Louis wore a single crown; it was his greatest source of strength. Spain and Austria were most vulnerable through their outlying possessions, with all the problems of control and strategy that these involved. France, in however an untidy and ramshackle way, was a political whole. Nineteen million subjects owed one allegiance. Her interests were undivided and she fought from interior lines. Her primacy was based upon the demonstrable facts: high population, taxable wealth and geographical compactness.

These facts are emphasised by the relative weakness of the scattered lands on her frontier. Two small states in particular could look forward to an uncertain tenure. The Swiss could live on in neutral repose behind their mountains; but for the Dukes of Savoy and Lorraine, political existence was less tranquil. The Duchy of Lorraine, lying west of Alsace, separated France from her new outposts on the Rhine. Since Richelieu, French diplomacy had worked hard to absorb the Duchy into France. Louis was never to achieve this, but it made little difference. The Duke was never a free agent and French armies could march at will across his indefensible lands. The Duke of Savoy, however, had room to manœuvre. Tutelage to France was represented by the French occupation of the fortresses of Pinerolo and, after 1681, of Casale. But Savoy's position flanking the mountain passes, whose control was vital to French strategy in Italy, gave successive dukes the opportunity to sell their alliance dear. They fluttered between France and her enemies. Victor Amadeus II was brought into the French circle by marriage with Anne, daughter of Philippe d' Orléans, but this did not stop him joining the allies in the War of the League of Augsburg and again in the War of Spanish Succession.

The cords of Hapsburg encirclement, which still looked menacing on the map, were now rotten and frayed. Of the lands belonging to Spain, Navarre, Béarn, Cerdagne and Rousillon had all passed to France. The south-west frontier therefore now ran through the mountain barrier of the Pyrenees. In the north and east were Spanish Flanders, Luxemburg and Franche-Comté. With the French already in parts of Alsace and controlling the Upper Rhine, able at will to sever the great artery, the prospects of these isolated provinces were dim indeed. There was no reason why the changes made in 1648 and 1659 should be final or definitive. The north-westerly course of the Rhine left a broadening belt of territory, including a part of the Lower Palatinate, Julich, all the Spanish Netherlands and the southern part of the United Provinces, without any natural frontier. This great wedge of indeterminate land had long been the strategic focus of the Hapsburg-Bourbon struggle, and it was to remain so during Louis' reign. The river valleys of the Moselle, the Meuse and the Scheldt, cutting across the frontier, provided ways of penetration rather than obstacles. The weakness of Spain and the artificial character of the north-east frontier presented a choice of two policies; either consolidation, by the methodical construction of a defensive line of forts; or daring aggression and the conquest of the wedge up to the Rhine.

Louis XIV's policy

Louis has been blamed for achieving neither of these objects, and for a messy sequence of marriages and sieges, for lack of realism and for wanton aggressiveness. Examples may be found to support these charges. A comparison between what seemed possible in 1661 and what had been achieved by the end of the reign seems to indicate that Louis' foreign policy did not pay the dividends which might have been expected from so large a capital expenditure. But this sort of balance-sheet reckoning was entirely foreign to the seventeenth century, whose statesmen did not, for the most part, account for towns and territories won, against *livres* spent and lives lost. War was for them a normal state of affairs, a natural activity for civilised men, almost an institution. Some wars were more desirable than others. The Crusade was still an ideal, although tarnished, to which one should pay lip service, while civil war, it was admitted, was unfortunate. The scheme which Leibnitz presented, in the name of the Elector of Mainz, to Pomponne, in 1672, has been lauded as an attempt to conserve the peace of Europe. But Leibnitz merely proposed that Louis should turn his arms against the Turk, and the intention behind his plan was to promote the Elector's policy of co-operation between the Emperor and the Dutch. This it was suggested would be a better way of damaging the Dutch and their commerce. It was the experience of the age that when wars between states ended, civil wars began. The Peace of Cateau-Cambrésis had been followed by the French Religious Wars and the Revolt of the Netherlands. The idea that foreign war provided an outlet for militant elements which might otherwise cause trouble at home was widely held. Henry IV and Richelieu both saw this; for them, the chief problem of statesmanship was to turn the militarism of their subjects to the constructive aims of the state. War was not discussed in moral terms of right and wrong so much as in tactical terms of timing and the allocation of resources. War was *ratio ultima regum*; one which they should not hesitate to use when other policies failed. When resources gave out and bankruptcy threatened, then diplomacy might take over. 'War', said Clausewitz, 'is a continuation of policy by other means'; diplomacy was a continuation of war by other means.

Louis was, in a real sense, his own foreign minister. From him alone came the daily directives which inspired the work of his ambassadors and ministers. When in 1667 Condé was put forward as candidate for the elective Polish throne, Louis wrote to his ambassador that he had decided that Condé should run for the office with the support of a force of 9,000 or 10,000 men. Lionne, in a covering note, added: 'the resolution of His Majesty is all his own; no one in the world would dare take it on himself to advise him'. Such evidence is hardly needed, for again and again we see the ideals and prejudices of the king reflected in his foreign policy. He was, of course, forced to rely, for the timing and details of his acts, upon his residents abroad, his *intendants* and Ministers at home. But these men knew the way in which the king's mind worked, and they studied his wishes.

The king's own statements tell us something about his views. His *Mémoires pour l'instruction du Dauphin* were supervised and approved, if not actually written by him. For 1666 we find these entries: 'the death of the King of Spain and the war of the English against Holland offered at the same time two important chances to make war. . . . I envisaged with pleasure the design of these two wars, like a vast field where might at any moment be great opportunities to make my mark. . . . So many of the brave people that I have seen aflame to serve one, seemed all the time to be asking me to give them some outlet for their talents, more advantageous than naval war.'

Louis was severely chastened by the end of his reign; he had tasted defeat, humiliation and personal griefs which seemed together to be a judgment of God upon his mistakes. But at his death he confessed, not to loving war, but to 'loving war too much'. That kings should love war he took for granted. He thought it pardonable that he should have sought for the laurels that history bestows upon the great captains. War was a means of attaining the legitimate ends of the state; an extreme view of these can be found in the passage of the *Mémoires* in which he says that Charlemagne had been the only true ruler of France and that the king of France must re-establish his empire. But war was also a glorious opportunity for distinction, for himself and his entourage.

It must be stressed that Louis was the king of a court which was, for sixty years, the boundary of his physical and mental existence. He was in honoured theory the 'father of his people'; in practice he often seemed to be only the 'head of the *noblesse*'. This class, whose *métier* was arms, for whom war was a sport and a way of life, looked to him for patronage. The paradox of Louis' reign is that the king who was so determined to strengthen the powers of the state and to reduce the independence of the nobility accepted, by and large, their ideas. He presided over an administrative revolution, but his personal values remained feudal. He lacked the greatness to insulate himself from the influence of the class which provided both his setting and his audience. So Louis, who wrote of '*la gloire*' as if it were his own invention, was more than he realised the slave of public opinion. The word which caressed the ear of the king was continually in the mouths of his courtiers. Even Colbert surrendered to its siren voice: 'What do the millions matter when your glory is at stake?'

The reason why Louis' preoccupation with *gloire* had devastating consequences is that it came at a time when the resources of the state had increased and were increasing. Louis' reign was to see the *étatisation* of war, the mobilisation of the total resources of the state, of the economy as well as of manpower. Militia fought alongside professional troops, there was massive public investment in war, matters of overseas trade became prominent and the struggle was extended overseas to the colonies of the contending powers. So war became more extensive and potentially more destructive. More than any man Louis was responsible for this development, although we may see that in the long run it was inevitable.

Louis was not always able to resist the lure of *une politique de prestige*. One authority, Zeller, even ascribes to this concern for the good name of France and Louis XIV, the determining role in his policies. Mignet sees in the struggle for the Spanish Succession the pivot of the reign. Sorel stresses his concern for 'natural frontiers', whatever they might be. To attempt to look for any sort of consistency in Louis' actions is however doomed to failure. On different occasions we shall see Louis concerned with prestige, with religion, with tariffs, with the frontiers, with the Spanish Succession. We shall see him acting the part of the good pupil of Mazarin and the careful student of European affairs, showing shrewdness and caution, as in the Treaty of Aix-la-Chapelle. We shall see him, four years later in 1672, toppling over in his pursuit of glamorous victory and easy advantage, when he attacked the Dutch and spurned their vast concessions. In this year, it has been said, he *dénatura* the foreign policy of France and undid the work of the Cardinals. Before condemning the king however, we must recognise the existence of a fundamental dilemma, which was most acute when he was most successful, one which goes beyond the common dilemma of the statesman, where to stop in the course of victory.

The treaties of Westphalia and the Pyrenees had laid down certain broad lines of advance. Especially they demonstrated that France's continued preponderance in Europe depended upon her successful presentation of the image of France as defender of the rights of the Princes against the Emperor. It is possible that this could have been reconciled with the pursuit of the Spanish Succession and with the expansion of the northern and eastern frontiers that France's security demanded. It is possible that if prestige issues had been played down, some compromise might have been found between these three conflicting objectives. But before we condemn Louis for the mistakes which provoked the formation of the coalitions which in the end defeated him, we must at least recognise that the dilemma existed. Louis' splendid inheritance in divided and jealous Europe brought with it the old and familiar problem of the balance of power. He could pluck the roses, but could he avoid the thorns?

Diplomatic preludes

In 1661, the war chest was empty. Events waited upon the work of administrative reform, of Colbert upon the finances, and the Le Telliers upon the army. The recent peace between France and Spain inhibited drastic action and there ensued a period of alliances and gestures. Intense diplomatic activity directed towards the end of isolating the Hapsburgs was thrown into occasional relief by 'incidents', arising usually from the strong assertion of the rights and precedence of France.

In the North the alliance of Sweden was strengthened by a subsidy, in return for the use of Swedish troops, if required, in Poland. A similar agreement was made with Denmark, but all hope of a northern alliance in the French interest foundered upon the jealousy of the two countries. Money was poured too into Poland, to facilitate the election of the young duc d'Enghien, son of the great Condé. But the Diet, fortified by money from Austria and Brandenburg, obstinately refused to elect, while the existing king still lived. Louis dabbled too with the Hungarian rebels and gave leave to courtiers to go and fight there, but shrank from open alliance with the crude insurgents. A treaty in 1663 with the Swiss Cantons replaced earlier agreements. French money was useful to their budgets while Swiss troops were invaluable to Louis' expanding armies. Louis was accused at the time of designs upon Calvinist Geneva, but without substance. French influence remained supreme in Switzerland until the Revocation of the Edict of Nantes aroused hostility. With Holland a twenty-five-year alliance was concluded in 1662. But on the crucial question of the Spanish Netherlands and on the division that should follow Louis' inheritance from Maria Theresa, no agreement was possible; both sides had too strong an interest in the matter.

The Peace of the Pyrenees had ended the war, but not the differences between France and Spain. At the root of all was the question of the succession. The sickly child, Charles, born to Philip IV in 1661, was not expected to live, and the clause, inserted by Lionne, tying Louis' repudiation to the payment of an impossible dowry, kept the question alive. In a series of negotiations at

Madrid, Don Luis de Haro refused to entertain the French claims either upon the succession or upon the unpaid dowry. Then, in October 1661, a violent fracas in London between the rival households of the French and Spanish ambassadors, in which several people were killed and the French were worsted, gave Louis a chance to publicise his case and at the same time to humiliate Spain. The memoirs of Colbert and Pellisson show that Louis attached the greatest importance to this incident, with the damage to his prestige that it might cause. The Spanish ambassador in France was expelled and a strong note sent to Madrid demanding a full apology. He required that the precedence of French ambassadors in every court in Europe should be accepted by Spain and then, in February 1662, added sudden menace to his request, by demanding an advance payment of the dowry, in the shape of Franche-Comté, Luxembourg, Hainaut and Cambrai! The Spanish ambassador then announced, in a special royal audience, that his master had conceded Louis' initial demands. In this brusque way, a technique which was to become familiar to Europe, the use of a small 'incident' to advertise the strength of France, was given its first trial. The incident of the Corsican Guards was used to impress a similar lesson upon the Papacy.

This affair arose in 1662 from a dispute between the duc de Créqui, French ambassador in Rome, and Pope Alexander VII, on the delicate subject of ambassadorial privileges. Créqui, an overbearing man, insisted upon so extending ambassadorial franchises in Rome, beyond the Embassy in the Palazzo Farnese, that street brawls occurred unchecked by the Papal police in a wide area around, under cover of letters from the French Embassy. Bad feeling came to a head when, on August 20, 1662, some of the Corsican Guards of the Vatican, revenging many insults and the personal grievances of the Pope's nephew Don Mario, attacked the embassy itself. In a rowdy affray, several people were killed and the ambassador's wife herself, returning from Mass, was bundled unceremoniously from her carriage. Créqui himself, when the Papacy seemed unwilling to atone for the outrage, left Rome. Louis determined to show the world that his servants were not to be trifled with and, encouraged by the active anti-Papalism of his ministers, especially of Lionne, sent troops under Marshal du Plessis-Praslin to take Avignon; thence they were to march on Rome itself. Alexander, shaken by this energetic action sent his nephew, Cardinal Chigi, to apologise; a mission without precedent. Eventually, by the Peace of Pisa, February 12th, 1664, Avignon was restored; but the Pope had to disband his Corsican Guard. He also had to erect an obelisk, recording the insult to the king and its humiliating sequel. It was wholly characteristic of Louis that he should take a personal interest in its design, insisting that the inscription should be of such a size that it should easily be read by the passer-by! The shameful stone was later removed, but its lesson was learnt. The effacement of the Papacy as a power in European politics had been publicised by Louis' overweening diplomacy.

The revolt of the Portuguese, which had been active since 1640, gave Louis the means of distressing Spain without coming to the open breach. One article of the Pyrenees settlement forbade military aid, but was ignored on the usual ground that Spain had already violated other clauses. Louis pursued this guerilla course under cover of his useful *entente* with Charles II of England, who was about to marry Catherine of Braganza and who had already engaged to supply the Portuguese with troops in return for his dowry of Tangier and Bombay. Charles was now in the pleasant position of being able to play the part of middleman and satisfy both allies without risk. Louis sent, through England, the money to pay for troops, and these, officered largely by French 'volunteers' and commanded by Schomberg, contributed largely to the success of the Portuguese. After the victory of Schomberg at Villaviciosa, the independence of Portugal was assured. It was finally granted in February 1668, during the War of Devolution, after a court revolution, engineered by the French queen, Isabella of Nemours, and assisted by the arrival of a French squadron in the Tagus.

Even England felt the whiplash of Louis' pretensions, and in a tender part, when he objected to French ships having to dip their flags to English ships met on the high seas. Charles was not prepared to give much away over this and to his instructions to English ships to salute the French in the Mediterranean he added a secret rider that they should avoid doing so when possible! Lionne also, aware of the importance of keeping Charles' friendship, instructed his ambassador to soften the tone of Louis' protest. He was justified by the important acquisition of Dunkirk, in 1662. Louis confided to his memoirs his belief that Charles would always be 'some two or three millions in debt', and it was debt that persuaded Charles and Clarendon to take the unpopular step of selling Dunkirk to France. Like Calais a century before, this recently won foothold on the Continent was not worth its cost of upkeep. For five million *livres*, the useless relic of Cromwellian imperialism was disposed of. In December 1662, Louis made a triumphal entry into the town, soon to be turned by Vauban into a show-piece of defensive engineering.

A bitter trade war between the English and the Dutch broke out in the spring of 1665; in Louis' words, 'the most extraordinary and embarrassing affair'. For if he executed to the letter the treaty of 1662, and gave full military support to the Dutch, he would ruin the useful friendship of England and promote the interests of a country for which he had a deep antipathy. It did not suit him to have Holland strong in trade, nor in a position to dispute the advances that he intended to make into Flanders. On the other hand he liked to be scrupulous about treaty pledges, and if he were to count upon the Dutch supporting him later, he must make some show of good-will. He formally declared war in January 1666, though he admitted afterwards that he had done so but 'on paper'. He sent Turenne with a small force to obstruct the hired mercenaries of the storm-trooper Bishop of Munster, Bernard Von Galen, but it did not come into action for Galen's men melted away. The French fleet was sent from the Mediterranean to the Atlantic, but with orders not to fight the English; a small expedition was sent to capture St. Christopher. While he made these gestures he was intent upon bigger game in Europe. In March 1667, he made the first of his secret agreements with Charles II of England. Charles's capital had been ravaged by plague and fire, and he had neither the will nor means to wage war against France, wanting only to extricate himself from his present war. He readily agreed, therefore, not to oppose a French invasion of the Spanish Netherlands on condition that the French fleet would not help the Dutch. This was the preliminary to the Peace of Breda between England and Holland, signed under the neutral auspices of Sweden, in July 1667. By then the War of Devolution was two months old, and Louis had already won his main objectives.

The War of Devolution

When Philip IV died in September 1665, leaving all his lands by will to his weakling child Charles, aged 4, and specifically excluding Maria Theresa from all or part of the inheritance, Louis' first inclination was to make immediate war for his queen's rights. Maria Theresa had renounced these by the Treaty of the Pyrenees, but the renunciation had been made dependent on the payment of a dowry within eighteen months, and was now invalid. Discretion led Louis to act less precipitately and to complete his preparations. He had already given advance notice of his intentions when in 1662 he made first claim to 'advance payment of his dowry', and it was in the negotiations over this claim that the term Devolution was first used. To Turenne's secretary, Duhan, has been ascribed the credit for discovering and working out the claim which was set out in the *Traité des droits de la reine Marie Thérèse*, the document which was despatched to Madrid by way of declaration of war, and then published as a pamphlet to 'inform Europe of the justice of his cause'. Inquest had shown that in Brabant and certain regions of Brabant and Flanders, property 'devolved' to the children of the first wife to the exclusion of those of the second. Therefore in respect of Flanders, Maria Theresa, daughter of the first marriage, had superior rights to Charles II and his sister who were offspring of the second. The juridical flaw in this contention was that the custom was not universal in Flanders and did not hold at all in Luxembourg. A more serious objection was that Louis was using a private law of property to justify his breaking the public peace of Europe. The pamphlet was very technical in form, texts being carefully cited in the margin. It claimed for Louis that 'as king he feels he ought to prevent injustice, as husband to oppose this usurpation and, as father, to assure this patrimony to his son'. In fact, Louis was putting up a façade of legalism to placate his conscience and as propaganda to Europe. Behind the façade his actions were those of military necessity. Turenne was impatient to resume the work of conquest in which he had been interrupted in 1659, Lionne's conception of diplomacy was essentially predatory and opportunist, and both men urged Louis to seize the chance to protect Paris by pushing his frontiers north and east. He was not reluctant to tread the path of glory so carefully mapped out by Lionne's diplomacy.

1666 was the 'year of reviews', great musters of troops assembled for the king's inspection; they made an outing for the court, appealed to Louis' taste for parades, and gave Louvois, son of Michel Le Tellier, the chance to check up on equipment and training. 'The projects of the war in Flanders', wrote Le Pelletier, 'have established M. de Louvois in great confidence and much intimacy with his Majesty. The court begins to keep its eye upon him.' In 1667, Louis had at his disposal over 70,000 effectives, only the nucleus of the huge army that Louvois was to build up, but already the best in Europe. In this year, too, the royal revenue was about double what it had been at the start of the reign. Castel-Rodrigo, the Spanish governor of the Netherlands, with only 20,000 men in his forts, wrote to warn lethargic Madrid: 'if the French attack in the spring, I do not see how these provinces can be saved, except by a miracle'.

There was no miracle. Turenne's invasion of Flanders has been called a military promenade. The Spanish commander was forced to blow up his exposed fortifications and retire; the only serious resistance was at Lille, and this only lasted a fortnight. As one town after another surrendered, Charleroi and Ath, Furnes and Armentières, Tournai and Douai, Courtrai, Oudenarde and Lille, as the French came up to the gates of Ghent and Brussels, the countries of Europe reacted in various degrees of alarm and resentment.

This revelation of France's strength and Spain's decrepitude had long been anticipated but was none the less a brutal shock when it came: to Holland, which saw the 'barrier' dissolve and did not behave in that complaisant manner that Louis expected of an ally; to England, for as Andrew Marvell said 'the Spanish Netherland has always been considered as the natural frontier of England'; to Austria, powerless to help because of the non-co-operation of the Rhineland states. These saw the pacifist aims of the League of the Rhine vanish in smoke; then Louis invaded Franche-Comté and the war concerned them more nearly.

There is no doubt that the hostile reactions of Europe made Louis undertake this new stroke in the depths of winter when it was not usual to take troops out of their billets. The talks between England and Holland which were to lead to the Triple Alliance were already started when, on February 4, 1668, Condé swept into Franche-Comté with 18,000 men. He was not opposed by the Emperor because of the secret treaty of partition completed the previous month. Plans had been made with the greatest secrecy, letters were sent to fake destinations, the army assembled only at the last minute. Even the king played his part in the deception. Two days before Condé was due to march, he left Paris; five days later he was at Dijon, receiving the surrender of Besançon; on February 13th he was present at the surrender of Dôle, the capital of the province. The *fleur de lys* floated over Franche-Comté, and Louis, having assured himself that Spain could neither strike at eastern France nor succour the Netherlands, was ready to bargain from strength. Already, before the campaign had been begun, the two bargains had been made which conditioned the terms of peace.

The Triple Alliance originated as a defensive compact between England and Holland. It had certain domestic causes, the fall for instance of Clarendon and the ascendancy of Arlington in England, but it represented broadly the common fear of the two countries for Flanders, and their desire to preserve it as a buffer between France and Holland. John de Witt expressed its sense clearly when he said that 'to abandon Spain is to make a present of the Low Countries to France: but to take her side alone is folly'. The Anglo-Dutch alliance, chiefly the work of William Temple, was completed at the Hague on January 23, 1668. A secret article affirmed the resolution of the two countries to make war upon France if she did not accept their mediation for the making of peace. Sweden, still bearing a grudge against her paymaster France, because of France's impartial attitude to Denmark, was persuaded to join the alliance in the spring. Louis' counter to this pressure group was the private partition treaty which was concluded with the Emperor a few days before the Hague Alliance. The Emperor, described by his own representative as 'unlike your king, who sees all and does all' but rather 'like a statue which one carries round where one wants', was at first dilatory. He was torn between his fears about the Turks and the revolting Hungarians, Condé's candidature for the Polish throne and the attitude of the Rhineland princes, but the sudden death of his only son, aged 3 months, speeded the talks. Six days later, on January 19th, the Partition treaty was signed and Louis hailed it in his *Mémoires* as 'a marvellous confirmation of the rights of the Queen'. The terms were that on the death of Charles II of Spain (always regarded as imminent), the Emperor was to have Spain, the Americas, and the Milanese, while Louis acquired Sicily, the Spanish Netherlands, Franche-Comté, Spanish Navarre, the Philippines and the Spanish possessions in Africa; terms soon obsolete.

Louis was therefore ready when the Spanish, dreading the renewal of war in Flanders, offered to treat for peace. The speed and weight of his armies had won their military objectives, and the Partition treaty had brought into view gains greater than could be won by the continuance of war. The Swiss were restive, the League of the Rhine dissolved, England and Holland wary and hostile, the feckless Charles of Lorraine offering to raise 8,000 troops for Spain. So, against the wishes of the war-party of Turenne, Condé and the younger Le Tellier, but urged by the more sober voices of Lionne and Colbert, he resolved to make concessions. At Aix-la-Chapelle, under the neutral auspices of Holland and England, in May 1668, peace was concluded. France restored Franche-Comté to Spain, and in Flanders kept only some isolated places, Charleroi, Douai, Lille, Courtrai, Oudenarde amongst others, enclaves of land not making a regular frontier. It was a valuable strategic extension, which gave Vauban something to work on in his task of creating an impregnable fortress-frontier, but it did not resolve the question of the ownership of Flanders. The queen's rights remained to be decided. But Louis deliberately sacrificed some immediate advantages for the large and peaceful gains which he trusted that the treaty of partition would bring him.

The Le Telliers

When Louis reviewed his troops before the border town of
Charleroi, on the eve of the attack upon Holland, he saw before him
the finest army in Europe. In a century in which war was a normal
state of affairs—there were only seven calendar years without
some war somewhere in Europe—and in which there had been a
steady increase in its scale, France now led the way. The Le
Telliers, father and son, who directed the reforms of the French
army, had made changes which were only the climax of a long
process, the Military Revolution as it has been termed, by which
the weapons, training and tactics of armies were being changed,
with effect, not upon the armies alone, but on the constitutions
and economies of the parent states. The fundamental change was
towards the strengthening of the state control over the armed
forces that fought in its name; in this the French played the greatest part. The work of the Le Telliers should be seen as an integral
part of the work of absolutism; the principles which guided the
extension of civil government applied equally to the military
sphere.

Michel le Tellier, the older, was born in Paris in 1603, into a
family of lawyers and *officiers*, and he rose by a succession of
typical steps, becoming *conseilleur, procureur, maître des requêtes*
and then, for three years, *intendant* with the army of Piedmont,
where he was able to study at first hand the problem of indiscipline
which crippled France's war effort. From 1643 until 1677, when
he succeeded Séguier as Chancellor, he was Secretary of State
for the army. He did not mean his work to die with him, and his
son Michel, later ennobled as marquis de Louvois, was carefully
trained to inherit his position, his first office being purchased for
him at the age of 14, in 1655. In his twenties, Louvois was his
father's confidant and aide, so that from the outbreak of the War
of Devolution, it might be said that Louis had two war ministers,
the old man being by then very much in the background. In 1672,
the son was admitted to the *conseil d'état*, in 1677 he became
officially Secretary of State for War, and from then until his death
in 1691, his was usually the dominant voice in Louis' councils.
It was a formidable partnership. To the father, subtle, discreet and
self-effacing, *le fidèle* as he appears in the private correspondence of

Anne of Austria and Mazarin, may be attributed most of the pioneer work in matters of recruitment and discipline. His son, an equally fine administrator and a more masterful personality, built upon his father's foundations the structure of the largest and best organised army in Europe. His ambition did not rest with the details of organisation which he understood so well, for he was determined to direct policy and to control the movements of his armies. He fought and defeated Colbert and his son Seignelay in the bitter dynastic war which split the council, and he did not hesitate to cross swords with the great Turenne. He was a great civil servant but a disastrous counsellor, for the army which he cherished and which was the source of his influence was also, for him, the last and strongest argument in all matters of state: equally serviceable for the devastation of a frontier province or for the suppression of heresy within the realm.

The feudal spirit

The lesson of the great wars of the century was that the state which could not control its armies was, in the last resort, impotent. The Emperor, Richelieu, Oxenstierna, all in turn learned this bitter lesson, as the Thirty Years War degenerated into a dog-fight of mercenaries and princely adventurers. Rich prizes went to the state which could keep a standing army upon a war footing for long enough to gain professional expertise and, at the same time control its movements by regular pay and a firm hand upon its commanders. Brandenburg, in its small way, was a portent of the shape of things to come, where the paramount need for money to pay his troops had caused the Great Elector to steam-roller the obstructive Estates, and where the *Intendantur der armee* appointed to maintain the ruler's authority over his army provided the nucleus of the civil administration. He found 2,000 men and left 30,000. By virtue of his efficient army, tested on the field of Fehrbellin in 1675, he came to enjoy a bargaining power among the German princes stronger than the size of his state would suggest. General Monk, who brought to an end the intervention of English armies in politics when he negotiated the Restoration, pointed to the strength of the Dutch army, where 'soldiers received and observed commands, but gave none'. For France, with her large population and ample revenues, the opportunity of improving upon these models was boundless.

To appreciate the character of the armies that were available to Richelieu and to other statesmen of his day, it is necessary to dismiss preconceptions which are implicit today in the very word army: uniforms, discipline, state direction. Even Wallenstein, at his most inflated, had only 100,000 under arms. Spain, whose troops were consistently the most efficient, had never more than 60,000 on the muster-rolls, and these never marched as one force. The finest recruiting-grounds, Castile and North Italy, were drying up; after Rocroi she could hardly pay for an army at all. The army of the Empire existed chiefly on paper, and it was the historic weakness of the Emperor that he fought with borrowed men. The French army of the period of Rocroi was archaic, decentralised and hardly recognisable as a national army. Nowhere had indiscipline, amateurism and local loyalties, the more disastrous relics of the feudal spirit, obstructed the state more than in France. In Le Tellier's words, the army was 'a republic, composed of as many provinces as there are Lieutenant-Generals'. The tactical improvements worked out by Gustavus and Wallenstein, the technical advances of Maurice of Nassau, the innovations of Cromwell in uniform and discipline, had not reached France. The French armies were little used to the large-scale operations of armies which had been advancing the art of war since 1618; nor had they learned the discipline required of an army like the Spanish which had always to fight far from home. Richelieu had been so sceptical of the native levies, produced by traditional methods, that he had raised Swiss and Germans, Scots and Irish to swell his ranks. Even so, the Swedish army was his best instrument in the Thirty Years War.

The policy of Richelieu had been rewarded with a great victory, but the *élan* of the army, and the flair of the young victor of Rocroi, did not in themselves constitute military power. Indeed, the high personal repute of Condé, and the way in which both he and Turenne exploited their fame during the Fronde, only served to emphasise the government's problem. True military power called for something more solid than the wayward genius of a *condottiere*, or the reckless dash of aristocratic cavalry squadrons. To create a reliable standing army which might enable France to play a part proportionate to her large resources, there must be radical alterations in the conditions of pay, recruitment and service. To make that army an instrument of state rather than the vested interest of the nobility, it was essential both to centralise its administration and to alter the attitude of its officers. The problem of authority began with the methods of recruitment.

The army at the beginning of Louis XIV's reign, the year of Rocroi and of the beginning of Michel le Tellier's administration, feudal in tradition and mercenary in composition, embodied the faults of both systems. It was not effectively a king's army at all, but a medley of armed levies, for which the king was only the chief of many contractors, the biggest among a number of shareholders. He enjoyed by virtue of his crown the right to lead, but since most of the regiments were not his property, he had little political control. The Secretary for War had none, and his principal anxiety was often to keep the army at the front, away from the metropolitan provinces before they caused a revolt. It was an irregular and shabby force, with only such discipline as could be imposed by floggings and hangings, held together by the lure of plunder, or the prestige of a great name; since plunder usually followed victory, these were not so very different. During the disintegration of the fifties, before Mazarin resumed some grip upon affairs, these weaknesses of the central government were given terrible documentation, in fire, sword and famine, and in the insolent independence of local commanders.

Recruitment and discipline

Discipline at every level would continue to be weak for as long as companies continued to be private and profitable speculations. Grants of commissions used to come, not from the king, but from two military viziers, the Colonel-Generals of Cavalry and Infantry. An officer's commission was a form of investment, like a tax farm or a block of Paris Municipal bonds, and, as on a stock exchange, prices rose and fell. With peace came reductions, so with rumours of negotiation towards the end of a war, 'the market' fell. But before or during a war, prices rose; a company of Guards might cost up to 80,000 *livres*. Such insecurity naturally encouraged speculation amongst the officers. When in 1661 the Colonel-General of the Infantry, the duc d'Épernon, died, Louis himself assumed his post; a first move towards reform. From then all infantry officers held their commissions direct from the king, and the document was countersigned by the Secretary for War. It is typical of Louis that he took his job very seriously, concerning himself with very minor appointments: (in 1676, for instance, after selecting the town major for a small Flemish town) 'I wish to have men from the Guards; but I have not yet chosen them'. Louis was not able to abolish the purchase of commissions, but he did try to restrict purchase to the wealthy who would not look on it solely as a money-making venture. Meanwhile a new ladder of promotion by merit was put alongside the old, with two new and unpurchaseable ranks, lieutenant-colonel and major. So even in the army, the preserve of caste privilege, the new man found room at the top. When in 1684 the king created twenty-seven new infantry regiments, there was not one of the new colonels who had not been either a major or lieutenant-colonel. A remarkable number of rankers rose in Louis' army, more than in the eighteenth century, when there was a reaction against this levelling tendency; two marshals, Catinat and Fabert, were *rôturier* in origin, and had started as ordinary soldiers. Saint-Simon, the most class-conscious of men, referred without disapproval to one Boissieux, a fellow-officer of the Royal regiment of Rousillon, 'who had started life as a swineherd, and risen by sheer merit; though old, he had never learned to read or write'. The slogan *'carrière ouverte aux talents'* smacks of the revolution, but it was, with certain qualifications, the principle upon which Louis' government was based.

Some old traditions, rooted in the purchase system, died hard; the worst was the *passe-volant*, or false muster, a time-honoured fraud which persisted, for all Louvois' efforts. If the captain of a company wished to draw pay for a company of a hundred, he might hire 'faggots' from another company to fill his ranks to the nominal strength. Soldiers were encouraged to inform against a corrupt officer; if they were detected acting as faggots, they were to be flogged and branded; after 1667, hanged. When the Minister heard of a *passe-volant* incident which had been hushed up by the governor of Belle-Isle, the governor forfeited a month's pay, the town major, three months; the captain was cashiered. It was by such firm measures that Louvois earned his reputation. He had been treated with disdain by the veteran Turenne, on his first appearances at the front, and reforms, such as the new table of precedence of ranks, were blocked till the latter's death in 1675. But he knew that he had the support of the king, who realised the importance of his work and was himself a stickler for detail; he could thus defy the complaints of those who looked back with nostalgia to slacker times, and those whom he had edged out of some private corner of fraudulence. He would be master, and he would take studied revenge upon the insolence of military men who objected to the interference of civilians. He concluded one interview with an idle officer with the words: 'you must do one thing or the other, sir: either declare yourself a courtier, or do your duty as an officer'. Dufay, defender of Philippsburg, had a soldier shot without reference to the Minister, who 'learned with the utmost surprise of the fact, so that it was necessary to remind the king of his past services, to prevent his being dismissed and put into prison'.

The example of the king, and the insidious force of feminine opinion at court, made war and service the fashion. When there was no fighting on the frontiers, officers would press the king for leave to go and fight further afield; in 1685, for instance, in Poland against the Turks. Reckless courage in battle was an admired and expected quality in the aristocrat; even in the disillusioning years after Blenheim, the Duke of Burgundy was despised for his alleged want of military ardour. War was the *raison d'être* of the aristocracy, the justification of their privileged position; it went at Versailles with the cult of the Roman and heroic in the arts, and it played its part in shaping and colouring the policy of the state. But along with this, and indeed all part of the officer tradition, went a sort of insouciant amateurism. Training was haphazard or non-existent, though an attempt was made with some success to establish cadet companies at frontier towns, such as Cambrai and Longwy. The tireless badgering of Louvois persuaded some incompetents to sell their commissions, while Marshals of France who questioned the reforms might be sent to their country estates to reconsider their attitude. Inspectors of Infantry and Cavalry were appointed to stiffen up discipline; one of the former, Martinet, with a vigour which has given his name to the English military vocabulary. One reform, by which a regular reserve of officers was created, seems to have been suggested by Louis himself. It was this reserve which enabled France to mobilise so swiftly in 1667; in 1668, when the war ended, the officers alleged to have been demobilised were secretly absorbed into permanent formations.

In order to recruit good men to the rank and file, Louvois was anxious to make the army a respectable calling. A soldier was expected to sign on for four years, to be unmarried, and to be physically fit. If he was destined for the *maison du roi*, he should be a Roman Catholic and, if possible, a gentleman. This was the wishful thinking of the bureaucrat; in reality, as successive wars of attrition strained France's resources of manpower, standards fell. Desertion was always a formidable problem. Of the 7,000 under Marshal Vivonne's command in 1677, some 4,000 deserted; in ten days, in the following year, the crack *régiment de Champagne* lost sixty-five men. During this war, Luxembourg complained that his troops were 'deplorable', a good half of them 'children whom I shall have to send back to France'. In 1689, at the outset of twenty years of war, Vauban urged a defensive campaign on the grounds that the infantry was very different in quality to what it had been in the last war. By 1703, Louis was reduced to offering five years' total exemption from tax to any man who would enlist on a three years' engagement. The recruitment of soldiers on a large scale was a problem in any European country that attempted it; only hunger would tempt the average French peasant to go soldiering, to 'follow the bread waggons'. But the needs of the state were for an ever larger army, as first the Dutch campaign developed into a general war, and then for a second and a third time France had to defend her gains against a European coalition. Though any such figure should be treated with caution, it seems that there were not less than a quarter of a million under arms in 1678. Even after the high casualties of the next war, the total in 1702 was still over 200,000.

The recruiting and maintaining of such a host was itself a miracle of administration; inevitably some measure of efficiency had to be sacrificed to size. There were always of course foreigners to be found in the ranks, during the Dutch War, some 20,000 Swiss, 10,000 Piedmontese, Genoese, Germans; at different times, Irish, Swedes, even Hungarians were to be found. When the Papal legate congratulated Louis on a victory in Flanders, he replied: 'in future, Sire, my enemies will not, I think, be happy to find themselves faced by an army of Frenchmen—but I am wrong to say Frenchmen, I should say a French army, for mine is made up of various nationalities, who all conducted themselves equally well'. There were some strange expedients. By 1690, the kidnapping of recruits in Paris had reached such proportions that the Lieutenant of Police was instructed to take severe action. More above-board was the idea of resurrecting the old feudal array. In 1675 Marshal Créqui received, without enthusiasm, an assemblage of some thousands of *hobereaux* from the fourteen provinces nearest the Rhine, armed with archaic weapons or with none at all. In 1688, Louvois went a stage further in starting a local militia, drawn by lot from every village, armed, equipped and drilled by the parish. By 1708, the state was turning the levy into a means of raising taxation, and parishes were allowed to send 100 *livres* in place of a man. But it was also becoming an essay in compulsory military service, a device for raising men for the regular army. Louis thought for a time of amalgamating with the fifty-six battalions of the army an equal number of militia units. The project came to nothing, but militia duty was no longer confined to garrisons; at Malplaquet and Denain, the militia played a heroic part. It may seem ironic that after all the work of the Le Telliers to create a great professional army, the salvation of France should have come even partly from the spirit of amateur soldiers; the legacy of their work was to be found, however, in the resilience of the army's organisation under severe strain.

In some respects, the army was the spoilt child of the state. A consistent militarist policy, the king's own pleasure in the incidentals of soldiering, and the jealous vigilance of the Le Telliers, all helped to give the army a special status in the community. When Huguenots were being 'compensated' in the period of the Revocation, Louvois negotiated special tariffs for the troops; at the bottom of the scale a private received twice as much as a peasant. It is perhaps surprising that he did not encourage the use of uniforms, compulsory for officers only after 1682, and introduced largely by the enterprise of individual colonels, for these have an important psychological effect in the establishment of discipline. But in small practical ways, and by small privileges, the lot of the soldier was improved. The fact that it was almost unique in being regularly paid attracted many foreigners to the army. A regular scale of pay was laid down by the government, and while the actual issue still came from the captain, after 1670 it was audited by civil officials, the army *intendants*. There were no decorations, but a characteristically practical reward for good conduct in the shape of tax-exemption. The king often showed concern for the soldiers' welfare, at one moment discussing allowances in billets, at another, ordering extra pay for troops stationed in the plague areas, or improved field hospital services. The Hôtel des Invalides founded in 1674 for ex-soldiers, was the first regular establishment of its sort; ex-servicemen were given a monopoly of sedan-chair traffic in the royal palaces. These small things throw light on

Louis' government; we see the state taking practical, if primitive, measures to fulfil its responsibilities to those whom its policies most closely affected. At the same time, from its priorities in the community, and no less from the prestige accrued from its victories, the army gained a certain *esprit de corps*. The troops who served under Vauban, Catinat and Villars anticipated in some ways the national and professional army of modern times; they were nearer to Napoleon than they were to Condé.

Tactics and weapons

Improvements in conditions of service did not alone make an efficient striking force, and the finest morale was wasted if the troops could not manœuvre or handle their weapons properly. It was a shock to Louvois to hear that many of the 'trained soldiers' in the Hungarian expeditionary force of 1664 could not fire a musket. Infantry training had been neglected because social values still lent to cavalry the *cachet* of distinction. The generals were mostly cavalry-minded; infantry were simply to soften up the enemy lines before the cavalry charge which won the battle. This was altered slowly by the great increase in the size of the army, by the introduction of better infantry weapons and the prevalence, in Flanders, of siege warfare. By 1691 there were ninety-eight infantry regiments, of which seventy-two had regular names; the proportion of infantry to cavalry was about five to one. The cavalry remained the smarter arm, and they were carefully trained and armed, their swords being replaced by sabres, carabineers attached to squadrons, and annual camps held for training in the field, the latter an occasion for fashionable jaunts for the king and court. Cavalry tactics altered during the reign, as with the development of a lighter, swifter breed of horse came a new momentum in the charge, with heavy sabre thrusts from a galloping line. But most of the great battles of the reign were won by the fire-power of the infantry fighting in line, with musket, *fusil*, pike and latterly bayonet. In the choice of weapons Louvois was oddly conservative, for the French army was still being rearmed with the musket, after the introduction of the more serviceable *fusil* with its flint-lock mechanism. The musket had to be loaded with ball and powder, raised to the shoulder, aligned upon a wooden fork stuck into the ground, and fired by a fuse which was itself lighted by striking tinder. Until the end of the century too, a third part of each company was still armed with the pike, to form a hedgehog of defence; it was always a clumsy weapon and was rendered quite obsolete by the development of the *baïonnette à l'aiguille*, needle shaped, with no cutting edge, which could be fitted to a musket by a socket, without interrupting fire. Frequent reports that the French soldiers threw away pike and musket and picked up the abandoned *fusils* of the enemy whenever they drove them back, did not apparently shake the conviction of the authorities that 'to change is to disarm'.

If infantry played an inferior part before the reforms of the Le Telliers, artillery and engineers had hardly belonged to the army at all. Until the siege operations of the Dutch War made the system impossible, the artillery was a civilian affair, provided by contractors who were paid for every gun that they brought into action. Louvois brought guns and gunners under straight royal control. Beginning with two companies of bombardiers, he rapidly increased the size of this arm until, by 1689, there were some twenty-four companies in the now-royal corps.

Vauban

The growth of military engineering is inseparably linked with the name of Sebastien Vauban, a name of importance in the history of armies, as in the history of France. In the craft of scientific warfare Vauban was not the only pioneer, for the study of Roman military methods had already borne fruit in the work of Justus Lipsius, who had taught at Leyden and there influenced his contemporaries, the brothers-in-arms Maurice of Nassau and William Louis. They had been the first to take pains over training their troops in digging and mining, while Maurice made good use of such inventions as the telescope and the hand grenade. It was he who persuaded the University of Leyden to add the art of fortification to its curriculum of studies, an art which became, in the age of Vauban, a normal part of the education of a gentleman.

Vauban rose to fame from humble beginnings, by his great practical ability and an abundant imagination. He had made his name first at Dunkirk, where he turned a wretched fishing-village surrounded by sand dunes into a fine fortified harbour. With his carefully schooled teams of engineers—a 'whole band of Archimedes' '—he pioneered and perfected new ways of fortifying and besieging towns. He laid siege to fifty places without a failure, and sieges under his direction became formal spectacles, immaculately staged and timed. He experimented continuously with new ideas. At the siege of Maastricht in 1673, parallel trenches were first used; the trench system of the 1914-18 war was only Vauban's brought up to date. At the siege of Philippsburg in 1689, he invented *ricochet* fire, which was so deadly that his delighted king made him lieutenant-general on the spot.

Vauban's life's work was the creation of a frontier which was to be the prototype of the modern frontier, conceived not as an area of sovereignty but as a hard-and-fast line. In Flanders, geography could suggest no clear boundary, so Vauban had to make good by his works the defects of nature. When the frontier was still an imperfect sketch, in 1673, he wrote to Louvois: 'seriously now, the king ought to give some thought to establishing his meadow square. This profusion of friendly and hostile forts does not please me at all, for you are obliged to maintain three for the sake of one.' Vauban conceived an unbroken defensive line from Lille to Briançon, from Mont-Louis to Bayonne and, on the coast, from Antibes to Dunkirk. At the end of the Dutch War he found himself in sole charge of this work, and Louvois encouraged him to spare no expense. The result was a web of fortresses, each with double or triple girdles, stone upon vast earth works, over deep ditches and steep slopes; angled forts and barbicans; great doors gilt with the *fleur de lys* opening on to buildings of severe splendour: works of utility, and at the same time works of art, in their grandeur and precision as typical of the age as the plays of Racine or the sermons of Bossuet. At Strasbourg, Vauban planned the most superb gates for the citadel, and when the king flinched at the expense, he was adamant: Strasbourg was the key to Germany, and the Germans were susceptible to display; they would judge the magnificance of the king by the beauty of these gates. Every place was suited to its terrain. At Neuf-Breisach he threw out bastion towers over the river; at Mont-Louis, on a high Pyrenean escarpment, he placed an eagle's nest to overlook the valleys around. From the Rhine to the sea he divided the frontier into sectors, according to the nature of the ground and the facility of communications. The northern region was well covered by two lines of works; the first from Dunkirk to Dinant, comprising fifteen forts, the second from Gravelines to Charleville, with thirteen; from Dunkirk to Escaut, the obstacle was continued with a tracery of trenches, ramparts and ditches, strengthened by redoubts. This plan made a strategy of that principle of defence in depth which he had already practised in his individual fortifications. At the same time it was no Maginot line of static resistance, but a fortified field of manœuvre. As defensive hedgehogs, his forts blocked an aggressor's path, while as pivots for a manœuvring army they covered its communications and guarded its ammunition and supplies. The value of these lines was proved in the war of the Spanish Succession when, after the defeat of the army in the field, the enemy were deprived of their advantage by the presence around them of French garrisons straddling their communications. After the great victory of Oudenarde, Marlborough could not advance upon Paris, but had to spend five months investing Lille. The work of Vauban in the years of victory saved France in the years of defeat.

The great victualler

Louvois was a superlative quartermaster, and it may be that his most important work was achieved in this field, in the building up, behind the armies, of vast *échelons* of supplies and transport. Exact ration scales were laid down for the armies and varied to meet their operational needs. Louvois realised, before Napoleon, that an army marches upon its stomach, and he was not called by the troops 'the great victualler' for nothing. By careful commissariat, he was able to increase the mobility of the army on campaign, though he could not end all at once the bad habits which came from generations of living on the land. There was negligence and indiscipline. When Boufflers surrendered Lille in 1708, he was forced to it by lack of food: but he had throughout the siege issued rations for the same number of men, regardless of the heavy casualties of the garrison. In 1673, the whole of Luxembourg's army had their pay stopped after the men had looted their own magazines. Faults in the contractor system, upon which Louvois depended for rations and carts, went unchecked by officers who were disinclined to undertake such clerkly work.

The introduction of the magazine made such an enormous difference to the striking power of an army that it is hard to realise that it was not used before Louvois. Well-maintained dumps of forage and ammunition enabled French armies to fight long campaigns far from base, and to reject the comfortable convention of winter quarters that had restricted western warfare since the day of Caesar. An army which did not need to hibernate till the spring herbage could supply forage for the cavalry, stood at a great initial advantage, one which was fully exploited in the early campaigns of the reign. But there is no patent to protect the military innovator; like all advantages on the field of Mars, this was short-lived. France more than any other country was responsible for the intensification of warfare during the second half of the century. Her example forced change upon the other states, and in the last and biggest war of the reign she was the victim of the very advances in war which she had done most to pioneer.

The means through which Versailles hoped to oversee the administration of the army was the *intendant*. These officials were first used regularly for this purpose by Le Tellier. He had himself been an *intendant* and it was natural for him to begin the process of army reform by putting the commander in the field under the eye of the agent of the crown. As the *intendant* was king in the province, so it was intended that the *intendant de l'armée* should be the king in the army; under his authority the army should belong really, and not by courtesy title alone, to the king. The *intendant*'s presence was resented and his mandate opposed by officers accustomed to independent ways. He operated in a milieu unsuited to a civil servant, so that he could not, if he were conscientious, avoid friction with the professional soldier. Louvois expected his agent to be treated with deference by all officers; but he was more likely to be regarded as a superior clerk, useful for the menial tasks below the dignity of the military staff—or cold-shouldered as the minister's spy. This was quite near to the mark; in 1678 Louvois wrote to the *intendant* in Rousillon; 'your first duty is to let me know everything that is said, projected and done in the army'. Without such commissars, the state could not be sure that its policies would be faithfully interpreted by its generals, or efficiently carried out. But victories could only be won by the uncramped initiative of the soldier in the field. Unfortunately the king and Louvois could not remain content with administrative control, but tried to order the tactics of the army in the minutest detail. The king's early experiences had taught him the menace of the semi-independent general and he was always tenacious of such lessons long after they had ceased to have any relevance. Easy success when he was a young man, and the flattery of courtiers, helped to convince him that he had a flair for soldiering, but although he would have made an admirable staff officer, there is nothing to show that he was a great strategist. The generals found his presence at the front embarrassing and assured him that he could exercise the supreme command as well from Versailles, and with less danger to his person. After the Dutch War he tended therefore to stay at home. Palace control became more strict and more detailed, until in the last war of the reign a general could hardly move from camp without sending couriers to the king to learn his pleasure. A large part of successful generalship is the ability to take quick advantage of a sudden development; risks never look the same to the commander on the spot as to the student of the wall-map; remote control, however intelligent, must mean time-lags. The failures of French armies in the war of the Spanish Succession must be partly ascribed to the king's strategic activities; a classic example is provided by the failure of Marsin and la Feuillade before Turin in 1706. Towards the end, Villars was given a relatively free hand however, and he repaid the trust with victory.

Colbert and the navy

The creation of the French navy—for nothing but a few rotten hulks remained from the regime of Mazarin—shows what could be done by a determined minister, given a free hand with the resources of the state. When it came to deciding upon priorities, Louis XIV was to neglect the fleet for the army; his own active interest was moreover slight, for he disliked the sea, and his acquaintance with ships did not go much beyond the manœuvres of miniature vessels on the artificial waters of Versailles. But he backed Colbert's work for long enough to make France a maritime power for the first time in her history. Richelieu had made a beginning and had used galleys effectively against the pirates of the Mediterranean; but the opportunities provided by an Atlantic seaboard were neglected till Colbert's day. Events of the naval war of 1652-4 between the Dutch and the English showed that, in a war of fleet actions, the converted merchantman and the privateer could no longer be any substitute for a regular navy. The developments in the naval world were not dissimilar to those of armies: tighter state control and greater professional efficiency. In the English navy, for instance, reforms culminating in the work of Pepys at the Admiralty laid down tactical principles and disciplinary rules which were to be the model for all subsequent advance. Progress amongst navies was stimulated by the commercial rivalry of England and Holland; now Colbert saw that a strong navy was necessary, to give effective backing to the tariff war, and to give substance to his dreams of wealth and autarchy. A measure of rebuilding was inevitable in any case for, since the appearance of sailing-warships in the Mediterranean, the galley was rendered obsolete. It was a task to his liking, and one that taxed to the full his talents for creating and organising.

Dockyards and arsenals were constructed at Toulon, Brest, Rochefort and Dunkirk, the latter Vauban's first work and 'the most grand and beautiful design of fortification in the world', in order that the new fleets might be built and equipped entirely in France. The resources of France were mobilised for the task, thoroughly and urgently. Forests were laid low and others replanted for ships' timber; a careful inventory was made of trees within reach of all rivers suitable for floating tree trunks to the shipyards. Sailors were recruited from the towns and villages of the long coastline from Bayonne to Dunkirk. From the haphazard injustices of the press, Colbert turned to a regular system of conscription which aroused many resentments, despite allowances such as exemption from the *taille*. A register was kept of all classes of seamen; the system proved so efficient that it has been retained to the present day. But a recent study of the class system shows that resistance came not only from fishermen, whose livelihood was threatened, or from naval officers, now listed in order of seniority, but from provincial *parlements*. The remaining galleys of Provence of course provided no manning problem, for there were always enough prisoners, and later Huguenots, for the oars. Colbert applied himself to the smallest details. The commander at Le Havre was ordered to see that his ships were kept very clean and gaily painted within and without, so that merchants should be attracted by them; the art of men as different as Le Brun and Puget was pressed into service. Prizes were awarded for naval construction, and for gunnery; schools were started for naval cadets; with the help of the *Académie des Sciences*, the reform of hydrography was taken in hand. Like his counterpart in England, Samuel Pepys, Colbert found his greatest problem to lie in discipline: how to instil the regular notions of a department of state, in place of the casual customs of the ex-traders, adventurers and inexperienced noblemen who commanded the new ships?

He was not helped by the independent attitude of early commanders such as Châteaurenaud, or Duquesne; the latter an
accomplished seaman who had begun life as a pirate. The solution
was the ubiquitous *intendant*; as with the army, the factory and the
remote province, the trained civil servant was brought in to
ensure obedience and loyalty. At the same time the formation of a
regular officer corps, the *compagnies des gardes de la marine* went
some way to meet the need. Parallel commands made for difficulties, but the point was slowly made; before Colbert's death, his
navy had won its first battles, and was a fighting instrument ready,
if properly appreciated by Versailles, to contest the seas with the
older-established sea powers. Duquesne twice defeated the Dutch
in a series of running battles off Sicily in January to April 1676;
the great de Ruyter was killed in the second action. The ability and
courage of de Tourville made the navy, for a brief but glorious
time at the start of the War of the League of Augsburg, a real
threat to Anglo-Dutch supremacy. Colbert found some twenty
ships; he left two hundred and fifty. After the death of his son
Seignelay, the navy was allowed to run down and reduced to the
subordinate role of commerce-raiding. Even this, in the hands of
adventurous seamen such as Jean Bart, was a large contribution
to the war effort, as may be seen in the insistence of the English
Parliament upon the destruction of the fortifications of Dunkirk,
which had alone commissioned about eight hundred corsairs at
the end of the war.

Peasants at a meal   *Louis le Nain*

ABOVE Le prévôt des marchands et les échevins de Paris
Philippe de Champaigne

OPPOSITE Henry IV   *Frans Pourbus*

ABOVE Nicholas Fouquet *Sébastien Bourdon*

OPPOSITE Cardinal Richelieu *Philippe de Champaigne*

ABOVE Cardinal Mazarin   *Philippe de Champaigne*

OPPOSITE *Left* Colbert *Right* Louvois   R. *Nanteuil*

ABOVE The Palace of Versailles, Salon de la Guerre

OPPOSITE The Palace of Versailles from the gardens

DEMOLITION
DU
TEMPLE DE CHARENTON
en No[v]embre 1685

S. le Clerc Inventit

ABOVE The demolition of the Temple of Charenton in November
1685 *Sébastien Leclerc*

OPPOSITE Louis XIV *H. Rigaud*

ABOVE Samuel Bernard *P. Drevet*

OPPOSITE *Left* The Duke of Burgundy *After Troye-Chéreau*
Right The Duke of Orleans *After Santerre*

ABOVE Raising the militia in a country parish
From an anonymous print of 1705

OPPOSITE Molière   *P. Mignard*

ABOVE Fénelon *J. Vivien*

LEFT Anne of Austria *P. P. Rubens*

The causes of the war

In 1672, France went to war with the United Provinces. It may be argued that this was a logical step from the first invasion of Flanders in 1667. It was nevertheless a clean break with the policy which had dictated the moderated demands of Aix-la-Chapelle. Then Louis had shown that he preferred the grand and distant hopes of Empire held out to him by the Partition Treaty; but now he staked his armies and his reputation upon snatching an immediate instalment. He had changed from the long to the short view. The invasion of Holland was in effect an armed burglary which could not be justified by any stretch of legal inventiveness; Louis could not now tell Europe that he was claiming his own. His action reversed the policy of the Cardinals and its effect was to push the Protestant Holland and—although he cannot be blamed for not foreseeing it—Protestant England into the arms of his Catholic Hapsburg foes. Further, it lost the moral vantage and repute of France in Germany. When Mignet said that 'the old political system suffered shipwreck in Holland', he had these results in mind.

Only four years separated the generous settlement of Aix from the invasion of Holland. Why in so short a time did Louis turn to outrageous bellicosity? The answer lies in the Triple Alliance, in the part played by Holland in checking Louis' aggression, in the clash of interests of the two powers which had become more apparent with the collapse of Spain, and in the actual terms of the peace of Aix which brought Louis only a moiety of the inheritance for which he had gone to war.

Louis had been mortified by the initiative taken by John de Witt in forming the Triple Alliance. In May 1668 the Dutch had acted as the arbiters of Europe and they had been able to boast that they had made 'five kings see reason'. How this rankled can be seen in the wording of that part of the Treaty of Dover in which Louis and Charles II agree 'to humble the pride of the States-General and to destroy the power of a people which has not only shown ingratitude to those who have helped to create its republic but has the insolence to set itself up as sovereign arbiter among other states'. The phrasing expresses Louis' political theology succinctly. After her original sin of being born out of rebellion,

I

Holland had twice treated her maker with disrespect and ingratitude: in 1648, when she had made separate peace with Spain, and
in 1668, when she presumed to arbitrate over Europe. There can
be little doubt that after 1668 Louis was set upon punishment.
In his *Mémoires*, he confided that the action of Holland had
'touched him to the quick' but that in prudence he put off the
'punishment of this perfidy'. There was provocation enough from
the outspoken Dutch press; a characteristic cartoon showed
Louis' sun obscured by a great Dutch cheese. But the essential
element in Louis' thinking was his own status as hereditary head
of the first state in Europe, responsible to God alone. To him and
to France was opposed not a respectable state at all but a com-
monalty of 'maggots', governed by 'business men and cheese
merchants'.

His ministers echoed their master's voice and added their own
special arguments. Lionne, who died in 1670 before he could see
his diplomacy consummated in war, examining the chances of the
death of the king of Spain 'which would change in an instant the
world situation', told Pomponne that it 'did not belong to merchants, themselves usurpers, to decide in sovereign manner the
interests of the two greatest monarchs in Christendom'. Louvois,
who had opposed the Peace of Aix, stressed the strategic side: 'the
only means of achieving the conquest of the Spanish Netherlands,
is to abase the Dutch and, if possible, to crush them'. The way to
Brussels lay through Amsterdam and The Hague. Reports that
the Dutch were setting up garrisons at points along the Rhine and
Meuse were used to give point to the arguments in favour of battle
practice for the new armies. De Witt's policy of the Barrier was a
defensive one: '*Gallum amicum sed non vicinum*'. His attitude is
understandable in face of the rising temper of French militarism.
Louvois' star was in the ascendant and war dominated the ideas
of the thrusting young war minister, who was convinced that
the French would carry all before them. Colbert, who was a
jealous critic of Louvois and opposed, on principle, the waste
and extravagance of war, might have been expected to take
a more moderate view. But he welcomed a trade war as the
natural extension of his commercial policy of prohibitive tariffs.
He had made plain in 1667 his determination to break the semi-
monopoly of the Dutch in the world's carrying-trade: 'as we
have ruined Spain on land, so we must ruin Holland at sea'. He
saw Antwerp as the tactical objective: 'once Antwerp becomes a

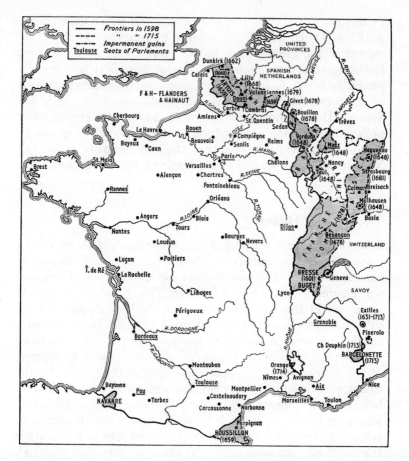

The expansion of the frontiers

French town, the closing of the Scheldt, on which depends the wealth of Dutch trade, cannot fail to be practical'. In short, the creator of the French navy had as great a part in the war on Holland as the war minister on whom historians have usually placed the blame. Colbert was not unaffected by the strident mood of the court, which was enhanced by the easy successes of the War of Devolution. He thought it the natural end of state policy to 'carry the glory of the king's name as far as can be imagined' and he spoke of war as 'the only means by which His Majesty could put an end to the insolence and arrogance of this nation'.

The isolation of Holland

Louis' tactics were a model of aggressive method. A prelude of intense diplomatic activity was in itself a formidable display of French strength—and wealth. First the acquiescence of England was assured by the Treaty of Dover. The episode is immensely important in English history, for Charles II's *volte-face* and the subsequent revelation of the religious plot, the treaty within a treaty, later brought the throne into jeopardy. Its value to France was that it destroyed the Triple Alliance and secured the support of the English navy for operations against the Dutch. By the treaty, negotiated in its last phase through the agency of Charles' beloved sister Minette, duchesse d'Orléans, Charles agreed to join with Louis in an attack upon Holland. Louis promised to respect the integrity of Flanders and to hand over to England the Isle of Walcheren with its useful ports of Sluys and Cadsand. Charles was also to receive subsidies through which he might hope to be independent of Parliament. Finally the English king promised secretly to do his utmost to bring back his subjects to the Catholic faith, if necessary with the assistance of French troops. Charles escaped with real advantages and some freedom of action; but he had come very near to a client relationship with the French king. In the discussions at Dover in June 1670, the survival of the United Provinces, of English Protestantism and of the Stuart dynasty were all at hazard. But to Lionne, the English alliance was only a part of the network of alliances with which he planned to isolate Holland, with all the dexterity of his long experience and with skilful agents empowered to offer lavish bribes. Sweden was easily bought; the nobles of the Council of

Regency were notoriously venal, and her Protestant sympathies now weighed little against the need for a strong patron against the rival power of Brandenburg. Catholic Bavaria promised to deny passage to the troops of the Emperor, while the Elector of Cologne and the Bishop of Munster both, perforce, opened their lands to the French. Brandenburg stood apart. The Great Elector was allied by family ties to the House of Orange; he certainly regarded the survival of Holland as essential to the independence of Germany. But no other German state could afford such defiance and they fell into line behind the paymaster of Europe or shrank into quiet neutrality. The Emperor could give them no lead. Looking anxiously towards his eastern frontiers and to Hungary in revolt, Leopold promised non-intervention so long as the war was kept out of the 'circles and fiefs of the Empire'.

The occupation of Lorraine, in 1670, gave a foretaste of Louis' summary method when his path was blocked. Charles IV of Lorraine had not met his 'obligations' towards Louis and in defiance of treaties binding him to France was pursuing a Francophobe policy; when threatened, he looked around for troops and allies. In August, French troops under Créqui moved into Lorraine and the Duke retired into Germany, where he received no support beyond the polemics of a few pamphleteers. 'Lorraine was the alarm clock of the princes,' declared Isola, the Austrian ambassador at The Hague. 'A very fine province to add to my kingdom,' was Louis' complacent comment. The annexation was of strategic importance to him, for it cleared his flank for advance into Holland and gave valuable field training to his troops. Until his appointment to Foreign Minister, Arnault de Pomponne, Louis' ambassador at The Hague, kept up formal negotiations with de Witt. Meanwhile, Louvois recruited energetically to bring the army up to strength and big troop movements caused nerve tremors throughout Europe. According to the English ambassador, Temple, few preparations were made in Holland, merchants did not hesitate to sell munitions to French emissaries, and the Pensionary himself, gloomily aware that the crisis would bring the Orange party again to the fore, offered to disarm. But Louis replied in braggart and menacing terms: 'we tell you that we will increase our estate by land and sea and that when it shall be of such strength as we intend, we will make such use of it as we think best suited to our dignity, for which we render account to none'. In the same month, January 1672, Louvois became a Minister of State. In March, Charles II, anxious for his subsidies, declared war. Then Louis, in train with Louvois and Pomponne, his confessor, and his tame historian, Pellisson, left Paris to review his troops massed on the frontier, and to conduct in person the campaign which promised such glory. There was no formal declaration of war.

The first campaign

The opening moves were rapid. The French armies, 110,000 strong, attacked from the lands of the Elector of Cologne and drove back the Dutch almost without a shot. The Dutch army was no longer the force it had been in the days of Maurice of Nassau. Condé and Turenne joined forces at Maastricht, on the Meuse, where the Dutch hoped that the fortress, with its garrison, of 10,000, would hold up the French advance. But the generals simply masked the town and pushed on to the Rhine, whose crossing, but lightly opposed, on a bridge of copper pontoons devised by Martinet, inspired the judicious Boileau to an admiring ode. The crossing was easy, but it turned the flank of the main Dutch army, which had to hurry back from the line of the Ijssel to defend Amsterdam. By the end of June, Overissel and Gelderland were in French hands, and when the king entered Utrecht in triumph and witnessed the Catholic re-dedication of its great Cathedral, the war seemed to be won. De Witt sued for terms. But at sea de Ruyter inflicted heavy losses upon the English and French fleets at Southwold Bay; then Condé, who urged a swift thrust forward to defenceless Amsterdam, was overborne by the caution of Turenne and Louvois. The English observer, Sidney Godolphin, thought that the generals would have been more effective if the king and Louvois had not interfered. Now they had to watch the waters rise over the level ground round Amsterdam, flooding the crops, drowning the cattle and turning the city into an island fortress. The action might have been foreseen, for the Dutch had used the same elemental weapon against the Spanish. In between the flooded polders (the land-strips between the rivers and canals) about 10,000 Dutch troops defended the principal roads into Holland. Meanwhile, the emissaries of de Witt were given discretion to accept any reasonable terms that might be offered. But Louis chose to fling at them demands which were harsh to the point of insult. The cession of provinces already taken, the cancellation of their measures of economic retaliation, an indemnity of 24,000,000 *livres*, might all have been swallowed. His demand for the acceptance of Roman Catholics to equal status in the country was unrealistic; but it was the request for an annual envoy to bring a medal to Louis in token of submission that conveys the spirit of arrogance which drove the Dutch to resume a war of survival. Because of his unnecessary rudeness, Louvois has been blamed for this cynical abuse of a strong position. But the terms show that loss of sense of proportion which Louis himself showed at critical moments of his reign, and which he admitted in his *Mémoires*: 'ambition and desire for glory are always pardonable in a prince, and particularly in one, young and so well-treated by fortune as I was'.

The first victims of these 'terms' were the brothers de Witt, who would have gone to any lengths for peace and who now faced a furious public opinion in search of a scapegoat for disaster. Already they had been compelled to promote the young William of Orange. In July he was proclaimed *Stadholder* by the estates of Zealand and Holland and vested by the States-General with the offices of Captain-General and Admiral for life and with sweeping powers. Once again the House of Orange had been recalled to its historic role of saving the state. On August 20th, John de Witt, who had been forced to resign his title of Grand Pensionary, and his brother Cornelius, charged with plotting against the life of William, were dragged out of prison and lynched by an excited mob. The pacific party of the great burgomasters was replaced in power by the militarist faction with its vital European connections. At its head stood the Prince of 22 who was to be Louis' most persistent and most effective enemy. William had been born a week after the death by smallpox, in 1650, of his father William II of Orange. He had grown up in obscurity in the republican regime of the Regents of Holland and seen the office of *Stadholder* grow rusty with disuse. Now severe and wary beyond his years, he took up the great task of his life. His object and his obsession was to be the defeat of the French king who trampled on the Netherlands and filched his own principality of Orange. Already he perceived that the grandeur of France could not be matched by any other single power and that he must work for 'a collective security' through a coalition of those states who were threatened by the 'universal monarchy' of France.

William hoped for a quick victory to justify the *coup d'état*. Valuable respite was gained when the Elector of Brandenburg appeared on the Rhine and French troops were detached to meet him. In December the *Stadholder* led an expedition to a surprise attack upon Charleroi. The attack was resisted and the French lines of communication remained intact, but the attempt served notice of the spirited resistance that the French might now expect. Already Louis had returned to Versailles with the historians commissioned to record his easy progress to The Hague. A very different sort of focus was perpetuated by the Dutch engraver Romeyn de Hooghe, whose depiction of the destruction of the Dutch villages of Bodegrave and Swammerdam aroused feeling in Europe about an unnecessary atrocity.

The war spreads

The next year, 1673, saw the elimination of the Elector of Brandenburg. Turenne advanced to the aid of the troops of Munster and Cologne in the depths of winter. By the spring, Frederick-William's troops had fallen back in disorder and in June, disgusted at the failure of the Emperor to lend him support, he contracted out by the Treaty of Vossem. The opportunist ruler showed scant regard for the binding force of treaties. In the following year, after the defection of England, he came back again; then, again defeated by Turenne, at Turkheim in January 1675, he made a second peace and turned his attention to the Swedes. The main campaign of the year in Holland turned upon the siege of Maastricht, a characteristic Vauban set-piece of logistics and engineering. The town was of strategic importance as assuring communications with the Rhineland princes; it fell early in July. The king attended with the court, announcing that 'big sieges please me more than others', and the final assault took place, as was customary, to the accompaniment of violins. In the siege, a tiny English force commanded by Monmouth, Charles II's illegitimate son, played a notable part, and in its ranks a young gentleman volunteer of fateful name—John Churchill.

Despite this success, Louis could not prevent the war from spreading. At the Congress of Cologne, convened under the mediation of Sweden, his peace terms were rejected with confidence. De Ruyter had defeated the French fleet off Zeeland in June, so thwarting a plan for an English expeditionary force to land behind the Dutch lines and relieve the stalemate in which Condé found himself, fretting before the wastes of floodwater. By the end of the year, Holland no longer stood alone for, by that time the Empire, Spain and Lorraine, alarmed and shaken by the ranging operations of Louis' troops, had come together in an offensive alliance. William joined forces with the Imperial troops at Bonn, and Condé was withdrawn from Holland to meet the threat of the new alliance, leaving Luxembourg to carry out a scorched-earth withdrawal. So Louis found himself committed to a European war, to defend his gains against a coalition which was now reinforced again by resilient Brandenburg and which had been expressly formed to halt the ambitions of 'the Christian Turk' of the pamphleteer's phrase. Charles II slipped out of his obligations to France under the double pressure of Protestant sentiment in Parliament and shortage of cash, and England made her separate peace with Holland in February 1674.

The last campaigns of Turenne and Condé

The entry of Spain tempted the French command to a lightning annexation of Franche-Comté. It had already been well rehearsed in 1668 and it now proved to be an easy affair; even the capital, Besançon, gave only a token resistance to the king and Vauban, and the whole province was in French hands by July. By then the Dutch affair had become a European war of two main fronts. In the Low Countries, siege warfare played the greatest part; but here the attempt of William of Orange to open up the way to Paris by attacking Charleroi gave Condé the opportunity for his last victory, at Seneffe, in August 1674. It was a murderous fight in which Condé, having three horses killed under him, showed perhaps more courage than discretion, and it was sufficiently even for both sides to give thanks to God for giving them the victory. In the Rhineland, where Turenne faced an opponent of his own mettle in Raimondo Montecucoli, the action was more fluid. In June, Turenne penetrated Germany and beat the Imperialists, Caprara and the old Duke of Lorraine, at Sintzeim, near Heidelberg. He then retreated, firing as he went an area of the Palatinate to make the country inhospitable to his opponents. His cousin, the Elector Palatine, reproached him with becoming cruel after his conversion to Rome, and challenged him to a duel. Such action was not rare—even Marlborough devastated tracts of Bavaria after Blenheim—and Turenne's effort was to be dwarfed by the more thorough devastation of the same parts in 1689. In the sullen state of German opinion it was untimely, and Turenne's own *commissaire* protested about its brutality. Allowing, however, for the military ethics of the day, it was an answer to the problem of defending a long frontier against several armies, by restricting their field of manœuvre. Turenne was hard pressed. In the winter of 1674-5 he faced superior armies in Alsace and Lorraine and rose to the challenge with campaigns of sustained brilliance. In months of rapid marches and bold offensive amongst the woods and snowy hills of the Vosges, he won engagements at Mülhausen, Altkirch and Turkheim (January) and threw the Imperialists back over the Rhine. But fate cut him short in his prime. On July 27th he was out reconnoitring the lines of Montecucoli at Salzbach, when he was struck by a cannon ball. The battle was won, but all was consternation. The 'great captain' had not won all his battles nor had he always been loyal. But his experience and judgment were unmatched and irreplaceable. With a gesture worthy of the *grand siècle*, Saint-Hilaire, lieutenant-general of artillery, who lost his arm by the same shot that killed Turenne, said: 'do not weep for me; weep for that great man'. Another comment on the death of Turenne was Montecucoli's swift re-occupation of Alsace. Condé was hastily called from Flanders to fend off danger. After a skilful campaign, he retired at the end of the year, crippled with gout and rheumatism—not helped by the 'prodigious height of the waters', as he described them in Holland—to a life of speculation and literary conversation at Chantilly. So in one year Louis lost his two finest soldiers, survivors of the tradition of the *condottieri* and great figures in their own right, who could afford to snap their fingers at the directives of Versailles.

In 1675 France lost also her last effective ally—for Bavaria was inactive. The Swedes moved reluctantly to fulfil their treaty promises and invaded Brandenburg. The Great Elector managed to re-organise the army which had been mauled at Turkheim and win, by himself, the fine victory of Fehrbellin. The defeat of the Swedish army was a significant blow to French diplomacy, which had leant upon Sweden since Richelieu called in Gustavus Adolphus to redress the balance in Germany. For all the eccentric exploits of Charles XII which lay in the future, Fehrbellin removed Sweden from a significant role in Europe. But for the moment

France had nothing to fear from Brandenburg, whose ruler was bent on wresting Pomerania from the Swedes.

The most important events of 1676 were the defeat of the Dutch fleet by Duquesne and the death of Admiral de Ruyter. While the armies in the Netherlands besieged towns or manœuvred watchfully, avoiding battle, Duquesne, a Protestant, reformed pirate but most capable seaman, engaged the Dutch and Spanish fleets in the Mediterranean. Successive victories at Lipari in January, Agosta, where de Ruyter was killed, in April, and Palermo in June, proved the value of Colbert's reforms of the navy and assured to Louis the mastery of the Mediterranean as well as the town of Messina, capital of Sicily.

Peace talks began, before the end of the year, at Nijmegen, where Charles II, treading a path of careful neutrality between his need for French money and the loud Francophobia of Shaftesbury's men in Parliament, was delighted to play the part of a patron. Louis' belligerence had been toned down by the years of attrition, despite his siege successes. His generals wanted peace. It had been necessary to call on the *arrière-ban*, the old feudal militia in 1674, and the experiment had been a failure. In 1675 Vauban lamented the state of the army—'garrisons defended by children or poor little wretches, the officers as bad'. In the same year, Bossuet, a reliable mirror of public opinion, reminded his master of his duty to his people, to heed their growing discomforts. France had never before been committed to a protracted war upon this intensive scale. Holland felt the strain even more severely and William could not afford to ignore the bitter complaints of burghers who saw their great trading empire crumble. At Nijmegen the elaborate and leisured ritual of the diplomats ignored these needs, and months were taken up with questions of precedence and status. Big differences of policy divided the coalition. The Emperor wanted to return to the situation after Westphalia, while Spain looked vainly back to the Treaty of the Pyrenees; the Dutch would be content with the Barrier and commercial guarantees. The war dragged on, an important part of the bargaining at Nijmegen in which towns taken and battles won were the counters of play. The capture of Valenciennes, St. Omer and Cambrai were reminders of French power. Then William was seriously defeated at Cassel in April by Luxembourg (Monsieur was nominally in command at this action and was never allowed near the front again!). In the winter Marshal Créqui took revenge for the loss of Philippsburg in the previous year by snatching Freiburg after a sudden crossing of the Rhine, while his enemy hibernated. These tactical successes were countered by William with a diplomatic *coup* of the first importance. In November 1677 he married Mary, daughter of James, Duke of York, brother of the childless king of England, who hoped by this marriage to quieten popular mistrust of Catholic James. The momentous consequences lay ahead; for the moment it was enough that the two great Protestant and maritime powers were linked by this marriage-tie and the first lines drawn for the pattern of the future. Louis' advantages in eastern Europe were trifling by comparison; peace between Poland and Turkey, intended to release John Sobieski of Poland for a war upon the Emperor which he proved reluctant to undertake, together with a new understanding with Hungary and with Tokoly, the new ruler of the struggling Magyars.

The Peace of Nijmegen

Slowly from the toils of Nijmegen separate settlements emerged. Louis advertised at once his might and his clemency when he launched 100,000 men into Flanders, took the important town of Ghent, published his peace proposals and offered the town of Messina for proof of his will for peace. Two positions were doggedly held. The Dutch were anxious to retain a workable barrier of frontier fortresses, and the French refused to sacrifice their ally Sweden. On this latter ground the conference nearly broke up, as the French king insisted that the Elector of Brandenburg should restore the lands he had won from Sweden. An Anglo-Dutch alliance was made in July and a renewal of war threatened if the French did not evacuate the Flemish towns without waiting for a settlement of the Swedish question. Meanwhile the French diplomats cunningly exploited the divisions of the Dutch: the rancour of the merchants against the Orange militants, who could afford to ignore the declining trade of Amsterdam. For the time the dispute was slurred over, the Swedes promising to accept the peace on condition that the Dutch promised not to help Brandenburg. The Peace of Nijmegen illustrated fully the resource and expertise of French diplomacy.

Holland was cleverly detached from Spain by separate and generous terms, thus leaving Louis free to bargain from strength for the Spanish possessions which he really wanted. The peace comprised, in fact, several separate treaties in which France settled her accounts in succession with Holland and Spain in 1678 and the Emperor, Brandenburg and Denmark in 1679. The terms reflected war-weariness in Louis. There was no talk now of religion nor of 'tokens of submission'. Colbert's policy was jettisoned with the tariffs of 1667 and mutual trade made possible again. Where, however, the more tangible interests of France lay, on her vulnerable north-east frontiers, there were solid gains. The outlying towns of Charleroi (gained at Aix), Courtrai, Oudenarde and Ghent were given up, but in exchange she gained a line of strong places up and down Spanish Flanders from Dunkirk to the Meuse, of which the foremost were Ypres, Cambrai and Valenciennes. So the frontiers were pushed out, filling the gaps left by Aix and giving Vauban further scope for his work of fortifying the 'meadow square' of France. France kept Franche-Comté, which Spain was obviously incapable of defending. Spain indeed suffered worst, but as her plenipotentiary Ronquillo recognised: 'better be thrown out of the window than from the top of the roof'. Since the Peace of the Pyrenees, his country had lost beside Franche-Comté, Cambrésis, part of Hainaut, part of maritime Flanders and the rest of Artois. The Emperor ceded two towns across the Rhine, Breisach and Freiburg. By the subsidiary treaty of St. Germain, Brandenburg was forced to give back to Sweden her conquests in Pomerania. Indeed, a French army was sent north to reinforce the argument. This arbitrary act of favour to an unsuccessful ally is an interesting commentary upon Louis' interpretation of prestige; the precise fulfilment of a diplomatic debt of honour was a powerful advertisement of the value of the French alliance. Its bitterness was palliated for the Great Elector by a diplomatic present of 900,000 *livres*. Louis could still afford to be both honourable and generous.

Louis' prestige stood at a remarkable level after Nijmegen. In the words of Voltaire, 'he spoke to Europe as a master while he acted as a statesman'. He showed a political sense, in his timing, and in his grasp of what was relevant and vital in diplomacy, that he was rarely to show again. But in the last resort his mastery was that of overwhelming military strength. Certainly he did not undervalue his success: 'I fully rejoice', he wrote in his *Mémoires*, 'in my clever conduct, whereby I was able to profit from every opportunity I found to extend the boundaries of my kingdom at the expense of my enemies'. The balance-sheet of history supplies a more exact picture but confirms the fact that France was, in the year of Nijmegen, the strongest and richest state in the world: a rare situation of pre-eminence. Spain had shown herself unable to impose upon events, and her troops could now hardly hold back the Moors from her African garrisons. Her possessions were held only by the sufferance of stronger states, each jealous of the gains the other might make, her policies were controlled by the Emperor and her very existence as a state was shortly to be a matter of bargain and contract between the powers. Austria was paralysed by the mounting pressure of Hungarians and Turks and was soon to be involved in the most alarming crisis of the century. Although Leopold I had not reconciled himself to the loss of influence in Alsace, even of the Three Bishoprics ceded in 1648, his hold over the Rhenish lands was only nominal. The Dutch were exhausted by a war in which they had preserved their frontiers only at the expense of the trade, shipping and capital which were the life blood of the state. England was sunk in the near-revolutionary disorders of the 'Popish plot' and the Exclusion bills, and the king's first aim was to survive. When he rode high again upon the royalist reaction of 1681 he pursued a tactful neutrality, and a pension assured his faithful alliance. The German states had shown again that their interests were local and that even if roused against France their separate strengths would only be effective as auxiliaries to a great alliance. There were resentments enough: with the Duke of Lorraine who preferred to wander stateless, rather than accept terms which he regarded as degrading, with the Elector Palatine, and above all at Berlin where Louis' snub to the Great Elector's pretensions was not forgiven. But for these diverse interests and hatreds to be fused in a common alliance there must be some great provocation. For the time Louis had a clear field; his future would depend upon the way he interpreted Nijmegen. Only if he behaved in such a way that a war seemed the only reply to his ambitions would the interested powers ally; only by such an alliance could he ever be defeated.

The origins of modern diplomacy

The Peace of Nijmegen was a triumph for Louis' diplomacy. Temple, the English ambassador in Holland and the doyen of diplomats, was struck by the expertise of the king's envoys and declared that he had never seen such skill in negotiation. The supremacy of France seemed to be as sure in the labyrinths of diplomacy as in the straighter passages of war. Like other splendours of the reign, something was owed to the training of the Cardinals, Mazarin especially, in the hard school of the Congresses of Westphalia and the Pyrenees. But the money made available by Louis' government and the expansionist trend of policy now gave French diplomacy new opportunities for distinction. It has since, as then, enjoyed a high reputation. How much was due to the excellence of the service? How much merely to the superior resources of the state?

Modern diplomacy was the product of the precarious equilibrium established by the Italian states of the Renaissance, and the natural egotism of political organisations with no other end than their own survival and enlargement. The words of Ermolao Barbaro might have served for a maxim of Louis' ambassadors two hundred years later: 'the first duty of the ambassador is the same as that of any government servant: to do, say, advise and think whatever may best serve the preservation and aggrandisement of his own state'. Outside Italy, Spain had been the first of the powers to have something like an organised foreign office with a nucleus of professional experts. For Henry VIII of England Wolsey created a network of resident ambassadors while, in the reign of his contemporary, Francis I, the *conseil d'affaires* functioned as a regular body in charge of foreign policy and there grew up an experienced corps of negotiators and observers. However, the long period of religious and civil war which followed the Treaty of Cateau-Cambrésis disturbed the growth of diplomatic conventions. Religious differences thwarted diplomatic contacts and everywhere, as one may see from incidents in England and Spain in this period, embassies were suspect as the centres of alien and subversive ideas. Of the Catholic rulers, only the Valois held to the policy of exchanging ambassadors with Protestant powers. When Henry IV came to the throne, he found that he had to rebuild the French service, like so much else; for some years, though he would have preferred a wider scope, his only reliable contacts were with England, Holland, Vienna and Venice. During his reign Villeroi was entrusted with all the correspondence with foreign governments and there was some degree of specialisation, but the improvement lasted only to his death, since sound diplomacy rests upon a stable state. When Richelieu took over the direction of foreign affairs, he was obliged to ask French ambassadors abroad for copies of their most recent instructions.

The new law of nations

When the Congresses of Westphalia and the Pyrenees had restored some sort of equilibrium of the states, the conditions of the first impulse of the Renaissance period operated again upon diplomacy. From this time can be traced the development of diplomacy as a distinct profession, with its own privileges and codes of ceremonial and conduct. The representatives of the state now worked in a world whose features had altered drastically in a century. No one believed any more in European unity. All that was left of the old ideal was the use of Latin in diplomatic documents and this was soon to go; at Rastadt, in 1714, French was used. Even Sully's pipe-dream, his *grand dessein* for a balanced federation of European states, had been strongly tinged with ambition for France. Grimmelshausen's plea for an international peace plan, coming as it did from the shambles of the Thirty Years War, was put appropriately into the mouth of a wandering lunatic. The Empire had ceased to hold the allegiance of Germans either by sentiment or by its institutions; after 1648, the German states had the right to send their own representatives to foreign states. The new situation in which the Emperor was important only as ruler of the family lands, in which the Pope's influence was so diminished that he was not even represented at the Peace of the Pyrenees, called for a new law of nations. Professors of law, like Gentili and Grotius, took for granted both the nation state and that unlimited sovereign right of the ruler which Hobbes and Bossuet were soon to define. Grotius, a Dutchman, living as an exile in France and employed as a diplomat by Sweden, in his *De Jure Belli et Pacis*, published in 1625, stressed the existence of a fundamental law of nature, above all dynastic and national ambitions, evolved from mankind's reserves of conscience and reason, which could take the place of the obsolete disciplines of Pope and Emperor. He asserted that no balance of power could work effectively unless nations recognised that certain principles higher than mere expediency should govern their acts. He accepted war as inevitable, the outlet for the passions of nations, magisterial in nature, playing the role of judge and executioner in the international order. Wars of ambition, conquest and propaganda were unjust. It would be a mistake to imagine that this book, or any like it, had any great influence upon the politics of the time, or that there existed anything more, in the way of international law, than a number of rules and bargains between jealous separate states. His work, with its realism and humanity, remains an interesting commentary however upon the situation in which, as he admitted, the sovereign state was subject to no human authority whatever outside itself.

War figured more largely than peace in Grotius' treatise, and we need not be surprised that in this century the usages of war attracted most attention. There were a few agreed rules. A country which was 'neutral', for instance, might expect to be protected from the worse ravages of war, but it usually had to allow belligerent powers to cross its territory, as the French crossed the Spanish Netherlands in their march against Holland in 1672. The exchange of prisoners again was usually arranged by exchange of equal ranks, an officer counting as several soldiers; those not claimed could be sent to the galleys. Belligerents had the right to exact contributions from the population in a theatre of war. Naval practices proved more contentious. The idea of freedom of the sea was not generally accepted. Grotius' *Mare Liberum* was not a general statement of principle but an attack upon the Portuguese claim to exclusive rights in the Indian Ocean. There was argument about 'coastal waters' as opposed to the 'high seas'. Colbert's naval ordinance of 1681 defined the *'mer littorale'* as that 'which the sea covers and leaves bare during the new and full moons and up to where the great tides reach on the beaches'; the definition based upon the range of cannon fire had to wait to the next century. But by far the most important question was that of the salute, the customary, and in the sixteenth century uncontested, courtesy of salvo, or dipping the flag, between the vessels of two different powers. It was a contributory cause of war between the English and the Dutch, while Colbert wrote in 1677: 'France claims that all other nations must bow to her at sea as at the court of kings'. These were not idle words, and the unlucky diplomat who drew up an agreement giving precedence to the English in the North Sea and to the French in the Atlantic was disavowed. The English were as obstinate as the French; in the end their ships had to avoid meeting at sea, even when they were allies. The Spanish could be more easily bullied and, in 1685, Tourville and Château-renaud attacked a Spanish fleet whose commander refused to salute the French colours. After the end of the Dutch War, Tourville twice demanded a salute from the Dutch fleet, the second time fighting a pitched battle for it.

Honour and precedence

Louis XIV, in Colbert's words, was 'extremely jealous about salutes and points of honour'. In this he was not alone. The history of the seventeenth century, and especially its diplomacy, cannot be understood unless it is realised how much importance was attached to ceremony and precedence. At all levels and in all countries, but especially in France and Spain, a man's status was judged by his clothes, his carriage and his retinue. No *seigneur* could hope to make a figure in French society unless he had a complete miniature court, a chaplain, a doctor and a master of ceremonies. At a lower level impoverished noblemen would starve rather than give up their *maître d'hôtel*. At the highest level, the king would not travel on any formal occasion without a retinue of hundreds. When he went to meet his Spanish bride, the procession was several miles long. Upon the same considerations of prestige his ambassadors abroad were expected to keep up a considerable pomp. Rome was an unpopular post since it inevitably ruined all but the very wealthiest. When they represented the king at congresses or on state occasions in foreign capitals, they were expected to guard his honour by attention to the minutest details of precedence. Because Louis would not concede the right of precedence which the Austrians accorded to the Spanish ambassador, his representative at Vienna had to be content with the modest title and limited privileges of 'Envoy Extraordinary'. The order of entry into a house, the placing of guests at a table, such trifles were an important part of the duties of an ambassador. They were held to be important; they were also of course used quite cynically to hold up deliberations when it was thought desirable. At Westphalia, questions of precedence held up the conference for months. To avoid deadlock, the conference had to be held separately in the towns of Munster and Osnabrück. In 1659, the Peace of the Pyrenees was only made possible by the discovery of a small island in the Bidassoa where the representatives of France and Spain could meet without prejudice to the rank of either country.

Royal diplomacy

When Louis came to direct foreign policy, there were already firm precedents to guide him. Richelieu had established the idea that negotiation must be a permanent activity, aiming at solid and lasting relations. He regarded a treaty, once signed and ratified, as something to be observed 'with religious scruple'. He assumed, of course, that the interest of the state must come before all other considerations. Allies must be chosen for their strategic value without regard to sentiment or ideology. Mazarin, both from inclination and from the weakness of his personal position during the Minority, ruled by the arts of diplomacy, and he made it his concern to see that Louis was well versed in these arts. After 1661, the diplomatic machine was directed by the king, all business passing through his hands. The ideal of omniscience that he set himself was unrealistic; but the vigilance, attention to detail and shrewdness of which we read in his *Mémoires* are attested to by outside observers. He followed his own precept: to hear much advice and deliberate without hurry and, after policy had been decided, to act on his own responsibility. He followed Richelieu in his meticulous attention to the letter of a treaty but he added nuances of his own: 'there is in no agreement in any clause so water-tight as not to allow some elasticity of interpretation'. He once went so far as to compare treaties to compliments, 'absolutely necessary for co-existence but of little significance beyond their sound'. This may seem to justify Lavisse's severe condemnation: 'he broke nearly every promise that he made'. In fact, he could be surprisingly scrupulous in his engagements when he thought that his honour was engaged, especially, as in the case of James Edward Stuart, when it was engaged to a fellow sovereign. In the Europe of the Great Elector, Victor Amadeus II and Charles II (of England) he can be made to appear, in the small change of diplomacy, a man of his word. But in the bigger issues, the policy of a king who looked upon diplomacy as the handmaid of war, as a sort of incessant campaign, was inevitably dishonest in spirit, however punctilious it might be in form.

Louis himself fixed the agenda for meetings of the Council, prepared and sometimes even worded his diplomatic correspondence, and always of course had the last word. He often wrote to his ambassadors without reference to his foreign minister and he would occasionally negotiate secretly behind his back, on some dynastic or family matter, or through another minister, as in the peace talks of 1708. But he was seldom irresponsible in the face of expert advice and he listened patiently to opinions. The '*secret du roi*' did not, as in Louis XV's time, confound official diplomacy. The king was careful too to get a memorandum from his ministers before giving audience to a foreign ambassador, advising him what subjects to avoid; on such occasions he was at his best, discreet and careful not to commit his foreign minister to an impossible course. He in his turn had many opportunities of influencing decisions. Such men as Lionne, Pomponne, Colbert de Croissy and Torcy were all experienced diplomats, professionals who knew the toils and tricks of negotiation, and they were in touch with the man on the spot. Under them they had no formal establishment, only a handful of cypher clerks and interpreters. But abroad the coverage was ambitious and far beyond the scale of any other power. By 1685 there were permanent embassies in all the more important capitals, special missions or ministers-resident in such places as Heidelberg, Hamburg and Genoa, and consuls, to represent French trading interests, mostly in the Levant.

The king's ambassadors

Louis drew largely, but not exclusively, upon the *noblesse* to serve him in diplomacy, for he believed them to be more capable of sustaining his reputation abroad by their style of living. A large part of diplomacy was an understanding of the conventions of polite society, and nobles were always preferred for Rome, Madrid and London. But a *bourgeois* served for Venice or The Hague. He tried to avoid using churchmen, since he suspected their equivocal loyalty to two masters. An ambassador was always provided with written instructions, which were not only a statement of policy but a full account of political conditions in the country, with comments on the character of its leading figures. The duc d'Aumont, on his appointment as ambassador to London, was given this advice: 'The English constitution is such that it is not regarded as offensive by the court of King James to have relations with the opposition. The duc d'Aumont need not therefore reject the society of the Whigs.' The ambassador was expected by Louis to be a constant advertisement for the faith and principles of his master. The king had observers to see whether his ambassadors attended Mass regularly, and even how they behaved there. Barrillon, d'Aumont's successor, was severely rebuked for carelessness in this respect in 1686, when Louis was closely supporting James's Catholic policy.

French diplomacy was served by some eminent men. We learn this from the despatches and *mémoires* of the time; Talleyrand, a good judge, testified to it a century later. The standard set by François de Callières, in his manual on diplomatic method published in 1716, was a high one; but there is no reason to suppose that it was meaningless. Callières was the son of a general, who served first as a secret agent, then as envoy in the Netherlands, Germany and Poland, then as representative of France at Ryswick. He abhorred the use of deceit in diplomacy, believing that, like a banker, the good diplomat should build up credit by inspiring trust. A lie 'may confer success today, but will create an atmosphere of suspicion which will make further success tomorrow impossible'; and again: 'the secret of negotiation is to harmonise the real interests of the powers concerned'. The ideal diplomat should be 'quick, resourceful, a good listener, courteous and agreeable. . . he should study history and memoirs, be acquainted with foreign institutions and habits, and be able to tell in any country where the real sovereignty lies'.

A diplomat's apologia must be treated with caution; he is trained to make a case and to destroy the pretensions of a rival's case. Callières would not be taken in entirely by his own phrases, any more than he would by the lofty language of the preamble to Westphalia; 'let there be for the salvation of the Christian republic a Christian peace, and a true and sincere friendship between the contracting parties'. He was one instrument of a *politique d'aventure* which destroyed a 'Christian peace' several times over. French diplomacy enjoyed its greatest successes at the great congresses (there were nine of them in Europe in Louis XIV's reign), and yet Callières himself admitted that these were often a façade. In times of necessity etiquette could be laid aside, as when Torcy met the Dutch in a farmhouse. Before Utrecht, the real business was enacted privately between Torcy and Bolingbroke. Nor were all ambassadors as intelligent as his model required. France had serious failures, notably in Poland, where Louis XIV was misled as to the real intentions of John Sobieski right up to the time of his famous march to Vienna to save the Hapsburgs. But it is not always easy to distinguish between the misjudgments of the ambassador and the myopia of Versailles. The routine attachment of France to the Swedish alliance inherited from Richelieu, for example, cramped the style of their diplomats in Germany. Then, in 1681, the seizure of the Duchy of Deux-Ponts, due to revert to the king of Sweden, wantonly alienated the ally upon whom such care and expense had been lavished. In one respect French ambassadors were well served: 'France', a Dutchman wrote in 1671, 'gives here and everywhere, buys what she cannot conquer.' But there was a serious lack to set against this: Richelieu had employed squads of writers to publicise his policy abroad but Louis neglected to do so. This was the great age of pamphleteers, and issues were not lacking: the Huguenot question, the Turkish menace, the liberties of Germany. Most of the publications of the time were anti-French, many coming from the presses of Holland, some, after 1685, from Huguenots. As defeats grew, and gold dwindled at the end of the reign the inadequacy of French propaganda proved serious.

Diplomacy was not disinterested, nor could it be; for all the talk of 'the balance of power' which was becoming fashionable as a new excuse for enlightened self-interest, it knew nothing of the idea of managing the affairs of Europe for the general good. Granted this, it is still possible to admire French diplomacy. The best of Louis' ambassadors showed an earnest sense of vocation and enjoyed an honourable reputation for being incorruptible, no small thing when it is remembered that part of their job was the payment of *douceurs* to individuals and governments. Torcy so far recognised the importance of this sense of vocation as to project, at the end of the reign, a seminary for young ambassadors where promising young men were to learn international law from Grotius and Pufendorf, and study the diplomatic history of their country. The project was abortive, but the rules of behaviour that guided French diplomats became part of the common stock of international dealings, surviving the rude shocks of Frederick the

Great, of the Revolution, even of Napoleon. The diplomats of the *grand siècle* would have been at home at the Congress of Vienna. They were not the least of the civilising influences of the century in which French replaced Latin as the language of diplomacy.

Government by spectacle

The palace of Versailles came to embody a form of government and court that was widely copied in Europe and admired where it could not be copied. The Emperor of Austria built Schönbrunn in imitation; scores of princelings in Germany planted out miniature Versailles to impress their authority upon their subjects. They were sometimes slavish in their imitation of the details of the palace; one prince, of impeccable morals, installed a nominal mistress in a wing of his palace because this, he thought, is what the great king did. The formal grandeur of Versailles represented an absolutism more pretentious than anything that had preceded it in Europe. The wisdom of posterity has condemned the palace on various grounds: that it was irrelevant to the real needs of France, that it isolated the king from his people, that it was artificial, foreign to the genius of the Frenchman. But to treat the palace as an extravagant whim of the king is to miss the most important point. Saint-Simon, writing late in the reign, might dismiss the whole place as a *folie de grandeur*. The stones burnt his feet in summer, but they saved him sinking into the black mud underneath; numberless springs made the garden damp and unhealthy; it smelled, as the palace smelled, because grandeur was considered more important than plumbing. 'Who could help being repelled and disgusted by the violence done to nature?' he asked. For him, the palace was a monstrosity for the very reason that most of his contemporaries admired it; it spoke of the power of the king, and this in Bossuet's view needed a large and spectacular frame. In his coronation sermon he had offered a prayer: 'May the glorious dignity and the majesty of the palace blaze out, for all to see, the splendid grandeur of the royal power.' If the effusive plea of Bossuet is thought to be untypical, the view of Colbert may be cited in support: 'Your Majesty knows that in default of resounding victories on the field nothing can add a greater glory to princes than buildings, and that all posterity will judge them by those great mansions which they have constructed in their lifetime.' Colbert admittedly was urging upon Louis the reconstruction of the Louvre; his own dream was the rebuilding of the whole capital city. But he thought that prestige was important. He wanted a palace that would provide a setting for a great king, and an opportunity to the artists and craftsmen of France. It was no mean vision.

At Versailles, where the court was finally installed by 1682, Louis practised the art of government by spectacle. Here was the establishment of France, the artificially concentrated centre of government and society. It was the centre of conciliar government as well as the way of life of a privileged aristocracy.

The estate of Versailles had been used by Louis XIII for hunting and seclusion and the 'little house of cards' that he built there was a simple building around whose pleasant gardens spread waste and swamp. In the first decade of the reign Versailles was developed as a country seat where parties could be held, such as the lavish *plaisirs de l'île enchantée* in honour of Louise de la Vallière. The king still then travelled from palace to palace, trailed by the *caravanserai* of courtiers, 'like some queen bee with attendant swarm', to Chambord, Vincennes, Fontainebleau, St. Germain, and when unavoidable, to the Louvre or the Tuileries in Paris. Colbert, in his capacity of *surintendant des bâtiments*, urged him to make the Louvre his principal palace. But Louis persisted in his design of creating a new centre of government away from the narrow streets and smells of Paris. He seems to have felt the need for a clean break with the past, to live in splendid isolation from the political brawls and the domestic discomfort which he remembered from his childhood. The political necessity to end the haphazard customs of an itinerant court and to create a palace to symbolise the new status of monarchy was reinforced by Louis' own taste for splendour. When in his *Mémoires* he reflected upon the value of display as a means of enhancing a monarch's standing, he did not omit architecture, and one note reads: '*Grands Bâtiments, leur magnificence*'.

The palace

When Louis set out to show at Versailles 'what a great king is able to do when he spares nothing to satisfy his wishes', he was very likely inspired by his visit to Fouquet at his palace of Vaux-le-Vicomte, for he employed the great patron's architect, Louis le Vau, his landscape gardener, André le Nôtre, and his painter, Charles le Brun. It was after the peace of Aix-la-Chapelle in 1668 that Louis decided to make Versailles his permanent seat; already by then a prodigious work of landscaping was making the frame for the constructions of Le Vau and Mansard, his chief successor. The eye might travel down long vistas of grass and stone, set with fountains and pools and adorned with sculptury, with here and there little classical temples, to the great canal which stretched to the horizon. All around trees were being planted, some uprooted from far parts of France to be replanted here. The water-works which fed the fountains and drained the marsh were a *chef d'œuvre* of engineering. Le Nôtre brought to perfection the art of gardening as an extension of architecture. His *jardin de l'intelligence* was designed to ease the rude shock of transition from art to nature, from the palace to the world outside, and the wilderness was made to yield a pattern which should reflect an orderly and regulated society. The symmetry of terraces and avenues, clipped yews and grassy walks has an affinity with Colbert's economics, Racine's plays and Bossuet's sermons. Nature was not defeated without loss; workmen died in scores of malarial fever and were carried away in carts to be buried at night so that no one should be disturbed.

The building was a continuous operation, and the pace did not slacken till the last years of the reign. New sculptures came daily to swell the host of amazons, bacchants, tritons and naiads; inside the palace, tapestries and chandeliers, paintings and plaster-work from the workshops of Le Brun. Before the palace itself was completed in 1711, more building was in train—the Trianon, which was to be a retreat for the king from the publicity of his official life; further away, Marly. The latter is unfortunately no more, but we know from engravings that it was a holiday palace; a central square block, flanked by small pavilions for the courtiers; an artificial village where a select few of the court could relax in comparative informality. Louis is said to have blanched when he read the accounts for building presented to him by Mansard and to have destroyed them; the cost for building altogether ran at about five million *livres* a year.

The first château of 1668 was Le Vau's masterpiece of classical architecture, a three-storeyed façade of twenty-five bays with coupled columns enveloping the Louis Treize château. Le Vau died in 1670 and his work was completed by a pupil, François d'Orbay. The most remarkable addition, the *galerie des glaces*, was the work of Jules Hardouin Mansard, who had already constructed Clagny for Mme de Montespan before he was given charge of the great extension planned by the king to celebrate the peace of

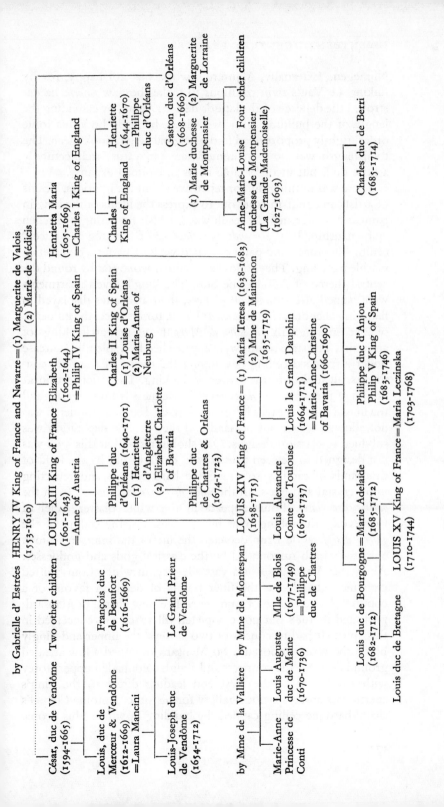

Nijmegen. Externally, Mansard's work was not happy, for by linking Le Vau's twin pavilions to make the new *galerie*, he destroyed the delicacy of the latter's design. Again, by extending the length of the building with two wings, he made Le Vau's Ionic order, rightly proportioned to the original height, look mean. The total length was now an immoderate 550 yards, architecturally a little dull, but incomparable in its disciplined expanse.

There was nothing dull or repetitive about the interiors. Teams of artists and craftsmen set out to express the ideals of the king in paint and plaster and the result was a lavish flowering of French craftsmanship. In the *grands appartements* of the king and queen, ceilings of stucco and paint crowned walls of patterned velvet or marble panelling. They followed a regular iconography round the central theme of Apollo, the Sun. The king's seven apartments were named after the seven planets, their attributes displayed in flattering allegories; in the *salon de Venus*, for instance, the influence of love on kings, in the *salon de Mars* the great warrior kings of antiquity. The state rooms were approached by a splendid staircase under a frescoed ceiling developing the theme of the four continents, all subject to the power of the king. The strict rectilinear design of the *galerie des glaces* saves its richness from vulgarity and the line of mirrors gives it light and grace. Extravagant detail was not allowed to get out of hand and the baroque decoration was subdued to classical designs. One should recall that this *salon* was not designed to be seen primarily in daylight but by the light of thousands of candles softening the hard colours and reflecting upon crystal and glass. In the *salon de guerre* leading off from the *galerie des glaces*, Louis appears in the white plaster panel of Coysevox, triumphing over his enemies. On the ceiling of the *galerie des glaces*, le Brun depicted the life of the king, in Roman emperor's garb surrounded by the classical gods and goddesses. Altogether Versailles was a vast allegory, in which Louis' gifted craftsmen abandoned the finer points of detail in favour of a comprehensive image of grandeur. The new chapel of Mansard, projected in 1688 but not completed till 1710, was conceived in this spirit. It had to consist of two storeys, the upper and kingly being the more important. So Mansard designed a low arcaded ground floor for the courtiers and a high colonnaded upper storey with royal pew at the west end leading direct to the king's apartments and a spacious gallery for his suite. Antoine Coypel's richly baroque ceiling capped the building in which 'this people

seemed to worship the prince and the prince to worship God'
(La Bruyère).

Pluribus nec impar

Louis regarded Versailles as his own achievement, and he loved
the place. He used to conduct tours of distinguished visitors
round the grounds and wrote a short guide-book to the gardens,
where the main beds were changed every day so that they glowed
with colour, even in winter. He was tireless in inspecting the plans
for new work, supervising the decorators and plasterers and
showing off its points to visitors who were confronted everywhere
by Louis in some edifying or strenuous guise. Here he was, as
seen by Mignard, presiding over the siege of Maastricht, on a
prancing horse *à la Romaine*, there resting in Coypel's sculpture,
after his labours at Nijmegen. The theme of all the artists was
Louis, not as an institution but as a person. Locke noticed when
he visited the Gobelins that 'in every piece Louis le Grand was the
hero and the rest the marl of some conquest . . . one, his making a
league with the Swiss, where he lays his hand on the book to
swear the article, and the Swiss ambassador in a submissive pos-
ture, with his hat off'. Apollo, the Sun, was everywhere, the very
statues being placed, not haphazard, but in relation to that deity.
Over the doors the words *Pluribus nec impar* engraved the spirit
of the building. Louis himself was the soul of the palace, whose life
was shaped into a strict ritual in which every act was designed to
emphasise him. Versailles was a temple of the cult of royalty and
those who attended had to conform to a discipline which was not
unlike a religious observance in its minute and ordered detail.

From eight o'clock when the duty valet drew aside the curtains
of the king's great bed—'Sire, it is time'—the king ceased to be a
private person; he was on parade. His court entered in waves,
controlled by the strictest rules of precedence; preceded by the
première entrée of the royal doctor and the bedroom attendants.
To wait upon the king in the first intimate moments of the day, to
watch him rubbed down with rose water and spirits of wine,
shaved and dressed, was the privilege of the highest in the land.
In a typical year, 1687, the Great Chamberlain, whose duty was to
drape the dressing-gown round the king, was the duc de Bouillon,
the Grand Master of the Wardrobe who pulled on his breeches
was the duc de la Rochefoucauld, and further dukes were required

to take off his nightshirt and put on his slippers. Some of his family were expected to be present and Monsieur himself might put on his shirt. These rare moments were a recognised time for confidential requests; when one was being made the rest would retire to a discreet distance. On the death of his father, Saint-Simon, wishing to be granted his father's title, arranged that Beauvillier acting gentleman of the bedchamber, should make representations for him. Beauvillier 'assured me of much good feeling on the part of the princes and promised that when he drew the king's curtains, he would ask the king to grant it'. Gradually the court entered, passing ushers who asked the name and qualification of unknown persons, bowed deeply and grouped outside the balustrade to watch the king receive the Holy Water, say his prayers, put on his peruke and tie his cravat. He would announce his plans for the day, 'in order that everyone might know to a quarter of an hour what the king was to do'. He might then disappear into a small study, for a time, to examine, perhaps, designs presented to him by Le Nôtre or Mansard, or some other private business. Before Mass, came one of these long slow processions along the gallery which counted so much in the courtier's day. Then the king could be observed in his 'terrifying majesty', equable but remote, smiling often but never laughing. Since the king usually reserved private audience for his ministers, ambassadors returned from missions and generals from campaign might be amongst the press of courtiers, competing for a royal glance, murmuring petitions or just gossiping. The king gave little away. 'I will see' had to satisfy most suitors, or worse, 'I do not know him', meaning that this unregarded person did not attend the court. If he looked irritated or flustered, courtiers knew that there was some major crisis of state. The Mass was a central part of the rite and it was rarely missed: a chance for pious reflection or further scrutiny and gossip.

The rest of the morning, unless it were Friday when his confessor claimed him, was spent in Council with his ministers. The king never flinched from this labour. All that the courtier would see of the workings of the state would be the entry and exit of ministers and secretaries, and it was a solecism for him even to talk about politics. The line between business and pleasure which the king passed so easily was, for the courtier, an emphatic barrier, for the price of his privileged lodging was exclusion from the affairs of the state. If he were lucky, however, he might catch a glimpse of his sovereign at dinner, when Louis ate prodigiously, usually alone and in silence broken only by a few words between courses to some prince or Cardinal standing behind his chair if he wished to confer some special favour.

The afternoon might be spent in hunting or in driving out; or the king might just walk in the gardens and inspect the new works, hat in hand, followed always by droves of courtiers, panting, for the pace was brisk. Usually further business followed, hearing the reports of ministers, signing despatches. In the evening there would be *appartements*, which were assemblies of the whole court in the series of *salons* that lay between the *galerie des glaces* and the Chapel gallery, where they danced or whiled away the hours at the gaming tables. Or there might be a play or concert. At ten, supper was served for the court at separate tables, the king supping in state with 'the sons, daughters, grandsons and granddaughters of France'. The long day ended as it had begun, with a sort of bedroom masque in the shape of the *couchée* when the minute procedure of the morning was re-enacted in reverse. While the high officers of the household undressed their master, the king's candlestick was solemnly passed from the hands of the king's chaplain to the great nobleman privileged to hold it for the night. These last obsequies, and the coveted right of the candlestick, symbolise the whole process by which the aristocracy was tamed. Louis understood perfectly the art of putting a premium on empty favours. Dealing from an endless fund of honorific trifles, he played a game in which he could hardly lose. A diplomatic incident was created when the candlestick was given to an English ambassador, the Earl of Portland, who did not fully appreciate the honour conferred upon him.

It has been pointed out that the scrupulous etiquette of Versailles, so different from the simplicity and *bonhomie* of the court of Louis XIII, where the king might be heard enjoying a slanging match with a groom, was Spanish in character and origin, like the king. This is only partly true. It was also the adaptation by the court of the ideals of the *salons* of Paris, where under the patronage of women like the marquise de Rambouillet, a cult of civility was established with firm rules about deportment and conversation. This was not as absurd as the pretentious antics of Molière's *Précieuses Ridicules* indicate. The pattern of elegance established was largely a feminine one, but its politenesses were not amiss in an age of crude ostentation. Its conventions were not all bad; for instance, the social prestige of men of letters, the elevation of women. But Versailles added rules of its own, for in place of the hostess of the *salon* stood a more exacting deity, and 'the awe which his presence inspired imposed silence and a sense of fear'. Nor was the purpose remotely cultural. The *salon* was concerned with the mind, but the art of the courtier is to be correct in externals; every word and gesture must emphasise his esoteric and separate status. The *salon* even at its silliest had a spontaneity which was wholly missing from the punctilious ceremonial of the court.

The courtier's life

Even though it was such a rich display of French art and technical skill, Versailles was an exotic and isolated society. Its life was one of sustained pretence. While, on the king's part, the ritual served the ends of the state, the round of flattery and dependence was necessary to the nobility because of their economic plight. By Louis XIV's time, the great nobility were no longer in a position to remain independent, or aloof from the crown. The Fronde had been the last occasion when great men practised blackmail on the king from their provincial estates; the bastard feudalism which persisted till then in a France of hereditary governorships and small private armies was no more. 'The time is very different now from when a son of the king of France would retire mutinous from the court and when one imagined, once he was three leagues from Paris, that the realm was threatened and in peril; everyone armed for his faction and the rebels raised their masks.' In these words the ambassador of Savoy inferred that Monsieur would be very ill-advised to leave the court in a huff. Louis was able to insist upon the nobility coming to court; only the unambitious, the philosopher, the *hobereau* would stay in the country for preference. Exile to one's estates was a dreaded punishment for, away from the fountain of honour, a man was worse than poor, 'he was ridiculous'. 'The masterpiece of Louis XIV, the complement of the system of Richelieu,' wrote Stendhal, 'was to create this *ennui* of exile.' There had always been a gulf between the capital and the provinces. Politically this was less dangerous, in the long run, than the new gulf that now opened up between the *élite* of the court and the *élite* of Paris, where *bourgeois* wealth and professional intelligence was the ground of a separate but flourishing culture.

So the nobleman was attracted to court; the life offered moments of luxury and amusement. More important, it offered a livelihood. For caught first by the effects of inflation upon static rents, then by the long agricultural depression, hampered by the caste prejudice against commerce and finance, he had the choice between a restricted life on his estates, the church, and a career in the king's service—soldier, diplomat or plain courtier. For most, the profession of arms brought more honour than gain; the price of a commission was seldom recouped and it was a point of pride to have an expensive equipage. This was the vicious circle of their existence. They came to court because all favours came from the king, in the form of commissions, sinecures and pensions, but the gambling and the competitive spending of the court might ruin them without recompense. The greatest were not exempt; the duc de la Rochefoucauld, author of the *Maximes*, was one of many who were pursued by their creditors and forced to lean upon some *bourgeois* financier, such as Gourville. Convention made the courtier play for high stakes when he gambled, and the king seems to have encouraged this. This prompts the question: did the king deliberately set out to ruin the old aristocracy as has been alleged? The most that can be said is that it suited him that they should be financially dependent, but not so bereft as to be unable to fulfil the social duties of their station. These Louis did not think unimportant, for no one was more sensible than he of the privileges and distinctions of rank.

There were social pressures at court for which the king cannot be held responsible, the toll of fashion, the necessity of being up to date in the world's centre of fashion and luxury goods. A nightmare of economic insecurity hung around the professional courtier, from daybreak in his squalid lodging through the anxious day in surroundings of gilt and profusion, hoping for some tit-bit of royal favour, to the night at cards. What a contrast between the heroic spirit of the building and the mean shifts of so many of its inmates, doomed to a life of licensed beggary! The Icarus who flew too near the sun could only hope to save himself and his family by a *mésalliance*, like Mme de Sévigné's grandson, married off to the daughter of a tax-farmer who promptly paid off half the family's debts. The fact that these *mésalliances* were becoming common in Louis' reign is evidence of the straits of the noble class. Reports made by the *intendants* for Colbert show that there was general poverty amongst the nobility and that the expensive life at court was the main cause of their debts. (He knew something of this, for all his daughters married dukes) At the foot of the ladder were the *gentilshommes indigents* who figure in the Treasury accounts as receiving grants of 15 or 20 *livres* to keep them alive. These pensioners may have been only the 'submerged tenth' of the court, but they represent an element in the great pretence, the hollow life of which a veteran spoke, advising a newcomer: 'speak well of everyone, ask for everything that falls vacant and sit down when you can!'

The values of the court can be seen in the waspish writings of Saint-Simon, who relieved his feelings in a full record of the daily scene. His journal is invaluable because he was both involved and detached; involved as a grandee whose life was centred upon the maintenance of his own rights as *duc et pair*, but detached as an artist in words and as a caustic critic who saw too clearly the disaster of his class. He drained the cup of social distinction to its dregs. He occupied one of the best garrets in a palace of draughts and discomforts; he was near to the king and he sometimes held the candlestick. He could be nowhere but at court. He might bite delicately at the hand that fed him (he thought Louis an 'ordinary man' though he conceded his remarkable politeness) and he might resent the *bourgeois* ministers who had the real power. But he swallowed the system whole, for he had no option. Sharpening his wits and his quill upon the drawing-room war of precedence, he well represents the collapse of the *noblesse de l'épée*. It mattered greatly to Saint-Simon who should have had the right of the *pour*, what ladies should be allowed to sit on *tabourets*. His was the inside view; from visitors one gets more naïve impressions. The sensible Mme de Sévigné was quite overcome by the spectacle. She conveys something of the enchantment that Versailles had for the uninitiated: 'all is great, all is magnificent, music and dancing are perfection. . . . But what pleases me most is to live for four hours in the presence of the sovereign, to be in his pleasures and he in ours; it is enough to content an entire realm which passionately loves to see its master.' Mme de la Fayette was more critical: 'always the same pleasures, always at the same time and always with the same people'. Mme de Maintenon, who was not one of nature's courtiers, made no pretence of her distaste for its boredom, the constraint and the futility of the daily round. There can be no doubt that, as an entertainment, court life deteriorated in the later years of the reign. But, even in the gayest years of Louis' youth, for the professional courtier it was always a serious business.

The theory of absolutism

The seventeenth century, except notably in England and Holland, witnessed a pronounced movement towards the strengthening of monarchic authority. Especially was this true of France where, by 1661, the Bourbons had achieved more than anyone could have thought possible in the last years of the Valois. The States-General had not been summoned again since 1614. The provincial governorship was no longer hereditary and the province was beginning to take notice of the mandates of the central government. Richelieu's successful campaign against the habit of duelling had been only one, spectacular, part of a gradual domestication of the nobility. The Peace of Alais had destroyed the military strength of the Huguenot state within the state; with it also the temptation of an aristocratic resistance movement. The Fronde had been a serious danger chiefly because of the leadership of great soldiers, the special circumstances of a long minority and the complication of war with Spain. But it was a minority movement and the realm did not disintegrate. Its follies even served the purpose of the crown by revealing the menace of social disorder and the weakness of the frontiers when the government failed to assert its will. In the sixteenth century the aristocracy had been most dangerous to the crown when it dressed up its opposition in 'constitutional' forms. The failure of its leaders in the Fronde to come to any working agreement with the leaders of *Parlement* showed how hollow these forms had become.

The wide acceptance of the principles of absolute monarchy clearly owed a great deal to the reaction of responsible and propertied interests against the disorders of the Fronde. The crown was supported as the guarantor of good order. But the emotional character of this support requires further explanation.

In the dawn of Louis XIV's personal rule there was an upsurge of loyalty to the crown which went deeper than the professional hyperbole of courtiers and clerics; nor was it aroused only by the personal qualities of the young king. Louis XIV aroused a spirit of devotion which was as old as the Capetian monarchy, as the fitting representative of a long dynasty of protectors. Louis himself subscribed to the traditional view which he did so much to destroy: 'there are nations in which the king's majesty largely consists in not letting himself be seen . . . but that is not the way with the French. . . . If there has been any unusual feature of our monarchy it has been the free and unlimited access of subjects to their prince. There is equality of justice between him and them and that keeps them together, so to speak, in sweet and open companionship.'

The claims of political theorists tend to rationalise an existing situation; they thus provide a useful commentary upon the facts of political power. As one turns to Locke for comment upon the situation in England after the Glorious Revolution, so one must turn to Bossuet, the high priest of the *ancien régime*, for a fuller picture of absolutism in Louis XIV's France. He was in many ways the representative Frenchman of his time. Even in his loftiest periods he never quite lost the common touch. The grandeur of his mind and prose should not be allowed to conceal the fact that he was primarily concerned with proving and improving upon a case which most of his fellow-countrymen believed to be true— the superiority of absolute monarchy over all other systems. It had been possible for a book published in 1611 to win approval for a programme of sovereignty for the people, based upon a contract between people and ruler and demanding power for the States-General. Such a book would have been suppressed instantly in 1661; but it is hard to imagine anyone even wanting to write it. Even where, as in the work of the Englishman Hobbes, a rational rather than theological approach was adopted, an absolute government emerged as the ideal. Hobbes' *Leviathan* presented a strong case for the concentration of sovereignty in the hands of one paramount authority. It had run to five editions by 1660 and even Bossuet found it serviceable. But the great churchman based his argument for Louis XIV's unlimited authority upon the special tradition of the French monarchy and the letter of Holy Writ.

Quod Principi placet, legis vigorem habet. If this maxim of the Roman Law be contrasted with the ideas of those lawyers in England who were at such pains to emphasise the sovereignty of the Common Law over the will of the king, it can be seen how important it was for France that the principal influence upon her lawyers was that of the Roman codes. In the long struggle between the crown and the Papacy, the lawyers had supported the crown and in so doing had stressed and clarified its sovereign rights. From the feudal complex of rights and duties a new view of royal authority had emerged: one that was within the borders of France indivisible. The clergy needed some good reason for according this specially independent status to the king and found it in the formula expressed by André Duchesne: 'the kings of France are so pleasing to God that He chose them to become His lieutenants upon earth'.

The origins of the theory of Divine Right can thus be found in the development of Gallicanism. But it owed its elaboration, in the favourable climate of opinion following the succession of Louis XIV, to the inspired exposition of Bossuet. He was convinced of the excellence of the polity in which he held so high a place: 'France can rightly boast of the finest political constitution that is possible', and again: 'What need is there to speak of the most Christian House of France . . . which alone and in all ages can consider itself, after 700 years, an established monarchy . . . the most illustrious realm there ever was on earth in the sight of God or man'. Patriotism to him was a sacred duty. He began his great polemic against the Protestants, *Histoire des Variations*, with a reproach for their sin of rebellion against their native land and against the principle of unity. This unity seemed to him to be embodied in the person of the king. 'Under Louis XIV, France learned to know herself.' Bossuet's phrase, uttered at the height of the reign, expresses the mood and expectation of his time. He saw France revealed in Louis, with all her pent-up capacity for greatness, a chosen people in a divided and heretical world. Mediaeval thinkers had held that power came from God but that it could be transmitted through the people. Such a view, as the Religious Wars had shown, invited resistance and could even be held to justify tyrannicide. In Bossuet's view, authority came direct from God and without intermediary. He did not reason, like the Renaissance thinkers, from Roman Law or classical precedent, or, like Machiavelli, from pure expediency. His *Politique tirée de l'Écriture Sainte* is grounded upon the laws, prophets and patriarchs of the Old Testament; he considered that this was verbally inspired and that it provided valid rules for statesman and lawgiver alike. The wide study of Hebrew and the knowledge of Jewish history had prepared people to accept the Monarch who was Divinely appointed to be God's instrument upon earth as the highest possible form of human government. Bossuet took this line of thought to its furthest extension: The royal throne was 'the very throne of God'. This was the sense of his famous exclamation, in a sermon preached before the king of Palm Sunday 1662: '*Vous êtes Dieu*'. It followed that resistance to a Superior power thus established by God was resistance to God; to question the will of the hereditary king was to commit a form of blasphemy.

On the face of it, the theory of Divine Right, as propounded by Bossuet and accepted by the king, left Louis free to believe that his power was sacred and unlimited. This seems to be borne out by the following passage in the *Mémoires* he composed for the Dauphin: 'However bad the king may be, the revolt of his subjects is always criminal. He who has given kings to men has required that they should be respected as his lieutenants, reserving to Himself alone the right to examine their conduct. It is His will that he who is born a subject should obey without question.' There could be no prouder statement of sovereign right; yet there remains one qualification, in the shape of his responsibility to God. In an age which was very conscious of the immanence of God, this moral obligation was much more than an empty form of words. Louis had a constant and lively sense of his moral responsibility as a ruler. The idea of rule as a sacred trust was central to his whole philosophy. It may be thought that the notion of responsibility to God alone put too great a strain upon the conscience of one man, and his confessor. But its real significance lies in the way in which it opened the way to the use of the state's authority. Louis identified sovereignty with complete ownership. He stated in his *Mémoires*: 'Kings are absolute lords and have by natural right the complete and free disposition of all goods, both of church and people, to use them according to the needs of their state.' This concept was given the force of law by an edict of 1692, in which he declared as an old-established crown right, the ultimate ownership of all property, of which subjects 'have only usufruct'. Second, it was possible for the king, in the name of '*raison d'état*', itself 'the first of laws', to violate the fundamental laws of his country. This was done, for instance, in 1714, when Louis obtained a decree qualifying his bastard offspring for the succession, in case of the legitimate line dying out.

Divine Right can be seen as a blank cheque upon which the king could write almost as he pleased. But one should not forget the tenacity of custom and tradition. When we consider what Louis might have done we may 'stand astonished' at his moderation. For Louis XIV never became the Oriental despot of hostile propaganda. He stood within the frame of custom, for the common good as he saw it, above the separate interests of class, province or *parlement*.

Métier du roi

The theory behind this authoritarian government was imposing; its claims were exalted. How did it work in practice? Since its unity resided in the person and will of the king, analysis must start with him. And Louis was in no doubt about the crucial importance of his role. It was 'To be informed about everything; listening to the least of my subjects; knowing always the number and quality of my troops and the state of the fortresses; giving my orders without respite for all their necessities; treating immediately with foreign envoys; receiving and reading despatches; composing one of the replies myself and giving the Secretaries the substance of the others; controlling the receipts and expenditures of my realm; requiring prompt reports from those that I put in important positions; keeping my business as secret as any other has done before me; distributing my favours by my own judgment and, if I do not deceive myself, keeping those who serve me, although loaded with benefits for themselves and their families, in a modest station far removed from the rank and power of first ministers'. Elsewhere he instructed his son that it was necessary 'to have one's eyes open upon the whole world, to learn every hour news from all the provinces and all the nations, the secrets of every court, the humours and weaknesses of all princes and foreign ministers'. His intention was that the king should be the brain as well as the heart of the country and to this end he was prepared to work as few kings had worked before. He valued a consistent routine before everything else; he was deliberate and thorough in everything that he did. 'Give me an almanack and a watch,' wrote Saint-Simon, 'and I will tell you what the king is doing even if I am 300 leagues away.' Colbert tells us that he worked for six to eight hours a day; in busy times he might see his ministers three times a day. Bishop Burnet, who first saw Louis XIV in 1663, admired the king for his passion for work, finding him 'diligent in his own counsels and regular in the despatch of his affairs', though he noticed already an inclination to view himself as more than mere mortal—which established the young historian of the Reformation in his 'love of law and liberty'. It was typical of Louis' approach that, in order to be able to read diplomatic documents, in the early years of the reign, he would shut himself up to study Latin. In 1662 the Dutch ambassador noted that the king was ponderiug the old maxims which had governed French foreign policy since the time of Henry IV and 'that he spoke so shrewdly and to the point that one could not help being struck by it'. Hugues de Lionne, Louis' foreign minister, wrote in a confidential letter, that he took pleasure in giving himself entirely to business, and described a typical session with his master. The minister read out some secret despatches and Louis conveyed to him his 'feelings and intentions as to the reply, on which I work in his presence, His Majesty correcting me when it did not conform exactly to his ideas'. Whatever their private reservations, his ministers knew that they must accept his direction. Obedience must be unqualified, as is shown by a cutting rebuke delivered to an unfortunate functionary in 1682: 'As the orders that I give are always prepared with my consent, I desire that they be interpreted literally and carried out without demur.'

The general chorus of approval was loud enough to flatter away any misgiving that he may have felt. A typical comment was: 'Your Majesty has need neither of masters nor directors. God has inspired you with the science of kingship.' But Louis had enough of the *bon sens* on which he prided himself not to be misled into believing that the *métier du roi* could be achieved without pains. Instinct, he knew, was no substitute for method and reason. And long after the timidity, to which he confessed in his *Mémoires*, had passed, he was circumspect in his judgments. The Cardinal's legacy was an immense private fund of prudence which tempered a personality by nature ingenuous. From the minister who had always looked on French affairs with the detachment of the diplomat and the foreigner, Louis had learned the diplomatic arts: subtlety in small things, graceful pretence, the valuation of men.

Was Louis anything more than competent? Did his infinite capacity for taking pains amount to genius? Perhaps the most balanced answer to these questions is contained in the account of Ezechiel Spanheim, the Elector of Brandenburg's envoy, writing in 1690. He spoke of his making an art of reigning less by science and by reflection than by method and habit and concluded: 'despite the extravagant eulogies of his panegyrists, he is not one of those minds of the first order who sees, who penetrates, who resolves, who undertakes everything on his own initiative. . . . He is content to know the surface of affairs without examining them sufficiently, and prone therefore to be prejudiced by people whom he trusts and whom he believes to be in some degree instructed.' Louis XIV was not another Richelieu. Even if he were, in Lord Acton's generous phrase, 'the ablest man born on the steps of a throne', it would be unreasonable not to expect him to lean heavily upon the expert advice of his ministers. Unfortunately the convention that the king ordered everything and his own concern for every detail made his ministers cautious. The work of two great ministers, Colbert and Louvois, concealed what became more obvious as the reign proceeded: this system did not encourage administrative initiative or plain speaking and could only be fully efficient under a ruler of great intellect and fine judgment. Louis' gift for the ordering of detail would have made him a good staff officer while his tact and his shrewdness would have served him well as an ambassador. As a king he was always impressive, sometimes heroic, but he was also to show faults which the system could not fail to exaggerate. In his concern for detail and for uniformity, he tended to lose sight of bigger interests. For all his shrewdness, he sometimes allowed prejudice to affect political decisions; *amour propre* played too great a part in the formulation of policy. This Spanheim saw: 'Jealous to the last degree of his authority, sensitive beyond measure to what affected or wounded it, he let himself be drawn easily into embracing advice given and measures taken to sustain it.'

Conciliar government

Louis' relations with his ministers rested upon two assumptions: first, that it was recognised that the king's word, literally interpreted, was law; second, the nobility, psychologically unfitted for the routines and loyalties of bureaucracy, were debarred from the key positions in the government. The crown could not simply ignore the claim of the great nobles to be the natural counsellors of the king. Louis' however, took the work of the Cardinals to its natural conclusion by evolving from the royal council, the *conseil d'état du roi*, which was still in form a single body on which the nobility might claim to be represented, separate small bodies with specialised functions. The change was considerable; in 1653 there were 24 persons in the *conseil d'état*, in 1661 only 3. The new system had several advantages: the specialist opinion and expertise of the professional administrator carried the greatest weight in the small council; it was flexible and could be convened easily; its members could be easily controlled, since they attended not by right but by individual summons to each meeting; it was unlikely therefore to consolidate itself into an institution with awkward traditions and vested interests. Although the professional element, for instance the *contrôleur général* in the *conseil des finances* or the Chancellor in the *conseil des dépêches*, was constantly present, the will of the king remained supreme.

Contemporaries seem to have accepted the idea that Louis, in this way, *was* the state, even if Louis himself never made that famous claim. Bossuet said 'all the state is in him', and the Huguenot pamphlet, *Soupirs de la France esclave*, attacked him on the same grounds: 'the king has taken the place of the state'. Such words seem to imply that the king controlled all. But it is legitimate to ask what such control amounted to. Much of the work of the councils was merely routine, and the acceptance, not the ordering of events. When the king, 'checked' the financial register read to him by the *contrôleur général* at the monthly audit, he enumerated the simple syllable: *bon*. It would have made little difference if he had not attended such meetings. As government became more specialised and more complex, an increasingly wide field developed in which the king's authority was no more than nominal.

The pattern of development in the constitution is not absolutely straightforward. In the early year Louis experimented towards the system which finally suited him. His task was to fit the new conciliar model into the discredited shell of aristocratic government without sacrificing appearances too much and causing dislocation and offence. Certain features of this—*la mécanique* of Saint-Simon's patronising phrase—were plain from the start and remained constant. A distinction can be made between councils concerned with government in the sense of high matters of policy and councils concerned with justice and administration. Of the former sort there were three, all of which the king would attend in person: the *conseil d'état*, the *conseil des dépêches* and the *conseil des finances*.

The *conseil d'état*, also variously called *conseil d'en haut*, because it was usually held on the upper floor of Versailles, near the king's apartments, or the *conseil secret* or just the *conseil*; each of these names reflects its prime importance. It consisted of four or five 'Ministers of State', who would usually include the Secretaries of State for Foreign Affairs, the Army and the Navy, and the *contrôleur général*. (The two latter were for some time the same person.) In addition one or two important 'outsiders' might be present. Turenne for instance, by virtue of his great experience, might be called in for advice on some military matter. Condé on the other hand was specifically excluded, great general and Prince of the Blood though he was, and the doors were barred to most of those great personages whose traditional right it had been to crowd into the royal council when they pleased. Even the king's brother was excluded, the poor man being doomed to trail ineffectively in the wake of the jealous king, a power only in the world of fashion. The *conseil d'état* dealt with all the big matters of state, but it concentrated on foreign affairs, holding normally three long sessions a week. Its discussions were secret and no official record has survived. Here, with his inner circle of ministers, Louis fashioned his policies for over fifty years.

The *conseil des dépêches* supervised the machinery of government, dealing with 'despatches from all parts of the kingdom'. Its business was varied and often humdrum; Louis found attendance tiresome. The Chancellor was joined in this council by those secretaries of state who did not hold the rank of minister and by one or two legal advisers, 'Councillors of State'. It spent much of its time considering the reports of the *intendants*, the men who wrestled in the provinces to apply the royal will. The other principal body, the *conseil des finances* was created in 1661 to replace the great office of *surintendant des finances*, last wielded by Fouquet. It met weekly and dealt with all questions of taxation and finance. For twenty years it was dominated by the towering genius of Colbert. With him and his successors as *contrôleur général* sat the Chancellor, two *intendants des finances*, an official known as the *chef du conseil des finances* and two Councillors of State. Beyond these three, on the perimeter of government, was the *conseil d'état privé*, a court of judicial appeal. Its title suggests a comparison with the English Privy Council, but they have little in common. It was a survival in that the nobles retained the right to sit with ministers and secretaries; but in fact the work was done by permanent 'councillors', after 1673 a statutory thirty in number, most of whom were drawn from the hereditary *officier* and lawyer class.

20 THE STRENGTH AND LIMITATIONS OF GOVERNMENT

The intendant

The new forms of centralised monarchy did not take the place of existing institutions; these were superseded or by-passed rather than destroyed outright. The States-General might easily have been given formal sentence of death, for its name still suggested the principle of consultation, even if it had not met since 1614; but it was allowed to survive, to play one last part before the end of the next century. The rights of *Parlement* were reduced till they were meaningless. In 1641, it had been forced to accept an edict forbidding the sovereign courts to consider affairs of state without special command of the king. The crown returned to this position after the Fronde; in 1654 the *conseil d'état* was recognised as the *premier compagnie du royaume*, a title to which *Parlement* had formerly aspired. In the provinces the *intendants* took over much of the former work of *parlements*. Finally, in 1673, letters patent of Louis XIV announced that the *Parlement* of Paris should make representations only *after* the edict had been registered. *Parlement* was entirely submissive during the reign of Louis XIV, but it survived to be active again in the regency which followed. The fate of the provincial governor was that of his class as a whole; from dangerous independence, he was transformed into a decorative nonentity. He was appointed not for life but for a three-year stretch and he was kept largely at Versailles while the Lieutenant-General and the *intendant* did his work in the province. His social status was high but his political power was negligible. The towns preserved many of the forms of local government and their fiscal privileges remained valuable. But a strong *intendant* could make his will felt in most towns. With the development of purchase of office, moreover, even the formal election of mayors and councillors was often stopped. The *pays d'état* were allowed to keep their envied privileges of levying their own taxes and paying their share of taxation to the central government in the form of the *don gratuit*, but when they came to negotiate this with the king's agents, they were no longer in a position to refuse his demands as they had been in more boisterous times. Meetings of the Estates of Languedoc might preserve, in their solemn debates, the forms of a parliament; but they were not even allowed to present their grievances before they voted their *don gratuit*. The *assemblée du clergé* was also entitled to pay its tax through the *don gratuit*. But the system by which all important appointments came from the king did not encourage the higher churchmen to display political independence.

The powers which the privileged classes had lost passed to the *intendant*; he was the instrument of the administrative revolution, the king in the province. There is some debate about his origins. The withdrawal of the *intendants* was prominent amongst the demands of *Parlement* in 1648, when Omer Talon, *avocat général*, addressed them upon the subject: 'it is not since the Regency that the *intendants* have been sent into the provinces. It is fifteen years since they were ordained, and for eleven whole years they have been in the provinces.' The *intendant*'s work does not seem to have been very prominent if the *avocat général* thought it necessary to remind his audience of these facts, but his first date, 1633, is of doubtful validity, for the representatives of the *parlements* were complaining about the 'new usage of *intendant de la justice*' in the Assembly of Notables of 1626. They were in fact used occasionally by Henry IV, before Richelieu extended their range of employment. The *trésoriers généraux* and *parlements* seem to have been roused by the developing role of the *intendant*, and the prospect that he would poach upon their preserves of justice and finance. He represented for them the tyranny of the state and there is a propaganda element in their protests. Richelieu's *intendants* were *commissaires*; their commissions were temporary and their instructions were specific. They were given powers of inquest and supervision, but they were not yet properly executive officers of the crown. In special circumstances they might have widespread powers. Barentin, designated *intendant de la justice* with the armies commanded by the comte de Soissons, in Saintonge, Aunis, Poitou and the surrounding provinces, was not confined in his duties to the surveillance of the army, but was necessarily occupied with the army's relations with the civil populations of the provinces through which it was dispersed. Much depended upon the initiative of the individual *intendant* and the position in which he found himself. La Rochelle after 1628 was a special situation and the official here, specifically named '*intendant de la police, justice et des finances*', would have wider authority than most. Richelieu's use of the *intendant* was *ad hoc*; he was concerned to keep the government going in the provinces in any way he could. There is no sign that he envisaged the regular institution of permanent and resident officials which developed in Louis XIV's reign.

It was the natural consequence of the centralising policy of Versailles that its agents in the country should grow more important. But the evolution of the *intendant* was slow and uneven; Béarn did not have one till 1682, Brittany till 1689, though, in the latter province, Pontchartrain had done equivalent work in the capacity of Commissioner of the Estates. Every conquered province was immediately given an *intendant*. 'The *intendant* gives constant intelligence of all things to the court'; he provided, as Locke saw, the information service upon which the government decided its policy. He had to keep a watchful eye upon influential persons in the province, the governor, the bishop, or some recalcitrant landowner. He presided over courts of appeal, and arbitrated in disputes over justice and finance. He was the exponent of Colbertism in his province, with powers to regulate agriculture and manufactures, to supervise markets and the supply of food. He was an indispensable part too of the 'military revolution', with powers to engage and supervise troops, which were of prime importance if his were a frontier province. He supervised many aspects of municipal administration and police, the poor law and problems arising out of epidemics and beggary. One of his more vexatious tasks was the verification and liquidation of communal debts, a matter of rancorous disputes and delays. As finance became the dominant concern of the government, he came to have control over taxation in the province and he was constantly reminded by Versailles that it was his responsibility to see that the *taille* was levied efficiently and fairly. 'Consider this work', wrote Colbert in a circular of 1670, 'as the most important of those which are entrusted to your hands', and in the same strain in 1672: 'it is of the greatest importance that you should have a particular and detailed knowledge of all the *élections* of your *généralité*'. Colbert, who always expected so much of the *intendants*, was always quick too to remind them of the limitations of their powers; they must respect the rights of the *élus*, for instance, and the *cours des aides*. He wished too to restrict the use of *subdélégués*, to whom an *intendant* was allowed to allot some of his work. But the accumulation of duties made some delegation inevitable; after Colbert's death most *intendants* had their *subdélégués* in the larger towns; since these were usually local men, they provided the essential link with the *officiers* of town and province.

In the deteriorating conditions of the later years of the reign, the *intendant* acquired further functions. An edict of 1692 stated that towns had to accept mayors approved by the crown, that is by the *intendant*; a further edict of 1697 gave him the right to inspect local *parlements*. In some provinces he became a kind of welfare officer, founding workhouses and co-operating with the church in the distribution of poor relief. He might have to find takers for new issues of *rentes* and for newly created *offices*. If there were a sizeable population of Huguenots in his province, he would have another pre-occupation, for he was the instrument of Louis' measures of constraint. For *intendants* of the stamp of Bâville, 'king of Languedoc', this was a fine chance to display efficiency and zeal in a cause which lay near to the king's heart. The *intendant* could judge, with two counsellors, cases which arose from the Huguenot legislation, and there was no appeal against sentences, which might range from confiscation of goods to service in the galleys, and even death.

No officials of a government had wielded such powers since the time of the Roman Empire. The post gave scope for men of ability and imagination. Some improved roads, with the forced labour that was available to them from the *corvée*, some improved the posting system of their province, some directed new ventures of town planning. De Muin supervised the rebuilding of the new town and port of Rochefort; Foucault founded a school of hydrography at Caen. They built themselves fine houses and enjoyed some of the influence which had slipped from the hands of the governor, the bishop and the mayor. *Intendants* were sometimes close to the inner government circle, married perhaps to a minister's daughter; an *intendance* was a recognised training for high office and most of Louis' ministers had climbed by this ladder. The conscientious *intendant*'s life had its frustrating side, for he knew at first-hand the limitations of seventeenth century government; the pedantry of provincial *officiers*, the chicanery of the *coq de paroisse*, the insolence of the *hobereau*, the tenacious conservatism of the *métayer*. We learn from the reports of the *intendants* how much, and yet by modern standards how little, the government was able to achieve.

Legal reforms

The confusions of French law were a standing challenge to the centralising state. The Canon Law of the church dominated marriage and related matters, and, at least in theory, business, for usury was still forbidden. Feudalism preserved its own worlds of private and privileged justice. The broad difference between the customary law of the more northerly provinces and the Roman Law of the south covered the variations to be found in four hundred local systems. New problems were being created by the extension of the activities of the state, especially in the field of commerce and manufactures, where changes were already taking place in the conditions of employment and the relation of master and man. This confusion of franchise and authorities was offensive to the rationalising spirit of Colbert, who was convinced that the king's writ would be effective only if there were 'one whole and perfect body of law'. In the pursuit of this ideal, he had one great advantage: the undisputed right of the king to make new law by simple edict alone. In many cases the edict was effective, as for instance that of 1667 which forbade the opening of a new religious establishment without the authorisation of the king. But positive action to improve a system was less satisfactory. The sheer number of edicts condemning the inefficiency or favouritism of local tribunals is witness to the difficulty of exacting even standards of justice from magistrates who might have no qualifications for office beyond family or a long purse.

The *Ordonnance Civile* of 1667 was the joint product of a commission of *avocats* and *maîtres des requêtes* and the critical scrutiny of *parlementaires* under the presidency of Lamoignon; it regulated some matters of civil procedure. The *Ordonnance Criminelle* of 1669 went far to standardise criminal procedure in the conservative spirit of Pussort, Colbert's uncle and a prime force in the work of rationalisation. A minority led by Lamoignon made some liberal proposals which anticipated the views of 'the enlightenment', for providing the accused with means of defence and removing the worst barbarisms, torture and the wheel. They were overborne by Pussort and the majority, who were adamant for the full severities of the law; so the subject was left with scant right or legal protection against the arbitrary will of the state. Other ordinances of the time, the *Ordonnance des Eaux et Forêts* of 1669, the *Code Maritime* of 1672, the *Ordonnance de Commerce* of 1673 and the *Ordonnance de la Marine* of 1680 made important contributions to the administrative law of the country in their specialised fields, but they should be viewed in the context of Colbert's managed economy rather than as reforms in the law. But in the *Code Noir*, produced after Colbert's death in 1685, the influence of Roman Law can be studied, as well as the spreading concern of the paternalist state—in this case for its black slave subjects. These were chattels and not accorded the status of persons; their master's rights however were restricted, for he could not kill or ill-treat them, and colonial *intendants* were given authority to protect their interests. Finally, as was appropriate in the year of the Revocation of the Edict of Nantes, the colonies were debarred to all not of the Roman faith; Protestants were not allowed to worship and Jews publicly expelled.

Police

A significant and novel extension of the powers of the state is to be seen in the institution of a new sort of police. None of the powers of the old institutions of municipality and *bailliage* was abolished. A bewildering complexity of police jurisdiction persisted, as in Normandy for instance, where an *intendant's* report reveals that it was executed in some towns by *lieutenant généraux*, in others by *vicomtes* (*prévôts* elsewhere), and in others by the officers of local *seigneurs*. These officers retained their functions— an important one was the fixing of wine prices. But the new police came at first under the direct control of the *intendant*. Then a new official was evolved, the *lieutenant général de police*, largely upon the instigation of Colbert; by an edict of 1669, it was made a purchaseable office in every town in the country. Needless to say, it was primarily a device to raise money, and the new official was often absorbed by the existing nexus of local government; in Lyon, for instance, the office was promptly bought by the *prévôt des marchands*. In many cases, however, the new man was independent of the existing authorities, and soon found himself in conflict with them. Far the most important of these was the *lieutenant général* in Paris, where two men of unusual ability, La Reynie (1667-97) and d'Argenson (1697-1715), made more of the position than its subordinate status would suggest. The *lieutenant général* took his instructions straight from the secretary of the *maison du roi*, and he was in close touch with the Chancellor, with the *procureur général* and with the *Premier Président*, after the elevation of Harlay to that office. He was sometimes closeted with the king himself, who busied himself in the latter part of his reign with every aspect of police work; a thing that would have astonished his predecessors and which tells us something about the changing character of monarchy. He had under him *commissaires* for the different quarters of the city (purchaseable offices) and some eight hundred sergeants and archers. His responsibilities included the water and food supplies of the city, the regulation of markets, the paving of streets, construction of fountains and of machines for cleaning the streets, fire-fighting, the protection of citizens against crime, prostitution and beggary, and the supervision of the vast *hôpital général*, at once hospital, asylum and prison. La Reynie saw to it that Paris was the best-lit capital city in Europe by means of 6,500 reflecting candle-lanterns. D'Argenson was always ready to intervene personally in riots and disputes, and by his own account, which Voltaire accepted, his door was 'open every day' to the unfortunate and destitute. A special problem for the police in their pursuit of crime was the large number of amateurs—soldiers and the lackeys of great families who swelled the ranks of the underworld. They were expected, too, to keep an eye upon the behaviour of more important persons. A young nobleman, de la Motte Aignan, was warned that if he could not behave himself in church, he would be deported from Paris. Stringent action was taken against notorious gamblers. The king was always paternally interested in the conduct of his well-born subjects, and in 1691 he ordered the lieutenant of police in Poitou to look into the scandalous debauches of the marquis de la Millière, which were distressing his family. Censorship was an important function, the *lieutenant général* being the agent of the government's determination to suppress 'subversive' ideas. He had to watch books printed in France, those as well as imported from abroad. Until about 1680, measures to control opinion by limiting the number of licensed printers and booksellers were successful, but before the end of the reign there was a flourishing market in banned books, from presses in Rouen or Lyon, or smuggled across the frontier. The government was increasingly sensitive about criticism of church and state in the later years of the reign, and Boisguillebert, *lieutenant de police* at Rouen, received a stinging rebuke on one occasion from Pontchartrain for his 'inexcusable' slackness in authorising a work which the Chancellor had found distasteful.

The great inquest

The *grands jours d'Auvergne* demonstrate vividly the lawlessness which existed in parts of France at the beginning of Louis' reign, and the urgent necessity for the installation of permanent *intendants*. This, the most remarkable of a number of similar inquests, was carried out in 1665-6, with a special tribunal of councillors of the *Parlement* of Paris, and the duty of inquiring into the behaviour of the nobility of the Auvergne and neighbouring provinces. Feudal privileges had survived in harsh, sometimes bizarre forms, especially in the remoter parts of Brittany, in the deep south and the border provinces, the new lands of Alsace, the Three Bishoprics, Franche-Comté, and here in the Massif Central. The record of this inquest is a case-book of the misuse of seigneurial rights, and a corrective to any idealised view of an unsophisticated French nobility living peaceably on their estates. Though these cases must have been exceptional they are numerous, and they stand as a shocking indictment of the provincial nobility. Many of those arraigned were found guilty of rape or robbery with violence. Two of the more eccentric cases may be noted. The baron de Sénégés had imposed his own taxes and collected them with a private army, established his own table of weights and measures, used his peasantry as slave labour and, the indictment ends: 'had already committed two or three murders and several ransomings'. Twelve towers on the estates of the marquis de Canillac housed his 'twelve apostles', nameless scoundrels, at whose head the marquis would roam, 'catechising' with sword and stick, burning down peasants' hovels or persuading some luckless traveller to pay him ransom. *Salus provinciarum repressa potentiorum audacia*: the words were inscribed on the medal that commemorated these grim assizes. Louis wished to show such uncouth *hobereaux* that his writ stretched to every corner of his land.

The limitations of government

Everywhere, to all outward appearance, the will of the crown was becoming supreme; no class or institution could offer any effective check to its machinery. It was not the overt resistance of any single element that opposed the work of administrative reform, but the inert force of abuses which time had disguised as custom, the 'order' that was the 'disorder of the state'. It should be remembered, too, that the *rationale* of absolutism, the claims that were made for it and the aims that it pursued were more advanced than the machinery for putting it into practice. France had reached a point along the road which all European states were travelling, when king and statesmen assumed responsibilities vastly greater than their real power. There is always some margin between theory and practice in the most imposing despotisms of modern times; much less did Louis' government, judged by the tests of its ability to secure uniformity, to enforce law, to raise money as it wished, match the lofty pretensions of Versailles. Words like absolutism or centralisation should not mislead us into thinking that this government was in any sense totalitarian. It was in fact closer to the Middle Ages than to the twentieth century and still at heart *seigneurial*; its view that of the great landowner of a complex estate. The king's own ideal was compounded of rights and duties; for the subject the idea of natural rights had not dawned, he was not yet *citoyen*. To king and subject, the sense of obligation to a natural law was still meaningful. The monarch's estate was fenced with moral limitations derived from this deeply felt superior law—whether it be described as divine or natural is immaterial. In practice, his land was so hedged and ditched with privileges, immunities and enclaves of private right, that he was less a free agent than he seemed. The provincialism of France reflected the manner of her growth over the centuries, by conquest and inheritance. Provinces differed in their weights and measures, their law, their taxation system; they might be divided by internal tolls and customs. Independent enclaves of territory persisted, such as Avignon and Orange. There were private jurisdictions, even private armies. The Clermontais, with its 40,000 inhabitants, still belonged to the prince de Condé, who collected and kept its taxes. The Boulonnais produced and officered their own army. Towns such as Marseilles and Bordeaux were virtually autonomous. Buonaparte, with the Revolution behind him, and greater power to reform than any minister of the *ancien régime* had dreamed of, had been astonished to find 'this chequered France, lacking unity of laws and administration, more like twenty kingdoms assembled than a single state'. If with this picture in mind we look back at the lame Leviathan of the seventeenth century, we shall be less surprised to find that it was weak when it came to invading directly the preserves of privilege. In some places and cases the authority of the state became more effective. The changes in the army and navy amounted to a revolution; justice reached further, and fiscal privilege, hydra-headed, was constantly attacked. The fact remains that the monarchy was never able to break the resistance of the conservative elements that stood in the way of radical reform. It remained a conservative force itself, driven to exploit the privileges which it could not destroy, indeed refurbishing them and creating new hierarchies out of the old. Colbert failed, as Turgot failed a hundred years after him, to abolish the tax-exemption of the nobility and office-holders which was a fundamental cause of revolution. All the time circumstance forced the crown to come to terms with feudalism and separatism in their various guises. It was saved from those revolutions which produced the 'crowned republic' across the Channel. But the irony of those complacent comparisons, between the unlimited and stable monarchy of France and its limited and unstable rival, is that the former was not really absolute. It could command the largest army and revenues in Europe, but the limitations were real and thwarting.

The 'administrative revolution' of Louis XIV's reign is usually associated with Colbert and Louvois because the biggest advances were made under the direction of these formidable ministers. These considerations may help to put their work into true perspective, without diminishing the importance of their efforts to reduce the vested interests which deprived the state of authority and revenue.

The minister

The greatness of Colbert does not consist primarily in his economic thinking, which was not original, nor in his planning, which was unduly rigid. He is noted for his prodigious labours to make France the wealthiest state in Europe, but these are not the limit of his achievement. He took as his field of action the whole state, for he realised that the problems of society and economy were closely related parts of the whole problem of government. He made it his life's work, through an unprecedented concentration of powers, to re-order the state; for he was as much concerned with its authority as with its wealth.

Jean-Baptiste Colbert (1619-83) was born at Reims, the son of a draper. He worked his passage in the royal service, first under Le Tellier, then, after 1651, under Mazarin himself. In the management of the Cardinal's vast concerns his appetite for planning had full scope. He gave the same painstaking attention to his master's wardrobe, or to his farm at Vincennes, as to lofty matters of state. He did not neglect his own interests; he became rich, a *conseilleur*, a *seigneur*. He was sensitive enough about his *bourgeois* origins to employ a genealogist to trace his family back to 'the valiant knight, Richard Colbert, called the Scot'. (He may have derived more solid satisfaction from the dynasty that he was able to create. His son Seignelay succeeded him as Secretary for the Navy, his younger brother Colbert de Croissy and Torcy his nephew were successively Secretaries for foreign affairs.) He knew how to make himself indispensable, and his position of trust gave him the opportunity to study at first-hand the ways and means of political life. Mazarin recommended him to Louis, 'for he is very faithful', and from the start of Louis' personal reign he pushed to the top with assurance and without squeamishness: it was he who supplied the most damning evidence against Nicholas Fouquet and planned the arrest of the *surintendant* whose personality and methods were the antithesis of his own.

'The north' of Mme de Sévigné's phrase was a graceless, absorbed figure who could write of himself: 'I take no holiday, I have no pleasure or amusements, my whole time is spent on the Cardinal's business, for what I love is work.' He was pragmatic, with little time for sentiment or style. But there was nothing mean about him or his aims, and he was enlightened before his time. In 1672, it was he who ordered that no more accusations of sorcery be received in France. He was an ardent patron of artistic and intellectual life, active in the foundation of the Observatory and the Academies. Through his agent Chapelain he organised the distribution of royal pensions to poets and playwrights. He may have been primarily concerned with the prestige value of such work, but he was not lacking in discrimination.

Colbert was the complete Cartesian, the incarnation of method, and he recognised no limit to the power of human reason to shape and control the human condition. His rules for work were simple and optimistic. For all matters, evidence and data must be collected and tabulated, historical antecedents studied. The minister's intelligence thus armed, he must think 'continually', with 'application' and with 'penetration'—the words are his. His work began with a great inquest, launched in 1663, which provided him with a new social and economic geography of the country. The *Bibliothèque Royale* was his creation, the *Académie des Sciences* his organ. He had an insatiable appetite for statistics, but he did not cherish them for their own sake. He was modern in his reluctance to base legislation upon guesswork. His scientific bent and method can be studied in the hundreds of volumes of letters, memoirs and directives in which he embroidered his themes of classification and regulation; they amount to a significant expression of the analytical spirit of the seventeenth century. His disciplined life was not so drab as it may have seemed to courtiers who remarked his ostentatious black, his beetling brows, his preference for water over wine, for his position and opportunity were unique.

Colbert's work carried the principles of absolutism into the economic field: planning from the centre and control by a single hand. To this end he was given an astonishing range of authority, for by 1669 he had added to his original posts of *contrôleur général* and *surintendant des bâtiments* the responsibilities of Secretary of State for the *maison du roi*, and for the Navy. Within the orbit of one man came finance and trade, the sea, colonies and the royal building programme: the authority over the economy which he required for his plans.

Colbert's was a personal mission, the expression of his own ideas about work, wealth and the community. He dreamed of a France rid of the *rentier* and the monk, a nation of well-ordered toilers, in which all good men strove to realise the abounding natural resources of the land, to increase the wealth of the nation and the prestige of the king. But his work may also be seen as a logical extension of the mercantilist ideas that were current, in one form or another, in seventeenth century Europe. For in one principle, the efficacy of state control of the economy, Colbert was strictly doctrinaire.

He was a man of his time in assuming that the state must act to protect and stimulate its trade and manufactures. Action might take two forms: regulation from within and protection from without. The ideas of the mediaeval guild were enlarged to serve the needs of the nation-state. As once within the smaller unit of the town, so now within the state the individual craftsman or trader had to accept a system of mutual aid. Elaborate rules fastened wages and prices, the conditions of sale and the movement of goods. In this way the individual was protected from the harsh uncertainties of free trade, while in return he accepted restraints and derived from the state his very right to work and wealth. The new monarchies, when they absorbed the sovereignties of the independent towns, had naturally taken over their responsibilities for trade their citizens' right to work for fair return, and their protection against the foreigner. Such protection had been a political imperative for the monarchies which had worked for social order in alliance with the trading community; it happened also to be the readiest answer to the most pressing needs of the states—ready money.

Mercantilism

Colbert was, to apply the convenient label of the economic historian, a 'mercantilist'[1]. The word has suffered in the course of controversy, from Adam Smith to Hecksher and Keynes in our time, and the body of ideas that it represents have been discredited, because of the obsession of some of its exponents with 'treasure'. This can be explained by the inadequacy of credit in an age of expanding trade, when there were no bills of exchange, and capital, in the form of bullion, was an urgent necessity. After the experiences of the sixteenth century, and the awful example of Spain, the spectre of bankruptcy hung close about the governments of Europe. Mercantilism, variously applied by merchants

[1] For a discussion of mercantilism see pages 28 ff.

and statesmen, was the natural evolution from the economic needs and political aims of the period. The success of the state depended upon the money that it could find to finance armies, navies and diplomats. Economists of the time did not believe that gold and silver could be eaten; they stressed as well the importance of material goods, timber and sailcloth, ropes and tar for ships, iron and saltpetre for guns and powder. Colbert, so far from being imbued with the Midas fallacy, held firmly that wealth lay in trade. But he saw, as he studied the chaos and poverty of Mazarin's regime, that France was suffocating through shortage of good coin. Much of the circulating coin was of debased silver or copper; he was not alone in being alarmed by the outflow of bullion in the Levant luxury trade, or gratified by the inflow from Spain. Agriculture was depressed by the end of the long price rise; though he could not foresee it, a period of stationary or declining grain prices was beginning. France's trade languished since at home there was not enough consumer demand to stimulate manufactures while exports abroad did not earn enough bullion. It was this state of affairs that led the minister to work out his programme for 'enriching the state by the state regulation of commerce', to borrow the words of Adam Smith. In his urgent hands, the aspirations of earlier writers such as Bodin, Laffemas, Montchrétien took shape, the hopeful regulations of earlier administrators were given new force in a coherent scheme.

The mercantilist assumed that the state was a community with a common wealth which could only be measured effectively in terms of gold and silver, of which there is at any given time a definite amount in circulation. It is in the interest of the state to increase its share of that fixed fund, and it must therefore take deliberate steps towards that end. 'A balance of trade' should be sought, by which was meant that the most desirable form of trade, and that which the government should foster, was an export of goods for which, in return, the purchasing country shipped gold and silver. 'The first principle to be adopted in our policy was to export fully manufactured goods in preference to partly manufactured goods, and goods in which the raw material values were as low as possible compared to the work done on that material. The more brains and craftsmanship we can export, the better for our balance of payments position.' The words are those of a post-war British Chancellor of the Exchequer, but they could easily be Colbert's.

France was not alone in wishing to increase her exports and her reserves of bullion. There must therefore be some degree of free trade. But here arose the dilemma: how to avoid a clash between the twin ideals of the reformer, protection of native industries from foreign competition, and expanding trade? Even France, which was better placed than any other country to supply its own needs, was never able to dispense with Dutch-supplied goods. Colbert put much trust in the tariff weapon, but he applied it at first with sensible caution. His aim was a double one: to simplify the baffling muddle of internal and external dues which were the legacy of generations of hand-to-mouth policy, and to use them to protect French, and to attack Dutch and English trade. He was never primarily interested in the revenue which might come from his tariffs. The tariff of 1664 actually lightened burdens, freeing raw materials and abolishing, where possible, internal tolls: a measure of simplification. In 1667, however, customs duties were raised to a point clearly intended to debar some imported goods completely; protective to the point of aggression. The duty on imported cloth was doubled, on tapestries it rose from 120 *livres* to 200. In 1669, Colbert worked for a trade agreement with England in the hope of increasing French exports of wine and silks, which were discouraged by the heavy English duty. The plan for both countries to relax their tariffs was abortive because he insisted that the English imports should conform exactly to the standards of French manufactures, minutely regulated, as was required by Colbert's policy—protection and subsidy. This was the effect of the dilemma in practice. Colbert certainly established a balance of trade in France's favour, so far as England was concerned; he believed that while France could keep up this annual inflow of bullion, she could afford to be an aggressive military state. But his tariff policy established a chain reaction. The preferential sugar duties of 1670-1, the tariff of 1672, went further than measures of trade to protect France's infant industries; they served notice of economic war upon England and Holland, and perforce their challenge was accepted. England put further duties upon French brandy and wine, while Holland banned the entry of French goods and waited for war; in John de Witt's words, 'there remained only the path of retaliation'. The temptation that came inevitably from these cut-throat policies was to take a short-cut to trade supremacy; so the military attack upon Holland was a natural, indeed, for Colbert, a desirable, consequence of the tariff war. From seeking to debar a trade rival from your ports it is a short step to destroying his trade by armed force.

Colbert's tariff policy has been much criticised; it was not even popular with the majority of French merchants, who saw benefits in the free interchange of goods which the minister ignored. At a general council held after the minister's death, to which representatives came from different towns, only the advocate from Rouen defended the policy which had been Colbert's; the rest declared for the reciprocal benefits of free trade. For him, it must be said that France, like America in modern times, was relatively well placed for a tariff war, as being very nearly self-sufficient. But against him it can be urged that his assumption that there was a fixed volume of trade, for which the nations had to contend, was out of date at a time when new areas and types of trade were being opened up in America and the East.

In fact, Colbert's tariffs should not be judged in isolation, nor on economic grounds alone. Mercantilism was not just an economic theory; rather it was a political approach to economic problems. Colbert was not, as has often been represented, a peaceful planner or would-be fairy godmother to the economy, thwarted in his civil purposes by an aggressive king. He was above all a statist who saw himself as the instrument of the king's glory. In England the government came to adopt a mercantile policy culminating in the Navigation Laws, from the continual pressure of private interests—so that Adam Smith could later refer to 'a conspiracy contrived by a minority for their own interests'. In France, by contrast, the impulse towards regulation came from the top. It was 'royal Colbertism', and while Colbert might consult the merchants, their interests and their advice might have little effect upon policy: 'they nearly always understand merely their own little commerce, and not the great forces which make commerce go'. Colbert's words reveal his limitations; his view of trade and wealth, not only as a good, but as a means to a further good, the might and impact of France. At heart he seems to have been convinced that manufactures were the true source of the contentment of society; he undoubtedly detested the effete and wasteful luxury of Versailles and he fought a stern battle to defend the main parts of his plan against the corrosion of war budgets. The fact remains that he subscribed fully to the notions of power which obsessed the king and his ministers. There is no sign that

he ever considered the 'condition of the people' or the destructiveness of war, except in the light of tax and trade returns. Colbertism
bears out the thesis of Schmoller, that mercantilism was primarily
concerned with the pursuit of power: 'in all ages history has been
used to treat national power and national wealth as sisters; perhaps
they were never so closely associated as then'. For Colbert the
creation of wealth was a sort of power-politics, 'state-making
and national economy-making at the same time'. He would have
agreed with Josiah Child that 'profit and power ought jointly to
be considered', and he would have sympathised with the thesis of
another Englishman, Yarranton, whose work of 1677, *England's
Improvement by sea and land* has the revealing sub-title: *How to beat
the Dutch without actually fighting.*

Financial reform

In 1659, Colbert presented Mazarin with a memorandum in which
he proposed remedies for the ills of the state: the purchaseable
offices should be reduced by twenty thousand, so that the numbers
exempt from tax might be diminished, fraud and illicit charges
prevented, the *taille* reduced and the condition of village and
peasant restored. Those who were dispossessed of office could
put their capital to better use in industry, working for 'the welfare
of the kingdom instead of for its destruction'. He was in line
with modern historians in fastening upon offices, and the accompanying exemptions from tax, as the root of the problem.
Richelieu, who was more concerned with survival than with sound
finance, had begun, as we have seen, with hopes of abolishing the
evil, but he ended by recognising the value of a system which
bound the *bourgeoisie* to the administration. Indeed he had little
alternative, for he had been driven to increase the number of
offices to finance his war. By 1633, returns from office were a third
of the entire revenue; before his death, the dues claimed by office-
holders came sometimes to be more than they paid in, while the
market in offices was so inflated that their value fell, some
remaining unsold. After the Fronde, with royal authority strong
again, there was less need for a minister to concern himself with
the feelings of the *bourgeoisie*. The questions for Colbert were:
could he find means of ridding himself of this most costly incubus,
and could he afford not to?

In the *généralité* of Rouen, Colbert found at the start of his

ministry that 41·6 per cent of the revenue was absorbed in payment
to the office-holders, who were still only receiving a third of their
dues. Had they received all, a million livres would have had to be
found by some form of taxation. This situation, widely reproduced, was critical. Exemption had grown to a point at which few
of the wealthier *bourgeois* paid any direct tax at all. His memorandum of 1664 showed that 46,000 office-holders enjoyed
exemption in the departments of Justice and Finance, all by virtue
of their office; 40,000 of these were unnecessary, created only to
be sold and bought for exemption or prestige. These offices
represented a steady haemorrhage of capital accruing from the
profits of trade and industry. When the rich could put half their
money into *charges* and half into *rentes*, they could not easily be
persuaded to invest in industry.

The other side of the unhappy picture was the failure of direct
taxation. The more exemptions there were, the more ministers
had turned the screw upon the unfortunate *taille* payer. Every
form of taxation had been increased clumsily during the past forty
years. The *taille* and the *gabelle* had been doubled since Richelieu
came to power. The *taille* was essentially a tax upon the peasantry,
since the inhabitants of towns often secured complete or partial
exemption. In the parishes, particularly in the *pays d'élection*, the
more influential often escaped lightly, the weak paid most and the
unfortunate collector might end up in jail for default. There were
discrepancies between provinces. Big landowners sometimes
secured concessions for their tenants, who could therefore pay
them more rent. Colbert himself was not above writing to an
intendant to thank him for reducing the *taille* levied on the peasants
of his son's estates. Locke singled out these inequalities for
criticism: 'when a *bourgeois* or tradesman that lives in the town,
if he have land in the country, if he keep it in his hand or set it to
rent, which is the common way, that pays nothing; but the peasant
who rents it, if he be worth anything, pays for what he has'. He
was writing of a province where the *taille* was personal, not on
land as in the *pays d'état*. The peasant in Languedoc or Brittany
was relatively fortunate. Even in Languedoc, however, Locke
noticed the working of privilege: 'to these 2,7000,000 (*livres*)
which this province is to pay this year, land of 100 *écus* per annum
will pay about 130 *livres*. The *levie noble*, which is about one-
twentieth, pays nothing. What was not anciently noble, but
ennobled by grant, pays one year's value every twenty or thirty

years, but the ancient doth not, and if a *roturier* or commoner buys it, it pays this year's value. Monks, when they get land by gift or purchase, if the Estates do not spare them, they usually get the king to ennoble them, and so the burthen still increases upon the rest.' As Locke observed: 'This is that which so grinds the peasant in France. The collectors make their rates usually with great inequality. There lies an appeal for the overtaxed, but I find not that the remedy is made much use of.' It should be remembered that the peasant also bore the brunt of the indirect taxes. The *gabelle* varied from province to province; it could be as heavy as the *taille*. The variation of prices between provinces led to smuggling, which was as dangerous as it was profitable; a man could be sent to the galleys for evasion of the tax. Customs duties were a constant nuisance. Tithe and feudal dues bore hard in this period of low prices, which hit landowner and peasant alike. Dues were often increased by landowners reconstituting their demesnes, and especially by new *bourgeois* landowners who expected their investment in land to be profitable.

There were some well-to-do peasants in France, a rural *bourgeoisie* with fair-size holdings, and the extent of poverty among the small proprietors and the *métayers* can only be guessed at. But it is hard to resist the conclusion that the majority of peasants lived close to subsistence level, that their taxes were a crippling burden and that the failure of a crop brought masses near to starvation. This is borne out by the peasant revolts which occurred throughout the reign. They were not, as we have seen, a new phenomenon; but they show that little was done in Louis XIV's reign to solve the peasant problem. In 1662, the introduction of new taxes in the Bourbonnais led to an armed revolt; in one pitched battle, nearly three hundred rebels were killed, wounded or taken prisoner. A revolt against the *gabelle* in Gascony and Béarn, which started in 1664, persisted for several years. A large military force was required to defeat a rising in the Vivarais in 1670; only brutal repression brought Bordeaux and Brittany to heel after the big risings of 1675. On one occasion Colbert wrote to the *intendant* at Limoges: 'You can give publicity to the fact that the king keeps ready, twenty leagues from Paris, an army of 20,000 men, ready to march into any province where there is a suspicion of a rising, in order to inflict exemplary punishment and to show the whole people the obedience they owe to His Majesty.' These revolts do not have much prominence in contemporary writings. Mme de

Sévigné must have known more about the reprisals in Brittany, where her estates lay, than her complacent comments would suggest, but the peasant's existence was not a matter of close concern to people of her class. There was no reporting of executions, and the movements of troops were only recorded in secret official despatches. There were no revolts on a national scale; in this the government was fortunate, but their regularity testifies to the incidence of periods of intolerable suffering for which the abuses of the tax-system were to some extent responsible.

Colbert was successful in reforms of detail. Though the operation of buying out all the *officiers* was too ambitious for a government bent on war, thousands of useless offices were abolished. He greatly increased revenues from crown lands, especially from the forests. He brought some order into the treasury accounts. He reduced the number of exemptions from tax-paying by checking the titles of nobility; over a thousand false ones were discovered in Provence alone. The leases of the tax-farmers were checked, many of them cancelled, while their commissions were docked. The *taille* was a wretched tax but gave the French king an income which was the envy of his fellow-princes. Charles II of England, struggling to survive on £1 million a year, was neither able to maintain a standing army nor pursue an independent foreign policy, and it is significant that his abortive attempt to increase his revenues, the Hearth Tax of 1662, was similar in principle to the *taille*. Colbert was very successful in increasing the tax's yield. When he started to apply his axe, he found that of 83 million *livres* paid by the tax-payer, only 31 millions reached the Treasury. By 1667 the gross revenue had risen to 95 millions, of which 63 millions were available for use. He had doubled the king's effective income in six years. He was not blind to the law of diminishing returns and he urged some reliefs upon his *intendants*: peasants were not to be squeezed too hard at harvest time, while, by an edict of 1666, those who married young and had large families were to pay less. Such paternalism did not last long under the pressure of war taxation, for to increase the *taille* was still the easiest way of increasing revenue. In 1679 Colbert had to write to suggest the use of troops to enforce the *taille*; in the same year, at Tours alone, we hear of over fifty peasant collectors languishing in prison for failing to collect the right amount. He had dreamed of extending the *taille réelle* to the whole country, but all in fact that happened was that the *taille réelle* was adjusted so that the *pays d'état* paid more. The most that can be said is that the *taille* was still 20 per cent lower when he died than it had been in the worst years of Fouquet.

The *rentes* had become, through the Crown's weakness, an exorbitant levy upon national revenue, for the benefit of a few rich financiers. Now, in the course of drastic 'conversion', interest rates were trimmed. In order to examine the titles of certain *rentiers*, he used the same special tribunal which had tried Fouquet; many claims were repudiated. The success of Colbert in forcing through these reforms in the teeth of influential opposition is witness to the change since 1649, to his courageous independence, and his confidence in Louis' support. He acted without scruple or favour in the Crown's interest, and neither riots in Paris nor threatening deputations could deter him. To Colbert, living on usury was anti-social, but he was driven to accept the necessity for a regular system of state borrowing, and during the Dutch War he set up a national loan bank, in which he proceeded to administer the *rentes* on a regular five per cent basis. As later happened in England, such a system could have grown to be a prop of the state; but in 1684 Louis abolished it—a triumph of prejudice over sense. So Colbert's successors had to rely again upon the speculators who provided long-term loans upon steep terms. War finance after 1688 presented golden opportunities to the bankers, tax-farmers and contractors, whose credit was so invaluable that they were protected by the state.

Planned production

In his compendious planning of the production and trade of the state lay the greatest part of Colbert's work. He was inspired by an idealised view of an earlier France, the supposed golden age of the beginning of the century, when French crafts and manufactures were booming, when money did not flow from the kingdom and when Spain and England sent their wool to France to be turned into cloth. Colbert believed that it was his mission to restore France to her pristine prosperity. His fiction was not wholly absurd, for the land of France was amply endowed, there were important established industries, and a long coastline with great harbours on the Mediterranean, Atlantic and the Channel. Compared to neighbouring Italy and Germany, there existed some degree of integration and maturity as a national unit. The thriving state of Holland presented him with an example of what a trading community could achieve by private capital enterprise. In the Dutch, Colbert descried a realistic community where trade was the first priority and capital was not thwarted by social taboos: 'there are no monks in Holland'. What more could the nineteen millions of France not do, when to the natural richness of the soil and the talents of her people was added the direction of the state, acting as its own *entrepreneur* and starting new industries with loans and imported labour?

Colbert did not, as is sometimes asserted, undervalue agriculture. Unlike Sully he was indeed little interested in farming for its own sake; agriculture gave, it seemed, fixed returns, while the manufacturing industries promised compound interest. But a poor and lethargic peasantry would create no demand for manufactured goods and such demand was to be the first stimulus to expanding production. Furthermore he had a horror of famine, the civil disturbances that accompanied it and the wastage of taxable wealth. Certain advances were made, drainage schemes were pressed forward and the scientific breeding of horses in stud farms subsidised. He favoured the industrial crops such as hemp and flax. Home industries were encouraged and peasants' wives in the Auvergne found wider markets for their delicate lace. To provide the large supplies of timber needed by the new navy, he re-organised the administration of the royal forests. (It is typical however, that this scheme was spoiled by local interests who bought up timber cheaply and sold it dear.) These were but marginal benefits and, overall, farming did not benefit nor the peasant's lot alter. Colbert, the man of the industrial north, looked grudgingly on the huge and vital wine industry of the south of France and even tried, characteristically, to destroy some vineyards and grow corn in their place, regardless of soil and climate—for 'wine hinders work'. But the corn producer did not gain from his solicitude. The failure to remove all the local customs barriers probably outweighed any gain from new roads and canals. In the last resort, the farmer was sacrificed to the dogma of the balance of trade. Colbert's ideal of a self-supporting country did not take account of the risks of the harvest. In bad years, rather than import foreign grain, restrictions were imposed on the movements of crops to keep down the price, while in plentiful years, elaborate controls prevented exports and thus caused waste and loss. Agriculture indeed responds badly to state interference and no amount of benevolent control could make up for the lack of interest and capital of the great landowners. Their untaxed rentals were rarely spent on estates which they might never see. Their peasants shrank from making any improvements which might catch the eye of the tax collector.

In manufactures, intensified by state aid, 'subject neither to the change of seasons, nor the fickle elements', Colbert saw the way to prosperity, for here was more scope for human intelligence; nature could be ignored, chance discounted and production planned. In an early memoir to Mazarin he outlined a programme. 'We must create or recreate all industries, even luxury industries; a system of protection must be established by means of a customs tariff; trade and traders organised into guilds. Transport of goods by sea and land must be restored, colonies developed and bound by financial ties to France; all barriers between France and India must be broken down and the navy strengthened to give protection to our merchant shipping.' In 1664, the year in which the *conseil de commerce* was formed, he was able to be more precise. By then he found, from the internal monetary famine which was causing prices to fall and business to contract, how urgent it was for the state to launch an export drive. He pointed to the examples of Venice and Holland, whose influence and fame had come simply from their success in exploiting the opportunities of trade, first the old Middle Eastern routes and then the seaways opened by the discovery of the New World, the new route to India and the Far East. France must now break into the restricted but not impenetrable markets of the world and manufacture for herself the goods which were at present bought from the English, Dutch, Hamburgers; at the same time the finer quality of French goods should draw purchasers from abroad. In new manufactures, a million subjects of the king, 'now languishing in idleness, will win their livelihood' and as many find work in the ports and in the marine. The king himself had a part to play, for he could 'show a special interest in the commerce of the nation and receive merchants at court with his favour'; and he might reduce the number of the religious 'who not only do no work for the community, but also deprive it of the children that they should be producing'. Colbert added: 'If Your Majesty could constrain all your subjects into these four kinds of profession, agriculture, trade, war by land or by sea, it would be possible for you to become the master of the world.'

The state could increase productivity in several ways: by creating and running new industries, or old ones which had lapsed, and by lending the capital and advisory officials; it could stimulate less directly by encouraging rich men to invest their money in industries, by issuing diplomas and supporting research. It could finance the importation of foreign workers with specialist skills. It could protect from the ordinary rigours of trading competition by granting monopolies and imposing tariffs and embargoes. It could control within by imposing special standards of quality, ordering the methods of production and enforcing its will through inspectors. All these methods played their part; but at the heart of Colbert's design was the state factory, designed and privileged to be the textbook and inspiration for lesser concerns.

Colbert's belief in the managed economy may seem absurdly rigid; the usual criticism is that he ignored human nature and the laws of supply and demand. He thought that 'we must resign ourselves to do the people good, despite themselves' and that 'the state must order the business of a great people on the same basis as the divisions of a government department'. Indeed his planning was naïve in some details. It is curious for instance to find that the state factories were expected to have a near-monastic discipline; no swearing nor irreverence, and only sacred chants were to be sung at work, in a low voice so as not to disturb one's neighbours. Some of his schemes too were impracticable, failures of planning which might have been avoided by the cautious, empirical approach of the private *entrepreneur* who risks his own capital. But it should be remembered that the introduction of a factory system had important advantages. Colbert's regulations made possible a greater division of labour and with it a saving in the cost of production. He was faced by a widespread reluctance in the monied class to invest their savings in industrial projects, by the dislike of the ordinary domestic worker for factory life and lastly by the jealousy and conservatism of the old privileged craft guilds. Against these obstructions he could best make headway by enabling the state to act as its own *entrepreneur* in certain selected cases, while it used the guilds as crown agents to enforce the new and comprehensive regulations. Colbert had to come to terms with these oligarchic guilds which controlled manufactures in such cities as Lyon, Tours, Reims; in order to get some response to his plans, he would even support their restrictive practices and allow wage reductions. But at the same time over 100 *manufactures royales*, specially sheltered and favoured, sapped their position. These concerns, of which the king was patron, whose patentees might bear the *fleur de lys* and whose workmen might even be exempt from the *taille*, were the *corps d'élite* of the industrial army. They were intended to be an advertisement of the quality of French goods throughout the world and so they were the special object of the minister's exact and solicitous rulings.

The tapestry industry, which was nearly extinct after earlier encouragement by Henry IV, was a special case which called for state patronage. Here patient skill and artistry brought slow rewards; but if French tapestries became famous again in Europe, what prestige would accrue! So the famous Gobelins workshops in Paris, where the artist Le Brun supervised the making of tapestries, furniture, gold and silver ware, was Colbert's pampered favourite. The place was as much a school of art and a showpiece as a factory, with its sixty apprentices and its huge commissions for decorative work in the royal palaces. The results adorn the great houses and museums of Europe today, but the cost of international fame was high, some 7 million *livres* in Colbert's time alone, when private industries were only given half a million a year.

Textiles were an important field of experiment, in which Colbert hoped to challenge the leadership of England and Holland. Where there was no industry in existence, flax and madder crops were grown to supply materials or, as round Lyon, mulberry trees planted for that city's expanding silk manufacture. At Abbeville, Van Robais, a Dutch capitalist, presided over the most modern cloth factory in Europe. Here the local *intendant* was expected to supply the minister with the fullest details, to visit every two months to discover 'particularly the number of workers in the factory, the bales of cloth that they produced and their quality' in order that he might 'make some monetary bonus to Sieur Van Robais, to keep him up to constant improvements, these manufactures being of the greatest utility to the state'. Practical instructions were laid down for making and dyeing the cloth and a civic stamp was only issued by the inspector when he was satisfied that the finished article complied to the high official standard. Within the mediaeval walls of Carcassonne the making of the finest cloth was supervised by Dutch experts in another of the *manufactures royales*. On his own estates at Seignelay, Colbert set an example of paternal despotism, for here the children of the poor were encouraged or forced to become apprentices in his model lace workshop. There was no shortage of cheap labour for the new concerns. When Locke visited a silk manufactory at Tours he saw 'the twisting and windeing of silke in one of their mills which is drove about by a maid and turns at once about 120 spools and windes the silk off them'. The girl worked 'from five in the morning till night, only rests twice in the day an hour at a time'. Most of the industries, such as the linen manufacture of Brittany, still depended largely upon domestic work; peasant families were ready to weave and spin for small payments to supplement their meagre incomes.

The importation of foreign labour played a big part in Colbert's schemes. From Holland came textile craftsmen and paper manufacturers, from Venice skilled glass-blowers to instruct the Parisians; by 1680, Colbert was able to boast that the royal manufactory of mirrors was depriving Venice of one million *livres* a year. Miners were recruited in Sweden to help in the development of the copper and lead mines of the south; engineers in England to construct the new dockyards and arsenals at Toulon, Rochefort and Brest. The royal ambassadors acted as recruiting agents and were empowered to offer tempting bribes. When an unfortunate cloth manufacturer of Rouen migrated to Portugal to establish his craft there, the ambassador at Lisbon was instructed to do all that he could by harassing the man and his family to induce him to return. Until the Revocation of the Edict of Nantes it was a one-way traffic.

Workers could be got more easily than capital; this was Colbert's greatest problem. Alongside the state-sponsoring of new projects went an incessant propaganda aimed at persuading the great financiers, bankers, tax-farmers, magistrates, even bishops, to give their money or moral support to the state plan to overcome 'difficulties that merchants by their own private efforts cannot surmount'. Colbert's constant theme for this 'money campaign' was that 'the trading companies are the armies of the king and the manufactures of France their reserves'. One important effect was to release for industrial purposes some of the capital that was locked up in the great commercial companies, notably the *merciers*, who had the right of selling to merchants and artisans certificates of mastery and controlled the corporations which monopolised trade in cloth, silks, gold and silver ware—in short, most of the crafts which Colbert wished to promote. This bore fruit in private capitalist enterprises without which many of his schemes would never have left the drawing-board: the work of men like Formont, lifetime collaborator with the minister, who interested himself in the manufacture of Dutch cloth, the receiver-general Claustrier, manufacturer of gold thread at Lyon, and Dalliez la Tour, whose interests were in armaments and mines. Help was enlisted too from foreigners, like Jabach, originally of Cologne, who financed the weaving of tapestries at Aubusson, and Van Robais of Abbeville. Colbert could usually get a good response from Huguenots who were debarred by their faith from public office, as for instance in bustling and prosperous La Rochelle. Office-holding had soaked up much of the available capital and with it business incentive, as can be seen in Dijon, capital of Burgundy and once the centre of a prosperous cloth trade, where the local *bourgeois*, growing rich in the hotel business and buying up offices and estates, had no time for new industrial projects. For all Colbert's efforts, too, interest rates remained high. When it was possible to get 6 per cent in safe investment, why risk money in trading companies?

To an extraordinary degree, the control of the economy stemmed from Colbert himself, inexhaustible and unbowed by checks and losses. Directives and memoranda flowed from his pen to the *intendants* and inspectors who were to carry them out. As well as the Inspectorate-general of Manufactures, with its travelling agents, regional committees were set up, on which sat industrialists and merchants. He used the guilds to enforce his regulations and even wished to increase their number, for they were a profitable source of revenue; through the mediaeval urban regime, he could enforce the social and economic discipline that was so dear to him. In 1669 a characteristic edict, one of a hundred and fifty, laid down the most stringent rules for the cloth industry; the texture and the dyes were specified, with the number of threads to the warp and woof, the length and breadth of every piece. For offences against such regulations, the unhappy manufacturer could be put in the pillory, with the offending article hanging round his neck, while ragged peasants might gape at a bonfire of faulty goods in the market square. The climax of the process of state control was reached with the promulgation of the great Ordinance of Commerce in 1673, in which rules were established for apprenticeships, contracts, bankruptcies, a blueprint for the whole of industry which swept away a mass of local custom and remained valid till the Revolution. This was intended to be only a part of a wider reform of the whole judicial system, 'this great work which has been reserved in its entirety for Louis XIV' but which in the end had to wait for Napoleon, despite all that was achieved in the Civil and Criminal Ordinances.

It did not need a comparison with the natural waterways of Holland to convince Colbert of the importance of improving internal communications. He ordered the repair and maintenance of roads and bridges. Between Paris and Orléans the first paved road was completed. A canal was dug between Orléans and Montargis, but the greatest enterprise was the canal of 'The Two Seas'. The principal engineer of the work was Riquet; when completed in 1681, 170 miles of waterway from the Garonne to the Aude linked Bordeaux on the Atlantic with Toulouse on the Mediterranean. It was begun with 12,000 workmen and a flourish of rhetoric; the work was 'to mark the grandeur, abundance and felicity of His reign'. Languedoc gained most from it, since the cost of transport was reduced by three-quarters. Colbert hoped that it would be used by foreign ships, but it was not wide enough and carried principally smaller craft with cargoes of grain and coal. The internal tolls of the country, so many and so intricate that only a few experts ever knew them all, were another target for the reformer. Many were mediaeval survivals and the river Rhône alone had more than forty toll stations. Some which could prove no right were abolished by edict in 1664. In the 'Five Great Farms', the central provinces of France roughly corresponding to the old Capetian domain, Colbert did establish uniform rates, but outside this area many trade-barriers remained. Throughout the reign the newly acquired province of Alsace could trade more profitably with the German states than with France!

Foreign trade and colonies

At the start of the century there had been only one colonial empire, that of the Spaniards and Portuguese. In the 1640's the rebellion of Portugal split again these unwilling partners; while Spain retained most of her lands, the Portuguese came near to complete dissolution and the richest parts of the east were lost to Holland. By Colbert's time, the Dutch, with the English, controlled the external trade of Arabia. The nucleus of their trading empire was in Indonesia; they held Malacca in the Malay Peninsula, Sumatra, Java, Borneo, New Guinea, Formosa, Ceylon and, nearer home, the Cape of Good Hope and Mauritius. The English had firm footholds in India, in Madras and, after the marriage of Charles II to his Portuguese wife, Bombay. But their settlements in North America were more important, stretching by 1664 from South Carolina north towards the Saint Lawrence. On the banks of this river French settlements had grown up early in the century, following the remarkable travels and discoveries of the pioneer, Samuel de Champlain. The struggles of the future between New England and New France could already be foreseen. The Dutch absorption of the Portuguese Far Eastern Empire had taxed her resources fully and three trade wars with England cost her dear in both ships and money. The initial impetus given by Puritanism to English colonisation had passed. From the living death of the Spanish Empire there was little prospect of new *conquistador* effort. Sustained French effort in North America might therefore give her the lasting control of those virgin lands explored by Champlain. The time was also ripe for a trade offensive into the ocean sea-lanes where the French flag was seldom seen.

Colbert foresaw that the trade wars of the future would be largely concerned with the possession of colonies and he wanted to give to the enterprise of traders and settlers overseas the full backing of the state. The view that colonies should serve their mother-country exclusively by providing natural resources that she lacked and acting as a market for her manufactures was common to all the colonising countries, whether it was Spain and the silver of Peru, Holland and the spices of the East, or England and the timber and furs of the North America. England had already advertised her brand of aggressive exclusionism with the Navigation Acts. But Colbert went further than any contemporary statesman in working out a science of colonisation. Each colony was to be a 'Little France', reserved for Frenchmen, living under French laws, reserving its products for the homeland and accepting only French manufactures. To make sure of this the haphazard proprietary arrangements were ended and, where possible, the colonial possessions were administered through monopolist companies, directly under the crown. In 1664 the first two companies of this type were founded; that of the West Indies, with its docks and offices at Le Havre, and that of the East Indies at Lorient. The Company of the North was founded in 1670, to dislodge the Dutch from their hold upon the trade in Baltic timber and naval stores: then the Levant Company in 1671, with twelve businessmen from Paris, Lyon and Marseilles in charge, and the grant of a state premium on every piece of cloth. Trading from the Mediterranean ports of Marseilles and Toulon, this company could compete on good terms with its English counterpart.

The problems faced by Colbert in starting these companies were daunting. There was no tradition of private colonial enterprise to compare with the sustained efforts of the great merchant adventurers of Holland and England. The country had produced great explorers and pioneers of the stamp of Cartier and Roberval, but the typical Frenchman was a reluctant emigrator. There was no community exodus in the seventeenth century to compare with those of the religious minority groups from England. The great activity of the religious orders had one unfortunate effect—of debarring Huguenots from the New World. This was also government policy. Consequently, when the Huguenots left France in the 1680's, they went to all parts of the world—except New France. The capitalist was unwilling to sink his capital in colonial schemes, the ethos of the nobility was hostile to projects of trade or settlement and the king was unconvinced of their importance. He might listen and subscribe dutifully to the projects for new companies, but they were of secondary importance and of little interest to him; his vision was bounded by the Rhine and the Pyrenees. Against this general indifference, Colbert's tireless planning could make small headway. In order to squeeze some money from the great fortunes immobilised in offices, *rentes* and seigneurial fiefs, glowing prospectuses were commissioned from the elegant pens of academicians such as Charpentier, who wrote of the brilliant future that awaited the East Indies Company, designed to wrest trade from the Dutch. But such appeals fell often upon stony ground. The minister's insistence upon monopoly and his apparent indifference to the experience of private merchants aroused irritation. The Chamber of Commerce, for instance, at Marseilles urged him to leave them alone, free from the monopolist companies which were 'odious to God and man'. Yet his economic imperialism bore some fruit.

In 1663, Canada had only 2,500 inhabitants. The expansion of this colony Colbert entrusted to the Company of the West Indies, which was granted a ten-year monopoly of trade. He sent out Jean Talon to be *intendant* of the colony and he proved to be a most ardent and capable administrator. The colony grew slowly, emigrants trickled out, and before long it had its own law-court, bishop and royal troops, the latter at the disposal of the *intendant* and governor. The lands of the Huron and the Illinois Indians were explored and 'concessions' staked out by adventurers like Cavalier de la Salle. With the pioneers went the intrepid Jesuits, who were in their element in these virgin lands, teaching the Indians the truths of the gospel and the advantages of the protection of the King of France. Talon thought in ambitious terms but he was cramped in his action by the control of the Company of the West Indies. Two years after the appointment of de Frontenac as Governor, the company's monopoly ended, and there began a phase of consolidation and more effective assertion of royal power. The new governor steam-rollered opposition, including that of the independent-minded Jesuits and Laval, bishop of Quebec, but despite the dislike of some of the inhabitants, his regime was beneficial. After his ten-year rule, ten thousand Frenchmen were settled in communities along the valley of the Saint Lawrence, principally at Quebec and Montreal, and more thinly in missions and forts along the route of the Great Lakes, at Fort Frontenac, on the lands of the modern Ontario and Niagara, between lakes Huron and Erie. Quebec was becoming an important port, with its superb natural situation and flourishing dockyard. A string of military posts protected the frontier against Indians and English. New France was still desperately underpopulated, but it looked now to be an impregnable redoubt from which the exploration and conquest of North America could be planned. In 1682, La Salle, with a handful of soldiers and Franciscan friars, made his astonishing voyage down the Mississippi. It had been provoked by a terrible massacre of the friendly Illinois by the Iroquois of New York State. On his way down the great river, he noted the junctions of the Missouri and the Ohio; for a month he was lost in a maze of small lakes and islands before he found the main stream again. This bore him down through the country of the Arkansas. On the 9th of April he arrived at the river mouth in the Gulf of Mexico, where his men set up a cross, sang a Te Deum and declared possession of all the land that they had traversed, in the name of the king, in whose honour they called it Louisiana. On the return journey, La Salle constructed a new fort, Saint-Louis, on a rocky escarpment, 600 feet high, dominating the river and plain around. When he returned to France, he offered the king a glittering prospectus of the great new empire, stretching from the Great Lakes to the Gulf of Mexico. The dreams of Colbert, Talon and Frontenac had been partially realised, but 'empire' was still a draft plan. To give it substance, inhabitants were wanted, money, forts, troops and above all ships; this meant more than the king's flattered interest for a few days—a re-direction of policy, unimaginable in the Versailles of the 1680's. The *réunions*, the Rhine frontier, Cologne, the Spanish succession, were the preoccupation of the king and the court. A little wooden fort in the swamps and forests of the New World, a rough handful of settlers and missionaries planting their forlorn flags and crosses, these things meant little; anyway it was Colbert's business.

Did Colbert do his business well? It has been customary amongst historians to explain the later failure of French effort in North America by the rigid application of state control as opposed to the relative freedom and immunity of the English settlements. Colbert was certainly absurdly obstinate in his trading policy. For instance, he refused to allow the West Indian planters to trade their molasses with the New Englanders who wished to sell their provisions in exchange, and he insisted upon excluding the foreigner altogether from French settlements. The imports of tobacco were granted to a syndicate which had a monopoly of the market. As a result, neither state nor producer benefited fully. But it must be emphasised that these were state projects, by default of private enterprise, in the face of prejudice and hostility. Colbert's views were characteristic of this xenophobic age of mercantilism, views which were in the next century to contribute to the greatest of all colonial wars. Louis' indifference and his policy of expansion within Europe, with its concomitant wars, was not compatible with colonial enterprise. In the last resort all was to depend on sea-power, and Colbert's new navy was already being neglected before the end of Louis' reign. In 1759 the English flag flew over impregnable Quebec, where Montcalm lay dying. The citadel was captured by Wolfe's soldiers, but it was a victory for sea-power intelligently applied. At Yorktown, in 1781, the French had their own revenge, but then the work of the French ships was to give victory to the Americans.

Colonies and companies were only means to the minister's ends of expanding trade. When the trader had secured a foothold it did not matter if the company later failed or was dissolved. Too much attention has been given to these apparent failures and too little to the increase of trading activity in the period. With vigorous action being taken against pirates from Naples and the Barbary coast and concessions to the merchants, profitable trade-links were established with Syria and Morocco, and Marseilles and Toulon grew rich. An entry was made into the spice market of the Far East and a precarious base established by the enterprise of François Martin at Pondicherry. France had started a profitable business in sugar, and the *fleur de lys* flew over some of the more important West Indian islands, Martinique, Guadeloupe, Saint Christophe and Antigua. The Company of Senegal shipped black slaves to work in the plantations, while in France itself, improved techniques of refining the cane created a new industry. The sugar was of course carried in French ships and by 1683 there were over two hundred in this trade alone. The busy docks and wharves of Nantes and La Rochelle were witness to the extent of this trade, at a time when Liverpool and Glasgow were insignificant and Bristol was still the greatest English port. In 1664 there were only about sixty merchant ships of over 300 tons; twenty years later, on Colbert's death, over 700, to play their part in the 'money war', to carry brandy, olive oil and cloth to the colonies and luxury goods from Colbert's factories to England, Spain and the Levant. At the end of Louis' reign, foreign trade was worth 200,000,000 *livres* a year, of which two-thirds was exports. This was indeed a transformation.

Militarism

When one contrasts Louis' pre-eminence in 1679 with the situation in 1689 when he was once again fighting against a coalition more united and determined than before, it is natural to look for some grand error of policy or disastrous act of pride; both the *réunions* and the Revocation of the Edict of Nantes have been seen as such. The thesis of the succeeding pages is that Louis and his ministers were principally responsible for the outbreak of the War of the League of Augsburg. But this is not to say that they were alone responsible or that there would have been no war if they had acted differently. Any account of these years which fails to stress the unforgiving pugnacity of Leopold I, the mortal and patient enmity of William of Orange, is unbalanced. Few people regarded Nijmegen as anything more than a temporary settlement or expected any golden age of co-operation between states to ensue. Most would rather have agreed with Montecucoli, who said of an earlier treaty in 1668 that within living memory in his part of the world there had been no peace which was not unreliable and suspect. Serious students of the international scene, such as Leibnitz, could think of no better solution than to unite Europe against the Turk and find an outlet for the passions of war in a new crusade. In 1672, the Elector of Mainz' chief minister had sent a letter to Pomponne, inviting Louis to turn from his designs against Holland to the Holland of the East. Pomponne's comment was the only one possible: 'You know that they (Holy wars) have ceased to be the fashion since St. Louis.'

Pomponne was perhaps the most reasonable and humane of Louis' ministers. In 1679 he was dismissed under a cloud, ostensibly for his Jansenist sympathies. The chief effect of his disgrace and supersession by Colbert de Croissy, Colbert's brother, was to give Louis closer personal control over foreign affairs. The king was taking a more important part in the formulation of policy, working voraciously in and out of council, taking more upon himself and insisting more upon his authority. Even routine requests from his ministers were liable to be refused, 'to show that he was the master and would not be governed'. The ministers accordingly showed less independence than those of the first generation; more serious than the dismissal of Pomponne in this respect was the death of Colbert in 1683 which left Louvois the pre-eminent figure. He was a fine administrator, but his political ideas were limited and his crude belief in force as the solution to political problems was always ready to support Louis' notions of grandeur. After 1683 he secured the exclusion from the Council of Seignelay, Colbert's son and Secretary for the Navy. Louvois himself took over Colbert's responsibility for Buildings and his friend Le Pelletier, a mediocrity, was made *contrôleur général*. Since his father had been made Chancellor in 1679, the faction could be sure of three voices out of four in the Council of State.

In this decade the king's behaviour was more arbitrary and provocative than in any other period. The influence of the Le Telliers is one explanation. But Louis would have been wise and strong-minded indeed to have remained moderate in these years. By 1682, he had settled finally upon Versailles as his permanent abode. Everything about the building spoke of splendour and glory; the whole palace was an idealisation of war, insidiously garbed in allegory and myth. Flattery enveloped the king. It might be absurd, like the essays of the duc de la Feuillade, but it was often unfortunately sincere. The attendant musters of the court, the studied modes of speech and behaviour, made up a tapestry world of unreal perspectives. The intrusion upon this world of disinterested advice or honest criticism was rare. The king could not help being affected by the idea of a personal transcendence which arose from his sharing in the qualities of the Divine state. This might have had little practical effect upon policy, for the dogmas of Divine Right did not absolve him from the necessity of acting as a politician. His authority was in theory fenced about with moral restraints which were the obligations due from his lieutenancy to God—and he took them very seriously. But in practice every influence worked to undo these restraints. Louis' strokes and gestures were performed before a rapt audience whose applause drowned independent views. The most intelligent were caught in the spell of the man and the system, and only a few had reservations which, like Saint-Simon, they kept to themselves. For all its splendours Versailles was stuffy, lacking the draughts of free discussion and criticism that freshened the air at Whitehall. The *milieu* which Louis had created was artificial and a little precious; its values could not escape being parochial and complacent.

So one sees a paradox. The king, who could be as subtle as any student of Machiavelli, could also make naïve misjudgments upon the largest scale. While he never failed to be competent and shrewd in daily matters of government, his orderly but unimaginative mind was unsuited to the situation created in this decade by the triumphs of his armies. For all his excellent information, he was insensitive to the repercussions of his policies and to the changing patterns of strength and opinion abroad. His principles only made matters worse because they lent a distasteful appearance of hypocrisy to his actions. He was perfectly sincere in rejoicing that the capture of Strasbourg had restored that city to the Roman faith; but Germany could see only the French bayonets on the Rhine. His alliances were lucrative, but they were made and unmade with an apparent indifference to the interests of smaller states. He made one especially grave error when he revoked the Edict of Nantes, failing to perceive that his treatment of the Huguenots, because of the international character of Protestantism and the 'wholeness' of Europe and European opinion, could not remain a simply domestic issue. By a series of aggressive actions, too, he alarmed the states into coalition against him. But one suspects that it was not his open aggressions only which embittered feeling, but his evident self-satisfaction and his patronising airs. This can be seen from contemporary comments: 'The grand doge, if we allow him, will soon leave to the German princes no throne but a tomb' (Sophia of Hanover); 'If we do not put things to rights, he will be the tutor of all Christendom' (the Elector Palatine, her brother and the man most nearly concerned).

The Réunions

After 1679, Louis kept his armies on a war footing, at the size, without precedent in peace time, of over 200,000 effectives. Even before the conclusion of the Treaty of Nijmegen, Temple had observed that he 'was of the prince's opinion (Orange) that he (Louis) will make with a design of a new war after he has fixed his conquests'. But the war had shown that there was a limit to actual aggression, a *ne plus ultra* beyond which lay retribution. Louis had learned the lesson that a blatant military offensive would force his rivals to ally against him. Now in the decade of 'cold war' between Nijmegen and the renewal of hostilities proper in 1689, he used more subtle means. The systematic expansion to which all the resources of his army and diplomacy were turned went on behind a camouflage of legalism. The *réunions* were carried out after exhaustive research into juridical rights, and because no state was in a fit condition to challenge Louis' armies, the annexations were peaceful. They were none the less alarming, for by these encroachments Louis seemed to be trespassing over those lines of conduct, variously expressed as 'treaty obligations', 'the balance of power' or even 'international law'. They added up to an impression of an insistent menace, of ambitions in Germany and perhaps upon the Imperial crown itself; a process entirely opportunist, taking advantage of weakness, not to be appeased, and to be halted only by armed force. Yet if studied in the context of the permanent needs of France rather than in that of the hostile pamphleteers, it becomes at least intelligible.

The policy of the *réunions* was in essentials simple. It was, to use the jargon of modern diplomacy, 'unilateral' action to rationalise the tangled mess of claims left by recent treaties. The eastern frontier was a chaos of conflicting authorities and, worse than untidy, it was indefensible. To bring order and coherence to her new territories and to fill out the frontier to the Rhine was the gist of the policy. To meet the needs of the modern state, feudal custom was invoked. By the treaties of Westphalia and Nijmegen, territories had been ceded with their 'dependencies'. Where such dependencies, however vague the customary tie, comprised towns or provinces of strategic value, they should be shown to belong to the King of France. To this end *chambres de Réunion* were set up.

The technique was probably inspired by Colbert de Croissy, Foreign Minister after 1679, irascible and authoritarian. Before he became a full-time diplomat he had been a conscientious *intendant* of Alsace and a councillor in the *parlement* of Metz, so he may have been working on the plan long before Louvois took it up. In one sense the problem was not new, but another aspect of the clash between the modern state and the feudal pattern of society. The centralising principle of the state demanded a new type of frontier: the idea of an area round a military or civil centre, a sort of marchland, must give way to that of the line. Such lines which, for perfection, had to wait the precision of the map-maker, only gradually became the accepted way of demarcation. As late as 1789 there was confusion because certain landowners in Alsace claimed that, as vassals of the Emperor, they were exempt from the revolutionary law abolishing feudal dues. This may have been sharp practice—but in 1680 such anomalies were numerous. In Alsace, for instance, Westphalia had given to Louis a scattered mass of sovereignties which was more like a landholding of estates than a province, and there was a genuine confusion about law and ownership. Everywhere there were privileged enclaves or clients owing embarrassing allegiance to a foreign ruler. The ten Imperial towns had a thorny strategic problem in the Dutch War—and this was the sort of consideration which influenced Louvois. Sedan provides the classic example of a problem of this type which had already been settled. It was a vital place, at a crossing of the Meuse, a centre from which roads went to Paris and Dijon, and into Germany, to Aachen, Strasbourg and Luxembourg. Nominally a *sub-fief* of France, it had come under the immediate lordship of the Dukes of Bouillon, who also held some lands from the bishop of Liège—and he was a prince of the Empire. It was finally secured by Mazarin in 1651, in exchange for other estates within France. It is proof of the ambiguity of its status that some writers have referred to this act as the annexation of foreign land and some as an addition to France! An equally striking case is provided by the principality of Orange, 100 miles inside the French frontier, from which Louis' principal enemy took his title. Seen from the standpoint of cases such as Sedan and Orange, the *réunions* were only an intensification of a long process: the nation mopping up the loose pieces of a feudal society which its advance had already made obsolete within its frontiers.

The execution of the *réunions* reflects the harsh and impatient character of the War Minister. At the end of the war Louvois had taken over the supervision of the frontier provinces of Alsace, Lorraine and the three bishoprics, in place of quieter areas, Saintonge, Limousin and Dauphiné. He travelled tirelessly in his new provinces and directed the researches of Roland de Ravaulx, *procurateur général* of Metz. He resolved the problem in simple military terms: the defensible line that had been achieved in Flanders would be extended to cover eastern France. Vauban had long been urging upon him the desirability of 'squaring the meadow' for economy and efficiency in the defensive war that the French have always to be ready to fight. Louvois was convinced, unlike many of his contemporaries who were still pre-occupied with Spain, that France should now turn all her energies towards Germany: 'the Germans ought now to be considered as our true enemies'. All the places absorbed in Alsace which he supervised in person had some strategic significance—such as Trarbach, commanding a loop of the Moselle, near which Vauban was soon to build the fortress of Mont-Royal. Strasbourg itself, commanding a bridge over the Rhine, was of crucial importance. In the Dutch War it had shown Imperialist sympathies, acting as a supply base for the Imperial troops, giving them passage over the river and even entering into alliance with Lorraine. So military necessity hurried along the lawyer's researches into rat-eaten folios.

Since 1668 the antiquarian Denis Godefroy had been working upon the charters in which the relevant claims were recorded. In 1678 Pomponne had over two thousand titles examined. At Metz in the following year de Ravaulx set the pace with a series of biased judgments; under Colbert de Croissy, the process gathered momentum. The treatment varied. At Besançon, Breisach and Douai, ordinary courts were given the power to decide questions of sovereignty; at Metz a special royal tribunal was set up; at Strasbourg there was no pretence of legal form. In all the courts the decisions might be guessed before the evidence was examined for the advocates knew what was required of them. In the first two years there were big annexations: the province of the Saare up to the Moselle, the Principality of Montbéliard, the county of Chiny and most of Luxembourg, many places in Flanders (under the specious pretext that they were still occupied and their restitution was not laid down in the text of Nijmegen), Orange, and almost everything left in Upper and Lower Alsace except Strasbourg. The territories of German princes such as the Elector of Trèves and the Duke of Wurtemburg were touched. When they went into Zweibrucken the French stubbed the toe of the King of Sweden, who promptly looked for an alliance with the Dutch. This Louis could afford to ignore since he had come to useful terms with Brandenburg and Saxony. In October 1679, in the second Treaty of St. Germain, the Great Elector and John George II promised their vote for Louis or the Dauphin at the next Imperial election. Bavaria was secured once more by the marriage of the Dauphin to a sister of Max-Emmanuel. One should not put too much emphasis upon these promises, for the German princes traditionally rallied to the Hapsburgs at election times, if only because they could rely upon them to be inefficient and undemanding. At the same time they wished to extract the maximum from the quarrel of the two dynasties—and Louis' diplomats paid well. No wonder that with these alliances and with the evidence of the disunity of Germany which such mercenary behaviour provided, Louis felt that he could go ahead with his most audacious raid.

Strasbourg

The burghers of Strasbourg negotiated with Louvois throughout the summer of 1681, hoping that they might preserve their status as a free town under French patronage. But Alsace was worth little to Louis without Strasbourg. It was really an independent republic, more like one of the Swiss cantons than any of the other Free towns of the Empire. The city fathers realised that they could not expect from the government of Louis XIV the majestic indifference with which Vienna had overlooked the fact that they were actually autonomous. They sent a deputation to Louis, which returned without satisfaction. After the Imperial Diet had voted for an army of 40,000 men and rumours had gone abroad that the Emperor planned to throw an army into the city, Louvois acted. He accompanied the army which seized the vital bridge, in person, then presented the citizens with the brusque alternative: to surrender their privileges, or to be put to the sword. The French army had some reputation in these matters, and the citizens had no choice but to surrender (September 30, 1681). The city was allowed to keep its privileges and its reformed religion, but Egon de Faustenbourg, long bishop *in partibus* only, returned to his cathedral—and the cathedral to the Roman rites. Louis crowned the event by a solemn entry in October, with the queen and the dauphin, to the music of three hundred guns. Some of the burghers who attended the Te Deum in the cathedral boasted that they had returned to sing *Super Flumina Babylonis* in the privacy of their houses. But the French entry was popular with many of the common people, who hoped for the end of the restrictions of the town oligarchy. Already four hundred barges had arrived laden with stone for use upon Vauban's new fortifications. Nor did the government waste time in striking a medal, bearing the proud legend: *Clausa Germaniae Gallia*. In these words lay the real significance and point of the *réunions*. The French frontier had been brought to a long front upon the Rhine—in French eyes a strategic necessity. But was it their final goal? Did they accept any limitation? After the fall of Strasbourg it was as clear to the Germans, as to Louvois, that western Germany was exposed and defenceless. The commander of the Imperial army, the Margrave of Baden, said that 'for Germany, the possession of this city means simply a guarantee of peace. For France it is a door through which she can invade German soil as often as she wishes.' Louis himself stated baldly that 'Alsace was a passage for our troops to Germany'. For the time the Emperor might abandon Alsace for more urgent calls in Hungary while Brandenburg obstructed the formation of an anti-French alliance so long as it suited her; but the threat could not be ignored for long. If the Rhine were to be the frontier of France, where did the Palatinate stand? Moreover, what of the king's designs upon the Empire itself, suggested by the terms of recent treaties? While the situation was being reappraised in the light of Strasbourg, Louis' actions did nothing to quieten his neighbours' fears.

Italy

The same day that Louis' troops entered Strasbourg, others marched into Casale, the capital of Montferrat, on the Po near Turin. This flamboyant stroke of policy ended a small saga of intrigue. Louis had long wished to have some base besides Pinerolo, in northern Italy, to counteract the Spanish garrisons on the Tuscan coast and in the Milanese and to stress to Italians the patent fact that France dominated the peninsula. Victor Amadeus II of Savoy had been left by his father virtually in the guardianship of Louis, Cosimo II of Tuscany was bound to France by marriage to the French royal house, and in the smaller states the French recruiting officers were accustomed to behave as if they were in their own country. The Papacy had been publically humiliated—though in the current struggle over the *régale*, Innocent XI was holding his own. Ferdinand-Charles de Gonzague, Duke of Mantua, debauched and absentee, having no male heir to succeed to the masculine fief of Montferrat, was prepared to sell the fortress of Casale. The first arrangements begun in 1677 had miscarried because Mattioli, the duke's agent, after taking ten thousand crowns commission on the sale, proceeded to betray the plan to the courts of Venice and Vienna. He was arrested by Marshal Catinat, Louis' commander in North Italy, and slipped into the undergrowth of history as one of several claimants to the identity of the 'Man in the Iron Mask'. At last by a second treaty the duke handed over the town for cash and a pension. It is questionable whether this important base was worth to Louis the resentment which Italians felt for his high-handed action. D'Estrades, his minister in Savoy, told him that 'there are few countries where the French are less loved than this one, or where Your Majesty's power causes more alarm and distrust'. Was Italy to be the theatre of the next war? Was Louis aiming to revive the Valois policy of direct intervention in Italy?

Louis is seen at his most insensitive in his handling of Italian affairs. A fussy concern for prestige, the rejection of the courtesies normal to relations between civilised states and perhaps also a bit of the Frenchman's innate scorn of Italians, can be seen in two further incidents of the period. In Savoy he played off the young duke, Victor Amadeus, against his mother and forced him finally to accept the presence of three thousand French troops in the country. After the Revocation of the Edict of Nantes in 1685, he attacked the Vaudois in their Alpine valleys, ordered the duke to help him on his side of the mountains and, when Victor Amadeus demurred, threatened to send French troops to help him. Victor played a waiting game, compromised and hid his real feelings. Later he was to show himself a resourceful enemy and play an important role in hostile coalitions, and the Vaudois fought bravely for him against the French. The wealthy little state of Genoa was treated with still less respect. She had been ordered to raise a regiment of Corsicans to fight for France in the Dutch War. French ships showed at the same time scant regard for Genoese neutrality. Though the old alliance between Genoa and Spain had long ceased to be effective, trading jealousies were bitter. Genoa was the trading rival of Marseilles and it was said of Colbert that 'he can hardly contain his anger when he hears of the arrival of a rich fleet at the port of Genoa'. In 1683, when France and Spain had broken off relations, Genoa armed galleys and allowed Spanish ships to refit in her harbours. Louis ordered them to desist; then, on meeting with refusal, sent the fleet to bombard the port. After ten days and huge destruction, Duquesne and Seignelay withdrew, but Louis was not content till the wretched Doge had come in person to Versailles to ask his pardon. Louis' Mediterranean fleet did find, however, more deserving targets for their guns than Genoa. The Barbary corsairs were making a profitable living from piracy and traffic in Christian captives and they had benefited from the decline of Spanish naval power and the recent embroilment of France and Holland. Since 1678, under Colbert's direction, squadrons based on Toulon policed the Mediterranean. On one occasion Duquesne went up to the Dardanelles, but Louis checked his zeal, not wishing to be embroiled in war with the Sultan himself. In 1684-5 Duquesne and d'Estrées bombarded Algiers, Tunis and Tripoli, treated with the local rulers for the release of Christians, and bound them to subsequent good behaviour.

The siege of Vienna

The Emperor was unable to oppose Louis' advance, owing to a revival of trouble on his eastern frontiers. Two elements were involved in the crisis which came to a head in the siege of Vienna in 1683: the militant revival of Turkey under the Kiuprili viziers, and the constant fight of the Magyars to free themselves from the rule of Vienna. When Toekeli allied his Magyars to the Grand Vizier Kara-Mustapha, the virtual ruler of Sultan Mohammed IV's Turkey, and marched upon Vienna, the two elements were fused in a single menace to the Emperor and to Christendom.

The position of the Most Christian King was equivocal. Earlier in the reign he had sent a contingent to assist the Emperor, but his hostile reception in Germany after the victory of St. Gothard in August 1664 had convinced him that he had been mistaken. Since then he had fostered the Hungarian revolt without actually committing his country by written treaty. Pomponne expressed in 1675 the deliberate vagueness of this policy: 'to encourage the rebels by some hope of succour and to force the court of Vienna to give greater attention to the revolt'. In 1677, however, the Hungarians secured a small subsidy for their army; Toekeli's soldiers called themselves 'the soldiers of France' and his coins carried the slogan: *Ludovicus XIV, Galliae Rex, Defensor Hungariae*. A stronger ally than Toekeli would have been the vigorous and able John Sobieski, elected King of Poland in 1673 with French support. But France would not second his attempt to create an absolute monarchy in Poland, and John, urged by his wife, Marie Casimir, who had a personal grievance against Louis because he had refused the title of *duc* to her father, began to detach himself from France. In 1677 he signed a treaty of neutrality with the Emperor. In Poland French diplomacy had one of its most costly failures.

When it was clear that Vienna was in peril, the Pope called upon the princes of Europe to go to the rescue; at Vessaillre, at the height of the siege, Bishop Bossuet spoke of the terrible trials of Austrian Christians and urged his congregation 'to do penance, to appease God by your tears'. But why should Louis have responded eagerly to such appeals? If Vienna fell, then he could march against the Turks as the undisputed master of Europe, protector of Germany, soon perhaps to be Emperor himself. Meanwhile he did nothing publicly to embarrass Leopold, who was still officially member of a league against him. His private hopes can be deduced from his dealings with Turkey. There was nothing new about an agreement between France and Turkey, where French merchants had enjoyed a privileged position since the time of Francis I. But Louis had recently taken pains to assure Mohammed of his friendship, dismissing a haughty ambassador and disavowing the actions of his naval forces in the Mediterranean against Moslem pirates. The new ambassador Guilleragues was urged 'to be careful above all things, to give these assurances in our name, and still more not to put anything in writing', and these assurances seem to have been a deciding factor in the Sultan's decision to campaign by land up the Danube.

Louis gained little from his tacit alliance. When the Turkish attack failed, Louis had forfeited his chance to stand forward as champion of Christendom. Prestige went rather to the King of Poland, whose action came as a shock to Louis. Sobieski was realist enough to know that Leopold would show no lasting gratitude, and have use for him only during the emergency, which was a grave one. By July 16th Vienna was completely invested by an army of more than 200,000 and the city became an armed camp, its garrison under Count von Stahremberg outnumbered ten times. The Turks dallied in their entrenchments, since Kara-Mustapha, who had boasted that he would stable his horses in St. Peter's but was now anxious for his personal share of the plunder, preferred starvation to storm. Sobieski made a formal alliance with the Emperor in March 1683, but not till September 11th did he and Charles of Lorraine reach the heights of the Khalemberg, overlooking Vienna. On the following day, in one of the world's decisive battles, the Turks, bombarded and demoralised, were driven from their trenches. John entered Vienna in triumph, and the feeling of many was voiced in the text of the celebratory Te Deum: 'There was a man sent from God whose name was John'. Leopold, however, received him coldly and gave poor support to his ensuing campaign which drove the Turks back along the plains of Hungary. He was unable to believe that John was disinterested, and feared that he would turn the victory to the advantage of Poland. Leopold's attitude helps to put Louis' conduct in the right perspective.

The Truce of Ratisbon

Before the Turkish peril overtook him, Leopold had joined the alliance formed at The Hague in September 1681 between William and Charles XI of Sweden. This was the third and feeblest of the series of coalitions against Louis. Spain came into the League, hoping to save something from the wreckage of her Empire. In October 1683, the Spanish king declared war, rashly but not without provocation, for in the previous month the French had made a preliminary foray into the Spanish Netherlands to support their claim upon Luxembourg. The futile gesture was followed by a predictable collapse. In succession Courtrai, Dixmude, Chinay and Bouvines fell to Louis' armies. The Spanish governor in the Netherlands bewailed a hopeless situation: 'no army, no crops, no resources'. Louvois ordered the salutary destruction of crops and cities; the *intendant de l'armée*, Robert, was instructed to 'see to these things with all possible severity'. After a four months' siege, the city of Luxembourg fell in June 1684 to Vauban and Créqui. Elsewhere an army had moved into Catalonia, while another waited on the borders of Navarre. Spain took the brunt alone, for Louis' diplomacy had been as active as ever and Brandenburg, Denmark and Savoy were his temporary allies. His subsidies satisfied Charles II of England, who was enjoying the last years of his reign in freedom from parliaments; his ambassador d'Avaux worked to immobilise Holland by playing upon the general fear of war. Though William of Orange had declared that he would rather lose his life than see Luxembourg fall, the States-General urged Spain to accept Louis' terms. The Emperor was being pressed to pursue war against the retreating Turks, recapture Hungary and gain control of the Danube, but Austria could not fight on two fronts at once. Under the auspices of Pope Innocent XI a 'Holy League' of Venice, Poland and the Empire was formed in March 1684, to exploit the victory of Vienna. The price that the Emperor paid for the alliance of Venice and Poland was the temporary abandonment of his position in the west. In August 1684, at the Dominican convent at Regensburg (Ratisbon), the

Emperor, Spain and France agreed to a twenty years' truce; for that time France was to keep Strasbourg, Luxembourg and the places secured by the *réunions* up to August 1681. 'Here', commented Saint-Simon, 'is the apogee of the reign and the height of its glory and prosperity'. Racine told the Academy that opposition to the king was futile: 'after many conferences, many projects, many useless complaints, his enemies were constrained to accept his law without having been able, for all their efforts, to move an inch beyond the close circle that he had traced around them'. In fact, many short-term advantages had been won; now the *contrôleur général* Le Pelletier looked forward to a lasting peace, to re-order the finances, 'to take sound measures concerning the Spanish Succession and to bring to an end the excessive hostilities aroused by the enterprises of M. de Louvois'.

23 GALLICANISM

The Most Christian King

Ecclesiastical affairs in Louis XIV's reign present a rich but confusing diversity of interests, aims and personalities. The richness is that of 'the great century of souls', the intellectual and spiritual grandeur of the age of Bossuet, Bourdalue and Fénelon. The confusion arises principally from the position of the king himself, intensely involved in all the great issues: the Gallican rights against Rome, the Gallican church against Huguenot heresy, the crown against Jansenist and Quietist unorthodoxies. These issues were rarely two-sided; usually a triangle or even quadrilateral of crown, Pope and one or more parties within the French church. Nor was the position of either crown or Pope fixed or predictable, for political pressures often dictated their attitudes. In Louis himself there was a fundamental ambiguity, between the conception of his duty as 'Most Christian King' to maintain the Catholicism of whose orthodoxy Rome was the recognised guardian, and his denial, on the other hand, of any implication that Rome could dictate to France upon any matter touching her traditional liberties. So when he needed the support of Rome in a question of doctrine, and when the political situation allowed, he was content to be a good 'ultramontane' Catholic. But when the need to assert the rights of the crown seemed paramount, or when Rome failed to comply with his wishes, he became a rampant Gallican. In a king who took his stewardship of church and state as seriously as Louis, there could be no consistency. Only one thing was certain: that no matter which concerned the French church would evade his paternal concern for order and orthodoxy.

Order was the natural concern of a responsible king who must consider what was good for the state. *Raison d'état* could be urged, too, for his interests in theology, especially in the tenets of Jansenism. But his interests in these matters came as much from his attitude to government as from his own passionate dislike of dissidence and novelty. For the explanation of the spectacular conflicts within the church we must therefore turn first to Louis' philosophy of ruling.

Louis was a *dévot* after his own unimaginative fashion, unquestioning and regular in his religious observances, even when he was having most difficulty with the sixth Commandment. It is hard to say what depths of feeling lay behind the impassive mask which he habitually presented to the world. But the feasts of the church were given solemn precedence and honour in court ceremonial; he took part in processions on Holy Days and listened to long, sometimes disconcertingly precise Advent sermons about the impurities and extravagances of court life. A bitter passage in a letter of Fénelon to the duc de Chevreuse, intended for the king, compared his religion to that of the Jews, 'consisting only of superstitions, of little superficial practices' and 'scrupulous about trifling details, unfeeling towards terrible evils'. Bossuet warned constantly about the dangers of absolute power and unceasing flattery. The Most Christian King could easily become a 'Nebuchadnezzar'. There was certainly something of the harem in Louis' circle in the hey-day of Mme de Montespan and Mme de Fontanges. But Louis never lost, in circumstances which would have demoralised a weaker man, his sense of sin. In 1675, on Holy Thursday, a brave parish priest refused the sacrament to Mme de Montespan. Louis was troubled, did not punish the priest, but sent his mistress away from court. He was only 46 years old when he turned finally to complete respectability of private life, with his marriage to Mme de Maintenon. The dignified piety of the last thirty years is commonly ascribed to the influence of Maintenon and the *cabale des dévots*, but it must also have owed much to his own will-power. His occasional surprising moderation and his self-dedication to exacting tasks surely reflect the steady influence of the rites and sacraments which he so conscientiously attended. Louis 'always made some conscience of what he did'.

Louis felt responsible for the well-being of the church in France because he stood as king in a unique relationship to God. The church was part of the estate of France which he was divinely appointed, *vice-Dieu*, to rule. These convictions were nourished by every influence that worked upon the king. The splendid coronation at Reims impressed upon a boy of 14 the sacerdotal nature of his function. The 'Royal Catechism', prepared for him by Godeau, placed the principles of absolutism on a sound theological footing. The most cogent Christian voice of the day, Bossuet's, developed the idea: 'The throne of kings is not that of a man, but the throne of God Himself. . . . God established kings as His ministers and He reigns by them. In the royal character there is inherent a sanctity which cannot be effaced by any crime.' These pronouncements accorded with Louis' own views, and he wrote himself: 'It is the will of God that he who is born a subject obeys without question. . . . Holding the place of God, the King seems to participate in His understanding.' The contemporary intellectual fashion for Divine Right, the drive of the absolute state to eliminate all rivals to its authority, and his own sense of stewardship of the realm and of the special tradition of the French church, together account for Louis' intense and intrusive surveillance of the affairs of the church.

The tradition of the lawyers

The Catholicism of the subjects of the Most Christian King was Catholicism with a difference, an historic native compromise between the claims of king and Pope. The Gallican tradition was older than Protestantism and reached back to that period of the Middle Ages when, after the Avignon captivity, the French monarchy was the spoilt child of the Catholic world. In the Pragmatic Sanction of Bourges (1438) had been expressed the Conciliar doctrines to which French clergy and lawyers were constantly to have recourse when the Pope's authority was in question. The Concordat of Bologna (1516), by which Francis I, in the year before Luther pinned his theses to the door of Wittenburg cathedral, received the right to nominate to benefices, was the framework of a half-way house between full schism, as in Henry VIII's England, and full acceptance of the Pope's sovereignty. Its effect had been to insulate France from the international Catholic movements of the century; while the dogmas of the Council of Trent were formally received, the disciplinary decrees were ignored. During the sixteenth century, while Huguenotism was being shaped in the crucible of the Religious Wars, Catholic France remained almost unaffected by the dynamic of the Counter-Reformation. The claims of the re-furbished Papacy were accepted only by the small Ultramontane group, and this was discredited by its connection with the Holy League, the anarchic tradition of the Guises and the ambition of Spain. So Gallican feeling became a sort of patriotism. The *Satire Ménippé* expresses it: 'What is the Papal legate doing here? He is Italian and the vassal of a foreign prince. There should be no rank or place for him here.' At the beginning of the seventeenth century, official majority Catholicism, taking its tone from the *politique* stance of the convert Henry IV and the humanism of Montaigne and his followers, was decidedly Gallican. To the old political claims of king against Papal authority was added the new appeal of a broad-based national church which should be a refuge for those who wearied of extreme religious attitudes of any sort.

Ever since the sallies of Philip the Fair against Pope Boniface VIII, lawyers had argued in *Parlement* and in pamphlets that the Pope was a temporal ruler with sovereignty only in his own land. Since kingdoms had been established by God long before the name of Pope had existed, 'the Pope is a usurper when he interferes with a dynastic question'. The theme had been reinforced by the activities of the Renaissance Papacy in secular Italian politics, and by French suspicion of the normally Hapsburg sympathies of Rome. Issues of church authority gave a new colour to the faded rags of constitutional sentiment, usually denied political outlet, and *Parlement* men, brought up on the Canon Law, could discuss Gallicanism and Ultramontanism with the same knowledge and verve that their common lawyer contemporaries in England applied to the struggle for political rights against the monarchy. *Parlement*'s role of arbitration in church affairs was further practised in the years of the *crise protestante* when it worked in harness with the Sorbonne, registering ecclesiastical laws along with those of the state. It became an axiom of *Parlement* that there could be no ecclesiastical exception to the authority of the king. The Gallican liberties, constantly re-examined and clarified, were made to enhance the spiritual and secular authority of the king. At the same time the lawyers lost no chance to stress the dependence of the church upon the protection of the king's court.

Ecclesiastical Gallicanism

The emphasis of the Sorbonne was naturally different from this. The Gallicanism of the bishops, many of whom were Sorbonne-trained, was based on the right of the bishops to regulate the affairs of the French church. The effect from the king's point of view was the same, for bishops and lawyers agreed that the king should be moral tutor, judge and master of the clergy. Cardinal du Perron had ascribed to the kings entire temporal sovereignty in which they 'depend upon God and recognise no power above them'. From this it was a short step to the lavish mandate of the French clergy to Louis XIV as 'patron and founder of the churches of France'. He was no mere layman for he 'had received an almost priestly unction and exercised a miraculous power'. However the Gallicanism of the bishops was more sentimental and more compromising than that of the lawyers because of the pull of conflicting loyalties. The old question of God or Caesar could not be overcome by formulae alone.

The fulsome rhodomontades of the church assembly in Louis XIV's reign should be read with caution. Behind the academic devices of an age of pulpit hyperbole, can be seen the sharper point of clerical designs against the Huguenots. Some bishops, such as the good Jansenist Zamet of Langres or Bossuet of Meaux, welcomed a theory which freed the jurisdiction of the church from the encroachment of foreign orders centred upon Rome. But a strong ultramontane current affected others who looked for the reform of a worldly church to the internationalism and *esprit de corps* of the religious orders, notably the Jesuits. Most churchmen adopted a compromise between intellectual acceptance of the doctrinal claims of the Papacy and recognition for practical purpose of the inescapable fact of royal power. Bossuet for instance, steeped in the work and thought of Carlo Borromeo, the saint of the Italian Counter-Reformation, yet born and bred in the *politique* tradition of the French *bourgeois*, borrowed from the 'ultra' exaltation of the role of monarchy as expressed by Bellarmine: 'the church is a monarchical society'. And he avoided the extreme conclusion of Suarez that 'the infallibility of the Pope is a Catholic truth taught up to our time by all doctors'. He saw clearly that the Reformation had made it impracticable to deny to the Pope theoretical powers and that the cause of unity was best served by recognition, in St. Thomas Aquinas' words, that 'the decisive authority of the Pope was the guarantee of unity of faith in the church'. He lived indeed in a different world from that of the Cardinal of Lorraine who declared before the Council of Trent: 'I am a Frenchman, brought up in the school of Paris, in which the authority of councils is said to be higher than that of the Pope.' In Bossuet's world the effective sovereignty was that of Louis *Dieudonné*, and under such a king 'unity of faith' could be for the devout more than a pious hope—a programme.

The contests of king and Pope during the reign have a slightly unreal appearance. A decisive body in the church looked to the king as head of a national church; the king however was obliged in the last resort to allow most of the Pope's claims to authority.

The parties who adopted such intransigent postures before the world could yet agree on essentials behind the scenes. Although he might play with the idea when it suited him, the king thought that the word 'schism' was 'too horrible to repeat'. Furthermore, the suppression of Protestants required at least the nominal approval of the Pope; the French church could hardly persecute Protestants while claiming Protestant rights for itself. Again, Gallicanism was not an attack upon material abuses. By the *appel comme abus* the victim of a decision by an ecclesiastical court could claim stay of execution from *Parlement*. Nor was the question of money serious, for the Pope drew little revenue from France. His only real hold on the French church lay in the Bulls of Institution which confirmed royal nominations. The king's Gallicanism was, more than anything, a protest against the intellectual subservience implied by the acceptance of a divided authority. It revolved round questions of prestige, a vital concern of any authoritarian government and a priority with Louis. His attitude may be interpreted as a sustained demonstration before the eyes of Europe of the power of France, the more impressive by contrast with the diminished moral standing of the Papacy.

The Régale

Louis felt his hand strengthened by the affair of the Corsican Guards, when anti-Papal feeling had blazed up in *Parlement* and the Sorbonne. The former's statement of the classic Gallican standpoint led to Alexander VII's Bull *Cum ad aures* (1665), and this in turn had been the signal for the Sorbonne and the Assembly of Clergy to protest. Only the king's involvement in a war with England postponed the trial of strength. Succeeding Popes, Clement IX, Clement X and Innocent XI, were at their election in the French interest. But it was in the pontificate of the last, a man of austere and crusading spirit, that the main conflict of the reign took place, over the *régale*.

The *régale* was an old right of the French monarchy by which, during the vacancy of a see, the king could appoint to benefices within its gift and receive its revenue. This double right, spiritual and temporal, was not universal but applied only to territories annexed before 1516. Many bishoprics in Languedoc were free from it and elsewhere exemptions had been bought. With the encouragement of Colbert, anxious as always to close loopholes and sweep away anomalies, Louis, in an edict of 1673, extended the *régale* to the whole of France. The usurpation was resisted only by two Languedoc bishops, Caulet of Pamiers and Pavillon of Alet, both Jansenist in sympathy. Their defiant stand was therefore complicated by the support of the Jansenists, who now emerged fortuitously as the champions of ecclesiastical rights, a role which intensified Louis' conviction that they must be proved heretical. Since the money was to be used for diocesan expenses and to start a new fund for compensating Protestant converts, the fight was clearly one of principle, the *rationale* of the state against the exemptions of the church. The storm burst when Louis presented, for a canonry at Alet, a candidate whom Bishop Pavillon promptly excommunicated. Pavillon's death in 1677 only intensified the battle in the other diocese where Caulet's obstinate stand was supported by the Pope, erratic in his political judgments but a man who, in Mme de Sévigné's words, 'did not tremble but threatened'. While royal agents worked in Rome and Papal agents in Paris, in the year of Caulet's death, 1680, Innocent XI quashed the king's nomination to the abbey of Charonne. So the king looked in exasperation to the Assembly of Clergy to give his claims definite and public support. The Assembly of 1681 was irregular, its members carefully chosen to give effect to the king's wishes, and it was dominated by the rival personalities of Bossuet and Harlay. Bossuet's purpose was constructive and moderate; he wished to define the Gallican principles in such a way as to make them a basis for sane negotiation. The wordly and astute archbishop of Paris was nearer to the mind of the king; while Bossuet preached movingly about the unity of the church, Harlay manœuvred to get the Assembly's support for a policy of duress which should bring the Pope to heel. A committee was set up under the chairmanship of Choiseul, bishop of Tournai, and produced the Four Articles of 1682, emphatic in essentials, tactfully ambiguous in detail. They affirmed (one) the king's independence in temporal matters and somewhat vaguely (three) the legitimacy of the Gallican customs. The second article revived, but in an inconclusive manner, the embattled theory of the superiority of General Councils over the Pope, while the fourth and most extreme could be taken to mean that Papal decrees were subject to the Assembly of Clergy, or by an invisible further stage, to the king. Bossuet's formula, that while the See of Rome was not infallible, it was indefectible and could not fall permanently into error, a typically fine-drawn yet valid distinction, gave shape to the view of the majority of the French clergy, who may have disliked the *régale* but were deferential to the king and resented the interference of the Holy See. But all depended upon the spirit in which these articles were interpreted; here Harlay's direction of the Assembly told; he secured that every candidate for theology should subscribe to the Articles. When the Pope protested the Assembly made brisk rejoinder: 'the Gallican church governs itself by its own laws'. Many felt at this time that France was poised precariously between her traditional place within the Roman church and a decisive step beyond it. Innocent accepted the challenge, refusing canonical institution to clergy who had taken part in the Assembly and had afterwards been promoted by Louis. The struggle was involved. The Jesuits, marshalled by Père la Chaise, who earned excommunication for his pains, supported the king against the 'Jansenist Pope', whose dislike for their order was notorious. Louis refused to ask for Bulls of Institution for those who had not taken part in the Assembly. This deadlock was the background to the events leading up to the revocation of the Edict of Nantes. The Pope, unimpressed by that display of royal piety, said that he would rather die than abandon his rights. In 1687 he abolished the franchises round the ambassadorial quarters; when the marquis de Lavardin, the French ambassador protested, he was promptly excommunicated. At Cologne in 1688, Innocent confirmed the appointment of Clement of Bavaria at the expense of Louis' candidate. Louis then seized Avignon while Colbert de Croissy mounted a virulent press campaign against the Pope, 'Jansenist, Quietist and supporter of the heretic William of Orange'. Innocent died in April 1689, by when more than thirty bishoprics were vacant, and both sides were anxious to end the affair. More cogent perhaps than any promptings of conscience or of Mme de Maintenon was Louis' desire to have the moral authority of Rome behind him in his grapple with the Protestant powers of the League of Augsburg. Both he and the Pope wished too to secure the neutrality of Italy in the widening international conflict. The vacancy of bishoprics was becoming an open scandal and a poor advertisement for the Gallican church to the cajoled remnants of Protestantism in France. So Louis was persuaded to ask for a Bull on behalf of Mme de Maintenon's confessor Godet des Marais, whom he had nominated to the archbishopric of Chartres. While he assured the Pope that the Four Articles would not be enforced, the bishops withdrew, in an official letter, anything said that could be interpreted as derogatory to the Papacy, for which they avowed 'their unspeakable grief'. In return Innocent XII gave his approval to some extension of the *régale*, and on this note of anti-climax Louis returned, without real concession, to the bosom of the church. He knew quite well that no letter could cancel an edict passed by the Assembly of the French clergy and registered by *Parlement*. The Gallican Articles remained a lively oracle, as Louis himself was to find, ironically, when he turned in unblushing orthodoxy to Papal support, in the nvolved mêlée over Jansenism in the closing years of the reign.

24 THE REVOCATION OF THE EDICT OF NANTES

The decline of Huguenotism

In October 1685, at Fontainebleau, Louis signed the edict which brought to a formal end the special and tolerated position which the Huguenots had enjoyed since his grandfather had signed the Edict of Nantes in 1598. In the eyes of the king and of the law the *religion prétendue réformée* ceased to exist in France. In fact, this was not the beginning of the persecution, nor was it the end of the sect. Louis' stroke was only the culmination of a long sequence of blows and pressures; it failed in its first purpose since the Huguenots were reduced but not destroyed. No historian can therefore defend the act upon the ground of success; most, upon moral grounds, have condemned it. Ranke, when asked against whom Prussia had been fighting in the war of 1870, replied: 'Louis Quatorze'. Taine thought that 'but for the Massacre of Saint Bartholomew and the Revocation of the Edict of Nantes, France might by the nineteenth century have had a liberal and parliamentary government'. David Ogg calls the act 'a crime noteworthy even in the sombre annals of religious bigotry'. The most sympathetic interpretation cannot conceal the cruelties and stupidities of the story. But it is surely inadequate to dismiss a policy which had the active sympathy of some of the best and most representative Frenchmen of the day in this way; nor should the twentieth century historian look at this matter through the hopeful spectacles of the nineteenth century liberal.

Huguenotism was a revolutionary movement, and a revolution cannot stand still; this may have been what Strowski had in mind when he wrote that 'the edict closed in on them like a tomb'. The militant Calvinism of the heroic days had given way, in this new political settlement, in the words of Le Cerf, to a 'worldliness, a cult of monarchy, and intellectual tastes, which killed a second time, more effectively than the dragonnades . . . the spirit of Calvin the master'. The optimists who 'waited for the coming decay of the Roman faith as if it were foreknown to them by express revelation' were gradually disillusioned. The leadership of the movement, too, had changed significantly since the Edict of Nantes. In the sixteenth century there had been a preponderance of country over town, reform had flourished in village communities under the feudal grip of the local *seigneur* and leadership had been aristocratic. The toughness of such communities survived, notably in the Midi, where old illusions of superiority lingered; nor had conversions been widespread, because the social coherence of the village made single apostasies difficult. But the independence of the southern Huguenots was discredited by the revolts of aristocratic rebels in the phase which ended with Richelieu's capture of La Rochelle in 1628. Political separatism under religious banners became a thing of the uncomfortable past as leadership of the sect passed from the *nablesse* to the town *bourgeoisie*. The Peace of Alais left the position of the 'separated brethren', as St. Vincent de Paul called them, intact but defenceless. Their tenure was precarious, their lease of tolerance conditional upon their good behaviour and the grace of their royal landlord. They were conspicuously loyal during the Fronde revolts and their reward was a soothing assurance of crown protection: they were to be maintained 'in the full and entire enjoyment of the rights of the Edict of Nantes'. This was however a measure of the crown's weakness rather than of its good will.

The Edict had not altered the attitudes of Catholic and Protestant towards one another, because it had been engendered in a spirit not of toleration but of impotent hatred. It was a federal settlement of convenience which neither side regarded as final or even entirely legal; a sort of armed truce. It remained controversial, and its clauses gave rise to tension and litigation, a cold war about the use of belfries and burial-grounds, fought by clergy, lawyers and congregations all over France. The Edict had merely entrenched a schism which all politically conscious Frenchmen recognised and deplored. Henry IV had accepted the Edict as a makeshift which assumed that the crown should remain neutral between the opposing creeds: 'we are all French and citizens of the same country'. But the crown in this century could be neither neutral nor agnostic but only Catholic, along with nine-tenths of the people. In England, where there was an analogous situation, where the king was head in England of the Anglican, and in Scotland of the Presbyterian church, the weak monarchy of Charles I had provoked a civil war by trying to impose upon Scotland the Anglican prayer-book. In France the situation was more complex because the schism was diffused, in every province and wherever there was a Protestant congregation.

Neither compromise nor toleration belonged to the political vocabulary of the seventeenth century; the accepted solution was still '*cuius regio eius religio*'. It was a Protestant, Benoît, who wrote that 'differences of religion disfigure the state'. Catholicism, moreover, gave to French monarchy its soul. Now that the tradition of Charlemagne and St. Louis shone again with lustre in the person of Louis XIV, the separate existence of the Huguenots was a sort of treason in itself, and an affront to all good Catholics.

In this situation the security of the Huguenots seemed to rest with those about the court who could make themselves indispensable, like Barthélemy Herwarth, Mazarin's *intendant* of finance, in whose *clientèle* alone there were about thirty of his faith, or the great soldier Turenne. Outward appearances at the start of Louis XIV's rule were not discouraging. There were some million and three-quarter Huguenots, about 630 'temples' and 750 ministers. Solid groups remained south of the Loire, in Guyenne, Poitou, the Dauphiné, Saintonge, Béarn and Languedoc. In Normandy, round Caen, an exceptional pastor was still making converts. But the influential and fashionable were drifting away, many Huguenots were defeatist and there was a severe pastoral crisis. The ideal of a native Huguenot culture had vanished and the Huguenot universities, such as Nîmes, had narrowed into theological seminaries. Behind the honourable façade and the strict discipline of the consistories there was a desiccated spirit and preaching was negative and tendentious. There was no inspiring translation of the Bible such as animated Protestantism in England. The canker of Arminianism had eaten into the Faith. The intellectual appeal of Calvinism lies in its uncompromising logic, and its spiritual strength primarily in its stress upon the individual, his state of mind and his relationship to God. Calvin had declared that his aim was 'to know the title and quality of God as creator and sovereign of the world' and he had affirmed the absolute dependence of man before his Creator. But Arminius and his followers both abandoned predestination and accepted the Erastian position of state control of religion. So they compromised Calvin's basic tenet of the single and absolute quality of sovereignty. When the rights of Caesar were allowed to infringe upon those of God, both the integrity of Calvinism and the right to existence of the Huguenot confession were called into question. Huguenot pastors reflected the hesitance of the theologians. In 1657 the delegates of the Reformed church assured their young king that they looked to him as to God, for his authority was as absolute in religion as in the state. The celebrated du Bosc of Caen declared that before Louis 'of the miraculous birth' a close scrutiny of the rights of God and Caesar must be irrelevant for they belonged alike to him. In the very year of the Revocation, Pastor Merlat stated baldly that 'sovereigns have no other law than their will'.

Movements towards reunion

The Catholics of the Gallican church also subscribed warmly to exaggerated notions of royal sovereignty, as they could well afford to. But this was the church of 'the great age of souls', of the devotional revival, of the dogmatic certainties derived from the Council of Trent. In the discussion between Bishop Bossuet and Paul Ferry, pastor of Metz, on the project of reunion, it was the Council's categorical defiance of heresy that stood in the way of compromise. The revival was grounded upon the authority of the hierarchy and the sacraments of the church. More important, in the work of men as different as Bérulle, founder of the Oratory, and the Jansenist Arnauld, can be seen a concern for the individual soul, an exploration of the implications of God's love, as strong as that of the first reformers. It is not too much to say that what Calvin's *Institution Chrétienne* did for the sixteenth, Bérulle's *Traité de l' Amour* and Arnauld's *Fréquente Communion* did for the seventeenth century. The position of Catholic and Protestant confessions had indeed altered profoundly since the Reformation. Now the Catholic view of the Real Presence and their insistence upon the authority of the Pope—not, in the view of the Gallican bishops of 1682, infallible—were the only fundamental differences left. Most Catholics were prepared to go half-way to meet the Protestants over Justification, whether by Faith or Works. The long battle over Jansenism revealed how close Catholic and Protestant views of Grace and Will could be, when Dominican, Jansenist and Calvinist could all make similar interpretations of St. Augustine. The Papacy, moreover, had already granted local concessions of the Cup, the right to Communion in both kinds. Even in the matter of the Real Presence, the Cartesian theory of extension seemed to offer a real hope of conciliation. The church which in one century harboured souls and intellects as various as Bérulle, François de Sales, Pascal, Vincent de

Paul, Le Camus and Fénelon, offered a tolerable refuge to those heretics who were unhappy about the claims of their isolated confession.

Turenne was the most important of these, and his reasons for adjuration may be cited for what they reveal of the dilemma of conscientious Huguenots. He had acquired a position of moral leadership in international Protestantism similar to that of Coligny in the sixteenth century, but he was also concerned for the unity and discipline of the nation. Perhaps he had a bad conscience after his ambiguous role in the Fronde; his decision may have been a political one, for all Bossuet's persuasive apologetics. But Turenne, who in 1661 refused the Constable's sword rather than abjure, was conscientious and devout. He was persuaded that Protestantism, in which 'every individual wishes to found a faith after his own inclinations and everyone who reads the Word of God wishes to interpret it according to his own fantasy', had no further theological justification. This sentiment was not peculiar to France. The ecstatic hopes aroused by the victories of Gustavus had been dimmed in the long anti-climax of a religious war which had lost all religious significance. After 1648 there were mass abjurations in Germany and talk of reunion became fashionable at Protestant courts. England went on its peculiar course; but hatred of Rome was accompanied there by the virulent persecution of sects who would not conform to a strictly defined Anglicanism. A few enlightened spirits searched for a more broadly based religion, not so much in tolerance derived from any positive view of human rights as in the latitudinarianism of disillusion. So Grotius, contemplating the wasteland of the Thirty Years War and the sectarianism of his native Holland, had envisaged a reunion of national churches of France, England and Scandinavia. This shows a misreading of the Gallican attitude in France; nevertheless he assured Archbishop Laud that there were in France 'many wise bishops who greatly approved the line of conduct of the Anglican church'. Leibnitz's work for reunion was of greater importance; he thought that it was the duty of Protestants to bring the schism to an end by negotiating reunion as a body. Under his influence, some Lutherans at Hanover signed articles of reconciliation which began by recognising the Pope's claim to be head of the church. Bossuet, who did not accept the common Catholic assumption that Protestant heresy sprang from intrinsic malice, and whose *Exposition de la doctrine Catholique* was so reasonable in tone that he was accused of watering down Roman doctrines to suit heretic taste, spoke for the moderates who were willing to come to terms. In his correspondence with Paul Ferry and later Leibnitz, we see that even his rational approach could not construct a bridge between Rome and Augsburg which all could cross. If Augsburg was difficult to approach, how much more would Geneva be!

Catholic approaches

Single voices of reason might speak of reconciliation, but the corporate opinion of the French church was different; the average French Catholic saw in the diffidence of the Huguenots only a signal for the final offensive. Though there might be disagreement about the methods employed by the government, almost all agreed about the principle upon which Louis eventually acted. The view of Augustine was widely quoted at the time: since error was a tyrannical oppression of feeble souls it was legitimate to appeal to the civil authority to free those souls. It is significant that in 1682 Saint Augustine's letter to a Donatist bishop, justifying the use of force, was specially published with the approval of the king. The gentle St. François de Sales had shown the way with the forcible conversion of the Chablais, and Bérulle, in a memoir to Richelieu, proposing a special crops of missionaries, had stated that these would be ineffective without political coercion. Now, Bossuet pointed out that the Protestants subscribed to the principle in their treatment of the Anabaptists. The young *abbé* Fénelon found the support of troops essential to his imaginative schemes of conversion. In its official assemblies the church had long been making outspoken demands for the suppression of the Huguenots and their 'synagogues of Satan'. Every meeting developed the simple theme: that the existence of a dissenting sect within France was a continuous treason to the king who embodied the ideal of unity, described by Fénelon in near mystical terms as the 'sacred bond which alone can hold the allegiance of souls, our heart-felt aspiration'. Thus the king and his ministers were conditioned to envisage revocation as an act of piety and patriotism. The crown was bombarded with *cahiers* of grievances against the Huguenots, who could not reply since, after 1659, they were not allowed to hold their national synods. In 1675 Louis was urged, typically, to show that he recognised the favour of God as revealed in his great victories by extirpating heresy: 'freedom of conscience is regarded by all Catholics as a precipice which yawns beneath their feet, as a trap prepared for their simplicity and as an open door to libertinage. Remove, Sire, this deadly freedom.'

Louis did not feel himself free to deal officially with the Huguenots till after the Treaty of Nijmegen which, in 1678, ended the Dutch War; but private enterprise had already achieved much. The Company of the Holy Sacrament, a pressure group of aristocratic *dévots*, had pioneered the way, preparing evidence for the massive case-books of the Jesuit Père Meynier[1] and the lawyer Bernard[2], an arsenal upon which bishops and *intendants* could draw in their dealings with the Huguenots. The skill of the casuist and jurist did wonders with the rambling and imprecise clauses of the Edict.

Since there was no explicit statement that Huguenots should be buried by day, they must be buried by night. Schools were permitted wherever the exercise of the religion was allowed, but since the subjects were not laid down, nor the number of masters who might teach them, they were restricted to the three R's, one master to a school, one school to a community; at Marennes, one master was left thus to the tender mercies of 600 children. The Edict had allowed exercise of the reformed faith where it already existed but since then, particularly in Languedoc, it had broken new ground. Now, after biased inquests, hundreds of 'temples' were destroyed, in Gex for instance, all except two, since this province had been gained by the crown three years after the Edict. There was duress too at less significant levels. In Calais, both inns were kept by Huguenots, so one was forced to sell out to a Catholic; in Paris, Huguenot master-embroiderers were forbidden to take apprentices of their faith. So the main lines of attack were defined: the schools, the congregations and the workshops. After 1678 the process was intensified. From 1661 to 1679 only ten edicts were registered; in the next six years there were eighty-five. By the gradual deprivation of the king's grace, the Huguenot was driven from public life, forbidden to act as judge, notary or advocate, to be a printer or doctor. He was banned from government office, even from the revenue department, the tax-farms and administration. He or she was forbidden to

---

[1] *L'Explication de l'Édit de Nantes* (1666).
[2] *L'Édit de Nantes exécuté selon les indications d' Henry le Grand.*

marry a Catholic. The special *chambres de l'édit*, created by the Edict to protect him, were abolished. By rigour, if not yet by violence, the Huguenot was being forced into an untenable position.

These measures gave insufficient material inducement to conversion. Then a pilot scheme launched in 1676 by the strenuous bishop of Grenoble, Le Camus, showed the possibilities of 'compensation'. His conversions amongst the Vaudois were backed by a special fund, the *'caisse de conversions'*, to compensate ministers for their loss of livelihood. It was run by Paul Pellisson with the revenues of Cluny and St. Germain, abbeys of which he was treasurer during their vacancy through the *régale* dispute between king and Pope. Pellisson had once been a Huguenot, Fouquet's right-hand man and disgraced with him in 1661. In 1667, after release and appointment to be royal historiographer, he was converted under Jansenist influence, promising to consecrate the rest of his life 'to the king and to God'. He was allowed to extend his fund until he was director of a vast network with agents in every province. There was a regular tariff of payments, ranging from 3,000 *livres* for a nobleman to 6 for a peasant, no small temptation to the miserably poor. He offered gratuitous advice to bishops and *intendants* and prepared regular statistical reports for the king. An entry in the *Gazette* of April 1678 ran: 'We have viewed with admiration the triumph of the king over the Vaudois, who have for centuries banned the Holy Church from their mountains.' Catholics as different as Bossuet and Fénelon approved of the system on the grounds that it was preferable to physical violence: God alone could cause a change of heart but material interest prepared man for the action of His grace. It is curious too to find Arnauld, later the first important Catholic to denounce the use of troops, championing the purity of their intentions in his *Apologie pour les Catholiques*—a Jansenist arguing that the end justified the means! But the Jansenists at the same time made a great missionary effort to instruct the *'nouveaux convertis'* in the faith, with translations of the liturgy and manuals of popular devotion such as that of the confessor of Port Royal, Le Tourneau, which set out to show that the liturgy offered deep spiritual consolation to the raw convert. The very success of Port Royal created its own problems. Their moderate approach and their vulgarisation of Holy Writ exposed them to the criticism of the regular orders, whose technique was less compromising. The deep divisions between Jesuit and Jansenist have indeed a cardinal importance in the story. The Society of Jesus had fought to check the insidious growth of the church within a church that was represented by Port Royal and its adherents. They were still smarting from the strictures of Pascal: 'the Jesuits have tried to combine God and the world and have only succeeded in gaining the contempt of both'. Were his successors now to be allowed to interpret the truth to Protestants in their own way and so to extend their influence?

The Jesuits urged more drastic methods. They were influential at court and in the *conseil de conscience*, through Père la Chaise, Louis' confessor, and Harlay, archbishop of Paris; they also had a sympathetic hearing from bishops who disliked the loss of their revenues to the *caisse*, and from officials who resented the growth of Pellisson's little empire. They pointed out to the royal ministers that the policy of bribery was slow and expensive; it was also wasteful and encouraged insincerity. Meanwhile Pellisson's work was hampered by his failure to get the support of Innocent XI, who had been elected in 1676, a Pope of strong and positive personality. He was at this time especially concerned with negotiations with the German Lutherans and with plans for a joint crusade of the European princes against the Turk. Innocent sympathised with the Jansenist position enough to earn himself the name of the 'Jansenist Pope', and he expressed a qualified approval of the conversions. But he was deeply embroiled with the French king over the rights of the Gallican church, he was concerned about the possibility of schism, and especially about the tendency of French bishops to make their own regulations in matters of dogma. As he was reported to have said in 1682: 'what use is the demolition of so many temples if all the bishops are schismatic? They will soon be like England.' He could not now tolerate the application of revenues arising from Louis' *régale* claim, even to convert heretics. This impasse of king and Pope played its part in the sequence of events that led to Fontainebleau. It was hard for Pellisson to answer his detractors without the formal mandate of the Pope, but he did enough to convince observers that Huguenotism was so rotten that a display of force and a categorical statement of royal will would destroy the sect. Arguments of force were indeed well received at this time, when the anti-Popish fury in England, stemming from the 'Plot', was arousing strong feelings amongst French Catholics. Every detail of the scurrilous trials was reported; a special number of the *Gazette* carried, for instance, the verbatim report of the scaffold speech of the aged Earl of Stafford. The 'Fury of Babylon', as the Co-adjutor of Arles called it, assumed an importance in French opinion beyond its real proportions.

The Dragonnades

In 1681 Marillac, *intendant* of Poitou, showed what could be done by the soldiers. There were precedents for the use of troops for non-military purposes and such billeting was a normal inconvenience of life in the frontier towns when no barracks existed. In 1675, Brittany had been successfully tamed, after the revolt there, by troops who treated it as foreign and occupied country. After the death of Bishop Caulet of Pamiers, the *intendant* Foucault lodged four companies of cavalry upon anti-*régale* men in his diocese. Now Marillac, anxious, in Burnet's nice phrase, 'to make his court' and jealous of the local bishop, Hardouin de la Hoguette, applied the method deliberately to the Protestant problem. He had experimented already with selective taxation; the *taille* rolls in his province were made out in three columns, 'Old Catholics', discharged from part, 'New Catholics', wholly exempt, and Huguenots, who made up the deficit. Now soldier missionaries promised better returns. In March 1681 he was authorised by Louvois to use a regiment of dragoons; within a year he was able to boast 38,000 conversions. Louis was shocked by the recital of cruelties in Poitou from a deputation led by a nobleman whose château had lodged a whole company of troops. Benoît, the first of a school of Protestant historians who specialised in the listing of atrocities, admitted that terror was more widespread than the violence which caused it. Stories of people being thrown on to fires or hounded by dogs to death were a commonplace of seventeenth century military behaviour. But abjurations at the point of the bayonet, men being declared Catholics after they had been dragged by the hair to the Mass and sprinkled with Holy Water, such blasphemies could not be ignored, nor the effect upon opinion abroad. Jurieu roused opinion in England and Holland with his '*Derniers Efforts de l'Innocence Affligée*', which was to be the model for a whole torrent of exilic literature. Neecassel, Vicar-Apostolic in the United Provinces, asked Bossuet to intercede with Louis for some curtailment of his missionary activities in view of their unhappy effects, in emigration and the loss of good-will to France. The hard-bitten Elector of Brandenburg assured the French ambassador that 'he looked with anguish at the persecution of people whom he regarded as brothers and the world as innocent'. Louis answered evasively that 'only chapels built since the Edict have been destroyed', while Pellisson was naïve enough to assure the Pope that force was being used only to strengthen the resolve of those who had 'fallen into the arms of the church'. Versailles in fact reacted sharply, for Louvois, though no humanitarian, was anxious about the discipline of his cherished troops, and Louis was realist enough to see that a domestic issue was becoming a European scandal which might imperil his relations with the rest of Europe. So Marillac was dismissed. De Muin, the *intendant* at La Rochelle who had improved the system by inducing the signing of false certificates, was checked at the same time by Seignelay, who was distressed to hear that some of the best seamen in France were emigrating. Louis had paused, to meet the needs of his foreign policy, but there was no re-appraisal. The method had shown its usefulness and might be used again, with greater control, when the time was ripe.

The Revocation

There was talk in Europe in the eighties of a *grand dessein*, as though Louis were carrying through a vast project, long prepared, stage by stage and with consistent purpose. This accords with his reputation in the years after Nijmegen and with the high-flown sentiment of the French themselves, who liked to attribute to Louis acts of classical grandeur. In fact there is no evidence for such a design. For all the posing and the propaganda, when decisions and their timing were in question, the king was an opportunist. As Picavet said: 'Great Designs are rare in politics; the king proceeded empirically and sometimes impulsively.' There is little pattern in the Huguenot legislation of the earlier part of the reign; indeed in 1669 it suited him to revoke earlier laws in an Edict worthy of Henry IV. *Le roi dévot* remained altogether *le roi politique*. The church was his ideology, the state his interest, and, like some modern autocrats, he acted most decisively when his ideology and interest seemed to coincide. He had invaded Holland in the interest of the Dutch Catholics. He had entered Strasbourg in order to recover that vital Rhine city for the Faith. Now again the Catholic ideal and political interest seemed to invite him to fulfil what he was encouraged to regard as his destiny. After the Truce of Ratisbon in 1684 had confirmed him in his frontier gains, conditions seemed to be favourable; the Huguenot question came again to the fore.

The ultimate responsibility for Revocation lay with Louis. What was in his mind during these last years? Actual cases of treachery, such as that of Ruvigny's secretary who betrayed to William of Orange in 1676 the terms of the secret treaty between Louis and Charles II of England, were few. Small things could weigh large however with Louis, who had always been irritated by the tendency of a few French Protestants to look to William of Orange as their patron. Suspicion of the potential role of the Huguenots, despite their massive and publicised loyalism, increased after 1672. With a strong pro-French party in the College of Electors Louis had dreamed of being elected King of the Romans and so heir to the Imperial title. But after the glory of 1683 and John Sobieski's repulse of the Turks from Vienna Leopold was popular in Germany; to oust French influence he was bidding for Lutheran support by patronising schemes for religious unity. So Louis put his trust in a carefully advertised orthodoxy. The capture of Strasbourg had already been hailed by Bossuet as a 'happy presage' of the destruction of Lutheranism. Louis now reproached the Emperor for failing to look after German Catholics oppressed by the Turks, while de Cornac informed a sceptical Europe that 'Holland and Germany served as a theatre, not for his victories alone but for those of Jesus Christ'. Then in 1683, the Most Christian king used his influence at the Vatican to have the greatest of all proposals for reunion, that of Rojas y Spinola, rejected. His agent told the Papal congregation that the scheme was 'incompatible with the purity of our faith and our principles'. By so committing himself to act as the champion of orthodoxy, he played into the hands of those who for different reasons wished to kill such pacific projects. When Bossuet wished to secure from Innocent the vital concession of the use of the Cup, which was a *sine qua non* for Protestants and one of their last insistent demands, he was not able to secure it. A lengthy negotiation with the Huguenots of Languedoc, initiated by Noailles and Daguesseau, governor and *intendant* respectively of the province, was repudiated by the king. Louis felt that the time had come for him to stand forward as the head of the Catholic party in Europe; a far

cry from Richelieu's support of Gustavus Adolphus against the
dévot Emperor Ferdinand. The great-grandson of Philip II and
the son of Anne of Austria, whose ritualistic court at Versailles
owed so much to Spanish influence, considered that France fitted
the place left by the decay of Spain. What better moment than now
to do what Philip had failed to do, to destroy heresy in Europe
and bring, perhaps, a new lustre to the name of Emperor? William
of Orange, a bitter but perceptive critic, considered in 1682 that
he was thinking in these terms: 'there is no doubt that it is the
intention of the King of France to make himself master of
Europe'. It is not irrelevant that the names of Constantine and
Charlemagne were bruited so constantly in France in these years.
Louis has been much criticised for pursuing these chimeras. But
his hopes were supported by the defeatist appearance of the
Protestants; were their current moves to reunion anything more
than admissions of defeat? When, in February 1685, the militantly
Catholic James II acceded to the throne of England, he immediately offered him troops to help him convert his subjects. He was
convinced that the religious balance had come down heavily upon
the Catholic side.

There is nothing to show that the king had any real misgivings
at any time after the Truce of Ratisbon in 1684. He basked in the
chorus of approval with which court and clergy met every
spectacular gain for the Faith. The few sceptics like Saint-Simon,
who confided to his diary that 'the king has the pleasure of an easy
repentance at the expense of others', were inaudible above the
clamour of the devout. There is no need to postulate a new seriousness of purpose in the king, or middle-aged qualms of conscience.
Nor is it very significant that about 1680 he finally gave up the
outrageous Mme de Montespan and in 1683 secretly married the
ex-Huguenot Mme de Maintenon. She figures prominently in the
demonology of Protestants, but her part has been exaggerated.
She was primarily interested in the education of Huguenot
children, and although her influence was earnest and bracing,
she seems to have acted at first rather as spokesman for the royal
conscience than as its director. None of her contemporaries accused
her of playing much part and the myth seems to have grown up
later when she busied herself so prominently in the Jansenist and
Quietist controversies, under the influence of her confessor
Godet des Marais. Maintenon complained in 1685 that 'Louis
thought so little about God'. A recent writer has described him

as having 'the faith of a nursery maid'. It might more fairly be said that his piety was constant, formal and unreflective. He was therefore the readier, though he may not have realised it, to accept the views of the experts around him: the *conseil de conscience*, for high-level decisions, the Ministers and the *intendants*, whose reports were the only guides to what was really happening in the provinces. The Papal nuncio wrote to his master, who was very ready to believe him: 'the King, who has never read or studied a book, lets himself be misled . . . and never lends his ear to anybody beyond these people'. Contemporaries were unanimous in ascribing his religious policy to the *conseil de conscience*, 'councillors of Babylon' in the eyes of the Pope, which now met every Saturday under the presidency of the king. Its two principal figures were Père la Chaise and Harlay. It was their task, representing as they did the advocates of extreme measures, to overcome the scruples of the king about the promise of his grandfather to his Protestant subjects; not to persuade the king that revocation was desirable, for of that he had no doubt, but that it was legal and honourable. La Chaise was essentially a courtier, 'intelligent, gentle and moderate' in Saint-Simon's view, his principal role was advising the king about church preferment. How effective his private insinuations were the historian can only guess, for he was careful to keep in the background. But as Bayle pointed out, the confessor alone 'could inform the king of what he could answer for in his conduct' and, he added, 'Monsieur de Paris acted in concert with the confessor'.

Harlay de Champvallon, archbishop of Paris since 1671, has been strangely neglected by historians, for there is reason to believe that his was the most influential single figure. He was worldly, scholarly, an assiduous courtier, a brilliant administrator. Saint-Simon catches something of the man in his description of the archbishop strolling in his garden with a duchess, followed at a fitting distance by a gardener raking over the gravel touched by their feet. He was in every way the opposite to Bossuet, who detested him. He had forced the bishop of Meaux, the 'great simplifier', to go further than he intended in the Gallican declaration of 1682. His firm principle was to serve the king, to defend his rights in the government of the church; in consequence he had become 'the sole minister of the king in ecclesiastical affairs and the repository of royal authority, which he disposes as he wishes'. By means of observers and agents he tested the pulses of clerical opinion and the king treated him as the oracle of the clergy. He worked in close concert with the pressure group of the church Assemblies whose demands were so swiftly translated into action. In the beginning of July 1685 the Assembly begged that the job of advocate should be barred to Huguenots; on the 11th of the month the demand was put into effect by edict. In this sort of work one can see also the hand of the aged Michel le Tellier, Chancellor since 1677 and an expert in such vexatious legislation. His son, the marquis de Louvois, now war minister in his father's place, may have been insensitive to the finer points of the Huguenot operation but he was ready to use his unemployed troops, take charge of the operation and make it his own. The Le Telliers had long supported harsh measures, if only to embarrass Colbert, who had always been a moderating influence; after the great minister's death, and despite the presence of his son Seignelay, they were the dominant party in the royal council. Their arguments seemed irresistible when the *intendant* Foucault announced from Béarn, in the spring of 1685, the conversion of 22,000 Huguenots. Boufflers was immediately ordered south with his whole army. When Daguesseau opposed the arrival of troops in Languedoc, where he was still parleying hopefully with the local ministers, he was replaced by the implacable Bâville.

The dragonnades brought prodigious results in the summer months of 1685; in Béarn, Montauban and Poitou there were mass abjurations. *Intendants* announced miracles and the court believed what they wanted to believe. Louvois wrote to Seignelay in September of 60,000 converts in the *généralité* of Bordeaux, where there had been 150,000 Huguenots: 'there are not ecclesiastics enough to receive the abjurations. Everywhere people demand new churches to hold the new converts.' To the archbishop of Reims, his brother, he declared excitedly: 'the last reports from the Saintonge and Angoumois convey that all is Catholic', but, his mood subdued for a moment by a sensible afterthought, 'His Majesty recommends that you be accommodating to the bankers and manufacturers'. For all the atmosphere of crusade, economic considerations were not lost sight of. When the matter was debated at the *conseil d'état* in October, Seignelay and Colbert de Croissy warned of the dangers of emigration to commerce. But more immediately pressing was the expense of conversions. The compensations, it was argued, were an intolerable levy upon the Old Catholics and upon the state; would it not be cheaper to drive out the remaining ministers? The king was now ready to believe anything. He was convinced that he could see the hand of God in all that happened: 'I cannot doubt but that it is the Divine Will that I should be his instrument in bringing back to his ways all those who are subject to me.' He was not deceived by the optimistic reports of his *intendants* into believing that 'heresy was no more', but he certainly thought that those who were left, deprived of temple, schools and pastors, would soon conform. As to those who were daily fleeing for conscience' sake—they were disloyal subjects anyway. Maintenon expressed another characteristic view: 'I well believe that many of these conversions are insincere, but God avails Himself of all ways to bring heretics to Him'; the children at least would be Catholic, even if their fathers were heretics, and their outward reunion would bring them within reach of the Truth.

In October the court was as usual at Fontainebleau for the hunting. There the Chancellor prepared the edict which brought to an end the guarantee of 1598 and abolished the legal existence of the *religion prétendue réformée*. It was Le Tellier's personal *Nunc Dimittis*, presented with senile joy. 'The best and greatest part of our subjects of the R.P.R. have embraced the Catholic faith; and as by reason of this the execution of the Edict of Nantes is useless, we have judged that we cannot do better, to efface entirely the memory of the troubles, the confusion and the evils that the progress of this false religion have caused in our realm . . . than to revoke entirely the above Edict.' So temples were to be abolished, Protestant schools closed, *curés* were to baptise the children of Protestant parents. Ministers who would not yield were to be exiled, while laymen who tried to escape the country were liable to the galleys. Only in Alsace, where Louis was anxious to show that he respected the terms of the Treaty of Westphalia, was the *status quo* respected. In the rest of France, Louvois instructed that the most draconian measures be taken against the stubborn, 'who should have no rest or quiet so long as they live in a religion which displeases His Majesty'.

Disillusion

Catholics everywhere greeted the Revocation with rapture. A few enlightened spirits were cynical about its efficacy, like Saint-Simon, or saddened by the waste. Vauban's protest is worth recording for his moral courage and good sense: 'Kings are masters of the lives and goods of their subjects but never of their opinions.' But criticisms were hushed in the general mood of euphoria. La Bruyère congratulated Louis on 'having banished a religion which was false, disloyal and hostile to the monarchy'. Lamoignon spoke for *Parlement*: 'the king has done in a single year what others have been unable to do in a whole century', and this, in the opinion of the Jesuit Robert, 'not by fire and sword, lawful means, but by his gentleness and wisdom'. Bossuet saluted the act in transcendent phrases: 'let us publish this miracle of our times; let us dote upon the piety of Louis; let our acclamations soar to heaven'. For all this exaltation, neither Louis' act nor his subjects' eloquence could solve the problem recognised in article 12 of the Edict: 'On condition that they do not practise their religion, Huguenots may live in the realm without abjuring until it pleases God to enlighten them.' The king was under no illusions about the extent of the miracle. He knew that Fontaine-bleau was only the start of the hardest phase of a campaign to win back the hard-core heretics and educate the 'New Catholics' whose case Mme de Sévigné put well: 'many people have been converted without knowing why. He (Père Bourdalue) will explain it to them and make them good Catholics. Up till now the dragoons have been good missionaries. The preachers that are being sent out will complete the work.' But what of the unconverted? Was article 12 to be interpreted by the missionaries or by the dragoons? Even the authority of Augustine and his *compelle intrare* could not reconcile all the protagonists of persuasion and reason to the coercion which was official government policy.

Harlay was entrusted with the control of missionary activities. Since it was recognised that the average village *curé*, probably ignorant of the Bible, was unfitted to undertake such delicate work, special squads were recruited from Parisian clergy and the regular orders. Money was available, 100,000 *livres* from the church, half a million added by the king. Translations of the New Testament, catechisms and breviaries were distributed, at least half a million volumes, by Pellisson, who still believed that the way to affect tender consciences was by moderation and reason. Le Camus, now a Cardinal, laid stress upon personal penitence and humility. He produced a daring formula for the remaining Huguenots of his diocese, was challenged by Robert, denounced at Rome for his indifference to images and relics and was promptly vindicated by the Pope. In Paris, conscience-saving formulas were devised by Seignelay and Harlay, for it would be impolitic to billet dragoons on wealthy Huguenots in the capital. In Saintonge, Fénelon found evidence of the disastrous effects of force. In his view the typical Huguenot was bound to his faith less by conviction than by habit; rather than arouse his spirit by argument or prod him with the bayonet, the priest should 'explain the Gospel with authority at once gentle and persuasive'. One-third of the ministers in his area were converted and it remained peaceful during the rising in the Cevennes. Fénelon found the civil authority useful principally for preventing evasions and emigration; also, since he believed that the emigration was often caused by economic distress, for giving pensions to those who lost their livelihood.

Undoubtedly many made sincere and lasting conversions. The letter of a Parisian to his minister son-in-law may stand for these: 'I have found the contrary of what I have been told, that I would hear of nothing but saints to whom one must address one's prayers. . . . I go every day to St. Barthélemy to hear a father of the Oratory, Père la Tour, who preaches the gospel admirably.' But the king's ministers, committed to the outward destruction of the sect, could not wait for every Huguenot to come to terms with his conscience. The government could not be made to look ridiculous by a few scrupulous churchmen. The initial effect of revocation was disappointing. Since it was widely assumed that the Edict of Fontainebleau meant the end of the dragonnades, many renounced their sword-point conversions, some affecting to appear more Huguenot than before. So Louvois ordered that 'those who want the stupid glory of being the last to resist, be pushed to the last extremity'. By way of example, Huguenots on his own estates were to be 'properly maltreated'. In December 1685 he ordered the destruction of all emigrants' houses in La Rochelle. The ablest exponent of his brisk policies was the *intendant* Lamoignon de Bâville, 'King of Languedoc', efficient and, to the heretic, implacable, as befitted the son of the prime mover of the *cabale des dévots* against Molière and *Tartuffe*. His draconian measures won 60,000 in three days and were supported by the bishops of Languedoc, who were confronted by compact and resolute communities, aggressive as later revolts were to show and not amenable to the missionary. But elsewhere officious *intendants* were resented; some set up their own inquisition for troublesome cases, claiming that they were responsible to the royal council alone.

Soon a party grew round those bishops who reacted against violence and were shocked by reports of blasphemy amongst forced converts. Matignon, bishop of Condom, protected the local Huguenots against the troops, and at Orléans, de Coislin lodged the soldiers at his own expense. Then Montgaillard, bishop of St. Pons, made an open stand against Louvois in February 1686. In two letters, gleefully published by Jurieu as evidence from inside the enemy's camp, he exposed the orders to drive all without exception to the altar, even those 'who spit and trample upon the Eucharist'. These prelates were concerned with the profanation of the sacraments; for if a Huguenot defiled the Host, who was the sinner, the unwilling communicant or the men who drove him there? The Jansenists, whose tradition was grounded upon the attacks of Pascal and Arnauld against the mechanical treatment of the sacraments, were also outspoken in criticism of the dragonnades. Harlay replied with a severe hint about Jansenist sympathies with the converted—and unconverted—and banned Le Tourneau's translations of the Breviary. Exiles rejoiced as Jurieu recalled the solemn promises of 1685; so this was the 'good faith' of their convertors, this was 'Catholic unity'!

More serious than feuds within the Gallican church was the equivocal position of the Pope. When Queen Christina of Sweden, herself perhaps the most remarkable convert of the period, certainly the most unorthodox, proclaimed that the dragonnades were worse than St. Bartholomew's Eve, Innocent reproached her, but with tears of embarrassment. Perhaps his main feeling was of relief, for Louis had at least shown that he was not prepared to come to terms with the Huguenots in order to create a native and schismatic church. But he was still not prepared to concede anything on the issue of the *régale* and he refused to make Louis' candidates Cardinals, preferring the independent Le Camus. As he became aware of the receding hopes of a pacific reunion of the churches, he returned to his original attitude of suspicion towards a prince 'who looked more to the advantages of his realm than to the kingdom of God'. So Louis was cheated of the salute which he felt was his due from Rome to the defender of the faith. He had gained nothing amongst the Catholics of Germany, who were more impressed by the Emperor's strenuous efforts against the Turks. Protestants were left with the impression that the head of the Church disapproved and mocked at Louis' discomfiture. Innocent XI rightly bewailed the setback to projects of reunion; for schism was now in the opinion of most judges irremediable. The Emperor was still concerned, for his own ends, with creating a union of the German princes, for which a condition of success was that the Pope would disavow the persecution in France. But haunted by fear of Gallican schism, Innocent could not do this. After 1688 the French were involved in a war for the Faith against William of Orange and the Emperor, and by then the German states, looking anxiously over the Rhine, had lost interest in reunion or the Pope's project for crusade against the Turks. In Holland the Jesuits were threatened with expulsion and appealed to Père la Chaise to use his influence to re-establish the Edict of Nantes!

The émigrés

James II would undoubtedly have found means to lose his throne without Louis' aid. But the Revocation was a wonderful weapon of propaganda for the enemies of a prince who wished to make England Catholic. To the judicious Evelyn 'the French persecution of the Protestants raging with the utmost barbarity seemed to exceed even what the heathen used'. More persuasive than the denunciations of Jurieu were the refugees who streamed across the Channel. The connection between these unfortunates and the policy of their king would have been noticed even without the tactlessness of the bishop of Valence: 'God seemed to raise the French king to this power and magnanimous action so that he might be in a capacity to assist in doing the same here (England).' William did not fail to exploit this situation. Already in his own country the Revocation had played a part in healing the division between the Stadholder and the Regents of Amsterdam, upon whose *bourgeois* caution Louis had relied for keeping the Dutch in safe neutrality; the Burgomaster of Amsterdam witnessed that 'it was the Huguenots who persuaded them to come to terms with the Prince of Orange'. So William, king after 1688 of both England and Holland, was able to rally support, not only as the defender of the frontiers but as the saviour of Protestantism. He had a new ally, too, in the Elector of Brandenburg, who defied Louis by making a treaty with the Dutch in 1685 and invited to his states all who fled from persecution. To the complaints of the French ambassador he replied that he could not be prevented from 'being as zealous for his religion as the French king was for his'. It is not surprising that in 1689, when Louvois was unleashing a 'preventive' war against the Emperor and William, that Bossuet was constrained to admit: 'your so-called Reformation was never stronger. All the Protestant peoples are now united in a single bloc. . . . Abroad the reformers have never been more united, arrogant, menacing.' So the revocation emphasised the moral division of Europe. 'Today it is virtually the North that is ranged against the South, the Teuton races challenging the Latin', wrote Leibnitz in 1692.

'My realm is being purged of bad and troublesome subjects': Louis affected to be complacent about the emigrations but they were the measure of the failure of his policy. Louvois wrote 'that the king is resolved to transplant all the people in the Cevennes if they continue to hold meetings'. But a policy designed to over-awe the rebels and expel the obstinate ministers was quite different from the voluntary exodus of whole communities which the government was powerless to stop. It can be inferred, despite the absence of statistics, from the evidence of receiving countries and the estimate of Vauban, who knew more about French social life than anybody, that at least a quarter of a million left. Many of these were workers, French and foreign, recruited by Colbert to further his plans for manufactures. Even making allowance for the effects of war upon industrial activity, it is plain that important industries were damaged seriously, if not irreparably. Towns like Reims, Tours, Nîmes and Rouen lost more than half their workers; Lyon all but 3,000 out of 12,000 silk-workers. Clothworkers, hatters, paper-makers, clockmakers, jewellers, shipwrights—the list is long. Perhaps most serious was the loss of bankers and merchants with their capital. Few peasants emigrated; the bulk of the exiles were townsfolk and many of them substantial citizens, pastors, lawyers, doctors, seamen. It was a small propor-tion of a country of 19 millions, but a serious haemorrhage of industry, of skills and capital that were desperately needed in an economy already starved of cash, with declining tax returns and mounting debts. Not all the exiles travelled empty-handed. Abraham Valéry of Languedoc was able to set up a large factory as soon as he arrived in Halle and one Paris merchant took 600,000 *livres* with him to Holland.

The loss to France can best be seen in the gain to the countries which were glad to give hospitality to this living wealth. In Holland they were given rights of citizenship, and Amsterdam accorded commercial privileges and three years' exemption from tax. A French agent estimated that 65,000 had arrived by 1686, principally textile workers. Some went even further, to the Dutch colonies; by 1691 there were 13,000 at the Cape of Good Hope. In England, Parliament voted funds and the public opened subscriptions; but James was reluctant to help and William was thwarted by Parliament in his desire to give them citizenship, which they did not achieve until 1701. 10,000 settled in London, and smaller communities in Norwich, York and Exeter. Several industries were started or improved, paper-making, tapestries, satin and taffeta. Emigrants found their way further to colonies in Massachusetts, the Carolinas, Boston and New York, to bring new life to Calvinism in the New World. At one such congregation, Benjamin Franklin used to recall from his childhood the preacher's violent denunciation of Louis, the 'anti-Christ'. Under the shadow of French power and vehement threats the Swiss could only shelter a few thousand Huguenots; in 1686, Catinat's army ravaged the Vaudois as an object lesson. But the handful of clockmakers who went to Geneva and Lausanne stayed to create a famous tradition. Some seamen ventured north to Scandinavia and a party of La Rochellais even took service in a corps recruited by the Genevese Lefort in Peter the Great's Russia. There were soon scattered settlements all over Germany, in Hesse-Cassel, Brunswick, Hanover and the Palatinate. The most important settlements, smiled on by the Great Elector, were in Brandenburg-Prussia. In Magdeburg, depopulated in the Thirty Years War, 1,000 evolved a complete community with pastors, surgeons, lawyers and army officers. At Berlin, alongside the little Brandenburg garrison town, a busy French township grew up, of 4,000 souls, the real beginning of the great capital city of today. The Prussian rulers thus gained industrious subjects and good soldiers from the intolerance of Louis XIV.

As early as 1685 Le Camus complained about the entry into France of the *Pastorales* of Jurieu, 'undoing in a day the work of months'. But the authorities were unable to prevent this sort of literature, inflammatory and treasonous, from reaching an eager public. From presses in Holland and Germany came a flood of pamphlets, ammunition for the greatest paper war since the Reformation. Bayle's style was magisterial: 'if people only knew the force and present significance of the expression, no one would envy France the distinction of "being wholly Catholic" under Louis the Great. The Roman church is nothing but a fury and a whore.' Jurieu, who included among his activities the organising of a spy-ring to operate in France, indulged freely in prophecy: the reign of Antichrist was soon to end, the true church would conquer and the Huguenots return to France. The date of the forecast tended to change, but the expectation of the event sustained Huguenot morale.

The Revocation stung the rival apologists into a fury of new activity. One significant consequence of Louis' policy had been to bring together, sharing common exile, the pastor Claude, Bossuet's old antagonist, Bayle, Gilbert Burnet, the English latitudinarian, and John Locke, former tutor to the earl of Shaftesbury, the last two finding the air of Holland good for their health in the years of royalist reaction in England. The influence of events in France upon many Englishmen is typified by Burnet. Already his *History of the Reformation* had justified the English schism; now he enlarged upon the dangers of Romanism. His work brought retaliatory rumbles from the Oratorian Joachim le Grand, then a thunderbolt from Bossuet. In the *Histoire des Variations*, at once history and apologetic, he condemned the 'variations', 'subtleties', 'equivocations' and 'artifices' with which the Protestants tried to repair their divisions and hide the error of their doctrines in the face of immutable truth. His charge could be answered; it was easy to point to the jealousies of Jesuit and Jansenist and show that Rome too had its 'variations'. Burnet declared that the Protestant church had not varied in essentials and Le Vassor pointed out that 'disunity was necessary to penetrate to the depths of truth'. The Catholic ideal, presented with such grandeur and logic, was discredited by the imposition of revealed truth upon a defenceless minority. So the ordeal of the Huguenots fertilised new religious and political ideas. Revocation was an act of faith, but it was also an act of state, and criticism of the idea led naturally to criticism of the authority behind it. Exiles like Claude and Basnage left France with a sense of grievance, not only against a church but against the establishment of which it was part. Their revolt went beyond the mandates of the church to the very nature of authority, personified in a king who, by the atrocities committed in his name, had put himself beyond the pale. It went beyond the person of Louis to the ideal of the unified state implied in his view of monarchy. So the exiles became organs of non-conformity, the 'mouth-pieces of heterodoxy', resistance took on a new meaning and liberalism stirred again in the womb of religious thought. The hack pen of Bayle, the genius of Locke served similar ends. The coincidence of the Huguenot dispersion and the Whig revolution against arbitrary monarchy gave rise to renewed speculation about the nature of faith and of sovereignty. The *avant-garde* of the Huguenots accepted the idea that the people had a sovereign power and that the prince was merely a delegate.

War in the Cevennes

As Louis' government grew more pre-occupied with the war of the League of Augsburg, conversion funds dried up, troops were sent to the front and policy became increasingly incoherent. The Huguenots who held out still were sustained by the *Pastorales* and believed that the League would save them. They clung to one straw after another; first it was the coming of the Dutch fleet, then the coming death of Louis XIV. But for the king it had become a question of *amour propre*. He still preferred to lose Protestant subjects rather than to tolerate them: 'the king will never renew the Edict of Nantes, even if the enemy are at the Loire'. He was supported by the introspective piety of the *dévots* at court, for whom spoke the Duke of Burgundy, Fénelon's *protégé*, and heir, after the Dauphin, to the throne: 'the recall of the Huguenots now would offer to the whole of Europe a pitiful inconstancy of principle'. But coercion was abandoned. In 1698, at the instigation of Cardinal Noailles and Pontchartrain, the council opened an inquest and the following January secret injunctions were given to the *intendants* and clergy to eschew all violent methods. In Languedoc, where clandestine organisations survived, Bâville encouraged his agents to ignore these instructions. 'The *curés* of Languedoc', wrote Villars, 'cannot lose their habit of browbeating their parishes.' One such priest, François du Chayla, stopped a convoy of refugees and imprisoned them; his house was surrounded by a peasant mob and he was killed. The trouble spread as old scores were paid off by desperate men. Preachers emerged to arouse their passions, guerilla bands quickly formed wearing white shirts—*camisards*—and in 20-year-old Jean Cavalier a leader was found. There had already been a small rising in the Cevennes in 1682 and there had been a gradual spread of 'prophesying'. Now insurrection raged in an extraordinary atmosphere of nervous excitement and Biblical fervour. The Protestants called their assemblies the 'Desert', an allusion to the Hebrews who waited for forty years in Sinai to enter the Promised Land. They were roused into a condition of mystical excitement by the passionate pamphlets of the *émigrés* and the apocalyptic imagery of their preachers. *Illuminés* appeared, as they did in Commonwealth England, men and sometimes children who foamed and fell into trances before delivering their message. Militarily the revolt posed grave problems in harsh and mountainous terrain. When the troops failed to come to grips with the skulking peasants they burnt their villages—Louis in 1703 ordered the destruction of 460. He had reason to be exasperated, for the revolt lasted three years, occupying in turn his best generals, Villars and Berwick. Versailles was forced in the end to make concessions, Cavalier was bought over (he subsequently sailed to England, where he later became governor of the Isle of Wight) and gradually the revolt petered out.

In the Cevennes, in open warfare against the state, Huguenotism recovered its soul. Royal policies had succeeded in destroying institutional and clerical Protestantism in France. They had destroyed at the same time in the remnant, perhaps three-quarters of a million, the respect for authority and the king which had been so marked before; above all any desire for a *rapprochement* with Rome. The hypocritical gestures which sufficed for the 'converted' at the Mass were a shock to those Huguenots who had been attracted to the devotional movement in the Catholic church: for what did the Catholic veneration for the Real Presence amount to if the sacraments could be treated as a civil test? So Huguenotism recovered that element of protest against the mechanical and formal character of the church which the work of François de Sales, Bérulle and the great Jansenists had done so much to dispel. The Huguenots had escaped from the doubts of a compromising theology; they were back in the heroic age again and issues were clearer. On August 21, 1715, Antoine Court presided over a Provincial synod, the first to take advantage of the edict of March. It was a new start. The new party rose round the tradition of 'resistance'. A third of the old pastors had abjured and few now returned from exile to lead their flocks. The conformists, the timid, the propertied, had no place in the new order, which was rural and democratic. As Vauban put it: 'the blood of martyrs has always been an infallible means of enhancing a persecuted faith.' An individualist confession, in which every man with his Bible was his own priest, could not be blotted out by the destruction of churches and the removal of pastors.

After the humiliation of Ramillies in 1706 Louis asked plaintively: 'has God forgotten all that I have done for Him?' In the subsequent disasters, bigotry softened into resignation. The Protestant issue had become largely academic and the authorities simply shut their eyes. The hope of the Huguenots, that the allies would include the re-enactment of the Edict of Nantes in their peace terms, was disappointed. It is a question whether toleration could have been imposed by foreign bayonets. It came in fact with the saving grace of time. In March 1715, the government recognised the facts: 'the Huguenots' long stay in France was sufficient proof that they had embraced the Catholic religion . . . without which they would have been neither suffered nor tolerated'. It was a limp formula and nobody was deceived. Nor by then were many interested.

The League of Augsburg

The Truce of Ratisbon was followed by a short interlude during which the great powers looked for causes and for allies for the renewal of war. The Truce had not satisfied the objects for which the League of 1681 had been formed and for which Spain had gone to war. Leopold was not reconciled to the loss of Strasbourg, nor to the waning influence of his House in Germany. Years of frustration had only sharpened William of Orange's conviction that Louis should be treated as a public enemy and met by a military coalition strong enough to defeat him in the field. The best basis for this—and here he adopted a plan long aired by publicists such as Lisola—was union between Holland and the smaller German states. Voices were not lacking in Germany to arouse ancient sentiments of patriotism; Leibnitz for instance, in his *Mars Christianissimus* of 1685, called for 'a union to defend the German Fatherland'. French moves in the Rhineland had already presented a painful challenge to the German states, and Louis' treatment of the Huguenots brought further shocks. Then, by his interference in the Palatinate and Cologne, he showed that he was still intent upon the management of western Germany in the interests of France. Finally, by misinterpreting events in England he allowed his greatest enemy to secure, without bloodshed, the throne of England.

Louis insisted on treating the Revocation as a simply domestic matter, and expressed himself indifferent about the emigrants; but these took with them to their new homes unhappy memories of France and loathing for its government. In England, Brandenburg and especially in Holland the emigrants helped to turn opinion against Louis. The Great Elector's minister Fuchs declared that only understanding between Brandenburg and the United Provinces, and their alliance with England, would be able 'to deliver Europe from the universal yoke of France'. The Elector was not wholly altruistic for he was angry at the time with the interference of the French navy in his colonial project in Africa. In March 1686, Brandenburg made a defensive alliance with the Emperor. In Holland the damage done by the revocation is attested by the letters of d'Avaux, who had worked so hard to sustain the pro-French party amongst the *bourgeois* at The Hague.

The gazettes and pamphlets of refugees informed Europe of the horrors of persecution and criticised every aspect of Louis' policy. This literature of atrocities was violent, sometimes revolutionary in tone. The author of the *Soupirs de la France esclave* did not hesitate to oppose to the power of kings that of the people, nor to defend the right to revolution. He branded the ambitions and defamed the character of the French king, who appears variously as 'the Beast of the Apocalypse' or 'the Antichrist'.

William exploited to the full the energy and bitterness of these expatriates and encouraged them with jobs and pensions. Fagel developed a regular propaganda machine which enlarged upon the menace of France. The same thing had happened at the beginning of the century when the ogre had been Spain, and especially Spinola; now it was France, Louvois and his master, with new notes of personal spite and caricature. William also got Huguenots to enlist in his army and navy, amongst them the admiral Duquesne and general Schomberg; according to Vauban, 9,000 sailors and 12,000 soldiers were in this way lost to France. The inexhaustible Jurieu ran a spy network which went for some time undetected. Of all this there could be only one result: the pro-French and pacifist party in Holland vanished, and William and Fagel were able to enlist the support of the States-General for the League of Augsburg.

Louis at first practised conciliation, aware of the advantages he had gained at Ratisbon and wishing to be free to manœuvre for the Spanish Succession should Charles the Sufferer, as was expected, soon die. In the Palatinate, he put forward the claims of Madame, his sister-in-law. She was herself the sister of the late Elector Palatine Charles, whose death without heir had left the succession in question. When in 1685 the Count of Neuburg, who was the Emperor's godfather, took possession, Louis then renounced Madame's claim, good as it was, and proposed the arbitration of the Pope. This was rejected by the German princes, perhaps unreasonably, since the Pope, in the year of the Revocation, would have been in no mood to further the interests of the French king. When the Succession question raised its head, Louis was less amenable. Leopold planned marriage for his daughter Marie-Antoinette to the Elector of Bavaria, a coup which threatened to detach Bavaria from her long-standing alliance with France, and tried to secure for her husband the Governorship of the Spanish Netherlands. Louis retaliated by massing troops on the Pyrenees frontier and made it known in Madrid that 'if His Majesty should give over any part of his states to one who had absolutely no claim', he might have some difficulty 'in preserving those lands which touch him most nearly'. The Spanish government could do nothing but accede.

Louis could not however prevent the deployment of Europe against him. The Catholic states began to look once more to the moral leadership of the Emperor, whose armies were winning victories on the Danube, a sequence which was to culminate in the capture of Belgrade in 1688, unassisted by Louis, who stood apart from the Pope's Holy League. The long-term consequences of the 'Eastern Question' which was to grow out of the disintegration of Turkey in Europe had not yet become apparent; meanwhile Leopold appeared in flattering light as the defender of Christendom against the Muslim Turk and the 'Lutheran' Hungarian. Spain, Savoy, Venice, Poland, Bavaria were all, for different reasons, ready to accept his lead. The Revocation, by contrast, had quite failed to give Louis the initiative in Catholic Europe that he expected. Instead, Catholic and Protestant for once acted together against him. At Augsburg in 1686, Spain, Bavaria, the Elector Palatine and Sweden all bound themselves to a League, on behalf of the various circles in which they had lands, to stop the intrusion of Louis into Germany, and to bind him to the treaties of Munster, Nijmegen and Ratisbon. Saxony and Brandenburg stayed out, but Brandenburg had already entered into a secret compact with the Emperor and guaranteed his rights in the Empire, especially in the Palatinate. The League of Augsburg was less formidable than it has looked in the light of later victories, but Louis feared encirclement and a declaration of war. He supposed that Leopold and William would use the League, though ostensibly defensive— 'to rescue any state attacked or troubled by unjust researches or illegal demands'—to wage war upon France when it suited their purpose. He may have been right, although some Germans, like Leibnitz, saw in the new Union of Germany the first real hope of peace. The Pope was more realistic, actually suggesting in a letter to Leopold that war against France might be 'the only prompt and efficacious means of bringing her to compensate all Europe for a part of the wrongs and injustices she has committed'. The long quarrel between Innocent XI and Louis now became of wider importance as Innocent threw the moral weight of the Papacy into the scales against the Gallican king.

The Cologne affair

When the affair of the Electorate of Cologne arose, Louis was already deeply in conflict with Rome over the privileges of his ambassador. It was the old dispute over ambassadorial franchises, never resolved, which now flared up at the appointment of Lavardin, a soldier and armed, as it was rumoured at Rome, with orders to maintain the traditional immunities of the French quarter. Innocent had announced that he would receive no ambassador till these privileges were renounced. Louis replied that, so far from his following the example of other sovereigns, God had established him as an example to others; they might be at least nominally appointed by the Pope, but he had a mandate direct from God. The incidents that followed were as trivial as they were scandalous. Two masterful men were at loggerheads. Innocent XI, opinionated and choleric, spoiled a good case by his discourtesy, while Louis allowed considerations of prestige to blind him to the ill effects of the squabble upon his delicate position in Europe. The Pope's support would have been invaluable over the question of Cologne. Here, more than prestige was at stake, for the little Rhineland electorate, through which Louis' armies had marched on their way to Holland in 1672, was of prime strategic importance. As a virtual appanage of the Bavarian Wittelsbachs, it had long been as amenable to the military requirements of France as Strasbourg had been to those of the Emperor. When the archbishop died in 1686, Cologne became something of a test case of the attitude of Pope, Emperor and King, a microcosm of the larger struggle. Louis put forward the complaisant client Bishop Faustenbourg whom he had already installed at Strasbourg; he was opposed by a brother of the Elector of Bavaria, Joseph Clement, aged 17. The chapter's profitable votes just favoured Faustenbourg, but he did not secure a two-thirds majority, so the Pope declared that he would confirm the Bavarian. This uncanonical act confirmed Louis' opinion that the Pope was in League with the Emperor and would stop at nothing.

Only by flaunting his military supremacy before the opposition was ready did Louis think that he could convert Ratisbon into a lasting settlement. In a letter to the Pope and Cardinals, he wrote: 'there is much to show that the conduct of the Pope is going to cause a general war in Christendom' and went on to threaten the Pope with the occupation of Avignon and Cologne. The private letter was followed by the public declaration of September 1688 intended to justify his resort to arms. This remarkable manifesto rehearsed the injuries which, since Ratisbon, had thwarted the pacific intentions of the King of France. His case rested upon the unwillingness of the Emperor to convert the truce into a permanent treaty, upon the unprovoked formation of the League of Augsburg, the denial of his rights in the Palatinate and intrigues over Cologne. The real argument lay with his troops, who acted with dramatic speed on the well-matured plans of Louvois. Avignon was seized, the Palatinate invaded and Philippsburg taken, with a sector of the left bank of the Rhine; measures too drastic to be the basis for any negotiation. Ratisbon became just another scrap of paper.

The devastation of the Palatinate

While Cologne was agitating Europe, the policy of James II was precipitating crisis in England. The birth of a son to James and Mary of Modena in June, 'the warming-pan baby', crystallised the opposition to his Catholic policy. William of Orange, linked to England by his marriage with James's daughter Mary, was approached by a group of magnates who represented roughly a majority, both of the gentry and the Anglican church, in their anxiety to end prerogative and pro-Catholic rule. William, who had for some time been in touch with the Whig leaders of the opposition, accepted their invitation to intervene. It may be that he did not expect to be placed on the throne, but reckoned that some form of regency would give him a useful influence upon English foreign policy. The capital resources of England and her navy together could alter the balance in Europe. Alliance between the two greatest maritime and commercial states was an alluring prospect, but the risk involved was correspondingly large. Invasion by sea in the late autumn, with a formidable English fleet at sea and James's army waiting to receive the expedition, was hazardous in itself. Louis could have made it impossible.

James II was sensitive about the French king's heavy patronage and his too friendly interest in the Catholic cause in England; he had briskly rejected Louis' suggestion that the French and English fleets should join in the Channel to bar William's way. But Louis could still launch an attack upon Holland and so force

N

William to abandon his invasion project. The issue was weighed at Versailles, where, despite the urgent reports of d'Avaux from The Hague, it was the fashion to mock at the idea of William's invading England. Marshal Villars re-enacted the debate: 'the court hesitated as to its policy, whether it should aid King James, about to be attacked, or should prevent the peace with the Turks which was being made and which would bring upon us the whole forces of the Emperor and the Empire. M. de Louvois, on his return from Forges, where he had been taking the waters, decided upon the second course. In effect, nothing was more important for us than to secure so powerful a diversion in our favour as that of the Turks. Besides, what prospect was there that so great a revolution could take place in England without great trouble and discord? This suited us better than settled government under King James; the more so that we had already seen England at peace and under the authority of King Charles II, a devoted ally, compel that sovereign to declare war against us.' So the French army marched against Philippsburg rather than against Maastricht. Philippsburg fell to the Dauphin and Vauban on October 29th, but on November 5th William landed unmolested at Torbay. By the end of the year James had fled his capital and William was master of his kingdom, in fact if not in title. England's 'Glorious Revolution', which gave to a landowning oligarchy wide political and social power and to William, if he could come to terms with the new ruling class, money, ships and troops for the continental war—this bloodless and unspectacular affair was the turning point of Louis' reign.

Louvois envisaged a defensive war, in which France, being encircled, must fight on several fronts and this is usually accepted as the strategic reason for the devastation of the Palatinate.[1] French armies could not hold the whole of the long eastern frontier; nor was Vauban's defensive system ever designed to be a Maginot line.

If the Palatinate were neutralised, this would both shorten the front and give a salutory lesson to the Emperor and his unfortun-

---

[1] There is another view. A letter from Chamlay to Louvois suggesting that the means he proposed would 'make the king absolutely master of the Rhine' has been interpreted by von Raumer as indicating that the traditional Imperialist policy was still very much alive and the purpose was not entirely or even primarily defensive. On the evidence of this letter it looks as if Chamlay must share responsibility for the Devastation.

ate client Philip-William, who had usurped the province despite the claim of Louis' sister-in-law. There were precedents for such action—and the Palatinate had suffered before. It had been an accepted convention of the Thirty Years War, when, for instance, the Imperialists had turned parts of Burgundy into a desert. But that had been as much a matter of indiscipline as policy. This was cold-blooded and deadly thorough. In the early summer of 1689, before the troops retreated, they sacked the riverside capital of the Electors, Heidelberg, with Mannheim, Spire and Worms, some fifty castles and innumerable villages. The standing crops were burned and thousands of homeless refugees carried their tales of distress into Germany. Saint-Simon, passing through Spire in 1694, noticed 'the few remaining inhabitants burrowing under ruins, or living in cellars'. The ruins of the palace at Heidelberg, where the Winter King of Bohemia and Elizabeth had briefly held splendid court, stand today to recall these wanton acts. The French commander, Tessé, had at first demurred at Louvois' order; by way of civility he sent some ancestral canvases to Madame, but she was inconsolable at the fate of her homeland. Louvois would have gone further, but Louis stopped the destruction of Trèves. The strategic point had been won; the scorched earth of the Palatinate could not maintain an army, Alsace could be left lightly covered and the French armies concentrated in Flanders and North Italy. Politically, however, it was an awful mistake, and evoked in Germany a display of public feeling unparalleled till recent times. Pamphlets and broadsheets, some crudely illustrated, described the atrocities of the French soldiery, the 'Huns' who had reduced warfare to armed robbery. Louis was represented as the complete monster, a blasphemer who claimed to represent God but really ruled on the principles of Machiavelli and on the model of the Turk. Some writers claimed too that his country was upstart and revived the old myth that the real descendants of Charlemagne were the Franks east of the Rhine. The moral drawn was that the German peoples had brought calamity on themselves by their good faith, *naïveté* and indifference to what was happening outside their frontiers.

The war which Louis had hoped to limit now inevitably spread. The devastation of the Palatinate brought in all Western Europe. In May 1689, the Emperor and the United Provinces entered into alliance. William, by promising his support to the Emperor over the Spanish Succession question, persuaded him to divert his main strength from the east to the Rhine. The two sovereigns engaged themselves to restore Western Europe to the position of Westphalia and the Pyrenees, to restore Lorraine to its duke and Pinerolo to the Duke of Savoy. Charles II of Spain, after the death of his French queen Marie-Louise and his subsequent marriage to the Emperor's sister-in-law, Maria-Anna of Neuburg, was clamped for the time being to the Emperor's party. When Louis sent an expedition to aid James in Ireland, England promptly declared war. Savoy joined the coalition in 1690. The German states—Brandenburg, Saxony, Hanover and Hesse-Cassel—were already pledged by their agreement at Magdeburg. Sweden later lent assistance to the coalition which, for all its divergences of aim, faced Louis with will and resources equal to his own.

The Nine Years War

Some historians have called 1689, the year in which England became once more fully involved in Europe, the start of a second 'Hundred Years War'. In this sustained contest, England and France battled for power and for the trade and wealth of the future—but few contemporaries would have seen the future so clearly. France continued throughout the eighteenth century 'to consult her traditions before her interests'. Marlborough's victories started a minor cult of 'glory' even in anti-militarist England. But the character of the 'Nine Years War', or 'War of the League of Augsburg' as it is otherwise called, was to prove different from that of previous wars. It was intense and 'total' in an idiom nearer to that of the modern war of nations. The economies of the leading protagonists were geared to their fighting efforts. Along with the military chess game of Flanders, with its standard moves and gambits, went a war of attrition, a war of resources fought on many fronts. The naval campaigns in the Channel, Irish Sea and Mediterranean assumed a new importance. When Savoy and Spain joined the Grand Alliance, Italy became a battleground, and a French army crossed the Pyrenees into Spain. The Holy League was fighting the Turks in Greece, on the Danube and on the Dnieper. There was scrapping in North America, in the West Indies and in India. The lingering tournament character of war, which the ordinary citizen was able to watch with detachment so long as he did not lie in the line of march, was almost lost in the vast mêlée. More than ever before, especially in France, subjects as well as kings were committed to the prosecution of war. This was a natural evolution of nationalism. For its rapid extension into Europe Louis was most responsible; the size of the army that he maintained and the apparently capricious way in which he used it as an instrument of policy, forced his enemies to answer in kind and with all their resources. When the diplomats met at Ryswick to discuss peace, the material condition of their respective countries was more significant as a bargaining factor than towns or territories taken. France did not lose an important battle but she unquestionably lost the war.

Louvois hoped at first, by supporting James's campaign in Ireland, to keep William out of Europe. James left St. Germain in February 1689, was escorted by French ships from Brest to Ireland and made a triumphant entry into Dublin to take the head of the ragged loyalists. 7,000 French troops joined him in May, and Chtâeaurenand dispersed the English fleet which tried to stop the disembarkation in Bantry Bay. The French fleet was effective in these months and easily eluded the English blockade. But in Ireland, where the French contingent found itself opposed by the expatriate Huguenot Schomberg, now in William's service, the Jacobite effort dragged out in dispiriting failure. D'Avaux, who had been recalled from The Hague on the outbreak of war, accompanied James as adviser; his letters fasten upon the lassitude of James and the unmilitary character of the Irish as the chief causes of failure. It was at least a useful diversion, and when the allies were shattered on the field of Fleurus in Flanders on July 1, 1689, William was still in Ireland, where he had taken over from Schomberg, in the hope of giving a speedy quietus to the rising. On July 10th William attacked James on the Boyne. The Irish were armed with nothing but their native valour and the French were able only to cover the retreat which followed James's defeat. He returned to the hospitality of Louis at St. Germain, but the French had little more to hope from this fatal prince. For a time he and his patrons continued to hope that William would succumb to the intrigue and opposition that surrounded him in England. But William was tenacious enough to hold together the war-party in England while he pursued the war in Flanders. Most of the leaders in political life, however much they disliked the man, had a vested interest in the revolution; since the Stuart alternative, Louis' pensionary, was impracticable, they were committed to making the settlement work. Louis' quixotic and persistent support of James's claim and his refusal to recognise William was the trump card of William's suit. Protestant indignation, trade rivalry heightened by Colbertism and all the irrational prejudices comprised in the mob-cry against 'Popery and Wooden Shoes' brought support, taxes from Parliament and loans from the City on an unprecedented scale. The credit revolution which this demand for money brought about, the formation of the Bank of England and the National debt, were to be vital factors in the defeat of Louis in the war of resources. The wealth which made London the chief emporium of Europe made England the banker of the coalition.

Beachy Head and La Hogue

On the same day that William was preserving his throne on the Boyne, Tourville won the naval battle which was the finest achievement of France's young navy. Off Beachy Head with some seventy ships he encountered a slightly smaller Anglo-Dutch fleet under Herbert, sank eight ships and then, thwarted by a change of tide, went off to destroy merchant shipping in the Channel. For a time Colbert's ships commanded the sea and put the possibility of invasion by sea into Louis' mind. By 1692, Louis had decided upon such an invasion, encouraged by reports of unrest in England, and an army was mustered at Cherbourg under Marshal Bellesfondes which Tourville was to convey across the Channel. The affair was poorly organised and Tourville's orders were vague. Seignelay had died in 1690, only 38 but worn out by hard work and dissipation; his successor Pontchartrain was a scrupulous civil servant but lacked technical knowledge. It was not his project originally but that of Bonrepas. Louis took little interest in sea affairs and was absorbed with the current campaign in Flanders. The thin hope of success lay in Tourville's being able to put to sea before the enemy or in his administering a crushing defeat. After contrary winds had kept him in harbour for a month, he sailed out with less than fifty ships, only to encounter an allied fleet of twice the size under Russell. The fight that ensued, on May 29th, was notable for the courage and seamanship of the outnumbered fleet. After twelve hours they were unbeaten, without a ship lost, while several allied ships were sunk and more dismasted; the carnage on the decks was terrible on both sides.

Battered and nearly out of ammunition, the French fleet split and made off at night for Brest and Le Havre. Owing to a pilot's mistake, Tourville himself, with twelve ships, had to make back for La Hogue, where, on the 2nd June, Russell found him and destroyed the ships. This unlucky disaster put an end to French plans for invasion and for carrying the war to the enemy's camp. It did not discourage Tourville, who in the following year gave the allied fleet the slip and wrought havoc with the Smyrna convoy, escorted by the English and Dutch, at the battle of Lagos, off Portugal. But the moral effect of the defeat was tremendous. Michelet hardly exaggerates when he says that La Hogue changed the course of history. It strengthened the hands of those councillors of Louis who argued that the navy was irrelevant to the real needs of a continental state and took resources that could better be used by the army. Colbert's vision of a great navy in the front line of a trading and colonising nation was lost in the smoke of Steenkirk and Nheerwinden. Vauban and Chamillart actually proposed in council that the fleet should be put out of commission. Louis resisted this, but there was no question of the navy's having priority and it was allowed to run down. Relative deficiencies in the necessary raw materials—timber, hemp, pitch and iron —have been advanced as a reason for France's naval decline at a time when England and Holland were securing larger supplies from the Baltic countries. But there was no difficulty which the French could not have overcome if the government had felt it sufficiently important. In fact, shortage of money rather than shortage of materials decided the king's policy—to concentrate upon attacking the enemy's merchant shipping; the natural weapon of the weaker party in a naval war, as it has been Germany's in the twentieth century. It had the advantage of making the cheapest use of local skill and private enterprise. The privateer was usually backed by a syndicate whose agent sailed with the captain to see that engagements were properly kept, and he carried a letter of marque from Versailles which legitimised his activities. Dunkirk, the main target of English resentment, kept as many as 100 privateers at sea during the Spanish War, ranging from lightly armed smacks which preyed upon fishing-vessels and coasters, to floating batteries ready to tackle any warship for the reward of 500 *livres* a gun which these prizes earned. Upon French sailors, Forbin, Saint-Pol, Duguay-Trouin and their like fell the mantle of Drake and Hawkins. Jean Bart, Flemish-speaking, fisherman's son from Dunkirk, a colourful and original figure, became a legend in his lifetime.

It is hard to judge the effect of this activity. The figures given by the English Admiralty for the main part of the Spanish War were a conservative estimate, given as part of the government's defence of its policy: 35 warships and 1,146 merchantmen (300 retaken). The losses were certainly high enough to cause an outcry from merchant interests in England and Holland and to rouse feeling against the war. Insurance rates rose, but not prices to any significant extent. Commerce-raiding was not by itself a war-winner. The French had a relative advantage in that merchant opinion played a greater part in shaping policy in parliamentary England than in France; the Tories were ready after 1710 to abandon continental war-aims so long as there was sufficient satisfaction for commercial interests, and the destruction of the harbour defences of Dunkirk was high on the list of their demands. But commerce-raiding was not all one-sided, nor could the French navy give much protection to its own merchant-shipping. The French India trade was nearly extinguished, the Baltic could only be reached through neutral vessels, and American waters were preyed upon by privateers from New York and Boston. Furthermore, the main effect of commerce-raiding was to enhance the importance of the English navy in English eyes. The pressure of public opinion, shocked by shipping losses, forced the government to spend large sums on enlarging the navy. For the first time the fleet was kept at sea during the winter. In 1694-5, an Anglo-Dutch fleet was sent to the Mediterranean and based on Cadiz, the French Toulon fleet was confined to harbour, and the foundation of a new English strategy was laid: control of the western Mediterranean, and the separation of France's Atlantic and Mediterranean fleets.

The victories of Luxembourg and Catinat

Flanders and Italy were the chief centres of land war. In the old prize-fighting ring of Europe, in laborious sieges and heavy collisions of infantry, Louis won some great but never conclusive victories. William's coalition was no match for Louvois' well-practised apparatus of war, and its commanders did not measure up to the French general Luxembourg. This ugly ardent little man, the posthumous son of the dueller Montmorency-Bouteville, had something of the great Condé's talents for war. He was quick to grasp a situation, to spot the chance for a breakthrough and he acted promptly, regardless of casualties. He signalled his arrival at the front with a victory at Fleurus over the pedantic Dutchman Waldeck, in July 1690, inflicting ten thousand casualties and sending home so many captured banners for the victory Mass that he earned the title of the '*tapissier de Notre Dame*'. The next two years saw two vast siege actions, planned by Vauban and presided over by Louis, who delighted in these ceremonious and predictable affairs. Mons fell in 1691 and Namur in 1692, celebrated by poets and rhetoricians. After the latter's fall, William retaliated with a sudden counter-stroke and achieved a genuine surprise near Steenkirk. On rough ground the French cavalry were not at first able to come into action and the infantry were driven back. But William lost control in the noisy mêlée and a counter-attack by the infantry of the King's Household saved the day for Luxembourg. The battle was notable for the careless gallantry of the aristocratic officers of the Household, who were too rushed to dress properly, fought with their cravats loosely knotted about their necks and so started a fashion at Versailles where cravats were soon being worn *à la Steinkirke*.

Louis seemed to rely upon the exhaustion of the allies and upon their differences, rather than upon an overwhelming concentration of force upon one front, to secure favourable peace terms. After the death of Seignelay in 1690 and Louvois in 1691 (his enemies murmuring of disgrace and suicide), Louis took more of the direction of the war upon himself. He had little confidence in Barbésieux, Louvois' son and successor, and leaned more upon the advice of Chamlay or one of the generals. He held fewer meetings of the *conseil d'état*, and took more decisions upon himself. After 1693, he embarrassed the soldiers with no further visits to the front, but ordered all from Versailles; and he was concerned always with securing short-term diplomatic advantages. This is the clue to the overall ineffectiveness of the French effort, the diffusion of their resources and the lack of plans to follow up victory. This ineffectiveness can be seen in the events of 1693. For this summer's campaign William was having serious difficulty in raising troops, and Luxembourg with over 100,000 might well hope for overwhelming victory. Louis however divided his effort. On the advice of Chamlay he sent nearly half his troops to the Rhine front, to follow up the capture of Heidelberg by de

Lorge and make a demonstration of power to the German princes. Even so, Luxembourg still had superiority of numbers when he attacked William's position by Nheerwinden, in the plain between Liège and Louvain on July 29th. This was again a victory of hectic courageous charges in the face of lethal fusillades gradually breaking down a stubborn linear defence. The allies lost over fifteen thousand men and seventy cannons, the French nearly as many. Notre Dame was draped again with captive standards and the court talked for weeks about the reckless bravery of the troops, for whose benefit Louis had recently instituted the Order of St. Louis, the first of modern decorations for valour. Luxembourg went on to take Courtrai, and William to defend his policies before the English Parliament and raise more troops. In the campaign of 1694 Luxembourg fought a defensive campaign of some skill, but nothing significant happened. Saint-Simon, who served under him, relieved his boredom by writing his own memoirs; fortunately this became a habit with him. In January 1695 Luxembourg died and his command went to Villeroi, the king's friend and a courageous man, but a fumbling commander. In this year, William was able to win a minor advantage with the recapture of Namur. On other fronts, too, the impetus of success had passed. Catinat had made his name in successful campaigns against Victor Amadeus. He defeated him at Staffarde in August 1690, then captured Nice and Montmélian. In 1692, he resisted the Duke's invasion of the Dauphiné, helped by the local peasantry who were roused by the depredations of the Savoyards and led by a heroic girl, Mlle de la Tour du Pin. In October 1693 he won victory and a marshal's baton at Marsagli, outside Turin. Catinat was not the typical soldier of this period. He had begun life as a lawyer, with no advantage of birth, and made his way by sheer merit. He was a careful general, thorough and sparing of the lives of his men, unambitious and something of a philosopher. After his failure in the Italian campaign of the next war, he retired to the country to cultivate his garden.

The last years of the war waited wearily upon the complex processes of international diplomacy. Both sides were anxious for peace; but the successes of French arms could not conceal the fact that the allies had time on their side. The reports of the *intendants* painted an alarming picture of the effect of war and over-taxation upon French society. The *capitation* which Vauban had originally urged as a substitute for all other taxes was now imposed as an additional emergency levy on the income of all classes, from Princes of the Blood, assessed for two thousand *livres*, to the peasant who paid one. This levy raised twenty-six million *livres*. but it did nothing to restore the over-worked tax system to health. The background to the war was one of deepening insolvency and social distress. As Voltaire put it: 'men perished of misery to the sound of the Te Deum'. Every year there were bad famines. Reports from the Auvergne in 1694 spoke of cannibalism; according to the Bishop of Montauban, 400 died every year in his diocese from starvation. In a remarkable letter, sent to Mme de Maintenon in order that she might convey it to the king, Fénelon accused the ministers of misguiding the king, of slurring over uncomfortable truths and sacrificing everything to the royal authority 'so that one only speaks of the king and of his good pleasure'. The indictment went on: 'since Nijmegen you have wished only to impose peace and its conditions in a spirit of mastery, rather than rule with equity and moderation. . . . Your peoples are dying of famine. . . . All France is no more than a huge hospital, desolated and without provisions. . . . Sedition grows slowly in all parts.' The prejudices of the aristocrat, the charity of the churchman and the exaggeration of the artist should be taken into account before this letter is accepted as evidence. That the wretchedness of the poorer part of the population, the ordinary hazards of peasant life, were increased by war conditions, was evident, however, not least to the king. Maintenon wrote in 1693, when the King of Sweden was first approached with a view to mediation, that 'the king will bring it (peace) about as soon as he is able, and wishes it as truly as we do'.

The Peace of Ryswick

For the last three years of the war both sides were simply concerned with securing advantages which would strengthen their hand at the conference table. There was no general able to defeat the French. The Duke of Lorraine who, in Louvois' estimation, had the stature to match Luxembourg, had died in 1690. Villars thought that Louis of Baden was 'a true soldier' and the Elector of Bavaria 'one of the Emperor's best soldiers'. The latter had fought successfully against the Turks, while the young Prince Eugène had shown promise in the campaigns of the King of Savoy. William himself had shown a certain pedestrian ability and his troops admired his dogged courage. But there lacked a Marlborough, a soldier-diplomat to rise above the stalemate and win the decisive battle. In 1695, William was encouraged by the capture of Namur, but only a great victory could have held the coalition together. The King of Sweden refused to send the soldiers he had promised for fear of retaliation upon his shipping. The Emperor was primarily interested in securing William's support for his Spanish claim and in pressing the war against the Turks on the Danube. Spain was unable to supply troops or money for Spanish Flanders, and the Dutch gradually took over the fortresses for the 'Barrier' which they regarded as essential. The Dutch themselves were anxious to contract out, for not only did they carry the heaviest burden of the land fighting but they were in no position to meet the attacks of the French corsairs at sea. The Dutch navy was already in decline and her commerce shrinking in relation to that of England. Amsterdam was yielding place to London as the financial centre of the world and many Dutchmen had good cause to long for peace. In England, gentry who paid the land tax and merchants who suffered losses at sea joined forces to demand a settlement.

It was Louis' policy to play on this lassitude and to split the coalition by separate negotiation. Throughout 1694, there were long discussions between the representatives of Louis and Leopold. As early as 1693 Daguerre, a French merchant, was employed in exploratory talks to sound Dutch opinion. Because Louis would not recognise William as King of England, or any of his ministers as representatives of England, William's interests had to be discussed through his Dutch officials, principally Dijkvelt, in an indirect way. As Louis still fondly imagined that he could impose succession terms upon England, progress was, not surprisingly, slow. William did not, as Louis imagined, wish for the continuance of the war to maintain his position in England and Holland; as his correspondence with Heinsius shows, the reverse was true. But he could not afford to let Louis escape with anything less than full recognition of his own rights. This became the principal issue of the negotiations.

Savoy offered Louis his first opening. The opportunist Duke made the most of his ambiguous position and the importance of his alliance to France. By the secret treaty of Turin, in June 1696, he deserted the League of Augsburg, became commander of the French-Savoyard army in Italy and turned with alacrity to conquer the Milanese. His eldest daughter Marie-Adelaide was promised to the Duke of Burgundy. Victor Amadeus gained much from his back-sliding: the restitution of Nice and the conquered parts of Savoy, Pinerolo and Casale (the latter to be handed over to the Emperor). The danger of tutelage to France represented by French occupation of those places was removed, and Savoy was left poised for the expansion into Italy which was to be her destiny. France, on the other hand, had broken the coalition at its hinge. The Emperor evacuated his troops from Italy and William pressed on with his own private negotiations. He could no longer afford to delay, for the threat of a new French offensive in Flanders, with the French reinforced by the army of Italy, was alarming. There was a severe bank crisis in London. From remote Canada came reports of Frontenac's victories which threatened the pre-carious English settlements. William admitted to Heinsius that he had no intention of fighting on merely to satisfy the ambition of Leopold. So he accepted the mediation of Sweden and formal peace discussions were started at one of his châteaux near Ryswick. He refused to accept the Emperor's proposal that the treaty should be used to confirm the right of the archduke to the Spanish Succession. So the Emperor's envoys were ordered to be obstructive and the real work of negotiation was done privately. As so often in this century the big congress was largely a façade. The French would still discuss nothing with the English, who were technically 'rebels', but Portland, William's trusted adviser, and Marshal Boufflers, two men who already knew and liked one another, prepared the ground for settlement in private talks. Louis, advised now by Pomponne, whose influence had grown since the death of Louvois and who had replaced Colbert de Croissy as foreign minister upon his death in 1696, was unexpectedly moderate. He clung to Strasbourg, rightly regarding this as the most important gain since Nijmegen, but offered up nearly all the other conquests since that treaty—Trier, Philippsburg, Breisach, Freiburg, most of Lorraine. The French were able, however, to insert a clause which guaranteed the religious status of surrendered lands. The Catholic party in Germany thus became the beneficiary and the defender of Louis' 'conquests for the faith', and the German front was split once again on the religious question. To Spain were returned Luxembourg, Ath, Charleroi, Courtrai and of course Catalonia. The disputes which had precipitated war, over Cologne and the Palatinate, were settled in favour of the Imperialist candidates, the Bavarian Joseph Clement and Philip-William of Neuburg respectively. The commercial tariff was mitigated in favour of the Dutch, who were also allowed to garrison a line of fortresses, the 'Barrier', in the Spanish Netherlands. Finally, William III was recognised King of England 'by the grace of God'. It was no longer possible for Louis to maintain publically the distinction between *fait* and *droit*. The treaties were signed in September 1697. Leopold, who by his obstinacy had lost his chance of getting Strasbourg, was forced to accede in the following month. The peace of Ryswick had been a personal triumph for William of Orange, who had consolidated his dynasty, thwarted Louis' designs upon Germany and furthered the security of Holland. He had drawn from Louis a significant change of policy and tone. As was said of him in the English Parliament: 'he had been given to England to hold the balance of Europe'. In reality the question of the balance of Europe was approaching its crisis in the palace of the Escurial.

The peace terms were received by the public in France with something like consternation. The victories of Luxembourg and Catinat had not prepared public opinion for such a diplomatic retreat. The king's ministers, Pomponne, Chamillart and Barbésieux, were blamed for the king's new moderation and they were lampooned in scathing rhymes.[1] Mme de Maintenon considered it 'a shame to restore what had cost so much toil and blood' while Vauban, writing intemperately to Racine, held it 'more infamous than Cateau-Cambrésis'. In truth, neither military stalemate nor economic stress alone account for Louis' apparent modesty. Charles II of Spain's tenuous hold on life was slipping; and what was 'Luxembourg and thirty-two towns' to even a fraction of that great inheritance? Round the sick bed of Charles the Sufferer was preparing the greatest of all dynastic issues.

[1] *Les Trois ministres habiles*
   En un seul jour
Ont rendu trente-deux villes
   Et Luxembourg
A peine ont-ils sauvé Paris
   Charivari.

The claims

It is impossible to exaggerate the significance that this problem had assumed for politicians at the close of a century whose beginnings had seen Spain still incontestably the greatest force in Europe. From its beginnings in the marriages of Louis to Maria Theresa and Leopold to Margaret Theresa, through its long brooding as Charles lived on childless in first and second marriage, to its crisis after the death of the infant Prince of Bavaria and its sudden *dénouement*, it grew in complexity and in tension.

The situation after Ryswick was that no arrangement existed for the disposal of the Inheritance amongst the heir-claimants except the Partition treaty of 1668, now obsolete, and the vague agreement made between the Emperor and Holland in 1689, by which Holland promised to support the Emperor's claim. This was clearly not satisfactory to the French king, whose family's claim was technically at least as strong as the Emperor's. Charles II being childless, right to the throne therefore went down through his sisters. The elder, Maria Theresa, had married Louis, himself a grandson of Philip III. She renounced her claim on conditions which were not fulfilled. Therefore, as Louis had claimed in 1667, it was valid still and lay with the Dauphin (1). The younger sister Margaret Theresa had married Leopold, also a grandson of Philip III, who by his marriage had only a daughter, Marie-Antoinette; she had married the Elector of Bavaria and had in 1698 a young son, Ferdinand-Joseph (2). Here again, however, Leopold had imposed a renunciation upon his daughter, Marie-Antoinette, since she was marrying out of the family. He himself intended the Spanish throne for a son. By his third wife he had two sons, Joseph and Charles (3); the elder was, of course, to be Emperor, the younger King of Spain. Such in outline was the tangle achieved by dynastic marriages of the rival houses; doubtful politics and bad genetics. On technical points alone there was no one solution. By seniority of daughters the Dauphin had the better right, as both son and grandson of an elder daughter. But if renunciations were to count, the Emperor's family had a better title for neither the Emperor's mother nor his wife had renounced their claim. These were only the technicalities of what was really a problem of the balance of power. It was objected that if the French candidate were favoured, since he was the immediate heir, he might some day unite the crowns of France and Spain. This seemed more likely at the time than the similar possibility of the Emperor's younger son uniting Spain to the Empire. (Actually the Dauphin was to die before his father, while Charles became Emperor after his brother's death in 1711.) Either way in fact the balance of power might be upset drastically; only a 'neutral' candidate or partition could avoid this.

The maritime powers could not disregard the matter. The great Empire of twenty-two crowns comprised, as well as Spain itself and the Low Countries, the greater part of Italy, the Milanese and Tuscany, the Two Sicilies, Sardinia and the Balearics; Holland could not approve French control of the Low Countries, nor did England want France to straddle the Mediterranean. In the New World there was Mexico and Central America, the biggest of the Antilles and all South America except Brazil; in Asia the Philippines, and in Africa the Canaries and the garrisons of the north, Oran and Ceuta. The transfer of this vast Empire from moribund Spain to Colbertist France was dreaded by England and Holland alike.

Not least concerned was Spain itself and her king. In 1689 his first wife, Louise d'Orléans, with whom he had been not unhappy, died and he had immediately remarried with Maria-Anna of Bavaria-Neuburg, daughter of the new Elector-Palatine, sister of the Empress and therefore aunt of the Emperor's preferred candidate Charles. This marriage had brought Spain closer to Vienna and, as we have seen, into the war of the League of Augsburg. Charles II recoiled before the fresh charms of this German girl, loud and greedy and bent on pushing the interests of Austria and her German friends at court. Charles himself was no fool; he had a sense of honour and of the needs of his country. But he was only half alive, the tragic victim of inbreeding. He had inherited from his father a constitutional disease. When he was 10 he was still really an infant; long before his death at 40 he was decrepit as an old man. He had chronic indigestion because a malformed mouth would not allow him to chew, and for the same cause he could not speak properly. He suffered constant fevers, he was epileptic and, towards the end, dropsical. His public appearances were an agony of shyness and mumbling irresolution. He habitually received foreign ambassadors in a long picture gallery, in semi-darkness, he sitting on the edge of a table, with only his profile visible. His morbid pleasure was to gaze upon the remains of his ancestors in the catacombs of the Escurial. This was the man, the incarnation of the decay of Spain, whose failing pulse agitated the chanceries of Europe.

The treaties and the will

The battle for the Succession was fought on two fronts: that of international diplomacy and the Partition Treaties, and that of the Spanish court and the Will of the king. It was alleged by critics of Louis, led by Bishop Burnet, the English Whig and historian, that he meant the partition treaties to be a mere blind and that he relied all along on obtaining the inheritance by will. There is little ground for the allegation. Louis made the partition treaties because he feared that he might lose the whole and, when the will was published, he found the choice between it and the Treaty a real embarrassment. He did indeed send to Madrid the marquis de Harcourt with the declared object of building up a French party at court, but in the following year, 1698, when the first partition treaty was made, little had been achieved. Louis hoped to avert a war and to secure some territory for France by coming to an agreement with the maritime powers. There were two other alternatives. First, to press his claim for the Dauphin; that would lead to war, which he felt was undesirable. The *intendants* were gloomy about the state of the provinces, while Harcourt in Madrid and Tallard in London, both soldiers as well as ambassadors, took the dimmest view of France's chance in another war. Second, to put forward one of his grandsons and renounce his own title to the French throne. The latter might open up a brilliant era for the House of Bourbon, but would add nothing to the frontier of France itself.

William had sent Portland to Versailles in March 1698 to complain of the hospitality still given to James II at St. Germain, and Pomponne and Torcy took the chance of discussing joint action by England and France to forestall the impending crisis. They stressed the danger that lay in Leopold's ambitions to re-create the Empire of Charles the Fifth, and guaranteed the Barrier in the Netherlands. Tallard, French ambassador in London, and Villars at Vienna, followed up these approaches. At Vienna, Villars could not make headway against Leopold's fatalist trust in the guarantee of the maritime powers in 1689. But in London, William and Heinsius, impelled by news of a popular movement in Spain for one of Louis' grandsons, were prepared to treat. At The Hague in October the terms were made. The prince of Bavaria, the neutral candidate, aged 8, was to have Spain itself and the greater part of the Empire. The Dauphin should receive the Two Sicilies and the *Presidi* (defended ports in Tuscany), Finale and Guipuscoa; the Archduke Charles the Milanese. Louis felt that he had made tangible gains which England and Holland would be bound to support against the Emperor's claim. He had served at once the interests of France and of Europe by his statecraft. All in vain, for the boy prince never knew the destiny planned for him. In February he died. The sick king, surrounded by soothsayers and exorcists, lived on and the question lay open again.

Again Louis took the initiative to save something from the wreck of the first Treaty. In the next round of negotiations with William he was almost obsequious in his approach, an attitude which served later as proof to his enemies that he did not take it seriously. In fact his haste showed something like panic at the prospect of the king's dying without settlement and Europe drifting into war. In June 1699, France and England agreed upon new lines of partition. The main part should go now to the Archduke Charles but France should receive in compensation Lorraine (whose duke was to be transferred to Milan!) or Nice and Savoy (if Milan were to be transferred to the Duke of Savoy). Louis hoped to get a quick signature from Leopold to show the Spaniards 'that it would be of no avail to oppose measures that have already been decided and that their forces are not big enough to stop them being put into effect'. It is interesting to see William and Louis, who represented opposite principles of kingship, abandoning those principles for which they had so recently fought. Louis had fought for hereditary monarchy in the person of James II of England, William for the right of a people to choose its own king, himself. Now both combined to impose upon the Spanish people a king who was neither evidently legitimate nor desired, and slice off part of the inheritance into the bargain. Everything that came from Louis was suspect to the Emperor and he sourly rejected the treaty that seemed to offer so much. He was old, inert and sunk in irresolution. He still believed that he would have the whole inheritance and would not think of sacrificing Milan and Naples to make sure of it. He would commit himself to nothing, decide

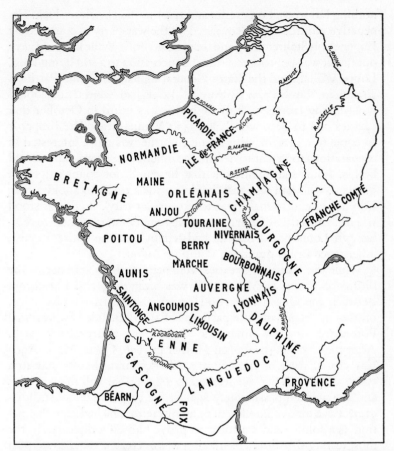

The provinces of France

nothing but to wait on events and trust to the Hapsburg luck. His negative attitude was encouraged by the war-party at court led by Eugene von Stahremberg and the archdukes. So while Leopold gave out that it was improper to rule the succession to a still living king, Louis, William and the States-General signed the second Partition Treaty, in March 1700. By August, Louis had heard that Leopold was sending troops to Italy. When it was heard in October that Charles had made a will, Kaunitz at Vienna urged the Emperor to come to an *entente* with France, but he was more interested in preparations for a war to defend the inheritance he was sure would be his. Louis meanwhile felt that he could not count surely on William, who had said that 'having made a treaty to avoid a war, I do not intend to make war to execute a treaty'. So things stood when Charles the Sufferer died, on November 1st, 1700. On November 9th Louis heard that he had left by will the entire Spanish inheritance to his grandson Philip of Anjou.

While the Partition Treaties were being fashioned to decide the future of Spain, at Madrid, all was wrangling and indecision. Between the Queen and von Harrach, the Austrian ambassador, on the one hand, and the partisans of the French led by Cardinal Portecarrero on the other, the king shrank and procrastinated. After the death of the Queen-Mother in 1696, Queen Maria-Anna was virtual ruler of the country. Charles could hardly stay in a room alone with her but seemed to defer to her will in all things; and she worked passionately against the French. Harcourt, however, was a man of intelligence and discretion; he had won distinction as a soldier and was now to prove himself a diplomat in the most testing situation. His mission was to create a party to support the French claimant, as unobtrusively as possible, in the very short time that the king had left to live. The overbearing nature of the queen and the pilfering habits of her circle at court gave him something to build on. But stronger than feeling against the German entourage of the queen, in swaying the patriot group, was the desire to find an heir to the throne with weight enough to hold the Empire together. Portecarrero urged that only from the Bourbons could such a man be found. The view was strengthened by the Partition Treaties and the bitter realisation that the other countries were taking it on themselves to decide the future of Spain. When the terms of the second treaty were made known, there was general indignation. The queen broke the furniture in her room and the Spanish ambassador in London used such strong language that he was requested to leave the country. Even the king was roused. He knew that he was dying, indeed longed to be dead. The previous November, visiting the tombs of his mother and first wife, he had prophesied that he would join them in a year. The exorcists abandoned their spells and potions. Even in his extremity, the issue was dimly visible to him: he must choose between family traditions, his natural preference for the House of Hapsburg, and Spain's need for unity. Leopold was feeble and distant, but Louis had strong armies. Neighbour to Spain and to her lands in Italy and Flanders, he could attack or defend her with equal facility. Under a French prince the Spanish Empire might remain intact and a bulwark against the heretic nations who had so coolly planned its dismemberment. Philip, Duke of Anjou, was separated from the French throne by both the Dauphin and the Duke of Burgundy, and it was to him that the choice narrowed. To ease lingering doubts, Charles applied to the Pope. Innocent XII had made his peace with Louis and feared to see the Emperor again at the gates of Rome. He therefore gave his approval, and on October 2nd Charles signed the will. Failing the Duke of Anjou, it should go to his brother Berry, next to the Archduke Charles and last to the Duke of Savoy. This one act of statesmanship completed, Charles sank, helped to his end by the prayers of Spain, troubled no more by the rude calculations of Europe. There was not enough money in his Exchequer to pay for the customary Masses for the soul of the dead king.

For two days and during several long meetings of the Council in Maintenon's room at the palace, the choice was debated. The Will or the Treaty? It was the gravest question of the reign. For the will were Torcy, foreign minister, the Dauphin and the Duke of Burgundy; for the treaty, the duc de Beauvillier. The latter argued that adherence to the Partition Treaty was the only way of avoiding another war against a European coalition; it would secure certain and solid advantages for France, whereas a Bourbon House in Spain would soon be independent and possibly hostile. If the will were accepted, France must give up all hope of advancing her frontiers in the direction of the Low Countries. Torcy's view, which may have been conclusive, was that France would have to fight anyway, for the Emperor would certainly oppose Partition. If the king refused the Succession, the courier had orders to go to Vienna and offer it to the archduke; then France would have to fight both the Emperor and Spain. He urged further the wonderful advantages which would follow a close connection with Spain and her Empire. The Dauphin's firm intervention on behalf of his son's rights surprised his hearers; a rare flash of political awareness in the fat and apathetic prince. His ministers could not agree, but for Louis there was really only one answer possible. Whatever the danger, he could not refuse this gift from heaven which surpassed the wildest dreams of Capet ambition and which came, it seemed, as the free wish of the Spanish people. The Spanish ambassador had already been informed privately when, after his levée on November 16th, he made the announcement to his court. Against all precedent the two folds of the doors of his chamber were thrown open and the crowd of courtiers called inside. Saint-Simon recorded the solemn moment: 'Gentlemen,' he said, indicating the Duke of Anjou, 'birth has called him to this crown, and the dead king also by his will. The whole nation wished for his succession and urged me to approve it; it is the will of heaven and I have agreed with pleasure.' Then to his grandson: 'Be a good Spaniard, this is now your first duty. But remember that you were born a Frenchman so that you may further unity between the two nations. This is the way to make them happy and to keep the peace of Europe.' Unfortunately this simple formula of conduct was not enough to keep the peace of Europe.

The formation of the Grand Alliance

For the moment peace and war were in precarious balance. It is argued by some that war was inevitable, by others that it was provoked unnecessarily by Louis' overbearing behaviour; the truth may lie somewhere between these assertions. War between France and the Emperor was almost inevitable, since Leopold and his sons believed that they had been robbed of their lawful inheritance and were anxious to save at least the Milanese from the wreckage of the Partition Treaties. But William was not a free agent and there were powerful interests in favour of peace in both England and Holland. Louis did nothing to give these interests any encouragement, everything to awake their prejudices against his policy. He need not be blamed for starting hostilities, but he should have been able to prevent the re-formation of the Grand Alliance, more united than it had been before. Because the war proved so disastrous for France, Louis' supposed mistakes have been brought into crude relief; yet each move is intelligible when examined in its context.

In letters sent round to the courts of Europe, Louis rehearsed his reasons and justified his decision. In his despatch to William he recalled how insistently he had worked to bring the Emperor to sign their treaty of partition, and with what ill success. He said that he was compelled by the Emperor's attitude to accept the will, although less advantageous to him than the treaty. English and Dutch shipping would have nothing to fear from Italy, now that the French were not to have Naples and Sicily and, the last vital assurance, Spain and France would remain quite separate. This latter, and the integrity of the Barrier, which was guaranteed to the Dutch at the same time, were the interests which would guide the actions of England and Holland and the tests by which they would judge Louis' sincerity. For the time being the maritime powers accepted the *fait accompli* and recognised Philip V King of Spain. Leopold protested alone, declared the will null and prepared for a war in which he could not yet count upon his former allies. Would the Emperor have carried on without allies? In the spring of 1701, after four years of intense diplomatic activity, Louis might with reason look forward to years of peace. And so thought Maintenon: 'all the wisest people are sure that we will have no war'.

But the dragon's teeth were already sown. William held his hand for the moment and moved with caution because of opposition in parliament. Most of the army had been paid off after Ryswick and there were noisy demands for lower taxes; he would gain nothing from rushing England into another Continental war before some real grievance arose. He himself, however, believed that war was inevitable and only a matter of timing. He did not regard his account with Louis as square. This apart, he thought that the maritime powers had everything to gain by war and relatively little to lose. As he wrote to Heinsius: 'I will drag this people in by prudent and gradual measures without their realising it.' Louis' actions soon provided him with propaganda to overcome the reluctance of his subjects.

Philip V went to Madrid in January and found the people disposed to welcome him. On the 1st of February, the *Parlement* of Paris registered letters patent reserving the right of Philip of Anjou and his descendants to the French throne. The wording was cautious: if Philip should become king of France, he should not cease to be king of Spain. It seems to have been Louis' intention, not that the crowns of France and Spain should be united but that Philip should be able to claim the French throne if the contingency arose. (He could little have guessed how nearly this was to happen.) Similar letters had been granted to an earlier Duke of Anjou who became King of Poland and afterwards Henry III of France. But Louis' letters seemed to challenge the stipulation of the will that the crowns should remain separate and, if only a formality, could have been delayed to a more propitious moment. Louis' next action was more serious. Without warning French troops suddenly entered the Spanish fortresses of the Barrier, took them over in the name of the King of Spain and held the Dutch troops as hostages until the States-General should reveal their intentions. The French argument was plausible; the Dutch troops should not be allowed to stay in Spanish garrisons if they did not recognise the Spanish king. The States-General promptly recognised Philip V and the troops were sent home in March. But the action was maladroit, and only excusable on the grounds that war was inevitable—in which case Louis should not have released his hostages. The Dutch were sensitive about the Barrier and grew apprehensive, while in England the *coup* was freely represented as the invasion of Flanders.

Though William's Tory ministers obliged him to express formal approval of Philip, there was growing backing for the king in Parliament. The complaints of the merchants were substantiated by the news that the French fleet had sailed to guard Cadiz and that the French Guinea Company had gained by treaty with Madrid the privilege of the *asiento*, that is of importing negro slaves into South America, coveted (and later gained at Utrecht) by the English. The merchants could not know that Louis' instructions to Harcourt for the new king were that Dutch and English ships should be excluded from the Indies and South America. But it looked plainly as though Louis intended to take over the Spanish Empire. Indeed, since it was incapable of looking after itself, he had little option. Spain had no effective force to defend the Milanese, any more than the Netherlands. If the Emperor intended war upon Spain and France, it was therefore a reasonable precaution of Louis to send troops under Catinat to defend the Milanese (in May). But this merely confirmed the view of the English and Dutch, that Madrid was to be managed from Versailles.

These events were the background to the formation of the Grand Alliance of The Hague in September 1701. William had been given by Parliament the power to conclude the alliances necessary for England's safety. The Emperor had already begun his campaign in Italy, where Catinat was retreating before Prince Eugène. The support of Brandenburg was assured. The contracting parties at The Hague, England, Holland and the Empire, stated their aims clearly. They would procure for the Emperor satisfaction of his claim to Spain; for the maritime powers 'particular and sufficient surety for their realms and for the navigation and commerce of their subjects'.[1] They would win back Flanders, in order to restore the Barrier, and the Italian possessions for the Emperor. They undertook to prevent for ever the union of the French and Spanish crowns and agreed to share any captures in the Spanish colonies between England and Holland. Louis was given two months to consider the terms, but they offered little inducement to negotiate and amounted to a manifesto of war; a manifesto which struck a nice balance between the dynastic imperatives of Austria and the commercial aims of the English and the Dutch. These were to prove discrepant interests, but at present were wedded together to the immediate task of destroying the power of Louis.

Louis and 'James III'

The Grand Alliance was completed on September 9th. Nine days later James II died at St. Germain; whereupon Louis, moved by the pleas of James's widowed queen and Maintenon, but against the advice of his ministers, recognised his son as James III, King of England, Scotland and Ireland. Louis' belated salute to heredity would have been more impressive had he not already defied the principle in the Partition Treaties. It was to some extent a political calculation. The French had been caught off guard by the Restoration of 1660; in a second restoration the returning king should have cause for gratitude to France. Louis may be forgiven for thinking that anything could happen in England, and it is true that the political barometer in that fractious country was unsettled, pointing down to stormy. But his action was of a piece with his

[1] After the conclusion of the main articles, when Louis formally recognised James Edward as 'King of England', a rider was added by which the allies bound themselves to secure satisfaction to England for Louis' insult.

whole handling of the Jacobite question, which shows his diplomacy at its least effective. He had gained nothing in the negotiations before Ryswick from his carefully advertised support of the Stuart exile. When he suggested James for the elective crown of Poland, vacated by the death of John Sobieski in 1696, he may have been making a serious attempt to be rid of an incubus. But the question of a pension for Mary of Modena was allowed to bulk large in the Ryswick negotiations. When after Ryswick he took no action to remove James from St. Germain, he caused unnecessary suspicion by a breach of what seems to have been an understanding, rather than a written compact, between Portland and Boufflers. He found it hard to view this matter objectively. It was for him a question of the honour due from one sovereign by Divine Right, to another. He was swayed both by principle and by the *amour propre* which was hurt by his abandonment of James at Ryswick—when Sourches wrote in his diary: 'we have abandoned the true king of England'. He probably lost face at court as much by this surrender of principle as by the cession of towns. The court, we know, revolved upon questions of status and precedence which Louis ordered down to the most trivial detail. In this very year he issued new instructions upon the status of *ducs et pairs* at court. Maintenon, who surely reflected her husband in this, continued to refer to the 'Prince of Orange', just as Anne was later to be the 'Princess of Denmark'. Louis was not uninfluenced by the values of the society which he ruled so meticulously. So by his chivalrous act he salved his pride. But it was a shocking blunder, for the English Parliament had just ruled the Succession to the Protestant line of Hanover by the Act of Settlement, and to see Louis dictating his own settlement of the throne now united English politicians as nothing else could. Their irritation can be seen in the protest of the City of London: 'The King of France gives himself a viceroy's status in conferring the title of sovereign upon a pretender prince of Wales. Our condition would be wretched indeed if we had to be governed at the behest of a prince who has used fire, sword and galleys to destroy the Protestants of his estates.' Parliament passed a measure attainting James of high treason for having assumed the title of king, which was largely the work of Henry St. John, later architect of the Tory peace and exile for Jacobitism! William then dissolved Parliament and secured a Whig majority, which promptly voted for 50,000 soldiers and 40,000 sailors. In the following

March he died. The frail body had collapsed, but his spirit lived on in the formidable coalition that he bequeathed to his successor. Versailles hoped that a change of ruler might bring a change of spirit, but they overestimated the personal authority left to the crown after 1688. By William's death war had become the policy of the dominant groups in Parliament, and this was as much due to Louis' tactical errors as to William's statecraft. Louis had not behaved with the reckless arrogance so often attributed to him but with that curious mixture of sagacity and *naïveté* which marks his conduct of affairs.

The state of the combatants

As the parties formed for the renewal of war, it was clear that Louis was again fighting Europe almost alone. On May 15, 1702, the English government produced a manifesto which laid upon him the responsibility for war and accused him of aspiring to 'universal monarchy'. At the Diet of Ratisbon in September, the Empire's declaration of war stressed French designs upon Germany: 'the king had done all that he could to enfeeble and entirely ruin the German people'. The Emperor was the stronger for having driven back the Turks and reconquered Hungary; now he was supported by most of the princes. One of them was given little option. The Duke of Brunswick-Wolfenbuttel was a mere figurehead, whose younger brother had collected, in his name but with French gold, an army of mercenaries in North Germany. In March, the Elector of Hanover, doubly bound by his new electorate, created in 1692, and by his claim upon the English throne, drove out this inconvenient prince and signed on his mercenaries for the Emperor. The Elector of Saxony, Augustus, had been supported by the Emperor when he obtained the Polish throne against the French prince Conti, in 1697; he was now fighting for this throne, with Imperial support, against Charles XII of Sweden. The Elector Palatine had not forgiven the disputed succession of 1685 and the subsequent ravaging of his lands by French troops. Frederick of Prussia, the son of the Great Elector, had been brought to the Imperial Alliance by his acquisition of a crown. In January 1701 he was crowned King of Prussia at Königsberg; now he furnished the Grand Alliance with 8,000 men. That most of the German princes were prepared to enter a war which was of little direct concern to them shows how successful Leopold had been in adapting Imperial policy to the growing self-importance of the states. Long offended by French insolence, these now saw an opportunity to enrich themselves upon allied gold and to wrest back some of the lands lost since 1648, Alsace and Strasbourg, the Three Bishoprics and Franche-Comté. Only the Wittelsbachs stood by France. Joseph Clement, Elector of Cologne, was anxious above all to prevent the occupation of his lands by foreign soldiers; besides the 10,000 troops that he offered to raise, Cologne had already, in 1672, shown its value as a corridor to the Low Countries. His brother Max-Emmanuel of Bavaria had indeed married the daughter of the Emperor, but she had been forced to renounce her claim upon Spain, and since the early death of his son, the King of Spain designate, he had supported Spain, and so now France. By a treaty of straight alliance signed in 1701, Bavaria undertook to ban the passage of Imperialist troops through her territory and to raise 10,000 troops. In return, besides money, Louis gave an assurance of help in case of an Imperial election. With two other powers whose alliance was vital to his strategy, Savoy and Portugal, he was less successful. Victor Amadeus II exacted the utmost from his position athwart the Alps. Louis, at the Treaty of Turin in 1701, promised, in return for troops, 150,000 *livres* a month and the marriage of Philip V to the Duke's second daughter. But the Emperor gave more, the greater part of Montferrat as well as fair subsidies. So after 1703, Savoy stayed in the allied camp, a factor of importance for the campaigns in North Italy. Portugal too at first favoured France, guaranteed Charles's will and closed her ports to the ships of England and Holland. But in 1703 the Methuen treaty with England placed her firmly in the Grand Alliance. In the north, Charles XII of Sweden was preoccupied with his struggle against varying combinations of the northern powers. He had left Stockholm in April 1700 at the head of an expedition to attack Denmark. In November of the same year he shattered the raw Russian army in a snowstorm at Narva. From then till 1706, when he defeated Augustus of Saxony and Poland at Fraustadt and imposed peace upon him, he was continuously at war. Denmark, after 1700, was nominally neutral, but sold valuable contingents of troops to Marlborough's army. The bare recital of these diplomatic engagements shows that France began this war at a serious disadvantage. But it should be remembered that the principal allies had very different aims. The Emperor fought primarily to impose his son upon Spain; especially after the serious development of the Hungarian revolt under Rakoczy, his interests and activity in the west were limited to Spain and Italy. The Dutch became increasingly defensive-minded as the war went on and their concern did not extend beyond the Barrier and the ruin of France's commerce. England was prepared to lavish gold upon her allies and to back the Hapsburg claim to Spain so long as this seemed necessary to maintain the balance of power, but her long-term interests lay in the extension of trade and the furtherance of naval power. A strong faction opposed continental involvement from the start, and this would have come to the fore long before 1710 if it had not been silenced by Marlborough's victories. One has only to imagine what would have happened in London had Marlborough been defeated at Blenheim to see that Louis had grounds for confidence in the outcome of the war. One great French victory would have splintered the Grand Alliance; and in 1702 Louis' armies had never been defeated in a full-scale battle.

France was, however, in poor shape for the prodigious exertions of a war on four fronts. Only five years had elapsed since Ryswick, scant time for the recoupment of army and treasury. Louis was aware of this, for his ministers continually reiterated the themes of poverty and disorder. From the start the doors of diplomacy stood open to proposals of peace, though the price lengthened, with successive defeats, beyond what Louis could or would pay. In 1702 France had over 200,000 men under arms, of which three-quarters were infantry; but many of these were raw levies, inexperienced and poorly fitted out, hastily mobilised and rushed to the frontiers. The cavalry were badly mounted and armed, and the shortage of horses was alarming. In the strains and improvisations of a war of defeats there was a steady decline from Louvois' high standards. After the terrible casualties of 1706, 20,000 militia had to be drafted to Flanders, and Louvois would hardly have recognised the gallant rabble which fought at Malplaquet in 1709, as an army of France. There was inexperience and inefficiency at all levels of command. Orders were always more efficiently executed in Marlborough's polyglot force, and his staff-work seems to have been consistently better than the French. This of course reflected inadequacies of generalship. It was Louis' misfortune that he did not have one really great commander. Vendôme displayed many of the parts of a natural soldier, but he was vain and culpably slack about matters of detail. Berwick, the natural son of James II and Arabella Churchill, and thus curiously Marlborough's nephew, was a careful general, but a little torpid. Villars was audacious and competent, but he was not liked at Versailles. He was indeed loud and coarse but, which was more serious in this war when Louis could not afford to offend neutrals, he was a notorious pillager, encouraging his troops to burn and loot; such a man was best employed against the Huguenots! Louis preferred safe men who would accept the strategic dictates of Versailles, such as Marsin, Tallard and, most disastrously, Villeroi. These were 'palace generals' on whom, as with his ministers, Louis thought that he 'conferred capacity along with his patent'. The problem of high command was aggravated by the extensive character of the war. So it happened that Vendôme was in Italy and Berwick in Spain when Tallard was losing Blenheim in Germany or Villeroi was being outmanœuvred at Ramillies in Flanders. Behind the commanders in the field was Chamillart, a conscientious toiler, trusted and liked by the king, but not the superman that the situation demanded. To avoid friction between the needs of the Army and the Treasury, Louis gave him charge of both departments, finance and war. Neither Colbert nor Louvois had had such nominal power; but in effect Louis himself closely supervised the conduct of the war, for which the unfortunate Chamillart had to find the ways and means. Twice he managed to restore shattered armies, but he could do little more than contrive expedients to stay the tide of calamity. Not till 1709 did Louis transfer the War Ministry to another, Voysin.

Spain herself was to be nothing but a liability to France, sunk in power but tenacious of privilege, a helpless and uncomfortable ally. Her territories were so dispersed as to make impossible any concentration upon defence. So French armies had to operate independently in Flanders, in the Rhineland, in Italy and in Spain. Could the Grand Alliance exploit these disadvantages? So large an alliance contained its own special problem of disunity. But the three vital men of the Alliance, Heinsius, Eugène and Marlborough, 'the *triumvirs* of the league' as Torcy called them, were not only remarkably able men; they all had in common a determination to destroy the power of France. Heinsius, as Grand Pensionary of Holland, had directed the affairs of the United Provinces in William's interests since 1688, and he had something of his master's gift for patient and shrewd diplomacy; he now carried on William's policies without break. In 1681, when he was on diplomatic mission to France, Louvois had threatened him with the Bastille; the harsh memory may have helped to sustain the quiet enmity with which he worked, first for war, and then for total victory. Prince Eugène was the great grandson of a Duke of Savoy, but as the son of the comte de Soissons and Mazarin's niece Olympe de Mancini, he was born a Frenchman. Since he had failed to find advancement under Louis, he had taken service in the Austrian army and won experience in the campaigns against the

Turks. He too nursed a lively grievance against the king who had passed him over. As befitted the nephew of Mazarin, he had a certain finesse; he was a thoughtful politician, an excellent general, with a single-minded passion for victory and fame. John Churchill, Duke of Marlborough, had a compromised political record and William, with some reason, had distrusted him. He was essentially the general of a faction, committed to and supported eventually by the Whigs, dependent too on court favour. So long as one faction or other of the Whigs retained a share of power, so long as his political ally Godolphin remained Lord Treasurer and so long as his wife Sarah remained Queen Anne's close friend, his position was secure. For Marlborough, then, politics and war were inseparable. He urgently sought victory, to justify himself and his friends at home. But he was no mere talented adventurer. After the death of William he became the soul and genius of the Grand Alliance. He displayed a statesman's grasp of the broader issues of the strategy of a war of four fronts. His generalship was not till 1704 proved in a great battle, but his diplomatic gifts were early shown in his dealings with the awkward Dutch Field Deputies and the princelings and commanders of the German states. It was Louis' greatest misfortune that the strings which tied the ill-assorted alliance of his enemies were in the hands of this great and magnanimous Englishman.

Blenheim and Ramillies

The results of the first campaigns were not too discouraging for Louis. On the Rhine, Catinat could not prevent the Margrave Louis of Baden from taking Landau, but in the following month, October 1702, Villars crossed the Rhine after a successful feint and defeated him in a spirited action at Friedlingen. He had rallied his troops with characteristic panache and they proclaimed him marshal on the field of victory. Had Villars been able to persuade Max-Emmanuel of Bavaria to march with him upon Vienna, almost empty of troops, he might have struck a more decisive blow. But they were at odds from the start and the opportunity was lost. The Elector tried to join forces with Vendôme, commanding in Italy, in the Tyrol—but without success. Villars, covering Bavaria itself, won a second victory, at Hochstadt, in September 1703, over the main German force, the army of 'The Circles', under Styrum, but was then recalled, at his own request and in pique with the Elector, to deal with the insurgent Camisards in the Cevennes. These events form the background to the great campaign of Marlborough in 1704. Marsin, who had been sent to replace Villars, was a lesser man. Bavaria, despite Villars' successes on the Danube, was easy prey and the French bridgehead which menaced Vienna was itself exposed. So Eugène and Marlborough decided upon a swift concerted thrust. Leaving Stahremberg and the Duke of Savoy to hold Vendôme in Italy, Eugène moved into Germany while Marlborough made his historic march from the Low Countries along the right bank of the Rhine, covered closely by Villeroi on the left bank, who was baffled when he suddenly swung off into the Palatinate, joined forces with the Prince of Hesse, retreating after defeat by Tallard and the Margrave of Baden (who subsequently went off to besiege Ingoldstadt) and marched to meet Eugène in Bavaria. On the previous year's battlefield of Hochstadt, on August 13th 1704, Marlborough and Eugène confronted the Franco-Bavarian army under Marsin and the Elector, reinforced now by Tallard who commanded the right wing in front of the village of Blenheim. The frontal attacks on the village itself were halted bloodily, but played their part in Marlborough's design by drawing the French reserves into the village; Tallard's left, the middle of the line, then gave way to Marlborough's central mass, Tallard himself falling prisoner by an unlucky accident. On the front attacked by Eugène, Marsin and Max-Emmanuel were left exposed by the collapse of the right wing and forced into bloody retreat. In the village of Blenheim itself 11,000 men, cooped-up and left without orders by the loss of their commander, capitulated. The French and Bavarians retiring towards Alsace left some 30,000 killed or captured behind them. The French regiment of Navarre proudly tore up and buried its colours at the surrender of Blenheim, Villars boasted that he could tame Marlborough, Saint-Simon pointed out that Tallard was notoriously short-sighted, and all joined in criticising his conduct of the battle. But no gesture or recrimination could mitigate the calamity of a day which changed the character of the war and altered the balance of power in Europe. Bavaria was lost; from now France fought to save her own soil from invasion. Old men could not remember when French arms had not been victorious, but now the reputation of invincibility passed to Marlborough, and with it the moral ascendancy that had played so great a part in French victories.

1705 saw no spectacular action on the eastern frontiers. Marlborough was twice deterred by his more cautious Dutch and German colleagues from attacking, first Villars, operating on the Rhine after a successful campaign against the rebels in the Cevennes, then Villeroi, who was defending the Low Countries. In 1706 however, on May 23rd, on the plain of Ramillies, he met and utterly defeated a French army of equal strength, about 50,000. The French commander, Villeroi, should not have fought alone when Marsin was moving up with reinforcements, and his tactics were deplorable. A large part of his troops were immobilised behind a marsh on his left wing which he reinforced excessively to meet Marlborough's feint attack. The main action then developed in the centre, where Marlborough achieved a crucial superiority of cavalry after drawing troops off from his right. Although he was at one stage unhorsed in a desperate mêlée, Marlborough never lost control of the action which was, perhaps, his tactical masterpiece. At the climax of the day, Marlborough's entire cavalry force was drawn up at right angles to the French, who were unable to meet its onrush in the spectacular action that ensued. The finest French troops, the *maison du roi*, suffered worst in the great cavalry encounter. The French army never took the field in such splendid array again. They left 12,000 killed or wounded upon the field, and another 6,000 were captured in the disastrous rout. For a month there was hardly the semblance of an army in the field, while the great towns of Flanders surrendered in turn to Marlborough: Louvain, Ghent, Oudenarde, Antwerp and Brussels. A town like Menin, fortified by Vauban, should have obstructed the allied advance for months and its fall in a previous war might have been held to justify a campaign; it surrendered to a ferocious attack in August, days before, in Marlborough's view, it was necessary. At Menin, Marlborough stood on French soil. The fruit of Ramillies had been the conquest of Flanders and the demoralisation of the French army. Villeroi was received gently and with dignity by Louis: 'at our age we must not expect good fortune'. But the king dismissed him and transferred Vendôme from the Italian front. When the new commander arrived he found that the allied ascendancy was complete: 'every one is ready to doff his hat at the mention of Marlborough'.

Italy and Spain

In Italy the French had repeated failures. As soon as the will was made public, Prince Eugène had occupied Spanish Milan with an army corps. Neither Catinat, in 1701, nor Villeroi who succeeded him, were able to find an effective answer to the ingenious plans of Prince Eugène, and Villeroi was actually captured in a humiliating manner during an Austrian attack upon Cremona. Vendôme replaced him and might have been able to take advantage of Prince Eugène's march into Germany in 1704 had not the defection of Victor Amadeus in the previous year deprived him of his Savoyard troops. In 1705, before the combined forces of Austria and Savoy, he had to retreat across the Adige. But at the start of the next year his position seemed hopeful. It is at this point that the lack of an intelligent overall strategy was disastrous to France. The loss of Flanders could have been countered by the winning of Italy. But Louis' reaction to the disaster of Ramillies was to direct reinforcements from other fronts to Flanders. The promising operations of Villars on the Rhine were therefore suspended, and the Italian commander Vendôme was transferred to the army of Flanders at the height of the summer operation. Vendôme had fortified the line of the Adige to hold Eugène, while Turin, Victor Adameus' capital, was being besieged by La Feuillade, Chamillart's son-in-law, a courtier as conceited as he was incompetent. No effort or expense had been spared; he had lavish siege equipment but not unfortunately Vauban, whose offer to serve him as a volunteer was brusquely rejected. His positions were amateur and while Vauban explained to his cronies at home what he should be doing, La Feuillade wasted valuable troops pursuing Victor Amadeus in the mountains. Marsin had come to replace Vendôme convinced that he was going to die; the duc d'Orléans was in nominal command but could do nothing to prevent catastrophe. Eugène, who had pierced the lines of the Adige without difficulty, attacked the French at Turin on September 7th before they had concentrated their troops, and gained a victory easier than Ramillies and no less important. The French, who were cramped in their choice of tactics by orders from Versailles to stay upon the defensive, lost 9,000 troops, their commander Marsin, all their siege equipment and, as it turned out, Italy. La Feuillade retired precipitately to the Alps, and in the following year the Austrians were on French soil, besieging Toulon.

Events in Spain at first brought no comfort to Louis. Here the problem was twofold: to bring some sort of order to the chaos and inertia of civil government, and to defend the throne of the young French king against the Archduke Charles and his allied troops. Philip V, only 17 when he came to the throne, had not, as a younger brother, been trained for kingship. Reserved and gentle, spending an inordinate amount of his time in bed, he could apparently neither see nor rise to the dangers of his weak estate. Rather he accepted timidly the clamorous advice of those nearest to him: his wife, the 14-year-old Maria-Luisa of Savoy, like her sister the Duchess of Burgundy a lively and intelligent girl; the princesse des Ursins, Camerar-Mayor and an expert and forceful courtesan, who had been appointed to take charge of the young monarch's household; the Cardinal Portecarrero, who had mobilised the pro-French faction for the battle of the will, and successive French administrators and ambassadors. By the death of Charles II Spain had been left with only the vestiges of administration, army, finance or justice; nor was there anyone in Spain who could give a new impulse towards reform. But as the government decayed, the pride of the grandees, the privileged separatism of the provinces, had grown. Portecarrero could only follow the usual courses of Spanish ministers: nepotism and inaction. There was frightful poverty, discontent in the country-side and steady migration. Even the court could hardly pay its bills. It was therefore reasonable that Spanish policy should be controlled by Versailles, for French troops were everywhere fighting for Spanish possessions; it was inevitable that French officials should be sent to supervise the running of the country which did not seem able to help itself. At first Louis ordered Harcourt to submit to the authority of the Spanish council; when this did nothing he was forced, not perhaps reluctantly, to accept the responsibility laid on him by the will, seeing himself, according to Torcy, 'as forced to enter into the details of Spanish government and its dependent states'. So Marsin, the new ambassador, entered the Council, Orry was sent to reorganise the finances and Louville to supervise the king. They and their successors in the Augean stables, Cardinal d'Estrées, Grammont, Amelot de Cournay, met with opposition at every point. The Spanish who wished at the accession to sit back and wait for miracles from Versailles did not relish the methods or the manners of the miracle workers. The *bourgeois* Orry offended the susceptible

Spanish by his presumption; the *grand seigneur* d'Estrées by his haughtiness. Within the French faction too there was jealousy and squabbling caused by the overlapping of authority. The Latin union of these years under the House of France was not, therefore, an unqualified success, and when Charles landed in Catalonia in 1704 he found support at all levels. The allied victories of the next two years were helped considerably by the weakness of the obstructed, resented Franco-Spanish government. In October 1702, an English fleet had destroyed the annual bullion fleet from America while it lay in Vigo bay, and with it most of a year's revenue. The naval power which Colbert had hoped to rival paid a further dividend to England when Admiral Rooke, by a lucky accident, found himself in possession of the rocky fortress of Gibraltar, then supposed and afterwards proved to be impregnable. In October a great naval armament of transports and men at war brought the Archduke Charles to Lisbon. The way had been opened for him by the *volte-face* of the King of Portugal in 1703. When the Austrian came to Catalonia to claim his inheritance there were popular risings for him. Barcelona opened its gates to his troops under the Huguenot Galway and the wayward genius Peterborough. Berwick was recalled at the request of the young queen, who could not bear his cold ways; in many towns there was an enthusiastic response to 'Charles III'. In 1706 Philip's attempt to recover Barcelona failed and for a few weeks he had to abandon Madrid itself. But 'the war of the two kings' was soon to take a different turn.

Oudenarde

As early as 1705 Louis had put out peace feelers towards the States-General of Holland but had found in Heinsius an implacable foe to any moderate settlement. In 1706 he was prepared, under the stress of his military disasters, to abandon the will and return to the idea of partition in order to save France. But the allies had swollen upon success. By the Grand Alliance it had been stipulated 'that the kingdoms of France and Spain should never be united or governed by the same person, that the dominions and commerce of the Dutch should be secured, and that a reasonable satisfaction should be given to the Emperor and the English king'. Now the scope of the war and its aims had both been extended. 'Reasonable satisfaction' was given a harsher interpretation and the Dutch claimed French towns as well as Spanish for their 'security'. At the end of 1707, the Whigs in Parliament carried a resolution to the effect that 'no peace can be safe or honourable for Her Majesty or her allies if Spain and the Spanish West Indies be suffered to continue in the House of Bourbon'. So the whole basis of the English policy was altered: the war, from being one to preserve the balance of power, became one to impose upon the Spanish people a king whom a majority were soon to show that they did not want. Under these conditions Louis could not find peace. In the events of 1707, and particularly in Spain, he had to find some hope in the continuance of a war of endurance. Although the year saw the abandonment of Naples to the Imperialists, there was no further setback. In the Low Countries Vendôme ceded nothing to Marlborough, while on the Rhine Villars fought dexterously, carrying the 'Lines of Stolhofen' and capturing Heidelberg, Stuttgart and Mannheim. Most important, in Spain, there was a revulsion of feeling for Philip. Hatred of Portugal, jealousy of the Catalans and loyalty to the successor chosen by their own king, these sentiments breathed life into a popular and priest-led Castilian movement which swept Charles out of Madrid and harassed his armies in retreat. In April 1707, Berwick, once more in command, won the battle of Almanza over Lord Galway (the former Huguenot Ruvigny) and Spain was saved for Philip V. In France itself, a large Savoyard-Imperialist army under Prince Eugène had invaded Provence and reached Toulon. But the Austrians had never been enthusiastic about the enterprise, which had been urged upon them by Marlborough. In the face of an opposition of peasants and militia, skilfully organised by Tesse Eugène, was driven back with much loss. Although the French shipping and installations were badly damaged by Admiral Rooke's bombardment, the allies lost their chance of dominating the Mediterranean from this vital harbour. Not till September of the following year did they achieve their aim of securing a Mediterranean base for winter operations by the capture of the island of Minorca.

The great struggle of the Northern powers hardly impinged upon France's war against the Grand Alliance. But for one anxious year it seemed that Charles XII, at the height of his military reputation, might come to terms with one or other of the contending powers and throw his army and his generalship into the scales. Such an intervention might not have been decisive; it could not fail to be important. In March 1707, the Swedish king encamped in Saxony. In a storm of aggression he had defeated the armies of Russia and Poland and imposed upon the latter country Stanislaus Leszczynski, in despite of Augustus of Saxony, the Emperor's candidate and King of Poland since 1697. In Paris that year the *Grand Dictionnaire Historique* appeared, depicting the lives of famous men. The second longest article in the work, 22 columns, was devoted to Louis XIV; the longest, 30 columns, to Charles XII, aged 25. It is a fair comment upon his reputation and upon the interest aroused by his every move. Now as he stood insolently upon German soil his first move was to force the wretched Augustus to recognise Stanislaus. Would he next, like Gustavus after the battle of Breitenfeld, sweep on to the Rhine? Would he take the side of France against the Emperor who had supported Saxony against him? 'The sword does not jest' he wrote once, and he only required the lightest pretext to take it from its scabbard. So a diplomatic tussle began for the support of this formidable prince. 'The king of Sweden', wrote Voltaire, 'received in his camp at Alt-Ranstadt the ambassadors of almost all the princes of Christendom.' Amongst them came the great Marlborough, apologising for the absence of Queen Anne on the grounds of her sex and the inconvenience of the journey. The French hoped that, if he would not give military support, at least he would act as arbiter for a general peace. Charles's grievances against the Emperor pulled him one way, his great ambition to humble the Czar another. The latter, more than the suave diplomacy of Marlborough, decided him. The gangling king in his old blue coat and soldiers' boots was more at home with his enormous sword than with the niceties of diplomacy. But he secured quick concessions from the Emperor, who rarely moved so fast: notably, Protestant rights in Silesia. Then, the very hour of the signature of the Treaty of Alt-Ranstadt in August 1708 with the Imperial representatives, the drums and fifes sounded for his march to Moscow. His hopes and the meteor greatness of Sweden were sunk the following June on the field of Pultava. By then France's hopes of an honourable peace had gone and her armies were stretched to prevent invasion.

1708 brought France military disaster as well as diplomatic setback. The negotiations of Mesnager, a Rouen merchant and special ambassador, had made no headway at The Hague, while in England the general election of May confirmed the power of the Whigs and their programme of 'No peace without Spain'. The allied war-plan was threefold: to restore Charles III to the throne of Spain, to conquer the realm of the Three Sicilies and to humiliate Louis by the invasion of France. The first aim was to prove impracticable; in the last lay the immediate peril for France. To meet the allied armies in Flanders Louis had concentrated his troops there; to encourage them, he sent his grandson Burgundy to share the command with Vendôme. It was an unhappy partnership of opposites, the fastidious prince and the uncouth soldier whom Saint-Simon portrays as lying with dogs all over his bed. Burgundy was thoughtful and circumspect—but his heart was not in the war. Vendôme boasted a long experience, but he was hasty and incurious. Their joint command was paralysed by quarrels and, when they came to action at Oudenarde on July 11th, the army was badly directed. The French were surprised by Marlborough and Eugène who had the tactical initiative throughout, their detachments came into the fight haphazardly and fought without spirit. Vendôme lost all sense of proportion, plunged wildly into a local action and fought at the head of his infantry when he should have been controlling the whole front. But if Burgundy had not, through a misunderstanding, prevented the French right wing from coming into action, Marlborough might have regretted his audacious crossing of the Scheldt, only seven miles from the French camp. As it was, he only had just sufficient troops to hold the French attack while he completed his deployment of Overkirk's Dutch infantry on his left wing. Their attack rolled up the French front and night closed upon a scene of confusion with the French army surrounded and demoralised. Most escaped under cover of darkness. But the road to France lay open. Six thousand French were left killed or wounded in the field, at least nine thousand captured. In the beaten army there was dismay and recrimination as the troops divided into Burgundians and Vendômists in their bitter post-mortem debates. The friends of Vendôme inundated Versailles and France with slander and ridicule of the young prince. When the allies besieged Lille, nothing was done to help the garrison of that city, which Boufflers defended inside Vauban's ramparts with 16,000 men. Two great convoys of siege equipment were allowed to trundle through to Lille unmolested. A third was attacked unsuccessfully at Wynendael, where the French suffered a sharp defeat. Louis felt that his prestige was involved at Lille so Chamillart was sent in person to order Vendôme, Burgundy and Berwick to seek a general engagement. Their failure to take advantage of Marlborough's exposed position while a large proportion of his troops were engaged in the siege is an indication of the extent of their defeat at Oudenarde. Had Marlborough marched direct upon Paris, as he wished, the French army might have been roused to resist. But Lille was left to its slow strangulation. Boufflers did not capitulate before December 9th—and the allies left some 15,000 men before its walls. With Lille fell also Bruges and Ghent. After the siege, Boufflers was made Marshal and peer of France, Vendôme recalled in disgrace.

Backs to the wall

Following upon the débâcle of the army of Flanders, the cruel frosts of 1709 seemed like the work of a vengeful God. Rivers froze, even the swift-flowing Rhône. Wine froze in the bottles, hares and partridges were found lifeless in the fields, and travellers on the roads. It was said at court that 'the common people were dying of cold like flies'. The fruit trees and the early sowings were caught, the water-mills were still and wolves roamed the countryside. The king strode round the gardens of Versailles followed by shivering courtiers, himself majestically indifferent to the elements. It was a time for greatness, but royal gestures were not enough. Wan Parisians chanted a bitter *Paternoster*: 'Our Father which art at Versailles, thy name is hallowed no more, thy kingdom is great no more, thy will is no longer done on earth or on the waters. Give us this day thy bread which on all sides we lack . . .' The common people shouted abuse outside the very windows of Versailles. The king reduced his table at Marly and sent gold plate to the Mint, but neither court nor people were impressed. 'He is reproached for his expenditure . . . they would like to take away his horses, his dogs, his servants. . . . There are murmurs at his very door, they would like to stone me (Maintenon) because they imagine that I never tell him anything unpleasant for fear of grieving him.'

Grim reports came from *intendants*, of famine, revolts, and taxes that could not be collected. The harvest of 1708 was poor, that of 1709 a catastrophe. So corn had to be imported from other countries at great cost. England tried to prevent this; in 1709 she made corn contraband and sent a squadron to the Sound with orders to stop exportation of grain in Scandinavian or neutral ships. The price of bread rocketed with scarcity and was held up by the unscrupulous grabbing of profiteers. In Picardy it quadrupled in the one year 1709, in Paris it rose for a time to eight sous a pound. At Lyon, shopkeepers and bakers were pillaged and there were similar scenes at Tours, Limoges, Orléans and La Rochelle. Religious houses suspected of hoarding were sacked by wandering bands of peasants, beggars and deserted soldiers. One of the most terrible reports from an *intendant* described savage bands 'squatting in the fields who scattered like wild animals when he approached'. In the province of Quercy in the south-west there were dangerous revolts in 1707 and 1709. Here the report of the *intendant* has undertones of panic: there were thirty thousand men under arms in Quercy, Cahors was besieged for ten days, he himself was held by a detachment in his coach and 'escaped only by a miracle'. He knew the authors of the trouble, but 'they are so many that it would be dangerous to make an example of them'. Parish registers of this time often show the laconic entry: *fame periit*. In the register of the village of Vincelles in the Yonne, the *curé* wrote this note: 'one sees men and women, children of all ages, faces and hands soiled, scratching the earth with their nails, searching for roots which they devour when they find them. Others less industrious scrabble the grass along with their animals, others completely broken lie along the roads waiting for death.'

Famine and poverty were reflected in the revenue figures. All the old and some new expedients re-appeared. To the capitation of 1695 was added the *Dixième* of 1710, designed to apply to all classes of society, but as usual falling most heavily upon the peasants. Chamillart and after him Desmarets lived from hand to mouth by the worst expedients, by loans, lotteries, the issue of government bills and paper money and by the sale of offices. Titles were sold and, most serious by any principle of sound finance, the coinage was depreciated. These various tax weights fell upon an economy already depressed; so the gap between revenue and expenditure yawned ever wider. In 1680 Colbert had deplored a deficit of 13 million *livres*. From 1700 to 1706 the total expenses were 1,100 millions but the ordinary revenues a mere 350 millions. From 1708 to 1715, expenses were 1,914 millions: receipts only 461. In the height of the famine of 1709, Desmarets despaired of collecting taxes at all, for 'it would be imprudent to exact the ordinary taxes from men who lack bread'. He summed up the plight of France in these terms: 'the armies cannot be properly paid, the subsistence of troops cannot be assured in so unfortunate a time, we are on the point of a total breakdown and may fear the most terrible uprisings . . . to all these evils no remedy can be found but prompt peace'.

For years there had been a party at court and in the council itself for peace at any price. They argued that it was wrong for France to be sacrificed for a decadent ally; to abandon Spain would be an act of generous policy which would save Europe from prolonged war. Successive defeats supported the arguments; the enemy seemed to be invincible. Chamillart, who best knew the situation of both the army and the economy, urged peace, backed in the Council by Beauvillier and Chevreuse. As early as 1706 Chamillart had been defeatist. 'It is a sorry thing', wrote Vendôme to him, 'that you are so hopeless about the prospects of campaigning. I am sure that the Dutch will hold their feet on our throats when they see that we are in no state to enter upon a campaign.' Outside the council Maintenon was always a Cassandra and her laments reflect the gloom of the court. 'How can you say', she asked the princesse des Ursins, ebullient in disaster, 'that God has not declared Himself against us, when He sends us a winter such as has not been seen for five or six hundred years?' Elsewhere she spoke of 'the hand of God which is so visibly against us. . . . Our king was too glorious, He wishes to humble him in order to save him. France was overgrown and perhaps unjustly; He wishes to confine it within narrower bounds and perhaps more solid. Our Nation was insolent and unruly; God wishes to punish it and to enlighten it.' Her mood was a pious despair, her policy capitulation. The same pessimism, shot through with contrition, can be seen in the letters of Fénelon, whose attitude was reflected in his protégé Burgundy. The eloquent bishop had been since the end of the Quietist affair confined to his diocese, but Cambrai lay in the path of the moving armies. He was visited by the great, and his restless pen could not be stopped. He now became a prophet for the little group at Versailles who talked of and planned for a better future. He argued for a bold stroke for peace. Considerations of honour and prestige should not stand in the way. 'It would be better to sacrifice Franche-Comté and the Three Bishoprics than to risk the whole of France'; again, 'I cannot hope for a victory such as can only flatter us with vain hopes and prolong our misery'. It is not surprising that his pupil, Burgundy, seemed pusillanimous to Vendôme and to his soldiers when he could argue about the loss of Lille: 'has not the state subsisted for whole centuries without this town, and indeed without Arras or Cambrai?'

Louis, who had hoped for victory to temper the terms of peace and had hoped with patience to divide the allies, now resigned himself to ask for peace. In the words of Torcy: 'it was the general opinion that the only way of securing peace was to approach Holland'. Feelers had been put out before, through unofficial ambassadors, such as Helvetius, Dutch in origin and Chamillart's private doctor. Chamillart had himself written to a Dutch politician that the realm was on the edge of a precipice and it was in the interest of the Dutch not to let it fall. In March 1709, Rouillé, President of the Council and an experienced diplomat, was sent to inquire the Dutch demands. The allies wanted their pound of flesh and the terms were not to be negotiated but dictated. When the Council debated these terms, Beauvillier is said to have painted so pathetic a picture of the state of the land that Burgundy burst into tears. 'It would be difficult,' said Torcy, 'to picture so melancholy a scene.' The ministers were all agreed that negotiations should continue and Torcy himself was sent to The Hague. It may have been a tactical error to send the man regarded by foreigners as the king's chief minister, for it confirmed the impression of the allies that France was in desperate straits. Torcy arrived in May; by that time the allies were starting their summer campaign. Heinsius was gratified by the humiliation of France, Eugène boasted that he would soon be in Paris, Marlborough was offered money but preferred victory. So the terms were actually stiffened, as each of the allies presented their bill in forty articles, 'the Preliminaries of The Hague'. Louis was prepared to abandon, on Philip's behalf, all the Spanish dominions; to allow the Dutch a new 'Barrier', including the French fortresses Lille and Tournai; to cede Strasbourg; to destroy the port and fortifications of Dunkirk and to give up Hudson's Bay and Newfoundland. But in two articles the allies overreached themselves. They stated that the Spanish crown should go to Charles with all the rights that Charles II possessed or ought to have possessed by the will of Philip IV. Then they required that Louis should himself, with his army, turn Philip from the Spanish throne if he did not accept the terms within two months! The first article threatened France with the loss of all the lands won from Spain at and after the Peace of the Pyrenees, Franche-Comté, Artois and Rousillon. The second was intended by the allies to be a guarantee that the French would act in good faith. They were also anxious to avoid the expense and hazard of conquering Spain. That this was recognised to be a serious problem can be seen from these words of Bolingbroke, written later, but representing the opinion of Stanhope who fought there: 'armies of twenty or thirty thousand men might walk about that country till Doomsday; wherever they came, the people would submit to Charles III out of terror, and as soon as they were gone proclaim Philip V out of affection'. They hoped to avoid this by securing an order from Louis to his grandson, but Louis understandably objected to a clause that was as impractical as it was offensive: 'since I have to make war, I would rather fight against my own enemies than against my own children'. There is room for debate about the responsibility for the breakdown of these peace negotiations. Neither Marlborough nor Eugène can escape their share; both expressed their misgivings about the fatal restitution clause, afterwards, but not at the time. Heinsius should perhaps have taken more note of the recent patriotic demonstrations in Spain, of Philip V's determination to die sword in hand rather than abandon Spain. But Louis was also responsible. His diplomatic record did not invite confidence. His attempts at negotiation during the war look either insincere or inept; the allies could be forgiven for suspecting his motives. From the start his agents, including both neutrals and Dutchmen, were putting out peace feelers. The Dutch naturally came to believe, from his using such agents, either that he wanted peace badly or that he was trying to divide the allies. The Dutch intelligence service was better than Louis perhaps realised and the activities of his agents were closely followed. He blundered in the choice of Rouillé, a man known to be unacceptable to the Dutch. Again, Louis would have done better to have left negotiation in the hands of Torcy. Instead Chamillart, minister of war, was supervising simultaneous separate negotiations. Torcy was exasperated and Dutch misgivings increased by such conduct. In 1709 Louis undoubtedly wanted peace but not so much that he would sacrifice to it the principle of Divine Right. The principle upon which he refused to turn out his grandson was the same as that upon which he refused to recognise Queen Anne of England.

Villars and the Battle of Malplaquet

Right or wrong, Louis could now claim for the first time in his reign a clear moral justification for war. He appealed to the patriotic instincts of his people. In an open letter to be read aloud in all the churches by the parish priests, he made known the case of France. The wording of the letter was paternal in the best Capet tradition: 'although my affection is no less than I feel for my own children, although I share all the sufferings inflicted by war upon my faithful subjects, and have plainly shown all Europe that I wish sincerely that they should enjoy peace, I am convinced that they themselves would scorn to receive it on conditions so contrary to justice and to the honour of the French name'. The simple dignity of these words may have evoked forgotten passions and memories of earlier wars. A ballad of the time of Joan of Arc had thus incited resistance: 'Let each of you village folk who love the King of France take courage to fight the English. Let each of you take a hoe, the better to uproot them; if they will not go, spoil their faces with your fists.' Now again the issue was simple, at any rate to the peasants of Artois and Picardy who were within range of the enemy's cavalry patrols. But Paris could not be saved merely by royal words or by a temporary mood of indignation. All depended upon Villars, guarding the north-east frontier with the last effective army in France. It might be called a national army, since the militia were now serving in the front line with the professional troops. Thousands of the new recruits were peasant volunteers attracted more by the food than by glory. To pay for the army, the king and his nobles melted down plate, ladies pawned their jewellery and peasants released their hoarded sous. Bullion was taken from the Spanish treasure fleet which put in at St. Malo. Villars had found hope and discipline abandoned, privates selling their weapons for food, subalterns parting with their shirts. He set himself to restore morale to the ragged soldiers who felt that they had been let down by their commanders. He had no doubt about his own capacity, and he revelled in the crisis; it was his hour and he could do as he pleased. He swaggered—but he also took pains over detail. The troops responded to his care for them and to his ribald scorn for the favourites and court officials who, he said, had landed France in this mess. Louis now backed him without reservation and provincial governors were set to find bread for the army at all cost.

Villars gave his troops bread on the days when they marched, and when in camp they fasted. Young peasants from the ravaged villages around followed the bread wagons and stayed to enlist. Villars' heroic humour and drive gave the troops a new will to fight; perhaps for the first time in the war the troops felt a real identity with their general and their cause. The supply problem remained grim—even after Malplaquet we are told that the horses died at the picquet ropes of hunger—but out of the hardships of frost and famine the army was re-born.

Villars relied upon an extensive trench system, and while Marlborough waited till June for the outcome of peace talks and extra troops which swelled his army to 120,000, the formidable lines of La Bassée, covering forty miles, were constructed. Had Marlborough attacked in April, nothing could have stopped him marching through to Paris; in June his reconnaissances deterred him from frontal attack. Instead, and the decision was to prove a critical one, he turned to attack Tournai, 'with not a foot of ground that is not undermined and casemated', reputed the strongest fortress in Europe. Villars would not be drawn out from his lines to relieve the town. But after its fall, on September 3rd, he edged forward and dug in to fight a defensive battle. On September 11th, where the gap of Malplaquet lies between the woods of Sars and La Lanière, his 100,000 men, drawn up in concave pattern, faced Marlborough's 120,000, upon what is nearly the line of the modern French frontier. The French held their ground with desperate courage against repeated attacks. Marlborough and Eugène turned the French left flank with a well-executed assault through the woods, but it fell back in good order, sustained by Villars' reserves from the centre. Meanwhile the Dutch were held up on the right despite the furious endeavours of the young Prince of Orange. When Marlborough was at last able to repeat his Blenheim tactic and carve a passage through the denuded French centre, he compelled a retreat. But his troops had lost too heavily to do anything more. The French fell back in good order and in good spirits, now under Boufflers, who had taken over when Villars was wounded in the course of the battle. In all the allies had lost some twenty thousand men, the French not more than two-thirds that number. The Dutch had suffered particularly for their stubborn heroism, the dead of their famous Blue Guard lying in heaps where they were first checked; then forced back by bayonet rushes. Marlborough and Eugène stood that night upon the reeking battlefield; but they knew that they could not afford another such victory. Efficient use of firepower at close range, the steady discipline of the infantry and cavalry masses, the failure of either side to achieve a breakthrough and compel surrender account for the carnage of this battle, unsurpassed till Borodino in 1812. One may compare the casualties of such an action with those of the actions of 1914-18, dominated by the machine-gun. But these were fought by conscript armies and spread over weeks. It is not too much to say that European society was shocked by Malplaquet. Orkney, one of Marlborough's lieutenants, summed up the affair: 'I hope in God it may be the last battle I may ever see. A very few such would make both parties end the war very soon. The French are very proud they have done so well. I do not believe they have lost as many as we. It is with us as it was with the French at Landen (Nheerwinden).... None alive ever saw such a battle.' Villars' return to Paris, on a litter, was a kind of triumph. Although the great fortress of Mons succumbed to Marlborough in October, Paris was saved.

The allies overreach themselves

In England, however, the City was still strong for 'no peace without Spain'. In Holland, Heinsius, Buys and van der Bussen, the directors of their country's policy, nursed hopes of winning the whole of Flanders. The alliance of the two countries was therefore riveted by the Barrier Treaty of 1709. Townsend signed it for England, but Marlborough would have nothing to do with it. England guaranteed Dutch claims in the Netherlands and agreed to share equally trade in the Spanish Empire; but was the Dutch were simply vassals of England. A separate peace with France, such as the Tories were later to gain for England, was always a danger to them. The English fleet could cut her off from the world trade which was her real wealth, and without English support she could not gain the Barrier which was her only security. Although the treaty seemed a good bargain for the Dutch, it contributed to the Tory reaction of the next year and the separate peace; also to the split of the allies, since Austria realised that the Dutch wished to get the entire Spanish Netherlands into their hands. In France the peace party was still urgent and clamorous and in the following March peace negotiations were resumed in the little village of Gertrudensberg. 'From the start,' wrote Torcy, 'the enemy showed more arrogance than ever, less readiness for peace.' For Louis the French principals, Huxelles and Polignac, offered almost everything; in one weary moment Louis indeed promised to pay a subsidy of half a million *livres* towards turning his grandson off the Spanish throne; but the allies persisted in demanding that he use his own army. The Dutch, by their unyielding rancour at this conference, which their historian Geyl describes as 'one of the most disastrous and truly humiliating episodes of all Dutch history', bared themselves to the consequences of the reversal of English policy the following year. The Dutch delegates who seemingly fulfilled the proud task of conducting the negotiations for the whole alliance, were in reality the puppets at this conference, in which England and Austria pulled the strings; all the Republic gained from them was the deep resentment of the French, who were at last cured of the delusion that it was through the States that the coalition could best be approached.

The allies were never to have such a chance again of negotiating from strength and unity, for Marlborough was unable to win any decisive advantage in 1710. He was not prepared to undergo another frontal assault upon prepared entrenchments. On at least one occasion he let slip a chance of battle which he would formerly have grabbed with confidence. He played military chess with his accustomed skill, but Villars did not make the fatal mistake for which he manœuvred. So four costly sieges gave him Douai, Béthune, St. Venant and Aire; but not Arras, which was his main objective. Between him and Paris still lay a great obstacle of siege works and inundations, Villars' *Ne plus ultra* lines. Across the Channel, he found himself deprived of the political props upon which his strategy depended; for in October 1710 the Tories, who represented all those who were discontented with high taxes and purposeless foreign campaigning, defeated the Whigs and their plans for war *à l'outrance*. By the end of the year these plans had been made to look ridiculous by Bourbon victories in Spain.

Spain, which had once seemed in hopeless case, now saved herself by her exertions and went far to saving France by her example. In 1708, Philip V had defied the diplomats of France and the allies: 'I would rather die at the head of my troops in the defence of my states, than weakly abandon them.' His brave words were rewarded by an upsurge of patriotic excitement. The towns paid for an army and the country sprang to life with priest-led partisans, who harried the Imperial troops and raided their convoys. In May 1709, Spanish troops defeated Galway and his Portuguese at the river Caya. In the following year, Stanhope beat the Spanish at Almenara and Saragossa. But in December, Vendôme, who had been recalled from resentful retirement at the request of Philip, caught Stanhope and Stahremberg apart and defeated them in successive actions at Brihuega and Villa Viciosa. The number of troops involved was small. But the consequence was the end of the allied effort to impose Charles III upon Spain.

The victory of Villa Viciosa delighted Louis XIV but depressed those at court who thought that the preservation of Spain was the greatest obstacle to the attainment of peace. In reality the keys of war and peace were held by the leaders of the new Tory ministry in England, Harley and Bolingbroke. The diplomacy of William and Marlborough had underpinned the Grand Alliance; now the defection of England was to break it up. Just before Christmas Torcy was informed that the English would no longer insist upon the entire restoration of the Monarchy of Spain to the House of Austria: 'we shall be content provided France and Spain will give us good securities for our commerce'. Bolingbroke perceived that the Whigs, by their insistence upon the reversion of Spain, entire, to the House of Austria, had given a twist to the direction of the war which had not been intended by William III and which was not in the interests of the English nation. He had been able to raise a loud outcry over the 'butcher's bull' of Malplaquet—although the English had only lost 2,000 there—and he was now able, with the judicious aid of Harley, to show that the war had been pursued for the private advantage of Marlborough and his clique. He was assisted by the death, in April 1711, of Joseph I, Emperor since 1705 and elder brother to Charles; this meant that in fighting to prevent one union of power under the French crown, the allies were now fighting to create another union. So England carried out a phased withdrawal which had two main ends: first, a military standstill in Flanders and Spain; second, a separate negotiation with France, in which the interests of England should be pursued without regard to the recent compacts made with Holland and the Emperor. French diplomacy was thus presented with an opening which her armies could never hope to secure.

The English first sounded French views unofficially through a private agent, the abbé Gaultier, one-time chaplain to Tallard, afterwards resident in London, working for Torcy and for the Jacobite Jersey. In July 1711, a few weeks after the death of Joseph I, he went again to Paris with Matthew Prior, who stated the English demands. For the allies, Bolingbroke, who now took over the negotiations, required satisfaction: Barriers for the Dutch and the Emperor, his lands returned to the Duke of Savoy, the separation of the Crowns of France and Spain, secure trade for the united Provinces. In England's special interests, Matthew Prior put certain extra propositions—those which were eventually embodied in the Treaty of Utrecht—which were to remain a secret. Bolingbroke and Torcy haggled fiercely; over two questions there was compromise. The matter of Lille and Tournai was deferred to the conference and Bolingbroke gave up his claim for 'cautionary towns' in the Spanish Indies, in return for an extension of the *asiento* for thirty years. On October 8th, Nicholas Mesnager, for the French king, signed the preliminaries.

In the summer campaign of 1711, Marlborough had to operate with a smaller army, because of the departure of Eugène to deal with the threat of French pressure upon Germany in the year of the Imperial election. After an elaborate bluff and a hectic night march, he pierced the *Ne plus ultra* lines, crossed the Scheldt, besieged and took Bouchain under the eyes of Villars. In order to provide cover for the besieging troops he had to construct a whole fortress ring round the city. In September he completed an operation which was acclaimed as a masterpiece of the military art. Villars had obeyed his orders not to fight a battle outside his entrenchments, but he had been outmanœuvred. The threat of invasion remained acute. At the end of the year however, Marlborough returned to his ungrateful island to face dismissal, followed by charges of corruption and even cowardice. We need not enter into the sordid details of the political scene, the calculated smears upon the character of the greatest soldier in Europe. It was, for Bolingbroke, a necessary part of the operation of making a separate peace with France, but to the French it gave new hope. Louis XIV's comment was apposite: 'the affair of displacing the Duke of Marlborough will do all we desire'.

The Treaties of Utrecht and Rastadt

The plenipotentiaries of the allies met at Utrecht in January 1712. When the English revealed that they had come to a preliminary agreement with France, the Dutch had no option, if they were to avoid being isolated, but to consider its terms. Huxelles for France presented these with the added suggestion that the Spanish Netherlands should be given to the Elector of Bavaria. This was unacceptable to both Holland and the Empire; so deadlock ensued. It seems remarkable that France should in this way take the initiative again, but Torcy now had certain advantages. First, Bolingbroke had made no secret of his dislike of the Dutch and he had compromised himself by his private engagements of the year before. Second, the tragically sudden deaths of the Dauphin, his eldest son and grandson, left only the duc de Berry (to die in 1713) and the sickly child, later Louis XV, between Philip of Anjou, *de jure* and now *de facto* King of Spain, and the throne of France. The Tories might yet find themselves placed in the same difficult position as the Whigs had been by the death of Joseph I. No one in England wanted to see Philip king both of Spain and France. So in the event England worked hurriedly towards her private solution and left her allies to find their own way out. Utrecht was intended to be a mere façade while business was done in direct parley between Torcy and Bolingbroke. The Tory propagandist Swift had prepared the way with a pamphlet entitled 'Some remarks on the Barrier Treaty'. By the summer of 1712, opinion in the country was so inflamed against the Dutch that any attempt to carry out this treaty obligation of only four years before would have been impossible. It was less easy to find a solution to the second difficulty, for Torcy told Bolingbroke that it was not possible in French law for the rightful heir to renounce the succession; Philip V rejected the other solution which would have provided him with a new kingdom in the north of Italy, his crown of Spain going to the Duke of Savoy. By July 1712 however, France and England had come to an armistice agreement; Ormonde, who had replaced Marlborough as commander-in-chief, had already received orders to 'avoid engaging in any battle or hazarding a battle', orders which were communicated to the French. Bolingbroke boasted that he had thus saved the French from 'being beat'. Villars responded with letters of abuse of the Whigs and the allies, Louis with assurances of sympathy and protection! The English ministers actually informed Villars in October, through Gaultier and Torcy, that Eugène was planning a surprise attack.

Holland and the Emperor rejected the Anglo-French armistice

and Eugène, who had already mounted what was to prove the last great campaign of the war, proceeded with the siege of Landrecies, as Ormonde marched away to occupy Dunkirk. The latter's 50,000 mercenaries were hired by the Dutch and swelled Eugène's army, which still made a very formidable show. Both sides yet hoped to win some advantage that would sway the peace talks in their favour. Louis appreciated the gravity of the hour. When he saw Villars at Marly before the start of the campaign, the old man spoke with fortitude of the loss, in one week, of his grandson, his granddaughter and their son. He then declared his trust in Villars: 'I hand into your charge the troops and the safety of my realm. I know your zeal and the valour of my troops, but eventually your fortune may come contrary. If there should be a disaster to the army that you command, what do you think my part should be?' He answered his own question: 'I know what the courtiers will argue; almost all will wish that I should retire to Blois and should not wait for the enemy army to approach Paris, which they could if mine were defeated. For myself I know that armies so large are not so badly beaten that a great part of mine could not retire behind the Somme. I know that river; it is very difficult to cross; it has strong places and I should count on being able to get back to Péronne or St. Quentin to rally what troops remain and make with you a last effort, perish together, or save the state.'

Villars was neither crushed by his responsibilities nor forced upon staid defensive. The fall of Landrecies would have opened to Eugène the valley of the Oise. So Villars, with a bare 70,000 against Eugène's 100,000, was ordered to save the town at all cost. By a feint he brought Eugène to concentrate his troops round Landrecies; then after a night march which might have come from Marlborough's copybook, he stormed the thinly held Austrian entrenchments and carried Denain at the point of the bayonet (July 24, 1712). Killed, captured and wounded, the allied casualties were about five thousand, the French not more than five hundred. The victory severed Eugène's long communication-line, ruptured his invasion plan and, in the words of Napoleon a hundred years later, 'saved France'. The old king was ecstatic: 'My troops displayed such courage as I cannot adequately praise; in it I recognised the whole valour of the nation.' Villars followed up his advantage with spirit, capturing town after town, with the supplies amassed for the invasion march; Marchiennes in July,

Douai in August, Quesnoy and Bouchain in October. Eugène's rashness and Villars' opportunism had altered the whole balance of military power. The Dutch were now more seriously disposed to peace. Slowly a settlement was unravelled from the twisted skeins of separate disputes, pledges and bargains. Bolingbroke was able to secure that Philip should renounce his reversionary claim to the crown of France, and that this should be registered by the *Parlement* of Paris and the *Cortes* of Madrid. In November, Louis gave way over Tournai, but the obstinacy of Heinsius still deferred the last stages. French attempts to secure either Belgium or Sicily for their unfortunate ally, the Elector of Bavaria, failed. A typical delay was caused by a quarrel between the lackeys of the French and Dutch envoys; few conferences passed without such incidents. England acted as arbiter to secure the *entente* of France with the lesser powers, Savoy, Prussia and Portugal. (Bolingbroke had to send an ultimatum threatening renewed war before Torcy would concede to Portugal her rights in Brazil against the encroachment of the French from Guiana.) It was after treaties had been signed with these powers, on the night of April 11th that Heinsius resolved, in his words, 'to drink the chalice of peace'. In England the news was brought to Bolingbroke by his half-brother, who was welcomed with ecstasy by the statesman whose individual triumph it was: 'it is the work of the Lord and marvellous in our eyes'. But France could not yet celebrate peace, for the Emperor, deserted by his allies, would not accept the *fait accompli*, and hostilities dragged on. Not until Villars had won further victories on the Rhine and taken Landau and Fribourg did he resign himself to peace. For two months Eugène and Villars negotiated; eventually, at Rastadt, was signed the last treaty, on March 6, 1714, significantly in French and not the Latin of Imperial usage. It was confirmed at Baden in September of the same year.

The Peace of Utrecht-Rastadt was not so humiliating to Louis as the war that it brought to an end. It was not the complete capitulation that had seemed possible in 1709, nor did France lose everything for which she had fought. When the terms are set against those of Nijmegen or Ratisbon, they mock the gains of those easier years; if put into account with the cost of the wars of the reign, in blood and treasure, they are bitter indeed. But France did not emerge without honour to solace defeat, nor without gain to show against her loss. Louis had gone to war to defend the right of his grandson to the Spanish throne and only for a few frantic months had he abandoned that war aim. Now Philip V was confirmed King of Spain and stood more strongly than in 1701, with the active support of his subjects. This was something to build on. Spain might still, with skilful management, become a client state, although for the present there was resentment in Madrid at the way in which Spain's Empire was dismembered. The acquisition of Gibraltar and Minorca assured England an extension of her sea power into the Mediterranean; these were henceforward prime objects of Bourbon aggression. In Italy, Naples, most of the Milanese and Sardinia (in 1720 exchanged with Savoy, for Sicily) were given to the Emperor. Sicily and a part of the Milanese went to the Duke of Savoy, whose family, in case Philip's line failed, was to inherit the Spanish throne. By the *asiento* insisted upon by Bolingbroke, England acquired the right to trade with certain towns in Spanish waters, a small beginning from which much would grow. England received also Newfoundland (subject to certain fishing rights) Hudson's Bay, Acadia and St. Kitts. Louis acknowledged the right of accession of the House of Hanover and banished James Stuart from France. (He could always be recalled if the circumstances, or Bolingbroke, required it.)

The need to secure her frontier was paramount in every war fought by France. It remained intact. Above all Strasbourg, with the province of Alsace, was kept; for this the victories of Villars in the last year of the war were an important bargaining point. The Spanish Netherlands were given to the Emperor, subject to the right of the Dutch to the military government of Furnes, Ypres, Ghent, Tournai, Menin, Mons, Charleroi and Namur, as their Barrier against France. But Lille remained to France, more than could have been hoped for in the winter of 1708-9. At Dunkirk, the fortifications were to be demolished, on the insistence of the English, who had suffered from the privateers of that port. In the south, Nice was restored to Victor Amadeus; in return France received Barcelonnette.

Utrecht-Rastadt represented an alteration in the terms of power which went further than any study of the text of the treaties themselves would suggest. The situation of the European states had changed greatly since the Peace of the Pyrenees. In 1659, the staring fact had been the decay of Spain as an international combination, its corollary the rise of France as a coherent and expanding nation. Now France was in turn checked in her aggressive course, and definite limits set to her physical advance. She did not, of course, sink to the position of a second class power. 'France had not arrived at the sovereignty of the world but she remained still the greatest country on the Continent' (Ranke). The serious disorders and discontents that lay beneath the surface are not the theme of this chapter, nor are they what the diplomats of Europe saw; rather they saw a country that was still pre-eminent in population, natural resources and efficient government; which had withstood the onslaughts of most of the rest of Europe, and survived intact.

Of France's rivals, Austria might seem to have secured most from the defeat of French militarism. But her winnings, Flanders, Milan, Naples, brought with them the problems which had hung so heavy round the neck of Spain. Austria belonged in the eighteenth century to the old and scattered type of international organisation whose disadvantages had been exposed in the wars of the past century. It is arguable that her very acquisitions at Utrecht, complicating as they did the question of whether she should concentrate on development in the east or in the west, prevented her from becoming a great power in the eighteenth century. The future lay rather with the compact, militarist nation of the sort being hammered out by the Hohenzollerns in Brandenburg-Prussia. The recognition at Utrecht by France of the new kingship of Frederick of Prussia was a portent of a new energy and ruthlessness of policy which was to startle the old dynasties in the person of Frederick the Great.

The climb of Prussia was matched by the decline of her neighbours. Sweden, which had long held for France the balance of power in Northern Europe but had completely given up that alliance in the late war, was never to recover from the reckless career of Charles XII and his defeat at Pultava. Saxony had little energy or prestige left after her defeats at the hands of Charles XII, and was reduced by 1714 to the level of a Polish province. Poland herself, whose crown had been tossed around by Sweden and France, was still reckoned worth playing for in the marriage stakes. Louis XIV however, we may be sure, would have regarded the marriage of his successor to Maria Lescinska with disfavour. The fate of Poland in the second half of the eighteenth century was to be the victim of a slow, cynical dismemberment. Hanover was no longer a mere auxiliary, but the new Elector's power lay mostly in his small army and in his prospect of succession to the throne of England. Max-Emmanuel of Bavaria had simply backed the wrong horse and had not therefore, like his fellow-elector of Brandenburg, won a kingdom. He paid the forfeit, at Blenheim and after, in diminished wealth and standing.

Outside Germany, the little power of Savoy had won considerable pickings, in parts of the Milanese and Sicily, from her political see-saw. But the diplomats of Utrecht may be forgiven for not discerning in this mountain country the matrix for modern Italy. The English ambassador in Spain, in 1715, thought that 'there is no nation that can raise itself more easily, and never more so than now', and Spain indeed gained rather than lost from the amputation of limbs into which so much of her blood had flowed. In the next decade, under the stimulus of Philip V's wife, Elizabeth Farnese, Spain played an adventurous life again in European politics, with a policy directed towards the recovery of the lost Italian crowns. 'Spain breathed again under Philip V'; but by the time Voltaire wrote this, the revival had proved to be an illusion.

England and Holland had been the twin props of the Grand Alliance, and of these the latter had given the most. At the time of the de Witts she had been a great maritime and commercial power and played the arbiter amongst the states of Europe. The brutal aggression of 1672 had created a spirit of recalcitrance which had given the militarists political control for forty years. The party of war had displayed to the finish a remarkable tenacity and they had made Louis and his diplomats bend and scrape for peace. But in 1713 they gained nothing for their pains except the right to garrison the forts of the Barrier. For this Barrier, which was proved militarily unsound and of little use in the French invasion of 1745, they had sacrificed their commercial supremacy. In 1700, the debts of the province of Holland alone amounted to 30 millions, in 1713, to 173 million florins. The direction of European policy passed largely to the English. A future Pensionary, Slingelandt, was to comment on this: 'the English, while amassing to themselves the advantages of Peace, left to the Dutch only the sad resource of complaining of the injustice and the infidelity of the court of London'.

England had most to gain from the war against France and least to lose; accordingly, and thanks to the foresight and trickery of Bolingbroke, she emerged with the greatest advantages. A war fought through the agency of a national bank, more upon loans than upon taxation, had enriched important classes in the community who were now able to turn their gains to account. As banker of the world, London outstripped Amsterdam. The country had gained from France a foothold in Canada, and from Spain the key to the Mediterranean. Already, in 1715, her foreign trade was worth £15 million a year; and this was only a beginning. The seventeenth century had belonged to France. The eighteenth century was to belong to England.

The monetary crisis

In 1701, twelve deputies of leading commercial towns made some strong criticisms of the government's protectionist policy to the *conseil de commerce*. Agriculture, they thought, had been sacrificed to manufactures, but it was unreasonable to turn all the resources of a great country to that one end. Everything was conceded to monopolies; the privileged companies had killed the spirit of enterprise; the policy of the favourable balance had been taken too far, and trade relations with other countries had suffered. It was necessary, in the opinion of a deputy from Languedoc, to abandon Colbert's doctrine that France could surpass the world in and by her trade, and that foreigners could be compelled to have recourse to her. These men were representatives of local interests and they could not be expected to appreciate Colbert's policies, and those of his successors, in the context of the needs of the state. They tested them, however, by the evidence of their balance-sheets, by the facts and figures of declining trade, and found them wanting; they were representative of a fairly general revolt against Colbertism amongst the business community. Criticising the restrictions imposed by the state, and looking forward to a larger liberty of trade, they anticipated the arguments of the *physiocrates* of the eighteenth century. The reaction against mercantilism had begun. It soon made its mark for, before the end of the Spanish Succession War, the government was so alarmed by the decline of trade that freedom of trading was restored to Dunkirk, Marseilles, Bordeaux and Bayonne. In 1712 Desmarets, *contrôleur général* and Colbert's great-nephew, wrote to Mesnager, who was charged with an important trade mission to England: 'I do not believe that we have to fear consequences prejudicial to the commerce of France in giving all countries reciprocal equality. My opinion is that the more facilities we give to foreigners to send their goods to us the more we will be able to sell of our own. Uniformity and freedom in commercial matters always creates wealth in the countries in which they are established.' It was in this spirit, so remarkably altered from that of the great-uncle of the *contrôleur général*, that the government signed with the Dutch the commercial treaty of Utrecht, and a similar treaty with Prussia. Only the opposition of

Whig merchants in London prevented Bolingbroke from carrying through the business on which Mesnager was engaged, the treaty with France which the Whigs were themselves to achieve after the Hanoverian Succession and the death of Louis XIV.

Businessmen habitually blame the government when trading conditions deteriorate, and in the managed economy this is not unfair. But they were less than fair in ascribing their plight wholly to protectionism. Colbert's tariffs had often been equal to, sometimes more than, the value of foreign goods that they attached to, while the privileges of his monopolist companies had driven foreign ships from French ports and prejudiced the prospects of French ships in foreign ports. Some of his enterprises had, however, borne fruit; there had been since 1661 a large growth in the country's productivity and in her foreign trade. There were other factors to consider: the bill for policies of aggrandisement and intolerance, the cost of war and the consequent increases of taxation, damage to trade and shipping, the expulsion of the Huguenots. Further, it should be recalled that Colbert's policies were conceived in the light of a deficiency of bullion and designed to remedy that deficiency. The monetary crisis would have been more acute without his measures; it is to this crisis, rather than to the system of protectionism, that we should look for explanation of the depression at the turn of the century. Colbert's successors, Le Pelletier, Pontchartrain, Chamillart and Desmarets, conscientious and sensible men, have attracted criticism for the financial decline of France. They could only find expedients to meet a trend largely beyond their control, which had nullified much of Colbert's work even in his lifetime. They were trying to meet the bills of war from resources attenuated by creeping deflation.

In the middle of the century the price rise, which had been continuous for more than a hundred years, was halted. From about 1650 to about 1730 there was, despite fluctuations, a discernible downward trend of prices, the consequence of a world-wide shortage of bullion. The flow of precious metals was not suddenly cut off in 1650: from 1601 to 1620 the world produced 422,000 kilograms of silver and 8,250 of gold; from 1661 to 1680, 337,000 kilograms of silver, 10,675 of gold. But these amounts had not increased relatively to the growing total; the percentage increase which had in the middle of the sixteenth century been 3·8, was by 1600 only 1, by 1700, 0·5. The great forward impulse of Western Europe, which had been started and fed by the bullion of the New World, was slowly pinched by its relative decline. No country had owed more than France to the original inflation, in the expansion of her manufactures and commerce to earn by her exports the money of Spain. Now, with England and Holland, she suffered from the contraction of world demand and from shortage of capital to expand her new-grown industries. Against this background the king's anti-Huguenot policy is seen to have been especially unfortunate, with its resultant loss of capital to the banks of Amsterdam and London. The steady wastage of capital tied up in *offices* was more serious than it would have been during a period of inflation. Finally, the failure of France to evolve a system of state credit as efficient as that of England was of crucial importance in the relative economic development of the two countries.

The problem was recognised by contemporaries. The Protestant pamphlet *Soupirs de la France esclave* spoke of a shortage of money so remarkable that transactions were everywhere stopped since 'those who have bread cannot buy wine nor those who have wine, bread'. Ministers could study the problem in more precise terms. The great inquest upon the state of the realm ordered for the Duke of Burgundy was only one of several. Colbert had had one made in 1663 which was the basis of his fiscal work. Further censuses were conducted in 1693 and 1709. The new use of applied mathematics is reflected in these conscientious works of statistics. Outside the government the works of the intelligent veteran Vauban and the magistrate Boisguillebert, *Dîme Royale* and *Détail de la France*, were clear analyses of France's economic plight which bore the mark of the monetary crisis. Both departed from the strict mercantilist idea in putting forward some other test for the richness of the community than precious metals alone: Vauban the size of the population and Boisguillebert the state of agriculture. But they each attributed to money the vital role in the economy; in Boisguillebert's phrase it was 'the valet of commerce'. One remedy proposed by *contrôleurs généraux* was the turning back of gold and silver into currency. The king led the way in this and the palaces were stripped of superfluous ornament, the gilding of mirrors, flagons, plates, even the silver throne at Versailles, were all sent to be melted down. Bishops were asked to contribute unused church ornaments. In the crisis of 1709 the king appealed for everybody's valuables; a few of the great families gave grudgingly, some like Saint-Simon may have gone on to porcelain but 'locked most of the silver away'. The *bourgeois* gave nothing and the total proceeds were less than 3 million. This sort of expedient was ineffectual; devaluation was called for, an operation beyond the resources of a seventeenth century administration. The crown, the greatest debtor and banker of the realm, could not afford such a devaluation and instead juggled with the exchange value of the *louis d'or* and the crown to favour its own transactions. (The crown was worth 3 *livres* in 1666; in 1690, 3 *livres* 6 *sous*; in 1709, 5 *livres*; in 1715, 3 *livres* 10 *sous*.) The necessity of making ends meet from day to day stood in the way of a sound policy, but in any case nothing could be done without an adequate credit system. Unfortunately this was crude, for banking hardly existed as a separate system and large-scale credit operations were simply carried on by great merchants, or by manufacturers whose business needs compelled them to be their own bankers. Many of these were Huguenots; nor did this necessarily sever their connection. The Legendres of Rouen, 'New Catholics', worked hand-in-hand with the older branch of the House of Legendre, still Protestants, in Amsterdam. Unfortunately, attempts to start a 'national bank'—on the lines of the Bank of England founded in 1694—all broke down; partly because of a confusion in the issue of notes, whether simply tokens of cash or interest-carrying; partly because the state could not provide them with enough backing in *specie*. In the correspondence of the *contrôleur général*, there are many references to the 'Royal Bank', but lack of technique, unhappy circumstances, public suspicion all played their part in delaying it. Samuel Bernard was the author of one plan that foundered, John Law, the Scotsman, of another. In the end he was allowed, after the death of Louis XIV, under the Regent Orléans, to go ahead. It was no chimerical scheme, although it was adventurous and doomed, in 1720, to founder amidst speculative mania.

The peasant problem

The effects of deflation were to be seen in all spheres of life. One writer has even gone so far as to attribute the sombre character of social and political life, so far at least as it was represented by the court, to this cause; he contrasts this new spirit with the boisterous gaieties of the Renaissance, an age of easy money and enterprise. It is true that there is an introspective quality about court life, but there were other causes for this besides declining rents: defeat in war, the middle age of the king, his growing pietism. It is more to the point to start at the source of these declining rents, in the countryside where nine-tenths of the population lived.

There is an element of truth in Taine's comparison of the state of the rural population to that of a man walking through a pond with the water up to his chin; if there is a slight fall in the economic level, he is submerged. But a caution is necessary, for conditions varied widely: between rich corn-growing areas and poor upland tracts; between the established wine districts and the marginal land where straggling vineyards defied the laws of supply and demand; between estates where the landowner was benevolent and those where rights and rents were grabbed with vigour and chicanery; between *pays d'état* and *pays d'élection*. Boisguillebert drew attention to the difference that this could make, in his *Détail de la France*, published in 1697. He was a native of Montauban and a government official in Rouen. Montauban was a poor hilly district but it paid the *taille réelle*; the peasantry enjoyed meat as well as bread, wore good linen smocks and lived in sound and well-tiled cottages. At Rouen, where they paid the *taille personnelle*, the land was good and should have been worth six times as much as at Montauban; but meat and wine were unknown, peasants' cottages were ruinous and land was going out of cultivation. The evidence is often conflicting and generalisations have to be made with circumspection. A principal source of evidence, for instance, is the reports of the *intendants*, upon whom the government relied for assessment of taxation and for their knowledge of conditions in the provinces. These tell frequently of starvation and misery; but it should be remembered that the *intendant* was concerned to obtain as low an assessment for his *généralité* as possible and it was not in his interests to understate the privations of his people. But there is an impressive unanimity about certain aspects of these reports which are born out by other sources of evidence; tax returns, population estimates, land values, besides the independent comments of other observers of the scene, bishops and *curés*, diarists and publicists.

Locke, travelling about the country in the seventies, found more evidence of want than of plenty. In Provence, for instance, an entry for 1676 describes 'five acres of poverty for one of riches'. Here he was nauseated by a typical Sunday dinner of 'slices of congealed blood fried in oile'. In the wine-district of Graves in 1678, he found a peasant family of five which had to exist on seven *sous* a day, with anything that his wife could earn to help out; for their windowless hovel they paid 36 *livres* a year rent, their *taille* came to 4 *livres*, together the wages of 114 days. Their diet consisted largely of rye-bread and water; meat 'seldom seasons their pots', but on some special occasion they might buy 'the inwards of some beast in the market'. Recently, 'the collector had taken their frying pan and dishes' in lieu of *taille*. 'Yet they say that in Xantonges (Saintonge) and several other parts of France the *paisants* are much more miserable than these, for these they count the flourishing *paisants* which live in Grave(s).' It was the class of the *métayers* who owned little or no land that suffered worse, and these were the first to starve if the harvest was bad, to join the marauding bands which terrorised some parts of the countryside and the peasant revolts which occurred sporadically throughout the reign. The decline of the peasantry does not seem to have been confined, however, to the dregs of the rural proletariat. Boisguillebert estimated that the value of leases had fallen by a half since 1660; Vauban, in his *Dîme Royale*, put the depreciation of prices in half a century at a third. In the same work he claimed that a tenth of France was reduced to begging. The taxes, whose returns form perhaps the most reliable index of peasant prosperity, fell steadily in the later years of the reign. The tax-farms, in an average budget of Colbert, would produce about 66 millions; by the end of the reign this had fallen to 47 millions. The population of France fell by at least a million in the last twenty years of the reign.

There was indeed serious over-population in rural France, so that the reserve of casual labour served to keep wages low and to depress the general standard of living. Too many people were trying to live off the land and trying therefore to farm marginal land which yielded poor rewards for their toil. The total production was not much increased by this, for there was not enough fertiliser to go round; this was owing to the shortage of livestock, which was in turn owing to the need for each area to be self-sufficient in arable crops. The peasantry were stubbornly conservative about their methods, often primitive and wasteful. A large proportion of the yield of the harvest went to provide seed for the next, and shortage of seed was often a prime problem. The *intendant* of Bordeaux wrote in 1708: 'most of the people have not the means to sow their fields. We have not judged it expedient to commit ourselves to supplying seed, for that would extend our resources too far.' An agrarian revolution was needed, but this would have required the active interest of landowners in new agricultural techniques, and the expenditure of capital. Neither was forthcoming. The lack of interest of the landowner may be attributed to the faults of the social system. The lack of investment was partly the consequence of the prevailing low prices which took the heart out of agriculture. Coin was everywhere short, in places there must have been hoarding, but the scarcity was genuine. Partly it was due to the oppressive taxes which fell always most heavily upon the rural producer, discouraging him from making any improvement to his land and depriving him of the means to do so. When in 1687, at the beginning of what was hoped would be a period of peace, the *intendants* carried out a detailed inquiry into the conditions of the countryside, their memorials were all agreed: high and unfair taxation was at the heart of the people's grievances. Two years before, Vauban had supported his arguments for the *'projet de capitation'* with the contention that the *taille* had fallen into such a state that 'the angels themselves could not reform it'.

Financial expedients

Some of the overflow of population from the countryside found its way into the towns, to provide labour for new manufactories. A large expansion of industry would have contributed towards the solution of France's economic difficulties. But from Colbert's death till the end of the reign there was actually a shrinkage of trade and manufactures. The chronic shortage of capital was made worse by the vicissitudes of government finance, especially its tinkering with exchange rates. *Entrepreneurs* could not be blamed, in the uncertain trading conditions of the war years, if they preferred to invest their money in the relative safety of the offices which the government was creating in ever-increasing numbers. The war was also responsible for shortages of raw materials, for losses at sea and closed overseas markets. The exact consequences of Louis' campaign against the Huguenots are impossible to assess but it is certain that many of Colbert's imported workers and much valuable capital was lost to the country, to the corresponding gain of those that received them. The textile industry, which had

P

grown fastest, suffered worst, in Flanders, Normandy and Champagne. We hear of the depression of the hat-making industry of Rouen and of the tapestry concerns of Paris and Beauvais. Lace, paper and deep-sea fisheries were three others to be particularly depressed. New outlets were however to be found in colonies and in the Levant, so that the picture is not one of unrelieved gloom. Nantes, with its sugar refineries, and Marseilles grew more prosperous at this time. The munitions industries of course flourished. During the war, harbours might silt up and merchant ships fall prey to enemy privateers, but French industry was resilient enough to look for new markets; with the peace there was a rapid expansion of trade again. In 1716, foreign trade was worth 200 million *livres* a year, colonial trade alone worth 40 million.

The depression of town and countryside meant falling returns to the *contrôleur-général*. Twenty of the last twenty-five years of the reign were years of war, and the tendency of war was to become steadily more expensive. The Dutch War of 1672 had been largely paid for out of current taxation; the War of Spanish Succession increased the country's debt sevenfold. Expenditure rose to new heights as income declined. In the last nine years of the reign, the expenses of the crown were approximately four times its income. The deficit of 3,000 million *livres* in 1715 is the measure of a fiscal calamity without precedent. Many expedients, some familiar, some banished by Colbert, some new, were tried. The titles of false nobles were chased and checked, a lottery was set up, new taxes, on tobacco for instance, were created. The church was pressed for higher *dons gratuits*; they gave 1,230,000 *livres* at the start of the reign, 6,400,000 at the end. In the form of the *capitation* of 1695, the government committed itself at last to a modest tax upon the rich. It fell upon all, from the Dauphin down to the *métayer*, in careful gradations. The first-class included the Princes of the Blood, ministers, farmers-general; the second, princes, dukes, marshals and great officers of the crown. The twenty-two grades were arranged characteristically more by class than by fortune so that bankers might find themselves in the tenth class, paying 120 *livres*, and merchants in the eleventh, paying only 100. The clergy contracted out for a lump sum of 4 millions. The *capitation* was introduced again in 1701, but on the bad system of lump assessment by *généralité*, upon the model of the *taille*, and with the same effect that the rich escaped lightly. In 1710, however, a drastic change was proposed: instead of an arbitrary classification, a uniform levy of one-tenth of all forms of revenue, regardless of class. The declaration of October 10th embodied an important change of principle. If its egalitarian spirit had been respected it would have been the fairest tax of the reign; if it had been accepted as the model for the future taxation there might have been no French Revolution. But it broke down upon the administrative front, for there lacked the personnel to carry out the necessary research into incomes and rights. Again one is reminded of the important difference between what the government willed and what it could perform. Critics of Louis' ministers have sometimes overlooked the fact that no seventeenth century government had evolved the machinery for the accurate assessment of income. It is also true that the administration was confronted with a revolt of the privileged, to whom it was plain that this was the thin end of the wedge of regular taxation. After numerous exemptions the tax gave the disappointing return of 20 millions a year. What it could have been is revealed by the fact that at the beginning of Orléans' Regency a company of businessmen offered 60 millions for the farm of the tax—on condition that the state should uphold them against the opposition of the privileged classes!

When taxation failed, the state had recourse to loans, which were often floated under the name of some other body with resources of its own for additional guarantee, the Assembly of Clergy, the Estates of Languedoc, the city of Lyon for example. Despite the risk that the *rentier* ran, these were well subscribed; in 1684 they procured for the Treasury 48 millions, in 1699, 310 millions. But the greatest standby of the impoverished state was the sale of offices and of patents of nobility. The traffic in titles did more than anything to alienate the old aristocracy of Saint-Simon's way of thinking and to foster criticism of the regime. But the sale of offices was a more significant abuse: 'every time your Majesty creates an office, God creates some sot to buy it,' observed Pontchartrain. It has been estimated that half a million people were involved by 1715, office-holders large and small, whose capital was thus lost to trade or manufactures or agriculture. By then few towns were without their hereditary grand criers of funerals, or inspectors of wigs. The administration was barnacled with controllers, receivers, checkers, weighers, registrars, sinecurists of every sort; an army of *petits bourgeois* who looked to the state to supply them with the symbols of status which raised them above the heads of the *roturiers*.

The financial needs of the state provided unprecedented opportunities for private individuals who were fortunate enough to be able to proffer aid. There is some irony in the fact that the king came to owe so much to the class of financier that he most despised; it did not escape the notice of the people, who began to associate the king with the iniquities of high finance. Several factors were at work in the enrichment of financiers and contractors: the complications of the taxes, the shortage of ready money, the lack of adequate banking facilities and the large-scale contracts for the supply of the armed forces. Their power was the measure of the state's administrative shortcomings, the price paid for the failure to develop a regular machinery of credit. They took risks for their profits; in war their offers could not be refused, but in peace the ministers might turn upon them, examine their accounts and force them to disgorge their gains. They acted as middle men between the state and its tax-paying subjects, as farmers-general of taxes or state-contractors, as private bankers making direct loans to a needy government, as brokers finding subscribers to the *rentes*, or applicants for new offices. Since one man might do all these things, the scope of an enterprising financier was considerable. La Bruyère, writing bitterly of these 'dirty souls', voices the general feeling about the type, and they play the villain in much contemporary literature.

Because of declining yields these years were not so rewarding for the tax-farmer as the period before Colbert, or after 1715; even so, between 1689 and 1697, tax-farmers took nearly 100 million *livres* from the 350 millon levied in taxation, much of which had to be disbursed among lesser agents. Le Riche and Romanet were two especially notorious figures among those who still contrived to make a fortune from their farms. Richer profits could however be made from the equipment, moving and foraging of troops, from naval contracting, privateering, speculation in the money market and in currency revaluation. After 1700 the Spanish Indies opened up a new field of profitable enterprise. Slaving and sugar-refining were two growing industries which offered large returns upon invested capital.

Those who made money could make themselves indispensable. They could perform valuable and patriotic service, like the brothers Paris who, in 1690, saved the province of Dauphiné from famine, and in 1712 pledged their credit to provide supplies for the army which conquered at Denain. These two were the sons of an inn-keeper; but they were destined to emerge as important persons in the state, presiding over the liquidation of the credit scheme of John Law which they had done their best to spoil. The wealthiest of all was Samuel Bernard. With interests all over the world, he made a fortune of sixty millions from grain dealings, exchange and munitions; he was diplomat-at-large and the confidant of successive *contrôleurs généraux*. When he was bankrupted in 1709 to the extent of 30 million *livres* he had to be propped up by the state, whose credit was inseparable from his own—but he survived to make another fortune.

The *noblesse de l'épée*, and indeed the *noblesse de la robe*, might affect to despise the new plutocracy, but they were often compelled to come to terms with it. An important feature of the period is the growth of interdependence and intermarriage of the nobility and the monied interest. There was nothing unusual about the marriage of the Comte d'Evreaux, son of the duc de Bouillon and grandnephew of Turenne, to the daughter of Crozat, Receiver-General and Treasurer of Languedoc, one of the richest men of France, and the son of a lackey. Between Paris, now once more the capital of finance, and Versailles, the gulf was narrower than the social taboos might suggest. Soon under the Regency the fountains of Versailles would dry up, the palace would be deserted, government, court and business interests merge in the capital of money and fashion.

Already the dealings of new high finance reached into every corner of the structure of absolutism. Some of the fortunes were as scandalous as they were spectacular. Bourvallais, who was the son of a Breton peasant and whose name appears in every sort of transaction, was forced in 1710 to pay 4,500,000 *livres* restitution. Morisset, son of a merchant of Châlons-sur-Marne, treasurer of les Invalides, farmer of taxes in Flanders and army contractor, protégé of Chamillart, was nevertheless compelled to disgorge a million in 1709. The very rich might be accepted even if they were unpopular. Beneath them, however, ranged a shabby host of prospectors, who flourished as commission agents in many lines of business, from the negotiation of mixed marriages to the sale of crosses of St. Louis. Even at court, at all levels there was profiteering and graft, known by experience to many and exposed to the public by successive inquests at which the government tried to make 'the bloodsuckers of the people' scapegoats for the country's destitution. These revelations reflected as much upon the crown as upon the individuals whom it had appeared to shelter. The decay of Louis XIV's ideal of disinterested welfare government was plain for all to see. In this manner material difficulties contributed to the moral crisis of the regime.

The spread of Jansenism

'The Peace of the Church' had been, at best, only a truce; after 1669 the issues remained alive, Jansenism was unabashed, the Jesuits unreconciled. The rival theories of Grace still glared out at one another over theology's no-man's land; if for twenty-five years antagonism was muted, it was only a matter of time before war was renewed, over the old grounds of belief and behaviour, but upon new issues. In this time, while the Protestant question came more and more to occupy the attention of all parts of the French church, the character of Jansenism changed perceptibly. Of the great originals only Arnauld lived on, the patriarch of a movement which, as it became accepted and even fashionable, lost something of its esoteric quality. From its original springs in Paris and Port Royal des Champs, Jansenism swelled out into the mainstream of French religious life, through certain parishes, in Rouen, Orléans, Toulouse and Grenoble notably, through religious institutions such as the Oratory of Saint Magloire in Paris, and the episcopacy, where men like Pavillon and Caulet were avowed Jansenists and Bossuet was openly sympathetic. As the movement became larger it became less coherent. New disciples were attracted for a variety of reasons; some by its stoical pietism, others by its heroic record of opposition to authority, others again by its advanced ideas about education and the translation of the Bible and liturgy into the vernacular. Inevitably some of the flavour of heroic unworldliness departed. The movement had been born out of the spiritual indignation of a few rare souls; now that its protest had been made it continued purposeful and busy but lost the sense of overriding spiritual purpose.

The exclusiveness that played so large a part in the character of the early Port Royals, too easily became an offensive sort of spiritual pride. One of the first Jansenists, Le Maître, who left a successful lawyer's career in Paris to join the solitaries of Port Royal, gave this pride its unconscious expression when he wrote a letter to his father beginning 'God having made use of you to bring me into the world'. Standards of sanctification were set which were nearly impracticable, and which could not be intended for the ordinary person. Fénelon asked once of Mère Angélique: 'would it not be better to catch smaller fish, and more of them?'

Their view of fallen man tended towards a cosmic despair. Arnauld's preface to the *Fréquente Communion* declares that the church 'will always be degenerating from its first purity as it advances towards the end of the world'. Pierre Nicole (1625-95), with Pascal and Arnauld the greatest of the Jansenist moralists, and a gentle moderate who tried to steer his followers away from controversy to the constructive work of education, shared this pessimism. In his *De la soumission à la volonté de Dieu* he described the past as 'little more than the history of the Devil and the Damned, because those who play the leading part on the stage of history are generally citizens of Babylon'. In the *Crainte de Dieu*, writing of the rigour and justice of God, 'which plunges men into the abyss of eternal torture', he went on: 'we pass our days in this spiritual carnage, and in a sense we swim in the blood of sinners. The world by which we are carried along is a river of blood; to perish one has merely to allow oneself to be carried along.' A few, the elect, gave themselves heroically to God and rose above the river of the damned in little jealous islands of sanctity. But how could even they be sure of it? Rigorous care could all too easily become morbid self-scrutiny—the familiar waste-land of Puritan souls.

Logical analysis of motives and feelings was characteristic of later Jansenism. Reasoning had always been encouraged at Port Royal, and the 'Logic' written for its *petites écoles* was famous. Nicole was mainly responsible for this handbook, and he was a thorough-going logician. The influence of Descartes on religious thought can be seen most clearly in his work. 'Never has the human heart been more clearly anatomised than by these gentlemen,' wrote Mme de Sévigné of Nicole and his followers. The mystical tradition in Jansenism started by Saint Cyran had been quickly choked, and the Jansenism of Arnauld and Nicole was severely pragmatical. The 'perfect union with God', self-annihilation in contemplation, these were distractions from the vital business of man, which was to work out his salvation reasonably and without sentiment. This was Nicole's contribution to the Jansenist controversy. In the *Réfutations des principales erreurs de Quietisme*, he attacked Mme Guyon's position of direct inspiration from God, and perfect union with Him, distinguishing in the process between love of God and the love of that love; only the former, he thought, came by Grace. Prayer and devotion, moreover, could be no substitute for living action. Pascal's mathematical approach persisted in Jansenism. To the true Jansenist, Christianity was not mysterious; it was all too agonisingly plain.

Sainte-Beuve described the period which followed the Peace of the Church as one of autumnal splendour. Abercrombie writes of the social and worldly prosperity of Port Royal. The coming and going of great ladies in their carriages shocked the fastidious Nicole. The house in Paris belonged to those who had accepted the principle of signature; those who had remained faithful to Saint Cyran had to be content with Port Royal des Champs. It was also a period of intense activity. They translated the scriptures into French—the Bible of Mons—developed their schools for the Christian education of laymen, worked out new and simpler rituals and joined in the war of apologetics against the Protestants (Arnauld's *Perpétuité de la Foi*, 1669). They basked in Papal favour, especially after the Jansenist bishops had declared for Innocent XI in the controversy of the *régale*, and so risked the unforgetting anger of the king. There was rumour in 1680 of making Arnauld a Cardinal, and Innocent XI was labelled by Jesuits the 'Jansenist Pope'. They threatened the Jesuit monopoly of education and, so far from remaining on the defensive, re-awoke controversy by supporting the anonymous publication of a series of tracts, at Cologne, on the 'Moral Practice of the Jesuits'.

The destruction of Port Royal

To some extent they prepared their own catastrophe by their truculence. In 1679 death removed their influential patroness, the duchesse de Longueville, and Pomponne, foreign minister and nephew of Arnauld, was dismissed. In the same year, Harlay, who had succeeded Péréfixe and continued his policy, visited the convent in person to tell them that they could take in no more novices. Their confessors were dismissed. Nicole and Quesnel left in turn for the Low Countries where they continued to state the Jansenist case, now in terms less academic than before, more easily understandable by the layman and so more dangerous from the Jesuits' standpoint, strengthening their determination to destroy the movement. Arnauld died in 1693, Nicole in 1695. Their restraining hands removed, the militant Oratorian Pasquier Quesnel, encouraged by the sympathy of the new archbishop of Paris, Noailles, who succeeded in 1695, brought their differences to the natural crisis. His book, *Réflexions Morales sur le Nouveau Testament*, was a classic of Jansenism; like the other classic, *La Fréquente Communion*, fifty years before, it provided the ammunition for a controversy which now shook the whole French church and echoed noisily abroad. Quesnel had published the work originally in 1678, but the Jesuits were now strong enough to challenge its extreme assumptions: the irresistible power of Grace and the futility of human effort; the identification of sin with self-love, the glory of persecution for righteousness' sake and the need for access to the Scripture for all Christians. Quesnel's work had an alarmingly democratic tendency: 'An unjust excommunication ought not to prevent us from doing our duty'. Already the Jansenist Jacques Boileau had come to the defence of the lower clergy against the jurisdiction of the bishop. The Jesuits could therefore count upon the backing of much of the hierarchy; also of course of the king, Mme de Maintenon, who had deserted Noailles, her former protégé, and finally of the Pope, reconciled after 1693 with the king. They were supported too by the persuasive pen of Fénelon, who had incurred disgrace for his association with the Quietists, and had clashed swords, in the course of that controversy, with Nicole.

The French church was now torn apart by all the theological questions at once: Jansenism, grace and will; Quietism, man's prayer relation to God; Gallicanism, the inevitable issue of authority; all this at a time when there was a growing difference of opinion over the tactics to be employed against the Huguenots. The situation was confused as prelates took opposite sides in the grand climacteric of the theological struggles of the *grand siècle*.

The Jansenists brought controversy into the open when they submitted to the friendly archbishop of Paris a definite *cas de conscience* from the case of a Parisian *curé*: could a confessor absolve an ecclesiastic who condemned the Five Propositions, but who refused 'with respect and silence' to attribute them to Jansen? The old hares of *fait* and *droit*, which had been lying up since the Peace of the Church, were thus started again and neither Bossuet nor Noailles could stop the Jesuits from giving chase. Clement XI, to whom the *cas de conscience* was referred, decided against the Jansenists. Quesnel was arrested in Brussels, at the Pope's orders; but he escaped. Louis demanded from Rome a Bull condemning the Jansenists and promised in return to use the secular arm to destroy heresy. A strange sight this, for Europe: Louis and the

Pope, dancing a solemn measure, perfectly in step, in the midst of the greatest of European wars. In July 1705 the Bull *Vineam Domini* condemned the Jansenist attitude of respectful silence; the formulary could now be strictly enforced, in letter as well as spirit, and the peace of 1669 was undone.

The Gallican question then raised its head. The articles of 1682 had stated the right of the French church to be consulted before the promulgation of Bulls in France, and despite the reconciliation of the king and the Pope the articles were very much alive. The successful assertion of the principle that the Pope could not make final pronouncement upon doctrinal questions, without the approval of a General Council, might yet save Jansenism. The position had altered since the time of the *régale*, when the Jansenists had made their ultramontane stand against the crown. Now with the king and the Pope working closely together they sheltered behind the Gallican view of the relationship of church and state. Noailles, who was himself in the most delicate position, searched for a compromise; he induced the clergy to accept *Vineam Domini*, but with the reservation that the Pope might be fallible on a point of fact. This left a loop-hole for Port Royal, since the right to adjudicate on points of doctrine was preserved. But Port Royal refused to accept the Bull, reservation or no. Noailles had to acquiesce in its destruction; in the year of Malplaquet the two houses were suppressed. The year after, in 1710, the very buildings of Port Royal des Champs were demolished and royal licence was given to the Jesuits to dig up the remains of notable Jansenists from their graves. There had been over 70 nuns in 1669; in 1709 there were only 19, and this miserable remnant was dispersed to other houses. The communal symbol of Jansenism was shattered. In one of the most critical years of France's history, the little domestic war of intolerance ended with a triumph for the Jesuits.

Unigenitus

The capture of the attenuated garrison of Port Royal had not however brought final success, for the heart of Jansenist doctrines remained intact. In 1711 Louis asked for a Bull condemning Quesnel's *Réflexions Morales*; in 1713 the Bull *Unigenitus* anathematised 101 propositions, extracted from the book. Noailles now had firmer ground to stand on; more than Quesnel's book, he was defending now the very ark of the Gallican covenant. From a cautious Jansenist he now became an ardent Gallican and he was widely supported, by the Chancellor Pontchartrain and foreign minister Torcy amongst others. Old alliances reformed, the *refusés* amongst the lower clergy, the *appellants*, a strong minority amongst the bishops, in parties in the Sorbonne and in *Parlement*—the latter being more active than it had been for fifty years. Père Le Tellier, who succeeded La Chaise as royal confessor in 1709, and Fénelon pressed for an ultramontane stand. Controversy flourished in the discontented state of society at the end of the reign, and a mass of pamphlets poured from the press. There was talk of a General Council, even of schism. Noailles was the hero of a popular resistance which seemed to the king to be becoming alarmingly political in its language. Opposition to the Jesuits merged easily with criticism of the crown in the last years of a discredited king. Louis had managed to have the best of both worlds during his reign. He had used Gallican sentiment to secure his political ends, he had become ultramontane in his anxiety to prove himself a good Catholic; now in the last weeks of his life he was forced to make a decision, between the claims of Rome and the traditions of the French church: if the monarchy were now to reject the latter they might become the instrument of opposition to the crown itself. No wonder that he hesitated, groaned and blustered. *Procureur général* Daguesseau came boldly out into the open with a denunciation of the 'idol of Roman grandeur' and saluted Noailles as 'the man of the nation'. Daguesseau had been told by his wife to face imprisonment rather than give in to Louis, who shouted to him that it was not far from his room to the Bastille: if *Parlement* resisted, he 'would make them crawl on their bellies'. Jansenism in this last phase became part of the voice of the underground opposition which had so long been a nightmare to Louis. Was his reign to end, as it had begun, with a *fronde*? Associating itself with the idea of a national church it threatened king and Pope alike. Despite Louis' dalliance with the Pope he had remained Gallican at heart; so now he wavered before accepting, in the last month of his life, the Bull *Unigenitus* on behalf of church and kingdom. He projected a national council which should obtain the submission of Noailles and the clergy. But on August 30th Louis died. It was grimly fitting that Jansenism, which had been such an obsession with him, should be the thorniest problem of his last days.

Parlement had to register the Bull in 1720, and only one bishop refused to conform. By the time that Noailles abandoned the cause it was hardly recognisable. But the exclusion of Jansenists from the Sorbonne helped to keep the spirit alive. Its struggle against authority in church and state played some part in the formation of liberal traditions in France, strengthened the *philosophe* attack of the eighteenth century upon obscurantist dogmatism and helped to discredit 'official authority'. It was one of the forces corroding the establishment of the *ancien régime*. As a spiritual movement it degenerated into an odd sect. The extremists took over, men such as the abbé Étémare, who believed that the Jansenists were the true church. There was a growing interest in the supernatural, in miracles and relics. Jansenists started to 'look for a sign'. The cemetery of Saint Médard, where the saintly Jansenist deacon Paris was buried, became the object of pilgrimage: the sick flocked to it and there were miraculous cures. Convulsionaries battered themselves with hammers or had themselves hung over fires to prove their immunity to physical hurt. Shakers and psychopaths are a sad epilogue to the genius of Port Royal. Something of Jansenism's arid theology indeed lived on, but it died as a movement, with the *grand siècle*, to which its heroic poses and its taste for theology in the grand manner truly belong.

Quietism

The precise definitions of the Council of Trent had been intended to stabilise Catholic doctrine, and in the matters of Grace and Will they marked, particularly as they were interpreted by the Jesuits, the reaction of the church to the theological determinism of Luther and Calvin. In origin Jansenism was a swing back to an Augustinian view from the opposite extreme of the Jesuits, and the same thing may be seen in the sphere of devotion. The Reformation had been in part a mystical revolt against institutional religion, substituting a direct approach to God: 'every man his own priest'. So the church, after Trent, looked askance at enthusiasm and its spirit was formal. In turn, in the seventeenth century came the reaction, in the form of a revival of mysticism amongst the Catholics; so Quietism was born. Jansenism and Quietism are related in that they are both part of what may be termed the counter-Counter-Reformation, and that both were opposed to the ecclesiastical orthodoxy of the time—but for different reasons.

As the controversy of Nicole and Fénelon shows, the precise spirit of Jansenism, with its concrete theology, was utterly opposed to the aspiration and sentiment of the Quietists.

Quietism was no new phenomenon. Since the time of Christ, spiritual adventurers had searched for the perfection of true union with their Maker through absolute passivity. The idea was not peculiar to the Christian religion, for the Buddhist monk and the hesychast of Mount Athos, who sat gazing at his stomach, would have found much in common. But the Christian forms of mysticism went far beyond this form of self discipline. When Mme Guyon made her bold appearance she had behind her a mystical tradition with its own literature, saints—and of course heretics. Saint Theresa and Saint John of the Cross, the greatest figures of the Spanish school of mystics who explored the ways and means of mystical union with God, had been accepted and canonised by the church. Bérulle and the Oratory that he founded owed much to their teaching; St. François de Sales and Saint Cyran—*Bérulle malade*—in their quite different ways contributed to the interest of Frenchmen in the mystical inner life. There was always a minority of Christians who wished to get nearer, in contemplation, to the mind and will of God, than they could through their formal devotions. This desire inevitably produced aberrations which the church watched with jealous care. The Illuminists of Seville and Cadiz who were condemned—some 7,000 of them—by the Inquisition in 1623 provide the classic example of the mystical approach which went too far; they claimed that mental prayer alone was necessary to salvation and that they could thus be perfected. The perfect, who saw God in a special light half-way between faith and glory, had no need of virtuous acts to show it, while a few had special grace which allowed them every indulgence. The evidence of the trials would suggest that they took it. The case and the condemnation scared the orthodox from dabbling in mysticism. To Richelieu, as later to Bossuet, the Illuminists were a real menace.

In an age which Bérulle called '*passionée pour la méthode*', mental prayer, following the lead given by Saint Ignatius in the *Exercitia Spiritualia* and numerous other authorities, was most elaborately directed. The object of Saint Ignatius had been to turn the careless soul, by deliberate psychological effort, to see itself in the light of eternity. A certain sort of mystic would by-pass this strenuous mental exercise in order to find 'loving attention to God present in the soul'. He could not help it, for he was called by supernatural voice to the 'prayer of quiet' in which God required the subject to adhere to Him. He suffered 'divine things' and his faculties were in a state of suspense. One such was Molinos. Round the controversial figure of this Spanish priest—holy man, false prophet or utter charlatan, who can tell?—condemned by the Inquisition in 1687, a small society of Quietists had grown up, devotees in small conventicles. Knox compares the position of Quietism in the Italy of 1680 to that of Buchmanism in England in 1930: 'the same spirited defence against literary attack, the same habit of whispering that people in the highest places are practically converted to its principles . . . the same fear of an undefined "group" which threatens to become a church within a church'. Of this 'group' movement Molinos was the darling and prophet; when arrested he had 12,000 letters from his devotees. Mme Guyon came to play something like his part in France. She had the same exhibitionism, the same belief that the ordinary conventions, even common moral prudence, were not for her, and the same sense of mystical death and rebirth in Christ. But she gave her own special qualities to the movement in France. 'Men make heresies but women spread them and make them immortal.' Mme Guyon—her maiden name was La Mothe and she was a remote cousin of Arnauld and presumably too of Fénelon—was born with tendencies to hysteria and a taste for interior prayer. She also had imagination and brains in plenty and a will of iron. After passing through all the trials of a mystic she had arrived by 1680, in her phrase, at the 'Peace of God'. She travelled round Europe upon a private apostolate, imperturbable in triumph or persecution. She was, as for instance in her association with Père Lacombe, a Barnabite priest who ended his days in a madhouse, naïvely indiscreet. She saw herself as a saint and claimed miracles, but always as the passive instrument of God. Bossuet's 'Account of Quietism' tells us that she sat opposite her friends in complete silence, acting as a reservoir through which grace flowed into them. In her *Spiritual Torrents*, a typical work, she seems to relate herself in a literal and sensuous way to God. She claimed in all her books that she merely moved her hand to write the words which God directed. Her ecstasies were accepted for a time; she had friends at court, where interest in mysticism was in vogue. Mme de Maintenon herself protected her, introduced her to Fénelon and took her to her girls' school at Saint Cyr. Why was Fénelon impressed by her? Something in her ingenuous style appealed perhaps to the sensitive and scrupulous prelate who was living with difficulty the double life of courtier and *dévot*. Why did she lose her favour at court? Mme de Maintenon may have been jealous of their *rapport*, the spiritual affiliation which Mme Guyon felt for Fénelon; in Saint-Simon's phrase: *'leur sublime amalgame'*. Bossuet's common-sense criticism of her excesses may have influenced her. Most likely Mme Guyon was sickening everybody by her assurance.

In 1693, while Louis was making his peace with the Pope, Mme Guyon accepted the articles drawn up by Bossuet with Noailles and M. Tronson, head of Saint Sulpice, which were an orthodox formulary of interior prayer. But, after further examination, while her morals were cleared her ideas were found unsound. She passed from the prison of Vincennes to the Bastille, whence she was released in 1702 to live another fifteen years in simple and unassuming piety. Long before her death, the affair had grown bigger than its author, for the battle of ideas had become a personal duel of the two greatest churchmen of the time, opposites in mind and temperament, Bossuet and Fénelon, the 'Eagle of Meaux' and the 'Swan of Cambrai'.

Bossuet and Fénelon

Jacques-Bénigne Bossuet (1627-1704), bourgeois and son of an unimportant official, who had risen in the church by his transcendent talents, bishop of Meaux since 1681 and lately tutor to the Dauphin, was in his late sixties when he was called on to examine Mme Guyon. The role of *fidei defensor* came naturally to him for he was orthodoxy itself, a good Gallican without ceasing to be a good Catholic. His theology was broad enough to have made him sympathetic to some of the ideas in Jansenism and prepared to correspond with Leibnitz on a plan for uniting the Catholic and Lutheran churches. His interests were encyclopaedic and he took the whole field of human knowledge for his province. Studies of the Bible, the Fathers and Abstract Theology, logic, Cartesian philosophy, political ideas, the history of the world, all these were grist to his mill. As he believed in the unity of knowledge as so many branches from the one tree of Christian Truth, revealed in the Scriptures and in the Fathers, so in the unity of history. In his *Histoire des Variations* he showed that the Protestant sects were discredited by the very fact of their differences, severed branches from the one tree and so cut off from the Truth. His *Discours sur l'Histoire Universelle* was planned to show how from the moment of creation, in 4004 B.C., God's purpose had worked in the histories of the various countries, and notably of course the Jewish, until the Christian era, that of Constantine and Charlemagne and now the climax—Louis XIV, the new Charlemagne, called to rule over a new chosen people. It was a pity that Bossuet's pupil, the Dauphin, for whom this supremely edifying book was written, was too dull and indifferent to take it all in. Fénelon was more fortunate in his pupil, but perhaps, too, he taught with a lighter touch.

In a society which was almost morbidly interested in religious argument and scandal, the bishop of Meaux was the accepted prince of debate. His style had a classical grandeur which, given a deep and simple theme to work upon, was able to rise to a height of rhetoric, contrasting light and dark, disturbing, now booming, now quiet. But his mind was not cloudy; above the cumulus of his imagination, the ideas were sharp and defined. Expansive, confident and clear, testing all by reason and by accepted authority, he interpreted the mind of God to his age and pronounced, upon those who disagreed with him, stately and crushing anathemata. Anything which did not admit of definition, whose premisses he could not accept, which he did not understand, he mistrusted and condemned. This was the limitation of his genius. He could not accept the manner or the conclusions of Mme Guyon, who declared: 'Neither can I give any reason for my conduct; yet I act infallibly so long as I have no other principle than the Infallible One.' She belonged to a world of inspiration quite foreign to the busy bishop, to whom 'mysticism was essentially a lamentable extravagance, a kind of spiritual failing tempting the odder saints'. To Fénelon, however, mysticism was the heart of true religion, 'the touch of God directly experienced in the human spirit.' He accepted her ideas, was won by her personality and, if later he modified his views, stood loyally by her at the cost of disgrace and some mockery.

François de la Mothe-Fénelon (1651-1715) was a southerner and an aristocrat. He was nearly twenty-five years younger than Bossuet. He was one of the most interesting men of the century, ardent, gentle, a man of sensibility; an original and subtle mind, a little 'unsafe'. Like Bossuet he was an educationalist. He earned a reputation as a convertor and as an instructor of the 'New Catholics' in the Saintonge. His ideas about teaching were advanced, but his royal pupil Burgundy did credit to his methods. Fénelon abhorred the cramming of knowledge for its own sake and tried by rousing the interest of his charge to train his intelligence. He was always ready to answer his questions with sympathy. He encouraged the use of French in writing in place of formal Latin themes, and he taught that the knowledge of trade and industry was useful to a prince. Where Bossuet wrote a universal history to ensure that the Dauphin grasped the facts of his heritage, Fénelon wrote for his son, *Télémaque*; this romance and allegory, with its critical references to the rule of Louis XIV, was sheathed of course but there was a cutting edge for the man who cared to feel it, as in Dean Swift's *Gulliver*. When in 1699 a servant got hold of the manuscript of *Télémaque* and published it without his permission, Fénelon's criticisms were noticed, although their point was not fully made till the disasters of 1701-14. In the same year his *Explications des Maximes des Saints* was condemned by the Pope.

This disgrace was the outcome of a struggle between Fénelon and Bossuet, as inevitable perhaps as that between Cardinals Newman and Manning in nineteenth century England. The case of Mme Guyon only brought their incompatible beliefs into the open.

Fénelon could have bought himself peace by disavowing the tiresome woman, but he was not a man to detach person from principle. He saw things subjectively and he was deeply involved in, and fascinated by, the whole question of disinterested love. His moods changed quickly; his writing was, like his thought, emotional, and from splendid indignation he could drop to a gushing humility which, as in his letters to Bossuet, had a hypocritical look. His attitudes were extravagant, even for the *grand siècle*, and there was about him a touch of the natural insincerity of genius. But he had also a magnanimity which makes Bossuet look an uncharitable old man—'if he replies,' Bossuet once declared, 'I will grind him into dust'. Innocent XI is supposed to have said of them that 'the bishop of Cambrai loved God too much, he of Meaux loved man too little'. They had a different sort of reverence and a different sense of humour.

The Articles of Issy in 1695 disowned Quietist doctrine and the prayer of simple regard, and disallowed any claim that extraordinary states of prayer were the only way to perfection. Fénelon, who had just been made archbishop of Cambrai, signed the articles as had Mme Guyon, but could and did interpret them differently from Bossuet. Each wrote books to illustrate his own point of view. Fénelon's *Maximes des Saints* attempted to define the authentic tradition of Christian mysticism; untimely in the circumstances. In Fénelon, chivalry was perhaps now replaced by the indignation of the author who feels that his work is misinterpreted, while Bossuet felt that the heresies of Mme Guyon were still visible in the spirit of Fénelon's writing. He wrote to save the state, but one may feel that a weary man was simply losing his sense of proportion. Fénelon appealed to the Holy see in 1697. While Rome pondered, the literary battle of the giants went on, tome after tome, till Fénelon reached the point of writing 'A reply to Bossuet's remarks on Fénelon's reply to Bossuet's Relation'. No wonder that the Pope mildly complained about the inexhaustible fecundity of the French genius! Fénelon, with infinite subtlety, elaborated his meanings while Bossuet 'the great simplifier' searched for their sense. The latter descended to using documents, entrusted to him privately, to incriminate their authors, and Mme Guyon's eccentricities were aired before a fascinated public. Meanwhile, at Rome, the *abbé* Bossuet, the bishop's ambitious nephew, badgered the faltering pontiff Innocent XII and distributed Christmas boxes amongst the Cardinals. Louis was persuaded to write five letters to 'sustain' the Pope. 'We have for us', wrote Bossuet the elder, 'God, Truth, our good intentions, the king Mme de Maintenon', etc.—it was magnificent, even if it was not Christianity.

Rome at last censured Fénelon, but gently, and the Bossuet faction was denied the Bull for which they had asked. The *Maximes* were condemned in general as misleading, but Fénelon's explanations tacitly accepted. Bossuet was dissatisfied and thought of calling for further censure, but Fénelon rose magnificently to the occasion. Laying aside his sermon at his cathedral of Cambrai, he announced to his congregation, in radiant terms, the news of his own defeat. He expressed the conviction of the sincere Papalist with the instinct of the great actor. If in his own mind he made reservations about the meaning of the condemned maxims—so may the Pope have done. Lord Acton quotes the incident with approval as evidence of the equivocal allegiance which Rome exacts and the Roman Catholic may give. Perhaps Fénelon knew that after the mild judgment of Rome he was the moral victor.

Bossuet had indeed been tilting at windmills. One may regret that the energies of two great churchmen were so long engaged in this war of definitions. But the subject and the manner were supremely characteristic of the age of the baroque; and the result was a work of art, such as controversy rarely is. Fénelon did not return to court again but devoted himself to his war-torn diocese of Cambrai, giving his money to the poor, looking after refugees and wounded, and attracting servants and nobility to his palace. He died in the same year as his king.

Louis XIV and Madame de Maintenon

It is not easy to discover the extent of criticism of the government and the system—and the king himself—in the later stages of the reign, because it was usually hushed or hidden. Nor is it easy to assess its force, when so many people had such varied reasons for opposing the regime. The evidence comes mainly from two sources; the few people who—to private papers, like Saint-Simon, or publicly, like Fénelon—aired their real views at the time; and the events of the period immediately after the death of Louis XIV, when the resurgence of *Parlement* and the experiment of the *Polysynodie* gave shape to some of the ideas which had been simmering under the surface. What is certain is that the last years of Louis' reign witnessed something far more serious for absolute monarchy than noble cabals or the restlessness of *fin de siècle*. In a period of intellectual turmoil, the most basic and cherished assumptions of absolution were scrutinised, from the outside of course, by men like Locke and Bayle, but also from the inside.

The régime was still, to a large extent, the king; Louis, self-controlled as ever in public and private calamities, remained the imperturbable centre of unchanging routines of court and government. Matthew Prior, the English agent, saw him as 'an Eastern Monarch, with good health for a man of sixty and more vanity than a girl of sixteen'. As much an institution as a person, he grew old without a trace of senility and continued to be as rigorous, exacting and methodical as ever. His massive egotism rose to a sort of sublimity under the shocks of military disaster. His fortitude and dignity at a time when the realm seemed, as in the years after 1708, to be on the verge of ruin, was truly Roman. His calm acceptance of misfortunes in war and the awful mortality of his family, without sentiment or hysteria, was truly kingly. It was ironic that in these years he came nearer to representing France and the sentiment of ordinary Frenchmen than ever in the pomps and triumphs of the earlier years. He was stiffened by his confidence in his own powers of kingship and his rectitude in the eyes of God. He imagined that he had served God so well in the pursuit of heresy that God must in the end recognise the justice of his cause. So armoured, he was prepared to ignore criticism and defeats, as sure that he was right in the continued persecution of Huguenots and Jansenists as in the pursuit of the war from which he was unable to retract.

The influence of Mme de Maintenon (1635-1719) on Louis' old age was unassuming but important. Born Françoise d'Aubigné, she was poor but of good family; her father had died in Martinique when she was 10. Her beauty and sense had attracted notice in Parisian society after her lucky marriage to the poet Scarron, comic poet and cripple. A chance connection led, after his death, to her leaving provincial poverty to act as governess to the bastards of Mme de Montespan. Her discretion was rewarded by the estate of Maintenon, while the stormy relationship of Montespan and her lover brought her into contact with the king himself. Louis, quite disenchanted with Montespan's rash temper, was attracted to the sedate beauty of her children's governess. The death of the queen made possible the secret marriage of the king and Maintenon, probably in 1683. The king would never publicly announce it, knowing too well the sentiment of the court who, like Saint-Simon, were prepared to accept the aristocratic mistress but were shocked by the near-*bourgeois* wife—'the deepest, most flagrant, enduring, unparalleled shame for that proudest of monarchs'. She was no ordinary woman who had such extraordinary fortune. She had poise and discernment, and a taste for power which her demure manner belied. Louis came to rely upon her sympathy and judgment. 'When the king returns from hunting he comes to me. They close the doors and no one enters. I have to sympathise with his troubles, if he has any, his sorrows and his vapours. Sometimes he is overcome by tears which he cannot master or he feels uncomfortable and there is no conversation. Then one or other of the ministers arrives': it is one of the rare indications of the lonely human being behind the royal front. Council meetings, often in the evening, took place in her room. Ministers knew her influence and took pains to study her views. Rightly or wrongly it was believed at Versailles that she was responsible for the disgrace of Louvois and later of Chamillart. She provided a cushion for the king in the discomforts of old age and in return she secured an influence which, like that of the confessor, must remain uncertain; it was probably most effectual in his religious attitudes, particularly concerning the Jansenists and Quietists. Courtiers tended to blame her for the dull respectability of later court life and to sneer at her interest in education, her finishing school at Saint Cyr and her serviceable piety. Her circle of *dévots* indeed contrasted strongly with the profligacy of a section of the court. She never shed the bossy habits of the governess and to Mme de Sévigné she was simply 'sniffy' (*l'enrhumée*). Saint-Simon detested her, but his comment has two shrewd touches: 'she had an evil passion for administration. It was incredible how much time she wasted over Saint Cyr and the affairs of a hundred converts . . . she saw herself as a kind of universal mother superior.' 'Diana of Ephesus made a much less figure than she,' thought Matthew Prior; he also saw her as 'an exceedingly able woman'. The king's life of public appearances left him with little privacy. To the end of the reign, all acts of state were his personal decisions—and final. In such a situation, the strong-minded woman who was his confidante for thirty years cannot be discounted.

The Duke of Burgundy

As the king grew older, more light fell naturally upon his heirs, from whom the future king would come. Critics of the régime as well as those who wanted to be near the seat of power in the next reign clustered together in loose groups and cabals. Under the robust presence and sharp eye of the king there could be no open disintegration, but there seem to have been pressure groups which were recognised at court and which busied themselves with planning and speculation about the future; with so much favour and patronage at stake the succession was a serious matter. When reform was in the air, intrigue was a tonic to the more politically conscious nobility, long starved of any genuine part in political life but still nostalgic for imagined halcyon days when the nobility helped the king to govern the country. At worst it was agreeable to have something interesting to divert the long hours of the courtier's days. Madame described the 'vastly pretty comedy of intrigue' to her fellow German, the Duchess of Hanover: 'the entire court is in ferment of intrigue. Some try to win the favour of the all powerful lady (Maintenon), others again that of M. le Dauphin, others again that of the duc de Bourgogne. He and his father have no love for one another; the son despises the father and would like to rule.'

There were three principal groups. The Cabal of the Nobles, who sheltered under the influence of Maintenon, represented roughly the orthodox courtier's outlook, of men like Marshal

Boufflers and the marquis de Harcourt, critical of the administration and joined by most of the fashionable. In the 'Cabal of Meudon', slightly *frondeur* in character, ambitious women like the princesse de Conti (bastard daughter of the king and Louise de la Vallière) and the duchesse de Condé (bastard daughter of the king and Mme de Montespan) vied for influence over the irresolute Dauphin. Their plottings ramified widely but their object broadly was to prevent the duc d' Orléans succeeding to the throne or to influence —which became more urgent after the deaths of the Dauphin and Burgundy in 1711 and 1712—and at the same time to secure the legitimisation of the bastard sons of Louis, the ducs de Maine and Toulouse. The whole situation is a pungent comment on Louis' policy of allowing rank and recognition to the royal bastards, who could not fail to be an uneasy element.

A third clique formed round the duc de Bourgogne (Burgundy). Aged 29 when his father's death made him heir he made more mark than the Dauphin in the latter's life of dutiful subordination. The strong-willed awkward child was given, with his younger brothers Anjou and Berry, a secluded and intensive education in the charge of Beauvillier and Fénelon. The duc de Beauvillier was high-minded, retiring and devout; of his nine daughters, seven took the veil in the same convent. Fénelon was at once instructing a prince in whom he saw the instrument of great reforms and conducting an educational experiment upon tractable human nature. The future bishop of Cambrai looked undoubtedly to see the prince grow up a mirror of his own high-souled intelligence. Under such pressure it was inevitable that Burgundy, as he emerged, should be a dedicated young prince with something of the laboratory about him. He was unnaturally solemn. 'Our three princes are very badly brought up', thought Madame, 'because they have not been taught to live.' Only the challenge of ruling could have answered such a charge—and this was denied him. He might have been ineffective; some contemporaries thought that his education had made him too scrupulous and paralysed his will. He could have been a Joseph II, a dogmatic and unrealistic reformer; or he could have found a happy medium between the administrative reforms that were so badly needed and the near-romantic conservatism that coloured the reformers of the period. If he had not, like Louis, been 'taught to live', he had at least been taught to think and 'to make some conscience of what he did'. Fénelon urged on him the view, which was a straight comment upon his father's ideals, that a king lived for his people, not a people for their king. Constantly in *Télémaque* he spoke of the burden of royalty and never of its grandeur.

Burgundy was uneasy in the society of Versailles, a detached and brooding figure. He was a philosopher prince before the attitude had become fashionable, an earnest dabbler in metaphysics and physics. He was devout, an unwavering supporter of anti-Huguenot measures, when many people were doubtful about their efficacy or distressed about their consequences. His social conscience made him avow a courageous and lonely pacifism which, after his ineffective part at Oudenarde, was construed by the average courtier as cowardice. Lacking a sense of humour, like most of the Bourbons, he seems to have been regarded as an uncomfortable prig. His human feeling was lavished on his wife only, Marie-Adelaide of Savoy, the charming and coquettish leader of court society and the favourite of the old king.

It was natural that Burgundy should be the focus of many who criticised the régime, and the hope of reformers. From Cambrai, after he had been disgraced for his part in the Quietist controversy, Fénelon continued to correspond with his disciple and to advise. When he heard that Burgundy was 'too content with his obscure life', he reminded him that 'the realm of God does not consist only in a scrupulous observation of minute formalities. A great prince ought not to serve God in the same way as a solitary or a simple individual.' He was expected to patronise a policy based upon the avoidance of war—and therefore of excessive taxation—which would bring to France some of the blessings which the archbishop attributed in *Télémaque* to his mythical republic of Salente, where all were engaged in agriculture and lived in peace and abundance, and where the legislator's purpose was to secure a regular increase of population, in proportion to the development of agriculture. In his *Examen de Conscience sur les devoirs de la Royauté*, which was drawn up for the Duke—the very title conveys its tone —and in his piercing *Mémoires* written in 1710 and depicting the miserable state of the country as he saw it in his own frontier diocese, he impressed on Burgundy his horror of war; this derived not only from the brutal physical facts of death and mutilation but from liberally unorthodox values. He contrasted for instance the lot of the beggar who steals a *pistole* because he is hungry, and that of conventional heroes who robbed neighbouring states of their liberty. Magistrates destroyed the hungry individual while poets lauded the feats of the army which injured thousands. He urged some limitation upon the will of the king: 'He should be all-powerful for good; but he should have his hands tied against evil'; and again: 'the king is only a man of the people and worthy of his crown only so far as he gives himself to their good.' Voicing sentiments like these, it is not surprising that Fénelon had to stay in remote Cambrai.

When Fénelon turned from the reforms to the reformers, the men who in the new dispensation should be responsible for these changes of policy—to whom in some measure the crown should be responsible—he revealed himself the aristocrat. For he diagnosed the ills of the realm as the consequence of the error of the crown, in abandoning its rightful advisers and excluding them from a share in government. He pronounced that the ideal state was an aristocracy, in which birth, the distinction which all could respect, should be the first qualification for political power. Though this was not borne out by recent history, he maintained that an aristocracy was more stable and resilient than absolutism, whose growth was artificial. Fénelon was therefore the philosopher of the revolt of the aristocracy which was to lead to the experiment of the regency. He rationalised the prejudices which can be seen in every page of Saint-Simon and were perhaps the common factor in all the cabals of the court against the bourgeois ministers and the levelling processes of Louis' monarchy. More extreme views were being expressed; the comte de Boulainvilliers, for one, constructed historical arguments to show that an ancient Frankish aristocracy had been ruined by the rise of royal despotism. Had Burgundy, with all his high promise, come to the throne of France, he might have found that the force of aristocratic reaction was incompatible with the programme of reform in which he was interested—which must have begun with taxation of the privileged, on the pattern of the *dixième* of 1710.

We cannot know whether he could have reconciled the reformers with the reactionaries, which was to be the great problem of the *ancien régime*, for in February 1712, a few days after his wife, he died of what may have been measles or scarlet fever—aided by the unspeakable court doctors. His death, followed quickly by that of his elder son the child duc de Bretagne, left only his younger son, aged two and his younger brother, the duc de Berry, as direct heirs to the throne. The future Louis XV was saved only by the refusal of his governess, the duchesse de

Ventadour, to let the doctors treat him. Anjou was debarred of course by the terms on which he accepted the crown of Spain and Berry died in 1714.

There is as much emotion as artistry in Saint-Simon's account of these mortal shocks, for he prided himself on being in Burgundy's confidence: 'Great God, what an example thou hast given us in him. I speak not only of death and suffering but of his gentle, tolerant outlook, his supreme unselfishness. In his death France suffered her final chastisement, for God showed her the prince she did not deserve.' Michelet, an historian who looked favourably on the Bourbons, writes of Saint-Simon's account: 'A hundred and fifty years after the event, we still weep as we read the harrowing pages. . . . History is disarmed before his memory.' 'In all his life,' said Madame, 'he never harmed a single person.'

The Duke of Orleans

The death of Burgundy put a new emphasis upon the personality and aims of the duc d' Orléans (1674-1723). The son of Monsieur, the King's inadequate brother, duc de Chartres till he inherited his father's title in 1701, this prince aroused justifiable hostility by his cynical behaviour. Nature was not unkind to him; he had a rapid brain and an easy manner, but he prided himself upon his sceptical attitudes, and his immoralities shocked the court. He was hopelessly unconcentrated and gave the impression of a dilettante: 'Never was man so gifted, yet no man's life was ever so flat, vain, empty', said Saint-Simon, who looked to him hopefully after 1712. He would turn restlessly from chemistry, to music, to painting, to some mistress in Paris. His mother recited, in a letter to her sister, his talents for music, languages, painting, science, and yet concluded: 'all that does not keep him from being bored by everything'. Perhaps his greatest crime in the eyes of the court was that he obviously preferred indecorous parties in Paris to the more formal occasions of the court. Like his father, he could not resist a chance to show off. He was seen once at the Midnight Mass on Christmas eve at Versailles, deeply immersed in what seemed to be a prayer-book—and afterwards announced that he had been reading Rabelais. He encouraged his family and friends to deride conventional morality, and the indelicate behaviour of his widowed daughter, the duchesse de Berry, shocked society. What is the importance of this almost futile person? His indifference and his obscenities were the reaction of a man of parts to a system which denied him, like his father before him, any practical outlets beyond a round of social duties. In 1707, he had displayed initiative and bravery in military operations in Spain on behalf of Philip V; but he had been promptly recalled, after being accused of plotting to supplant his cousin on the Spanish throne. Like Burgundy, only in his own perverse and mocking way, he rebelled against the stifling ordinariness of the court and the jealous monopoly of the king. Louis had despised the father—he detested the son. Some courtiers—encouraged perhaps by the faction of the duc de Maine—actually suspected him, at the time of the sudden deaths, of poisoning his way to the throne.

He could not have been accused of the death of Berry, who fell from his horse. But this death did mean, if power over the young future king were not to come into the hands of the bastards Maine and Toulouse, that Orléans must bestir himself. Round him therefore ranged disgruntled courtiers, conservatives who cast hereditary right in the face of the illegitimates and lawyers of *Parlement* who hoped to use the opportunities of a new reign to claim privileges that they had lost or never possessed. Their claim, as it was expounded during the eighteenth century, to be the guardians of an assumed body of public law and their right of registration of edicts as a safeguard against the *fiat* of the king was as controversial as it was to prove ineffective. In 1714 they registered without murmur a royal edict declaring Maine and Toulouse fit to inherit the throne, in default of legitimate princes. This extraordinarily bold step, which shocked the court, was an extreme statement of the notion that royalty was a caste apart, following logically from Louis' idea of the relation between king and subject, royal blood and mere noble; nothing that Louis did aroused more dislike amongst the aristocracy. Birth and precedence were of transcendent importance, holy, immemorial. Saint-Simon wrote of the clique of the bastards 'making a mockery of the crown and trampling on this nation'. The king, as 'head of a unique line', should have been doubly anxious to preserve its sanctity 'since he was king solely by right of inheritance' but was caused 'to dishonour and overthrow its most ancient laws in order to make possible the crowning of the offspring of a double adultery'.

The legitimisation of royal bastards was a considered act of policy, part of a compromise by which he hoped to ensure a tranquil succession. Peevish nobles could afford to see the succession question in terms of caste and legitimacy, but Louis was responsible for the stability of the realm. Within a century there had been two minorities and two regencies, each a time of constitutional disorders. His own memory of the Fronde must have been lively when he thought of the prospects of the little duc d' Anjou—who was, as it happened, destined like him to come to the throne at five years of age. What if he died? He had to take into account the character of Orléans and the discredit that his notorious habits might bring upon the throne. Although there were still seven possible heirs, the unnatural mortality had disquieting effects; and the king grew lonely as one by one his confidants disappeared, Boufflers, Chevreuse, Beauvillier. Maine and Toulouse showed him affection and it was natural that he should turn to them in the hope of balancing Orléans, even if it were not sound politics. So he was persuaded, after the legitimisation, to draw up a will (August 1714) which provided for a Regency council of 24, in which all should be decided by a majority. Orléans who, by established custom, might expect to be sole regent, was only to be President of the Council and would not therefore enjoy unfettered liberty of action. Not only would Maine and Toulouse be on this council but the former would have control of the young king's household—a key position. Villeroi was to be the governor under his authority and all the household was to take an oath of allegiance to him. Conforming to usage this will was entrusted to the *Premier Président*. The king had no illusions about the way in which this last testament might be executed for he recalled how *Parlement* had treated his father's will. The authority of the *grand monarque* would die with him: 'I know how futile it is. We do what we choose while we are alive, but after we are dead, we have less power than ordinary individuals,' he is supposed to have said.

The death of the king

Louis kept up a stiff front to the end. There was no relaxing of ceremonial, or giving in to old age or failing digestion. He made a great occasion of the visit of a supposed 'Persian ambassador', perhaps bogus, which became in effect the last great dress parade of his court, a wearisome orgy of protocol. Coypel's painting of the scene hangs today at Versailles. By the right of the haggard king stood the duchesse de Ventadour with the little Dauphin, the Princes of the Blood and the royal dukes grouped around him; a sad tableau of departed glory. He worked steadily upon the absorbing question of Jansenism, perhaps the keenest interest of his last years, and the making of a new foreign policy from the wreckage of the old. His ministers worked after 1714 for a *rapprochement* with Austria and a pacification between Vienna and Madrid. But there the French cause did not prosper, for after the marriage of Philip V to Elizabeth Farnese, soon to show Europe her termagant spirit, the princesse des Ursins was pushed out of court—a poor reward for all her services to Philip V and to France. The king could find some solace in the outcome of the war and some pride in his own part in rallying the nation. There is an echo of the old *hauteur* in his rejoinder to the English ambassador who complained that the French were not properly fulfilling their guarantee to destroy the works at Dunkirk: 'Mr. Ambassador, I have always been the master in my house, sometimes of others, too. Do not cause me to remember it!' He was still able, too, to think of war. One of his last letters dealt with a plan to assist the Jacobites to recover the English throne. His death was timely for the English, since the '15' revolt failed largely because the French withdrew their aid.

On Friday, August 9th, 1715, Père le Tellier instructed the king about the registration of the Bull *Unigenitus*. That afternoon he went stag-hunting for the last time. On the 11th he walked to the Trianon—he never went out again. On the 13th he received the supposed 'Persian ambassador' who had already had a ceremonious court reception. Even after this he was able to hold the *conseil de finance*. The next day he was able to attend Mass and hold the *conseil d'état*. But he was a dying man. After a life of large eating, tempered by regular emetics and bleeding, his digestion failed him; then a gangrene set in, in the leg. Despite pain he continued to hold the council from his bed and there was no deviation from routine. The drums and fifes stationed outside his window still saluted him when he woke. He received Extreme Unction on the 25th, the feast of Saint Louis. Saint-Simon says that he then completed the codicil to his will, giving Maine the entire control of the child-king's household. The same witness recorded Louis as saying to the courtiers round the bed: 'I ask your pardon for the bad example I have set you. It grieves me that I have not done all I could have wished for you; the fault lies in the hardness of the times. I shall ask you to show the same attachment to my great-grandson; that child may right my wrongs.' Then to the Dauphin: 'My child, you are about to become a great king. Do not imitate my love of buildings nor my liking for war. Always follow good councillors; try to comfort my people, which it grieves me I was unable to do'. Louis did not trifle or deceive himself upon his death bed. Madame witnessed to his 'courage beyond description. He gave his orders as if he were only going on a journey.' On the 29th he startled listeners in the chamber by referring on the Dauphin as the young king. On September 1, 1715, at about 8 a.m., three days before Louis' 77th birthday, an officer of the king's household came out on to the balcony to cry '*le roi est mort*', then re-appeared: '*vive le roi Louis XV*'. Monarchy continued without formal break. But the age of Louis XIV died with the great king, who boy and man had reigned for 72 years. He had lived on into a generation of courtiers who were too concerned with their future to regret his departure.

Outside the court pent-up hatreds came to the surface. On the road to Saint-Denis, wrote Voltaire, the funeral *cortège* passed little tents, outside which men were drinking, singing and mocking. Bitter little songs were bandied about the streets.[1] Paris had no reason to love Louis. But Paris was not France. The great king had burnt up some of the material resources of the monarchy. Opportunities for administrative and social reform had been squandered. Royal authority was being questioned by the sophisticated. But in the eighteenth century most nobles and *bourgeois* came to look back on the years of Louis XIV as a time of heroism and grandeur. His kingship was respected by contrast with that of Louis XV. The simple mass of Frenchemn still venerated the monarchy. Louis XV himself was to be the *bien-aimé* before his career disillusioned them. Louis had not used up the deep fund of devotion of the ordinary people who lived still sufficiently in the past to imagine God and king as supreme in the natural order of things—and not to be shaken.

---

[1] This one for example:

> '*Ci-gît le roi des maltotiers,*
> *Le partisan des usuriers*
> *L'Esclave d'une indigne femme*
> *L'Ennemi juré de la paix*
> *Ne priez point Dieu pour son âme*
> *Un tel monstre n'en eût jamais*'.

The seventeenth century witnessed the final destruction of the systems of thought of Aristotle and Ptolemy and their replacement by new values and by a new approach to the problems of the universe. There was nothing new about destructive criticism nor about fruitful experiment and inquiry. But there had been lacking any coherence, direction or purpose. Leonardo da Vinci, for instance, had experimented brilliantly in many things, but contributed little to the sum of ideas because he lacked experimental method. The astronomer Tycho Brahe made some vital observations in his detailed study of the heavens, but lacked the mathematical skill to make use of them. Even Francis Bacon, who in his own words 'rang the bell which called the wits together', whose influence in French thought at this time is attested by the numerous translations of his work and who urged the importance of broad, exact and organised experiments, did not influence his age as he might have done because he failed, where Newton later succeeded, to ground empirical research upon mathematical procedure.

The century of mathematics

The intellectual developments of the seventeenth century were coloured throughout by the achievements of the mathematicians; indeed, the 'century of genius' might more specifically be called the 'century of mathematics'. At the start of the century logarithms were being brought into use, a calculating device which can be used without understanding the principles on which it depends. The slide-rule was invented, and notation, with most of the signs familiar to us, was being simplified and extended. The Frenchman, François Viète (1549-1603), had already established the use of letters to represent numbers. The way was clear for the great break-through, in the matter of handling mathematically the motions of bodies in curves, and—the great achievement—the calculus. At the start of the century, Galileo was urging a mathematical approach to the problems of the universe for, he said, its book was written in mathematical language and its alphabet consisted of triangles, circles and geometrical figures.

If men of his age wanted to discover at what angle a gun should be in order to fire its furthest, they worked it out by mathematics; experiment came afterwards, to test the theoretical answer. They believed, too, that science should confine itself to those things which could be calculated and measured: shape, size, quantity and motion. For this mathematics provided the tools— 'the general science', in Descartes' words, 'which should explain all that can be known about quantity and measure, considered independently of any application to a particular subject'. Kepler's creation of an orderly system from the observations of Tycho Brahe, his discovery of the laws of planetary motion, were made possible only by his study of conic sections. At the end of the century, Newton and Leibnitz were demonstrating that the direction and acceleration of movements on a curve could be described by arithmetic. At the centre of the advances of the age lay the work of Descartes. If the century seems to be ruled by *l'esprit de géométrie*, it is not only because of his contributions to mathematics and science, though these especially, in the field of the relation of algebra to geometry, were vital. In fact, Newton's *Philosophiae Naturalis Principia Mathematica* established a new view of the universe which departed in important ways from Descartes' principles, rejecting for instance the Cartesian view of the ether, vortices and light. But he remained faithful to Descartes' fundamental view of the mechanism of the universe and its causation. Newton, like most other important thinkers of the age, was dominated by the Cartesian concept of the world as a machine, describable in terms of mathematics. 'Sometimes one great man,' wrote Fontenelle of Descartes, 'gives the tone to a whole century.'

René Descartes was born in 1596. At the age of 8 he was sent by his father, a *conseilleur* of the *parlement* of Brittany, to a Jesuit college, where he found himself 'so embarrassed with so many doubts and errors that it seemed that the effort to instruct myself had no other effect than the increasing discovery of my ignorance.' After some unsettled years during which he 'studied the great book of the world' and saw service as a volunteer in the Thirty Years War, he settled in Holland in 1629 and stayed there for twenty years. To this period belongs his *Discours de la Méthode*, published in 1637, and the *Méditations*, published in 1641. He had already conducted a long correspondence with Elizabeth of the Palatinate, instructing her in ethics and mathematics. Then, at the invitation of Queen Christina, he went in 1649 to Stockholm, where he died in the following year.

He was first a mathematician, who contributed to geometry

the idea of the property of the curve and its use, in relation to fixed lines at right angles, and in equations which fixed that relationship. From this idea, coupled with the previous application of algebra to geometry, came both co-ordinate geometry—the use of the graph which was soon the stock-in-trade of the statistician —and the completion of earlier discoveries, through the work of Leibnitz and Newton, by the system of the calculus.

Mathematics was impressive to Descartes, as it was to Pascal, not only for its own sake but for the keys that its orderly and related truths, its exactitude and its straight suppositions, seemed to provide to the mysteries of the mind, of nature and of the universe. Philosophy, in his view, must proceed from what is clear and definable to the explanation of what is complex and uncertain. He rejected Bacon's notion that new knowledge could be got by amassing facts and proceeding thence to general laws. He believed that learning might impede reason by implanting conscious prejudice, and he himself read little. He chose to write his *Discours de la Méthode* in French because 'I hope that those who use only their natural reason will better judge my opinion than those who believe only in old books'. The study of history and languages were of no assistance in the search for truth: 'to know Latin is to know no more than Cicero's daughter when she emerged from the nursery'. This was a clean break with the past and with Bacon's development of the ontological pattern of the mediaeval school-men—'systematically arrange all that is known and then argue from it'. The first part of Descartes' novelty consists in his starting, not from what was known, but from the fact of knowing. He accepted that it was legitimate to doubt everything, but he postulated an 'intuition' which was the 'undoubting conception of an unclouded and attentive mind and springs from the light of reason alone'. Deduction was a train of such intuitions along which thought moves, guided by the natural light of the mind. Starting thus from the doubt, not of despair but of caution, Descartes searched for truth along a route lit by flares of intuition. Where was he to start, if all ideas were suspect? In the mind there was one thing that could not be doubted: its own existence, as something which was aware, which willed and thought. This is the famous first principle, *cogito ergo sum*, the basic intuition, dependent on nothing else. From it there follows: first, the quality of mind, simply a thinking thing; second, the universal criterion of certainty, that whatever is clearly and distinctly conceived is true. But how to establish the existence of things outside the mind? By the necessary existence of God, the first cause which no seventeenth century thinker, even Hobbes, could dispense with. 'God alone can be the author of my idea, which I, as finite, cannot have manufactured, of an infinite and perfect being, pure spirit and pure thought, omnipotent.' This notion gave Descartes a passport out of the circle of his own consciousness. Two realities were now established: ourselves and God. But, he asserted, consciousness of the outside world cannot be due either to God or to our own minds, so that something else must exist. His immortal and veracious God would not deceive his own creatures. Here was proof that the external world existed *really* and was not merely an illusion of his mind. Its qualities were geometrical and its essence was to exist in space, to have length, breadth, and depth. In this external world of substance there are bodies, animal and human, in which mind and matter interact; how?

The vigour with which Descartes accepted the challenge presented by this contrast of mind and matter 'in the stimulus that it gave to further thought' is more important than the terms of his solution. He defined matter and mind as two substances, each with one essential attribute, extension in the case of matter, thought in that of the mind. Both substances were quite distinct, could exist without the other and 'need only the concurrence of God in order to exist'. Movement he defined as the 'transference of one part of matter or one body from the vicinity of these bodies that are in immediate contact with it and which we regard as in repose, into the vicinity of others'. From these geometric elements, extension, divisibility and mobility, Descartes framed a wholly mechanical theory of nature. God is the *primum mobile* and since He is unchangeable, the quantity of movement in the universe is also unchangeable. Gravitation and the planetary system he explained by circular movements of vortices. Any idea of final causes was rejected on the ground that human beings cannot know the purpose of an infinite being.

Unwilling to accept any connection between the exclusive substances of mind and matter, but forced to admit that in man mind and matter were in some way indissoluble, he evolved a theory of the pineal gland where, in the centre of the brain, the mind and 'vital spirits' met and communicated. (Animals, he thought were mere automata and not sentient at all: 'doubtless when the swallows come in the Spring they act like clocks'.) In these wild guesses he was stretching contemporary knowledge of physiology beyond recognition, but he was looking in a direction which others were to follow. And the great geometer did more: he gave to all philosophy a new method and direction. Its character was from now rationalist, with here and there off-shoots of a mystical nature; of all the systems, Cartesianism had most hold upon educated minds. Christopher Huygens, the Dutch savant who knew Descartes, said, 'What has above all commended his philosophy is not that he has debunked the old ideas but that he has dared to substitute for them causes from which one can comprehend all that there is in nature.'

Descartes had put a formidable query against accepted views of the universe and of God. He constructed his system, however, at a time when religious men seem to have been hankering after a universe that was rational and consistent in order to justify the existence of a rational and self-consistent Deity. In expounding his theory of the machinery of the universe he had been careful to stress the role of the Divine Mechanic; but it was easy for later generations to forget him. It is not surprising therefore that the Jesuits banned the teaching of their most brilliant pupil, nor that, in 1667, Louis XIV forbade a funeral oration in honour of his memory, after representation by the Company of the Holy Sacrament, fresh from their success in stifling Molière's *Tartuffe*. The academic world was split. A party in the Sorbonne tried to hold the faculty of Theology to the exclusive study of the unfashionable Aristotle, but they received no support from *Parlement*. In 1675, the university of Angers held a course on Descartes and aroused the king's censure. After the Oratorians, in 1678, had adopted a formulary based upon the physics of Aristotle, the government, influenced by Harlay, supported them with a general ban on Cartesianism. But the defence of the traditionalists was unsuccessful, for it was being undermined from the inside.

Groups of disciples formed in Paris round the Minim friar and mathematician, **Mersenne** (1588-1648), whose role as correspondent and general clearing-house for the master's ideas is important. Mersenne, whose conferences brought together the mathematicians and physicists—Gassendi, Roberval, Pascal and Descartes—may have been more than any other Frenchman responsible for the primacy of Paris in the intellectual world in the middle of this century. From these informal meetings came later the scientific societies—the Royal Society in England, the *Académie des Sciences* in France—whose discussions, researches and publications cross-fertilised the scientific world, contributed to its international character and assisted the communication of ideas and discoveries.

The work of **Malebranche** (1638-1715), a priest of the Oratory, made Cartesianism respectable in some clerical circles and introduced it to a wider intellectual public. In the process of reconciling the faith to Cartesian principles, he subtly changed their spirit. From his austere cell came the *Recherche de la Vérité*, 'the last essay in Christian philosophy', but he ended by seeing everything contained in God, mystically, almost pantheistically conceived. By making God subservient to the all-powerful Reason, he deprived Him both of His prerogatives and of the *raison d'être* with which Descartes had provided Him. So the gentle Oratorian earned Fénelon's criticism: 'You did not see that what you were really doing was to subordinate religion to philosophy.' Malebranche began his work as a refutation of Spinoza, the Dutch Jew, whose Ethical system gave Descartes a new twist. Spinoza's reputation as an atheist was a grotesque libel; for he regarded God alone as real, all finite things being *sub specie aeternitatis*. In absorbing God into his entirely coherent system of the universe he did not eliminate Him. His offence in the eyes of the orthodox was that he so built God into his natural order that the whole apparatus of the Revealed God, miracles especially, was dismissed as irrelevant superstition. Spinoza was widely misinterpreted both by admirers and by detractors; it is the fate of philosophers that they are most influential when they are half-understood. It was Descartes' especial fate to become fashionable in the *salons*. Like Jansenism and Quietism later, Cartesianism was table talk; Molière makes the women in *Les Précieuses Ridicules* talk of the Cartesian '*tourbillon*'. With its stress upon ideas and its rejection of the drudgery of learning, it could not fail to appeal to those who were as incapable of sustained reading as they were confident of mastering the new dialectic, so deceptively simple. So the duc de Luynes held a Cartesian academy in his château; under the shelter of Condé, the *abbé* Bourdelot directed a study group. Mme de Sablé's brilliant group, which included Mme de Sévigné, La Rochefoucauld and some Port Royalists, chattered about Descartes in Paris, and the libertine exile Saint-Évremond interpreted him to polite society in England. His more serious followers were not uncritical; for instance, many Jansenists were unhappy about the clash that they saw between his view of extension and transubstantiation. Nor were his main tenets unopposed by his contemporary and fellow-countryman, Gassendi (1592-1655), for instance, who preferred a pragmatic outlook founded upon probabilities and whose teaching profoundly affected both Locke and Leibnitz, so that he may claim to be the founder of the 'Empirical' school of philosophy. But the method for a time swept all before it—the *Éloges* of Fontenelle (delivered by him as Secretary of the *Académie des Sciences*) speak of case after case of men converted, almost in a religious sense, to geometry: Louis Carré, for instance, training to be a priest but enticed away from a prospect which he thought disgusting by his discovery of the philosophy of Descartes. The adulation of the master of *l'esprit de géométrie* had its unfortunate side, for the idea that inspired the disciples that a few fundamental principles would provide the basis for a rational explanation of all natural phenomena was not conducive to the toils of original research. Education was captured by it and the Jesuits, who had all the best schools in provincial France, based their method—it is still the same—on the precept that man must first understand how to order his thoughts. The Port-Royal *Logique*, edited by the Jansenists Arnauld and Nicole, enshrined the principles of the method. It enlivened the universities, though slowly. (Here one is struck by the fact that all the great thinkers of the century worked and found their audiences outside the academic institutions, a sign of the decline of the universities in this period.) It almost captured the church or, as Bossuet thought perhaps with justification, threatened to destroy the church. The Protestant Jurieu remarked spitefully, in 1684, that 'the disciples of Aristotle must be feeling themselves in a disagreeable quandary when they perceive that the Eternal Word has turned Cartesian'.

Blaise Pascal[1] (1623-62) was, like Descartes, a great mathematician. He also shared his belief in reason as the only true guide to the conduct of life. But where Descartes was content to accept doubt as the initial situation of the philosopher, Pascal knew it as the constant torture and stimulus of his life. Pascal the philosopher cannot be separated from Pascal the Jansenist. From Descartes he learned how few assumptions are capable of proof; from his fellow-Jansenists he learned how few Christians were capable of salvation. Port Royal taught him too that Christianity, demanding certain states of mind, conflicted with the human physiology;

---

[1] For details of Pascal's life, his relations with Port-Royal and his *Lettres Provinciales*, see pages 97-102.

while demanding adherence to certain dogmas, it conflicted with human reason. The *Pensées* were concerned with the conflicts of this intestinal war between reason and the passions. Rather than surrender to authority, or stifle his doubts, Pascal applied deductive processes to the data of his personal experiences. He ranged against his own beliefs all the arguments of the sceptical scientist. The anguish of the struggle between the believing heart and the unbelieving head is that which the twentieth century has called existential; the struggle was necessary for him to remain true to his faith that 'the whole dignity of man lies in his thought', while accepting that 'the heart has its reasons of which the reason knows nothing'.

Many of the eight hundred and forty 'thoughts' are rough jottings; they belong to the last period of his life, after the second 'conversion' of 1654, and are therefore the work of a committed but still uncertain Christian. They are in the form of a debate in which the believer's case is built up from a mass of converging opinions, all pointing towards the same truth. They were too fondly drawn, too various and numerous to amount to a system. He never therefore attained the certainty, and with it the influence, of Descartes. He was essentially a solitary, and a reading of the *Pensées* is as much a reading of a man's soul as the receiving of a philosophy. They were intended to be an answer to the libertinism of Montaigne and his followers, who put faith beyond the bounds of reason, and who offended by their unconcern about the soul. They represent one reaction to the discoveries of Copernicus, Kepler and Galileo, who had destroyed the traditional picture of a universe centred upon man and his world, and replaced it by one in which the earth revolved humbly amongst planets round the sun. He admitted to moments of despair: 'man is equally incapable of seeing the nothingness from which he came and the infinite in which he is engulfed'. He was overawed by the new cosmology: 'the eternal silence of those infinite spaces strikes me with terror'. Was there room in them for the individual soul? The question was for him not one to be evaded. Revelation, in the two-hour ecstasy of his vision, had assured him that God cared for his soul. In the *Pensées*, therefore, he strove to prove to the satisfaction of the mathematician what the Christian knew by intuition to be true. The attempt was impossible. His standpoint is revealed in his own words: 'you would not look for me if you had not found me'. His methods were those of *l'esprit de géométrie*; but his arguments were those of *l'esprit de finesse*, religious arguments stemming from religious conviction about the greatness of God and the misery of man. His achievement may seem to be negative, for he succeeded in proving only two things: that the world is not limited to those things for which we have the evidence of our senses, and that Christianity cannot be proved in the same manner as a mathematical proposition. But the *Pensées* are more important for what they suggest about the human condition than for what they prove about the nature of God.

The victory of rule

Latin was already losing its vigour as the intellectual language of Europe when Descartes, by writing his *Discours de la Méthode* in French, broke away from the tradition of scholarly literature, and Pascal showed in his *Lettres Provinciales* the possibilities of a living language as a vehicle for exposition and controversy. They were not without their precursors, notably Calvin, who translated his own Latin text into the lively French of the *Institution*. Indeed, two years before this, in 1539, the Edict of Villars Cotteret had enacted the use of the vernacular for judicial debates and state papers. When Gassendi, the opponent of Descartes, wrote in Latin, he was clinging to a tradition which had no hope of survival. The future, as in England, lay with the vernacular. During the course of the century which was hailed by contemporaries as the supreme flowering of French genius, French became the accepted language of diplomacy and polite society throughout Europe. In no sphere was the ascendancy of France more prominent or more lasting. This was of course a reflection of her political strength and consequent prestige. To what extent was it also due to the qualities of the language and the talents of its writers?

It is usual to entitle the literature of the seventeenth century 'classical', and the term is justified by the tendency of the greatest writers to look for their inspiration and for their rules to the 'classical' writers of Greece and Rome. But the victory of 'rule' was not won without a struggle. Until 1660 at least, in the 'pre-classical' period, there was plenty of creative and spontaneous writing which did not conform to the rigorous laws later established by the critics. No great figure stands out, if we except Montaigne, whose urbane and easy writing conforms to no rules but those of good sense and who belongs in time to the end of the sixteenth century. The poets Régnier (1578-1613), Théophile de Viau (1590-1626), Saint-Armant (1594-1661) and Tristan l'Hermite (1601-53) were enjoyed in their time but were not to be read again for their rich and imaginative phrasing until the romantic revival of the nineteenth century. Scarron (1610-60), first husband of Mme de Maintenon, and most famous for his scurrilous sallies against the Cardinal—the *Mazarinades*—gibed in his parodies and epigrams at the stiffening conventions of classicism; but his was a moderate talent. Cyrano de Bergerac (1619-55) was an incoherent minor genius, who achieved little more by his fantasies than to give ideas to Swift and Fontenelle. The exuberant facility of Alexandre Hardy (1570?-1631) was his downfall. This rapid but negligent artist, who claimed to have written over 600 plays, was famous in his day. But he was a living exemplar of the faults, the want of discrimination and incoherence which critics such as Malherbe and Boileau wished to correct.

It is more than a mere coincidence that the classical period proper begins with the assumption of personal power by Louis XIV in 1661, for there is a common tendency towards stability and order in the arts as in politics at this time. The literary struggle between the romantic and the classical schools of thought in the early part of the century may be said to reflect the see-saw of disorder and authority within the state. The desire for strong authority, which Louis fulfilled in his personal rule, has its counterpart in the ready conformity of the arts to hierarchy and order. But the general concurrence in the dictates of the self-appointed critics of taste and form argues that one must look beyond politics for the causes of this victory of 'rule'.

The new stability of thought is important. **Pierre de Bérulle** (1579-1629) founder of the Oratory and author of the *Discours de l'estat et des grandeurs de Jésus*, and **François de Sales** (1567-1622), bishop of Geneva, the most famous spiritual director of his day and subsequently canonised, two leaders of the devotional movement, are the two most important names in this respect. The latter, through his manuals, *Introduction à la vie dévote* and *Traité de l'amour de Dieu*, touched the hearts and minds of thousands of his fellow-countrymen. He wrote, as did Pascal, of the true piety which consisted in the abandonment of the creature to the love of God, but no intellectual difficulties furrowed the course of his charity and good sense. By his own tenderness and humility and the simplicity of his language, he taught an ideal of unaffected holiness, and with it the humble and unquestioning acceptance of authority, in the shape of the will of God. The spirit of Port Royal was more austere; there was nothing gentle or delicate about the writing of Antoine Arnauld (1612-94) or Pierre Nicole (1625-95). But the polemics of these writers, engaged in the defence of their ascetic ideals, were fired by the same inspiration as that of Bérulle and Saint François. They put more stress upon the grandeur than upon the charity of God, but their theme was still obedience to His will. How important Port Royal was in the history of French literature can be seen from the expression of their values in the work of Pascal, their greatest associate, and Racine, an early pupil of their *petites écoles*.

A different but equally significant trend of the time was the evolution of an intellectual concept of the gentleman. This is the *honnête homme*, who represents the adaptation for social purposes of the fashionable rationalism which was the aftermath of Descartes. The phrase was popularised by the work of Nicholas Faret, who used it as the title of his treatise on correct deportment or *bienséance*. His subtitle was *l'Art de plaire à la Cour*; but the notion went further than a mere code of manners and polite conversation since it was designed to make possible an interest in ideas and in literature within the framework of the *salon*. The *honnête homme* '*ne se pique de rien*' and the open-mindedness that he was supposed to cultivate matches the rationalism that now displaced pedantry, and the 'mean' which was one of the aims of classicism. The ideal is that of the *salon*, which is the distinctive expression of upper-class French culture. The *salon* is inseparable from the name of the marquise de Rambouillet (1588-1665), whose house near the Louvre was the focus for many years of the social and intellectual life of Paris. Lesser *salons* might be the scene of idle scandal and intrigue, or the pretentious nonsense guyed by Molière in *Les Précieuses Ridicules*. But in her boudoir of blue velvet and silver, this remarkable hostess had an ascendancy so complete that historians can write of her following as 'a movement'. Here, where Richelieu might meet Corneille, the ruler of France and the ruler of the drama, there was a free-for-all of the talents, subject only to the rules of *honnêteté*. No subject was barred in these regular meetings, to which a talent for good talk was the only passport required. Themes were set for discussion upon the most difficult questions of language, ethics or love. When Madeleine de Scudéry (1607-1701) took upon herself the mantle of Mme de

Rambouillet, her own interests as a romantic novelist gave a strong moralising tone to discussions. The character of love was discussed endlessly and with as many refinements as amongst the selfless heroes and heroines of her novels. Such conversations may have been often absurd and to the Anglo-Saxon precious (an inadequate translation of the *salon* word *préciosité* which may be defined as a delicate refinement of feelings). The *salons*, with their emphasis upon the manners and methods of conversation, certainly lent themselves to superficiality. The cultivation of wit for its own sake and the necessity of pleasing might seem to have discouraged creative thought. But they provided a milieu for free discussion, amongst very different sorts of talent, which might not otherwise have been possible in a caste-ridden society. When the two sexes met and talked in an atmosphere of complete equality, the way was open to that feminisation of French culture which was so strong an influence in the *grand siècle*, with its idealisation of love, worship of heroism and exaltation of language. At the same time, the concern of its arbiters for precision in the use of words ensured that the *salon* made a real contribution to the formation of the language.

This was the role of the *Académie Française*, founded by Richelieu in 1635. It was intended to hold a watching brief over the language, to preserve its purity by its decree and publications. This aspect of its work was to be crowned by the publication of a Dictionary, but not in the event till 1694. Its authority grew swiftly until it came to be accepted as the public guardian of taste; as such, inevitably, it encouraged orthodoxy and thus furthered the efforts of those who were already trying to dictate the taste of the age. Of these the first was Malherbe (1555-1628), poet and prose translator, who was so favoured by Henry IV and Marie de Médicis that he enjoyed the status of an unofficial laureate, writing therefore principally for the court. His doctrine was simple; echoing Horace, he taught that poetry was a craft: the poet must always preserve balance and avoid vulgarity; form is the goal and originality does not matter; the laws of grammar must never be sacrified for the sake of poetic felicity. His work, like that of his disciples Jean Bertail (1552-1611) and François Mesnard (1582-1646), can be more pleasing than his austere doctrine would suggest. A gentler critic than Malherbe was Vincent Voiture (1597-1648), an *habitué* of Mme de Rambouillet's *salon* and the acknowledged master of the art of conversation. His verses and letters show something of that irony and tact in the choice of words which made so great an impression upon contemporaries and which have led later critics to compare his skill to that of Voltaire. While Voiture and other drawing-room poets were setting new standards of delicacy and *finesse*, grammarians were inquiring into the nature and proper use of words, with the end of eliminating the obscurities of the language and fitting it both for the converse of society and for the clear expression of ideas. Besides the self-imposed task of purging the 'vulgarities' of idiom from the language, there was the problem of assimilating the new abstract and technical terms, usually Latin-derived, which must be used since the demise of Latin as the language of scholarship. (Against this we may set the natural advantage that French enjoys as a medium for expressing ideas, over English for instance, in its subjunctive forms which enable the writer to pass from the statement of opinion to the statement of fact, from the hypothetical to the categorical, simply by changing a few letters in a word, without fear of being misunderstood.) The central character in this process of bringing the language under the control of *les règles* was Jean Chapelain (1598-1674), literary adviser to Richelieu, and as such responsible for drawing up the regulations of the *Académie*. He held that an artist could only achieve beauty by conforming to the rules which he derived entirely from classical writers but which, he held, were firmly based upon reason. Upon these grounds he earned the ridicule of posterity by criticising *Le Cid* of Corneille for breaking the three dramatic unities, and defying probability, unity of place and moral decorum. His own epic, *La Pucelle* was cumbrous and tedious, though it hardly deserved the cruel strictures of Boileau, and perfectly illustrates the dangers of too academic an approach to the arts.

Claude de Vaugelas (1585-1650), in his *Rémarques sur la langue Française*, the fruits of a lifetime devoted to the discussion of the niceties of the language in the *salons*, simply equated good writing with the modes of polite society. Upon this assumption that good usage belongs to an *élite*, he disallowed any claim to influence of *Parlement* or, more surprisingly, of the universities. The consequence of such doctrine was that literature became, like painting and sculpture, almost exclusively an expression of aristocratic values. The Prince de Condé (father of the general) and Gaston d' Orléans used, we are told, to have a censor in their houses so that if any of their family spoke any word that savoured of the

Palais (*Palais de Justice*) or the Sorbonne, he should incur a fine! Corneille even went so far as to revise his earlier plays in order to eliminate archaic words. Words which were considered plebeian or crude, such as *cracher* or *vomir*, were eliminated. When the *Académie* finally pronounced its verdict, in the Dictionary of 1694, whole classes of words were banished. Those that were left were typically hierarchic; the words suited to society were distinguished both from those of the *bourgeoisie* and the *lie du peuple*. There was also a distinction between the 'higher forms' of literature which must have a noble diction, and mere comedy, satire and fable which might draw from everyday life. These restrictions of language accorded well with the values of the *salon*. They led to the death of lyricism; unmourned, since the display of personal emotions was now thought vulgar. There are few references to nature in the poetry or prose of the time, except in the most stylised way. It is an urban literature, concerned, as the *salons* were, more with man than with nature. Insight into the human predicament is the common feature of all the great writers of the day. This concern with general themes and the relative absence of local idiom and colour gave them an immediate influence. No language has proved more suitable for export abroad than the French of the seventeenth century. Its best exponents had no sooner become classics than they became textbooks.

The *salon* and the *Académie* helped to create an environment in which literature echoed the accepted attitudes of society. The system of patronage completed the dependence of the writer. The seventeenth century was an age of patronage in all fields. There were some, either noble or wealthy, who needed no patron. But the great amateurs were few; even they—as Fénelon found when he wrote *Télémaque* and as Saint-Simon knew when he kept the secrets of his diaries to himself—were limited in their choice of subjects by a censorship which forbade all criticism of authority in church or state. Most writers had to consider the wishes of a patron. Within the conventional scope of comedy or tragedy this need not be cramping, but it could not be entirely healthy, especially when the patron was a government which could not afford to be disinterested. Richelieu was a discerning patron of men of letters, who aided struggling writers with gifts and pensions. No one quite took his place, though Fouquet spent his vast fortune freely and earned the gratitude of some of his pensionaries during his brief period of splendour. Lytton Strachey's picture of the superb and brilliant Louis, gaining 'true immortality' as the patron of Racine and the protector of Molière, should be treated with caution. Louis saw literature as an adornment to his court and his kingship, but his appreciation was sincere, for he shared the taste of many of his courtiers for music and plays. It is to his credit that he shielded Molière against the more bigoted of his clergy. Colbert's initiative, too, made patronage more systematic than it usually is, by drawing up lists of poets, playwrights, scientists and scholars. It is impressive that foreigners appear on these lists. But Colbert and his master saw patronage as a form of advertising and it was run on strict business lines. Colbert envisaged something like a civil service of the arts, whose beneficiaries should pay for their keep by providing a running commentary on the glories of the reign. Even where the king's glory was not a set subject, a flattering reference made the work more acceptable. The propaganda element was indeed quite blatant, for Chapelain, Colbert's agent, made it clear in his letters to foreign grantees that pensions would only be granted so long as they continued to eulogise the king. Even domestic pensions were on a cautious year-to-year basis, paid out, with the builders' and decorators' bills, by the *surintendance des bâtiments*. They had a low priority; when expenses rose in the seventies because of the demands of building and war, the pensions of men of letters were the first economy. Only a favoured few continued to receive them: Racine, Boileau who worked hard for his with his almost indecent flattery, Quinault, the author of the *libretti* of Lulli's operas; Corneille, however, received nothing from 1673 until just before his death in 1684. Later in the reign, Louis conceived a pious distaste for such worldly activities as the theatre, and the trickle of patronage dried up altogether. It had never been more than a small tributary of the broad river of expenditure. He had always preferred to see the money of the state spent on sculptures and paintings, which accorded better with his passion for building, and gave more solid returns for his outlay. The court provided an incomparable setting for writers who were already established, but it was not one in which new talent was likely to emerge. In proportion as the buildings of Versailles grew more magnificent, its literary life shrank. Before the end of the reign we can see a new situation. A new public for books and plays was coming into existence amongst the literate *bourgeoisie* of the larger towns. By then could be foreseen that clean break between the regime and the writers, which was characteristic of the eighteenth century, as they became emancipated from the court influences and more critical of the old order.

Many of the tendencies of French literature at this time can be seen in the work of **Pierre Corneille** (1606-84), the real founder of the art of tragic drama in France. Malherbe's linguistic discipline, the *salon* concept of ideal love, fashionable theological problems of Grace and Will, the cult of the military hero, even fashionable opposition politics in the Fronde period—all in turn influenced his work. He began with refined comedies such as *Le Menteur*; but it was in tragedy that he excelled. In *Le Cid* he made free with the dramatic unities, although he bowed to that of time by cramming a rich story into twenty-four hours. But more important, he grasped the basic principles of Greek drama, the necessity of action, and the importance of developing the action from within the characters. The incidents are complicated, the rhetoric powerful, but the psychological study is superbly simple. In subsequent plays such as *Cinna* (thought by contemporaries to be his best), *Horace* and *Polyeucte*, he confined his plots to narrower limits, so that the conflict between passion and duty which is the theme of his greatest plays is even more stark. From these conflicts, between love and patriotic obligation for instance, or between different sorts of political expediency, there emerges an ethic of self-mastery. This is true virtue, to serve some sublime ideal higher than self; it might be honour, loyalty, chastity, even revenge. His heroes are scarcely real persons but embodiments of intellect, pride and will, so placed in relation to events and to fate that their qualities are revealed. The drama comes from argument rather than from atmosphere and it is built up logically, without the aid of images of sense. The great tirades should be heard aloud to be appreciated, for their cumulative eloquence. At his best there is a nervous strength and a clarity about his writing which saves it from being pompous. But when inspiration flagged and passion cooled, he became a theatrical bore, his heroes merely declaiming puppets. It is a pity that the economics of authorship—at most he received 200 *livres* for a play, and he wrote more than thirty—compelled him to write beyond the means of his imagination.

In the work of **Jean Racine** (1639-99) it is possible to see less of the faults and more of the virtues of the neo-classical drama, for within his chosen limits he achieved a perfection of form and style that has never been surpassed. He was orphaned early in life and educated at Jansenist schools. For a time he was the only pupil at *l'école des Granges* near Port Royal, and his education must have been intense. He learned from it a minute knowledge of the Greek drama which he made the model for his own work. His plays follow Corneille in their concern with human passion and their disregard for the intricacies of human personality. At their root is the explicit psychology of the age, that the human mind can be most accurately perceived when it receives a formulated expression. But here the likeness ends, for where Corneille's heroes are disembodied souls, Racine's live, lust and suffer. *Andromaque*, a tragedy of passionate love (written in 1667), first brought him fame. Love was his constant and overmastering theme, conceived as a sort of drunkenness of the mind that deprives it of freedom and balance. The restraint of his language is all the more effective when it conveys the cruelty and blindness of unreasoning passion. The Cartesian precision of his thought makes his analysis of wild emotion the more intense and penetrating. In 1677 came *Phèdre*, one of the world's great plays and the product of two years' labour, a study of passion which, in its *genre*, is almost flawless. But the jealousy and obstruction of private enemies, marshalled by the obnoxious duchesse de Bouillon, killed the play; Racine then, with the approval of his Jansenist mentors, retired from the stage, married a girl who never read a word of his plays, and was appointed, with Boileau, historiographer to the king. He was a man of parts and he played the courtier with detachment and success, to earn the accolade of Saint-Simon: 'nothing of the poet in his conduct, everything of the *honnête homme*'. Later, at the request of Mme de Maintenon, he wrote two further plays, *Esther* (1689) and *Athalie* (1691), for her schoolgirls of Saint Cyr. The themes are now Biblical and the writing is more concerned with the creation of character than with the analysis of passion: in *Athalie*, for instance, that of the queen, ruthless, criminal, but weakening with remorse and middle age. This last play was performed in Mme de Maintenon's private apartments and it never reached Saint Cyr. Some have detected in *Esther* an allegory in which Esther is Mme de Maintenon, Vashti, her rival, is Mme de Montespan and Aman, Louvois. Aman's words in one place would seem to refer to his relations with the king, and in 1689, the year of the devastation of the Palatinate, they could hardly have been interpreted otherwise by a court audience. 'He knows that he owes everything to me and that for his glory I have crushed under foot remorse, fear and shame; and that wielding his power with a heart of brass, I have silenced the laws and caused the innocent to groan.' After *Athalie* there was another long silence until his death: he was not popular at court and he may, like others, have been disillusioned with the king and the regime that he had once praised so unreservedly.

The English reader, brought up on the careless splendour and rich characterisation of Shakespeare, finds it hard to appreciate Racine. Indeed, nothing more different from the English or German style can be imagined. He was of course derivative; the plot of *Phèdre*, for instance, follows the *Hippolytus* of Euripides very closely. But it is from the restrictions of the dramatic unities of time and place that his depth comes; and in this depth of treatment lies the originality which makes some of his classical models look like pale and flimsy sketches by comparison. The plot of *Bérénice* is drawn from five words of Suetonius: '*Titus Berenicem dimisit invitus invitam*', and the whole tragedy takes place within her bedchamber. Yet he succeeds in conveying, out of her personal crisis, the turbulence of the outside world. The mind in his view must be concentrated upon the crisis for its full intensity and the reaction of its victims to be felt; concentration is achieved by the ruthless paring of everything superfluous in words and characterisation. No poet has written from a smaller vocabulary, yet he avoided flatness. His verse is devoid of imagery, although it constantly suggests it; understatement is given point by the rhythm of his verse, full of precise antitheses. So his calm has its own depths and contrasts of light and shade. If there is such a thing as Jansenism in art, this is it: intense feeling, purified by the most self-critical and rigorous discipline.

Racine called Molière '*le contemplateur*'; his subject was man, not like Racine's man in all time, but man in his own time. Comedy was his medium, but tears are never far from laughter, for he used comedy as later writers used the novel, to convey life and manners in the round. Racine tells us a great deal about the psychology of the thinking *élite* of the seventeenth century; but, with Molière, we leave high fashion and high thinking and visit the ordinary Frenchman. If Racine is more French of the *grand siècle*, Molière has represented to millions the foreigner's idea of France.

Molière (J. B. Poquelin, 1622-73) was born the son of a well-to-do upholsterer and educated at a Jesuit school. He was for some time an actor and an actor-manager, so he always saw theatre from the stage end and his aim was always to entertain. His approach was not in the least academic, nor was he ever primarily interested in the plot or construction of the play. In 1655 *l'Étourdi* first revealed his power of comic invention. In 1658, *Les Précieuses Ridicules* exploited the ideal subject for comedy, for only a little caricature was needed to reduce the pretensions of the *salons* to absurdity. In his disconcerting nearness to the truth lies one reason for his success with social comedies such as *Le Misanthrope* (1606), *Georges Dandin* and *l'Avare* (1668), *Le Bourgeois Gentilhomme* (1670) and *Les Femmes Savantes* (1672). The approval of the king gave him an assured position, but it could not save *Tartuffe* (1664), a play about a religious confidence man, from censorship at the instigation of the *Compagnie du Saint Sacrement*. After the success of the *Lettres Provinciales*, devout people were afraid of the demoralising barbs of ridicule when they were aimed at the broad target of casuistry. But such opposition was misconceived, for Molière's purpose was not primarily didactic; morality triumphs as his plays move to their expected conclusions, but it is the essential flaw in a character that brings accumulated disaster and final retribution. He was more interested in the weaknesses of human beings than in the misdirection of institutions, although, as in *Le Malade Imaginaire*, he could make a damaging indictment of a class that he disliked. Some doctors may have thought it only poetic justice when he died after a seizure on the stage while playing the part of the hypochondriac Argon in this last play.

The genius of Molière lies in his sympathy for the characters that he pillories. His disillusionment was that of a sensitive, honest and very scrupulous man. He did not create 'types' so much as characters, mean or snobbish or hypocritical. He was essentially the observer of man in his social relationships and the setting of most of his plays is the homely intimacy of family life. His audiences could laugh with the author, a little uncomfortably perhaps, but always in situations that they recognised, at real follies and vices which did not lose their sting for being familiar. His racy and vigorous prose was perfectly suited to his purpose of making his characters come alive, and no obscurities or artificialities came between the players and his meaning. His repartees might be brilliant, but they never interrupted the logic of ordinary dialogue. It was always the anti-social vices which he satirised and those especially which offended against common sense. He stressed the merits of moderation and naturalness at a time when these common qualities of life were in danger of being overlooked. He tilted at the pushing crowd at the entrance to a *levée*; did the courtiers who laughed at the titled boobies on the stage think of the artifices of their own life at Versailles? Did the climbers wince at the efforts of Monsieur Jourdain to climb the ladder that led to social acceptance? It is a tribute to Louis' confidence, as to his taste, that he could countenance this comic genius whose sallies went so near the bone. He himself was safe, of course, and in Molière's day he was still successful. But what might Molière's pen have made of the great king himself? Here was the subject of the greatest of all comedies, but it could not be touched.

Another writer who seems to have owed relatively little to the literary fashions of the society which lapped up his verse was **Jean de la Fontaine** (1621-95). He was a son of a forestry official and his intimate knowledge of wild life was the material of his best-known work. After a fortunate introduction to society, however, he showed no sign of wishing to return to his native haunts, and his 'wood notes wild' were subdued to the polite measure of an *honnête homme*. He was kept by a succession of aristocratic ladies and lived an agreeable Skimpole-like existence; having cast off his family, he devoted his ample time to the cultivation of the genre of fable writing, in which his friends were right to call him 'inimitable'.

Nature is both the field and the morality of this sophisticated person. His allusive little studies of herons and hares, swallows and tortoises are characterised by the minute accuracy that is typical of the writers of the century; but he was a natural poet and, for all his careful pruning and revision, they retain a certain *naïveté* and spontaneity which is their principal attraction. His technique can seldom be faulted and he was the master of a wide range of metre and a full vocabulary. He did not scorn to use archaic or peasant words when it suited him for he could afford to disregard the edicts of fashion. Attempts have been made to prove that his *Fables*, of which the first came out in 1668, had some political intent. His *Obsèques de la lionne* is almost certainly a sharp satire on monarchy and his donkeys may well be simple peasants. But he was the most unpolitical of beings, as he was the most amoral. His avowed intent was to please and, if an animal morality of self-preservation emerges from his stories from nature, it is surely rather an expression of his own outlook upon life than of any urge to convert his fellow-men. He is in many ways the Horace of seventeenth century France, in his 'art of concealing art' and in the mastery of form which enables him to handle ideas with nonchalant daring. But more than Horace he followed the promptings of his heart. It is not the nature of the Romantics that he describes, but his portraits, recollected from the life in the tranquillity of the drawing-room, have, as Mme de Sévigné said of *Le singe et le chat*, the quality of painting. His effortless lines are a pleasant oasis in this age of artifice. In their dilettante way, they look forward to the time of Watteau and the Dresden Shepherdess.

La Fontaine, who was clearly very good company, used to meet regularly with Molière, Racine and Boileau, for convivial discussion of each other's work. The penalty for a breach of the conventions was to read a verse or a page of Chapelain. We may be sure that in this company the verdict of Boileau was as much respected as the verse of poor Chapelain was derided. But the reputation of critics tends not to outlast their lifetime, and that of **Nicholas Boileau-Despréaux** (1636-1711), the author of *l'Art Poétique*, does not loom so large now as it did then. He was trained in law and theology, and he brought to literature the combative spirit of the lawyer and the reverence of the theologian. His *Satires* first brought him fame and broadcast his hatred for ugly writing and his instinctive sense of style. In them he did not hesitate to attack the greatest names: Mme de Scudéry, the fashionable romancer, Quinault, even Chapelain who was at this time, advising Colbert on the giving of pensions. Chapelain produced his dreary epic *La Pucelle* in 1665; an unfortunate piece of mistiming. Boileau had little difficulty in explaining to a public who had feasted on Pascal and were having their first taste of Racine that the grandiose epic was out of fashion. It would not be true to say that Boileau led a new fashion; rather he set the seal of his deserved critical reputation upon the classical ideal. He also gave it a new look and rescued it from the pedantry of the 'Dramatic Unities' school of thought. His approach was wholly Cartesian and the first commandment of *l'Art Poétique*, published in 1674, was: think well, if you wish to write well. Good thought he defined as proceeding from one certitude to another. Since beauty and truth are so strictly related, the strictest obligation of the writer is to be true to his subject matter. Extravagance was banned, the unusual was frowned upon. The hallmarks of good poetry were lucidity and elegance, to secure which long and devoted labour was necessary. The craftsman poet is familiar to us from the writing of Horace and only in his insistent stress upon the quality of *bon sens* was the Frenchman adding significantly to the ideal of Rome. His own elegant alexandrines, not unlike the work of Pope who was his great admirer, were a fair exemplar of his own precepts. But the strength of his code stands proven in Racine, rather than in anything he wrote himself. It stands or falls upon his dictum: '*qui ne sait se borner, ne sait jamais écrire*'. It falls if one thinks that poetry should never be entirely subservient to good sense. The Romantics were later to accuse Boileau and his followers of thwarting the spirit of poetry by fitting it into an arbitrary and rigid system of aesthetics. His critics may have overestimated his importance, when they attacked the *législateur du Parnasse*, but they aimed in the right direction. In the age that stretched ahead from Bossuet to Voltaire, his rules and his spirit held sway.

It is inevitable that from Boileau one turns to Bossuet, from one high priest to another. **Jacques-Bénigne Bossuet**[1] (1627-1704) served God in the same spirit of reasoned devotion as Boileau served the cause of literature. His contribution to history and theology is dealt with elsewhere. Here we are concerned with him as an original artist, in a medium which was near to the heart of the *grand siècle*. The historian of the universe, the Catholic controversialist, the political philosopher have receded into the shadows under the impacts of new knowledge and new criticism; this is the penalty he pays for being so completely a man 'who saw all round his age but not beyond it'. But the writer has survived. God was allowed by the taste of the age to be a great subject and sermons were expected to rise to the subject with elevated imagery and lyrical periods. Bossuet's gifts were perfectly suited to the requirements of this convention. He was a man of method, in spirit and in words; in his grandest periods he was always direct and lucid. He could evoke awe and pathos without disturbing the even tenor of his argument, or the natural rhythm of his prose. He rose to his greatest heights in the *Oraisons Funèbres*, which were set pieces, performed before the most discriminating audience in Europe, at the funeral obsequies of a great person—Condé, Le Tellier, Henriette d'Angleterre. His theme on these occasions

[1] For Bossuet's contribution to political thought and for his part in the Quietist controversy, see pages 278-80 and 446-53.

was seldom original; essentially it was the nothingness of our dust, the infinite possibilities of our spirit and the victory of the Cross. He had difficulties to contend with in a society which found it hard to accept the equality of all men before God, and he had to recognise the privilege of the great even in death. But contrast served his genius well, for he excelled in the delineation of light and shadow. His best sermons in this style still read well. When, as in the case of the much loved Henriette d'Angleterre, there was a real pathos which needed no abstract development, his audiences were greatly moved. They appreciated especially his capacity for rising to *le sublime*. Mme de Sévigné however preferred the sermons of **Père. Bourdalue** (1632-1704) to those of Bossuet, and he was the more generally admired of the two. When it was known that he was going to preach at court on Good Friday 1671, people sent their lackeys on the previous Wednesday to keep seats for them. The sombre Jesuit seems to have answered to the public taste for moral analysis. His standards were stern, and he did not shrink from denouncing the aristocratic vices of extravagance, gambling and social pride. His sermons lacked the imaginative grandeur of Bossuet and their hold came from the psychological insight of the experienced confessor, and from his remorseless logic. Bishop Fléchier (1632-1710), whose funeral oration upon Turenne is a fine specimen of this form, had a gentler manner and a more elegant style than Bourdalue. These men deserved the praise of their devotees, but the rapture of fashionable crowds calls for some further explanation. It is possible that to courtiers, amongst whom piety was so normal as to pass unremarked, who for the most part confessed and communicated regularly, but who were at the same time members of an exceedingly worldly society and had a lot of time on their hands, the sermon provided a periodic moral purge. They took their medicine with good grace when it contained such qualities of form and substance that they could forget their ills in their admiration of an artistic performance.

The depth of French culture can be studied in the artistry of three writers, none of whom was professional, in the sense that literature was the centre of their existence or that their living depended on their efforts. The fame of each rests upon a single work; that of La Rochefoucauld on his *Maximes*, Mme de la Fayette's on *La Princesse de Clèves*, Mme de Sévigné's on her *Lettres*.

François de Marcillac, **duc de la Rochefoucauld** (1613-80), like so many of the old aristocracy, had joined the opposition to Richelieu and Mazarin. In Louis XIV's reign he lived in half-retirement, but was a constant guest in the *salons* of Mme de Sablé and Mme de la Fayette. He recalled a career that had been nearly as spectacular as that of de Retz, but by comparison with the dash and warmth of that reprobate's *Mémoires*, his are cold and dull. He expressed his experience and philosophy more aptly in the *Maximes:* pointed remarks worded as briefly as possible. The shaping of miniature 'characters' and 'sentences' was a fashionable exercise in the *salons*, and La Rochefoucauld brought the mode to perfection, realising fully its possibilities for epigrammatic statement. In about five hundred diamond-polished *sentences*, he presents a view of life that could see nothing but *amour propre* at the heart of all social behaviour: 'what we take for virtues are often nothing but a collection of diverse actions and interests'. Man is ruled by his temperament, his *humeur*: here La Rochefoucauld borrows from the psychology of Descartes. His 'bitter love of truth' does not lead him to say anything beyond the commonplace about the natural depravity of man. But it was left to this melancholy grandee, who had slept with the duchesse de Longueville and been desperately wounded in the service of the duc de Condé, who afterwards had little to do except to live with style, to arrive at the perfection of the classical ideal, in the slight compass of these miniatures.

The friend of La Rochefoucauld's old age and a woman of fine sensibility, **Mme de la Fayette** (1634-93) was a leading hostess of the *salons*. After the failure of her married life, she turned to the novel. It was not wholly original, for Madeleine de Scudéry and Honoré d'Urfé had already used the form for picaresque romances. But, in the *Princesse de Clèves*, she produced the first psychological novel, in which the scrutiny of characters and moods is as important as her tale of unfulfilled passion. Her characters are heroic and, like Corneille's, they are types rather than individuals; but they are developed with a subtlety worthy of Racine. The style is easy and unpretentious, strong in its understatements. If her novel is a precursor of the romantic movement, her own feet are firmly upon the calm ground of the seventeenth century.

We have seen the tendency of all these writers, in their own ways, to the deliberate study of the inner life. **Mme de Sévigné** (1626-96), who was a frequent visitor to Mme de la Fayette's house, was the least deliberate of artists and made no parade of descriptive talent; she was not writing her letters for publication but to please herself and her friends. The great events and ideas of the time rest lightly upon her and yet she is the child of her age, cultivated, balanced and wonderfully clear-headed; her portraiture may seem casual but it is very perceptive. She was left an orphan during her childhood, then a widow at 26, when her husband was killed in a duel. The heart of her work is the correspondence with her married daughter, whom she loved to distraction. The letters are a commentary upon Louis XIV's reign, seen from the angle of a woman on the fringe of the court, sufficiently in touch to be accurately informed, but never so close to events as to become *blasé*, or to lose her sense of fun. From her detached and lively pen we learn about the fall of Ghent, the first performance of a new Racine play; the birth of a son to the Dauphin; or—an incomparable event for this most honest of women—Mme de Sévigné dancing a minuet with the king. Or, in Brittany, it may be the *gaietés* of provincial society, the horrors of a peasant revolt, or a solitary walk in the woods round her château. She was unusual in her love of nature and her eye for landscape, but she was in most respects a typical upper-class Frenchwoman of her day. She accepted the hierarchy of birth, she was stirred by French triumphs in battle, she had little sympathy for the peasants who were strung up after the Brittany revolt. She reminds one of Jane Austen, in her candour and modesty and sharpness of observation. What would Jane Austen have made of the social drama of Versailles? And what might Mme de Sévigné have made of the novel, if she had chosen to express herself in that way?

Reason and research challenge authority

The classical doctrine still ruled the world of letters to the end of Louis' reign: but the intellectual assumptions upon which it had rested secure were being abandoned. The process was neither so dramatic nor so revolutionary as is conveyed by Hazard's celebrated aphorism: 'One day the French were thinking like Bossuet; all of a sudden they began to think like Voltaire.' But it was Bossuet himself who perceived most clearly the force and drift of the new thinking; the last years of his life were spent in a strenuous defence of his threatened positions of belief. He perceived that reason, which had been hitherto on the side of authority, was changing its allegiance. His *Discours sur l'Histoire Universelle* had stated with confidence the traditional view that the world was founded in 4004 B.C. Some unorthodox thinkers had suggested that it might be 4000. Now some, like the Englishman John Ray, were working upon the disturbing evidence of fossil remains. Seventeenth century thinking was not yet ready for anything remotely resembling a theory of evolution and a considerable 'theological geology' was expounded to prop up the *status quo*, attributing dates to such phenomena as the flood (November 18th, 2349 B.C. in the view of William Whiston) with an extraordinary mixture of scholarship and fantasy. Locke supported Whiston's thesis, and even Leibnitz fitted his Cartesian view that primitive matter was fluid, because of the tremendous heat, into the framework of *Genesis*—Seven Days' Creation and the Flood. Travellers' discoveries could be less easily ignored and Bossuet, in the 3rd edition of the *Discours*, accepted the view of Fr. Perron that a difference between the Vulgate and Septuagint Editions of the Bible made 5500 B.C. a possible date, thus accommodating his work to the recent discoveries about early Egyptian and Chinese history, which made nonsense of the later date. The fixed frame was beginning to crack. The method of Descartes had shown potentialities which the philosopher's own prudence and faith had veiled; he had educated thinking men to follow the dictates of logic and some of his followers were less cautious than he. As authority came to be discredited by its abuses and failures, notably in the sphere of religious controversy, champions of reason became more critical too of the established rules of life and politics. Cardinal Bérulle, who first directed the young Descartes towards philosophy, would have been horrified if he could have seen the results; reasoned faith becoming reasoned humanism, leading men back to the libertinism which he had sought to destroy.

'All the ills that affect a man proceed from one sole cause, namely that he has not learned to sit quietly and contentedly in a room.' Pascal's pronouncement exactly describes the inward-looking classical state of mind; one that is reluctant to travel, content to accept definition and rule, and prefers to search for truth in the human mind than in the outside world. Such an approach was bound to induce a sort of claustrophobia, for sentiment and curiosity must find ways of release if they are not to be extinguished. 'The climate of opinion,' wrote Lecky, the eighteenth century historian of rationalism, 'is created, not by the influences arising out of any one apartment of intellect, but by the combination of all the intellectual and even social tendencies of the age'. That it changed so rapidly is due to the fact that thought knew no frontiers. Europe had a small aristocracy of intellect, which was not at this time divorced from the *élite* of wealth and power that dominated opinion. So a scientific discovery, one day, was a fashionable way of thinking, the next. Science was enlarging its frontiers rapidly. We have seen the contributions of Descartes and Pascal. To these should be added: Newton's coherent system of dynamics, which marked an epoch in the study of the action of force upon bodies; Boyle's work in chemistry which he limited to the study of the composition of substances; Harvey's work in the field of physiology and the impulse that this gave to biological studies. Germs of thought upon lines suggested by the work of such men were soon coursing through the blood-stream of European culture. The foundation of observatories and academies, botanical and zoological gardens, and the patronage of kings helped the process: for instance, the Royal Society in England, the *Académie des Sciences* (1667) and the *Jardin du Roi* in France. A consequence may be seen in changing views of nature and reason. The Cartesian reduced nature to a system, a set of habits, a world of rules; the new attitude had to take accidents and circumstances more into account; observation and experiment show that nature is untidy and unpredictable, a mass of conflicting forces. Reason was supposed in classical theory to be common to all men, its laws to be immutable; but now it was to become a quickening urge to discover and an impatience with general abstractions.

Accompanying these significant alterations of ideas was a new tendency towards Deism. Travellers' tales have a certain vogue at this time; from Colbert's sponsored colonies, news arrived of the great American lakes from Capucin or Jesuit missionaries of the pagodas of China. In 1683, Alain Manesson-Mallet published his *Description de l'univers*, a comprehensive study of the geography, governments, societies and cultures of the world. This ambitious work was profusely and fancifully illustrated; it was translated into several languages and widely imitated. La Bruyère understood the meaning of this: 'some complete their demoralisation by extensive travel and lose whatever shreds of religion remain to them. Every day they see a new religion, new customs, new rites.' Notions of relativity develop when practices that are thought to be based on reason turn out to be merely custumal. It was disturbing to be assured by the Jesuits that the morality of the Chinese was in many respects superior to that of the westerner. Idealised types find their way into the European imagination: 'the noble savage', 'the refined Russian' and 'the Chinese philosopher'. In the hands of Bayle, travellers' observations became ammunition for his gospel of doubt: 'M. Bernier, in his interesting account of the Great Mogul, etc. . . . ' Travel books answered to the restlessness of intellectuals; *voyages imaginaires* start to appear. The reported wonders of distant lands or imagined Utopias can be used to insinuate criticisms of society or faith which could not yet appear without disguise. In one country disguise was not necessary, at least after 1688. Traffic across the Channel was still two-way, for England was still influenced by French manners and fashion. But French ascendancy in thought was passing. The names of Newton and Locke were becoming familiar to Frenchmen. If one has to name one writer who above all influenced the philosophers of the next century, and so helped to prepare French opinion for the Revolution, it is surely Locke, author of the *Treatises on Civil Government* and the *Essay on Toleration.*

'The year 1688 marks the apogee of the reign of Louis XIV, the height of his glory and prosperity.' Saint-Simon's date has a significance in literature too. The great writers were almost silent. A poem by Charles Perrault, *Le Siècle de Louis le Grand*, had extolled the age of Louis XIV as greater than that of Augustus. In the 'quarrel between the ancients and the moderns' which followed, even the dogmatic Boileau was forced to concede that the ancient models were not the only ones, that classical rules were not immutable. In this year, **Jean la Bruyère** (1645-96) published his *Caractères*. He began his book with the words 'tout est dit' and what he went on to say is new, in subject and in manner. He cast his characters in the traditional mould, after Theophrastus. His writing is deft, balanced, classical without pedantry; he was not a *libertin* and on occasion he praised the king. But he was an observer of conduct and manners rather than of character, and his portraits, real and imaginary, are drawn from the outside, warts and all. His caricatures are recognisable as Frenchmen, and they are allowed no masks. His minute observation is true moralising, though he seldom labours a point.

La Bruyère thought that since French prose had reached perfection, the artist must now put more of himself into his writing— *mettre l'esprit*. 'He belonged to two centuries,' said Sainte-Beuve, 'he ends the one, and one might say that he begins and introduces the other.' His writing was disturbing, more because of his values than because of the manner in which he wrote. He presented ordinary people who could be virtuous and self-sacrificing, rich people who could be idle and vicious. His art crossed frontiers of birth and wealth as it sketched the vanities of the human race. His humour was agreeable enough when he was describing the obsessed grower who could think of nothing else but his tulips, but it was less comfortable when it turned to the staleness and hypocrisy of the courtier's life. He could be terrible and mordant without resorting to false colour. His peasants are probably no more real than Hogarth's Gin Alley layabouts, but they have the same hint of truth under the exaggeration: 'one sees certain wild animals, male and female, scattered about the countryside, black, livid and cracked with sun, bound to the soil that they till with invincible obstinacy; they have an articulate voice, and when they get up on their feet they reveal a human face, and in fact they are men. They retire to hovels where they live on black bread, water and roots. . . .' La Bruyère once declared that the important topics were forbidden to writers of Louis XIV's reign. One can guess from this what he meant by 'important topics' and how he would have dealt with them. As it was, through the meticulous writing of the *Caractères*, he contrived to voice criticisms which were all the more effective for being so unimpassioned.

There is a double interest in the writing of **François de Salignac de la Mothe-Fénelon**[1] (1651-1715): the unfolding of an original and sensitive mind, and the informed criticisms of a man who lived, until his retirement to Cambrai, near to the centre of affairs. *Télémaque*, like *Gulliver's Travels*, could be read by children for the story, which is engaging, though a little obviously didactic. But in the Republic of Salente, where the population was engaged in farming, and the ruler sought ways to increase the population and the wealth of the land, avoiding wars and high taxation, adult readers could see a studied rebuke to the ideals of the king. His protégé, the Duke of Burgundy, was meant to see the book in this light. His *Dialogue des morts* contains a noble passage which may be chosen to summarise his views of human rights: 'Each individual owes incomparably more to the human race, which is the great fatherland, than to the particular country into which he is born. As the family is to the nation, so is the nation to the universal commonwealth; therefore it is infinitely more harmful

[1] For Fénelon's career and his part in the Quietist affair, see pages 447-53.

for nation to wrong nation than for family to wrong family.' But his political ideas do not concern us here. Even if they were valueless, there is still enough left in his writing to interest the critic. Fénelon was a man of sensibility, as the eighteenth century understood the word; oceans of tears are shed in *Télémaque*. He longed to escape from convention. In his *Lettre à l'Académie*, he pointed the way, with the proposal that taste rather than dogma should be the guiding principle in the art of writing, and the plea for a richer vocabulary. His criticism of the school of Boileau was that they had 'impoverished and desiccated' the language. There was a wholeness about his criticism, for these are the very words which he would have applied to the government of Louis XIV. He saw the same artificiality and the same consequent lack of imagination in Louis XIV's aristocratic government and in the literary school of Boileau. Whether he is writing about Quietism or the education of women, or composing tutorial exercises for the Duke of Burgundy, it is the quality of imagination in him which attracts notice. In the *grand siècle* he is outstanding as the man who thought for himself, whose values were his own.

Louis duc de Saint-Simon (1675-1758) had little in common with Fénelon except noble birth and inclination to criticise the regime. Nor do his *Mémoires* belong strictly to our period, for he did not begin to write them out till 1723. But they were reconstructed from earlier and copious notes and they give us an elaborate picture of the court in the last years of the king. Saint-Simon would have been shocked to hear himself classified as a writer, since his only profession, apart from short excursions into war and diplomacy, was to be a duke. His style was indeed unprofessional and impressionistic, for his interest was not in composition for its own sake but in conveying his feelings to paper while they were still warm and unconfused. He cannot be relied upon for accuracy, as he was not an impartial witness and his talents were those of a journalist. He was a master of movement, of the quick strokes and daubs which delineate three-quarters of a character, of the unfairness which contains just enough truth to make it sting, or amuse, or arouse one's curiosity. It was fortunate that he was placed, by his station in life, in constant attendance at the best spectacle in Europe, the perfect field for his talents.

His pages are rancorous with the prejudices of a mediocre man who never rose to the height which his birth seemed to warrant. He was in an ambivalent position; perhaps many shared the feelings which he made articulate. On the one hand he was the complete courtier, wrapped up in the ceremonies and the gossip of the court, and ungrudging in his respect for the person of the old king. The other part of him resented the system which was ostensibly based upon the privileges of birth but yet denied the well-born any share of the government. So his diary is of unique interest as the record of a society in which he was at once accepting, sharing and disapproving. He was an unsparing critic of absolute government, but his comments are personal: upon the royal bastards who came between the king's legitimate family and his hereditary nobility, or the great ministers who carried on the business of the state, for which their business did not fit them; Mme de Maintenon, isolated in her eminence as wife of the king's old age, or upstart bishops. His hostility is always entertaining, but it is usually petty. He is at his best when he is detesting, but his passionate curiosity and prejudices lifted him on occasion to the level of great events. He admired the Duke of Burgundy, and sympathised with his projects of reform, and his account of the duke's death, shrouded as it was by the accompanying deaths of his wife and son, is a memorable elegiac. There are tender portraits, too, as well as malicious—the duc de Beauvillier or Marshal Boufflers, for instance. Great men, churchmen particularly, challenged his art; his portraits of Fénelon and Harlay are, of their sort, incomparable.

The classical equilibrium could not survive for ever whilst inquiry and invention went on unabated amongst philosophers and scientists. **Bernard de Fontenelle** (1657-1757) was a nephew of the great Corneille, but he was the most unenthusiastic of men and far removed from the heroic mood which to him was 'simply bombast'. He spent his life avoiding draughts and the more exacting of his friends. He was so successful in preserving his delicate frame that he lived to be a hundred, but it was not to this that he owed his reputation in his day. He was a new phenomenon, the popular scientist. In method he was the last word in Cartesianism, advocating the order and precision of the geometrical method in all things. 'The geometric spirit is not so attached to geometry that it cannot be disentangled and carried over into other areas of knowledge. A work on politics, on criticism, perhaps even on eloquence will be better, all other things being equal, if it is written by the hand of a geometer.' His philosophy was based on two things: 'one, that we have inquiring minds; two, that we have very short sight'. His tastes were wide and ran to elegiac conceits, madrigals and comedies, but he was most influential as a populariser of new ideas and discoveries. From 1699 to 1741 he was the secretary of the *Académie des Sciences*, which enabled him to keep in touch with the results of contemporary research. A typical work was the *Histoire des Oracles*, a contribution to the debate about the relationship between the pagan oracles and Christianity. His *Dialogues des Morts* (1683) was perhaps the most sensible contribution to the literary controversy between the Ancients and the Moderns. His simple but telling point, that the Moderns could start where the Ancients left off, and draw on a cumulative tradition, opens the door to the eighteenth century, since it introduced a new view of civilisation: no longer a descent from memorable heights of revelation, but an ascent towards light. Obstacles had to be removed in the course of this process of enlightenment, and his technique of exposure is worthy of Voltaire. But he was a prudent man, and careful to spare the susceptibilities of the orthodox. The *Entretiens sur la pluralité des mondes* (1686) was designed to bring the new astronomy 'within the grasp of the feminine intelligence'. He only hinted at the possibilities of life on other planets, just as in his *Oracles* he did not go beyond implying the possibility that some miracles could be ascribed to natural causes. But his writing had the same effect as Bayle's fiercer onslaught upon accepted ideas in his studies of comets, for it appealed, as the eighteenth century *philosophes* were later to appeal, to the wide audience of common sense, and it was aimed against tradition and the human frailties that supported it.

He was responsible for a new fad in fashionable society. 'Anatomy', he wrote, 'hitherto confined to the schools of Medicine, now promises to come out into the *beau monde*.' Paris in the eighties was full of foreigners who came to observe the demonstrations of scientists: the chemist Lémery or the anatomist Dr. Verney. In 1686, *Mercure Galante* reported that a young lady refused an eligible suitor on the grounds that he would not give her any plausible ideas about 'the squaring of the circle', another made the construction of a telescope her *sine qua non*. More important than this dilettante astronomy was the new outlook that his work encouraged; men were becoming once again more interested in facts than in causes.

Fontenelle's law—'make sure of the facts before you bother about their cause'—was also the guiding principle of the life of

Pierre Bayle (1647-1706), son and brother of Protestant ministers, himself first a renegade convert to Catholicism and then a heretic again in reaction to Jesuit teaching. In 1675 he became Professor of Philosophy at Sedan but went to Rotterdam in 1681 when the Protestant academies were suppressed. Because of his brother's death—in 1685, after five months in prison, where he had been sent on the score of Pierre's attacks upon Jesuit doctrine—he became a caustic critic of religious bigotry of both varieties: Roman and, as in the case of the orthodox Jurieu, Protestant. His life was spent in the pursuit of knowledge for its own sake. Reason in his hands came to be synonymous with irreligion, for as he himself put it: 'the champions of reason and the champions of religion are fighting desperately for the possession of men's souls'. Voltaire called him the 'first of the sceptical philosophers', but he was never in fact the complete agnostic. If anything firm can be discerned amongst the shifting sands of his encyclopaedic labours, it is rather a sort of Deism, concerned with the separation of morals from religion, rather than disbelieving the existence of God. His ideas come incidentally from his works of reference and propaganda, and form no coherent system. They have nothing in common except a hatred of all forms of dogma, Protestant as well as Catholic. He was more of a collector than a scholar, and his faith in the power of facts to overwhelm superstition is sometimes naïve, for he was not always critical of his own sources. He was more of a publicist than a philosopher, and he could not resist the temptation to shock, by indecent or irreverent asides.

His *Pensées sur la Comète* (1682) is a classic of the sort of criticism that rests upon weight of facts and patient analysis. It was written supposedly to disprove the fear that Halley's comet, which appeared in 1680, was a portent of evil. It broadens out into a review of other fallacies in history, theology and politics, and even goes to the point of propounding a moral existence independent of dogmatic faith. Discussing miracles, he presents his view of God: 'miracles are against all reason. There is nothing more consonant with God's infinite greatness than his maintenance of the laws which he himself established; there could be nothing more unworthy than to imagine him intervening to interrupt their regular operation.' He found a wide audience through two great undertakings: the *Nouvelles de la Rèpublique des Lettres* and the justly celebrated *Dictionnaire Historique et Critique*. The first was a monthly review, produced in Rotterdam by his single-handed efforts, during the vital years 1684-7, when events in France and England were creating a favourable climate of moral indignation. It was banned in Paris which probably did something to increase its circulation. The *Dictionnaire* was intended as a corrective to an earlier dictionary, but it grew into a monument of learning and cost him, incidentally, the Chair of Philosophy which had been specially created for him, and his pension from William III, because of 'the impiety' of his comments. It set out to re-interpret, in terms of new standards, the records of ancient and modern civilisation and to present them plainly, without the colour or bias which came from theological assumptions. With its combination of erudition and curious facts, many of them culled from travellers' reports, its snippets of scandal and invective, and its solid and honest reasoning, the *Dictionnaire* became the sceptics' bible. His admirers considered that a statue should be erected in his honour, alongside that of Erasmus. His talents and graces hardly merit this comparison, but he had this in common with the sixteenth century humanist: the beaver labours of Bayle were ennobled by a single-minded passion for truth. Ironically it was not always the sceptic who provided food for the enlightenment of the next century. Sébastien de Tillement, a Jansenist and friend of Mabillon, collected and edited the documents relating to the first six centuries of the Christian church and the Roman Emperors; it was a labour of piety and of scholarship and with zestful impiety Gibbon was to use the material to abuse the church which de Tillement hoped to vindicate.

A very different sort of émigré and sceptic was **Charles de Saint-Denis de Saint-Évremond** (1616-1703). He was an aristocrat, he was a general in the French army until he went too far in his criticisms of the Peace of the Pyrenees and he spent the more creative part of his life in London. Charles II and William III patronised him and he rode the Glorious Revolution with the ease of a man who had long given up the sordid concerns of the world. He was indeed the fine flower of gentlemanly scepticism. With all the finesse of the *grand siècle*, he maintained the ideals of the age that ended with Descartes. Mathematics and physics were vulgar and the man of breeding should concern himself only with ethics and polite letters: an attitude which ensured him a position of splendid isolation amid the cross-currents of argument of the time. He was in short an engaging epicurean, who made it his aim to live according to the laws of nature. He was inevitably cosmopolitan

R

in outlook: 'the salt of the earth are the French who do the thinking and the English who put it into words'. He tried to transplant the ideal of the *honnête homme* in English soil, but there was nothing of the missionary about this temperate man who studied the classics, wrote a comedy in the English manner entitled *Sir Politick Would-be*, and came to rest in the Poet's corner in Westminster Abbey. He may be credited with some effective essays in a new art, that of appreciation, in pursuit of his ideal: to say little but to say it well. He contributed, like Fontenelle, to the removal of the barriers which came between the scholar and the drawing-room. But his interest lies principally in what he hints of the future; of Montesquieu in his *Réflexions sur les divers génies du peuple romain*, and of Rousseau in his essay on religion, when he longs for the time when faith will shift from 'the curiosity of our spirits to the tenderness of our hearts'.

Some painters and sculptors

Painting in the seventeenth century is as much an expression of contemporary life and thought as literature. The painter could not, as he has later been able to do, isolate himself from society and ignore current fashion. His work was almost inevitably influenced by the preferences of his patron. In this period patronage became more discriminating, and so more demanding. At the same time academic standards were imposed and the painter's freedom of subject and manner to some extent curtailed. So it is possible to talk about the *style Louis Quatorze* as covering a period when the painter and sculptor were drilled to perform their part in the cultural production of the state. In some ways the earlier period is of more interest, when there is no one school of thought, and before academic virtues of correctness came to dominate the scene. If a date is wanted to divide the two periods, it can be supplied by the foundation of the *Académie de Peinture et de Sculpture* in 1648. But it was more the state patronage exercised by Colbert and for the new royal palaces which channelled the creative talents into court painting.

At the beginning of the century, when painting in Paris was of mediocre quality, there was an important group of artists working in Lorraine, celebrated beyond the Duchy, the best of whom is probably Jacques Callot (1592-1635). He found his *métier* in engraving his favourite subjects in crowd scenes which show a close and sensitive scrutiny. He was commissioned by Richelieu to depict the capture of La Rochelle, a work which tested his fine powers of composition. The Cardinal's invasion of Lorraine in 1633 introduced him to the grimmer features of war and must have influenced his best known work—*Les Misères de Guerre*—a series of war studies.

The influence of Flemish painters can be traced back to the commissioning of Rubens for the decoration of the gallery of the Luxembourg for Marie de Médicis (1622), and to the work of Frans Pourbus who was the principal portrait painter in Paris during the period of Henry IV and Marie de Médicis. It can be seen best in the painting of **Philippe de Champaigne** (1602-74), who was appointed painter to the Queen-Mother in 1628. *Louis XII offering his crown to Christ at the foot of the cross* and the fine portrait of Cardinal Richelieu which is now in the National Gallery belong to this period. The pose of the Cardinal is that often used by Van Dyck and Rubens, but the modelling of the robes belongs to classical sculpture. Champaigne modified a baroque style to a more sober and classical form. Like many serious minded people of his time, he was attracted to the Jansenists. From about 1663 to the end of his life he was in close touch with Port Royal, and Jansenist ideals came to permeate his work. There is a complete rejection of the vivid emotionalism of the baroque and, instead, a simplicity which can be uncomfortably cold but is most powerful when the theme is suitable. The picture of the curing of his daughter, a nun at Port Royal, in its simple composition, and plainness of blacks and greys, with a ray of light between the figures to convey the miraculous, is a perfect illustration of the Jansenist idea of miracles. Champaigne's portraits of this period, mostly of Jansenist friends and bourgeois patrons, are somewhat apart from the manner of the *grand siècle* and the method of any other painter. They are the French equivalent to the Hals-Rembrandt school of Dutch domestic painters, in their sharp observation and sombre colour. It may not be too fanciful to see the rationalism of the period of Descartes expressed in these portraits, with their severely ordered design and their disregard of any ornament that is irrelevant to the subject.

Other artists in this period were influenced more by Italian masters, especially by Caravaggio. Vouet (1590-1649) brought with him from Italy a style of compromise between the ecstasy of baroque and the firm lines of classicism which was ideally suited to the religious aspirations of the period of Bérulle and St. François de Sales. He was principally employed upon altar-pieces and large schemes for panels and ceilings, and he may be considered the real founder of the French tradition of decorative painting. Georges la Tour (1593-1652) preserved idiosyncrasies of style amid the Italian influences on his work. He lived most of his life in Lorraine and his more important painting is religious, influenced somewhat by the Franciscans who were prominent in the religious revival in Lorraine. He borrowed Caravaggio's naturalism without any of his violence or drama. There is a stillness and simplicity about his best paintings, such as the *Christ and Joseph* (in the Louvre), which is in the recognisable French manner of Champaigne and Poussin. His peasants too are clearly French peasants, with torn and dirty trousers, and not the idealised swains of court painting. The brothers **Le Nain** (the eldest born 1588, the youngest died 1677; their work is not easily distinguishable) specialised in the depiction of real life at a time when this was still permissible. The second brother, Louis, is the one to whom the family owe their reputation for his wonderful peasant groups, for example, *Peasants at a meal* (in the Louvre). The figures are poised, the canvas is uncluttered; there is no satire or caricature, and the people look more real than Brueghel's; they are poor, but neither brutish nor demoralised. The same naturalism can be seen in the work of two engravers of the time. Abraham Bosse (1602-76) depicted well-to-do unromantic bourgeois life in his well-ordered compositions. Robert Nanteuil is best known for his minutely observed studies of the great men of the period. His *Louis XIV* (1664) (in the British Museum) may be the most accurate representation of the monarch.

It is odd that the two best-known and best-loved French painters of the century should have spent most of their active lives in Rome. Italy was still the centre of gravity for the artistic world. But the work of Poussin and Claude in portraiture and landscaping gave as much to succeeding French artists as they took from Italian. Little is known about **Nicholas Poussin** (1593-1665) beyond the fact that he was born in a peasant family in Normandy and that he worked with Champaigne at the Luxembourg. Rome shaped him; he lived there for forty years and was only once tempted away to Paris for two years' work on decorative scenes. Many of his patrons however were French, such as the civil servant Chatelon, and his work is the embodiment of French classicism. One can never forget that he is the contemporary of Descartes and the fellow-countryman of Racine. He passed through several phases. From a period of experiment with the baroque, he went on to explore themes of classical mythology, such as *The Bacchanals*, painted for Richelieu. But, during the central period of his art, he concentrated upon the great subjects which were considered appropriate by patrons who went to the plays of Corneille. *The Crucifixion*, the *Holy Family*, *Coriolanus* were typical compositions. His method should be noticed, for it throws light upon the artistic values of the time. He believed that the processes involved in a work of art were essentially rational. Imagination, which he took for granted, must be moulded, by rules of reason, into forms of absolute clarity. Every subject demands a particular method of treatment if the artist (cf. Boileau) is to be true to its spirit. If an artist paints a harsh and solemn subject, his technique must eliminate any suggestion of sweetness and charm. Poussin always preceded a painting by reading all he could about the subject; he then made a sort of puppet show of wax figures to get his composition right; from these he made larger models. Since he never painted from life direct, and since the figure always had to fit into the pattern which conformed best to his canons of design, it is not surprising that there is a cold and marble character about his style. It has the qualities of architecture and classical sculpture; the appeal, as the artist intended, is to the mind more than to the heart. In one of his lectures to the Academy, Le Brun traced the ancient models for each figure in Poussin's *Gathering of Manna*.

Claude le Lorrain (1600-82) made the painting of landscape his means of artistic expression and again his inspiration came from Italy, the Naples coast and the Roman *campagna*. His importance lies in his departure from the conventions of the Mannerist school, their stylised trees and hills. He is a master of light as he saw it in the Italian landscape of ruins and olive groves, pines and poplars. There is a classical tendency; ruins recall the greatness of Rome, and there is meticulous care for proportions. But his painting is not essentially heroic. Vivid light-effects convey balm more often than storm. The atmosphere is pastoral poetic. If the glories of Rome are invoked, it is the Rome of Virgil and Catullus rather than that of Coriolanus and Cato.

Under the heavy hand of the *Académie de Peinture et de Sculpture*, the method of Poussin became the required standard for any painter who wished to be accepted. Under the guidance of 'reason, rules and the best masters', the *Académie* laid down laws of perspective, proportion and composition. Nature was barred, for from its wildness and beauty the artist could choose only such subjects as accorded with reason. To adapt Keats only slightly (but completely to alter his meaning): 'reason is beauty, and beauty reason'. The painter should give more attention to form and colour, and he should only choose 'noble subjects'. He must observe the 'proprieties' of the subject. He must not copy the Venetians, for they were too garish, nor the Netherlandish, for they were too undiscriminating. But he might choose from the Ancients; Raphael and his followers were most acceptable. The unhappy consequences of this narrow code can be seen in the acres of decorative painting at Versailles, a weariness of the flesh and interesting only where some impatient painter broke the rules. It is a scheme of art suited to mass production, for it could only produce a sort of copying, and suited to the scenic effects of the interior decorator. The two greatest names associated with the *Académie* or Colbert style are Le Brun and Mignard, for both have a talent for magnificence which raises them above the level of mere competence.

Charles Le Brun (1619-90) was the king of decorators and the artistic foreman of the Gobelins and of Versailles. His *Family of Darius before Alexander* (1661) was the foundation of his success with the young king, who owned to some likeness to the great Alexander. His pictures are most successful when he broke away from the rules that he insisted upon with his pupils of the Academy. The portrait of *Chancellor Séguier* and the *Entry of Louis XIV and Maria Theresa into Paris in* 1661 are essentially baroque compositions. In the large canvas of *Louis XIV adoring the Risen Christ*, discreetly placed, appears the small figure of his paymaster Colbert; when Colbert died Le Brun's supremacy was at an end, for Louvois typically supported a rival painter, **N. Mignard** (1612-94). This most bombastic of painters specialised in the allegory. The comte de Toulouse appears as Cupid asleep, the marquise de Seignelay as Thetis, Louis XIV, at the siege of Maastricht, as a Roman emperor. His manner was admirably suited to the mood of his patrons in these years of easy victory, but does not appeal much to admirers either of strict classicism or of the baroque, for it lacks the restraint of the former and yet misses the drama and flow of the best baroque.

A reaction from the grand manner was inevitable. The last decades of the reign show the same ferment of changing values that we have seen in the writing of the period. The same factors are at work: disillusion with the king's policies and a more questioning attitude towards faith and authority. After the battle of Blenheim, Caesar and Alexander were out of place. **Charles de la Fosse** (1636-1716) went back in his later years to the freedom and colour of the Venetian painters. The central composition of his dome for the Invalides (1692) has a typical subject: *Saint Louis presenting to Christ the sword with which he has vanquished the enemies of the Church*, and the faithful could see in Saint Louis a striking resemblance to Louis XIV; but the composition is slight. His paintings for the Trianon are gay, and his nymphs are slender and rosy-coloured. The same leaning towards the baroque can be found in **Antoine Coypel** (1661-1708). As a young man he conformed to academic taste in his *Louis XIV resting after the Peace of Nijmegen*. But the ceiling for his gallery at the Palais Royal is one of the most complete baroque schemes, with a fine piece of false perspective, and his ceiling of the Chapel at Versailles has another melodramatic *trompe-l'œil*. 'It seems to me that the subjects are too serious. Something youthful must be mingled with future works.' With these words Louis XIV gave the licence of royal approval to the painters who were working in the more sprightly veins of the baroque and rococo, for the younger members of the royal family. In this case he was commenting on the projected decorations for the *Ménagerie*, for the Duchess of Burgundy. **Santerre** (1658-1717) was a leader in this new mode. His *Saint Theresa*, for the chapel of Versailles, created a scandal and his *Susanna* (now in the Louvre) is a classical nymph, if anything nearer to the shepherdesses of Boucher than to the saints of Poussin. It looks forward to the poetry and fantasy of Watteau (1684-1721), the favourite painter of the Regency.

Another feature of these later years is the return to the straight portrait, based on the formulas of Van Dyck, which combined the impressive with that sense of ease which was the goal of the artists who wanted to escape from the formalism of the Académie. **Hyacinthe Rigaud** (1659-1743) became almost entirely a court painter. He could do grand paintings of generals standing against the background of a battle. But he could also show liveliness and elegance, as notably in his *Louis XIV*, one of the greatest of royal portraits (the Louvre). The conventions of setting and pose are completely baroque, but the outlines are sharp, the colour strong but cold. The effect is splendid; the man is not lost in the symbolism of majesty. His dignity and his pretensions are both in the painting, the grave strong face, the wedged shoes and ballet pose of his feet. From **François Desportes** (1661-1743) Louis commissioned portraits of favourite dogs and rare animals. But with this painter, who used to wander round the countryside with a portable easel, painting his landscape backgrounds from life, we truly leave the seventeenth century!

Sculpture had an ancillary part to play in the artistic scheme of Colbert and Le Brun. It was seen as the complement to architecture, and its role was to embellish the gardens and rooms of Versailles; the emphasis was thus inevitably on quantity as well as quality. But several men stand out from the ruck as individual artists. **François Girardon** (1628-1715) collaborated closely with Le Brun; he embodied the classical theories of the *Académie*, which were perhaps more suited to sculpture than to other arts. His fame rests today on his groups, for example *Apollo tended by his nymphs* for the grotto of Thetis at Versailles. During his execution of this group, the artist paid a special visit to Rome to refresh his memory. Faithful to the precepts of the *Académie*, the nymphs are grouped symmetrically round the central figure of Apollo; monotony is avoided by the variety of their poses and gestures. Girardon was pure classic. But **Antoine Coysevox** (1640-1720) leaned always towards the baroque. His garden ornaments for the palace were lifeless; but, working on the interior, he allowed his imagination a freer rein. The stucco relief of the victorious *Louis XIV* in the *salon de guerre*, full of violence, embodies the spirit of the *grand siècle*. His individual busts, such as his *Louis XIV* (Wallace Collection), are remarkable for their freedom and technical brilliance. Like the painter Rigaud, he was able to adapt his style to the wishes of the younger patrons. His *Duchesse of Burgundy* is a most engaging essay in the lighter vein. She appears as Diana, but she is convincingly the real woman whom Louis XIV admired so much. **Pierre Puget** (1622-94) had only a short-lived success, for he would not fit into Colbert's schemes, and so worked most of his life at Toulon and Marseilles. He is interesting as an example of the outsider amongst artists, though he could never entirely throw off the clutches of the state. His finest work, *Milo* (1670), was executed from a block of marble discovered abandoned at Toulon docks to use which he had to secure, with difficulty, Colbert's permission. He was eventually taken up by Louvois, as Mignard had been, and he executed various groups for the palace in his free baroque style. His last years were embittered by the rejection of his *Saint Charles Borromeo* and he had difficulty in securing payment for his work. He was no courtier; when he told Colbert the terms on which he would work for the king, the words *je veux* appear with a frequency unknown at Versailles. There is something of the elder Mansard in his independence and his refusal to accept the artistic tyranny of the managed economy.

Classical and baroque architecture

Architecture is always interesting as a commentary on the conditions which produced it. A classical, cosmopolitan or pretentious style may be held to indicate a royal and aristocratic age. It may not be an accident that the baroque style is least to be seen in England, where patrons were practical and realistic men, who looked for solid value for their investment. These suggestions should not be pushed too far. It is certain, however, that the emergence of a native school of architecture in France, which was able to dispense with the tutelage of Rome, and whose qualities of measure, harmony and grace were exported all over Europe, owed much to the increasing wealth and power of the state. Private patronage and taste, too, played their part; the taste formed by the pervasive influences of classicism, by heightened religious sentiment and, in the secular buildings, by the desire for ampler and more comfortable living. Before Louis XIV's reign had begun, the reconstruction of Paris had made it the most splendid capital in Europe.

The period of the Religious Wars was hardly favourable to building, but there was a vigorous resumption under Henry IV, with an inclination to massive plainness. The buildings in the Place Dauphine and the Place Royal by Châtillon (1547-1616) are typical, with their massive arcades and brick walls surmounted by tall slated roofs. A more important architect was Salomon de Brosse (1560-1626), whose Palace of Luxembourg, designed for Marie de Médicis, anticipates Mansard in its emphasis upon the central block, the *corps de logis*, subordination of the wings and the delicacy of classical detail. His successor as royal architect was

R*

Jacques Lemercier (1585-1654), who brought from Rome the academic style of the period just before the full flowering of the baroque. Two Paris landmarks, the great domes of the churches at the Sorbonne and Val-de-Grâce, are his memorial. But he also designed the Palais-Cardinal for Richelieu (later to be known as the Palais Royal) and extended the sixteenth century buildings of the Louvre, where he left his mark in the square-domed clock tower. This characteristic square-dome design recurs constantly at Richelieu; the château has disappeared but the 'new town' survives as an interesting example of early town planning, on a severe rectangular design. It was also a *folie de grandeur* on Richelieu's part, for there was—and is—no economic justification for a town on that site.

By the side of **François Mansard** (1598-1666), Lemercier appears a little pedestrian. It is fortunate that there were *nouveaux riches*, tax-farmers such as Brûlart de Sillery, who were intelligent as well as rich enough to give this original artist scope for the full development of his ideas, for he was an obstinate and opinionated person who would never have flourished under Colbert's regime. He learned little from foreign contemporaries, but brought the French tradition to perfection. The house which he built in 1635 for La Vrillière, the tax-farmer, was the model for the *hôtels* of the time: severe classicism, almost without ornament but with a perfect harmony of design. The Château of Maisons is the most complete surviving example of Mansard's work, with its fine front wings projecting in unbroken sections from the main block, and its tremendous staircase of four flights. He was a perfectionist. His plans for the completion of the square court of the Louvre have flaps incorporating possible variations for every possible sector, so that for some parts of the building there might be sixteen combinations. In his combination of ingenuity and restraint he is worthy to stand with Poussin and Racine as an exemplar of the finest qualities of French classicism. It is not surprising that he appealed to the fastidious taste of Voltaire, for his achievement was related to a new refinement in society. So one finds the grand staircase moved to one end, giving space

---

[1] These lines of Voltaire are supposed to refer to Maisons:

> *Simple en etait la noble architecture;*
> *Chaque ornement en sa place arrêté*
> *Y semblait mis par la necessité*
> *L'art s'y cachait sous l'aide de la nature.*

for a range of reception rooms *en suite*, facing a garden, and separated by courts from the filth and hubbub of the streets. For the large households of his rich patrons, the 'mansard roof' was convenient, having the lower part steeper than the upper and thus providing good attic rooms.

Louis le Vau (1612-70) seems to have been temperamentally better suited to the exacting demands of his patrons than Mansard, since he was less touchy and less of an individualist. Le Vau headed a term of craftsmen, painters, sculptors and plasterers; he could leave the details to them and concentrate upon the general effect. With his father he had done some land speculation in the Île Saint-Louis, where his earlier buildings were commissioned. He was brought by Fouquet, who could afford to patronise more lavishly than the crown itself, to design a new palace for him; thence after Fouquet's fall he was taken over, with his team, to design for the king. The way in which architect and painter worked together can be seen in the Hôtel Lambert, where a theatrical staircase creates a series of splendid baroque impressions as it winds up to a rich Le Brun ceiling. Vau-le-Vicomte is of course his masterpiece. It is extraordinary that the building, commissioned in 1657, was roofed by 1658 and decorated by 1661. Characteristic of Fouquet, and ironic in view of his fate, was his provisions of two great *appartements* in each wing, one for the owner and one for the king. Le Vau gave the building his characteristic trade-mark, the triple-arched portico carried right through the building. In the king's bedroom a novelty appeared which was to be used a lot at Versailles: the combination of stucco gilding and painting which Le Brun seems to have learned from the rooms in the Palazzo Pitti. This represents the compromise which was to endure, between the French classical spirit and the baroque.

The term *boroque* is widely used as an adjective to suggest flamboyance, richness or luxuriance, perhaps too widely; when applied to tendencies of thought or to literature, the word is imprecise to the point of meaninglessness. It is correctly used to describe a tendency of artists and architects of the seventeenth century to elaborate upon the formalities of classicism, to allow imagination to find expression in more daring shapes by impressionism, by lighting effects, even by illusionism—*trompe-l'œil*—or by richer use of colour to convey the idea of movement, with emphasis upon curves rather than symmetry. Classicism is essentially static: emotion is subordinated to reason; whereas baroque is more concerned with decoration and less with the design. It is fluid and seeks to convey passion, awe and mystery. The spiritual home of the baroque was Rome, where it expressed the religious fervour of the Counter-Reformation. There Bernini and Borromini celebrated in stone and plaster the triumphs of the Papacy and stressed in their figures of the saints, their reliquaries, reredoses and baldacinos the efficacy of prayers to the dead, the mediation of saints and the mystery of transubstantiation; in Rome Claude and Poussin learned their craft, celebrating not as in the Renaissance the mastery of man over things, but his aspiration to the joys of paradise. The Romans, with the assurance that they were building upon dogmatic certainties, took over Classical Rome and embellished its Renaissance monuments. They moved columns and obelisks to suit their grandiose plans, and crowned them with crosses to mark the triumph of the church over old pagan and new humanist alike. They dared to interpret in buildings, paintings and sculpture ideas which classical design could not contain. Bernini's sculpture, the *Ecstasy of Saint Theresa*, almost brought off the impossible, the ecstatic fusion of a human being with the Divine Spirit. Vignola's and Tristano's work in the majestic *Gesu*, the new church of the Jesuits in Rome, marks the advent of a new style of building, basically the Latin cross with large transepts and flanking side chapels, which was to be so widely copied in Europe that it is now thought of as the characteristic Counter-Reformation pattern. In the seventeenth century, the Greek cross favoured by Renaissance architects was abandoned in favour of the traditional Christian form, suitable to large processions, to the cult of the saints and their relics. In the typical church of the seventeenth century, the eye is drawn to the high altar, at least where it is not distracted by the richness of side altars or the splendour of a fresco portraying some exalted theme, such as the majesty of God, or as in the *Gesu*, the apotheosis of Saint Ignatius. Although there were many local variations of style and design, the international ramifications of the order, and their liturgical requirements (they were not bound to the daily offices) led to a diffusion of the Jesuit style throughout Europe, most notably in those parts of central Europe where they were the pioneers in the recovery of the Roman faith. The baroque has therefore been fathered on to the Jesuit order. This view is one-sided and ignores other important factors in the supremacy of the style in Europe.

The Jesuits did not have the monopoly of religious fervour, nor of the wealth to express it in architectural form. The great abbeys of South Germany, for instance, like Melk and Ottobeuren, masterpieces of the baroque, show the appeal of the style to the religious sentiment of the time. Again baroque expresses the ideals of the age of absolutism; it can be called aristocratic in its values, its lack of inhibition, its delight in splendour for its own sake. It may be held to express the values of the courtier who was taught, as by Bossuet, to accept ostentation in palaces: 'God forbade ostentation that springs from vanity, and the puffed-up folly of a court intoxicated by riches, but he was well-pleased that the court of the king was brilliant and magnificent, to inspire respect among the peoples'. The same argument could apply to churches. A peasant might resist rational argument but his heart could be touched by sumptuous reliquaries, his understanding engaged by allegories in paint and carving. Many of the missionaries of the Counter-Reformation were themselves of peasant origin and understood this. It is no accident that the baroque is to be found at its most luxuriant and delightful in South Germany, Bohemia and Austria, where the church was ministering almost entirely to peasant congregations, and where in many cases, after the havoc of the Thirty Years war, the priests were starting almost from the beginning, with new churches and semi-pagan congregations. There the plastic arts became predominant; architecture and painting, sculpture and music made greater appeal than books or laboratories.

It can be seen then, that the baroque had affinities with king, aristocrat and peasant; it engaged their mind and sensibility; it was popular art, as well as court art. It made less appeal, however, to the *bourgeois*. It is to be found in restrained style in France, where the *bourgeois* were a substantial element of society, and where an intellectual élite was disposed to logical processes of thought which supported classical canons of taste. The sophistication of simplicity is not confined to the Jansenists, who were more interested in arguments about Grace than in the adornment of reliquaries. To the influence of *bourgeois* taste and thinking may be ascribed the compromise between the classical spirit and the baroque which is characteristic of French art in the seventeenth century.

This compromise was threatened when Colbert turned to Bernini for the development of the Louvre as the principal royal palace, after Mansard had refused to be tied down to a set plan. Colbert considered that the new monarchy for which he laboured required something better than the cramped quarters of the old palace of the Louvre; at the same time he knew the limits of the king's coffers and wanted value for money. Bernini, the master of the high baroque, whose work was ingenious and infinitely adaptable, prepared a series of plans which have survived in the engravings of Marot. He came to France in 1665, to work out on the spot the aesthetic and practical problems of the rebuilding. Louis was gracious to him, treating him almost as an equal, as the 'king of art' and he lived up to the part without modesty. 'The horrid deformity' of the rooftops of Paris, the irregularities of the Fontainebleau Renaissance style, he found shocking; at the same time he was surprised at the degree of artistic conformity that he found in France: 'submission is necessary only in matters of faith; otherwise man has complete freedom in all spheres of life'. Colbert, whose outlook was the very antithesis of this, wished that 'he would spare others a little'. Courtiers mocked at his uninhibited gestures and his passionate way of speaking, but they admired his bust of Louis, a perfect study of the young king. French architects questioned the exuberance of his designs and lobbied the minister. Colbert, who took immense pains over the project, was characteristically concerned over practical matters of detail, the siting of the lavatories, the providing of a private passage for the king to the chapel. Bernini, however, professed a lofty disregard for such matters and did not appreciate the minister's point—an interesting one to set against exaggerated conceptions of royal power—that it would take several years to get rid of tenants of the properties scheduled for demolition: 'you can't just throw people out overnight; whatever you do in Rome, it is not usual in France'. So Bernini left France with nothing but a bust of the king to show for his visit, and a few plans which show that the king could have had a worthy palace in his capital. Two years later Louis gave the job to Le Vau, Le Brun and Claude Perrault. French architecture had come of age.

The consequence is known to the millions who go to look at the paintings of the Louvre; its great colonnade in the manner of a peristyle of a Roman temple, the coupled columns under a flat skyline. Christopher Wren watched the building in progress and declared that 'it was the best school of architecture in Europe'. Before the colonnade was completed, however, Louis

XIV had decided that he would make Versailles his principal seat.

Le Vau was in more ways than one swallowed up by Versailles. Like his successor, J. H. Mansard (1646-1708), he was primarily a civil servant with a state function to perform; namely, to produce a setting for the court, titanic at Versailles, pastoral at Marly. Louis did not understand, and his architects therefore ignored, subtleties in the use of orders, proportions and mouldings. To create an impressive whole, the artists sacrificed the detail. They were rewarded by fame and grandiose achievement. Others like Libéral Bruant (1637-97), who designed the Invalides, with its formal arcaded courts, received little of the manna which dropped from royal patronage in this great age of buildings, because he lacked not talent so much as the sense of the spectacular which Versailles demanded.

In public works the influence of **J. H. Mansard,** the great nephew of the earlier and greater Mansard, was paramount. His extension to the palace, trebling its length without variation of height, was unhappy; Le Vau's original Ionic border looks out of proportion in a front of six hundred yards. His work on the chapel of the Invalides shows the tendencies of official taste. The lower part, with rectilinear columns, builds up towards the centre by means of a number of breaks forward. The great dome is a variant of Saint Peter's; gilt trophies fill the space between the ribs. Inside there are vast free-standing columns and a high altar with black marble columns. Mansard solved the problem of the chapel of Versailles (completed 1711) that was posed by the need for two storeys, the upper containing the royal pew being the more important, by a low arcaded ground floor and high colonnaded first storey. The great height in relation to depth makes this quite unclassical in feeling; over it all the ceiling of Antoine Coypel is an illusionary fresco. These chapels are baroque in sentiment because they embody the autocratic rule and heightened religious atmosphere which usually give rise to this style. But by comparison with buildings which were exploring the possibilities of light and space in Italy and South Germany, this is modest baroque; walls and pediments are straight and plans are simple. Coloured marble is eschewed and sculpture and painting remain distinct; the tendency towards baroque is always restrained by the classical tradition, kept intact by the *Académie*, where a strictly rationalist doctrine was still preached by such men as

François Blondel and practised in his Porte Saint Denis. Mansard could, we have seen, flout the rules, but there was little disagreement about essentials.

Saint-Simon followed contemporary gossip when he accused Mansard of using the work of talented assistants as his own. He has been accused since of being too willing a victim of the taste of his generation. But he did something to shape the taste of the next. He showed imagination in his designs for the Place Vendôme, and the Place des Victoires, the latter the eccentric duc de la Feuillade's private homage to the king. Meanwhile contemporaries, like Pierre Bullet (1639-1716), were building houses, such as that for the rich financier Crozat which come near to the daring of the eighteenth century. The work of Mansard and Bullet, developed by a younger school, was to evolve from the austerities of classicism and the heavy richness of the baroque, the lightness and elegance associated with the word rococo.

BIBLIOGRAPHY

The compiling of a bibliography in a book of this sort is bound to present difficulties. The reader who wishes to make any special study will look elsewhere. The average person, on the other hand, will only wish to know of a few of the more accessible works for further reading. I have listed the books which I have found most useful and a selection of specialist articles which deal with matters which cannot otherwise be pursued. It will be noticed that I have confined my list to books in French or English. This is merely a reflection of my own linguistic limitations.

The most copious bibliography is E. Bourgeois et L. André, *Les Sources de l'histoires de France, dix-septième siècle*, 8 vols. (1913-35). There are full bibliographies attached to the volumes of the (old) *Cambridge Modern History* and E. Lavisse et A. Rambaud, *Histoire générale*. The handbook of E· Préclin et V. L. Tapié, *le XVIIe siècle*, vol. vii of *Clio: Introduction aux études historiques* (1949) is invaluable. It gives a bare summary of the facts, followed by extensive bibliography and a statement of '*l'état actuel des questions*'.

GENERAL HISTORIES OF EUROPE

Henri Hauser, *La Préponderance espagnole*, 1559-1660, vol. x in the series *Peuples et Civilisations* (1935).

P. Sagnac et A. de Saint-Leger, *Louis XIV*, 1661-1715 (1949), vol. x in *Peuples et Civilisations*.

Roland Mousnier, *Les XVIe et XVIIe siècles*, in the *Histoire générale des Civilisations* (1949).

David Ogg, *Europe in the Seventeenth Century* (7th ed. 1959), still the best in the sparse field of textbooks of European history in this century, in English.

Sometimes useful still are the *Cambridge Modern Histories*, of which vol. iii, *The Wars of Religion* (1904), vol. iv, *The Thirty Years War*, and vol. v, *The Age of Louis XIV* (1908) are the relevant volumes.

Of the more valuable new series which is designed to replace these, only vol. v, *The Ascendancy of France*, 1648-88, ed. F. L. Carsten (1961) has so far appeared for the 17th century.

A useful account is to be found in the volumes of E. Lavisse et A. Rambaud, *Histoire Générale*, vol. v, *Les Guerres de religion*, (2nd ed. 1917), and vol. vi, *Louis XIV* (2nd ed. 1912).

American surveys include: C. J. Friederich, *The Age of the Baroque,* 1610-60 (1952); F. L. Nussbaum, *The Triumph of Science and Reason*, 1660-1685 (1953); and J. B. Wolf, *The Emergence of the Great Powers* (1951). (All these are also in a paperback edition).

Amongst other studies of the century, special note should be taken of G. N. Clark's *The Seventeenth Century* (2nd ed. 1945), a wise and stimulating series of studies of different aspects of the period.

HISTORIES OF FRANCE

E. Lavisse, ed., *Histoire de France depuis les origines jusqu'à la révolution* (1900-4), is still valuable; for this century, vols, VI, 2, VII, 1-2 and VIII, 1.

G. Hanotaux, ed., *Histoire de la Nation Française*, 15 vols. (1920-7), is divided according to subjects: political history, 1515-1804, by L. Madelin is contained in vol. IV; vols. VII and VIII by J. Colin and F. Raboul deal with military and naval history; vol. IX by R. Pinon, diplomatic; vol. x by G. Martin, economic and financial history. The volumes are well illustrated and are useful books of reference; the system of partition, however, has obvious disadvantages.

Amongst short studies mention may be made of:

Marie Martin, *Histoire de l'unité Française* (1948), (trans. by North, *The Making of France*, 1951) a synthesis of the idea of France in French history.

P. Gaxotte, *La France de Louis XIV* (1946).

BIOGRAPHIES

There is a surprising shortage of good biographies in this period. For instance, there is no satisfactory life of Mazarin.

G. Hanotaux, *Richelieu*, 6 vols. (1893-1947, later vols, compiled by the duc de la Force). A history of the age as well as a biography, it is a monumental work but still incomplete.

D'Avenel, Vicomte, *Richelieu et la monarchie absolue*, 4 vols. (2nd ed. 1895). Despite its name, less a biography than an account of France in the early 17th century.

L. Batiffol, *Richelieu et le Roi Louis XIII* (1934).

L. André, *Michel le Tellier et Louvois* (1942), with the earlier *Michel le Tellier et l'organisation de l'armée monarchique,* a most important study of the creator of the modern army.

P. Boissonade, *Colbert* (1932).

M. Boulenger, *Fouquet* (1933).

D. Halévy, *Vauban* (1933).

P. Lazard, *Vauban* (1934).

M. Langlois, *Madame de Maintenon* (1932).

M. Weygand, *Turenne* (1929). Interesting as the study of one soldier by another.

V. Sackville-West, *Daughter of France: La Grande Mademoiselle* (1959). The best of several lives of this lady.

C. V. Wedgwood, *Richelieu and the French monarchy* (1949). A short but skilful introduction.

Maurice Ashley, *Louis XIV and the Greatness of France* (1948). In the same series. Another useful introduction.

H. Carré, *l'Enfance et la première jeunesse de Louis XIV* (1944).

L. Bertrand, *Louis XIV.* Uncritical to the point of worthlessness.

D. Ogg, *Louis XIV* (1933). Another short biography; more of an abridged history of France in this period.

W. H. Lewis, *Louis XIV* (1959). An informal portrait.

Louis XIV still has not found a biographer to do him justice. The difficulty is that a life of him must also be a history of France in this period. French studies, such as Jacques Roujon's two volume essay, are coloured to a surprising degree by the author's political sympathies; in this case the views are those of *Action française*.[1]

G. Montgrédien, *Louis XIV* (1963). Not strictly a biography but a very useful approach to him through eye-witness accounts.

Voltaire, *Siècle de Louis XIV* (1731). Last, but not least. An account not of 'the actions of a single man but the spirit of men in the most enlightened age the world has ever seen'. Still essential as well as interesting.

POLITICAL, ADMINISTRATIVE, DIPLOMATIC AND MILITARY

C. Almeras, *La révolte des Camisards* (1959).

L. André, *Louis XIV et l'Europe* (1950). A study of Louis XIV's foreign policy.

L. André, *Michel le Tellier et Louvois* (1942).

G. Ascoli, *La Grande-Brétagne devant l'opinion française au XVIIe siècle*, 2 vols. (1930).

L. Batiffol, *Richelieu et le roi Louis XIII* (1934).

M. Beloff, *The Age of Absolutism*, 1660-1760 (1954). A comparative essay on institutions of government.

E. Bourgeois, *Manuel historique de politique étrangère*, I, 1610-1789 (1892).

P. A. Chéruel, *Histoire de France pendant la minorité de Louis XIV*.

G. N. Clark, *The Dutch Alliance and the War against French Trade*, 1688-1697 (1923).

G. N. Clark, *War and Society in the 17th century: six lectures* (1958).

G. Castellan, *Histoire de l'armée* (1958). A brief account in the *Que sais-je?* series.

J. Dedieu, *Le rôle politique des Protestants français* (1921).

L. Dollot, *Les Cardinaux-ministres sous la monarchie français* (1952).

P. R. Doolin, *The Fronde* (1935).

E. Kossman, *La Fronde* (1954).

G. Lacour-Gayet, *L'Education Politique de Louis XIV* (1898).

G. Lacour-Gayet, *La Marine française sous Louis XIII et Louis XIV* (1911).

G. Livet, *L'Intendance d'Alsace sous Louis XIV*, 1648-1715 (1956).

G. Mattingley, *Renaissance Diplomacy* (1955).

R. Mousnier, *L Vénalité des offices sous Henri IV et Louis XIII* (1945).

H. Nicholson, *Diplomacy* (1930). A general study.

G. Pagés, *La Naissance du Grand Siècle*, 1598-1661 (1948).

G. Pagés, *La Guerre de Trente Ans* (1939).

C. Picavet, *La Diplomatie au temps de Louis XIV* (1930).

[1]Since writing this I have read *Louis XIV* by Vincent Cronin, a good biography, though sympathetic to a degree which some readers may think excessive.

Richelieu, *Le Testament Politique du Cardinal*, ed. L. André (1947).

O. Ranum, *Richelieu and the Councillors of Louis XIII* (1963).

P. Sagnac, *La formation de la société française moderne, vol.* 1, 1661-1715.

M. C. Trevelyan, *William III and the Defence of Holland* (1930).

J. M. Wallace-Hadrill and J. McManners, ed., *France, Government and Society* (1957). Two relevant essays: M. Prestwich, 'Making of Absolute Monarchy; J. S. Bromley, 'Decline of Absolute Monarchy'.

C. V. Wedgwood, *The Thirty Years War* (1938).

G. Vast, *Les Grands Traités du règne de Louis XIV* (1893-9).

G. Zeller, *L'organisation défensive des frontières du nord et de l'est au XVIIe siècle* (1928).

M. Marion, *Dictionnaire des Institutions de la France aux XVIIe et XVIIIe siècles* (1923) is a fundamental work of reference.

SOCIAL AND ECONOMIC

P. Boissonade, *Le Socialisme d'État*, 1559-1661 (1927).

P. Boissonade, *Colbert, le Triomphe d'Étatisme*, 1661-83 (1932)

C. Cole, *French mercantilist doctrines before Colbert* (1931).

C. Cole, *Colbert and a century of French mercantilism* (1934).

H. Hauser, *La Pensée et l'action économique du Cardinal Richelieu* (1944).

F. Hayek, *Capitalism and the Historians* (1954).

E. Hecksher, *Mercantilism* (trans. by Schapiro—2 vols. 1935).

W. H. Lewis, *The Splendid Century* (1953). A series of essays about French life.

J. Locke, *Travels in France*, 1675-9, ed. J. Lough (1953).

J. Lough, *An Introduction to Seventeenth Century France* (1954).

E. Magne, *La Vie Quotidienne au temps de Louis XIII* (1948).

G. Montgrédien, *L'Affaire Fouquet* (1956).

G. Montgrédien, *La Vie Quotidienne au temps de Louis XIV* (1948).

J. Nef, *Industry and Government in France and England* (1940).

G. Roupnel, *La Ville et la Campagne au XVIIe siècle* (1922). A study of economic and social life in and around Dijon, of value far beyond the local confines of the subject.

J. Saint-Germain, *Samuel Bernard* (1960). A study of the great banker.

J. Saint-Germain, *Les Financiers sous Louis XIV: Paul Poisson de Bourvalais* (1950).

W. C. Scoville, *The Persecution of Huguenots and French Economic Development*, 1680-1720 (1960).

H. Sée, *L'évolution commerciale et industrielle de la France sous l'ancien régime* (1948).

H. van Dyke, *Boisguilbert, Economist of the reign of Louis XIV* (1935).

S. Vauban, *Projet d'une dîme royale* (ed. E. Coornaert, 1933).

POLITICAL THEORY, SCIENCE, RELIGION

N. Abercrombie, *Origins of Jansenism* (1936).

J. W. Allen, *History of Political Thought in the Sixteenth Century* (1938.)

M. de la Bédoyère, *The Archbishop and the Lady* (1956). A study more serious than the title would suggest, of Fénelon and Mme de Guyon.

A. E. Bell, *Christian Huygens and the Development of Science in the 17th Century* (1947).

H. Brémond, *l'Histoire litteraire du sentiment religieux en France depuis les guerres de religion* (12 vols. the first appeared in 1916). A classic in the field of popular exposition of Catholic spirituality.

J. Bronowski and B. Mazlish, *The Western Intellectual Tradition* (1960).

M. Brown, *Scientific Organisations in 17th Century France* (1934).

R. H. Butterfield, *The Origins of Modern Science, 1300-1800* (1949).

G. N. Clark, *Science and Social welfare in the Age of Newton* (1946).

L. Cognet, *La Jansenisme* (1961). Short study in the *Que sais-je?* series.

E. Daniel-Rops, *L'Église des Temps Classiques* (1958).

G. H. Dodge, *Political Theory of the Huguenots of the Dispersion* (1947).

J. N. Figgis, *Studies of Political Thought from Gerson to Grotius, 1414-1625*.

A. Gazier, *Bossuet et Louis XIV* (1914).

A. R. Hall, *The Scientific Revolution, 1500-1800* (1954).

P. Hazard, *La Crise de la Conscience Européene, 1680-1715* (1935) (trans. by May, *The European Mind,* 1953). An interesting development of the theme that the roots of the Enlightenment lay in travel, scholarship and challenge to traditional beliefs.

A. Huxley, *Grey Eminence* (1941). The subject of this 'study in religion' is Father Joseph. Judgements suspect because of psychological guesswork.

R. A. Knox, *Enthusiasm* (1950). Especially for chapters on Jansenism and Quietism.

E. Léonard, *Le Protestant Français* (1955). An invaluable study.

E. Mortimer, *Blaise Pascal* (1959).

J. Orcibal, *Louis XIV et les Protestants* (1951). The best work on the Revocation.

J. Orcibal, *Louis XIV contre Henri IV* (1911) *Innocent XI* (1949).

J. Pannier, *L'Église réformée de Paris sous Henri IV* (1911).

E. Préclin et E. Jarry, *Les Luttes Politiques et Doctrinales aux XVIIe et XVIIIe siècles* (1955).

Sainte-Beuve, *Port Royal,* 7 vols. (1930 edn).

H. Sée, *Les idées politiques en France au XVIIe siècle* (1923).

H. F. Stewart, *The Holiness of Pascal* (1940).

H. F. Stewart, *The Secret of Pascal* (1935).

B. Willey, *The Seventeenth Century Background* (1934). Especially valuable for his treatment of Descartes.

A. Wolf, *The History of Science, Technology and Philosophy in the Sixteenth and Seventeenth Centuries* (1935).

ART AND LITERATURE

A. Blunt, *Art and Architecture in France, 1500-1700* (1953).

G. Brereton, *Racine: A Critical Biography* (1951).

G. Brereton, *A Short History of French Literature* (1954).

L. Cazamian, *A History of French Literature* (1955).

E. Henriot, *XVIIe siècle: courrier litteraire* (new ed. 1959). A series of essays.

A. Lagarde et L. Michaud, *XVIIe siècle* (1962). In the series, *Textes et Litterature*, admirably illustrated and presented.

J. Lough, *An Introduction to Seventeenth Century France* (1954). Uses texts to illustrate the social, political and literary character of the period.

J. Palmer, *Molière: His Life and Works* (1930).

G. de Reynold, *Synthèse du XVIIe siècle* (1962). A survey of the cultural tendencies of France in the century.

V. L. Tapié, *Baroque et Classicisme* (1953) (trans. by Ross Williamson, *Age of Grandeur*, 1960).

G. Ziegler, *Les Coulisses de Versailles* (1963). A study of the palace as it appeared to contemporaries.

ARTICLES

I have found the following articles especially useful or interesting.

E. Armstrong, 'The Political Theory of the Huguenots' (*Eng. Hist. Rev.*, 1889).

G. N. Clark, 'The Character of the Nine Years War' (*Cam. Hist. Journal*, 1954).

Descloseaux, 'Études critiques sur les économies royales de Sully' (*Revue historique*, 1887).

P. Goubert, (trans. P. Rudé) 'The French Peasantry of the Seventeenth Century: an example from the Beauvaisis' (*Past and Present*, 1956).

J. Meuvret, 'Comment les français voyaient l'impôt (*Bulletin de la Société d'Études de XVIIe siècle*, 1955).

J. Meuvret, 'Circulation monetaire et utilisation économique de la monnaie dans la France du XVIe siècle et du XVIIe siècle' (*Revue d'histoire moderne et contemporaine*, 1947).

R. Mousnier, 'Comment les français voyaient la France au XVIIe siècle' (*Bulletin de la Société d'Études du XVIIe siècle*, 1952).

R. Mousnier, 'Études sur la population de la France au XVIIe siècle' (*Bulletin de la Société d'Études du XVIIe siècle*, 1952).

R. Mousnier, 'Recherches sur les soulèvements populaires en France avant la Fronde' (*Revue d'histoire moderne et contemporaine*, 1958).

R. Mousnier, 'Quelques raisons de la Fronde: les causes des journées révolutionnaires parisiens de 1648' (*Bulletin de la Société d'Études du XVIIe siècle*, 1949).

R. Mousnier, 'Le Conseil du roi de la mort de Henri IV au gouvernement personnel de Louis XIV' (*Études d'histoire moderne et contemporaine*, 1947-8).

G. Pagés, 'La vénalité des offices dans l'ancienne France' (*Revue historique*, 1932).

G. Pagés, 'Essai sur l'évolution des institutions administratives en France du XVIe siècle à la fin du XVIIe siècle' (*Revue d'histoire moderne*, 1932).

G. Pagés, 'Autour du "grand orage" Richelieu et Marillac, deux politiques' (*Revue historique*, 1937).

E. Porschner, 'The Legend of the Seventeenth Century in French history, (*Past and Present*, No. 8, 1955).

A. Rebelliau, 'Bossuet et les débuts de Louis XIV' (*Revue des Deux Mondes*, 1927).

A. Rebelliau, 'Un episode de l'histoire religieuse au XVIIe siècle: la Compagnie du Saint-Sacrement' (*Revue des Deux Mondes*, 1903).

M. Thompson, 'Louis XIV and William III' (*Eng. Hist. Rev.*, No. 298 1961).

M. Thompson, 'Louis XIV and the Grand Alliance' (*Bull. Inst. Hist. Research*, No. 89, 1961).

H. Trevor Roper, 'The General Crisis of the Seventeenth Century' (*Past and Present*, No. 16, 1959).

INDEX

Surnames and names of places beginning with the definite article are indexed under 'L' (as, La Rochefoucauld, La Rochelle); names of works beginning with the definite article are indexed under the name succeeding (as *Misanthrope, Le*). Surnames sometimes or always preluded by 'de' or 'du' or 'des' are indexed under the name succeeding (as, Avaux, d'; but Van Tromp).

Hapsburg, House of, 52-3, 57, 136,
210, 212, 216, 221, 245, 266, 337,
392; and Northern Italy, 59, 115-18,
127, 129; and Germany, 64-55; and
Thirty Years War, 115, 118, 127,
155, 158, 162, 173, 175, 179, 181-2;
and War of Spanish Succession,
401 (see also Austria, and Empire,
Holy Roman, and the Emperors)
Harcourt, marquis de, 389, 392, 396,
408, 460
Hardy, Alexandre, 477
Harlay, Achille de, 293
Harlay, Archbishop, 340-1, 351, 356,
359-61, 445, 472, 498
Harlay, family of, 48
Harley (Earl of Oxford), 422
Haro, Don Luis de, 185, 222
Harrach, von, 392
Harvey, William, 494
Hauranne, Duvergier de, see Saint-
Cyran, abbé de
Hautefort, Mme de, 131
Heidelberg, 375, 381, 410
Heinsius, Grand Pensionary of
Holland, 384-5, 390, 403, 409,
416-17, 420, 426
Helvetius, 416
Henrietta Maria, Queen of England,
115, 118, 120
Henriette d'Angleterre, see Orléans,
Henriette d'
Henry III, King of France (1574-89),
1-4, 13, 16, 42, 72, 201, 396
Henry IV, of Navarre, King of France
(1589-1610), 74-5, 84, 105, 136, 166;
in the last days of Henry III, 1-3;
character of, 3-4; and the League,
4-11; changes his religion, 8-9, 336;
and the Huguenots, Edict of
Nantes, 11-15, 344; court of, 16,
19; economic and agricultural
policy of, 28-36; government of,
40-44, 289; and sale of offices 50;
diplomatic policies and operations

of, after Peace of Vervins, 52-67;
and the *Grand Dessein*, 57-9; designs
of, in Italy, 58-62; anti-Hapsburg
policy of, 59; arranges Treaty
between Spain and Holland, 62-4;
policies in Germany, 64, 72;
and Affair of Clèves-Julich, 65-7;
assassination of 68, 72, 93; never
summoned States-General, 71;
Episcopal appointments of, 83;
admits Jesuits, 85-6; and Père
Coton, 15, 67, 88; and Carmelites
85, 104; view of war, 218; and
national diplomacy, 259-60;
artistic patronage of, 479, 503, 509
Herbert, Admiral (earl of
Torrington), 378
Hérouard, family of, 120
Herwarth, Barthélemy, 345
Hesse, Prince of, 405
Histoire des Oracles, 499
Histoire des Variations, 281, 365, 452
Hobbes, Thomas, 280, 471
Hochstadt, battle of, 404-5
Holland (United Provinces), 217,
218, 220, 226, 332, 362; navy and
shipping of, 28, 55, 63, 166-7,
173-4, 213, 242-4, 255, 261-2,
378-80, 384, 395-6, 401; truce with
Spain (1609), 62-4, 70, 117, 153;
and Affair of Clèves-Julich, 67; and
Treaty of Compiègne, 115, 118,
163; and Thirty Years War, 152,
155-6, 171, 173-4, 179; signs Peace
of Munster, 180, 213, 246; policy
of, after 1648, 213; alliance with
France (1662), 221, 224; trade war
with England, and Peace of Breda,
224; joins Triple Alliance, 227;
war with France, 235, 238, 242,
244, 245-58, 261, 302, 325-6, 353;
peace with England (1674), 253;
alliance with England, 256; trade
of, 302-3, 309-10, 312-13, 315-7,
380, 433; Huguenots in, 364, 369;

S

James II, King of England, 256, 265,
355, 362, 364, 373-4, 377-8, 397
James Edward Stuart, 'James III',
397-8, 427
Jankau, battle of, 180
Jansen, Cornelius, 89-90, 92, 95-6,
103, 446
Jansenism, 80, 321, 334, 340-2, 346,
350-1, 361, 367, 452, 458, 466,
473-4, 484-5, 503, 513; origins and
early history of, 88-103; Louis XIV
and, 443-50
Jardin du Roi, 494
Jarzé, comte de, 194
Jeannin, 4, 7, 63, 72, 74
Jersey, earl of, 423
Jesuits, 52-3, 68, 72, 79-80, 145, 153,
158, 200, 318, 338, 341, 349, 351,
362, 443, 472, 474, 490, 494, 500,
512-13; organisation and work of,
85-9; struggle with the Jansenists,
91-3, 95-7, 99-103, 107-9; and
the destruction of Port Royal,
446-9
Jésus, Catherine de, 103
John IV, King of Portugal, 174, 177
John, Don, of Austria, 53, 55
John, Don, illegitimate son of Philip
IV of Spain, 185
John George I, Elector of Saxony,
65, 152, 161-3
John George II, Elector of Saxony,
326
Joinville, Treaty of, 1
Joly, Guy, 195
Joseph I, Emperor (1705-1711), 387,
411, 422-4
Joseph Clement, of Bavaria, see
Clement of Bavaria, Elector of
Cologne
Joseph, Père, 108, 112, 114, 118, 130,
144, 159-60, 165, 171
Joyeuse, 10, 61
Juliers, 69-70
Jurieu, 352, 361-2, 364-5, 370, 474, 500

Justice, administration of, 46 (see
also Courts of Law, and Law)
Kara-Mustapha, Grand Vizier of
Turkey, 330-1
Kaunitz, 392
Kepler, 469, 475
Knox, John, 13

Labardemont, 145
La Bruyère, 24, 359, 440, 494-6
La Chaise, Père, 341, 351, 356, 362,
La Chapelle-Marteau, 2-3
Lacombe, Père, 451
La Fayette, Mme de, 131, 133, 278,
490-1
La Feuillade, duc de, 242, 322, 407,
516
Laffemas, 28-9, 31-3, 120, 301
La Fontaine, Jean de, 209, 487-8
La Force, 79, 120
La Fosse, Charles de, 507
La Garde, de, 33
Lagos, battle of, 379
La Hogue, battle of, 378-9
La Hoguette, Hardouin de, 352
Lamboy, 134
La Meilleraye, 141, 165
La Millière, marquis de, 294
Lamoignon, 292, 359
La Motte Aignan, de, 294
Landrecies, siege of, 425
Language, purity of the French, 479-
481
Languedoc, 305, 315, 439; Rohan in,
120; revolt in, 128, 132-3, 141-2;
dragonnades in, 357, 360, 366
Lansac, Mme de, 133, 201
La Porte, 201
La Reynie, 293-4
La Rochefoucauld, Cardinal de, 84
La Rochefoucauld, duc de, 273, 277,
473, 490-1
La Rochelle, 13-14, 28, 79, 289, 320,
360; siege of, 119-23, 127, 129, 155,
159, 344